"*Migration and the Making of Global Christianity* is an outstanding book. Jehu J. Hanciles has made an enormous contribution to our understanding of how Christian faith and practices moved cross-culturally and trans-regionally through their first 1500 years. The book disrupts the dominant historical narrative that reduces Christian missions to expressions of imperial power and the work of hierarchs of the churches. Recasting mission history as the history of migration has implications not only for how we understand the Christian past but also for how we understand the world of Christianity today."

— DALE T. IRVIN
New School of Biblical Theology

"Contrary to what is widely assumed, the role of migration in the global diffusion of Christianity is not a peculiarity of the last half-century. Jehu Hanciles's ambitious study of Christian history to 1500 shows that it has been at the heart of the Christian story from the beginning. He makes a convincing case that historians of Christian expansion who are preoccupied with structures, institutions, and imperial power are looking in the wrong place. Rather, they should turn their attention to the traders, exiles, and pilgrims who took the faith with them on their travels."

— BRIAN STANLEY
University of Edinburgh

"In *Migration and the Making of Global Christianity* Jehu Hanciles takes the reader across vast regions, through centuries of time, and from one world empire to another to show how Christianity became a global faith by 1500 CE. Migration, he insists, is 'a defining feature of human existence' and a major force for change. Migrant Christians, not organized missions, played the primary role in the spread of Christianity. In its essence, then, Christianity is not a top-down, imperially shaped religion, but the dynamic faith of people on the move. This is a hugely important book. It will force us to rethink the history and character of Christianity in our own time no less than in the past."

— JOEL A. CARPENTER
Calvin University

MIGRATION *and the* MAKING *of* GLOBAL CHRISTIANITY

JEHU J. HANCILES

WILLIAM B. EERDMANS PUBLISHING COMPANY
GRAND RAPIDS, MICHIGAN

Wm. B. Eerdmans Publishing Co.
4035 Park East Court SE, Grand Rapids, Michigan 49546
www.eerdmans.com

27 26 25 24 23 22 21   1 2 3 4 5 6 7

ISBN 978-0-8028-7562-4

Library of Congress Cataloging-in-Publication Data

Names: Hanciles, Jehu, 1964– author.
Title: Migration and the making of global Christianity / Jehu J. Hanciles.
Description: Grand Rapids, Michigan : William B. Eerdmans Publishing
    Company, 2021. | Includes bibliographical references and index. | Summary:
    "A socio-historical study of the spread of Christianity through the lens of
    human migration and intercultural exchange"—Provided by publisher.
Identifiers: LCCN 2020037428 | ISBN 9780802875624
Subjects: LCSH: Emigration and immigration—Religious aspects—Chris-
    tianity. | Globalization—Religious aspects—Christianity. | Christianity and
    culture.
Classification: LCC BV639.I4 H275 2021 | DDC 261.8/38—dc23
LC record available at https://lccn.loc.gov/2020037428

To Biffoh,
my fellow sojourner

For [Christians], any foreign country is a motherland, and any motherland is a foreign country.

—"Epistle to Diognetus"

Contents

PART TWO
HISTORICAL ASSESSMENT

Contents

Maps

Foreword

Among the many stories recounted by Jehu Hanciles, we hear the celebrated tale of Ireland's Saint Patrick. Abducted into slavery, Patrick escaped and returned to his native Britain. Soon, though, he returned to Ireland, both to serve other British captives and to evangelize the pagan Irish. But however well known the story might be, it points to certain historical realities that we so often neglect, above all about the nature and purpose of religious mission. For all the tracts ever written about heroic and committed missionaries, a great many key figures find themselves in a particular place despite their own wishes and, at least at first, they have no particular intention of becoming missionaries. They are migrants and merchants, captives and travelers, exiles and deportees, students and seekers. They move between countries and continents, willingly or otherwise, and—perhaps reluctantly—they find themselves bearing the torch of faith into new lands. Christianity itself grew out of a Judaism that had been utterly transformed by its own experience of exile and diaspora.

In varying forms, that pattern has recurred in every era of our Christian history, although it very rarely receives the attention it merits. Jehu Hanciles himself published an exemplary study of this theme in his 2008 book *Beyond Christendom: Globalization, African Migration, and the Transformation of the West*, which established him as a key scholar in the field. Beyond the theme of migration, that book reinforced yet again the critical lesson about the truly global and worldwide nature of the Christian faith, which is today returning to the transcontinental character it possessed in earlier centuries.

In *Beyond Christendom* and other writings, Hanciles did much to define an emerging field. Now, it is wonderful to see him applying his insights about migration and mission to an earlier era—nothing less than the first three-quarters of Christian history, the years before 1500. This is a remarkably ambitious goal, which he accomplishes with great success. Throughout, we must be impressed by his range of scholarship, and his acuity, as he roams through so many diverse eras and locales. He never lets us forget the links and parallels that bind those early centuries to our own day. This is an adventurous transnational history, which demands to be read and cited.

The book has so many takeaways that it is hard to single out any particular one, but let me focus on one lesson that scholars of Christianity need to learn. Whatever era we are studying, we must be careful with the language of "mission," with its implications of planned and intentional ventures into the pagan darkness. On occasion, that is indeed the model by which religion spreads, but by no means always: just think again of Patrick. Never underestimate the power of happenstance, or dare we call it Providence? Commonly, ordinary people move from one area to another, sometimes reluctantly, and they take their religion with them, with no particular intention of sharing it beyond their own community. The Aquila and Priscilla we encounter as such key characters in the book of Acts would never have lived in Corinth had they not been kicked out of Rome by an intolerant regime.

Yet however humble the conditions in which they arrive, such people created (and create) a bridgehead for their faith. They build churches originally to serve the highly practical needs of their own communities, but over time, those congregations attract interested seekers from the wider host community. After some years, the same thriving churches become the bases for newly arrived and more committed believers, who define themselves explicitly as missionaries. Believers arrive first, and the missionaries follow. And sometimes, the new mission churches write the history to emphasize the deliberate decisions of churches and institutions, at the expense of ordinary grassroots endeavors.

Reading Jehu Hanciles's new book, I often find myself nodding enthusiastically as he touches on topics that for so long I have regarded as crucially important, but which were seldom treated properly in the literature. To take one example of many, he is absolutely right to place so much emphasis on borderlands and frontier states, those territories that stand uncomfortably between the great empires and states, and which so often prove vital for the preservation and transmission of faith. By all means tell the story of faith and faiths in the Roman or Persian Empires, but many vital developments actually occurred in the contested lands between their shifting borders, from the Caucasus to the Arab Gulf. Literally, Hanciles redraws the historical maps by which we understand the Christian story.

It would be tempting, but misleading, to read the present book as a reflection of recent postmodern and postcolonial literatures. Hanciles is after all addressing such themes as borders, literal and metaphorical, and the mixed and fluid nature of societies in an age of migration and global consciousness. In every sense, he is discussing border crossers, people with feet in two or more cultural camps, people who of necessity circulate easily between languages and identities. Yet however pivotal such ideas might be in scholarship in the strictly contemporary world, Hanciles shows beyond doubt that these are essential realities of Christianity and Christian growth in every age of the church. That is a provocative and fundamentally necessary insight.

After praising this excellent book so much, I will end by mentioning the one negative reaction it inspires in me. I am sad to reflect that I did not write it!

Philip Jenkins

Acknowledgments

This book has been some seven years in the making, with the bulk of the writing completed during the summer months. The idea for the project materialized soon after the publication of my last monograph, *Beyond Christendom* (2008), which analyzed the impact of global migratory flows on the reshaping of world Christianity in the present era. Countless conversations with audiences across the country (in church and academy) evoked persistent questions about the significance of migration in the life and formation of Christian communities worldwide and the implications for historical assessment. After fits and starts, work on the project began in earnest in the fall of 2013. My initial expectation that it would be completed in three to four years evaporated quickly. The absence of major funding meant that progress was subject to a perennial struggle for time and space. I wrestled with the scope of the study continuously. It was all too apparent that, without fastidious crafting and constant calibration of content, the undertaking was liable to become unmanageable. My intellectual fascination with the subject matter never flagged. But it was not always enough. The requisite help and support came from many quarters.

I had the privilege of working with three outstanding research assistants (promising scholars in their own right) for varying periods of time. Diana Rodriguez Click worked closely with me throughout the project; Jennifer Aycock served for five years; and Janelle Moore (née Adams) put in a one-year stint. I am deeply grateful to all three (all of whom, at this time of writing, are doctoral students in Emory's Graduate Division of Religion) for their extraordinary resourcefulness and diligence. Each handled a mountain of data across a wide range of fields and made exciting discoveries that bolstered the work. This project would have been even more protracted and infinitely more demanding without their help.

I am grateful to many colleagues (too many to name) who, over the years, affirmed the importance of the project in personal conversations or offered stimulating insights that aided my assessment. I am especially indebted to Dale T. Irvin, Douglas G. Jacobsen, Klaus Koschorke, and Joel Carpenter, who graciously read an early draft of the manuscript and provided valuable feedback. Andrew Walls, my mentor, strongly affirmed the project from its inception and spurred the endeavor with constant encouragement. My esteemed colleague Philip Jenkins readily agreed to write the volume's foreword and has enlivened the end product with his insightful endorsement. This small group of renowned world Christianity scholars stimulated my writing in a variety of ways, though the book's blemishes are my responsibility alone.

Institutional support was vital and took many forms. Candler School of Theology provided small research grants that made the hiring of research assistants possible, and I am very grateful to Jonathan Strom (academic dean) for his unwavering support. I benefited enormously from the dependable efficiency of Candler's staff, especially those who directly support faculty endeavor or serve in Pitt's Theological Library. But I owe special thanks to Deborah van der Lande for incomparable service and many acts of kindness. Emory's Center for Digital Scholarship (ECDS) agreed to provide the illustrative maps included in the volume, and I am indebted to cartographer Michael Page, Emory University, for producing maps of stunning vibrancy and detail.

James Ernest (editor-in-chief, Eerdmans Publishing) was possibly the first person I shared the idea for this book project with, when we first met in Boston in January 2011. His enthusiastic response and unwavering interest over the years has been a source of valuable affirmation. The entire Eerdmans team that worked with me on the book project (from proposal to publication) exemplified the highest standards of expertise and efficiency. I am most grateful to David Bratt (my editor), for his ardent support and candid feedback; Jennifer Hoffman (project manager), for her responsiveness and excellent supervision of the production process; Laurel Draper (copyeditor), for her meticulous and intuitive revisions of the manuscript; and Laura Bardolph Hubers (director of marketing and publicity) for her excellent work in the book's promotion.

In every major academic undertaking I have embarked on, the active support (and sympathetic understanding) of family and friends has made a world of difference. I want to convey my heartfelt appreciation to Desmond and Eunice Terry and Isata Momoh (my close friends and Bible study partners) for prayerful support and sustained encouragement. I thank Sade and Shola (our college-age children) for their willing accommodation and oft expressed appreciation for the endeavor, even when it meant wondering aloud why a particular chapter was taking so long! To my wife, Biffoh, the best confidante and companion that a man can ask for, I owe more than I can ever say. This book is dedicated to you.

Introduction

Church history in its hallowed place in the theological curricu-
lum plunges us into the deep end of classical Christian thought,
too much so to be serviceable as we try to follow the tide of
Christianity's global growth. Church history is too closely tied
to the old historiography, too deeply embedded in a top-down
view of God in history, to take in the landscape of an emergent
world Christianity.

—Lamin Sanneh[1]

This study provides a historical assessment of the global spread of Christianity,
with migration as the central lens or explanatory key. It argues that migration
has been an indispensable element in the advancement of the Christian faith
from the earliest beginnings and a prime factor in the plural frontiers of cross-
cultural engagement that mark the world Christian movement. Migration is
a constant feature of human existence and a key driving force of historical
change; so it is no surprise that migrants have literally been prime movers of
Christian expansion. As this treatment makes clear, *every Christian migrant
is a potential missionary*! This fundamental reality is scarcely acknowledged
in the vast troves of published material produced by historians. I contend
that a major reason for this is the "top-down" orientation of much historical
study of Christianity, exemplified by a principal focus on structures of power,

1. Lamin Sanneh, "World Christianity and the New Historiography: History and
Global Connections," in *Enlarging the Story: Perspectives on Writing World Christian
History*, ed. Wilbert R. Shenk (Maryknoll, NY: Orbis Books, 2002), 102–3.

institutional life or resources, and great men. My assessment determines that the church in every age has been decisively shaped by the movement and experience of migrants (drawn from all ranks of society).

It is important to clarify at the outset that I am not claiming an outright correspondence between migration and the spread of the Christian faith down the centuries. That would be wildly inaccurate. Generally speaking, human migration in its variety of forms has had a mixed impact on the fortunes of the church. There are countless instances in which migration has advanced the cross-cultural spread of Christian teachings and practices into new contexts. But history also provides ample evidence that migration can inhibit Christian expansion or even reverse Christian presence. Some Christian migrants abandon their faith or convert to other faiths. On occasion, substantial emigration by Christian communities due to any number of precipitating factors can also significantly decimate the church in a particular place. The line of inquiry I pursue in the pages that follow is fairly precise: namely, that the migration *of Christians* has typically contributed to the spread of Christianity and represents a predominant element in the globalization of the faith.

The study's approach is sociohistorical, a mode of analysis characterized by a number of key elements such as "a substantial focus on groups out of power," a conviction that "non-political activities and beliefs warrant serious analysis in their own right as part of understanding the past," and an emphasis on "patterns or processes of culture, power relationships and behavior rather than a series of events."[2] These analytical commitments have the whole of society in view and add up to a "bottom-up" perspective.[3] Sociopolitical structures and the activities of privileged elites are not ignored, but there is conscious effort to integrate the experiences of ordinary people or neglected social groups in the historical account.

2. Peter N. Stearns, "Social History and History: A Progress Report," *Journal of Social History* 19, no. 2 (Winter 1985): 322.

3. On the "bottom-up" perspective of the sociohistorical method, see, among others, Raphael Samuel, Keith Hopkins, John Breuilly, Joyce Youings, David Canadine, Royden Harrison, and J. C. D. Clark, "What Is Social History?," *History Today* 35, no. 3 (1985): 35; also, Clarke A. Chambers, "The 'New' Social History, Local History, and Community Empowerment," *Minnesota History* 49, no. 1 (1984): 17; Louise A. Tilly, "Social History and Its Critics," *Theory and Society* 9, no. 5 (1980): 668; Donald M. MacRaild and Avram Taylor, *Social Theory and Social History* (New York: Palgrave Macmillan, 2004).

OLD AND NEW CONCEPTUAL MODELS

The last three decades have witnessed ample scholarly critique of the Western ethnocentrism that has long defined the academic discipline of church history and the historical study of Christianity.[4] The fixed periodization of church history into "early," "medieval" ("middle ages"), and "modern" is an obvious case in point. As a historical construct, "medieval" is bereft of meaning and relevance outside the European experience—it is bizarre to talk of medieval Islam—and the label "modern" is tied to Western notions of progress and standards of achievement (by which the rest of the world, the Christian world in this case, is judged). The fact that professional guilds, scholarly publications, major textbooks, and academic appointments are structured around these outmoded and deeply Eurocentric categorizations hints at the entrenched nature of the problem. For now, at least, the unapologetic promotion of Western intellectual paradigms, limited geographical focus, and tacit assumption of the primacy of the Western theological heritage are increasingly acknowledged and challenged.

The growing World Christianity scholarship maintains that the study of Christianity as a global faith must be pluralistic and incorporate the voices, experiences, and expressions of Christians worldwide in all their social, ethnic, and generational diversity.[5] A world Christianity approach is inherently inter-

4. Among others, Andrew F. Walls, "Eusebius Tries Again: The Task of Reconceiving and Re-Visioning the Study of Christian History," in *Enlarging the Story: Perspectives on Writing World Christian History*, ed. Wilbert R. Shenk (Maryknoll, NY: Orbis Books, 2002), 1–21; Wilbert R. Shenk, ed., *Enlarging the Story: Perspectives on Writing World Christian History* (Maryknoll, NY: Orbis Books, 2002); Andrew F. Walls, "Structural Problems in Mission Studies," *International Bulletin of Missionary Research* 15 (October 1991): 146–55; Dana Robert, "Shifting Southward: Global Christianity Since 1945," *International Bulletin of Missionary Research* 24 (April 2000): 50–58; Philip Jenkins, *The Next Christendom: The Coming of Global Christianity* (Oxford: Oxford University Press, 2011); Lamin Sanneh, *Whose Religion Is Christianity? The Gospel beyond the West* (Grand Rapids: Eerdmans, 2003); Wilbert R. Shenk, "Toward a Global Church History," *International Bulletin of Missionary Research* 20 (April 1996): 50–57; Jehu J. Hanciles, "New Wine in Old Wineskins: Critical Reflections on Writing and Teaching a Global Christian History," *Missiology: An International Review* 35 (July 2006): 361–82.

5. For coverage and critique of the world Christianity approach, see, among others, Dale T. Irvin, "World Christianity: An Introduction," *Journal of World Christianity* 1, no. 1 (2008): 1–26; Paul V. Kollman, "Understanding the World-Christian Turn in the History of Christianity and Theology," *Theology Today* 71, no. 2 (2014):

disciplinary and lends itself to a plurality of models and methods. So it is not one thing! Also, no region or epoch is precluded from its purview—though it does invite greater attentiveness to underrepresented or marginalized communities globally and emphasizes the polycentric and multidirectional nature of global Christianity's development. The impact of this growing field is noteworthy; but the enduring dominance of the old historiography must not be ignored. All too often, the label "global" or "world" is applied to church history courses that treat the stories of non-Western peoples as supplements to the main diet. This has contributed to a common perception that the study of *world* Christianity is a post-1500 endeavor, with the sixteenth-century Reformations and Western colonial expansion as inflection points.

To counter the limiting effects of the "church history" model requires close conceptual scrutiny of Western interpretative assumptions and methodologies. This study draws attention to a dominant explanatory frame in historical analysis that I term the "empire argument": an allusion to the predilection among Western scholars for a "top-down" view of historical processes that centers on political authority, structures of power, dominant (or elite) segments of society, and institutional forms. As Philip Curtin pithily surmises, "[Western] historians . . . have often concentrated on the doings of great men, top nations, or great civilizations, unconsciously setting aside the activities of women, the ordinary run of men, or societies whose achievements failed to attract Western admiration."[6] Such is the pervasiveness of the empire argument in Western thought that even "postcolonial" critique, which sets out to challenge the "master discourses of imperial Europe" and analyze processes of hegemonic dominance, unwittingly promotes "empire" as a central model for thinking about historical experience.[7]

164–77; Klaus Koschorke, "New Maps of the History of World Christianity: Current Challenges and Future Perspectives," *Theology Today* 71, no. 2 (2014): 178–91; Joel Cabrita, David Maxwell, and Emma Wild-Wood, eds., *Relocating World Christianity: Interdisciplinary Studies in Universal and Local Expressions of the Christian Faith* (Boston: Brill, 2017); Shenk, *Enlarging the Story*; Ana Maria Bidegain, "Rethinking the Social and Ethical Functions of a History of World Christianity," *Journal of World Christianity* 1, no. 1 (2008): 88.

6. Philip D. Curtin, *The World and the West: The European Challenge and the Overseas Response in the Age of Empire* (New York: Cambridge University Press, 2000), xii.

7. Bill Ashcroft, Gareth Griffiths, and Helen Tiffin, *The Post-Colonial Studies Reader*, 2nd ed. (New York: Routledge, 2006), 1–3.

The empire argument or rationale has analytical value. Indeed, empire (in a literal sense) is a prominent factor in historical development. But historical interpretation centered on a "top-down" view comes with major blind spots and leaves much unaccounted for. In this case, the focus on human migration shows that attentiveness to "nonpolitical" activity, multidirectional cultural processes of change, and the agency of disempowered groups produces a more complete understanding of the making of global Christianity. At the very least, an explanatory framework that emphasizes ways in which mundane events, marginalized persons, and commonplace experiences shape historical development is deeply subversive of master narratives and constructs centered on use of power.

The sociohistorical approach is not free from the limitations or preconceptions that afflict all historical interpretation. Social historians can unwittingly succumb to a reflexive anti-institutional bias, while the wide-ranging nature of their concerns and coverage can elicit blind accumulation of facts.[8] Analysis is also prone to prize experience over explanation or confuse contexts with causes.[9] Furthermore, since the whole-society approach greatly widens the scope of historical research and assessment, hermeneutic coherence can suffer. Conversely, the fact that historical records heavily favor the activities and testimonies of dominant groups or prominent individuals means that data on the actions and experiences of ordinary people or underrepresented groups are typically scanty. This conceivably opens the door to greater speculation on the part of the social historian. More positively perhaps, it renders the subjectiveness of all historical interpretation more evident.

The advantages and shortcomings of the sociohistorical approach are readily apparent in this volume. It extends the range of historical inquiry and offers conceptual tools that provide a more intimate understanding of particular historical developments. A "bottom-up" perspective with a singular focus on the lives and actions of ordinary people also yields unique insights into the fluidity and plotlessness of major historical developments, especially cross-cultural religious encounters. Yet, the scantiness or inadequacy of the historical records poses particular challenges to our understanding of the nature, scope, and types of migrants in earlier epochs. Regardless of the period or era

8. Samuel et al., "What Is Social History?," 39.
9. Francis G. Couvares, "Telling a Story in Context; or, What's Wrong with Social History?," *Theory and Society* 9, no. 5 (1980): 675.

under examination, analysis is constrained by the nature and quality of the data.[10] Long-distance migrants in every age have constituted a tiny segment of the societies they come from. Yet, their numbers, and the networks that facilitate their myriad activities, progressively expand in scale and scope over time. There are enough data to construct a general picture of migration and travel in many specific contexts;[11] but records of individual migrants are uncommon. With very rare exceptions, the massive hordes that thronged the roads and seaways in the pre-1500 era left no trace of their movements or activities.

To make a compelling case for the centrality of migration in the cross-cultural expansion of the Christian faith thus requires close reading of the available data with a focus on individuals and groups whose identity and contribution were often peripheral even to the culturally conditioned gaze of contemporary writers or historians. This was true not only of migrant-outsiders but also of whole segments of any given population, notably females. Regardless of the strength and substance of relevant primary data, historical reconstruction frequently requires deductive reasoning and a disciplined imagination, with "the authenticating conventions of scholarship" acting as guardrails.[12]

Approach and Structure

This project is located within the emerging field of world Christianity in terms of approach and appraisal and adds to the growing list of monographs that provide a historical study of global Christianity. But its primary focus on the facility and importance of human migration means that it is not a general survey. The treatment it provides is illustrative rather than comprehensive, and decidedly selective. The central aim is to assess key episodes and major historical transitions in the history of Christianity that demonstrate the pivotal impact and profound implications of human mobility for the cross-cultural

10. In one sense, migrant data are always incomplete due to the variability of the phenomenon.

11. Such data are provided by Lionel Casson, *Travel in the Ancient World* (Baltimore: Johns Hopkins University Press, 1994), 190–218; Stephen S. Gosch and Peter N. Stearns, *Premodern Travel in World History* (New York: Routledge, 2008), 36; Jerome Murphy-O'Connor, "Traveling Conditions in the First Century: On the Road and on the Sea with St. Paul," *Bible Review* 1, no. 2 (1985): 38–45.

12. Keith Hopkins, in Samuel et al., "What Is Social History?," 38.

and transnational expansion of the Christian faith. Foremost attention is given to the initial Christian encounter with non-Christian peoples or the spread of Christian ideas and practices into non-Christian contexts, and also to missionary encounters that reflect or illustrate expanding global linkages and escalating movement. For the most part, evangelistic enterprise confined in scope and impact to a particular nation or territory receives less attention, even when such efforts involve migrant movement and agency.

These preferences and the limitations of a single volume account for notable exclusions, some more defensible than others. The Byzantine Empire, eastern Europe, and India receive only passing mention. More could have been done to explicate the role of migration in the establishment and spread of Christianity in Africa, especially Ethiopia and Nubia (present-day Sudan). The notable contribution and impact of the Nine Saints in fifth-century Axumite Ethiopia is one example. However, other notable developments such as the purposeful contacts and growing connections between Ethiopian rulers and Christian Europe from the fourteenth century fall outside the study's purview because, however fascinating, they do not represent missionary expansion.[13] Although this study provides numerous and detailed examples of the link between monastic missions and migration, Franciscan and Dominican missionary efforts in the wake of the Crusades are not covered. Despite these strategic (editorial) exclusions, the embeddedness of the world Christian movement in migratory processes and the deepening interconnectedness of the world's peoples are fully demonstrated.

Research and writing for this project required considerable use of primary sources. But the extensive historical coverage means that secondary material, rather than forensic textual analysis, forms the mainstay of the overall assessment and particular arguments. The breadth of the material and the scope of analysis also dictate intersection and engagement with a variety of fields of scholarly inquiry and subspecialties—including migration, biblical, and Persian studies. I have been as scrupulous as possible in my intellectual engagement with key ideas or arguments within these different fields without being drawn into intramural fights or debates. And where helpful or relevant, I have been at pains to make my own assumptions or approach plain to avoid

13. On this, see David Northrup, *Africa's Discovery of Europe, 1450–1850*, 3rd ed. (New York: Oxford University Press, 2014), 3–6, 45–50.

sailing under false colors. Ultimately, by providing a thoroughgoing historical assessment of the varieties of Christian migrant movements as a primary form of missionary mobilization and a critical factor in the globalization of the Christian faith, this study breaks new ground.

The first section of the book (part 1) is specifically devoted to a detailed overview of the concepts and theoretical constructs that frame the study and inform my assessment. Each of the three chapters in this section is devoted to a foundational set of issues or questions. Chapter 1 delves into a historical and conceptual overview of migration, with particular attention to theories and typologies. Chapter 2 conducts a thoroughgoing examination of religious conversion, with a focus on definitional complexities and challenges for historical study, as well as the two central theoretical constructs (the translation principle and modes of social conversion) that inform the study. Chapter 3 examines how the profound role that migration plays in biblical religion (as a metaphor for the life of faith and a critical element in "missionary" encounters) informs Christian theological understanding. It also assesses the intimate interconnection between migration, Christian identity, and missionary encounter, with a focus on the theological and missiological implications of the vulnerability and marginalization of the migrant-outsider status.

The remaining chapters (4–10), which constitute part 2, explore specific historical periods and contexts that are illustrative of significant cross-cultural expansion of the Christian faith. Most chapters in this section include a summary overview of the types of migrants as well as the scope and patterns of migration characteristic of the era under consideration. Chapter 10 provides a detailed assessment of the "empire argument" and contrasts its conceptual limitations with the centrality of the migrant factor in the formation of global Christianity. Taken as a whole, this study debunks the centuries-old view that the global spread of the Christian faith is largely the work of institutional entities (ecclesiastical or political) and their trained agents.

Part One

Conceptual Overview

CHAPTER ONE

Migration in Human History: A Conceptual Overview

> There comes a moment to the patient traveler (and there are
> many such that wander far afield) when the road ahead of him
> is clear and the distance so foreshortened that he has a vision
> of his home, he sees his way to it over land and sea, and in his
> fancy travels there and back so quickly that it seems to stand
> before his eager eyes.

> —"Jason and the Voyage of the Argo"
> (from Apollonius Rhodius, *The Argonautica*)

For many years, there were two competing hypotheses among scientists that explained the origins of modern humans.[1] The first, known as the "multi-regionalist" theory or Candelabra model, maintained that modern humans have multiple origins or evolved from isolated groups in different regions. In this view, our most recent ancestors (*Homo erectus*, or "upright man"[2])

---

1. Among the many sources, see Brian M. Fagan, *The Journey from Eden: The Peopling of Our World* (New York: Thames & Hudson, 1990), 15–22; John Haywood, *The Great Migrations: From the Earliest Humans to the Age of Globalization* (London: Quercus, 2008), 12–21; Russell King, *Atlas of Human Migration* (Buffalo, NY: Firefly Books, 2007), 16–19; David Christian, *Maps of Time: An Introduction to Big History* (Berkeley: University of California Press, 2004), 176–82; and Nayan Chanda, *Bound Together: How Traders, Preachers, Adventurers, and Warriors Shaped Globalization* (New Haven: Yale University Press, 2007), 2–8.

2. The earliest representative of the genus *Homo*, to which all modern humans belong, *Homo habilis* ("handy man" or "tool-making man") emerged in the African savanna about 2.3 million years ago. The first specimen was discovered in the Olduvai Gorge in northern Tanzania in 1960 by paleoanthropologists Louis Leakey and Mary Leakey. *Homo erectus* also migrated out of East Africa (David Christian, *Maps of Time: An Introduction to Big History*, The California World History Library [Berkeley: University of California Press, 2004], 164).

emerged and flourished in Africa about 2 million years ago and began to migrate into Asia and Europe about 1.9 million BCE.[3] The dispersed groups developed independently but comparably in Africa, Europe, and Asia, adapted to their different environments over millions of years, and eventually evolved into modern humans (*Homo sapiens*, "knowing man"). Proponents theorize that present-day variations in skin color and facial differences reflect the impact of the disparate physical environments on regional heritage.

The alternative explanation, popularly known as the "Out of Africa" theory or the "Noah's Ark" hypothesis, rejects the view that *Homo erectus* were our direct ancestors and contends that diverse populations living in disparate environments separated by considerable distances could not have evolved separately into the same species. Proponents claim that humans evolved in one place, as a single species, *before* they began to migrate and colonize the world. This happened long after *Homo erectus*, "the first intercontinental travelers," had died out. In essence the homogeneity of modern humans (*Homo sapiens*)—all humans are 99.9 percent similar—indicates that global migration was a rather recent occurrence.

Neither of these competing views gained ascendancy until the 1980s when the development of DNA testing allowed geneticists to compare genetic differences among populations in different parts of the world and reconstruct the migration movement of their ancestors. In particular, cutting-edge analysis of the mitochondrial DNA (mtDNA), which is inherited only through the female line, revealed that the mother of all modern people lived in Africa about 200,000 years ago. This is not to say that she was the only woman alive at the time, only that her progenies survived while the lines of descendants of the other women became extinct. This mitochondrial African Eve "is the 10,000th grandmother of every human on the planet."[4] Subsequent research also established that the Y chromosome, which determines male sex, also originated in Africa.

The evidence indicates that our ancestors first migrated to different parts of the African continent. Then, some 100,000–60,000 years ago, a small group of migrants, all of them Eve's descendants, all closely related and sharing her mtDNA, migrated out of Africa. These African migrants numbered any-

3. The Americas and Australia remained beyond their reach.
4. King, *Atlas of Human Migration*, 19.

where from 150 to 2,000 people, out of an estimated population of 10,000.[5] In a process lasting around 50,000 years, their descendants "colonized every corner of the world except for Antarctica, the high Arctic, and some oceanic islands."[6] They successively occupied the Fertile Crescent and southern Eurasia (by 90,000 BCE), Australia (about 58,000 BCE[7]), Europe and northern Eurasia (ca. 40,000 BCE), and eventually the Americas as far as Chile in the southern tip (about 13,000 years ago).[8] "One of the amazing things about this global journey," notes Nayan Chanda, "is that it was undertaken almost entirely on foot, with occasional use of rafts or dugouts over waters."[9]

The dating of this global migration shows that for at least half our history modern humans lived exclusively in Africa, and that variations in skin color (derived from a minuscule particle of our DNA) emerged within the last 60,000 years, or very recently in evolutionary terms.[10] Most important for our discussion, the "Out of Africa" account establishes that the tremendous diversification of the human race is *fundamentally rooted in migration*, an understanding that is unequivocally endorsed by the Hebrew Bible.

Human migration is a fact of history; and the history of humans is one of migration. In a quite literal sense, "humans are born migrants."[11] When our ancestors first became fully human, writes historian William H. McNeill, "they were already migratory, moving about in pursuit of big game."[12] Archeological remains of human ancestors like the iconic "Lucy" (who supposedly walked the earth 3.2 million years ago[13]) highlight the critical

5. Christian, *Maps of Time*, 143; also Chanda, *Bound Together*, 5. Haywood suggests that they may have been as few as a few dozen (*Great Migrations*, 20).

6. Haywood, *The Great Migrations: From the Earliest Humans to the Age of Globalization*, 19.

7. Until the end of the last glacial period about 10,000 years ago, Australia formed part of a large continental mass incorporating New Guinea and Tasmania, named Sahul by paleogeographers.

8. Christian, *Maps of Time*, 191–94. Up to 10,000 years ago, the Bering Strait that now separates Russia from Alaska was dry land (Haywood, *Great Migrations*, 26).

9. Chanda, *Bound Together*, 19–20.

10. Haywood, *Great Migrations*, 14.

11. King, *Atlas of Human Migration*, 8.

12. William H. McNeill, "Human Migration in Historical Perspective," *Population and Development Review* 10, no. 1 (March 1984): 1.

13. Christian, *Maps of Time*, 156; Patrick Manning, *Migration in World History*, Themes in World History (New York: Routledge, 2005), 14.

role of mobility for our species: her remains indicate that Lucy was on the move when she died! For good reason, migration has been described as "an irrepressible human urge."[14] The migrant impulse aided human evolution and has played an indispensable role in human development throughout the ages. The various forms of migration "provide one of the major forces for historical change."[15] In other words, migration is not just a prominent feature of one stage or the other of human history. Migration has been a constant feature of human existence, embedded in the complex transformations that shape our world.

The tendency to associate human migration exclusively with crises perhaps helps to explain why its influential role in human history and development is often overlooked or greatly underestimated. Conversely, the pervasiveness and near ubiquity of migration in the present era can foster the view that the centrality of the phenomenon to human existence and world affairs is a recent development. There are good grounds for calling the last six to seven decades "the age of migration";[16] such is the extraordinary volume and diversity of migration since the mid-twentieth century. But such a claim also belies the new constraints or paradoxes that mark current migratory flows.[17] Due to advancements in technologies of travel, the reach and rate of migrant movement have never been greater; at the same time, efforts to control or regulate cross-border movement have expanded tremendously. Consequently, compared to a hundred years ago, people are generally less free to migrate, as the increasing measures by Western governments to regulate or stem the unremitting tide of unauthorized (or "illegal") migrants indicate. Even more important, while it is true that there are more migrants in the world than ever before, the transformative impact of migration on human development is perennial, and the past offers important lessons for the present. This is particularly true of the role that migration plays in the globalization of religion.

14. W. R. Böhning, "International Migration and the Western World: Past, Present, Future," *International Migration* 16, no. 1 (1978): 18.

15. Manning, *Migration in World History*, 7.

16. Stephen Castles and Mark J. Miller, *The Age of Migration: International Population Movements in the Modern World*, 4th ed. (New York: Guilford, 2009).

17. See King, *Atlas of Human Migration*, 8.

HISTORIOGRAPHICAL CHALLENGES: CONTEXTS, SOURCES, AND MODELS

It is only in recent decades that historians have begun to give detailed attention to migration as a fundamental feature of human development. Even so, historical treatments of migration are beset by major limitations:[18] these include a primary focus on Europe and the Atlantic region, the dominance of the bipolar analytical approach ("voluntary" vs. "involuntary," "free" vs. "forced," "legal" vs. "illegal," etc.), the centrality of the nation-state in the research methodology, a preoccupation (notably among American immigration scholars) with particular ethnic groups, and the fact that the period of study is seldom longer than five hundred years. Dirk Hoerder's landmark study of human migrations in world history from 1000 to 2000 CE, titled *Cultures in Contact* (2002), represents a major breakthrough; but a fixation with European movements and initiatives is detectable in his analysis. However, there is now a small but growing list of historical treatments of migration from a global perspective, including Jerry Bentley's *Old World Encounters* (1998); Richard Foltz's *Religions on the Silk Road* (2010, 2nd ed.); Stephen Gosch and Peter Stearns's *Premodern Travel in World History* (2008); Christiane Harzig and Dirk Hoerder's *What Is Migration History?* (2009); and Patrick Manning's *Migration in World History* (2005), which among other things offers a much-needed typology of migration.

To be sure, the study of human migration in history presents particular challenges to historians.[19] Historical studies, notes Hasia Diner, place great stress on "context" as marker of a particular time and place. Since "contexts

18. For details, see Jan Lucassen, Leo Lucassen, and Patrick Manning, "Migration History: Multidisciplinary Approaches," in *Migration History in World History: Multidisciplinary Approaches*, ed. Jan Lucassen, Leo Lucassen, and Patrick Manning (Boston: Brill, 2010), 6–14; also Hasia R. Diner, "History and the Study of Immigration," in *Migration Theory: Talking across Disciplines*, ed. Caroline Brettell and James Frank Hollifield (New York: Routledge, 2000), 31, 37–39.

19. See Diner, "History and the Study of Immigration," 27–42; also Nancy L. Green, "The Comparative Method and Poststructural Structuralisms: New Perspectives for Migration Studies," in *Migration, Migration History, History: Old Paradigms and New Perspectives*, ed. Jan Lucassen, Leo Lucassen, and Patrick Manning (New York: Lang, 1997), 58; Richard Foltz, *Religions of the Silk Road: Premodern Patterns of Globalization* (New York: Palgrave Macmillan, 2010), 20–22.

differ from place to place, and change over time" historians generally eschew typologies and models that account for variations over long periods of time and across regions. Also, she adds, the "sources" that historians depend on for assessment "have been grounded in particular moments in time, anchored to particular spots on the globe, and embodied in the experiences of particular people even as they moved from one of those settings to other new ones." This limits the study of the human experience to "periods and places for which [historians] have written records."[20] Dependence on written texts becomes a major impediment for the historical exploration of migration, which encompasses periods, places, and persons (nonelite men and women) that are not represented in recorded history. Migration is "one of the defining characteristics of the human race";[21] but for many epochs and periods, the scantiness of the historical record and the necessity of extracting important conclusions from fragmentary and inconclusive material are an ever-present dilemma.

The problem is compounded when there is interest in specific dimensions of human migration, such as its links to religious or cultural expansion. Foltz warns that the tendency to depend on key texts as the authoritative representation of a particular tradition or belief system reinforces artificial boundaries and elevates particular voices or experiences. "We should recognize," he warns, "that an overly text-centered approach not only tacitly supports elite, often hegemonic views at the expense of the nonliterate majority, it also does little to help us reconstruct what it is that the majority actually did and believed."[22] The modern preoccupation with periodization and categorization can also impose rigid boundaries on major movements, enforce distinctions (based on preconceived notions of religious adherence, for instance) that overlook the fluidity of religious allegiance and expression in local contexts, or misrepresent religious transformation. Additionally, the dense fog that often inhibits full grasp of the dynamics and extent of migrant movements in some contexts can also impede efforts to probe complex issues like the nature and direction of cross-cultural change or, for that matter, the extent of religious conversion and pluralism. These challenges underscore the interdisciplinary

20. Lucassen, Lucassen, and Manning, "Migration History," 17–18.
21. Haywood, *Great Migrations*, 8.
22. Foltz, *Religions of the Silk Road*, 21; also Michael David Coogan, "In the Beginning: The Earliest History," in *The Oxford History of the Biblical World*, ed. Michael David Coogan (New York: Oxford University Press, 1998), 17–18.

nature of migration studies and inspire increased calls for historians to incorporate or learn from the approaches of other scientific disciplines in the study of migration.[23]

In this regard, the sociohistorical approach adopted in this study is quite germane to an assessment of the historical impact and contribution of migrants, because of its distinctly "bottom-up" perspective.[24] Peter Stearns identifies three interrelated features of social history:[25] first, "substantial focus on groups out of power, with the concomitant belief that these groups display some capacity to change and therefore some capacity to influence wider historical processes"; second, "a fascination with aspects of life and society in addition to politics, which entails a belief . . . that non-political activities and beliefs warrant serious analysis in their own right as part of understanding the past"; and third, an emphasis on "patterns or processes of culture, power relationships and behavior rather than a series of events." The conscious effort to integrate the experiences of ordinary people or neglected social groups in the historical account has obvious advantages for exploring the migrant experience and cross-cultural religious encounters.

DEFINITIONS AND TYPOLOGIES

Migration may be a fact of human existence; but the nature of mobility, the forms of relocation, and major types of migrants vary tremendously through the ages. For instance, whereas slaves and captives represented a quite prominent category of migrant in the ancient world, this is hardly the case in the early

23. Cf. Lucassen, Lucassen, and Manning, "Migration History," 3–35; Caroline Brettell and James Frank Hollifield, "Migration Theory," in *Migration Theory: Talking across Disciplines*, ed. Caroline Brettell and James Frank Hollifield (New York: Routledge, 2000), 1–26.

24. On the "bottom-up" perspective of the sociohistorical method, see, among others, Raphael Samuel, Keith Hopkins, John Breuilly, Joyce Youings, David Canadine, Royden Harrison, and J. C. D. Clark, "What Is Social History?," *History Today* 35, no. 3 (1985): 35; also Clarke A. Chambers, "The 'New' Social History, Local History, and Community Empowerment," *Minnesota History* 49, no. 1 (1984): 17; Louise A. Tilly, "Social History and Its Critics," *Theory and Society* 9, no. 5 (1980): 668; Donald M. MacRaild and Avram Taylor, *Social Theory and Social History* (New York: Palgrave Macmillan, 2004).

25. Peter N. Stearns, "Social History and History: A Progress Report," *Journal of Social History* 19, no. 2 (Winter 1985): 322.

twenty-first century world.[26] Similarly, the distinction between international migrants and "internally displaced peoples" (used from the 1990s) is a product of the modern world and one not easily applied to ancient societies. Also, regardless of the time period under examination, analysis is constrained by the nature and quality of the data. In one sense, migrant data are always incomplete due to the variability of the phenomenon. But the paucity or inadequacy of the historical records poses particular challenges to our understanding of the nature, scope, and types of migrants in earlier epochs, whereas ideological considerations and the varying classification applied to migrants by different countries in the modern period can impede analysis of the surfeit of data.

In any case, the unprecedented levels of interconnectedness and mobility that mark the present era of globalization have rendered forms of human mobility more complex and diverse than ever before. Across all major academic disciplines, these complexities have spawned numerous typologies aimed at providing an analytical framework that clarifies or explains vital aspects of the phenomenon.[27] The prevalence of the nation-state as a unit of analysis and the overwhelming tendency to conceptualize migration as a one-directional or linear process greatly limit the explanatory potential of most theories or models. More long-standing theories of migration that attempt to explain the phenomenon in terms of human behavior or social processes typically produce a bipolar framework of analysis that draws sharp contrasts between "voluntary" and "involuntary" migration, "free" and "forced" movement, "push" and "pull" factors, "receiving" and "sending" society.[28]

26. In 2016, for instance, some 40.3 million people—70 percent of whom were women and children—were estimated to be victims of forced servitude around the world. Undoubtedly, this is a staggeringly high figure but a small fraction of the global migrant population. See "Findings: Executive Summary," Global Slavery Index, 2018, accessed July 22, 2019, https://www.globalslaveryindex.org/2018/findings/executive -summary/.

27. Most—such as Brettell and Hollifield, "Migration Theory," 1–26; and Karen O'Reilly, *International Migration and Social Theory* (New York: Palgrave Macmillan, 2012), 39–65—highlight either the dynamics of immigrant settlement (the receiving end) or the factors that shape emigration (with a tendency to focus on migration as a problem to explain).

28. See Anthony H. Richmond, "Sociological Theories of International Migration: The Case of Refugees," *Current Sociology* 36, no. 2 (June 1, 1988): 7–25; Caroline Brettell, "Theorizing Migration in Anthropology: The Social Construction of Networks, Identities, Communities, and Globalscapes," in *Migration Theory: Talking*

While these dichotomies offer useful insights, they impose a rigid framework on a phenomenon that is exceptionally fluid and dynamic. The motives and impetus for migration, and the compound of calculations, pressures, and opportunities that attend the process, are much too complex to allow a priori distinctions between "choice" and "compulsion." Even the commonplace distinction between *migrant* and *refugee* is misleading, in part because it ignores "the relation between structural constraints and individual choice."[29] As Anthony Richmond argues, "all human behavior is constrained."[30] More specifically, the choices available to migrants "are not unlimited"; "degrees of freedom" vary.[31] Ultimately, migrant autonomy (individual or group) is situationally determined, which is to say that the ability to migrate is inhibited or enabled by wider forces (such as preexisting networks or immigration policies in the destination society) that limit the degree of freedom or choice.[32] In this study, human migration is viewed as a phenomenon *subject to constant change, marked by varying degrees of compulsion (or freedom), and shaped by wider structures and historical processes.*

The existing literature is replete with definitions of migration that support detailed analysis of particular historical periods or contexts. In his monumental study of migration in the ancient world, for instance, Peter Bellwood adopted the basic definition of migration as "the permanent movement of all or part of a population to inhabit a new territory, separate from that in which it was previously based."[33] Bellwood's focus on "the large-scale *permanent* translocations of population that changed prehistory" (italics added) means that his analysis focuses wholly on *colonization*, which he defines as "migration into territories previously devoid of human inhabitants." He intentionally excludes the type of migrants who subsequently returned to home territory.

---

across Disciplines, ed. Caroline Brettell and James Frank Hollifield (New York: Routledge, 2000), 97–136; Lucassen, Lucassen, and Manning, "Migration History," 9–38.

29. Richmond, "Sociological Theories of International Migration," 14, 15; see also Lucassen, Lucassen, and Manning, "Migration History," 9–10.

30. Richmond, "Sociological Theories of International Migration," 17.

31. Thus, refugee movements "are only an extreme case of the constraints that are placed upon the choices available to an individual in particular circumstances" (Richmond, "Sociological Theories of International Migration," 14).

32. Richmond, "Sociological Theories of International Migration," 20.

33. Peter S. Bellwood, *First Migrants: Ancient Migration in Global Perspective* (Malden, MA: Wiley-Blackwell, 2013), 3.

This understanding of migration is much too restrictive for our purposes. The expense and travails of travel in the ancient world meant that many migrants (or types of migrants) only made a one-way trip; but many also "traveled back and forth across borders . . . and maintained transnational lives."[34]

Since this study is concerned with all major forms of human migration in history, the concept has to be framed as broadly as possible to allow consistent application across historical periods, yet not so broadly that analytical utility is compromised. As a case in point, the basic description of migration as "cross-border movement" is simply too generalized as an analytical category.[35] Dean Snow's definition—"the intentional long-term or permanent movement of human beings across space and over time"[36]—is more refined but equally open-ended, and the emphasis on "intentional" movement undermines its usefulness in my view. Far more compelling is historian Leslie Moch's definition of migration as *"a [short-term or permanent] change in residence beyond a communal boundary, be it a village or town."*[37]

The explanatory worth of this definition is evident in three areas. First, as Moch indicates, it is "designed to capture the full range of historical change." Second, by invoking the need for "residence," the definition attests to the need for some degree of social insertion for the migrant experience to have analytical significance; this requirement effectively rules out more transient forms of human mobility such as tourists and most pilgrims. Third, the basic prerequisite of the crossing of a communal boundary allows application to a wide range of geographical movement, ranging from rural-urban displacement to the wider regional and international migrations of the modern pe-

34. Michael C. Howard, *Transnationalism in Ancient and Medieval Societies: The Role of Cross-Border Trade and Travel* (Jefferson, NC: McFarland, 2012), 4.

35. For this definition, see Ian Goldin, Geoffrey Cameron, and Meera Balarajan, *Exceptional People: How Migration Shaped Our World and Will Define Our Future* (Princeton: Princeton University Press, 2011), 2.

36. Dean R. Snow, "The Multidisciplinary Study of Human Migration: Problems and Principles," in *Ancient Human Migrations: A Multidisciplinary Approach*, ed. Peter N. Peregrine, Ilia Peiros, and Marcus W. Feldman (Salt Lake City: University of Utah Press, 2009), 9.

37. Leslie Page Moch, "Dividing Time: An Analytical Framework for Migration History Periodization," in *Migration, Migration History, History: Old Paradigms and New Perspectives*, ed. Jan Lucassen, Leo Lucassen, and Patrick Manning (New York: Peter Lang, 1997), 43.

riod. It also captures the important fact that all human migration is framed by the existence of a social community, as the typology below confirms.

Types of Human Migration

Historians of migration generally identify four main types of human migration:[38] (a) home-community migration; (b) colonization; (c) whole-community migration; (d) cross-community migration. Each type is predicated on the existence of a community, which can be broadly defined as a group with a common language and a shared set of customs residing in a specific locality. A community can be of any size, though Manning suggests that a language community "must maintain a minimum size of several hundred speakers in order to survive over the long term."[39]

Home-community migration entails movement of people from one place to another within their own community. It is the most common type of migration, present in all human societies. The best-known example involves marriage and reproduction, when young men and women move from one family to start a family of their own. In societies with land-based economies, inheritance customs typically determined which members of the family must move; but female migrants were likely to dominate since (with the exception of matrilineal systems) male children normally inherit the land. Modern humans typically make several home-community migrations in the course of a lifetime, prompted by divorce, employment, upward mobility, or even higher education.

Colonization refers to the departure of individuals from one community to establish a new community modeled on the home community.[40]

---

38. Haywood, *Great Migrations*, 10–12; Manning, *Migration in World History*, 4–10. Cf. Christiane Harzig, Dirk Hoerder, and Donna R. Gabaccia, *What Is Migration History?* (Malden, MA: Polity, 2009), 10–11. Rather less compelling is Roger Sanjek's alternative classification, which breaks down human migration throughout history into a set of seven processes—namely, expansion, refuge-seeking, colonization, enforced transportation, trade diaspora, labor diaspora, and emigration ("Rethinking Migration, Ancient to Future," *Global Networks* 3, no. 3 [2003]: 315–36).

39. Manning, *Migration in World History*, 4.

40. It is helpful to note that "the original Greek meaning of a colony implied an outward migration from a mother city or metropolis to settle in a new place" (Philip D. Curtin, *The World and the West: The European Challenge and the Overseas Response in the Age of Empire* [New York: Cambridge University Press, 2000], 1).

Colonization-migration can take variable forms: movement into previously unoccupied territory (a process by which the various continents of the world were occupied), movement followed by the forcible expulsion of previous inhabitants in the new locality, or movement and settlement involving the total subjugation of the resident population. Colonization invariably reflects the dynamics of unequal power: the forcible domination or control of relatively weaker communities by groups with superior methods of production or more advanced (military) technology. In cases involving large-scale settlement, similarity of the physical environment in the new territory to that of the colonizers' home community is a key to success, since this allows the migrants to preserve or impose their way of life with minimal acclimatization or adaptation to an alien culture. In the initial stages, colonization efforts often involve small numbers of migrants (chiefly young adult males) followed by successful large-scale settlement of the migrant population. European colonization of the temperate regions in the Americas, South Africa, New Zealand, and Australia is a case in point.[41] Outside a few areas, European colonization efforts in tropical Africa and the islands of the Caribbean ended in failure due to high mortality and poor adaptability to tropical conditions and diseases.

Whole-community migration involves the movement or dislocation of all the members of a community. This form of migration was normal in prehistory—at least prior to the age of agriculture—when whole groups moved in search of more fertile land or in response to drastic ecological change. Migration of whole communities is far less common in human history. It occurs mainly among communities such as hunter-gatherers or nomadic pastoralists that are habitually mobile and need to migrate seasonally, literally taking their homes (animals, tents, and other belongings) with them, in search of new food sources or fresh pastures. This phenomenon is known as transhumance. Otherwise, human migration as whole communities is invariably associated with major catastrophes. These include escapement in the face of natural disasters such as famine or the forcible expulsion of an entire community from its place of habitation by powerful aggressors. The biblical story of the exodus is a well-known example of whole-community migration.

41. Though the genocidal impact on the indigenous population of the diseases imported by the European colonizers, combined with the high birth rates among the latter, also played a major role in this unparalleled saga of rampant colonization (Bellwood, *First Migrants*, 26–28).

Cross-community migration involves select individuals or groups, typically young adult males, leaving one community to join another community. Like home-community migration, this pattern of migration is prevalent in human history; indeed, it influences or intersects with the other types of human migration. Out-migration by some members of a community to join another community is a universal human experience. It is exceptionally rare in human history for any community to exist in complete isolation without experiencing either out-migration of at least some of its members (even if to escape punishment) or in-migration of members from other communities who seek short- or long-term settlement. Cross-community migration is occasioned by diverse factors and encompasses a wide spectrum in terms of distance and duration. It also takes a variety of forms, including trade diasporas, enslavement, exile, military service, missionary endeavor, or population transfers linked to imperial expansion (often reflected in the mass deportations of conquered peoples).

In all its multiplicity, cross-community migration plays a more prominent role in human development than any other form of migration. Intrinsic to its impact is the distinctively human trait of language communication or the "linguistic complexity" of human interactions.[42] Among other things, migrating humans introduce new languages and practices, as well as new ideas and technologies, when they settle in other communities. Cross-community migration is the main reason why migration is "one of the great driving forces of world history."[43] It is the dominant type of migration reflected in this study.

Migrant Categories

With the obvious exception of whole-community migration, migrants are typically a small fraction of their community. In fact, migrants "have always been a minority of the human race."[44] Yet, the multiplicity and ceaselessness of human migration in history mean that no typology of migrants is ever

42. Bellwood, *First Migrants*, 57. Cross-community migration is rare among other species of mammals because lack of language differentiation means that other animals (such as wolves, whales, or elephants) "encounter almost exactly the same society when they migrate from one community to another," which means that "their migrations bring few benefits and, indeed, few results at all" (Manning, *Migration in World History*, 6); see also Christian, *Maps of Time*, 145–48.

43. Haywood, *Great Migrations*, 8.

44. Haywood, *Great Migrations*, 6.

conclusive. To start with, the diversification in forms of human mobility over time, exceptionally so in recent decades, has cumulatively increased the varieties of migrants. Moreover, migration is embedded in social processes marked by considerable flux and dynamism. In reality, the distinction between migrant and nonmigrant can be blurred and the boundaries that distinguish different kinds of migrants are often permeable. For that matter, legal frameworks notwithstanding, the status of "foreigner" or "outsider" is locally determined and therefore subject to norms and attitudes that not only vary from one context to another but can also shift over time within the same society. In some instances, the migrant status is indiscriminately applied to entire groups of people (such as "ethnic minorities" in the modern context) or equated with prominent social categories such as religious affiliation.[45] When this happens, the "foreigner" or "immigrant" label has less to do with the act of (im)migration than with predetermined notions of outsider within the majority population.

But perhaps the greatest challenge to mapping kinds of migrants is terminological. Contemporary English words like "immigrant" or "resident alien" embody a semantic range or have application that is not always matched in the written languages or records of the ancient world. David Noy notes, for instance, that Latin lacks a term that matches the full range of meaning associated with the word "foreigner" in English.[46] A variety of terms—including *peregrinus/a* ("someone who was free but not a Roman citizen"),[47] *provincialis* (applied to inhabitants of provinces outside Italy), and *alienigenus/a* (someone born elsewhere, i.e., an alien)—were commonly used. Latin also has no comparable word for "immigrant"; and Romans did not distinguish between temporary and permanent residents. In Hebrew, different terms, with

45. In some modern European countries, for instance, members of the Muslim population are persistently branded as "immigrants" or "foreigners" even though, after half a century of immigration, these communities now span at least two to three generations. Some estimate that by 2005 about 50 percent were European-born nationals. See David Masci, "An Uncertain Road: Muslims and the Future of Europe" (The Pew Research Center, October 19, 2005), 11.

46. David Noy, *Foreigners at Rome: Citizens and Strangers* (London: Duckworth, 2000), 1–3.

47. Noy intimates, however, that by the fourth century *peregrinus* came to be applied more broadly to "'foreigners' who were periodically expelled from Rome" (*Foreigners at Rome*, 1).

some overlap of meaning, are used to represent the "foreigner," "stranger," and "sojourner"—with corresponding Greek translations. Some scholars allow, however, that the Hebrew word *gēr* (plural, *gērîm*), meaning "stranger," is a general term that incorporates other categories of migrant—including the resident alien, foreigner, seasonal laborer, and sojourner.[48] Similarly, the Greek word *paroikos* (meaning "one who does not belong," or "the other") is believed by some to cover every category of migrant: the stranger, the alien, the foreigner, the sojourner, the displaced or uprooted person, even the legally classified resident alien.[49]

Given these complexities, the best approach requires an analytical framework that utilizes broad categories to denote the most significant differences between types of migrants (individuals or groups). Cross-community migration has been the most significant and consequential form of migration in human history, "the basic pattern underlying most major movements of humanity."[50] It therefore fully embodies the complex dimensions of the phenomenon and affords the best basis for identifying categories of migrants. Manning proposes four main categories of migrants in connection with cross-community migration: (1) *settlers* who "move to join an existing community that is different from their own, with the intention of becoming permanent residents"; (2) *sojourners* who "join a new community, usually for a specific purpose, with the intention of returning to their home community"; (3) *itinerants* who move from community to community and have no single home to which they expect to return; and (4) *invaders* who arrive as a group in a community with the objective of seizing control rather than joining.[51]

Manning's categories are useful; but his descriptions impute a high level of volition and clear intention on the part of migrants. This reduces migration to rational proactive choice and ignores the role that wider forces or structural

48. See Bernhard A. Asen, "From Acceptance to Exclusion: The Stranger in Old Testament Tradition," in *Christianity and the Stranger*, ed. Francis W. Nichols (Atlanta: Scholars Press, 1995), 19.

49. For a helpful treatment, see John Hall Elliott, *A Home for the Homeless: A Social-Scientific Exegesis of 1 Peter, Its Situation and Strategy* (Eugene, OR: Wipf & Stock, 2005), 24–26.

50. Manning, *Migration in World History*, 105.

51. Manning, *Migration in World History*, 8–9. Manning distinguishes between "settlers" (migrants whose intent is simply to join a different community) and "colonists" (migrants who occupy new territory on behalf of their home community).

constraints often play in migrant movements (see "Definitions and Typologies" above). In order to conform to the conception of migration that frames this study—namely, as a phenomenon *subject to constant change, marked by varying degrees of compulsion (or freedom), and shaped by wider structures and historical processes*—I have taken the liberty of making modest revisions to Manning's descriptions while retaining his categories. My revisions are italicized, and possible kinds of migrants are given in parentheses:

(1) **Settlers** move to join an existing community that is different from their own *and become permanent residents.*
(captives, slaves, diasporas, refugees)

(2) **Sojourners** become part of a new community, usually for a specific purpose *and for a limited duration, after which they usually return to their home community.*
(seasonal laborers, merchants, diplomats, exiles or deportees, refugees, asylum seekers)

(3) **Itinerants** move from community to community and have no single *place they regard as permanent residence.*
(nomadic tribes or transhumance, wandering monks)

(4) **Invaders** arrive as a group in a community with the objective of seizing control *or displacing the inhabitants* rather than joining them.
(colonizers, invading armies)

Such are the complexities of migration that these distinctions often break down in reality: sojourners such as exiles sometimes become settlers; settler-migrants may increase in number and displace (or absorb) the original population, and even become colonizers. At the same time, some types of migrants are prominent in certain domains. Prior to the sixteenth century, the period covered in this study, when the categories and numbers of migrants began to multiply in unprecedented fashion, certain types of migrants featured more recurrently than any other in connection with *religious expansion*—namely, captives or slaves, government administrators or agents, the military, merchants, and religious specialists or devotees.[52] These deserve brief comment here, since they feature prominently in my assessment.

52. John Foster makes the case that "sailors" were influential in the spread of the gospel. But while sailors might be considered a category of migrant, data about their activities and numbers are lacking. See John Foster, "The Sailor's Share in the Spread of the Gospel," *Expository Times* 70, no. 4 (1959): 110–13.

Captives/slaves: The creation of empires and the emergence of successive world orders, not to mention inevitable conflict between rival groups or societies, made large-scale violence a pervasive reality in human history. Until more recent times, captivity and enslavement were prominent features of human societies. Recurrent warfare, widespread insecurity, and the heavy reliance on human labor rendered servitude a common condition. In ancient societies, notably within major empires, the slave population was massive.[53] Some were born slaves, others made so (including free individuals who sold themselves into slavery, often temporarily, to pay off debts). But the supply and size of the slave population was mostly a product of conquest and capture. The trade in slaves was also hugely lucrative; the seizure of as many captives as possible, along with immense booty, was a primary objective of marauding raiders and pirates. Of necessity, most of the slaves in major cities were foreign and mostly casualties of imperial expansion.[54] Put differently, a substantial proportion of the immigrant population in ancient societies consisted of slaves, former slaves, or descendants of slaves.[55] Until the early nineteenth century, at least, slaves or captives remained the most prominent category of migrants.

Government administrators/agents: As far back as 3000 BCE, government agents were the most frequent travelers, and they remained a prominent category of cross-cultural migrant well into the fifteenth century. In the ancient world, where overland travel was often hazardous, expensive, and dangerous, government officials and their entourages (and military escorts) dominated long-distance travel. The demands of administering large political realms,

---

53. For a comprehensive overview, see J. P. V. D. Balsdon, *Romans and Aliens* (Chapel Hill: University of North Carolina Press, 1979), 77–113; also Richard L. Smith, *Premodern Trade in World History* (New York: Routledge, 2008), 79, 80–81. Smith notes, for instance, that slave dealers followed in the wake of the Roman army when it embarked on the conquest of Gaul, a region whose most important export was slaves.

54. Naturally, the creation of empire guaranteed a sizeable and growing slave population. "During four centuries of wars of expansion," notes George La Piana, "the victorious armies brought to Rome thousands of captives of all races from all the conquered lands" ("The Roman Church at the End of the Second Century: The Episcopate of Victor, the Latinization of the Roman Church, the Easter Controversy, Consolidation of Power and Doctrinal Development, the Catacomb of Callistus," *Harvard Theological Review* 18, no. 3 (1925): 189. See also Smith, *Premodern Trade in World History*, 80–81.

55. La Piana, "The Roman Church at the End of the Second Century," 188–91.

not to mention the complexities of diplomatic relations with foreign powers, meant that from the earliest civilizations to the age of empires, tremendous efforts and resources were devoted to facilitating the movement of government officials over land and sea.[56] The extensive road networks of the Assyrian, Persian, and Roman Empires were primarily built to serve administrative needs, to facilitate rapid communication and military movement.[57] The "royal road" built by the Persians, primarily to serve government couriers, was 1,600 miles long. Much later, government officials were prominent agents in the establishment and administration of overseas empires. Throughout the ages, by virtue of their central role in the internal management and external relations of political states, government agents interacted with a greater variety of cultures and peoples than virtually any other category of migrant (except possibly merchants). Regardless of whether they formed part of an official effort to propagate a particular religion, or whether their encounter with foreign cultures was sporadic or limited, government representatives often functioned as agents of religious expansion or exchange.

The Military: Soldiers were often required to travel great distances and settle in distant places either in the service of a government or as mercenaries. As was the case with government agents or administrators, militaries were the primary beneficiaries of investments in transportation infrastructure and, all the way down to the present era, military needs often determined or influenced major advancements in travel technology—from the chariot to ships and airplanes. In the context of empires or major states, regular deployment to protect borders, "pacify" unruly subjects, or safeguard long-distance trade at frontiers made soldiers more mobile than most sectors of society. In societies where religion was fused with political structures and cultural identity, the military functioned as a powerful emblem of religious allegiance or patriotism. Needless to add, military action was necessary for forcible conversions associated with empire building or efforts to enforce state religion.

Merchants: Undoubtedly merchants were the most mobile segment of the ordinary populace in preindustrial societies. In the ancient world, notes Lionel Casson, "traders, journeying regularly year in and year out . . . made up the

---

56. See Lionel Casson, *Travel in the Ancient World* (Baltimore: Johns Hopkins University Press, 1994), 28–29, 35–43, 50–54.

57. Casson, *Travel in the Ancient World*, 50–54.

biggest number [of travelers] both on land and water."[58] That said, in agrarian societies where the vast majority of people worked the land, merchant specialists were a small minority.[59] The merchant profession was also derided in some cultures, in part because it was associated with greed and dishonesty. Thus, the combined status of foreigner and trader meant that merchants engaged in cross-cultural trade were liable to be viewed with extra suspicion or suffer from double opprobrium.[60] Regardless, specialist merchants were motivated to travel further than anyone else and found ways to maintain cultural traditions in distant lands. A multitude of merchants immersed in ever-expanding networks of international trade or associated with trade diasporas were vital to the globalization of major faiths, most conspicuously so in the case of Islam and Buddhism. It is no coincidence, attests Richard Foltz, "that throughout history ideas and technologies have spread along trade routes, and that merchants have been among their prime transmitters."[61] Perhaps more so in previous eras than now, trade and religion were tightly interlaced (see chapter 8).

Religious specialists/devotees: These encompass a wide range of actors, including monks, missionaries, scholars, clerics, nuns, and holy men and women. In this study I contend that all migrants are potential missionaries. But for certain groups of migrants the willingness to confront the dangers and privations of long-distance travel was rooted in religious devotion or purpose. Religion, as Nayan Chanda affirms, continually inspired individuals "to set out for long journeys that reinforced [intercultural] connections."[62] In the ancient world, massive throngs of religious devotees and pilgrims who set out on pilgrimages to visit shrines or celebrate religious festivals outnumbered all other groups of migrant travelers at certain times of the year.[63] With the emergence of the major religions (Christianity, Islam, and Buddhism), the numbers of pilgrims multiplied; and religious practitioners (monks, scholars, specialist missionaries, and holy men and women) now joined the world of long-distance travelers

58. Casson, *Travel in the Ancient World*, 76.

59. Philip D. Curtin, *Cross-Cultural Trade in World History* (New York: Cambridge University Press, 1984), 5.

60. Curtin, *Cross-Cultural Trade in World History*, 6.

61. Foltz, *Religions of the Silk Road*, 8.

62. Chanda, *Bound Together*, 158.

63. See Casson, *Travel in the Ancient World*, 31, 76–85. Like other groups of migrants, those who were so minded had ample opportunities to sample the local culture and its diversions.

and numbered among the most indefatigable migrants. Specialist missionaries dominated in Christianity, but by the tenth century CE, Islamic Sufi masters and Buddhist monks were also energetic foreign missionaries.[64] The dedicated zeal of millions of these religious specialists who traversed great distances to convert others (through preaching, personal charisma, performance of miracles, acts of charity, etc.) were indispensable elements in the sustained cross-cultural engagement required for new ideas and practices to penetrate new communities.

In truth, these four categories (government officials, military, merchants, and religious specialists) often overlap or blur into one another. Government agents may form part of the military complex; merchants were often missionaries (and vice versa);[65] merchants also served on many an occasion as government officials;[66] and it was not uncommon for monks to participate in military action or for soldiers to be pressed into "missionary" service.

The Costs of Migration

The understanding that migration has played a crucial role in human development since earliest times should not obscure the fact that migration or the act of migrating is also attended by significant costs—regardless of the degree of choice or individual freedom involved.[67] In most cases the community of origin experiences deprivation to some extent, since the migrants take with them not only their knowledge and skills but also their emotions, inventiveness, and spirituality. The trauma of displacement and the perils of travel (including hunger, adverse weather, disease, armed conflict, piracy, and pillage) expose migrants to risks of dying that are often greater than those faced by the community they left behind. Moreover, those who survive the journey must contend with social marginalization or loss of status, economic vulnerability, and

---

64. Foltz, *Religions of the Silk Road*, 12.

65. So integral was commercial activity to the mission of the Syrian Church (centered in the Sassanid or Sassanian Empire) that, among Syrian Christians, the word "merchant" became a metaphor for "missionary."

66. In ancient Sumer, records Richard Smith, the words for "envoy" and "merchant" were used interchangeably (*Premodern Trade in World History*, 28).

67. See Manning, *Migration in World History*, 8, 93, 109; Harzig, Hoerder, and Gabaccia, *What Is Migration History?*, 11; Stephen S. Gosch and Peter N. Stearns, *Premodern Travel in World History* (New York: Routledge, 2008), 4.

the long process of inculturation (acquiring a new language, new customs, and a new diet) in the destination society. Inevitably the migrants' own cultural heritage changes in some way as part of this intercultural dynamic. Under the impact of large-scale migration, entire languages or dialects (especially if unwritten) and traditions could disappear over time through innovation, expansion, or hybridization.[68]

Human migration inevitably contributes to the spread of deadly diseases. Historically, as the scale and scope of migration increased, extending the range and extent of human contact, the transfer of microbes into new human environments triggered disease epidemics and widespread death. The fourteenth-century Black Plague, which ravaged populations in China, India, Persia, Syria, and Egypt and killed a third of the population in Europe, is a notable example; the transfer of the highly infectious smallpox to the Americas in the sixteenth century by European migrant colonizers is another. In the latter case, it is estimated that some 6 million of the indigenous population in North America fell victim to the disease. All told, the proportion of the entire population in the Americas that succumbed to European imported products, practices, and diseases ranged between 50 and 99 percent.[69]

Cultural encounters can also be destructive in more insidious ways. In human history, cultural difference has frequently been a root cause of friction, conflict, and confrontation between the world's tribes, peoples, and civilizations. Perceptions of the "other" (cultural, ethnic, or racial) are seldom free from ethnocentric prejudice. Writing in the fifth century BCE, for instance, the Greek historian Herodotus (ca. 484–425 BCE) observed of the Persians: "Themselves they consider in every way superior to everyone else in the world, and allow other nations a share of good qualities decreasing according to distance, the furthest off being in their view the worst."[70] Such ethnocentrism was quite common and

68. Bellwood, *First Migrants*, 23–24, 27–29. Bellwood contends that because "people do not give up native vernaculars lightly," substantial immigration—rather than the simple act of colonial conquest—is usually necessary for a foreign language to take hold in a territory. Even then, the new language tends to become part of a multilingual mix.

69. See H. McKennie Goodpasture, *Cross and Sword: An Eyewitness History of Christianity in Latin America* (Maryknoll, NY: Orbis Books, 1989), 14; also Bellwood, *First Migrants*, 27.

70. Herodotus, *The Histories*, trans. Aubrey De Sélincourt (Baltimore: Penguin Books, 1954), Book I, pp. 69–70.

unabashedly strengthened by political or economic supremacy. The use of the term "barbarian" (or variants thereof) to describe other tribes or nations deemed backward in comparison to a particular urban civilization attests to this fact.

With this in mind, it is hardly surprising that migrant encounters with unfamiliar cultures invariably trigger instinctive judgment of the "other" as strange or bizarre. Over time, global migrations brought into contact peoples with radically different physical appearances and modes of cultural existence. These encounters intensified notions of "otherness" beyond the common depiction of outsiders as backward or strange. Entire societies or categories of people were deemed by other migrant groups encountering them for the first time as not only "weird" but also inherently inferior, even subhuman. This was the case among Europeans, whose deep contempt for non-European cultures and peoples contributed to colonial aggression and fertilized the soil that produced modern racism. But we are getting ahead of the story.

ANCIENT EMPIRES AND MIGRANT MOVEMENT

The known world of the biblical writers, which centered on Egypt and the Fertile Crescent, was marked by a significant range of travel and cultural exchange. A brief overview of the interplay between empire building, expanding trade networks, and migrant movement is in order. By 2300 BCE, there is evidence of trade between Mesopotamia and the Indus Valley (western Pakistan), regions separated by well over 1,000 miles by land or sea.[71] Around 2300–2200 BCE, Harkuf, an Egyptian official (and the first long-distance traveler known by name), conducted three trade missions as far south as Darfur in modern Sudan, a distance in excess of 900 miles.[72] Merchants from other lands occa-

---

71. Gosch and Stearns, *Premodern Travel in World History*, 12–13; Smith, *Premodern Trade in World History*, 26–28; Howard, *Transnationalism in Ancient and Medieval Societies*, 30–33. Under the Akkadian king Sargon (d. 2215 BCE), writes Smith, "Mesopotamia was the hub of a system that stretched from India and Central Asia on one side to northeast Africa and the borderlands of Europe on the other" (*Premodern Trade in World History*, 28). Casson adds that "cargo laden sailing vessels navigated the waterways of the Mediterranean region, the Persian Gulf, and Indian Ocean"; and "from the second half of the third millennium ships made their way down the Arabian Gulf to Saudi Arabia and along the coasts of Iran and Pakistan as far as the northwest coast of India" (*Travel in the Ancient World*, 21, 30).

72. Casson, *Travel in the Ancient World*, 28–29; Gosch and Stearns, *Premodern Travel in World History*, 14–15.

sionally made it to the Nile Valley; trade caravans became a common sight in Mesopotamia; and, early in the second millennium BCE, flourishing trade developed between Assur (the Assyrian capital in northern Mesopotamia) and Kanesh, a flourishing city-state in Anatolia 600 miles away.[73]

The centuries immediately preceding the biblical patriarchal age (linked to the early twentieth century BCE) witnessed major political upheaval and instability caused by the collapse of the Akkadian Empire (under the Third Dynasty of Ur), the dissolution of the Old Kingdom in Egypt, and the disintegration of major urban centers in Palestine. By the time of the patriarchs, however, the period of anarchy and disintegration had given way to political and economic revival. Long-distance trade resumed, independent city-states (notably Assyria, Mari, and Babylon) emerged in Mesopotamia, and urban life flourished in Palestine and Syria. It was possible for individual travelers or groups to move around freely. The *Tale of Sinuhe* (ca. 1920 BCE), for instance, relates the adventures of a high-ranking Egyptian official who fled Egypt, traveled eastward as far as Byblos and Qedem (east of the Jordan) to put himself beyond the pharaoh's reach, and found refuge with a group of Semitic pastoralists returning to Canaan.

Over the centuries, the rise of successive empires, invariably attended by considerable violence, generated recurrent upheavals and displacements of peoples. Many imperial projects were short-lived, such as the powerful Hittite Empire in Anatolia (1340–1200 BCE) or the rise of Babylon, as a regional power, under the Amorite ruler Hammurabi (reigned ca. 1792–1750 BCE). Even the neo-Babylonian Empire, which reached a height of economic and cultural dominance under Nebuchadnezzar II (r. 604–562 BCE), only lasted about eighty years (ca. 626–539 BCE). Many others—like the small and relatively obscure Kingdom of Israel, under the united monarchy (1020–931 BCE)—barely made an impact on the wider region.

Occasionally, large-scale migration was the cause rather than the consequence of political turbulence. This was the case with the "Sea Peoples," a loose confederation of tribal groups whose fleets "wreaked havoc along the eastern Mediterranean seaboard as they searched for new lands to settle."[74] From ca. 1200 BCE, these invaders produced widespread ruin and devastation

73. Gosch and Stearns, *Premodern Travel in World History*, 13.
74. Haywood, *Great Migrations: From the Earliest Humans to the Age of Globalization*, 38; see also, Casson, *Travel in the Ancient World*, 44.

in many cities (including Syria and Canaan), wrecked the Hittite domains, and caused widespread terror through numerous pirate raids. Their invasion of Egypt met with resounding defeat but left the Egyptian power weakened. Thereafter, large remnants of the Sea Peoples settled in Egypt and Canaan; others took advantage of declining Egyptian control from the late 1100s to "set up independent city-states at Ashdod, Ashkelon, Ekron, Gaza, and Gath."[75] In Canaan, their expansion efforts were blocked by the emerging Israelite kingdom, and they became the Israelites' most formidable foes. Readers of the Hebrew Bible know them as the Philistines.

PHOENICIANS, ASSYRIANS, AND PERSIANS

Empire building greatly expanded the reach of trade networks, revolutionized long-distance travel, and ushered in a new era of international exchange in which the nation of Israel fully participated. From ca. 1100 to 700 BCE, Phoenicia, a nation of traders and extraordinary seafarers, monopolized the Mediterranean and contributed more to the expansion of trade and travel than any other nation.[76] By 1000 BCE the Phoenicians had established a network of far-flung trading colonies that stretched from their homelands along the coasts of modern Lebanon and Syria throughout the Mediterranean to western Europe (the limits of the "known world") and the Moroccan coast. Phoenician merchants dominated the trade in both finished goods and raw materials and met the "booming demand in the fast-growing Assyrian Empire for iron, copper, tin and exotic products."[77] Around the mid-900s BCE, Hiram of Tyre, the most famous of the Phoenician kings, supplied the Israelite King Solomon (r. 971–931) with timber and craftsmen for his building projects (1 Kings 5). Most famous for their seafaring prowess, Phoenician ships reportedly completed the amazing feat of circumnavigating Africa (clockwise) by 600 BCE. The voyage lasted three years.

The lucrative Phoenician trade colonies were conquered and absorbed by the bellicose Assyrian power (in 734 BCE). Emerging out of the chaos and turmoil generated by the invasions of the Sea Peoples, the Assyrian Empire

75. Haywood, *Great Migrations*, 41.
76. Casson, *Travel in the Ancient World*, 45–46; Haywood, *Great Migrations*, 42–43; Gosch and Stearns, *Premodern Travel in World History*, 22–23.
77. Gosch and Stearns, *Premodern Travel in World History*, 22.

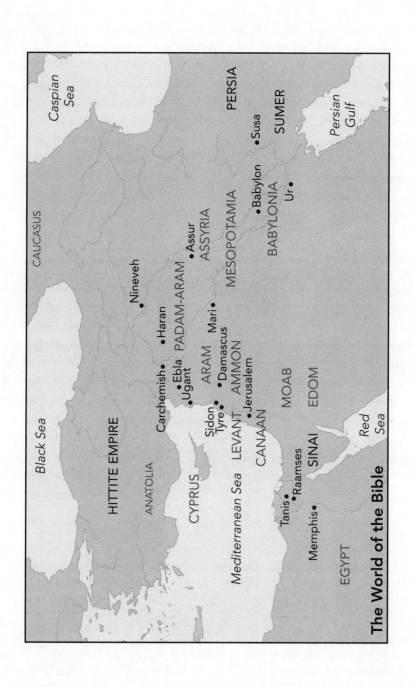

The World of the Bible

Caspian Sea

Black Sea

CAUCASUS

Mediterranean Sea

CYPRUS

ANATOLIA

HITTITE EMPIRE

Nineveh

Carchemish

Haran

PADAM-ARAM

Ebla

Ugarit

ARAM

Mari

Assur

ASSYRIA

MESOPOTAMIA

BABYLONIA

Babylon

Ur

SUMER

Susa

PERSIA

Persian Gulf

Sidon

Tyre

Damascus

AMMON

Jerusalem

LEVANT

CANAAN

MOAB

EDOM

Raamses

Tanis

Memphis

SINAI

Red Sea

EGYPT

(which lasted from the 1100s to early 600s BCE) was "the greatest empire the Near East had ever seen."[78] The rulers of this immense multiethnic empire embarked on extensive road building to aid rapid communication between its vast territories and facilitate the movement of the fearsome Assyrian army, especially its chariots. The massive road network incorporated road signs, guard posts at regular intervals, and permanent stone bridges. These and other construction projects were financed by extensive trade, tributes, and pillage.

The formidable Assyrian military was the mainstay of the empire; but administrative leadership mattered. In the eighth century BCE, the Assyrian ruler Tiglath-Pileser III (r. 745–727 BCE[79]) implemented the practice whereby conquered populations were deported to different regions within the Assyrian Empire in an effort to weaken ethnic identity and communal unity.[80] Foreign peoples, including Assyrians, were also introduced into captured provinces. This practice of population transfer produced changes in the ethnic configuration of the region and led to "the blending of two of its larger ethnic groups, the Akkadians and Amorites."[81] Under Tiglath-Pileser and his successor Shalmaneser V, the northern Kingdom of Israel (identified in Assyrian records as "The House of Omri") was subjugated and finally conquered (in 722 BCE). The Israelite population was deported to Assyria, in two major waves (2 Kings 15:29–31; 17:3–4), and resettled throughout the vast empire (2 Kings 17:6). Israel along with its capital Samaria became an Assyrian province repopulated by Assyrians. The dispersed Israelite tribes disappeared from history; but the Assyrian inhabitants of Samaria subsequently adopted the Jewish religion and became known as the Samaritans.

Assyrian power was crushed by the Medes, who united with the new Persian invaders (under Cyrus II, r. 559–530 BCE[82]) to form the largest empire

---

78. Casson, *Travel in the Ancient World*, 44; also Howard, *Transnationalism in Ancient and Medieval Societies*, 35–37.

79. Tiglath-Pileser III is also known as Pul or Pulu (see 2 Kings 15:19).

80. Howard, *Transnationalism in Ancient and Medieval Societies*, 36; also Iain W. Provan, V. Philips Long, and Tremper Longman, *A Biblical History of Israel* (Louisville: Westminster John Knox, 2003), 270–71, 377n80. It is estimated that in the three centuries this policy was in force, Assyrians deported a total of 4.5 million people—see Daniel L. Smith, *The Religion of the Landless: The Social Context of the Babylonian Exile* (Bloomington, IN: Meyer-Stone Books, 1989), 29.

81. Howard, *Transnationalism in Ancient and Medieval Societies*, 36.

82. Cyrus II, or Cyrus the Great, "was of joint Parsu and Mede ancestry" (Howard, *Transnationalism in Ancient and Medieval Societies*, 39).

in the world to that time (lasting 550 to 330 BCE), comprising some 40 million peoples of diverse nationalities.[83] With the rise of the ancient Persian Empire "all of the Near East was in the hands of a single well-organized and powerful state" for the first time in history.[84] The Persian rulers expanded the Assyrian road networks and government posts and created a governmental courier service of unprecedented speed and efficiency. The 1,677-mile "royal road" (from Susa to Sardis) included rest houses and inns for officials at regular intervals of 10 to 15 miles, as well as forts and ferries.[85] Mail couriers could cover the entire distance in about a week, while ordinary travelers who could only average about 18 miles a day took ninety days to traverse the entire distance. The Persian investment in transportation and communications infrastructure facilitated travel throughout the Middle East. It is estimated that the empire's extensive road network totaled about 8,000 miles. The Persian rulers even built roads "across parts of Afghanistan to improve communication with India."[86]

MODES OF TRAVEL AND THE LIMITS OF MIGRATION

These developments, however, must be put in perspective. Well beyond 500 BCE, even during the age of the Persian Empire, long-distance travel was slow, laborious, expensive, and dangerous for most. The main categories of regular migrants remained government envoys, merchants, soldiers, nomadic pastoralists, and religious pilgrims. Government posts or hostels appear in Mesopotamia by 1500 BCE; and inns, generally run by women, became increasingly common.[87] But in many parts of the ancient world ordinary travelers "had to

83. At its greatest extent, "the empire included portions of Afghanistan and Pakistan (e.g., the Punjab) to the east; adjacent areas of Central Asia to the north; Iraq, Turkey, Bulgaria, parts of Greece, Armenia, and the Caucasus to the west; Syria, Lebanon, Jordan, Israel, northern Saudi Arabia, much of Egypt, and as far as Libya to the southwest" (Howard, *Transnationalism in Ancient and Medieval Societies*, 39.

84. Casson, *Travel in the Ancient World*, 56.

85. Casson, *Travel in the Ancient World*, 53; Howard, *Transnationalism in Ancient and Medieval Societies*, 40–41.

86. Howard, *Transnationalism in Ancient and Medieval Societies*, 40.

87. David A. Dorsey, *The Roads and Highways of Ancient Israel*, The Asor Library of Biblical and Near Eastern Archaeology (Baltimore: Johns Hopkins University Press, 1991), 43–47.

depend on haphazard private hospitality and trust to luck they would escape being molested."[88] Dependence on private hospitality remained widespread even when inns proliferated to meet the needs of increased movement.[89] Partly due to these hazards, the quickest way to travel was by sea;[90] but this option was mainly the preserve of merchants. For ordinary travelers the only options were wagons, carts, donkeys, horses, or camels. During their wilderness sojourn, for instance, the Israelites were able to provide six wagons and twelve oxen for the transportation of the dismantled tabernacle (Num. 7:3–8).

If the volume and scope of travel increased over time, this was due less to the availability of new forms of conveyance than to improvements in infrastructure. Like the donkey, the dromedary (single-humped) camel was known in the ancient Near East as early as 3000 BCE; but its use (for transportation over long distances and riding) was mainly confined to nomadic peoples inhabiting desert and arid regions outside urban civilizations (see Judg. 6:5; 7:12). However, its capability as a beast of burden—"perhaps five times the capacity of the donkey"[91]—saw increased usage. The queen of Sheba is depicted "arriving at Jerusalem with a very great caravan; including camels carrying spices, large quantities of gold, and precious stones" (1 Kings 10:2, NIV). Under the Persians, "the cross-desert caravan" using camels became a key feature of Near Eastern trade. But "by far the most common means of transport was the donkey";[92] there are numerous references to its use for transportation (of

88. Casson, *Travel in the Ancient World*, 49. In the book of Judges (chapter 19), the Ephraimite Levite traveler who stopped over at the Benjamite town of Gibeah for the night (with his concubine, a young servant, two donkeys, and self-sufficient provisions) was forced to camp in the town square because "no one had taken me in for the night." The old man who eventually offered him hospitality was a foreigner (also from Ephraim). The story ends horrifically when a band of lawless men descended on the house with vile threats, and the Levite's concubine was handed over to them to sexually abuse. The fact that the narrator notes that this happened at a time when "Israel had no king" does little to ameliorate the ghastly event; but it hints at the fact that the establishment of strong government authority provided a level of safety that bolstered travel.

89. Casson, *Travel in the Ancient World*, 87.

90. Casson, *Travel in the Ancient World*, 45; also Maribel Dietz, *Wandering Monks, Virgins, and Pilgrims: Ascetic Travel in the Mediterranean World, A.D. 300/800* (University Park: Pennsylvania State University Press, 2005), 13–14.

91. Dorsey, *Roads and Highways of Ancient Israel*, 15.

92. Dorsey, *Roads and Highways of Ancient Israel*, 13.

goods and persons) in the Old Testament. The availability of various pack animals for conveyance is illustrated in the report that Israelites "from as far away as Issachar, Zebulun and Naphtali came [to David] bringing food on donkeys, camels, mules and oxen" (1 Chron. 12:40).

Horses were also draft animals. But once the horse-drawn chariot came into use around 1600 BCE, horses were used almost exclusively for warfare.[93] Horseback riding spread from the nomads of the steppe lands and was adopted by the Assyrians for military purposes in the early ninth century BCE. But horses were "expensive to buy and maintain" and beyond the reach of all but the very wealthy.[94] For the most part "kings and princes rode mules."[95] Chariots were implements of war, though members of the ruling class occasionally used them for personal travel (as did Absalom, 2 Sam. 15:1).[96] Wagons and carts were also used extensively in the ancient Near East. But only the reasonably well-off could afford wagons and the servants to go with them. Carts (pulled by cows or oxen) are widely referenced in the Old Testament and notably feature in efforts to transport the "ark of the covenant" (1 Sam. 6:7–14; 2 Sam. 6:3).[97] Significantly, Isaiah prophesied that the Jewish exiles

93. Casson, *Travel in the Ancient World*, 51; Manning, *Migration in World History*, 82–83.

94. Casson, *Travel in the Ancient World*, 52; see also Dorsey, *Roads and Highways of Ancient Israel*, 7. The earliest references to horseback riding in the Old Testament appear in the wake of the divided kingdom, i.e., after 930 BCE (see 1 Kings 20:20 and 2 Kings 7:13–16). Incidentally, horseback riding did not become widespread until the Middle Ages (Casson, *Travel in the Ancient World*, 52, 181).

95. The first reference to mules in the Old Testament dates to the time of David; and Dorsey speculates that it was "used primarily by royalty, at least at first" (*Roads and Highways of Ancient Israel*, 7).

96. Casson, *Travel in the Ancient World*, 49; Dorsey, *Roads and Highways of Ancient Israel*, 9–12. Chariots remained the dominant military weapon throughout the Near East. Dorsey notes that they "fill[ed] the scenes of warfare in Mesopotamia, Syria, Anatolia, and Egypt," and that "kings, whether Egyptian, Assyrian, Hittite, Mitannian, or other, rode out to battle or set out on campaigns in their royal chariots, accompanied by armies containing all-important chariot units" (*Roads and Highways of Ancient Israel*, 9). They feature prominently in the Hebrew Bible and became a dominant element in the Israelite army from the time of David. Solomon maintained a chariotry of 1,400 and even sold surplus chariots to the kings of Syria and the Hittites (1 Kings 10:28–29).

97. Dorsey explains that the reference in 2 Sam. 6:6 is probably to a two-wheeled cart, since the stumbling of the oxen threatens to overturn the ark (*Roads and Highways of Ancient Israel*, 16).

would return from all the nations "on horses, in chariots and wagons, and on mules and camels" (Isa. 66:20). But few traveled in such style. Even the commonplace donkey "was used as a riding animal most often by women and children or by men who were old . . . or infirm."[98] With the exception of high government officials or dignitaries, men traveled *on foot*.

By standards of the modern world, travel was tremendously time consuming. Each of Harkuf's trips (from Egypt to Nubia) lasted between seven and eight months; and the trip from Assur to Kanesh, which involved caravans of two hundred or so donkeys, took at least a month. Due to the limited road network and challenging terrain, wheeled traffic had "an average speed of 2½ to 3½ miles per hour."[99] Government officials and couriers, who had access to regular posting stations with fresh horses and riders, traveled the fastest. As noted above, Persian messengers could traverse the 1,677-mile "royal road" in seven days or so, averaging over 230 miles a day! But ordinary travelers in a chariot or carriage could only expect to cover 25–30 miles in a single day—or up to 45 miles when pressed.[100] Even with heavy loads of up to 500–1,000 lb. (227–454 kg), camels averaged 25 miles (or up to 60 miles if forced to) in a day, but they were mainly used for trade. Depending on the terrain and road conditions, "a typical day's journey by foot was probably 20 miles."[101]

So, well into the first millennium CE, travel by sea afforded the quickest and least strenuous means of long-distance travel, though it had considerable dangers.[102] The quality of roads and road networks gradually improved and, at least within the compass of major empires, road usage increased and became well-nigh indispensable. As early as the fourth century BCE, Alexander's army traveled great distances (using mules, horses, and camels), and perhaps covered a total of 20,000 miles.[103] But increased range was not matched by better

---

98. Dorsey, *Roads and Highways of Ancient Israel*, 7.

99. Casson, *Travel in the Ancient World*, 26.

100. Dorsey, *Roads and Highways of Ancient Israel*, 13.

101. Dorsey, *Roads and Highways of Ancient Israel*, 13.

102. See Casson, *Travel in the Ancient World*, 45, 66–76. "The traveler in Greece of the fifth and the fourth century BC," writes Casson, "thought twice before taking along any vehicle, light or heavy, since roads that could handle wheeled traffic were by no means to be found everywhere" (Casson, 68). But sea voyages exposed travelers to capture by pirates no less than travel by road was rendered hazardous by the activities of bandits and highwaymen.

103. Gosch and Stearns, *Premodern Travel in World History*, 34.

speed. For all the ingenuity of Roman engineering, the speed of travel remained largely unchanged from the period of the Hebrew patriarchs (roughly 2000–1500 BCE). When they migrated into the Roman Empire in the late fourth century CE, the Visigoths traveled mainly on foot, accompanied by thousands of wagons.[104] Ships were built for capacity and safety. Sailing vessels had limited maneuverability and lacked techniques to manage speed—the top speed was about six knots.[105] With prevailing winds, the voyage from Rome to Alexandria, a distance of some 1,000 miles, took ten to twenty days; but on the return (against headwinds) the journey lasted "as much as two months or more," or the same as the overland route.[106]

But this is the world in which our story begins—a world that witnessed some of the most dramatic developments in the history of humanity. As is the case throughout the history of human existence, cross-community and other forms of migration play a pivotal role in all major transformations, even though the vast majority of migrants were on foot and literally made their move one step at a time!

104. See Dietz, *Wandering Monks, Virgins, and Pilgrims*, 21–22; Ian Wood, *The Merovingian Kingdoms 450–751* (New York: Longman, 1994), 6–8.

105. Casson, *Travel in the Ancient World*, 66, 152.

106. Casson, *Travel in the Ancient World*, 151–52; see also Gosch and Stearns, *Premodern Travel in World History*, 41.

CHAPTER TWO

Migration and the Globalization of Religion: Understanding Conversion

Everyone without exception believes his own native customs, and the religion he was brought up in, to be the best; and that being so, it is unlikely that anyone but a madman would mock at such things. There is abundant evidence that this is the universal feeling about the ancient customs of one's country. . . .

—Herodotus, *The Histories*

The influential role that human migrations play in historical developments is acutely manifest in the rise and spread of major religions, reflecting the basic axiom that migrants carry their religious beliefs and practices with them. Evidence of religious life from prehistoric times is sketchy and elusive, in large measure because religion in primal societies is indistinguishable from other human activities. But there is general acceptance that "religion has permeated human life since obscure and early times."[1] Well before the ancestors of modern humans dispersed from Africa, they already possessed religious instincts, including realization of their "dependence upon higher powers beyond [their] control."[2] Successive migrations and worldwide dispersion contributed to the immense diversity and complexity of religious beliefs and practices that mark human societies. As Herodotus recognized, religious ideas were deeply held in

---

1. Ninian Smart, *The Religious Experience*, 4th ed. (New York: Macmillan, 1991), 23; see also Joseph Mitsuo Kitagawa, *The History of Religions: Understanding Human Experience* (Atlanta: Scholars Press, 1987), 112; Mark Juergensmeyer, "Thinking Globally about Religion," in *The Oxford Handbook of Global Religions*, ed. Mark Juergensmeyer (New York: Oxford University Press, 2006), 4.

2. Smart, *Religious Experience*, 18 (also, p. 39); see also Morris Jastrow, *The Study of Religion* (Chico, CA: Scholars Press, 1981), 196.

ancient societies. Yet, the designations and developments of religious systems in human history attract contentious debate. The focus here, however, is on the role of migration; and I have chosen to draw on earlier scholarship, with a few caveats.[3]

Religion is notoriously difficult to define; and exploring its meaning is rendered more difficult by the fact that many societies and languages lack a word for it. In the assessment that follows, religion is viewed as a multivalent phenomenon generally focused on divinities or otherworldly powers and the mysterious Other as well as entangled in myriad human rituals, needs, and aspirations.[4] Scholars identify several stages or periods in the religious history of humankind, each of which ostensibly coincides with a major stage of human development and large-scale migrations.[5] It is necessary to stress, however, that these processes were less developmental than cumulative.

The religious life of the earliest humans, for whom "religion" was fully integrated into all social existence and undifferentiated from other daily pursuits, is often described using unflattering or pejorative terms such as "hunting religion," "animism," or "primitive religions." The label "primal" is arguably less objectionable while also conveying the "basic, elemental status" of these religious forms in the human experience.[6] As a concept, *primal religions* refers

---

3. My own reasoning is that religious systems that have spread globally over time generally purvey a universal message (or at least allow that the particular system of beliefs and practices connecting the human and the transcendental or divine is not constrained by "tribal" or national identity) and demonstrate a capacity to appeal to indigenous spirituality. At the very core of religious traditions like Islam and Christianity, writes Juergensmeyer, "is the notion that their religion is greater than any local group and cannot be confined to the cultural boundaries of any particular region" ("Thinking Globally about Religion," 6–7).

4. This is important to clarify because in recent years, the academic study of religion has taken on a heavily material and functionalist bent. In his introduction to a major study, Graham Harvey maintains that the phenomenon is principally concerned with "health, wealth and the pursuit of happiness," adding for good measure that "it is a considerable mistake, however, to see beliefs and practices about deities as definitive of or central to religion." Graham Harvey, introduction to *Indigenous Religions: A Companion*, ed. Graham Harvey (New York: Cassell, 2000), 1, 3.

5. Robert S. Ellwood, *Readings on Religion: From Inside and Outside* (Englewood Cliffs, NJ: Prentice-Hall, 1978), 37–49; Smart, *Religious Experience*, 16–22; Kitagawa, *History of Religions*, 30–46.

6. Andrew Walls, *The Missionary Movement in the Christian History: Studies in the Transmission of the Faith* (Maryknoll, NY: Orbis Books, 1996), 121. The use of

to "the universal, basic elements of humanity's understanding of God and of the world" or "the most basic forms in the overall religious history of [human]kind."[7] That said, the tendency to view the incredibly diverse primal religious forms as representing an outmoded, more rudimentary, stage of human development is misconceived.[8] Due to the worldwide dispersal of the earliest humans, primal religions "have been widely distributed across all continents and have preceded and contributed to all other known religious systems of mankind."[9] Nor are they static and unchanging. A number of scholars insist that not only do they "continue to claim the allegiance of a good proportion of humanity" but that they also "underlie all other religions,"[10] and "many of [their] motifs . . . continue to flourish as much as ever with somewhat transmuted meanings."[11]

The development of agriculture and permanent large-scale settlements produced religious systems that placed prominent emphasis on "mother-earth" or a mother-goddess, the spiritual/ritual importance of the seasons, and fertility cults linked to animal or human sacrifice. Agricultural knowledge

---

"religions" (plural) indicates that, since primal religions cannot be separated from society as a whole, each primal religion incorporates unique features peculiar to the social group. Critics of the term "primal" argue that it is overly broad and unscientific—cf. James L. Cox, "The Classification 'Primal Religions' as a Non-Empirical Christian Theological Construct," *Studies in World Christianity* 2, no. 1 (1996): 55–76. The suggestion that "the term compromises efforts towards understanding, dialogue and mutuality between people" is mystifying (Harvey, introduction to *Indigenous Religions*, 9). The term "indigenous religion," suggested as an alternative, seems problematic because it can be used to describe all religious forms in specific local contexts, including Christianity or Islam.

7. John V. Taylor, *The Primal Vision: Christian Presence Amid African Religion* (London: SCM Press, 1963), 23; John B. Taylor, *Primal World-Views: Christian Involvement in Dialogue with Traditional Thought Forms* (Ibadan, Nigeria: Daystar, 1976), 2. See also Phillipa Baylis, *An Introduction to Primal Religions* (Edinburgh: Traditional Cosmology Society, 1988).

8. See Robert S. Ellwood, *Many Peoples, Many Faiths: An Introduction to the Religious Life of Mankind* (Englewood Cliffs, NJ: Prentice-Hall, 1976), 31; Gillian Bediako, "Christianity in Interaction with the Primal Religions of the World—a Historical and Global Perspective," paper presented at Calvin-FTS Religious Plurality Project Consultation (Pasadena, CA: 2005).

9. Taylor, *Primal World-Views*, 2.

10. Walls, *Missionary Movement*, 119.

11. Ellwood, *Many Peoples, Many Faiths*, 30; see also Harvey, introduction to *Indigenous Religions*, 4.

and techniques, as well as religious ideas and tradition, dispersed through extensive migrations. In instances of cross-community migration, the local communities adopted agricultural practices and absorbed the immigrants. But in situations where the immigrants were sufficiently numerous or powerful, their movement led to the colonization of new territories and the imposition of their language and culture on the destination society.[12] The global spread of agriculture was produced by an extended pattern of migrations that inevitably contributed to the expansion of particular religious systems.

Relatively more "sophisticated" forms of religion developed in the larger political units or states that emerged out of urban civilizations (10,000–4000 BCE). These religious systems incorporated at least three notable elements: (1) the concept of sacred kingship in which the ruler was associated with the divine order; (2) complex organizations comprising temple cults, specialist priests, and religious writings; and (3) a highly developed polytheism purportedly reflective of the diversity of peoples and cultures as well as the compartmentalization of human skills and activities. By incorporating an array of ethnicities and nationalities within a single administrative system, empires were by definition centers of religious diversity and interaction. But in their effort to impose order over extensive realms, imperial governments sometimes upheld particular cultural forms and institutions with the aim of fostering integration and loyalty. The identification of a particular religious system with the state created an intimate link between the extension of political authority (over vast territories and a multiplicity of peoples and nations) and religious expansion.

The emergence of the so-called world (or great) religions marked a major stage of religious development. The list and classification vary considerably but typically include the three monotheistic faiths (Judaism, Christianity, and Islam) as well as Zoroastrianism, Buddhism, and Confucianism. The term "world religions" (a designation of obscure origins) for these belief systems is now often criticized as an academic label rooted in a Eurocentric discourse with undue focus on literacy, written texts, and hierarchical authority.[13] I single out these six faiths based on relevance to my study rather than any assump-

---

12. Patrick Manning, *Migration in World History* (New York: Routledge, 2005), 68.
13. Harvey, introduction to *Indigenous Religions*, 6–8; Tomoko Masuzawa, *The Invention of World Religions, or, How European Universalism Was Preserved in the Language of Pluralism* (Chicago: University of Chicago Press, 2005), 2–13.

tions about qualitative importance. From a historical perspective, the nature and rise of the great religions owes something to the development of writing, as well as their locus within major centers of civilization (in the Middle East, India, and China) and the transcontinental reach of international trade.[14] All are built on the teachings of religious founders whose ideas have had a profound influence on sizeable segments of the world's population. Uncritical assumptions about the degree to which they either serve as a benchmark for understanding all religious life or are deemed exhaustive of the religious imagination must be avoided. But the great religions are recognized as being among "the most powerful and significant forms of the globalization of culture in the pre-modern era."[15]

Generally speaking, the basic creedal convictions enshrined within a particular religion or faith system also help to determine the energy and resolve with which migrant adherents proselytize or maintain religious ideals across cultural frontiers. The global spread of the "missionary" faiths (mainly Christianity and Islam; also Buddhism to a lesser extent) has been attributed to three major traits:[16] "presenting a single [person] as a means of access to God and salvation"[17]; emphasis on "the compassion of God for all people and the offer of salvation to every individual"; and a remarkable capacity "to gather and organize people," leading to the formation of both local communities and international networks. Christianity and Islam, the world's most dominant faiths, have benefited the most from migration movements in part because they both espouse a universal vision that not only mandates worldwide outreach but also imagines a single global community.

The presentation of religious development in human history in terms of stages inevitably conveys a sense of linearity, or consistent improvement over

14. Cf. Ellwood, *Many Peoples, Many Faiths*, 22.

15. David Held et al., *Global Transformations: Politics, Economics and Culture* (Stanford, CA: Stanford University Press, 1999), 333.

16. Cf. Robert L. Montgomery, "Conversion and the Historic Spread of Religions," in *The Oxford Handbook of Religious Conversion*, ed. Lewis R. Rambo and Charles E. Farhadian (New York: Oxford University Press, 2014), 167–69.

17. Dan Smyer Yü, "Buddhist Conversion in the Contemporary World," in *The Oxford Handbook of Religious Conversion*, ed. Lewis R. Rambo and Charles E. Farhadian (New York: Oxford University Press, 2014), 467. However, it has to be said that in Buddhism, unlike Islam and Christianity, converts can attain the same essence of spiritual state as the historical Buddha.

time. But the notion that each successive development replaced or superseded the previous system, resulting in progressively "superior" forms, is unwarranted and flawed. As Robert S. Ellwood argues, the history of religion is "largely cumulative"; for "when a new period, or even a new religion, comes it does not so much replace what went before as just add another layer on top of it, while the former still continues to live, perhaps with changed name and role."[18] For the most part, major elements of each developmental stage have endured in human experience and coexist or intermingle with others. In the historical study of Christianity, the terms "pagan," "ancestral religion," "heathen," and "pre-Christian" are frequently used, usually in contexts of conversion, to describe the religious systems that potential converts come from. These labels, which are seldom applied to the "great" religions, typically convey sweeping judgment and reflect an either/or approach that usually offers little insight into the religious traditions in question (see "Religious Conversion in Historical Perspective" below).

CROSS-CULTURAL ENCOUNTERS AND RELIGIOUS CONVERSION

Migrants cannot carry everything with them, but they do take a lot: their language, ideas, knowledge of technology, religious beliefs, customs, cuisine, and much else. Also, the history of humanity is replete with evidence that "relatively small numbers of migrants can have a disproportionately large cultural impact on their host communities."[19] This capacity to transform human societies is one reason why migration is a major source of historical change. This is not to suggest that such cultural encounters are benign. Many involve violence (in the case of conquest, for instance), inspire conflict, or even result in the demise of particular cultural traditions. The fact remains, however, that cross-cultural interactions and engagement represent an engine of cultural change, positive or negative.

But the penetration of cultural boundaries raises complex historical questions.[20] How is the long-term impact of cross-cultural interaction to be assessed, particularly when it involves large-scale religious conversions? What

18. Ellwood, *Readings on Religion*, 19.
19. John Haywood, *The Great Migrations: From the Earliest Humans to the Age of Globalization* (London: Quercus, 2008), 8.
20. For a broad overview, see Jerry H. Bentley, *Old World Encounters: Cross-*

considerations influence the appropriation of foreign ideas and practices (especially those that are integrated within a religious system) by a cultural group or some section thereof? Since the impact is seldom one-directional, what critical elements shape the dynamic of transmission, reception, and incorporation? Are there particular conditions that favor meaningful interchange or reciprocal transformation? What are common forms or causes of cultural resistance?

IMPERIAL POWER AND RELIGIOUS EXPANSION

The most common response to these questions takes the form of what I have termed the "empire argument," a form of historical analysis that emphasizes structures of power, political ambition, instruments of large-scale mobilization, superior resources, efforts by institutional elites, and economic self-interest. In truth, almost all the great religions were intimately associated with one or more major empires in the course of their history; and military conquest or the colonization of extensive territories enabled them to achieve dominance in societies and cultures well beyond their original context. Zoroastrianism, for instance, was instituted as the state religion of the Persian Empire by the Sassanid Dynasty (lasted from 224 to 651 CE) in their effort to restore the ancient Persian civilization. Farther east, Asoka the Great, emperor of the Maurya Dynasty (r. 273–232 BCE) and a convert to Buddhism, promoted Buddhism within an empire that encompassed almost all of the Indian subcontinent.

Aided by imperial expansion and military domination, the religion of an Arabian tribe expanded to incorporate a multitude of peoples, ethnicities, and cultures around the world within *dar al Islam* ("house of Islam"). Already by the ninth century (during the Umayyad Caliphate, 661–750 CE), the Islamic empire created by the vigorous expansion of Islam incorporated some 62 million people (nearly 30 percent of the world's population) comprising distinct nationalities. At its height in the twelfth century CE, Islamic rule stretched from Iberia and Morocco in the west to sub-Saharan Africa in the south and as far east as northern India, already penetrating Indonesia.[21] For Christianity

---

Cultural Contacts and Exchanges in Pre-Modern Times (New York: Oxford University Press, 1993).

21. The globalization of Islam received further boost with the rise of the Ottoman Empire (which lasted from the fourteenth century to the end of World War I). The

too, early global expansion coincided with its establishment as state religion within various empires: the Western Roman Empire (from the conversion of Constantine I to its collapse in the fifth century CE), the Byzantine Empire (330–1453 CE), and the Frankish (Carolingian) Empire (770–888 CE).[22] However, by the fifteenth century, significant territorial losses following the spread of Islam,[23] and culminating with the conquest of the Byzantine Empire by the Ottomans, reduced Christianity to a largely European religion.

But, as a basic unit of analysis, the "empire argument" confuses correlation with causation. The central role of economic expansion and the projection of political power in the integration of diverse societies is undeniable; imperial interests do play a role in the transregional spread of religion. But the dynamics of unequal power relations and the lure of political (or economic) interests do not adequately account for religious transformation in new societies or widespread conversions to a new religion. For one thing, the focus on structures of power often reduces religious change to a material function. Also, a top-down perspective overlooks the multifarious array of social movements, cultural processes, ordinary experiences, and nonelite activities and decisions that contribute immensely to religious encounter and exchange.

RELIGIOUS CONVERSION: CONCEPT, VARIATIONS, AND CONTEXT

It is self-evident that the global spread of the great religions required religious conversion. For this reason, a meaningful assessment of the role of migration in wide-ranging cross-cultural religious transformation requires a critical appraisal of processes of religious conversion. Yet, analyzing conversion or religious transformation as a process derived from cross-cultural encounter and

---

largest and most influential of the Muslim empires of the modern period, the Ottoman Empire controlled territories spanning southeastern Europe, the Middle East, and North Africa.

22. By 600 CE, the obscure religious movement that emerged in first-century Palestine had spread as far west as present-day Portugal, northwestward to Ireland, eastward into China and South Asia, and in Africa at least as far south as present-day Sudan.

23. As many as half of the world's Christians were under Muslim political rule by the end of the seventh century. Dale T. Irvin and Scott Sunquist, *History of the World Christian Movement*, Vol. 1, *Earliest Christianity to 1453* (Maryknoll, NY: Orbis Books, 2001), 270.

contact is a complex issue. The concept of religious conversion is attended by considerable debate. Religious adherents defend it vigorously; but critics associate it with coercion, religious intolerance, propaganda, psychological manipulation, self-deception (on the part of converts) and even loss of religious freedom. Furthermore, what constitutes "genuine conversion" varies among religious traditions and across historical contexts, and variations of meaning emerge even within the same religious tradition in different times and places. The assertion that "conversion is what a group or person *says* it is" has much to commend it.[24]

Despite the multiplicity of definitions across disciplines, there is general agreement that conversion connotes major change or transformation in the life of an individual or group. To what degree and how long the change must last to warrant the claim of conversion is a thorny issue. But the long-standing view of religious conversion as an instantaneous, wholesale, and permanent transformation is now considered problematic, though not ruled out altogether.[25] More recent scholarship views religious change as a process frequently marked not only by multiple decisions and shifting motivations but also by both continuities and discontinuities with the past—a process, in fact, that is often incomplete! Until fairly recently, also, major treatments of the concept by Christian scholars depicted religious conversion as essentially an *individual* and *psychological* (i.e., "interior") experience with scant attention to the role of social elements. In a seminal assessment, A. D. Nock stated that conversion involves "the reorientation of *the soul of an individual* . . . , a turning which implies a consciousness that a great change is involved, that the old was wrong and the new is right" (italics added).[26] This understanding offers little insight into group conversion and obscures the significance of the sociocultural context.

In a highly regarded study of conversion, Lewis Rambo argues that religious conversion is a process over time that is influenced by contextual factors

---

24. Lewis R. Rambo, *Understanding Religious Conversion* (New Haven: Yale University Press, 1993), 7.

25. Lewis R. Rambo and Charles E. Farhadian, introduction to *The Oxford Handbook of Religious Conversion*, ed. Lewis R. Rambo and Charles E. Farhadian (New York: Oxford University Press, 2014), 6–8; also Rambo, *Understanding Religious Conversion*, 1.

26. Arthur Darby Nock, *Conversion: The Old and the New in Religion from Alexander the Great to Augustine of Hippo* (Oxford: Clarendon Press, 1933), 7.

and produced by multiple (interactive) elements.[27] Rambo makes the case that even though religious conversion is a universal phenomenon, there is no single, universal process of religious conversion and that the conversion process and its consequences are different in different times and places in history.[28] Even the profile and motivation of converts can vary as a new movement becomes more established or spreads to new regional contexts.[29] Similarly, conversions in a setting where the new religion is the dominant faith and well known tend to be quite different in nature and outcomes compared to conversion in situations where the new religion is unfamiliar or is being encountered for the first time. As Rambo stipulates, "there is not one cause of conversion, not one process, and no one simple consequence of that process."[30]

The understanding that there is "a range of types of conversion" and that "no type is normative" is critical for historical inquiry. The main types of conversion that Rambo identifies are as follows:[31]

> *apostasy* or *defection*, the repudiation of a religious tradition or its beliefs by previous members (in essence, deconversion)
>
> *intensification*, the revitalized commitment to a faith with which the convert has had previous affiliation, as when members move from indifference to fervor
>
> *affiliation*, the movement of an individual or group from the absence of a faith system or no religious commitment to full involvement with an institution or community of faith
>
> *institutional transition*, the change of an individual or group from one community to another within a major tradition, as in switching from one Protestant denomination to another
>
> *traditional transition*, the movement of an individual or group from one major religious tradition to another

27. Rambo, *Understanding Religious Conversion*, 4, 5.

28. Rambo, *Understanding Religious Conversion*, 12, 16. Marcia Hermansen also endorses this view in her examination of Islam. Marcia Hermansen, "Conversion to Islam in Theological and Historical Perspectives," in *The Oxford Handbook of Religious Conversion*, ed. Lewis R. Rambo and Charles E. Farhadian (New York: Oxford University Press, 2014), 364.

29. As a case in point, "the nature of conversions on the frontiers of expanding spheres of Islamic influence" are thought to have differed significantly from those that occurred within stable boundaries (Hermansen, "Conversion to Islam," 639).

30. Rambo, *Understanding Religious Conversion*, 5.

31. Rambo, *Understanding Religious Conversion*, 2, 12–14.

Of these, *traditional transition* is the most germane to this study. As a matter of fact, this type of conversion is predominantly cross-cultural. Rambo explains that it entails "moving from one worldview, ritual system, symbolic universe, and lifestyle to another," and that it is a complex process that "often takes place in a context of cross-cultural contact and conflict."[32]

In a similar vein, Robert Montgomery argues that the basic criterion for all conversions associated with the global spread of religions is "the acquiring of a religious identity not previously held."[33] He adds that variations in this type of conversion mainly reflect "levels of volition" (the degree of individual choice involved), which range on a spectrum from high to low. Thus, group conversion to a new faith (such as may occur through foreign invasion, for instance) involves low volition, whereas conversions in a situation of religious plurality, when an individual makes a conscious and voluntary commitment to a new faith, are marked by high volition.

However, to use degree of individual choice as a rubric for analyzing cross-cultural conversion is unhelpful and appears to impose a modern Western value on the issue. An emphasis on volition is also problematic. In many communities throughout history, religious identity is inseparable from other aspects of cultural life or social existence. Adopting a new religious identity has huge and immediate implications for morality, social institutions, political allegiance, and even cultural identity. This means that, whether or not it involves a single dramatic event, the conversion process is typically prolonged and often linked to historical change. Such long-term transformation is typically subject to innumerable variations or motivations and is attended by an extended, intergenerational process of negotiation and adaptation. This is one reason why cross-cultural conversions are more likely in situations either where there is some degree of congruence between the two cultures or where the potential converts identify areas of affinity that provide rationale for embracing the new religious tradition. All said and done, cross-cultural religious conversion demands the most significant change.

Rambo captures this complexity when he asserts that the process of religious conversion is a product of the interactions among (a) the potential converts' aspirations, needs, and orientations, (b) the nature of the group into which they are being converted, and (c) the particular social matrix in which

---

32. Rambo, *Understanding Religious Conversion*, 14, 38.
33. Montgomery, "Conversion and the Historic Spread of Religions," 165, 166.

these processes are taking place.[34] These three variables elucidate the diverse nature of religious conversions, since they vary tremendously across historical periods and between localities. A brief examination of these three elements with specific reference to cross-cultural religious expansion and "traditional transition" is warranted.

Contexts of Conversions

Rambo proposes a *sequential stage model* of conversion in which the phenomenon is depicted as a "process oriented" phenomenon involving a sequence of (seven) stages: context, crisis, quest, encounter, interaction, commitment, and consequences.[35] These stages "are interactive and cumulative over time" and do not necessarily follow a particular sequence. *Context* captures the vast array of factors in particular settings that impede or facilitate conversion; the *crisis* stage examines the tensions, dilemmas, or predicaments in the lives of potential converts that activate a turning point; *quest* describes the motivations, aspirations, and emotional and intellectual considerations that set potential converts on the path to transformation; *encounter* refers to the interaction and interplay between the religious advocate and the convert that leads to rejection or acceptance; *interaction* signifies the period of formal (or intensive) contact between the potential convert and the religious group—with obvious relevance to migrant encounters—during which the former becomes more acquainted with the group's rituals, teachings, expectations, and so on; the *commitment* stage refers to the decision-making point at which the potential convert shifts loyalties (often a profound experience that entails "surrender" to a new authority); and *consequences* evaluates the nature, extent, and impact of the changes (initial and progressive) in the convert's life—emotional, moral, intellectual, social, religious, and so on—as well as the sociocultural implications for the converts' group (of origin).

For Rambo, *context* comprises social, cultural, personal, and religious dimensions.[36] It is comprehensive in that it represents "the total environment in which conversion transpires" and "embraces an overall matrix in which the force field of people, events, experiences, and institutions operate on conver-

34. Rambo, *Understanding Religious Conversion*, 7.
35. Rambo, *Understanding Religious Conversion*, 16–17.
36. Rambo, *Understanding Religious Conversion*, 22–35.

sion."[37] Importantly, it not only forms the initial stage but also "continues its influence throughout the other stages"; it "shapes the nature, structure, and process of conversion." In its totality, context encompasses two overlapping entities: *macrocontext*, which covers the broader (global) elements such as political domains, economic systems, or transnational organizations; and *microcontext*, the local setting in which more immediate influences such as social identity, ethnic rivalries, and family ties are at work. In different settings, as we shall see, the patronage of local authority (or absence thereof) and the distance of the context from the missionary's homeland all factor into the conversion equation.

Within each context are forces that "facilitate conversion or act powerfully to prevent it." Rambo hypothesizes, among other things, that "indigenous cultures that are in crisis will have more potential converts than stable societies," although whether the crisis was created externally or internally also has bearing on patterns of conversion. Furthermore, the greater the degree of consonance between the two cultural systems, the more likely it is that conversion will transpire from one to the other.[38] From a different analytical perspective, Montgomery asserts that the degree of choice (or tolerance of religious plurality) within the society to which the religion spreads and the capacity of the missionary religion to cultivate "inter-societal relationships" (as opposed to depending on domination and coercion) directly affect the prospects of conversion.[39]

In this study, cross-cultural contacts facilitated by migrant movement are of paramount consideration in assessing the role of the "context" in conversion. In other words, how the various contexts have significant bearing on the conversion process will be analyzed with primary reference to two major elements: first, the global reality in which expanding human migrations of great variety bring increasing numbers of the world's peoples and cultures into each other's orbit and form the basis for cross-cultural contact and exchange; and second, the specific developments instigated by migrants or associated with migrant movement within particular settings that have critical bearing on the encounters, interactions, and responses central to cross-cultural conversion.

---

37. Rambo, *Understanding Religious Conversion*, 20.
38. Rambo, *Understanding Religious Conversion*, 41–42.
39. Montgomery, "Conversion and the Historic Spread of Religions," 169–76.

The Converts' Agency

The reference to the convert's needs and aspirations provides an important corrective to studies of conversion and missionary accounts that explain the process wholly in terms of missionary intention and activity or the use of force. Rambo insists that most converts "are active agents in their conversion process," although he admits that the degree of agency ranges from very active to relatively passive.[40] In the Christian tradition, the key role that the convert's perception and receptivity play in the conversion process is often captured in the prolonged agonizing internal struggle that many prominent converts experience before they make a final decision or commitment. Augustine of Hippo (354–430 CE) records in his *Confessions*:

> When I was deliberating upon serving the Lord my God now, as I had long purposed—I it was who willed, I who was unwilling. It was I, even I myself. I neither willed entirely, nor was entirely unwilling. Therefore was I at war with myself, and destroyed by myself. . . .[41]

Motives for conversion can never be fully accounted for; but some are more accessible to historical inquiry than others. All too often, the process of conversion is attended by both constraints and aspirations. Clearly, the potential for elevation of status or the possibility for economic advancement (even the desire to live a better life) can influence the receptivity of individuals or groups to a new religion. This nineteenth-century Igbo prayer conveys the socioeconomic considerations that informed one group's response, while also hinting at the sense of constraint:

> *Our great ancestors, we greet you.* The world is changing with us. What used to be the norm when you were here on earth no longer obtains. Civilization, Christianity and *travelling* are forcing us to adjust ourselves to the new way of life. Our neighboring villages which were inferior to us in battle, trade and farming are now growing in strength because they have

---

40. Rambo, *Understanding Religious Conversion*, 44–46.

41. Augustine, *Confessions* 8.10. *The Confessions of St. Augustine*, trans. J. G. Pilkington (New York: Boni & Liveright, 1927).

taken to the new ways. . . . Very soon, but God forbid, they will become our master if we pay no heed to the changing situation and the new ideas which we feel are not entirely bad.[42] (italics added)

It is well recognized that some form of crisis at the individual or societal level often acts as a catalyst for religious transformation. In this regard, the trauma and unsettledness associated with migration (note the reference to traveling in the above quotation)—not to mention situations of mass relocation or population transfers—can intensify religious consciousness or "trigger a religious quest."[43] This dimension is fairly conspicuous in biblical accounts (see chapter 3). Conversely, in societies served by well-organized religions, and underpinned by political and economic stability, resistance to conversion tends to be stronger.

Rambo observes that when potential converts have little or no prior knowledge of the new religion (as opposed to contexts where it is already established and well known), they are greatly dependent on the missionary and consequently more passive.[44] He reasons that, in such situations, the foreign missionary or religious advocate tends to control the processes of conversion, though potential converts retain the ultimate power of resistance or rejection. It seems obvious, however, that in situations of cross-cultural engagement ("traditional transition") the converts' capacity for resistance is especially strong since a cultural frontier is involved. Even when advocates of the new religion can make claims to cultural prestige or political patronage, the convert's needs and orientation remain crucial. As the principle of translation makes explicit (see "The Translation Principle and Syncretism" below), and I explain in subsequent chapters, foreign missionary agents are cultural outsiders to the society of reception, and transmission of the message requires adaptation to the latter's norms.

Clearly, the convert's agency is severely limited in situations of forced conversion or conversion through conquest, which is why such efforts are the most likely to elicit forms of resistance and to require many generations for

---

42. Cited in Cyril C. Okorocha, "Religious Conversion in Africa: Its Missiological Implications," *Mission Studies* 9, no. 18 (1992): 172.

43. Rambo, *Understanding Religious Conversion*, 47.

44. Rambo, *Understanding Religious Conversion*, 44–45 (also, pp. 87–101).

the conversion process to be completed (beyond external conformity or observances), as was arguably the case in the conversion of Scandinavia (see chapter 7). Ultimately, the convert's capacity to resist is generally overlooked in conversion studies. Rambo points out, however, that resistance "is *the normal or typical reaction* of both individuals and societies to conversion attempts"[45] (italics added). As noted above, even in situations of mass conversion or contexts in which coercive structures are present, the majority of people generally repudiate the new religion. All this is to say that pre-Christian religious traditions must not be viewed as passive systems of beliefs and custom.[46] Everywhere, the spread of Christianity elicited active responses that covered the spectrum from adaptation to hostile resistance.

The rise and spread of Islam led to the erosion or complete eclipse of Christianity in large swathes of western and central Asia. But, generally speaking, the great religions have been most successful in converting peoples from primal religions or societies. This is decidedly the case in the global expansion of Christianity.[47] At least two explanations can be given.

The most common rationale holds that conversion was often a coping mechanism in the face of the rapid social change and profound dilemmas caused by sustained encounter with the more advanced civilization and the universal claims of the Christian religion—often, though not always, in situations of conquest or invasion. The Christianization of the peoples of northern and western Europe in the fourth to twelfth centuries CE and the conversion of various peoples in non-Western societies in the modern period are major examples.[48] For both, it is argued, Christianity afforded resources to cope with traumatic change and furnished "a new set of values" for a more complex

45. Rambo, *Understanding Religious Conversion*, 35.

46. This is a point that John-Henry Clay makes in connection with the medieval German context. John-Henry Clay, *In the Shadow of Death: Saint Boniface and the Conversion of Hessia, 721–754* (Turnhout: Brepols, 2010), 347.

47. Walls, *Missionary Movement*, 68–69.

48. However, as Norwegian historian Sverre Bagge points out, the gap between Christians and non-Christians, especially in terms of technology and culture, was considerably less in early medieval Europe than was the case between Europe and the vast lands Europeans colonized in the non-European world. Sverre Bagge, "Christianizing Kingdoms," in *The Oxford Handbook of Medieval Christianity*, ed. John Arnold (New York: Oxford University Press, 2014), 122.

world. It also provided "a universal point of reference, linking the society with its traditionally local and kin-related focus to a universal order."[49] Robin Horton argued more controversially that the dramatic transformations of the post-1500 world generated by the advent of colonialism engendered strong receptivity in the traditional societies of Africa to monotheistic religions. This was because modernity exposed the limitations of the lesser spirits in African cosmology (who are primarily concerned with the local community) and accentuated the role of the supreme being whose power extends to the whole world. The beliefs and practices of Islam and Christianity were thus accepted in Africa "where they happen to coincide with responses of the traditional cosmology to other, non-missionary, factors of the modern situation."[50]

In the case of Christianity, an alternative explanation makes the case that primal religions have constituted the religious background of the majority of Christians of all ages and places precisely because the Christian message and Scriptures embody concepts that appeal strongly to the primal imagination. New Zealander missionary-scholar Harold Turner identified six broad areas of affinity between the biblical and primal worldviews that help to account for the receptivity of primal religions to the preaching of the gospel:[51] first, a sense of kinship with nature in which the natural environment is used with respect and reverence; second, a consciousness of human weakness and the need for a power beyond one's own; third, the conviction that ours is a world

---

49. Walls, *Missionary Movement*, 69.

50. Robin Horton, "African Conversion," *African Affairs* 41, no. 2 (1971): 85-108. As such, the beliefs and practices of Islam and Christianity were accepted because the arrival of the two religions coincided with the reorientation already taking place within traditional cosmologies. Critics challenged the assumption that adherents of African traditional faiths would interpret and respond to changes in their society in a particular way. Moreover, Horton's thesis does not successfully account for the persistence of the African cosmological worldview alongside Christian missionary doctrine well into the process of modernization. See Humphrey J. Fisher, "Conversion Reconsidered: Some Historical Aspects of Religious Conversion in Black Africa," *African Affairs* 43, no. 1 (1973): 27-40; Robert W. Hefner, *Conversion to Christianity: Historical and Anthropological Perspectives on a Great Transformation* (Berkeley: University of California Press, 1993), 3-46.

51. Harold W. Turner, "Primal Religions of the World and Their Study," in *Australian Essays in World Religions*, ed. Victor C. Hayes (Bedford Park, South Australia, 1977), 27-37; quoted in Kwame Bediako, *Christianity in Africa: The Renewal of a Non-Western Religion* (Maryknoll, NY: Orbis Books, 1995), 93-96.

of spiritual powers or transcendent powers who may be ambivalent, malevolent, or benevolent—so human beings are not alone; fourth, the belief that it is possible to "enter into a relationship with the benevolent spirit world, to share in its power and blessings and receive protection from evil forces"; fifth, an intense belief in the afterlife, or sense of continuation beyond this life, that is reflected in the conception of ancestors as the living dead; and sixth, a sense of "living in a sacramental universe where there is no sharp dichotomy between the physical and the spiritual."

This is not to suggest that Christian beliefs and practice were one and the same with primal or ancestral religions. The latter, for instance, lacked either monasticism or the bureaucratic clerical structure of the church.[52] Moreover, as noted in the next section, the claims of the Christian message are exclusive and unique. Obviously, the closer the missionary lived to potential converts, the greater the likelihood of shared religious or cultural understanding, not to mention linguistic affinity. But the conspicuous and pervasive accounts of miracles and other supernatural events in narratives of conversion in Europe and Asia referenced in this volume attest to the shared worldview of Christian missionaries and potential converts. This element is overlooked in Horton's analysis, which focuses on functional imperatives.

It is also worth noting that vernacular translation of the Bible in Africa allowed direct interaction between indigenous understandings and the biblical message in a way that bypassed or undermined foreign missionary transmission of the Christian message sheathed in European culture and Enlightenment assumptions.[53] To put it more plainly, the indigenous cultural heritage provided important reference points for response to the message of the gospel and shaped motivations for conversion often beyond the understanding of the foreign missionary. The most conspicuous example is the recognition and use of the indigenous name for God to represent the God of the Bible, in striking contrast to medieval Europe where the pagan gods were displaced.[54]

---

52. Cf. J. N. Hillgarth, *Christianity and Paganism, 350–750: The Conversion of Western Europe*, rev. ed. (Philadelphia: University of Pennsylvania Press, 1986), 6.

53. It is said, for instance, that "Africans reading the Bible in their own languages do not have far to go before they discover that they are treading on familiar ground" (Humphrey Waweru, *The Bible and African Culture: Mapping Transactional Inroads* (Eldoret, Kenya: Zapf Chancery, 2011), 107.

54. Cf. Walls, *Missionary Movement*, 70–72.

The obvious implication that the Christian God was active in a people's past tacitly shifts the terms of comprehension and application to the minds and world of the converts.[55] As Lamin Sanneh notes, "Africans best responded to Christianity where the indigenous religions were strongest, not weakest, suggesting a degree of compatibility with the gospel."[56]

Nature of the Religious Group

Conversion is central to Christianity, and the concept is laden with notions of radical change. In the New Testament, the Greek term (*metanoeō*) translated *conversion* literally means "to think again." Theologically, the act of conversion entailed repentance from sin and a turning to God: to wit, "repent, then, and turn to God, so that your sins may be wiped out" (Acts 3:19). It also carried the expectation of major transformation, conveyed by the ideas of "new birth" (rebirth) or "new creation" (made possible not by self-effort but through faith in Christ): "Therefore, if anyone is in Christ, the new creation has come: The old has gone, the new is here!" (2 Cor. 5:17). Most important, the Christian faith, in sharp contrast to the various primal or ancestral religious systems it encountered throughout the world, demanded exclusive allegiance. There may be affinities between old and new, and (as we shall see) the precepts of the old religion were instrumental in shaping reception to the claims of the new. But conversion or faithful allegiance to the new faith required the dethronement of all other gods or competing centers of spiritual power, for Christians claimed to worship "the only God" (1 Tim. 1:17) and that "salvation is found in no one else" (Acts 4:12).

From the very beginning, however, the experience of Christian conversion showed great variety in form, expression, and duration. Some were mass conversions (Acts 2:41; 5:14; 11:21); others involved entire households (Acts

---

55. See Walls, *Missionary Movement*, 75; Lamin O. Sanneh, *Translating the Message: The Missionary Impact on Culture* (Maryknoll, NY: Orbis Books, 2009), 36.

56. Lamin O. Sanneh, *Whose Religion Is Christianity? The Gospel beyond the West* (Grand Rapids: Eerdmans, 2003), 18, 31–32. For more on this, see Andrew F. Walls, *The Cross-Cultural Process in Christian History: Studies in the Transmission and Appropriation of Faith* (Maryknoll, NY: Orbis Books, 2002), 116–35; Walls, *Missionary Movement*, 79–101; Bediako, *Christianity in Africa*; Kwame Bediako, "Understanding African Theology in the 20th Century," in *Issues in African Christian Theology*, ed. Samuel Ngewa et al. (Nairobi: East African Educational Publishers, 1998), 56–72.

16:15, 33) or a single individual (Acts 8:38). Some, including the apostle Paul, experienced the baptism of the Holy Spirit before receiving the rite of water baptism (Acts 9:17–18; 10:44–48). For others, the sequence was reversed, with a long interval in between (Acts 19:1–6). Still others were only baptized with water (Acts 16:33; 18:8), and on occasion no mention of baptism is made in connection with the act of conversion (Acts 11:21). It is noteworthy, however, that all the conversion experiences appear instantaneous. However, the accounts of the Ethiopian eunuch and Cornelius the Roman centurion suggest that the conversion event was the culmination of a process.

David Kling observes that "the phenomenon of turning from former attitudes and loyalties to a new allegiance to God's saving activity in Jesus Christ forms the basic story line in Christian history."[57] Yet, Rambo's five types of conversion (see above) are amply represented in the history of the Christian movement—including apostasy or defection. Inevitably, the meaning and forms of conversion in Christian thought and life became tremendously complex as the local groups, ritual practices, and theological orientation multiplied around the world. The "nature of the religious group" is easier to identify in some places and times than in others. In medieval Europe, both Latin Christianity and its Byzantine counterpart appear as cohesive (though distinctive) blocs or traditions, each with a dominant center. With the demise of Arianism in the West and the expulsion of non-Chalcedonian groups from the East, a relatively stable conception of the community of faith emerged in these rival forms of Roman Christendom. By contrast, the plurality of confessional groups (Armenian, Jacobite, Monophysite, East Syrian, and Chalcedonian) present in Arabia, in the Persian Empire, and to a lesser extent in Mongol realms represented competing theological understandings and diverse notions of what kind of Christian community converts joined.[58]

---

57. David W. Kling, "Conversion to Christianity," in *The Oxford Handbook of Religious Conversion*, ed. Lewis R. Rambo and Charles E. Farhadian (New York: Oxford University Press, 2014), 598.

58. Later still, in the wake of the Protestant Reformations, "intra-Christian" conversion from one form of Christianity or denomination to another prevailed, while subsequent reform or revival movements (including the Puritan, Pietist, and Wesleyan) emphasized the "new birth" and inward transformation. See M. Darrol Bryant, "Conversion in Christianity: From Without and from Within," in *Religious Conversion: Contemporary Practices and Controversies*, ed. Christopher Lamb and M. Darrol Bryant (New York: Cassell, 1999), 185–87.

Again, our main concern is with conversions in the context of cross-cultural encounter, up to 1500 CE. In this regard, it is striking to note that in the book of Acts conversions in the form of "traditional transition" (to use Rambo's typology) were marked by two distinct elements. First, the prompting and activity of the Holy Spirit is conspicuous. In the account of Philip and the Ethiopian eunuch, missionary action is prompt and motivation for the convert's decision is unmistakable; but the entire encounter is predicated on the initiative of the Spirit (Acts 8:26–39). Similarly, the conversion of the Roman centurion Cornelius and his household is wholly orchestrated by the Holy Spirit (Acts 10). Importantly, the apostle Peter also experiences a "conversion" of sorts in the Cornelius episode: the spontaneous outpouring of the Holy Spirit on a gentile household forces him to rethink and turn from his earlier conviction (that God's plan of salvation was restricted to Jews) to a new affirmation of the universal scope of the gospel. In these and other instances involving the crossing of cultural frontiers—including the missionary movement into Europe (Acts 16:7–10)—the Holy Spirit is consistently depicted as the primary agent in the mission of the church (also Acts 13:2; 14:27).

The second notable feature in the cross-cultural spread of the gospel in the Book of Acts is the recurrent demonstration of supernatural power—so much so that questions about the distinctiveness and authenticity of gentile mission are partly laid to rest by accounts of "the signs and wonders God had done among the Gentiles" (Acts 15:12). At the start of the gentile phase of his ministry, Paul preaches the gospel to Sergius Paulus, the Roman proconsul in Cyprus, who becomes a Christian believer after a well-known Jewish sorcerer is afflicted with blindness in his presence at Paul's command (Acts 13:8–12). The outcome of the conflict between two opposing spiritual forces apparently left the proconsul in no doubt as to the way of salvation. During the mission in Europe, the casting out of a spirit of divination landed Paul and Silas in jail; but the supernatural opening of the prison doors and chains at midnight prompted the conversion of the jailer and his household (Acts 16:25–34).

At Ephesus, the special miracles of healing and deliverance performed by Paul contrast sharply with the abject failure of Jewish exorcists to accomplish the same (Acts 19:11–16). But there is a strong hint here that the demonstration of spiritual power alone was not sufficiently compelling in a context where sorcerers, magicians, and exorcists were a familiar sight. It took the humiliating downfall of the seven sons of the Jewish chief priest to produce unequivocal acclamation of "the name of the Lord Jesus"—and many "believed." As if to leave readers in no doubt about the complete triumph of the Christian savior over other powers, Luke is careful to note that "a number who had practiced sorcery brought their scrolls together and burned them publicly" (Acts 19:19).

This very brief review of the Acts record is additionally relevant because the gentile mission—which opened the door to the spread of the Christian message among the diverse nationalities and cultures of the Greco-Roman world (and beyond)—represented the first major shift in the history of the Christian movement in which cross-cultural missionary movement produced phenomenal conversions (in the mode of "traditional transition") among primal peoples or societies and changed the face of Christianity.[59] As we shall see, in these and subsequent transitions, extensive migrations were pivotal.

RELIGIOUS CONVERSION IN HISTORICAL PERSPECTIVE

Rambo's analysis does not attempt a comprehensive historical overview. For this, we must turn elsewhere. In an assessment of treatments of conversion by historians, Marc Baer identifies four major types: acculturation, adhesion or hybridity, syncretism, and transformation.[60] *Acculturation* signifies religious conversion as cultural change: it is equated with Christianization or Islamization and involves the "incorporation or integration [by subordinate groups] of the customs, habits, and language of a conquering civilization." *Adhesion* (or *hybridity*) occurs when individuals or groups "adopt new beliefs and practices alongside the old." In this case, continuities between old and new religious traditions are as important as, if not more important than, discontinuities for understanding the conversion process.[61] *Syncretism* takes place when "the

---

59. Kling, "Conversion to Christianity," 610–14. For Kling, the second was the conversion of the peoples of northern and western Europe (from the fourth to the fifteenth centuries); the third, and by far the most extensive, were the accessions to the faith from among societies in Asia, the Americas, the Pacific, and Africa (from the sixteenth century). There is a case to be made that the rise of Persian Christianity and the phenomenal missionary expansion across central Asia was also historical.

60. Marc David Baer, "History and Religious Conversion," in *The Oxford Handbook of Religious Conversion*, ed. Lewis R. Rambo and Charles E. Farhadian (New York: Oxford University Press, 2014), 25–47.

61. Nock, by contrast, famously distinguished between conversion and "adhesion,"

convert(s) reconcile or fuse old and new beliefs and practices to create a new religious synthesis." (The difference between syncretism and adhesion in this analysis is quite hypothetical, and the two are often lumped together.) *Transformation* is depicted as the culmination of the process, "when converts attempt to completely replace the old with the new."

This typology raises as many questions as it solves. Baer recognizes that acculturation generates cultural resistance; but he fails to explain how or under what circumstances such resistance recedes sufficiently for indigenous societies to adopt "the predominant religion of the new empire into which they are incorporated."[62] "Adhesion" and "syncretism" are also depicted as impermanent states that are "often abandoned over time" and give way to full piety as converts overcome their former indifference and reject past beliefs and practices.[63] This assumes that the new religion passes seamlessly into the new cultural environments (of potential converts), unchanged and unchangeable. Moreover, if old and new religious elements are already reconciled to create a hybrid or new religious synthesis (the "adhesion"/"syncretism" phase), what exactly do the converts reject in the final phase characterized as *transformation*, and what makes the latter more permanent compared to the previous state? Furthermore, insofar as this "final" stage presumes a fixed or ideal outcome for the conversion process, we are left with an additional question: how does a community leave its past behind?

These queries highlight the conceptual dilemmas that historians grapple with when assessing the process of conversion in different historical contexts and periods. Efforts to understand conversion in pre-1500 settings encounter many challenges:[64] the scantiness of sources that document pre-Christian

---

associating the latter with experiences in which the old spiritual home is not abandoned for a new one in a single movement, but rather there is "an acceptance of new worships as useful supplements and not as substitutes" (*Conversion*, 7).

62. Baer, "History and Religious Conversion," 26.

63. Baer, "History and Religious Conversion," 32.

64. For details, see Alphonse Mingana, *The Early Spread of Christianity in Central Asia and the Far East: A New Document* (Manchester: University Press, 1925); Hillgarth, *Christianity and Paganism*, 1–8; James Thayer Addison, *The Medieval Missionary: A Study of the Conversion of Northern Europe, A.D. 500–1300* (Philadelphia: Porcupine, 1976), 140–54; Anders Winroth, *The Conversion of Scandinavia: Vikings, Merchants, and Missionaries in the Remaking of Northern Europe* (New Haven: Yale University Press, 2012), 128–37; I. N. Wood, *The Missionary Life: Saints and the Evangelisation of Europe, 400–1050* (Harlow: Longman, 2001), 3–24; Clay, *In the Shadow*

religion;[65] the pejorative nature of the meager descriptions of pagan religion in conversion narratives by Christian writers who are reporting beliefs and practices they strongly oppose; the near absence of accounts that convey the insights or responses of the pagan tribes themselves; and the sketchy reports on the style and content of the missionaries' evangelistic preaching (the primary emphasis in sources being on the piety and heroic deeds of missionary agents). Archeological discoveries (of burial sites, for instance) provide valuable clues; but even these are often inconclusive and, like all archeological findings, open to interpretation and conjecture.

The presentation in conversion narratives of "Christian" and "pagan" as stable diametric entities is obviously simplistic. But the historian must also contend with the fact that the terms "paganism" or "pre-Christian" religion are shorthand for a vast assortment of belief systems and religious traditions that varied greatly from one setting or context to another. Worship of various gods, ancestral veneration, and the practice of sacrifice were widespread; but some bore little evidence of a priesthood or temples. Moreover, religious life was inextricably bound up in social institutions and daily routines, so that itemized listings of pagan religious practices were stereotypical or simplistic. Also, in the medieval European context, missionary endeavor arguably sought to supplant the pre-Christian sacred landscape as well as to convert the pagan inhabitants.[66] The same could not be said of mission among the nomadic tribes of central Asia. Ultimately, paganism in all its forms was everywhere underpinned by a world of superstitious beliefs and oral folklore that endured in daily life and the collective consciousness long after the change in religious allegiance.

For medieval historians, who study an era and environment that gave rise to the notion of a Christian nation (Christendom), a deceptively simple question inevitably crops up: *when is conversion complete?* (This question is immaterial in the multitude of situations outside the European context in

---

of Death, 283–94; Christopher Haas, "Mountain Constantines: The Christianization of Aksum and Iberia," *Journal of Late Antiquity* 1, no. 1 (Spring 2008): 101–26.

65. The meagerness of historical records regarding Christian mission and conversion is a greater issue for missionary endeavors in contexts of insecurity and political volatility. Sources are even more negligible with regard to the informal interactions and seepage of intercultural exchange enacted through migration. The vast majority of Christian migrants left no testimony or trace of their missionary encounters.

66. Clay, *In the Shadow of Death*, 279–397.

which long-standing Christian communities were a minority, or Christianity coexisted with other *great* religions.) A number of medieval historians draw a distinction between "conversion" and "Christianization."[67] In this understanding, with variations, the "conversion" stage is associated with the initial missionary encounter and involves the preaching of the Christian message, confrontation with paganism, destruction of pagan temples and shrines, and baptism of converts. Alternatively, "Christianization" describes institutionalization, encompassing "the long term arrangement for pastoral care"; the establishment of "an enduring parochial system," including dioceses; incorporation of Christian ritual practice such as church attendance on specific days; and in some settings the emergence of a Christian political class.[68]

This categorization is germane in situations where Christian expansion was linked to political hegemony or bound up in processes of acculturation. But, aside from the fact that the focus on formal initiatives minimizes or ignores the importance of religious encounters and exchange facilitated by varieties of migrants,[69] the tacit assumption that the process is straightforward and sequential (in a fixed sense) is questionable. A firm division between conversion and Christianization may be encouraged by the fact that whole tribes were frequently brought into the church; but wholesale baptisms also precluded thorough knowledge of the new faith among new or prospective converts. More to the point, the confrontation between paganism and Christian ideals continued long after the establishment of formal Christian structures and rituals. The multiple decisions and motivations of potential converts and local pagan authorities, the multifaceted missionary approaches and modes of conversion, prolonged resistance by many pagan groups, incidents of mass reversion, and the ample record of efforts by ecclesiastical authority to root out entrenched pagan traditions or reinforce Christian precepts and practice long after the organization of a "national" church all point to a persistent and

---

67. Hillgarth, *Christianity and Paganism*, 170; Winroth, *Conversion of Scandinavia*, 103–4; Clay, *In the Shadow of Death*, 347; Wood, *Missionary Life*, 3–6. Winroth uniquely characterizes the initial infiltration of Christian ideas and practices (through migration) as Christianization and the institutional process of replacing pagan temples with churches as "conversion."

68. Clay, *In the Shadow of Death*, 347.

69. As we shall see in subsequent chapters, historically the spread of Christian ideas and practices typically precedes formal missionary action, and Christian immigrants often constitute the nucleus and embodiment of the church.

dynamic overlap between conversion and Christianization. A more comprehensive view suggests that even if conversion may be described as complete in some settings, it was never *final*.

In this study, the terms "conversion" and "Christianization" are used interchangeably (especially in chapter 7) to signify the multifaceted process of religious change. For analytical purposes, "Christianization" is frequently used when the transformation of a whole society, not just individuals or groups, is in view, but without any assumptions of finality or completeness. In any case, taking migrant experiences and encounters into consideration radically alters the frame of assessment and throws significant light on the notion that the conversion process and its consequences are different in different times and places in history.[70] From a global and historical perspective, two very different concepts provide what I consider the most meaningful framework for understanding conversion when the role of migration in the cross-cultural spread of Christianity is in view: first, the "translation principle" propounded by mission historians Lamin Sanneh and Andrew Walls, which I evaluate here in connection with the vexed question of syncretism; and, second, the "social conversion" approach advocated by the historian Jerry Bentley.

The Translation Principle and Syncretism: Strange Bedfellows

As an analytical tool applied to cross-cultural transmission, the translation principle places premium emphasis not on the values of the missionary but on the *recipient culture*. In other words, it accentuates local response or indigenous appropriation. Conceptually, Andrew Walls depicts translation in terms of "incarnation"; but he also draws on "linguistic" categories. The Christian story, he argues, begins with translation; for the incarnation (when God in Christ took on human flesh) was an act of translation: "Divinity was translated into humanity," becoming "*a person* in a particular locality and in a particular ethnic group, at a particular place and time."[71] The spread of the gospel (the word of God) to the different nations and societies of the world represents "re-translations," or a "succession of new translations," as Christ

---

70. Rambo, *Understanding Religious Conversion*, 12, 16.
71. Walls, *Missionary Movement*, 27.

becomes "flesh" in different cultures and territories through conversion.[72] This produces a diversity of translations, none better than any other, no one a normative standard for anyone else; for God has no favorite culture! In linguistic terms, writes Walls, translation "involves the attempt to express the meaning of the source from the resources of, and within the working system of, the receptor language." This is to say, he adds, that "something new is brought into the language, but that new element can only be comprehended by means of and in terms of the pre-existing language and its conventions. . . . [For] none of us take in a new idea except in terms of the ideas we already have."[73]

For Lamin Sanneh, "mission as translation is the vintage mark of Christianity."[74] He clarifies the point by contrasting mission by *translation* to mission by *diffusion*.[75] Mission by *diffusion* requires assimilation or adherence to the "founding cultural forms" of the missionary faith. As such, conversion is "a matter of cultural adoption"; membership of the new religion requires cultural change, including adhesion to a specific language and practices.[76] Mission by *translation*, on the other hand, entails no such deference to the originating culture and, in fact, challenges "the idea of [any one] culture as the arbiter of the truth of God." By establishing the compatibility of the Christian faith with all cultures, he insists, translation provides an antidote for cultural absolutization or idolatry, for the simple reason that "other cultures count equally before God."[77] Thus, "contrary to much of the prevailing wisdom . . . , [Christian] mission implies not so much a judgment on the cultural heritage of the convert . . . as on that of the missionary."[78] Sanneh insists, moreover, that "cultural hegemony violates the gospel by giving primacy to conveyance over the message."[79] But even in situations of conquest or imperial domina-

---

72. Walls, *Missionary Movement*, 27, 28.

73. Walls, *Missionary Movement*, 28, 35.

74. Sanneh, *Translating the Message*, 34.

75. Sanneh, *Translating the Message*, 33–34, 37.

76. In the case of expanding Islam, which Sanneh cites as a prime example of mission by diffusion, "adherence to the sacred Arabic of Scripture in law and devotion" is assumed. Cultural identity is fused with religious status—to be an Arab, for instance, is to be a Muslim (*Translating the Message*, 42).

77. Sanneh, *Translating the Message*, 56, 58, 93.

78. Sanneh, *Translating the Message*, 29.

79. Sanneh, *Translating the Message*, 34, 35.

tion, missionary pioneers must "concede the primacy of indigenous influence and materials."[80]

In their writings, both Walls and Sanneh point to the gentile breakthrough depicted in the book of Acts, whereby the gospel message (still encased in a distinctive Jewish heritage) spread across the cultural frontiers of Palestinian Judaism into the wider pagan gentile world, as a major example of translation. Gentile converts to faith did not have to adopt the norms and traditions of Judaism to become followers of Christ. Rather, their conversion required the Christian message to be expressed in the ideas and concepts of the Hellenistic cultural and religious environment they belonged to. Jesus the Messiah (a Jewish concept) was now presented pre-eminently as "the Lord Jesus" (Acts 11:20)—the term "lord" having unique meaning and application in the polytheistic Roman world with its cult of divinities—and "Jesus the Jew became the Christ of the Gentiles."[81] This process of translation gave rise to "an indigenous Hellenistic Christianity." Thus, for the gentile mission, the originating language of Hebrew and Aramaic that formed the basis of Jesus's ministry gave way to ancient Greek as the dominant language of proclamation and formation (see chapter 3).[82]

Lamin Sanneh concedes that the two ways of doing mission (*diffusion* and *translation*) often overlap, sometimes inseparably, in the spread of the Christian movement. The conversion of Germanic tribes, for instance, involved the suppression of local vernaculars and the imposition of Latin as the language of religious life.[83] But Germanic conversions also required translation and were not entirely free of cultural appropriation. The Anglo-Saxon missionaries had perforce to learn South German or use interpreters;[84] and elements of pre-Christian religion survived the Christianization process in the form of cultic

80. Sanneh, *Translating the Message*, 29.

81. Walls, *Missionary Movement*, 34; Sanneh, *Translating the Message*, 30.

82. Sanneh, *Translating the Message*, 36. For more on how the gentile mission "saved the Christian faith for the world," see Walls, *Missionary Movement*, 16–19; see also Sanneh, *Translating the Message*, 56–79. As I explain in chapter 3, migrant believers who were at home in both the Jewish and Hellenistic worlds played a critical role in this momentous development that saved the fledgling Christian movement from cultural captivity and ensured its survival.

83. Sanneh, *Translating the Message*, 57–59; also Walls, *Missionary Movement*, 69.

84. Hillgarth, *Christianity and Paganism*, 169; also, *The Letters of Saint Boniface*, trans. Ephraim Emerton (New York: Norton, 1976), 15–16.

observances, saints' days, festivals, and the very notion of Christendom.[85] Even though mission among the Slavs in the medieval period operated under the leadership of the Byzantine emperor, with the imposition of Greek culture firmly in view, vernacular translation was integral to the missionary strategy; for, as Richard Sullivan explains,

> the adoption of a native liturgy and the development of a written language for liturgical and instructional purposes facilitated the progress of barbaric society toward filling its need for Greek culture. Its use reveals the inspiration moving Greek missionary thought and practice. Christianity was not to be presented as a religion foreign to the pagans, but as a means for the attainment of ends already desired.[86]

In real life, the translation principle takes a variety of forms, is laden with ambiguity, and has no fixed outcome or end point; for "as social life and language change, so must translation."[87] Moreover, not only is the message more relevant than the missionary, but the missionary also has much to gain or learn from the gospel's encounter with another culture. For each act of translation, as the word about Christ interacts with new traditions and worldviews, has the potential "to reshape and expand the Christian faith."[88] In other words, crossing cultural frontiers is not only a prerequisite for the spread of the Christian movement; it is also the means whereby the worldwide community of faith increasingly experiences the fullness of the gospel. As Walls states else-

---

85. See R. W. Southern, *Western Society and the Church in the Middle Ages* (Harmondsworth: Penguin, 1990); Isnard Wilhelm Frank, *A History of the Medieval Church*, trans. John Bowden (London: SCM, 1995); James C. Russell, *The Germanization of Early Medieval Christianity: A Sociohistorical Approach to Religious Transformation* (New York: Oxford University Press, 1994); Richard Fletcher, *The Barbarian Conversion: From Paganism to Christianity* (New York: Holt, 1997), 228–84. A major example of such appropriation was the ninth-century Saxon poem titled *Heliand* (Savior), which recounts the life of Jesus in the style of a Germanic saga: Jesus is portrayed as a "guardian of the land" and "lord of the peoples" who gathers around him "youths for disciples, young men and good, word-wise warriors" (like the retainers of a Saxon lord).

86. Richard E. Sullivan, "Early Medieval Missionary Activity: A Comparative Study of Eastern and Western Methods," *Church History* 23, no. 1 (1954): 27.

87. Walls, *Missionary Movement*, 29.

88. Walls, *Missionary Movement*, 28.

where, "the representations of Christ by any one segment of human society are partial and impaired"; "all the representations are needed for the realization of the full stature of Christ.[89] Migration, therefore, does more than facilitate the cross-cultural expansion of the Christian movement; it often provides the impetus for historic transformations of the faith.

The translatability of the Christian message has bearing on the complicated question of *syncretism*. For Sanneh, syncretism in the Christian tradition "represents the unresolved, unassimilated, and tension-filled mixing of Christian ideas with local custom and ritual."[90] More broadly, the term is used to describe the process, in situations of cross-cultural penetration, whereby converts adopt or appropriate specific elements of a new religion (say, Christianity) and combine them with preexisting beliefs or practices in a way that makes sense within their cultural heritage. It is important to note that this concept is mainly applied to non-Western religious forms, often in judgmental fashion. This has met with strenuous objections. If it means "a mixing of ideas and practices from different sources," writes J. D. Y. Peel, a well-known scholar of Yoruba Christianity, syncretism "is by no means peculiarly African. For no adherent of the world religions anywhere derives all the furniture of his mind from his religion. [Human] beliefs are nearly always syncretistic, in that their content shifts in response to new experiences, and that some attempt to harmonize old and new."[91]

Not only is the term "syncretism" uncomplimentary, but it is also rarely, if ever, used as a self-reference. No individuals or groups describe themselves as "syncretists"! The translation principle, however, affirms syncretism not as an aberration or transitional (undeveloped) phase in the conversion process but as integral to the transmission of the Christian gospel. The syncretic motif is embedded in the Christian story because translation involves "the concrete embodiment of the faith in relevant cultural forms."[92] The incarnation, the original act of translation, involved not the abolition or replacement of humanity (made in God's image) but a confounding synthesis. The new religious

89. Andrew F. Walls, "Scholarship, Mission and Globalisation: Some Reflections on the Christian Scholarly Vocation in Africa," *Journal of African Christian Thought* 9, no. 2 (December 2006): 35.

90. Sanneh, *Whose Religion Is Christianity?*, 44.

91. Quoted in Elizabeth A. Isichei, *A History of Christianity in Africa: From Antiquity to the Present* (London: SPCK, 1995), 4.

92. Sanneh, *Translating the Message*, 59.

movement that emerged out of Jesus's ministry was unmistakably Jewish but formed of both old and new ideas—somewhat reflective of Jesus's claim that he came not to abolish the Law or the Prophets but to fulfill them (Matt. 5:17). The conversion of gentiles, who were "foreigners to the covenants of the promise" originally given to Jews, required neither the abolishment nor the subordination of either heritage but rather the creation of "one new humanity out of two" (Eph. 2:12, 15).

Christianity's "syncretist potential," writes Sanneh, is manifest in "an enormous appetite for absorbing materials from other sources."[93] The recurring acts of translation down through the ages as the Christian message encounters living cultures have given rise to a multiplicity of adaptations and a plurality of indigenous expressions. This process is always fraught with tension and danger, not least because the many cultural systems that make room for the Christian message also add to the Christian story in some way. But the greatest danger lies in that form of adaptation whereby the faith becomes fully and exclusively enshrined in a particular culture as the final or normative expression; for Christ speaks to all the nations as the Word made flesh.

This is not to imply an unqualified wholesale endorsement of the recipient culture. In the encounter with the gospel some features of culture are weakened or rejected, others are preserved or bolstered, with much ambiguity in between. But this is possible because the gospel spreads without the presumption of cultural rejection. In fact, observes Sanneh, "the degree to which Christianity became integrated into a particular culture [is] important for assessing the success of Christian preaching."[94] It is this full penetration of culture that allows the message of the gospel to mold and transform that culture or society; and it is worth bearing in mind that the encounter between old and new also takes place out of sight in the minds of converts where faith in Christ informs life's decisions. By and large, therefore, conversion from the viewpoint of translation is not about "substitution" of something new for something old nor about "addition" of something new to something old; it is rather "the turning, the re-orientation, of every aspect of humanity—culture-specific humanity—to God."[95] This process is never free from risk or compromise but always full of promise, and it has consequences for both the recipient culture and the Christian faith.

93. Sanneh, *Translating the Message*, 49.
94. Sanneh, *Translating the Message*, 43.
95. Walls, *Missionary Movement*, 28.

Social Conversion

From a historical perspective, Jerry Bentley provides a thoroughgoing examination of cross-cultural encounters and conversion in *Old World Encounters: Cross-Cultural Contacts and Exchanges in Pre-Modern Times* (1993). The book's coverage ends around 1400, and the term "pre-modern" in the title hints at a Eurocentric view of the world. Moreover, Bentley intentionally minimizes treatment of religious conversion, which he perceives as an individual (mainly psychological) experience. His main focus is on what he terms *social conversion*, "a process by which pre-modern peoples adopted or adapted foreign cultural traditions" resulting in the transformation of whole societies over three to five centuries.[96] This means that, in Bentley's assessment, the main distinction between "social" and "individual" conversion lies principally in the time frame: the former involves a process of change lasting over centuries while the latter is primarily associated with sudden spiritual or religious transformation.

As we have seen, this view of religious conversion is problematic. It ignores the significance of contextual factors in religious conversion and misconceives the phenomenon as essentially instantaneous and private. But Bentley's analysis is valuable because it pays close attention to religious change and expansion, not least because religious elements were integral to cultural traditions and interwoven with social life.

Bentley identifies three modes of (social) conversion that recurred frequently in premodern societies: (1) "conversion through voluntary association"; (2) "conversion induced by political, social, or economic pressure"; (3) "conversion by assimilation."[97] Inevitably, migrant movement and activities are integral to each category, since all are based on cross-cultural contact.

Conversion through voluntary association was typically instigated by merchants engaged in long-distance trade. Foreign merchants represented a source of great wealth to local elites, who consequently did everything possible to accommodate them. Traveling merchants were allowed to establish diaspora communities in the lands where they traded and brought with them cultural traditions from their homelands. Over time, these trading diaspora communities

96. Bentley, *Old World Encounters*, 8.
97. Bentley, *Old World Encounters*, 9–15.

73

also added religious institutions and authorities, such as priests. Since the foreign merchants transacted their business cross-culturally, those who dealt extensively with them often came to recognize that voluntary association with the merchant community and adoption of their (foreign) ways offered significant benefits; it smoothed business dealings and, for ruling elites, also offered "opportunities to establish political, military, and economic alliances with foreign powers."[98] In many instances, Bentley argues, the ruling elites or local monarch eventually embraced the faith of the foreign merchants. This repeatedly occurred in encounters between Muslim merchants and rulers in West Africa.[99]

Major incentives for conversion by voluntary association included access to the wider commercial world, political legitimization (through the establishment of Islamic rule under the local ruler's auspices), and the prestige imparted by alliance with other Islamic states. Whether or not the use of force or state sponsorship was brought to bear, transformation of the larger society frequently followed. The extent to which individuals or the society as a whole adopted the vast array of new customs and practices associated with the new religion—from language and cuisine to family relationships and observance of new laws—is not always easy to determine. As we shall see, it is hardly ever the case that the embrace (or imposition) of the new faith and cultural practices is accompanied by the complete abandonment of indigenous culture and traditions. Bentley is strangely silent on the issue of how communities in trade diasporas in turn appropriated or were co-opted into the culture of the host society, such as when foreign merchants married local women.[100]

Conversion induced by political, social, or economic pressure is typically associated with mass migrations of peoples or military conquest. None of the missionary religions (Christianity, Islam, and Buddhism) officially condones or recognizes conversion by coercion. But various measures can be utilized by conquerors or imperial authorities that, consistently applied over long periods of time, eventually produce the social conversion or religious transformation of an entire society or people group. These measures included increasingly punitive taxation; the extension of privileges enjoyed by adherents of the

98. Bentley, *Old World Encounters*, 10.

99. The story of Mansa Musa (1312–1337) of the Mali Kingdom, who became a devout Muslim and presided over one of the greatest empires in Africa, is a remarkable case in point.

100. See Philip D. Curtin, *Cross-Cultural Trade in World History* (New York: Cambridge University Press, 1984), 247.

majority or favored religious system to new converts (such as exemption from conscription and forced labor); the destruction of temples, churches, or shrines associated with minority faiths; the deployment of state resources and use of the full weight of the political apparatus to bolster the official religion; the prohibition of religious practices associated with the preservation and transmission of the minority faith/cultural tradition; and the passing of discriminatory regulations that deepen social and economic exclusion.

Such methods often meet with enduring resistance and remarkable efforts at cultural retention. Bentley argues correctly, however, that when these measures are unremittingly applied over several generations or centuries the potential for large-scale conversion from one religious system or cultural tradition to another increases dramatically. Indeed, even if "conversions" are insincere or opportunistic to begin with—a case of outward conformity that masks sustained allegiance to the old gods or traditions—over several generations such external conformism can result in de facto social conversion.[101]

Conversion by assimilation refers to "a process by which a minority group adapted to the cultural standards of the majority and eventually adopted its beliefs and values." Here too, mass migrations provide the context. Bentley reasons, for instance, that Germanic peoples who invaded the Roman Empire from the early fifth century were inclined to adopt Christianity (by then the dominant faith in Roman domains) because they were attracted to the more advanced political and economic life of the empire. In other situations, migrants who were cut off from their homelands and native culture for extended periods of time also experienced unwitting assimilation into the foreign culture of the destination society, as they adopted the language, married indigenous spouses, and raised children who were socialized to a society very different from their own. In Bentley's thinking this can even happen to groups of missionaries who lose regular or close contact with their fellow believers back in the homeland and, at the same time, fail to establish a permanent religious community by attracting significant numbers of converts.

As with the other types of cross-cultural conversion, "conversion by assimilation" is presented as a long-term process effected on a large (or societal) scale. Presumably because of his view that individual conversion is a spontaneous experience, Bentley insists that conversion by assimilation tends to be incomplete at the individual level. "Even in cases where individuals consciously and

101. Bentley, *Old World Encounters*, 13.

energetically sought assimilation," he writes, "signs of their original cultural orientations would inevitably persist," so that individuals are "rarely or never thoroughly converted."[102] But, however partial, such individual conversions can provide the foundation for large-scale social conversion as subsequent generations experience the new ways as native culture.

This reasoning is curious. The argument appears more credible when turned on its head. Culture is fundamentally social. The preservation of even basic elements like language represents a significant challenge for isolated individuals, for whom greater dependence on the host society and the need for social acceptance naturally intensify the pressure to assimilate. In effect, the individual migrant who experiences cultural isolation is much more likely to experience full incorporation (or social conversion) into the foreign culture, even with conscious resistance. Conversely, large groups of migrants, such as the Germanic tribes in Bentley's example, have a greater capacity to preserve their cultural traditions in a foreign environment over extended periods of time. Loss of contact with the homeland matters less because the group is usually quite capable of re-creating the institutions and structures that support native culture, thus providing the means for socializing the next generation. This does not preclude some degree of assimilation or acculturation. Some aspects of indigenous culture will be transformed or eroded as the migrants adapt to the new environment; participate in new institutions; acquire new skills, knowledge, and language; and even marry foreign spouses. And adoption of new religious traditions inevitably intensifies the process. But the capacity for cultural retention or resistance is less blunted, and continuities between old and new are more likely to be enduring.

These two theoretical models—the "translation principle" and "social [cross-cultural] conversion"—inform the assessment of the role of migration in Christian expansion in this volume (specifically chapters 4–9). In a few instances one or the other is more applicable, or provides greater analytical traction, than the other. But, combined or separately, they yield the critical insights needed to investigate the missionary significance of migrant movements and initiatives, historically and globally. At first glance, Bentley's three modes of social conversion appear to have greater utility value for the study of the impact of migration on religious change across cultures. But, in some ways, the trans-

---

102. Bentley, *Old World Encounters*, 14.

lation principle carries even greater meaning and application. This is because the focus on migration underscores the outsider status of the missionary agent, whether linked to a superior power or not; and this, in turn, allows greater attention to the society of reception as well as the modes of indigenous appropriation that prioritize the needs and aspirations of potential converts.

But as important as these models are, they do not constitute the most basic analytical tools for our study. Ultimately, the historical study of mission and migration in the Christian experience requires theological understanding and insights. From a biblical perspective, human migration is more than a matter of historical happenstance; it is intrinsic to faith and religious identity. The next chapter explores the body of ideas, beliefs, and historical experiences (dating back to the biblical period) that constitute foundational conceptions for full appraisal of Christian migration as an instrument of religious transformation.

CHAPTER THREE

Theologizing Migration: From Eden to Exile

> As for the foreigner who does not belong to your people Israel
> but has come from a distant land because of your name—for
> they will hear of your great name and your mighty hand and
> your outstretched arm—when they come and pray toward
> this temple, then hear from heaven, your dwelling place. Do
> whatever the foreigner asks of you, so that all the peoples of
> the earth may know your name and fear you, as do your own
> people Israel. . . .
>
> —1 Kings 8:41–43

From a historical perspective, the primeval history recorded in Genesis 1–11 reflects the understanding that the ancient Near East produced one of the earliest civilizations in the history of the world and was home to the earliest humans. But the Genesis account offers little concrete insight into the nature and extent of the multiple millennia that preceded recorded history. What it offers is a compact account of human beginnings that conveys consciousness of a long past.[1] The opening chapters of Genesis permit no exactitude of time spans: "In the beginning . . ." (Gen. 1:1) hardly corresponds to an ascertainable date or determinable epoch. The subsequent genealogical references also provide little guidance, since in the Hebrew tradition *sons* or *children* (as in "sons of" or "children born to") are not necessarily literal references and "can include grandsons and great-grandsons."[2] Indeed, such conventions remind

---

1. By the 1900s BCE, explains Egyptologist K. A. Kitchen, the ancients already knew that "their world was old, very old"; and this consciousness of a long past was preserved in oral traditions. K. A. Kitchen, *On the Reliability of the Old Testament* (Grand Rapids: Eerdmans, 2003), 439.
2. Kitchen, *Reliability of the Old Testament*, 440–41.

us that even if the distinctiveness of the Hebrew Bible is well attested,[3] its materials (including the stories of creation and the flood) bear the imprint of the motifs and cultural forms of the ancient Near Eastern world in which they were produced. All in all, while the biblical tradition is definite about the role of divine action—"to which we are invited to listen and respond in faith," notes John Goldingay[4]—its creators fully utilized or adapted the perspectives and concepts of their contemporary environment, with all its limitations.

The available extrabiblical data only fill some of the gaps. Despite the increasing gains of archeological endeavor, our knowledge of prehistory, the entire period in human history for which there are no written sources (before ca. 3000 BCE), remains quite limited. Scientific understanding of human existence prior to the Neolithic period (roughly 10,000–9,000 BCE), when there were already an estimated six million humans on the planet, is incredibly sketchy. Considerable imagination or guesswork is required to compensate for the paucity of archeological evidence.[5] In fact, the tremendous gaps in our understanding of primordial history invite a reticence about its exact details that is often absent in the copious literature.

THE ORIGINS OF ISRAEL DEBATE: MUCH ARCHEOLOGY, LITTLE CHEMISTRY

This chapter examines the integral role of migration in the biblical tradition (especially the Torah) and highlights its theological significance. This line of inquiry requires meaningful attention to the complex tapestry of polit-

3. Neither the Hebrew Bible's chronologically formed storyline nor its arrangement of documents into a single, largely sequential and coherent corpus has any equivalents in the ancient Near East. See A. R. Millard, "Israelite and Aramean History in the Light of Inscriptions," in *Israel's Past in Present Research: Essays on Ancient Israelite Historiography*, ed. V. Philips Long (Winona Lake, IN: Eisenbrauns, 1999), 129. See also William W. Hallo, "Biblical History in Its Near Eastern Setting: The Contextual Approach," in *Israel's Past in Present Research: Essays on Ancient Israelite Historiography*, ed. V. Philips Long (Winona Lake, IN: Eisenbrauns, 1999), and Long's introductory comments in the same volume (pp. 70–71).

4. John Goldingay, "The Patriarchs in Scripture and History," in *Israel's Past in Present Research: Essays on Ancient Israelite Historiography*, ed. V. Philips Long (Winona Lake, IN: Eisenbrauns, 1999), 490.

5. See David Christian, *Maps of Time: An Introduction to Big History* (Berkeley: University of California Press, 2004), 171–82, 197–99.

ical developments, undulating cultures, societal relations, recurrent invasions, and varieties of human migration that characterized the ancient world within which the biblical texts and tradition are set. The question immediately arises of how well the story of ancient Israel, as depicted in the Old Testament books, correlates with the broader history of the Near Eastern world. There is no simple or straightforward answer to this question; and it is well beyond the scope of this work to review the contours of the complex debate surrounding the historical credibility of the Hebrew Bible.[6] The brief and greatly simplified overview that follows serves mainly to clarify the approach that informs my assessment of the migrant motif that pervades the biblical material.

The debate around the historicity of the Hebrew Bible is mainly between two groups or camps: *minimalists*, who question or unequivocally repudiate the historicity of the biblical texts; and *maximalists*, who uphold the historical credibility of the biblical record and make a case for the plausibility of the biblical tradition.[7] Many, perhaps most, occupy "the middle ground of sweet reasonableness."[8] The fact that proponents in both camps rely heavily on archeological data and discoveries for their respective views and arguments clearly highlights the latent ambiguities of archeology and its limitations for

6. The specialties involved encompass Old Testament studies, archeology, Egyptology, Assyriology, ancient Near Eastern history and languages, etc.

7. For a comprehensive representation of the various points of view in the debate, see V. Philips Long, ed., *Israel's Past in Present Research: Essays on Ancient Israelite Historiography* (Winona Lake, IN: Eisenbrauns, 1999). From the 1980s, after decades of maximalist dominance, the tide swung in the direction of minimalism and widespread skepticism. However, maximalists remain sufficiently well represented within the Western academy to sustain an insidious tug of war between the two positions. A recent example of minimalist scholarship is *The Bible Unearthed: Archaeology's New Vision of Ancient Israel and the Origin of Its Sacred Texts* (New York: Free Press, 2001), by leading archeologists Israel Finkelstein and Neil Asher Silberman; while the most rigorous case for the maximalist view to date has been made by renowned Egyptologist Kenneth A. Kitchen in his 2003 volume *On the Reliability of the Old Testament*. See also Stephen E. Fowl, "Texts Don't Have Ideologies," *Biblical Interpretation* 3, no. 1 (1995): 15–34; Iain W. Provan, "Ideologies, Literary and Critical: Reflections on Recent Writing on the History of Israel," *Journal of Biblical Literature* 114, no. 4 (1995): 585–606; William W. Hallo, "The Limits of Skepticism," *Journal of the American Oriental Society* 110, no. 2 (April–June 1990): 187–99; James K. Hoffmeier, *Israel in Egypt: The Evidence for the Authenticity of the Exodus Tradition* (New York: Oxford University Press, 1997), 13–17.

8. Hallo, "Limits of Skepticism," 187.

establishing historical truth. More to the point, archeological material is "mute," which is to say, "archaeological remains do not speak for themselves but must be interpreted creatively both by the archaeologist and by the historian."[9] This means that individual preconceptions, ideological suppositions, and even undeclared agendas are more fundamental in the dispute. In fact, biblical scholars "are fiercely divided and in deep disagreement" on every important issue of interpretation pertaining to the Hebrew Bible.[10] Ultimately, therefore, the polemical debate over the historicity of the Hebrew Bible is not so much between heresy and orthodoxy but "essentially a disagreement about the relative merits of *different* ideologies."[11]

The survey of migration in the biblical material that follows assumes the historical reliability of the biblical texts, broadly speaking, and pays close attention to the ancient Near Eastern context in which the biblical material is set. This also requires recognition that the texts reflect the worldviews, conventions, and convictions of that world; and these have inherent limitations. The role played by subsequent generations in the preservation and transmission of the traditions they received raises awkward questions. However, I share the view that the historical value of the biblical record is not diminished by later redactions or subsequent updates. Proximity to narrated events is not an indication of a text's historical reliability.[12] Most important, whatever our presuppositions, "the biblical writings demand a readiness to read them in their own terms,"[13] as well as an acceptance that "we receive the text from the hands of these last writers, and they are the ones whose voice and message we have to hear first."[14] Thus, I take the position that in areas where the available

9. Provan, "Ideologies, Literary and Critical, 593.

10. Robert P. Carroll, "Exile! What Exile? Deportation and the Discourses of Diaspora," in *Leading Captivity Captive: "The Exile" as History and Ideology*, ed. Lester L. Grabbe (Sheffield: Sheffield Academic, 1998), 70. He adds tellingly that "there is no route that takes us away from disagreement."

11. Provan, "Ideologies, Literary and Critical," 600.

12. As others explain, the so-called sanctity of proximity argument has ensnared proponents in both sides of the debate. For more on this, see Iain W. Provan, V. Philips Long, and Tremper Longman, *A Biblical History of Israel* (Louisville: Westminster John Knox, 2003), 56–62, 111–12.

13. Millard, "Israelite and Aramean History," 137.

14. Rolf Rendtorff, "The Paradigm Is Changing: Hopes—and Fears," in *Israel's Past in Present Research: Essays on Ancient Israelite Historiography*, ed. V. Philips Long (Winona Lake, IN: Eisenbrauns, 1999), 67.

extrabiblical data are ambiguous or inconclusive, the historical worth or intention of the biblical record must be granted until it is shown to be *unhistorical* (rather than the other way around).

As John Bright acknowledged, "the Bible need claim no immunity from rigorous historical method."[15] But the latter has its own limitations. To start with, it is the historian's reconstruction that gives the available records (in themselves only a fragment of the past) meaning and significance. Clearly also, "the transcendent interpretation which the Bible gives [major] events" is not subject to historical investigation.[16] As it happens, the biblical texts were produced and preserved in an environment in which every community, indeed every adult, worshipped one god or another. Human existence was defined by an all-pervading religious consciousness; and the divine or otherworldly was perceived and experienced as active in the physical world. Moreover, while the biblical texts paint a portrait of Israel's past, that is not their only purpose. There is theological intent and inspiration, an effort to depict Israel's faith and portray an understanding of God that is deeply intertwined with Israel's history. From a theological perspective, "Israel's history cannot be severed from Israel's faith in the God who delivered, sustained, and constituted Israel as a people."[17] Whether archeology authenticates the historicity of Abraham's pilgrimages may be of less importance than the fact that his sojourn was also an act of faith; and this, it is correctly observed, is "something that archeology will never be able to verify or falsify."[18]

THE CITY OF BABEL AS A PARADIGM OF ANTI-MIGRATION: "LEST WE BE SCATTERED"

The story of Babel in Genesis 11:1–9 forms part of the biblical tradition that portrays primeval history and represents the culmination of the story of human beginnings presented in Genesis 1–11. In other words, its function is etio-

---

15. John Bright, *A History of Israel*, 4th ed., with an introduction and appendix by William P. Brown (Louisville: Westminster John Knox, 2000), 68.

16. Goldingay, "Patriarchs in Scripture and History," 489. For some, this raises serious questions of historical factuality—see, for instance, John J. Collins, "The 'Historical Character' of the Old Testament in Recent Biblical Theology," in *Israel's Past in Present Research: Essays on Ancient Israelite Historiography*, ed. V. Philips Long (Winona Lake, IN: Eisenbrauns, 1999), 150–69.

17. William P. Brown, introduction to John Bright, *A History of Israel*, 4th ed. (Louisville: Westminster John Knox, 2000), 22.

18. Brown, introduction to *A History of Israel*, 22.

logical—it seeks to explain human origins. The Babel episode, in fact, is said to mark the climax of the creation story.[19] Essentially, it provides an explanation for the irrevocable cultural diversity that marks our common humanity; and it leaves readers in no doubt that this dimension of human existence is rooted in migration and global dispersion. It also provides major theological insights into the formation of human societies and cultural pluralism.

Throughout the history of the Christian church down to the present day, interpretation of the Babel story has been dominated by the "pride and punishment" tradition.[20] In this understanding, the story describes the ungodly spirit evident in the actions or ambitions of a group of migrants who settled in Babylon (Mesopotamia). In defiance of God's explicit postflood command that humans "increase . . . and fill the earth" (Gen. 9:1, 7), this group decided to settle in one place and build a permanent, self-contained city with an enormous tower. The assumption that this project reflects human hubris or sinful rebellion is based on two assertions found in Genesis 11:4 (noted with added italics):

> Then they said, "Come, let us build ourselves a city, with *a tower that reaches to the heavens*, so that we may *make a name for ourselves*; otherwise we will be scattered over the face of the whole earth."

In this hermeneutic, the first phrase, "a tower that reaches to the heavens," is regarded as an egregious attempt on the part of the builders to challenge God's supremacy. Indeed, in popular understanding, the entire episode turns on this phrase—so much so that, in much of the literature and virtually every English translation of the Bible, the story is titled "The Tower of Babel"! The second phrase, "may make a name for ourselves," is interpreted as a striving for fame, prominence, and long-lasting recognition, further indication of overweening pride. Some even consider it an aspiration to divinity,[21] or, at the very least, a determination to carve out a destiny apart from God. The sum total of this perspective is that the diversity and diversification of human

---

19. E. J. van Wolde, *Words Become Worlds: Semantic Studies of Genesis 1–11* (New York: Brill, 1994), 105; Bernhard W. Anderson, *From Creation to New Creation: Old Testament Perspectives* (Minneapolis: Fortress, 1994), 167.

20. For a recent example, see André Lacocque, *The Captivity of Innocence: Babel and the Yahwist* (Eugene, OR: Cascade, 2010), 40–68.

21. Wolde, *Words Become Worlds*, 91–92.

existence is a needless drawback inflicted on humanity by a displeased deity in response to an act of prideful rebellion by our primeval ancestors. By implication, the divine intention at creation was for a culturally homogenous human population, speaking one language and occupying a single location. As such, the extraordinary cultural pluralism that marks the human condition is a contravention of the ideal, a hallmark of divine disfavor.

In a revision of the "pride and punishment" approach, contemporary scholars who read the text through the lens of liberation or postcolonial hermeneutics see a powerful demonstration of divine liberation from evil empire. *Babylon*, some note, means "gate of the gods" and symbolizes not primeval aspirations but efforts by contemporary entities to usurp powers that belong to God. The story thus highlights the human propensity for imperial or universal domination commonly manifested in the ambitions of nation-states or the actions of tyrannical regimes.[22] The powerful are wont to build economic or political towers of Babel that "perpetuate the unjust economic order of the world and control the destiny of humanity."[23] God's action not only thwarts the "project of false unity of domination" but also liberates "the nations that possess their own places, languages, and families." In other words, "the act of defeating the 'imperial project' is at the same time an act of deliverance: the peoples can return to their own nation, place, and language!" The divine action is retributive (directed at a segment of humanity) *and* restorative (it reestablishes the creation ideal of pluralism).

Like the more commonplace "pride and punishment," this "imperial domination" reading also fixates on the "tower" as the hermeneutic key. That aside, this understanding suffers from a major weakness: it *reads into* the account elements that are absent. There is "no suggestion of royal or imperial motivation" in the story, and the text "gives no intimation that the project was under the leadership of a king."[24] Nor is there any "hint that the builders surrendered

---

22. José Míguez-Bonino, "Genesis 11:1–9: A Latin-American Perspective," in *Return to Babel: Global Perspectives on the Bible*, ed. John R. Levison and Priscilla Pope-Levison (Louisville: Westminster John Knox, 1999), 15; see also Theodore Hiebert, "The Tower of Babel and the Origin of the World's Cultures," *Journal of Biblical Literature* 126, no. 1 (2007): 30–31, 34–35.

23. Choan-Seng Song, "Genesis 11:1–9: An Asian Perspective," in *Return to Babel: Global Perspectives on the Bible*, ed. John R. Levison and Priscilla Pope-Levison (Louisville: Westminster John Knox, 1999), 31–32.

24. Anderson, *From Creation to New Creation*, 172.

their primitive democracy to an aggressive ruler like Nimrod who promised political security and imperial renown." If anything, the narrator highlights the consensual nature of the decision (v. 3, "they said to each other"). Similarly, "a name for ourselves" more likely underscores the collective's determination to preserve its unity and unique identity (epitomized by one language) rather than the aspirations of a despot.

The durability of the "pride and punishment" interpretative tradition belies its flaws. The first thing to note is that the Babel story forms a narrative unit that is observably out of sequence.[25] There is obvious dissonance between the preceding sentence at the end of Genesis 10, "from these [clans] the nations spread out over the earth after the flood," and the opening statement in Genesis 11: "The whole world had one language and a common speech." So Genesis 11:1–9 takes us back to the beginning, to an earlier time when our human ancestors spoke the same language and shared the same location. Tellingly, the human actors in the passage are anonymous; "they are not presented with a personal name or collective identity" but are depicted as undifferentiated humanity.[26] At the same time, the nameless category ("the people" or "one people") identifies them as "a kinship society with a common ancestry and a single, shared culture."[27] In this regard, it is the *city*, not the tower, that holds the key to understanding the story. For the decision to build a city reflected decidedly human concerns for settled existence, stability, and security.

"There is something very human," notes Bernhard Anderson, "in this portrayal of a people who, with mixed pride and anxiety, attempted to preserve primeval unity."[28] The builders' strivings, adds Ellen van Wolde, "seem not to be directed vertically but rather horizontally."[29] At the heart of the story, therefore, is not sinful human rebellion but rather a natural human resistance to migration and the forces of dispersion, evidenced in the expression "lest we

---

25. The divine mandate that humans must "be fruitful and increase in number and fill the earth" is stated twice in Genesis 9; and the "Table of Nations" in Genesis 10 captures the diversification and dispersion of the human race into the known world, with the multiplication of languages and ethnicities that this implies. Kitchen correlates the list of nations in Genesis 10 to known entities identified in ancient records from the third to first millennia BCE (*Reliability of the Old Testament*, 430–38).

26. Wolde, *Words Become Worlds*, 96, 101–2.

27. Hiebert, "Tower of Babel," 43.

28. Anderson, *From Creation to New Creation*, 173.

29. Wolde, *Words Become Worlds*, 100.

be scattered abroad on the face of the earth" (Gen. 11:4, KJV). One could say that the builders were motivated not by the spirit of pride but by a spirit of *anti-migration*, induced by the fear of losing cultural homogeneity and tribal identity. In biblical usage, making a name is "essentially the act of establishing an identity that will endure."[30] Thus, the aspiration to "make a name" also reflects the striving for unity, the desire to preserve the status and solidarity of kinship for posterity. The builders of Babel were motivated not by prideful ambition or an aspiration to divinity but by a determination to preserve what they had—one language and one location—by building one city with one tower.[31] This is a story more accurately titled "The City of Babel."[32]

What then of the tower? As it turns out, this is a rather mundane reference. Indeed, more careful reading suggests that the tower is inconsequential, perhaps relevant only as a testimonial to the builders' religiosity. Due to the region's lack of natural stone the builders were forced to "make bricks and bake them thoroughly" and use "tar for mortar" (Gen. 11:3). The phrase "a tower that reaches to the heavens" was a popular cliché in the ancient Near East for "impressive height"; and it "appears often in descriptions of fortifications and cultic installations," which typically include towers.[33] In Mesopotamia, in fact, "this idiom is ubiquitous on the descriptions of the height of ziggurats and temple complexes."[34] The tower simply captures the realities of ancient Mesopotamia.

All this is to say that the divine response in this story is *corrective*, not retributive. Clearly, the condition of having the same language and location was not of the builders' making; it was "the earth's original situation."[35] To attribute hubris or sinful pride to the building project is therefore dubious; and this fosters a misreading of the divine action. Most translations of Genesis 11:6 are worded in such a way as to conform to the entrenched view that God's response was motivated by apprehension about "unrestrained human pride" or sinister human intentions:[36] "The Lord said, 'If as one people speaking the

30. Hiebert, "Tower of Babel," 40.
31. In the Hebrew language, the expression of this desire for a "name" (*šem*) and a single location (*šam*) is semantically more arresting.
32. Cf. Hiebert, "Tower of Babel," 37.
33. Hiebert, "Tower of Babel," 35 (see notes), 37–38.
34. Hiebert, "Tower of Babel," 38.
35. Wolde, *Words Become Worlds*, 98.
36. See Hiebert's insightful examination of the original Hebrew ("Tower of Babel," 43–46).

same language they have begun to do this, then nothing they plan to do will be impossible for them'" (NIV). Old Testament scholar Theodore Hiebert explains, however, that the Hebrew word translated "if" is more commonly and consistently rendered "behold" in the Hebrew Bible (conveying a simple statement of fact). With this understanding, the sense of Yahweh's entire speech is better conveyed thus:

> [Behold] there is now one people and they all have one language. From what they have accomplished already, it looks like their plans to remain one people, with one language in one location, will succeed.[37]

The divine response is corrective because human intent (non-migration and universal cultural sameness) collided with divine purpose. The builders' self-preoccupation (v. 4, "for ourselves") contrasts sharply with the divine purview (vv. 8, 9, "the whole earth").[38] This clash of perspectives is embedded in the storyline: preservation versus propagation, tribalism versus pluralism, singularity versus multiplicity. From this perspective, the divine plan for humanity is not one language but a plurality of languages, not one location but global dispersion, not a single name or cultural identity but a multiplicity of cultures. In this regard, the divine rejection of a single location—"from there the Lord dispersed them over the face of all the earth" (Gen. 11:9, ESV)—is strikingly evocative of the modern "out of Africa" explanation of human origins.

The "City of Babel" story, then, establishes that the multiplicity of languages, peoples, and nationalities dispersed throughout the world reflects divine purpose, not divine punishment. That this central truth mattered to the ancients is striking, since linguistic diversity was even greater in the ancient world than it is today.[39] Down through the ages, the hostility and tensions between migrants and settled groups, foreigners and native populations, outsiders and mainstream societies have been a dominant and recurrent theme of human existence. It is etched in the entire biblical narrative and under-

37. Hiebert, "Tower of Babel," 45.

38. Wolde notes that the catchphrase "the whole earth" brackets the story and provides a critical reference point for both human action and the divine response (*Words Become Worlds*, 95–96).

39. Until multicultural empires facilitated use of a lingua franca, "most people . . . could not communicate with those living across borders" (Michael C. Howard, *Transnationalism in Ancient and Medieval Societies: The Role of Cross-Border Trade and Travel*, 20.

girds the cross-cultural expansion of the Christian movement down to the present day.

From a biblical perspective, however, human migration is not only integral to the pluralism that marks the human condition but also, theologically speaking, quite compatible with divine purposes. It is of great significance, therefore, that the biblical drama continues with the story of Abraham (Gen. 12:1). In sharp contrast to the builders in Babel, Abraham was willing to leave his homeland and exchange the comfort of cultural homogeneity (and linguistic familiarity) for the uncertainties of nomadic existence. It is as the quintessential migrant-itinerant that he becomes a paradigm of the people of God. (See "The Hebrew Patriarchs" below.)

Migration and the Biblical Tradition

We encounter every major form of migration in the biblical record. The four types of human migration and the major categories of "cross-community migration" (see "Types of Human Migration," chapter 1) are fully represented in all their complexity and incalculable impact. The Hebrew Bible narratives are replete with references to "home-community migrations"—that is, movement of people from one place to another within their own community—undertaken for a variety of personal reasons (including weddings, funerals, searching for a bride, attending a banquet, procuring food for one's household, and relocation from one town to another). There can be little doubt, as David A. Dorsey notes, that "during the Iron Age [1200–600 BCE] the highways and byways of Israel were bustling with activity."[40] Our main interest, however, is in the long-distance travel ("whole-community" and "cross-community" migrations) that involved either the dislocation of an entire community or the departure of select individuals or groups.

Taken as a whole, the biblical tradition and message would be meaningless without migration or migrant activity. The migrant experience not only pervades biblical material but also forms bookends of sorts to Scripture: expulsion from Eden marks the opening act while exile on the island of Patmos casts a long shadow over the final chapter. As Frank Crüsemann puts it, "from

---

40. David A. Dorsey, *The Roads and Highways of Ancient Israel* (Baltimore: Johns Hopkins University Press, 1991), 3.

Abraham's departure—and fundamentally even from Cain—to the child in the manger, in its main lines the Bible is a story of people who depart, set out in search of bread, land and protection, wander about and return."[41] The theme of migration is particularly pervasive in the Hebrew Bible: the book of Genesis could sensibly be renamed the book of migrations (significantly, the following book is titled "Exodus");[42] the corpus known as the Pentateuch or Torah is dominated by migrant activity; and Israel's existence as a nation is indissolubly linked to the memory and experience of migration. Equally significant is the fact that migration is also imbued with profound religious and theological significance in the biblical text.

Biblical Migrant Categories

There are three major categories of migrants depicted in the Bible, with some overlap of meaning and application: (1) "stranger" or "alien"; (2) "foreigner"; and (3) "sojourner."[43] A "stranger" or "alien" (Hebrew *gēr*, Greek *paroikos*, Latin *peregrinus*) was a person who did not belong to the community, nation, or territory in which he or she permanently resided (or was a long-term resident).[44] In the ancient Near Eastern context, strangers and aliens were commonplace; their numbers constantly swelled due to famine, military conquest,

41. Frank Crüsemann, "'You Know the Heart of a Stranger' (Exodus 23:9). A Reflection of the Torah in the Face of New Nationalism and Xenophobia," in *Migrants and Refugees*, ed. Dietmar Meith and Lisa Sowle Cahill (Maryknoll, NY: Orbis Books, 1993), 96; see also Robert P. Carroll, "Deportation and Diasporic Discourses in the Prophetic Literature," in *Exile: Old Testament, Jewish, and Christian Conceptions*, ed. James M. Scott (New York: Brill, 1997), 64.

42. Andrew F. Walls, "Mission and Migration: The Diaspora Factor in Christian History," *Journal of African Christian Thought* 5, no. 2 (2002): 3.

43. See James K. Hoffmeier, *The Immigration Crisis: Immigrants, Aliens and the Bible* (Wheaton, IL: Crossway, 2009), 48–52; M. Daniel Carroll, *Christians at the Border: Immigration, the Church, and the Bible* (Grand Rapids: Baker Academic, 2008), 99–102; Crüsemann, "You Know the Heart of a Stranger," 101–2; Peter C. Phan, "Migration in the Patristic Era," in *A Promised Land, a Perilous Journey: Theological Perspectives on Migration*, ed. Daniel G. Groody and Gioacchino Campese (Notre Dame: University of Notre Dame Press, 2008), 48–49.

44. Crüsemann counsels, however, that "even within the territory on which one's own people is settled, one is a stranger where one is not at home and has no social roots" ("You Know the Heart of a Stranger," 101). In other words, the term "stranger" is not strictly restricted to the nonnative.

enslavement, nomadic existence, or the need for refuge from punishment (as was the case for Moses in Midian).[45] The other two labels, "foreigner" and "sojourner" (Hebrew *nokrî* or *zār*; Greek *allotrios*), typically applied to someone whose permanent residence was in another nation, therefore wholly "other" (with unfavorable notions of incompatibility), and whose stay was only temporary.[46] The Hebrew *zār* applied to one who was "passing through the land with no intention of taking residence"—such as a merchant, seasonal worker, or mercenary—or one who had only recently taken up residence. The term *nokrî*, however, appears to have religious connotations. It was mainly used to indicate "that something or someone is non-Israelite"—the religious other (i.e., someone who worships idols or belongs to another religious tradition). The term was frequently applied to the "foreign woman" in this negative sense; thus, Jews were forbidden from marrying *nokrî* (Deut. 7:1–6).

For our purposes, the "stranger" (or "resident alien") and the "foreigner" are the main categories of interest. The meaning and application of these biblical terms are laden with ambiguities. Some scholars suggest that the Hebrew *gēr* (pl. *gērîm*) or the Greek *paroikos* (pl. *paroikoi*) are broad descriptions of the "other" that encompass the stranger, resident alien, foreigner, or sojourner.[47] Others, however, insist on a sharp distinction between the "resident alien" and the "foreigner" in connection with Israel's legal tradition.[48] But, as I explain

45. See Frank Anthony Spina, "Israelites as Gērîm, 'Sojourners,' in Social and Historical Context," in *The Word of the Lord Shall Go Forth*, ed. Carol L. Meyers, Michael Patrick O'Connor, and David Noel Freedman (Winona Lake, IN: Eisenbrauns, 1983), 324–25; see also Aaron A. Burke, "An Anthropological Model for the Investigation of the Archeology of Refugees in Iron Age Judah and Its Environs," in *Interpreting Exile: Displacement and Deportation in Biblical and Modern Contexts*, ed. Brad E. Kelle, Frank Ritchel Ames, and Jacob L. Wright (Atlanta: Society of Biblical Literature, 2011).

46. See André Lacocque, "The Stranger in the Old Testament," in *The Newcomer and the Bible*, ed. André Lacocque and Francisco Ruiz Vasquez (Staten Island, NY: Center for Migration Studies, 1971), 9–10.

47. See Bernhard A. Asen, "From Acceptance to Exclusion: The Stranger in Old Testament Tradition," in *Christianity and the Stranger*, ed. Francis W. Nichols (Atlanta: Scholars Press, 1995), 19; Thomas M. Horner, "Changing Concepts of the 'Stranger' in the Old Testament," *Anglican Theological Review* 42, no. 1 (1960): 49–53; Yu Suee Yan, "The Alien in Deuteronomy," *Bible Translator* 60, no. 2 (April 2009): 112–17.

48. Hoffmeier, *Immigration Crisis*, 48–52; Crüsemann, "You Know the Heart of a Stranger," 101–2.

below, the latter view seems partly influenced by modern conventions and perhaps overlooks the fluidity of everyday existence in the ancient world. In English translations, the two terms are often used interchangeably; thus Isaiah 1:7 proclaims, "Your country lies desolate, your cities are burned with fire; in your very presence *aliens* devour your land; it is desolate, as overthrown by *foreigners*" (NRSV; italics added); or "Your country is desolate, your cities burned with fire; your fields are being stripped by *foreigners* right before you, laid waste as when overthrown by *strangers*" (NIV; italics added). Incidentally, the same is true of "foreigner" and "sojourner," as is evident in Abraham's declaration to the Hittites when negotiating purchase of land to bury his wife Sarah (Gen. 23:4): "I am a *sojourner* and *foreigner* among you..." (ESV; italics added). In what follows, these terms ("stranger," "foreigner," and "alien") are synonymously applied as referential categories for the migrant-outsider.

Migration and Biblical Faith

Andrew Walls offers what might be termed a twofold biblical typology of migration:[49] the "Adamic" and "Abrahamic." The *Adamic* model, he explains, stands for "disaster, deprivation, and loss," exemplified by the expulsion of the first couple from the Garden of Eden or the Babylonian Exile. This model is "punitive." The *Abrahamic* model represents "escape to a superlatively better future," epitomized by the call of Abraham to leave his Mesopotamian city for the land of promise. This model is "redemptive." Walls admits, however, that the two models can overlap, for within the divine economy, disaster can have redemptive purpose.

The recognition that migration often serves a redemptive purpose is central to this study. My assessment, however, analyzes migration in the biblical tradition based on two hypotheses. First, that migration—more specifically the experience of being an outsider, alien, or foreigner—emerges as a metaphor for the life of faith and often proves to be "a theologizing experience."[50] Second, that divine purposes and designs are recurrently disclosed (or providentially unfolded) within the experience of migration and dislocation.

49. Walls, "Mission and Migration," 3.
50. Timothy L. Smith, "Religion and Ethnicity in America," *The American Historical Review* 83, no. 5 (December 1978): 1174.

How migrant movements facilitate cross-cultural encounters and interaction is vividly portrayed in the biblical texts. But, repeatedly, the experiences of displacement, exile, or being refugees are depicted as providential. In other words, the tragedy and trauma associated with human migration is often given transformative significance or transcendental meaning. Joseph says of his captivity, "God sent me ahead of you to preserve for you a remnant on earth and to save your lives by a great deliverance. . . . It was not you who sent me here, but God . . ." (Gen. 45:7–8). This understanding does not legitimize human suffering. Rather, it suggests that the vulnerability, powerlessness, and marginalization integral to the experience of migration allow divine purpose and promise, rather than human effort, to be directly perceived. Human migration, then, serves as a prism through which we apprehend "the redemptive acts of God"; and this, rather than the heroic acts of Israel's ancestors, is invariably the most decisive factor.[51]

The Hebrew Patriarchs, Migration, and the Foundations of Biblical Faith

The world contemplated by the biblical writers extended "from Spain in the west to India in the east, with sporadic references to parts of North Africa west of Egypt, to Ethiopia, and to Arabia."[52] But it is Egypt and the Fertile Crescent (encompassing Palestine, Syria, and Mesopotamia) that dominate the biblical narrative. It is this geographical area and its rich history, spanning a period of almost two millennia, that command our attention.

The overall data (biblical and external) situate the Hebrew patriarchs in the period roughly spanning 2000–1500 BCE.[53] By this patriarchal age

---

51. J. Alberto Soggin, "History as Confession of Faith—History as Object of Scholarly Research," in *Israel's Past in Present Research: Essays on Ancient Israelite Historiography*, ed. V. Philips Long (Winona Lake, IN: Eisenbrauns, 1999), 217.

52. Michael David Coogan, "In the Beginning: The Earliest History," in *The Oxford History of the Biblical World*, ed. Michael David Coogan (New York: Oxford University Press, 1998), 4.

53. Kitchen, *Reliability of the Old Testament*, 313–72; Provan, Long, and Longman, *Biblical History of Israel*, 109–19; Bright, *History of Israel*, 47–103; Roland de Vaux, "The Hebrew Patriarchs and History," in *Israel's Past in Present Research: Essays on Ancient Israelite Historiography*, ed. V. Philips Long (Winona Lake, IN: Eisenbrauns, 1999), 470–79; Goldingay, "Patriarchs in Scripture and History," 455–91. Kitchen

(as explained in chapter 2), long-distance travel and transnational exchange (commercial and cultural) were major features of the ancient Near Eastern world. However, the biblical book of Genesis, our sole source for the story of the patriarchs, provides only indirect hints of the extensive migrations and constant flux of peoples and cultures that marked the period. The story of the patriarchs fits well into a world in which the juxtaposition of sedentary dwellers (in villages and large urban centers) and substantial nomadic populations was a major and enduring feature. Relations between settled inhabitants and pastoral nomads were complex and prone to conflict.[54] But the relationship was also symbiotic, "each providing goods that were necessary to the other" and both antagonistic to political domination by large cities' authorities.[55] In any case, the proximity of nomadism and sedentary existence allowed many tribal groups to fluctuate between the two modes of existence based on need and circumstances. The biblical narratives place the Hebrew patriarchs (Abraham, Isaac, and Jacob) in this milieu.

Importantly, the religious life and identity of the patriarchs were profoundly linked to the experience of migration. The clan headed by Terah (Abraham's father) consisted of either city dwellers in the ancient city of Ur in southern Mesopotamia or members of a pastoralist tribe temporarily settled around the city.[56] Apart from the obscure observation that they "worshipped other gods" (Josh. 24:2)—quite likely including the moon god *Sin*—we know

---

contends that "in terms of content, these narratives give a picture of real human life as lived by West Semitic pastoralists, derived mainly from conditions observable in the early second millennium, with a very moderate amount of minor retouches in ... later periods" (*Reliability of the Old Testament*, 365).

54. Howard, *Transnationalism in Ancient and Medieval Societies*, 29. The precarious relations between nomads and settled populations are strikingly depicted in the book of Judges, where the Israelite population settled in Canaan is systematically terrorized by the periodic migrations of vast numbers of nomads—described as "the Midianites, Amalekites and other eastern peoples" (Judg. 6:1–6).

55. Wayne T. Pitard, "Before Israel: Syria-Palestine in the Bronze Age," in *The Oxford History of the Biblical World*, ed. Michael David Coogan (New York: Oxford University Press, 1998), 75.

56. In the recurring debate over the identification of Abraham's birthplace as Ur (also Urfa) in northern or southern Mesopotamia, the case for the latter appears much stronger. Cf. Alan R. Millard, "Where Was Abraham's Ur? The Case for the Babylonian City," *Biblical Archaeology Review* 27, no. 3 (May/June 2001); also, Kitchen, *Reliability of the Old Testament*, 316.

little of their religious background.[57] Nor are we afforded any insights into Abraham's "conversion" from worshipping "other gods" to the worship of Yahweh. But the narrative details suggest that while the change was momentous, it was by no means instantaneous. This can be inferred from the fact that Abraham's first recorded act of worship took place after three divine revelations spanning a considerable period. The first occurred "while he was still in Mesopotamia" before the entire clan migrated to the city of Haran over 1,000 miles away (Acts 7:2; cf. Gen. 15:7; Josh. 24:3). The second came in Haran, some sixty years later, in the wake of Terah's death.[58] By then sufficient time had elapsed for Abraham to accumulate substantial possessions and acquire servants (Gen. 12:5). This second encounter included the well-known divine directive (Gen. 12:1–3):

> The Lord said to Abram, "Leave your country, your people and your father's household and go to a land I will show you. I will make you a great nation . . . ; I will make your name great, and you will be a blessing. . . . And all the peoples of the earth will be blessed through you."

The third divine revelation came after Abraham had completed the long journey from Haran to Canaan, an event that prompted him to build an altar "to the Lord, who had appeared to him" (Gen. 12:7).

In Abraham's story, the fusion of migrant existence and divine election is irrevocable. The biblical writers leave us with no doubt that Yahweh initiated his divine plan for the nations by choosing a migrant. Whether or not his family were nomad pastoralists in Ur, Abraham was a migrant when he received and acted on the divine promise that shapes the rest of the patriarchal narratives and forms the basis of Israel's religion.[59] We will never know the precise considerations or religious instincts that triggered his exemplary faith.

---

57. Ur was a major center for the worship of the moon god Sin, as was Haran, which may partly explain Terah's decision to settle there (Gen. 11:31), aborting his original plan to go to Canaan. Several names of members of the clan (including Terah, Laban, Sarai, and Milcah) were associated with the cult of the moon god (Bright, *A History of Israel*, 90).

58. Based on the details provided in Gen. 11:26, 32; 12:4. See also Miguel A. De La Torre, *Genesis* (Louisville: Westminster John Knox, 2011), 45.

59. See Walls, "Mission and Migration," 3.

But we know the circumstances and social condition that framed his response and commitment.

He became "Abram the Hebrew" (Gen. 14:13), the perpetual outsider. Though of uncertain origin, the term "Hebrew" in the Hebrew Bible is virtually synonymous with "foreigner" or "outsider."[60] It is used by non-Israelites to describe Israelites, often disparagingly: "this Hebrew has been brought to us to make sport of us!" cried Potiphar's wife (Gen. 39:14).[61] Its affinity with *'apiru* (a term widely applied in the ancient Near Eastern context to diverse groups of people who were landless refugees) remains an open question.[62] Regardless, prior to settlement in Canaan (the timing of which is vigorously debated), the Israelites are clearly represented in the biblical account as troublesome migrants, in fulfillment of the prediction that Abraham's descendants would become "strangers in a country not their own" before they entered the promised land (Gen. 15:13–16). Indeed, as in much else related to the link between migration and divine election, Abraham's life provided the blueprint. It imbued migration with theological significance.

To one who was a foreigner and resident alien, thus accustomed to alienation and marginalization, the divine promise of land and social recognition ("I will make your name great," Gen. 12:2) no doubt had special appeal. That same promise also impelled Abraham to "wander from my father's household" (Gen. 20:13) and embark on a lifelong state of nomadic migration. This is to say that, due to Abraham's worship of Yahweh, his life—albeit indelibly shaped by his cultural heritage (notably evident in his family life) and social environment—was defined by a migrant-outsider status. Abraham's story also exemplifies the juxtaposition of privation and promise inherent in biblical faith: he was brought out from his people to become the ancestor of a new people; his landless existence formed the basis of his faith in the divine prom-

60. The ancient Jewish philosopher Philo asserted that "Hebrew" means "migrant"—see José E. Ramírez Kidd, *Alterity and Identity in Israel: The גר in the Old Testament* (New York: de Gruyter, 1999), 124.

61. Other examples include Exod. 2:6; 1 Sam. 4:6, 9. The term was also used by Israelites but typically in situations where they identify themselves to foreigners or non-Israelites (Gen. 40:15; Exod. 3:18; 5:3). See Bright, *History of Israel*, 94–95; Provan, Long, and Longman, *Biblical History of Israel*, 170–72.

62. However, Frank Spina argues that the Israelites fall in this category and were certainly joined by such groups (Spina, "Israelites as Gērîm," 130–31); see also Bright, *History of Israel*, 94–95; Provan, Long, and Longman, *Biblical History of Israel*, 170–72.

ise of a specific land; his perennial state of not belonging was inseparable from his sense of belonging to God (divine election); he was removed from his father's household in order to become the father of the house of Israel (Exod. 19:3–7) and the spiritual ancestor of the universal household of faith (Gal. 6:10; 1 Pet. 2:5; 4:17).

Crucially, it was as a migrant that Abraham grew in faith. As explained above, migrant existence in the early second millennium BCE world was fraught with incalculable risks and dangers. Long-distance travel, especially by merchants, was not uncommon. But travel was exceedingly precarious, and a foreigner or outsider was vulnerable to grievous exploitation and countless threats. The patriarchs were perennial outsiders, who did not belong to the societies in which they sojourned or sought refuge. As foreigners, they had perforce to contend with grave dangers, tensions, indignities, and conflicts.[63] They were repeatedly pushed by famine and economic insecurity to become refugees, which rendered them dependent on the host society and its leaders for their safety and well-being.

Much has been made of the fact that Abraham, out of desperation—having migrated with his family to escape the danger of famine—felt compelled to lie and put his wife at risk as part of an elaborate ploy to enter Egypt (Gen. 12:10–13). Some commentators, with the privilege of modern Western sensibilities, label this a dreadful betrayal committed by a feckless man who "sells his wife for riches."[64] Many others lament Abraham's lack of faith. Viewed through the lens of migration, however, it is perhaps easier to understand why Abraham purposely deceived the authorities in an effort to ensure the survival of his large family. (During this period, Egyptian authorities were often hostile to Semitic-speaking immigrants, who were driven to Egypt in search of food; and they made great effort to secure Egypt's borders.[65]) Abraham's actions reflect the suspicion and distrust of authorities that mark refugee experiences down through the ages and are readily understood by twenty-first-century immigrants.[66] As Daniel M. Carroll R. observes, "modern accounts of border

---

63. For a brief summary, see Timothy Lenchak, "Israel's Refugee Ancestors," *Bible Today* 35, no. 1 (January 1997): 10–15.

64. De La Torre, *Genesis*, 153.

65. Hoffmeier, *Israel in Egypt*, 53–60.

66. Jean-Pierre Ruiz, *Readings from the Edges: The Bible and People on the Move*

crossings are full of such stories of danger and duplicity in order to survive."[67] In any case, the perplexities and travails of the migrant are inseparable from Abraham's distinctive faith. The writer of the New Testament book of Hebrews celebrates him as a model of faith precisely because he "went, even though he did not know where he was going . . . , [and lived] like a stranger in a foreign country" (Heb. 11:8).

In the final analysis, the theme of migration dominates the patriarchal narratives. The patriarchs were transhumant migrants (and occasional refugees) who constantly traveled in the region and borderlands of Palestine, with longer journeys to Mesopotamia and Egypt. They were not wanderers, isolated and perennially displaced, but rather seminomads who frequently pitched their tents close to towns or cities (Gen. 12:8; 13:12; 33:18) and sometimes settled in one place long enough to grow crops (Gen. 26:6, 12). They were also on occasion forced by adverse circumstances such as famine to seek refuge within settled populations (Gen. 12:10-20; 20:1-18; 26:1-2, 6). That said, the patriarchs are also depicted as "wealthy sheikhs"[68] or heads of large clans with numerous livestock. Abraham was hailed as "a mighty prince" (Gen. 23:6); and the placatory gifts Jacob sent his brother Esau included "two hundred female goats and twenty male goats, two hundred ewes and twenty rams, thirty female camels with their young . . . , and twenty female donkeys and ten male donkeys" (Gen. 32:14-15). Their substantial wealth afforded them a certain self-reliance and bargaining power in difficult situations. But they owned no land, were compelled to buy plots for burying their dead (Gen. 23:3-4, 17-20; 50:5), and did not settle permanently in cities.

As refugees among the Philistines, both Abraham and Isaac experienced serious conflict with the local authorities and population around the security issue of water rights (Gen. 21:25-31; 26:12-18). In both cases, a pact with Abimelech, the Philistine king, was necessary to ensure peace. Even so, Isaac was subsequently expelled from the land he had cultivated and forced

---

(Maryknoll, NY: Orbis Books, 2011), 66-68; Daniel L. Smith-Christopher, *A Biblical Theology of Exile* (Minneapolis: Fortress, 2002), 82.

67. M. Daniel Carroll R., "Portraits of People on the Move in the Bible," in *Thinking Christianly about Immigration*, ed. M. Daniel Carroll R. (Denver, CO: Grounds Institute of Public Ethics, 2011), 5.

68. Kitchen, *Reliability of the Old Testament*, 318.

to start over elsewhere. Similarly, Jacob spent much of his life as a fugitive, repeatedly forced to take flight as an individual or with his entire family in tow. Some of the most poignant episodes of his life reveal the insecurity and travail of a wanderer, such as his deeply emotional reaction when a chance encounter with strangers far from home revealed a family link (Gen. 29:12). When he met Pharaoh, he claimed the identity of a sojourner—"my life has been spent wandering from place to place" (Gen. 47:9)—and he spent his last days as a resident alien in Egypt where his descendants were subsequently enslaved.

As was commonplace at the time, the patriarchs mainly traveled on foot. Abraham's lengthy journey from Haran to Egypt, a distance of over 600 hundred miles, was conducted on foot with perhaps a few beasts of burden.[69] The gift of donkeys presented to him by Pharaoh (Gen. 12:16) represents the first time that this animal is mentioned in Scripture. An aged Jacob and his entire household traveled from Canaan to Egypt (a roughly 150-mile journey) "in the wagons [carts?] Pharaoh had provided for them" (Gen. 46:5). But such a mode of travel was far removed from the life of nomadic pastoralists. Jacob journeyed on foot for his reunion with Esau (Gen. 33:3), which made his newly acquired limp (see Gen. 32:25, 31; 33:3) even more significant. As he made clear to Esau, he was forced to travel at the pace of the children in his large entourage (Gen. 33:14).

Centuries later, the poignant (and somewhat enigmatic) pronouncement "My father was a wandering Aramean,"[70] enjoined on Israelites at the first fruits ceremony (Deut. 26:5), fittingly evoked the sharp contrast between settlement in a fertile land and the famine-induced migrations of their ancestors. Its association with a sacred ritual also points to a religious understanding of migration or, at the very least, suggests that the migrant experience was deeply enshrined in the community's religious consciousness.

---

69. Peter Farb also suggests this. Peter Farb, *The Land, Wildlife, and Peoples of the Bible* (New York: Harper & Row, 1967), 30.

70. For a probing of the rather confusing depiction of Jacob as an "Aramean," see Yair Zakovitch, "'My Father Was a Wandering Aramean' (Deuteronomy 26:5) or 'Edom Served My Father'?," in *Mishneh Todah: Studies in Deuteronomy and Its Cultural Environment in Honor of Jeffrey H. Tigay*, ed. Nili Sacher Fox, David A. Glatt-Gilad, and Michael J. Williams (Winona Lake, IN: Eisenbrauns, 2009), 133–37.

Israel in Egypt

The Joseph saga, the exodus, the wilderness wanderings, and the Israelite oc-cupation of Canaan are inarguably the most vigorously debated episodes in the Hebrew Bible. Growing extrabiblical data remain sufficiently inconclu-sive to keep the partisan wrangle between minimalists and maximalists fully energized. But, notwithstanding evident limitations and enough ambiguities to justify purposeful debate, a reasonable case can be made for the histori-cal reliability of the texts in question. Data supportive of the view that the biblical material coheres with the Near Eastern context in which it is set are fairly strong.

Egypt's well-watered delta was an attractive destination for a variety of migrants seeking temporary or permanent refuge, especially during periods of famine and economic hardship. Included in this constant influx of immigrants were Asiatics or Semitic-speaking groups from the Syria-Palestine region who moved in search of "pastoral sanctuary, or a better life in Egypt's wealthier and more sophisticated civilization."[71] The size of the influx varied over time, moderated in part by the levels of tolerance exhibited by different Egyptian rulers and the vigor with which they enforced border policies.[72] In the event, the Twelfth Dynasty (1938–ca. 1750 BCE) witnessed swelling Canaanite mi-grations into the Nile Delta in northern Egypt.[73] There is evidence to suggest that the patriarchal and Joseph narratives fit in this historical period.

The story of Joseph (Gen. 37–46), who rose from foreign slave to the high-est office of state (Pharaoh's "second-in-command"), is gripping by any stan-dard.[74] At a deeper level it describes a personal spiritual odyssey that sets the

71. Carol A. Redmount, "Bitter Lives: Israel in and out of Egypt," in *The Oxford History of the Biblical World*, ed. Michael David Coogan (New York: Oxford Uni-versity Press, 1998), 100; see also Kitchen, *Reliability of the Old Testament*, 343–44.

72. Under foreign rulers such as the Hyksôs, a Semitic race from Asia who reigned ca. 1648–1540 BCE and oppressed native Egyptians, the immigrant population rose considerably.

73. Pitard, "Before Israel," 56–57.

74. Foreigners, including Asiatic immigrants, who rose to high positions of power in Egypt are not unknown. In the New Kingdom (ca. 1300–1100 BCE), a Semite named Aper-el, who rose to the position of vizier, "oversaw the king's affairs in Lower Egypt during the final years of Amenhotep III and well into the reign of Akhenaten." Hoffmeier, *Israel in Egypt*, 94. See also Redmount, "Bitter Lives," 102, 103.

stage for momentous developments in the history of Israel.[75] Most important, how migration, with all its predicaments and unpredictability, serves divine purpose is a prominent theme. The biblical writers repeatedly discern the divine hand working through human machinations and complex political developments. In the Joseph saga, the narrator provides no indication that Joseph had a personal encounter with God; but Joseph repeatedly acknowledged God's power, and Pharaoh pointedly asserted that "the spirit of God" was in Joseph (Gen. 41:38).

Significantly, we encounter the phrase "the Lord was with Joseph" only after he was enslaved and taken down to Egypt (Gen. 39:1-2), supporting the link between migration and divine action. Like other prosperous Asiatic immigrants, Joseph became fully assimilated into Egyptian society.[76] He was given an Egyptian name, Zaphenath-paneah (Gen. 41:45) and he also married the daughter of an indigenous priest (which made him a member of the priestly class and perhaps incorporated him into the Egyptian religious system). He became so thoroughly Egyptianized in appearance, speech, and custom that he was no longer recognizably Hebrew, at least to his brothers (Gen. 42:8; 43:32); and the burial procession he organized for the death of his father Jacob looked to outsiders like an Egyptian affair (Gen. 50:11). Yet, like all migrants, Joseph remained conscious of being a foreigner despite social elevation and integration; and religious understanding of his own experience grew with time. The Hebrew (or Hebrew-sounding) names he gave his two sons indicate durability of a core religious identity (Gen. 41:51-52),[77] as does

---

75. Much about this story is unusual; and many details are impossible to verify historically. For a few scholars, the historicity of the story is affirmed by key elements of the narrative such as his sale price, his titles and offices, and the details of the Egyptian investiture ceremony, all of which point to a setting in the second millennium BCE. The price of twenty shekels that the Midian merchants paid for the young Joseph (Gen. 37:28) places the transaction in roughly the eighteenth century; and his spectacular rise from prison to palace was not at all unusual in the ancient Near East during this time. Before this period, observes Kitchen, "slaves were cheaper, and after it they steadily got dearer" (*Reliability of the Old Testament*, 344). See also Hoffmeier, *Israel in Egypt*, 83–84, 98.

76. Successful Asiatics in Egypt, writes Redmount, "adopted Egyptian names and portrayed themselves in Egyptian style and dress"; and "often the only hint of their foreign origin was their Semitic name" ("Bitter Lives," 102).

77. These were Manasseh ("because God has made me forget all my trouble") and Ephraim ("because God has made me fruitful in the land of my suffering").

his insistence that his bones must not be left in Egypt (Gen. 50:25). Above all, the assertion (to his brothers) that "it was not you who sent me here, but God" (Gen. 45:8) conveys a deepening of religious temperament.

Reconciliation with his brothers sets the stage for the migration of Joseph's extended family to Egypt. Joseph's prominent political status afforded them unique privileges (Gen. 45:17–18; 47:5–6) and presumably insulated them from the travails and hardships experienced by other Asiatic foreigners, whose numbers swelled in Egypt in the early second millennium BCE through enslavement, captivity, and immigration.[78] Yet, from the start, entrenched ethnic and cultural differences condemned the new arrivals to segregated existence from mainstream Egyptian society (Gen. 43:32; 46:34). Some degree of assimilation was inevitable as generations succeeded each other—Ezekiel 20:7–8, for instance, recalls religious compromise and integration. But cultural rejection (Gen. 43:32) and social separation (Gen. 46:34; cf. Exod. 3:22; 11:2) helped to solidify the Hebrews' status as perennial outsiders.[79] As part of Egypt's burgeoning immigrant community, the Hebrews were susceptible to the vicissitudes of political life.

In the long run, numerical growth and increasing visibility only served to accentuate their foreignness. For, even after long-term settlement, the descendants of Israel remained a distinctive community. This distinctiveness was perhaps partly rooted in a religious tradition centered on reverence for the deity who revealed himself to their migrant ancestors, a deity whose mighty deeds and covenantal promises presaged a special destiny for those who chose to follow him.

We are not told how much time transpired between the death of Joseph and the regime change that marked a dramatic reversal of fortune for his family's descendants. But latent antiforeign resentments, linked to grave doubts about their loyalty to the Egyptian state (Exod. 1:10)—perhaps inspired by their close association with a foreign regime[80]—erupted in state-sanctioned

78. Kitchen, *Reliability of the Old Testament*, 247.
79. Kitchen is suggestive—*Reliability of the Old Testament*, 298.
80. It is argued that Israelite settlement coincided with the gradual Hyksôs occupation of Egypt (ca. 1720–ca. 1527 BCE), during which "Semites replaced Egyptians in high administrative offices" (Nahum M. Sarna, "Exploring Exodus: The Oppression," *Biblical Archaeologist* 49, no. 2 [June 1986]: 70). If true, this explains heightened Egyptian concern about the dangers of foreign invasion and the fears evoked by the proliferation of the Israelite immigrant population.

xenophobic oppression. The Hebrew males were pressed into slave labor in imperial building projects as well as "all kinds of work in the fields" (Exod. 1:14).[81] Degrading and oppressive enslavement eventually culminated in state-sponsored infanticide. The exceptional courage of the lowly midwives (presumably non-Israelite Asiatics), who defied the decrees of Pharaoh because they "feared God" (Exod. 1:17), highlights the central role of female actors in the unfolding events.[82]

This forms the backdrop to the story of Moses, the individual with whom "Israel's distinctive faith begins."[83] Whether Moses's name has Egyptian or Hebrew origins is much discussed;[84] in either case, it identifies an individual in whose extraordinary life migration, exile, and otherness are defining features. Born to Hebrew parents and nursed into early childhood by his mother, but adopted by an unnamed Egyptian princess, Moses grew to adulthood in the rarified environs of the royal court. The biblical record indicates that he was thoroughly schooled in the Egyptian system, and there is strong suggestion that his education included extensive military training and accomplishments in the Egyptian army (Acts 7:22).[85] Moses's incorporation into the Egyptian ruling class was not unusual. Not only did large numbers of foreigners serve at the Egyptian court (as courtiers, administrators, attendants, etc.), but many (including Asiatics) also served in the Egyptian army. This was notably the case during the Ramesside era in the thirteenth century, a period also marked by vast building projects for which foreigners were conscripted.[86]

---

81. Redmount, "Bitter Lives," 89, 99.

82. Midwives were apparently held in high esteem in ancient Egypt and the two midwives mentioned in Exodus were likely heads of two guilds or groups of practitioners. For obvious reasons, they were unlikely to be Israelites, though the Semitic names (Shiphrah and Puah) used to identify them reduce the likelihood that they were Egyptian (Sarna, "Exploring Exodus," 78).

83. Bright, *History of Israel*, 128.

84. The name is commonly thought to be derived from the Egyptian word *Mose* (meaning "child"/"to give birth"), which, according to Kitchen, was pronounced *Masu* in Egypt during the fourteenth and thirteenth centuries BCE. Alternatively, it has roots in the Hebrew term *Moshe* ("he who draws out") in the light of the Exodus event—see Kitchen, *Reliability of the Old Testament*, 296–97; Provan, Long, and Longman, *Biblical History of Israel*, 126; Hoffmeier, *Israel in Egypt*, 140–42.

85. See Redmount, "Bitter Lives," 101.

86. Kitchen, *Reliability of the Old Testament*, 297, 310; Redmount, "Bitter Lives," 101; Hoffmeier, *Israel in Egypt*, 126, 142–43; Sarna, "Exploring Exodus," 71–74. Hoff-

In any case, Moses's advanced training is a crucial feature in the exodus narrative. As K. A. Kitchen observes, the formatting and stipulations of the Sinai covenant (depicted in the books of Exodus, Leviticus, and Deuteronomy) required firsthand knowledge of treaty protocols, legal conventions, and formal agreements that was only available to high-level government officials.[87] Such know-how was beyond the cognizance of runaway slaves; someone with Moses's learning and knowledge of the desert was indispensable for the extraordinary religious odyssey that awaited his people.

The biblical material is silent on the details of Moses's growth into adulthood in the Egyptian court, and we cannot be certain that he retained ties with the Hebrew community. But there is indication that he spoke his mother tongue and remained deeply conscious of his Semite identity (or his foreigner origin). A strong sense of affinity with "his own people" spurred his murder of an Egyptian and forced him to flee Egypt. It is important to reiterate that refugee movement and displacement of individuals or groups were common features of the ancient world. As the Egyptian *Tale of Sinuhe* (second millennium BCE) attests, it was not unusual for a high-ranking official desirous of putting himself beyond Pharaoh's powerful reach to flee in the direction of Syria-Palestine. Such were the political realities.

In Moses's case, however, exile and the distinct travails of the foreigner-outsider had theological significance. The experience of migration once again takes prominence in the unfolding of divine purposes. It appears lost on most readers that at the time he witnessed the extraordinary spectacle of a bush that was on fire but "did not burn up" (Exod. 3:2)—erroneously titled the "burning bush"—Moses was a refugee-exile sheltered by nomadic Midianites. The fact that his divine commissioning comes only after he has experienced the pain and predicament of being a foreigner-outsider reaffirms the link between migration and divine election. The traumatic impact of migration on Moses's self-understanding is evocatively captured in the naming of his first child: *Gēr-*

---

meier explains that the increase of foreigners at the Egyptian court was also triggered by the colonial policy, initiated under Thutmose III (1457–1425 BCE), of bringing the children of foreign rulers to be trained in Egyptian ways.

87. Kitchen, *Reliability of the Old Testament*, 295, 297–98. In truth, the "legal" content of the Sinai Covenant lacks Egyptian provenance; but, as Kitchen explains, someone in Moses's position would have been well acquainted with the treaties crafted between Egyptian rulers and Hittite kings. See also Christiana van Houten, *The Alien in Israelite Law* (Sheffield: Sheffield Academic, 1991), 23–36.

shom, so named because "I have become a foreigner [*gēr*] in a foreign land" (Exod. 2:22; 18:3). It requires no stretch of the imagination to comprehend that the personal experience of "not belonging" was a key ingredient in the formation of a man called to lead perhaps the most famous (certainly most debated) migration in human history. His personal exile was preparation for the exodus event. There is also striking parallel with Abraham. Moses, Israel's greatest prophet (Deut. 34:10), abandons service in the "household of pharaoh" (Gen. 45:2) to become "a servant in all God's house" (Heb. 3:5).

Exodus

Hasty whole-community migrations, such as the Israelite exodus from Egypt, were not uncommon incidents in the ancient (biblical) world.[88] The "exodus" of captive groups or immigrants determined to escape conditions of oppression, notes Kitchen, "is well attested from at least the eighteenth century BC onward."[89] As the eighth-century prophet Amos tartly reminded the Israelites, theirs was not a unique experience: "Did I not bring Israel up from Egypt, the Philistines from Caphtor and the Arameans from Kir?" (Amos 9:7). That said, the deliverance of the Hebrew captives from Egypt, in the wake of a series of phenomenal plagues (depicted as a "cosmic confrontation" between Yahweh and Egypt's gods—Exod. 3:19, 20; 6:1),[90] has distinctive features and significance. From this epic event springs the nation of Israel. The centrality of the exodus to Israel's faith and self-identity is affirmed by copious references to the episode throughout the Hebrew Bible. Yet, as most readers already know, no other biblical episode has attracted more contentious debate across a wider array of scholarly disciplines—even the term "event" is deemed objectionable by some since it implies a historical occurrence.

On this issue the ideological divisions that pervade biblical scholarship, and the limits of archeological data to resolve such divisions, are painfully manifest. There is no mention in the Egyptian records of Hebrew slaves, a figure named Moses, or an Israelite exodus. Moreover, in the biblical material, puzzling details and apparently contradictory references, combined with com-

---

88. Kitchen, *Reliability of the Old Testament*, 254, 301–2.
89. Kitchen, *Reliability of the Old Testament*, 254.
90. Hoffmeier, *Israel in Egypt*, 149–51.

plete silence on the names of any of the pharaohs, provide ample grist for the mills of scholarly disputation and speculation.[91] By the nature of things the historicity of the exodus cannot be established beyond all doubt. All verdicts must ultimately rest on unproven or unprovable assumptions.

The ambiguity of the biblical record is epitomized by the conflicting data on the vital questions of exactly how many people left Egypt and when. The implausibly large group implied by the assertion that the migrants included over 600,000 fighting men (Exod. 12:37; Num. 1:46; 26:51)—which indicates a total of some 2 million people, including women and children—long caused consternation. Even other biblical texts either contradict such an estimate (Num. 3:46) or outright exclude such a massive group (Exod. 1:15–22; Deut. 7:7). More recent scholarship emphasizes that the Hebrew word translated "thousand" (*'eleph*) can also mean "clan," "military squad," or "leader" depending on context. Thus, the number of Hebrews who left Egypt can be calculated as 20,000 (if *'eleph* refers to clans or military squads) or 140,000 (if the term applies to leaders).[92] To these, presumably, must be added the mixed multitude of non-Hebrew fugitives who accompanied the Hebrews (Exod. 12:38; Num. 11:4). Colin J. Humphreys, a British physicist whose appraisal of the Exodus numbers using a mathematical approach is often cited, estimated a total of 20,000–22,000 emigrants.[93]

The considerable debate surrounding the dating of the Hebrew exodus, even among those who accept its historicity, reflects the inconclusiveness of archeological data. The most that can be said with reasonable certainty is that a group by that name was settled in Canaan by 1210 BCE—based on reference to Israel in the Merneptah stele.[94] The biblical assertion that the exodus took

91. However, Hoffmeier points out that the omission of Pharaoh's name in the Exodus narrative reflects practices of the New Kingdom (ca. 1550–1070 BCE), when it was also "normal . . . not to disclose the name of Pharaoh's enemies" in inscriptions (*Israel in Egypt*, 109).

92. Kitchen, *Reliability of the Old Testament*, 264–65; Provan, Long, and Longman, *Biblical History of Israel*, 130–31; Bright, *History of Israel*, 133–34.

93. Colin J. Humphreys, "The Number of People in the Exodus from Egypt: Decoding Mathematically the Very Large Numbers in Numbers I and XXVI," *Vetus Testamentum* 48, no. 2 (1998): 196–213; Colin J. Humphreys, "The Numbers in the Exodus from Egypt: A Further Appraisal," *Vetus Testamentum* 50, no. 3 (2000): 323–28.

94. Discovered in 1896, the Merneptah (or Israel) stele contains inscriptions celebrating the achievements of the ancient Egyptian pharaoh Merneptah (reigned ca. 1212–1202 BCE). Its allusion to the king's decisive victory over "Israel" during a

place 480 years before the fourth year of King Solomon's reign (1 Kings 6:1) gives a date of ca. 1446 BCE. But this assumes a literal reading, which many scholars reject in favor of a symbolic understanding. The alternative view that 480 years refers to twelve generations is contested, but this would place the exodus in the thirteenth century.[95] Interestingly, the prevailing consensus, based on available archeological evidence from Palestine combined with the biblical data, does support a Hebrew exodus in the thirteenth century—most likely in the Ramesside era (1279–1213 BCE).[96] Yet, such are the ambiguities and complexities of the data that a thirteenth-century exodus remains, in Kitchen's words, "the least objectionable dating."[97]

For our purposes, it is important to recognize that the exodus episode extends the prominent and recurrent intersection of migration, divine action, and religious transformation that dominates the Torah. The flight of the Hebrews from Egypt, along with a diverse group of non-Hebrew fugitives— the entity that became Israel was not derived from a "single social organism," though all were migrants[98]—places migration and displacement firmly at the heart of Israel's origins as a nation. Without this epic migration event there would be no nation of Israel.[99] Little wonder then that the Hebrew exodus remained a primary point of reference for Israel's unique character and religious identity, from the earliest period of settlement ("I brought you up out of Egypt and . . . I will never break my covenant with you," Judg. 2:1) down to Babylonian captivity ("My Spirit remains among you, just as I promised when you came out of Egypt," Hag. 2:5). Indeed, its theological significance extends beyond the nation of Israel to the long-expected Messiah whose emergence is distinctly marked by a similar act of migration, anticipated in the prophetic declaration, "When Israel was a child, I loved him, and out of Egypt I called my son" (Hosea 11:1). Later still, this period of exodus and nomadic existence became a metaphor for God's people as a mobile community of faith guided by his promises.

---

military campaign in Canaan represents the earliest reference to Israel as a tribal or national entity outside the Bible.

95. For a thoroughgoing assessment, see Kitchen, *Reliability of the Old Testament*, 307–8, and Hoffmeier, *Israel in Egypt*, 125.

96. Hoffmeier, *Israel in Egypt*, 126; Sarna, "Exploring Exodus," 68–80.

97. Kitchen, *Reliability of the Old Testament*, 310.

98. Spina, "Israelites as Gērîm," 322.

99. Bright, *History of Israel*, 134.

The Sinai Covenant

Few passages in the Old Testament capture the theological significance of migration more evocatively than the Sinai covenant—the composite of treaty, law, and covenant enacted in Exodus-Leviticus and reaffirmed in Deuteronomy. The antiquity of the Sinai covenant has been the subject of discussion for over two centuries. Those who reject its historicity generally view it as a seventh-century creation, instigated by King Josiah's reforms (in 621 BCE).[100] Some scholars, such as K. A. Kitchen in his *On the Reliability of the Old Testament*, have argued for its origins in the late second millennium (fourteenth or thirteenth century) BCE.[101] Apart from consonance with a thirteenth-century exodus under the leadership of an individual matching Moses's upbringing and training (see "Israel in Egypt" above), other major considerations include the similarities between the covenant material and the ancient treaties or law codes of the ancient Near Eastern world as well as the widespread use (by the thirteenth century BCE) of the technology used to construct the mobile tabernacle. These considerations, however, do not preclude redactions or refinements (of language, for instance) in the process of transmission, with a finalized form emerging in the seventh century BCE or later.

What is of major interest here, however, is the fact that the Sinai covenant is intimately linked to the experience of migration and provides a vital theological framework for the migrant concept. Here we find an approach to the stranger-outsider category that imbues it with deep religious significance and lays a theological foundation for thinking about migration as inextricably connected to a life of faith or being a people of God.

Before we explore this issue, it is important to note in passing that settlement in the promised land did not abrogate the migrant consciousness at the heart of Israelites' identity as the people of God. The "nomadic origin" of the Israelites, explains John Flight, remained a taproot of religious life and thought, one that "exerted a great influence upon all subsequent development

---

100. From this perspective also, the Sinai material is typically viewed as comprising three major traditions or texts composed at different times in Israel's history: the book of the covenant (Exod. 20:22–23, 33); the Deuteronomic law (Deut. 12–26); and the Holiness Code (Lev. 17–26). See Asen, "From Acceptance to Exclusion," 24–27.

101. See Kitchen, *Reliability of the Old Testament*, 274–306; also Provan, Long, and Longman, *Biblical History of Israel*, 133–35; Bright, *History of Israel*, 124–29.

in Israel . . . too strong to be obliterated by the entrance into Canaan, the development of civilization and culture, [or] the contact with other peoples and other religions."[102] Indeed, Yahweh enjoins his people that *the land is mine and you reside in my land as foreigners and strangers*" (Lev. 25:23). Furthermore, in a manner reminiscent of the patriarchs, migration played a formative role in the faith of prominent figures like David, who spent an extended period of time as a fugitive-migrant before he became Israel's second king.[103] David's faith in Yahweh was distinctly shaped by his refugee experience.[104] In his fervent prayer before the assembly of Israelites, when plans for the building of the temple finally took concrete shape, he intoned: "We are foreigners and strangers in your sight, as were all our ancestors" (1 Chron. 29:15). A similar outlook emerges in the psalms: "Hear my prayer, Lord . . . , I dwell with you as a foreigner, a stranger, as all my ancestors were" (Ps. 39:12).

Also, the election of Israel—a nation founded on the experience of migration, and formed by landless refugees—invited dependence on Yahweh's sovereignty (Deut. 8—note especially verse 17). Yahweh's love of the foreigner was not limited to Israel (Deut. 10:18; Amos 9:7). Indeed, the Sinai covenant also affirmed that divine election or chosenness had nothing to do with the Israelites' intrinsic worth (Deut. 4:38; 7:7; 9:4-5; Amos 9:7). Chosenness was a divine prerogative; and it invited a religious identity marked by a continued sense of dependence on God's provision and protection—in contradistinction to other nations that espoused the trappings of political power and putative security afforded by a standing army. Israel's subsequent clamor for national sovereignty ("a king . . . such as all the other nations have," 1 Sam. 8:5) was therefore tantamount to a rejection of Yahweh, who "delivered you from the

102. John W. Flight, "The Nomadic Idea and Ideal in the Old Testament," *Journal of Biblical Literature* 42, no. 3/4 (1923): 197.

103. His entire household, along with other discontented Israelites, joined him on the run (1 Sam. 22:1-2). At one point he lived in Philistine territory for a year and four months (1 Sam. 27:7); but, as an outlaw-fugitive, he constantly moved from place to place (1 Sam. 23:13-14).

104. The psalms purportedly composed by him while on the run (such as Psalms 52, 54, and 59) express fearless confidence in God under oppressive circumstances or evocatively appeal to God's sovereignty and protection in the face of powerful enemies. It could also be argued that David's experience as the "commander" of a growing band of discontented Israelites who joined him on the run (1 Sam. 22:1-2) provided some training for kingship.

power of Egypt and all the kingdoms that oppressed you . . . , who saves you out of all your disasters and calamities" (1 Sam. 10:17–19).

The point at issue is that the Sinai covenant concretized the migrant status as a critical feature of Israelites' religious life and a central component of their national identity. This legally binding arrangement, which established Israel's relationship with Yahweh, involved a mixed group of displaced migrants among whom the Hebrews were but one component (as 1 Sam. 14:11–12 indicates). At Sinai, the Israelites were not yet citizens in possession of their own territory, and not even a cohesive social entity. They were a diverse group of wanderers or pastoral nomads (Num. 14:33; 32:13). The Torah never describes them as "sojourners" or "resident aliens" (terms that imply permanent or short-term residence within another nation or community) during the forty-year period in the Sinai wilderness.[105] Thus, the Israelites, like their ancestors, were migrant-outsiders (strangers and foreigners with no homeland) when they allied themselves with Yahweh. This view of Yahweh as a God of the migrant-foreigner framed Israel's religion.

To reiterate, the biblical world teemed with migrants of all stripes. Official documents from the ancient Near East contain copious allusions to strangers and foreigners, and some show marked similarities in form and content to the covenant. There is one major exception: the legal codes of the ancient Mesopotamian societies contain no reference to foreigners or resident aliens (apart from material dealing with the sale of slaves and regulations that distinguished between resident aliens and fugitives).[106] No laws or rulings appear in the legal collections of the Egyptians, Babylonians, Assyrians, Persians, or other ancient Mesopotamian societies that regulate the treatment of outsiders by the citizens of the land. In striking contrast, despite the fact that the Israelites shared the basic perception of foreigners prevalent in the ancient world (i.e., as a potential threat), the law codes of the Sinai covenant incorporate specific instructions governing the treatment of the foreigner.[107] Moreover, the

---

105. Hoffmeier, *Immigration Crisis*, 66.

106. See Ramírez Kidd, *Alterity and Identity*, 110–12; van Houten, *Alien in Israelite Law*, 23–42; Carroll, *Christians at the Border*, 102.

107. Ramírez Kidd, *Alterity and Identity*, 115. Indeed, the repeated injunctions in Deuteronomy calling for the elimination of the Canaanite nations reflects this general hostility to foreigners, albeit strongly linked to fear of religious corruption. See Yan, "Alien in Deuteronomy," 113.

legal provisions in question were primarily aimed at marginalized migrant-outsiders, not immigrants who had been integrated into the Israelite community through acceptance of its religion.[108] Under the terms of the covenant, foreigners and migrants were

- to benefit from the gleaning law that allowed the poor to receive crops left in the field by harvesters (Lev. 19:10; 23:22);
- to be allowed to rest on the Sabbath (Exod. 20:10; 23:12)—an acknowledgment that they were allowed to seek employment to support themselves;
- not to be deprived of their wages (Deut. 24:14–15);
- along with orphans and widows, to receive the special (produce) tithe collected every three years (Deut. 14:28–29);
- subject to the penalties of criminal laws (Lev. 24:22), though with strong injunctions against treating them unfairly or subjecting them to discrimination (Deut. 1:15–17; 24:17–18);
- if circumcised, to be given full access to Israel's religious life (including the Passover meal and other festivals) (Lev. 16:29–30; Exod. 12:48; Deut. 16:11, 14);
- to be present at the periodic reading of the law (Deut. 31:10–13).

To be sure, the law allowed the purchase of slaves from among the foreigners residing in Israel while prohibiting Israelites from purchasing other Israelites as slaves (Lev. 25:44–46). At first glance, this appears to be a departure from the unique safeguards it provided against the exploitation of the foreign resident. However, this stipulation also anticipated that impoverished Israelites might voluntarily "sell themselves to the foreigner" (Lev. 25:47), a remarkable acknowledgment that, even though they numbered among the poor and needy in Israelite society, foreigners and strangers could also become rich and self-sufficient. In fact, the prosperity of foreigners in their midst, at the expense of the Israelites, was included among the dire consequences (or curses) that would result from disobedience of the covenant: "The foreigners who reside among you will rise above you higher and higher, but you will sink lower and lower. . . . They will be the head, but you will be the tail" (Deut. 28:43–44).

108. Asen, "From Acceptance to Exclusion," 27.

Interpreting the Covenant

My assessment of ancient Israel treats the stranger (*gēr*, pl. *gērîm*) and the "foreigner" (*nekhar* or *zār*) as overlapping social categories that represent otherness—roughly equivalent to the modern usage of the term "immigrant," which covers a range of statuses. But some scholars insist that in ancient Israel "stranger" and "foreigner" were separate categories. Egyptologist and biblical scholar James Hoffmeier argues that Israel's legal tradition distinguishes between "alien" and "foreigner" and only makes provision for the former.[109] In his view, the *gēr* (as portrayed in the legal section of the Torah) was a person who "had legal standing in the community and therefore was afforded protection and had rights," whereas the foreigner lacked legal status and "is not mentioned anywhere in the Law as having these benefits."[110] For Hoffmeier this biblical concept of "foreigner" can be equated with the "illegal" immigrant in the contemporary American context; and he contends, based on this rationale, that unauthorized immigrants have no legitimate claims to social benefits or governmental support.

Regardless of the legitimacy of Hoffmeier's reading of "foreigner" in the Hebrew Bible, the fact that it is used to support a conclusion dictated by contemporary concerns raises acute questions of ideological bias—not to mention the dubious benefit of instituting congruency between two radically different historical contexts separated by over three millennia. But there are also biblical grounds for questioning the validity of Hoffmeier's reading. The strict distinction he insists on is difficult to reconcile with the spirit and intent of the law codes. In the first place, it would be quite odd if Israel's legal codes excluded from consideration the very kind of migrant that they themselves were at the time that same law was given to them. For in the Sinai desert, as noted earlier, the Israelites were neither citizens nor alien residents but rootless migrants with no legal status.[111] The notion that the provisions and protections stipulated in its legal tradition did not apply to "foreigners" (as a separate group) severely distorts the notion of Yahweh's impartiality and care for the most vulnerable in society implied in its statutes. It is hardly a system of justice if one marginalized group ("foreigners" such as the temporary res-

109. Hoffmeier, *Immigration Crisis*, 48–52.
110. Hoffmeier, *Immigration Crisis*, 71–89, 95–96.
111. Interestingly, this is a point that Hoffmeier affirms (*Immigration Crisis*, 97–99).

ident or a seasonal laborer) is denied the timely payment of wages, produce tithe, or Sabbath rest that enabled another marginalized group (the "resident alien") to survive.

Second, even assuming that there was strict adherence to provisions demanded by the law codes—a matter in which Israel failed abysmally[112]—to stipulate a rigid dichotomy between the migrant categories rather ignores the fluidity of migrant status in most social settings, ancient as well as modern. The fact that most versions of the Bible translate or apply "stranger" and "foreigner" interchangeably is telling; and imposing an inflexible application assumes meticulous differentiation in the minds of the biblical writers that lacks justification.

The use of migrant categories in the story of Ruth is a case in point. Food insecurity forces the Israelite family of Elimelek to migrate and settle as "aliens" (*gērîm*) in the country of Moab. The two sons marry Moabite women, one of whom, Ruth, returns with her mother-in-law to settle permanently among the Israelites. Is Ruth a "stranger" or a "foreigner"? As the widow of an Israelite man, Ruth certainly qualified for legal protection on two counts: as a "widow" and as an "alien." She was an "alien" because not only was she seeking permanent settlement (and protection), but she had also pledged her allegiance to the Israelite faith in that memorable declaration to Naomi, her mother-in-law, "Your people will be my people and your God my God" (Ruth 1:16). Yet, the biblical writer labels Ruth not an "alien" but a "foreigner" (*nokriyya*—Ruth 2:10). This may reflect ethnocentric bias, a subtle hint at the stereotype of the foreign woman liable to lead the God-fearing Israelite into idolatry, though the text is silent on the tensions between Moabites and Israelites. Carroll also suggests that the "foreigner" label makes sense because it is often applied to someone who has recently arrived and not yet integrated.[113] But this does not change the fact that Ruth was legitimately a resident alien, as the rest of the story attests. The point at issue is that in actual usage, and often for contextual reasons, migrant categories frequently overlapped.

Third, the unique stipulations and provisions in the covenant regarding migrant-outsiders (whether aliens or foreigners) were based on three

112. Indeed, as Spina points out, the emphasis on specific provisions in the legal codes implies that these were not the normal course of action ("Israelites as Gērîm," 323).

113. Carroll, *Christians at the Border*, 100.

important rationales that account for the distinctiveness of the Israelites' legal framework:

1. the Israelites themselves were once foreigners in Egypt (Exod. 22:20; 23:9; Lev. 19:34);
2. Yahweh loves the foreigner (Deut. 10:17–18; also Ps. 146:9);
3. there was no difference in the divine purview between the foreigner and the native-born (Lev. 19:34; 24:22; Deut. 10:17–18).

The Israelites were uniquely enjoined "to love those who are foreigners, *for you yourselves were foreigners in Egypt*" (Deut. 10:19). Indeed, they were to love the foreigner as themselves (Lev. 19:34). To love someone as oneself implied dissolution of the boundaries that foster rejection and discrimination. Yahweh's love for the foreigner—a reflection of his special regard for the most vulnerable and disadvantaged in human society (Ps. 146:9)—precluded the foreigner's oppression: "You are to have the same law for the foreigner and the native-born" (Lev. 24:22). As full recipients of God's love while they were themselves migrant-outsiders, the Israelites were now expected to embody love of the stranger and foreigner. At the very least, the covenant makes it clear that being a people of God is incompatible with rejection or exploitation of the outsider (Lev. 19:18; 19:33–34; 24:22; Deut. 10:19).[114]

For other scholars, the extensive rights and protections offered to foreigners—sometimes labeled the "*gēr*-tradition"—could only have applied to Israelites who were alienated from the covenant community, rather than to non-Israelite outsiders. One view is that the alien resident or residents (*gēr* or *gērîm*) referred to in Deuteronomy are "Israelites from the northern kingdom who ha[d] migrated and settled in Judah" (following Assyrian invasion in the eighth century BCE).[115] The belief that the book of the covenant dates to the exilic period forms the main basis for this reasoning.[116] But the claim

114. See Crüsemann, "You Know the Heart of a Stranger," 101.

115. Yan, "Alien in Deuteronomy," 112–17. It is estimated that by the end of the eighth century BCE, more than half of Jerusalem's population comprised refugees fleeing the Assyrian assault of the northern kingdom (finally conquered in 720 BCE). Burke, "Anthropological Model," 48–51.

116. Additionally, fellow Israelites are occasionally identified as *gēr*, typically when they settle within a different tribe (Judg. 19:16); the humanitarian elements in the legal codes suited the conditions of a massive refugee influx; and the conviction that

that the covenant and its legal codes were contracted with a subsection of the Israelite nation long after they had settled in the land is deeply problematic. In the Hebrew Bible, Israelites as a group are only described as *gērîm* in the pre-settlement period (Ezra 1:4 excepted); more often than not the term applies to non-Israelites.[117] David had the Amalekite who confessed to taking King Saul's life executed presumably because as a *gēr* ("the son of a foreigner," 2 Sam. 1:13) he was subject to Israel's laws and ought to have refrained from killing the king. In any case, as Frank Spina also points out, the view that the *gēr*-tradition dates to the exilic era is weakened by the fact that "the exilic literature is so silent on the subject." Moreover, a number of provisions—especially those related to religious life (Sabbath observance, circumcision, the reading of the law, etc.)—are difficult to explain if the reference is to fellow Israelites.

Migration and Mission: The Paradox of Election and Universal Inclusion

How human migration serves a "redemptive" purpose is also evident in the impetus it provides for universal inclusiveness. Contrary to the commonplace Christian view that the old covenant was erected on a system of works needed to achieve salvation, the purpose, notes M. Daniel Carroll R., was to show the Israelites "how to live as a redeemed people." The law codes were given to the Israelites *after* they had been chosen and redeemed (2 Sam. 7:23); as such, their observance was clearly not a precondition for redemption.[118] The observance of these distinctive provisions, in fact, potentially served a missionary purpose; for Israel's diligent observance of these "righteous decrees and laws" would demonstrate to the surrounding nations its exemplary way of life and its special relationship with Yahweh (Deut. 4:5–8). Explains Carroll:

> We should recognize that the way [the law of the Hebrew Bible] deals with the foreigner says something very important about the heart of Israel and of its God who gave them these rules. . . . It is not just that specific laws serve as a model for other nations. The laws reflect something deeper: Is-

the demise of the northern kingdom was caused by spiritual apostasy may have encouraged Judeans to view the refugees as "outsiders."

117. Spina, "Israelites as Gērîm," 329.

118. Carroll, *Christians at the Border*, 99.

rael's stance toward the foreigner was part of the larger fabric of its ethical life. It was part of the ethos of what it meant to be a people of God.[119]

The requirements and mandates enshrined within the Sinai covenant also point to the principle of universalism (or inclusion) at the heart of Israel's chosenness as a people of God. This is implicit in the divine view that the Israelites "are to have the same law for the foreigner and the native-born" (Lev. 24:22). Crucially, covenant provisions were to be applied without any requirement for integration or assimilation. In essence, the purpose of divine election was not to produce a closed, inward-looking, ethnically defined theocracy but rather to create a community of faith that was open and welcoming to all who chose to join.[120] As André Lacocque observes, "it was not a matter, even in part, of turning outsiders (the '*gērîm*') into Israelites, but of making them together with the Israelites into *Israel*." We see this same principle at work in the Abrahamic covenant. When God introduces circumcision as a sign of the covenant with Abraham, Abraham is instructed to have "every male among you . . . circumcised . . . whether born in your household or bought with your money" (Gen. 17:10, 13).[121] Abraham, the migrant-outsider, is chosen by God to become the head of a new household of faith that is universal because full membership is open to the outsider who chooses to join.

In the Torah, then, the people of God appear as foreigners and strangers chosen to form a community of faith whose boundaries are to be constantly expanded by the inclusion of migrant-outsiders (i.e., those from other nations). Divine election thus implies missionary responsibility: the call to make room for those who do not belong. Theologically speaking, at least, the terms of the covenant indicate that particularism and chosenness hold the potential for pluralism and serve as the basis for universal inclusion. In this equation, migration or the migrant experience serves to activate the transition from one mode to the other.

The history of Israel was one of persistent covenant disobedience, so this ideal was stifled or obscured. Indeed, antagonism to foreigners or outsiders (as

119. Carroll, *Christians at the Border*, 99.

120. For a similar argument, see Lacocque, "Stranger in the Old Testament," 11–12.

121. Interestingly, even Hoffmeier acknowledges that "here circumcision applied to all Abraham's household and any servants, including the foreigners among them" (*Immigration Crisis*, 90).

the story of Jonah, discussed under "Exile and Redemption" below, indicates) was a recurrent theme. But that does not lessen the theological import of the experience of migration. Interestingly, Israel's religious failings were adeptly exposed through accounts in which immigrants or foreigners—such as the Shunammite woman (2 Kings 4:8–37), Naaman the Syrian (2 Kings 5:1–19) or even Obed-Edom the Gittite[122] (2 Sam. 6:11)—became beneficiaries of God's power. The same is also true of situations in which outsiders, such as Rahab and Ruth, professed faith in Yahweh. The healing of Naaman the Syrian stands out for two reasons: first, because the testimony to the power of the God of Israel by an Israelite girl held captive in a foreign land contrasted sharply with the obliviousness of the Israelite king in Samaria (2 Kings 5:6–8); second, because a foreigner was healed from a terrible disease (leprosy) that afflicted "many in Israel" (Luke 4:27). The dating of this incident is obscure—though Elisha was active in the late ninth century BCE—but the outcome is not. The witness or religious devotion of an Israelite migrant sets in motion a series of events that led a prominent non-Israelite to confess, "Now I know that there is no God in all the world except in Israel" (2 Kings 5:15). Whatever the intention of the writer(s), this story foreshadows the more momentous experience of exile among the nations and its "redemptive" possibilities.

Exile and Redemption

It is important to note that the exile of the Israelite nation was preceded by Yahweh's "exile" from his people. Centuries of recurrent spiritual corruption and a history of breaking the covenant produced alienation between God and Israel. From the perspectives of both the exiles in Babylon and the remnant in Palestine (represented by the prophets Ezekiel and Jeremiah respectively), Yahweh had departed from the land and temple prior to the Babylonian invasion. In the distressing visions of the priest Ezekiel, God became "utterly transcendent . . . distant, terrifying and unreachable."[123] Jeremiah offered a pithier perspective. The contamination of the land and temple, he declared,

---

122. Obed-Edom was the individual from Gath (possibly a Philistine) whose entire household was blessed during the three months the ark of the Lord stayed at his house.

123. Carolyn J. Sharp, "Sites of Conflict: Textual Engagements of Dislocation and Diaspora in the Hebrew Bible," in *Interpreting Exile: Displacement and Deportation*

had forced Yahweh to leave his dwelling place, to go into exile! Yahweh had become a stranger (*gēr*) to his people: to wit,

> You [i.e., Yahweh] who are the hope of Israel, its Savior in times of distress, why are you like a stranger in the land, like a traveler who stays only a night? (Jer. 14:8)

Given that exile was the most dreadful consequence of covenant disobedience (Lev. 26:33; Deut. 28:36; Jer. 25:8–11), its coverage in the biblical record is surprisingly limited. The biblical account incorporates multiple perspectives of the horrific events and their aftermath;[124] but it also raises unanswered questions, among them: what was the duration of the exile, or when did it end; what happened to those who never returned; is "exile" both a geographic and religious reference? Among modern scholars, extreme positions and the paucity of archeological data preclude any consensus.[125] The term "exile" is itself contested;[126] and its usage raises troublesome questions, such as its applicability to the descendants of the original captives who *chose* not to return. At the same time, some recent assessments of the "exile" use insights from migration studies and other social-scientific disciplines to elucidate its historical and theological significance.[127]

---

in Biblical and Modern Contexts, ed. Brad E. Kelle, Frank Ritchel Ames, and Jacob L. Wright (Atlanta: Society of Biblical Literature, 2011), 369, 373.

124. See Smith-Christopher, *Biblical Theology of Exile*, 58–65, 70.

125. Not surprisingly, minimalists dismiss the Babylonian exile as a myth or "historical fiction" with only tenuous connections to the world outside the biblical text.

126. Irish scholar Robert P. Carroll denounces it as a deeply ideological concept, reflective of "a Jerusalem- or Palestinian-oriented point of view" and intended to silence other groups or understandings ("Exile! What Exile?," 62–79). See also Philip R. Davies, "Exile? What Exile? Whose Exile?," in *Leading Captivity Captive: "The Exile" as History and Ideology*, ed. Lester L. Grabbe (Sheffield: Sheffield Academic, 1998), 128–38. The reference to "songs of Zion" in Psalm 137 arguably captures a Judean point of view or simply connotes Temple worship, by then no longer possible. Adele Berlin, "Psalms and the Literature of Exile: Psalms 137, 44, 69 and 78," in *The Book of Psalms: Composition and Reception*, ed. Peter W. Flint and Patrick D. Miller (Boston: Brill, 2005), 68–70.

127. Among these, see Robert R. Wilson, "Forced Migration and the Formation of the Prophetic Literature," in *By the Irrigation Canals of Babylon: Approaches to the Study of the Exile*, ed. John J. Ahn and Jill Anne Middlemas (New York: T & T Clark, 2012), 125–38; Berlin, "Psalms and the Literature," 65–78; Smith-Christopher, *Biblical*

It is impossible to address the major issues of the "exile" discourse here. My sole aim, in keeping with the general thesis that migration was often a theologizing experience, is to examine how the exile served "redemptive" purposes. I contend that the exile provided impetus for cross-cultural missionary engagement or witness and that the reconstruction of religious community in foreign lands elicited profound understanding of the universal nature of Yahweh's salvific purposes.

After a prolonged siege of its capital, Samaria, the northern kingdom of Israel fell to Assyria in 722 BCE (2 Kings 17). In keeping with Assyrian policy, conquest was followed by mass deportation (Assyrian records claim 27,290 Israelite deportees) and the transfer of foreign peoples into Samaria. What became of the northern Israelite exiles is unknown. But large numbers of Israelites undoubtedly fled to neighboring lands, joining the swelling tide of refugees triggered by the Assyrian military incursions. It is estimated, for instance, that the influx of Israelite refugees into the southern kingdom of Judah more than doubled the population in Jerusalem by the late eighth century.[128] In the turbulent period that followed, a declining Assyrian power allied with Egypt to confront the rising neo-Babylonian Empire. King Josiah's ill-fated attempt to oppose the powerful Egyptian forces, perhaps to assert Judean independence, led to his demise and Egyptian subjugation of Judah (2 Kings 23:29–35). This state of affairs proved short-lived, however. Under the command of Nebuchadnezzar II (r. 604–562), the neo-Babylonian army crushed Egypt and swept into the Syria-Palestine region.

In 597 BCE the tiny kingdom of Judah quickly succumbed to the Babylonian forces. Jerusalem was plundered; and King Jehoiachin, other members of the ruling class, military officers, and skilled citizens were deported to Babylon (2 Kings 24:13–17). A vassal king, given the name Zedekiah, was appointed to the throne. Zedekiah's ill-judged revolt against Babylonian rule prompted the return of the Babylonian army under Nebuchadnezzar in 576 BCE (2 Kings 25). This time Jerusalem sustained massive destruction; the temple, symbolic of Yahweh's presence, was left in ruins; and the majority of the population was deported, with only "some of the poorest people of the

---

Theology of Exile; Daniel L. Smith, *The Religion of the Landless: The Social Context of the Babylonian Exile* (Bloomington, IN: Meyer-Stone Books, 1989).

128. See Burke, "Anthropological Model," 47–50.

land" left behind (2 Kings 25:12). The archeological data point to roughly 80 percent devastation and depopulation.[129] The Jewish state (and monarchy) disintegrated. Thus began the Jewish exile.

Subsequent periodization of the history of Israel into pre- and postexilic attests to the magnitude of these fateful events. Untold numbers perished by sword and famine, and the land was left in ruins (see Ezek. 5). The exact number of the Judean exiles who ended up in Babylon (see 2 Kings 24:14–16; Jer. 52:28–30) is subject to speculation—the biblical figures are difficult to harmonize—and estimates range from several thousand to 80,000. The total figure was clearly substantial.[130] Inevitably, untold numbers of Judeans fled to surrounding nations to escape the Babylonian menace. Fairly large numbers ended up in Egypt. From the perspective of the writer of 2 Kings, the destruction of the nation was total: "Judah went into captivity, away from her land" (2 Kings 25:21b). But, while the size and significance of the remnant in Palestine is debated, it is evident that many stayed. The book of Lamentations, possibly produced in the immediate aftermath of the horrific devastation, paints a vivid picture of their experience:

> Our inheritance has been turned over to strangers, our homes to
>   foreigners.
> We have become fatherless, our mothers are widows.
> *We must buy the water we drink; our wood can be had only at a*
>   *price.*
> *Those who pursue us are at our heels; we are weary and find no*
>   *rest. . . .*
> Joy is gone from our hearts; our dancing has turned to mourning.
> *The crown has fallen from our head. Woe to us, for we have sinned!*
> *Because of this our hearts are faint, because of these things our eyes*
>   *grow dim.*
> For Mount Zion, which lies desolate, with jackals prowling over it.
>   (Lam. 5:2–5, 15–18)

---

129. William M. Schniedewind, *How the Bible Became a Book: The Textualization of Ancient Israel* (New York: Cambridge University Press, 2004), 143–44; see also Smith-Christopher, *Biblical Theology of Exile*, 47.

130. See Smith, *Religion of the Landless*, 29–35.

For the migrant community that ended up in the Babylonian and Persian Empires also, the sense of loss, shame, and degradation would have been unbearably intense. But their situation was far more complex; and opinion about their experience varied considerably. As the books of Daniel, Esther, and Nehemiah indicate, some of the exiles (possibly the cream of the crop) were well treated, overcame major hazards, and attained high social standing. But exilic literature also provides clear indications that the exiles experienced adversities, conflict with other groups, threat of violence, and state repression.[131] In the royal court tales of Daniel, Esther, and Nehemiah, fear of the authorities is evident (Neh. 2:2; Esther 4:16; Dan. 1:10); exile is repeatedly characterized as humiliation or bondage at the hands of foreign rulers (Ezra 9:7; Dan. 9:7). The visions and prophetic declarations of divine judgment on foreign nations or powers (Dan. 7; Isa. 49:7, 23) also reveal the deep resentments fostered by powerlessness and oppression. Nehemiah attested to "the hardship that has come on us, on our kings and leaders, on our priests and prophets, on our ancestors and all your people, from the days of the kings of Assyria until today. . . . We are slaves. . . . They rule over our bodies and our cattle as they please. We are in great distress" (Neh. 9:32b, 36, 37). Ezra insisted that "though we are slaves, our God has not deserted us in our bondage" (Ezra 9:9).

For the Jewish exiles, life in foreign lands deepened religious consciousness (linked to an abiding sense of shame for the sins of their ancestors that led to "sword and captivity") and fostered a stronger sense of community identity or religious distinctiveness—one that in its most extreme forms bordered on an exclusivist nationalism (Isa. 49:25-26). But, paradoxically, separateness from others (an expression of divine election—Lev. 20:26; Isa. 52:11) was tied to

131. In a detailed analysis that draws on modern refugee and disaster studies, sociologies of trauma, and archeological data, Smith-Christopher challenges the benign view of exile as one of relative ease and freedom. Among other things, he highlights the brutal and oppressive nature of both Babylonian and Persian rule, the dominant control of minority/immigrant groups (evident in references to "decrees" or the need for letters of permission), the "forced subservience" of even high-ranking Jews like Nehemiah, and the frequent occurrence of metaphors of imprisonment (chains, fetters, "sight to the blind") in the literature. See *Biblical Theology of Exile*, 21–72. Yet, "forced subservience" does not tell the whole story; for embedded within these narratives is "a subversive theology, a hidden transcript, that reserves recognition of authority to God alone, while maintaining a necessarily polite demeanor to the imperial representatives." *Biblical Theology of Exile*, 45.

missionary function and served redemptive purpose. In the Daniel tales, the piety and religious devotion of Jews at the royal court, in the face of assim-ilative pressures and life-threatening conflict, repeatedly provided powerful witness to Yahweh's sovereignty. It even led to worship of Yahweh by the monarch (Dan. 2:46–47; 3:28–29; 4:34–35; 6:26–27).[132]

Even more strikingly perhaps, the prophet Jeremiah made it clear that the future of God's people lay not with the remnant back in the promised land (Je-rusalem) but with the exiles in a foreign land (Jer. 24:3–10; 29:11–19)! Yahweh exhorted the Babylonian exiles to "seek the peace and prosperity of the city [of exile, and] . . . pray for it" and assured them that "you will seek me and find me" (Jer. 29:7, 13). This message was tantamount to a theological bombshell, for, astonishingly, it instructed the displaced migrants to transfer their prayers and prospects from Jerusalem to the pagan city. They had become foreigners in a strange land, away from the land of their ancestors and the place of worship; but they were still enjoined to pray to Yahweh, call on his name, and "seek [him] with all your heart" (Jer. 29:13). So, Yahweh was not a tribal or national god, confined to a particular territory (like other gods). He could be approached and could be found, indeed fully worshipped, anywhere—even (from a Jewish point of view) in a pagan land, the place of exile and captivity!

The tale of Jonah, variously dated to the monarchy, exilic, or postexilic pe-riod, captures the tension between election and mission. If it was indeed pro-duced in exile, as some suppose, Jonah very possibly becomes "a symbol of the Israelite people themselves in exile."[133] Either way, the call to deliver a message to Nineveh, the capital of the brutal Assyrian Empire, is striking. So absolute was the prophet's rejection of this outreach mission that he became bitterly offended, not because he was "hurled . . . into the deep" (Jon. 2:2)—argu-ably a metaphor of exile[134]—but because Yahweh (Israel's redeemer) forgave Nineveh. Jonah would rather face death than see God's salvation, as opposed to the long-anticipated divine judgment, extended to reviled foreigners!

132. For a critical appraisal see W. Lee Humphreys, "A Life-Style for Diaspora: A Study of the Tales of Esther and Daniel," *Journal of Biblical Literature* 92, no. 2 (1973): 211–23.

133. Smith-Christopher, *Biblical Theology of Exile*, 132.

134. Smith-Christopher suggests that Jonah 2 contains "a number of images rem-iniscent of images of exile," including going into deep darkness (v. 2), being away from the land and missing the temple (v. 4), and allusions to "prison" (v. 6) (*Biblical Theology of Exile*, 133).

The message of Jonah also implied a deep awareness of the strong tensions between universal redemption and nationalist retribution in the theological reformulation taking place within the exilic community. On the one hand, there is expectation of universal salvation: foreigners will "bind themselves to the Lord" (Isa. 56:3, 6); the nations will acknowledge Yahweh as the only true God and turn to him for salvation (Isa. 45:20–24). On the other hand, foreign nations and rulers are portrayed in utterly negative terms. In a manner that presumably reflects "the voice of an oppressed and resentful people . . . [who] dream of a reversal of fortune,"[135] foreign nations and rulers are condemned in the divine plan; they are expected to experience catastrophe and "lick the dust" (Isa. 49:23). This mixture of images perhaps indicates the internal theological struggle within the diaspora community.

But, all things considered, the bold universalism of these passages is compelling.[136] And this recognition that Israel's relationship with Yahweh had universal dimensions was a product of diaspora existence. At the very least, dispersal among foreign nations opened the way for the recognition that Israel's fortunes were tied with the history of the nations.[137] This development had missionary implications. By virtue of living as God's people in foreign lands the Jewish people comprised "a confessional community open on principle to outsiders."[138] This also fostered a pluralistic vision of faith: "You are my witnesses, says the Lord" (Isa. 43:12); "I will . . . make you a light to the nations" (Isa. 49:6). Israel's witness to God's sovereignty and power would lead foreigners to say "I belong to the Lord" (Isa. 44:5), for Yahweh "will gather still others to them besides those already gathered" (Isa. 56:8). In the prophetic vision, gentiles and foreigners become part of the new, reconstituted people of God, the new Israel. Indeed, nonbelievers will be selected "to be priests and Levites" (Isa. 66:21).

Israel's election, then, was inseparable from its migrant identity and lineage. Its chosenness crystallized and exemplified Yahweh's love for the migrant-outsider. The universal implications of this became clear only with time. But

---

135. Joseph Blenkinsopp, "Second Isaiah—Prophet of Universalism," *Journal for the Study of the Old Testament* 41 (1988): 89.

136. See Smith-Christopher, *Biblical Theology of Exile*, 125–30.

137. Johannes Verkuyl, *Contemporary Missiology: An Introduction* (Grand Rapids: Eerdmans, 1978), 91.

138. Blenkinsopp, "Second Isaiah," 92.

its radical theological implications were made manifest in the lives of Israel's ancestors (who developed in faith and received God's promises as migrants) and in the "migrant" provisions within the Sinai covenant that reflected Israel's unique history as a people of God redeemed through migration. For Israel and its ancestors at least, migration was a theologizing experience because the migrant (outsider, stranger, foreigner) status exemplified the experience of dispossession, vulnerability, and exclusion that gave potency to faith and sharpened consciousness of divine action or protection (Ps. 146:9). The election of migrant-foreigners or outsiders was not only conducive to faith; it also made Yahweh's unconditional love and redemptive grace manifest. In these respects, the old covenant effectively foreshadowed the new: the people of God.

Migration and Mission in the New Testament Period

When exactly the Jewish exile ended is a question to which there is no single response.[139] One particular view maintains that the commencement of Jesus's ministry in Galilee (in fulfillment of Isaiah's prophecy), his announcement of the "kingdom of God," and his frequent quotation of exilic passages (some of which he claimed to fulfill—most notably Isa. 61:1–2[140]) marked the close of the period of exile and the beginning of a new phase of restoration.[141] Douglas S. McComiskey reasons that even if Jewish hardness in the face of Jesus's message of the kingdom "indicates a continuing state of exile," his preaching also "enabled the individual Jew to exit exile . . . through a faith response" to his ministry. Thus, Jesus's invocation of Isaiah 56:7 ("My house will be called a house of prayer for all nations") during his cleansing of the temple (Matt.

139. Some point to the rebuilding of the temple (completed under Persian rule in 515 BCE [Ezra 6:14–17]) and the subsequent restoration of Jewish worship in Judah under Nehemiah; others insist the exile technically lasted until the foundation of an independent Jewish state in 1948.

140. "The Spirit of the Lord is on me, because he has anointed me to proclaim good news to the poor. He has sent me to proclaim freedom for the prisoners and recovery of sight for the blind, to set the oppressed free, to proclaim the year of the Lord's favor" (Isa. 61:1–2). Others include Isa. 6:9–10; Mic. 7:6; and Dan. 7:13.

141. See Douglas S. McComiskey, "Exile and the Purpose of Jesus' Parables (Mark 4:10–12; Matt 13:10–17; Luke 8:9–10)," *Journal of the Evangelical Theological Society* 51, no. 1 (2008): 673–96; Douglas S. McComiskey, "Exile and Restoration from Exile in the Scriptural Quotations and Allusions of Jesus," *Journal of the Evangelical Theological Society* 53, no. 4 (2010): 675–79, 682.

21:13; Mark 11:17; Luke 19:46) affirmed the prophetic inclusion of the gentiles associated with postexilic restoration. The exploration of exilic theology in Jesus's ministry cannot be fully taken up here, but it raises important questions about the extent to which it exemplified the link between migration and divine action.

"I Was a Stranger"

To start with, Jesus's life and ministry are marked by the migrant motif in profound ways. Migration frames the circumstances of his birth. Joseph is a Nazareth resident whose place of birth or extraction is Bethlehem (Luke 2:4). Whether this renders Joseph an immigrant or a member of an immigrant community is unclear; but the inescapable theme of homeland versus residence means that an outsider identity cannot be ruled out. In any case, the fact that Jesus's family ends up as refugees in Egypt immediately after his birth means that their earliest memories as a family unit included the experience of living as strangers in a foreign land where their daily life was bounded by unfamiliar languages, customs, sights, and smells. That this episode was perceived as reminiscent of Israel's captivity and exodus (Matt. 2:14–15)—though in this case, Egypt only functions as a land of refuge—further strengthens the point. Jesus, uniquely God's Son, personified the people of God; and in his life, like the people of Israel, the migrant experience was linked to divine purpose.

But the act of migration was integral to Jesus's unique mission in an even more fundamental way, if we consider that the incarnation—whereby the divine took on human flesh and "made his *dwelling* among us" (John 1:14)—was a veritable act of migration or relocation. This is to say that when "he made himself nothing by taking the very nature of a servant, being made in human likeness" (Phil. 2:6–7), the God of the universe went into voluntary exile, so to speak—an experience of alienation encapsulated by the agony of the cross (Matt. 27:46). In one sense, this represented a striking reversal of Yahweh's desertion of his people prior to their exile (Jer. 14:8). In other respects, however, God remained "a stranger in the land," a fact interestingly attested to both at the beginning and at the end of Jesus's earthly ministry. The Gospel of John notes that "he came to that which was his own, but his own did not receive him" (1:12); and in the Emmaus Road discourse the resurrected Jesus is bemusedly queried: "Art thou only a stranger [*paroikos*] in Jerusalem, and hast not known the things which are come to pass there in these days?" (Luke 24:18, KJV).

The intersection of migration and divine action is evident throughout Jesus's earthly ministry. Regardless of any connections to the exile, it is striking that the public ministry of the long-awaited Messiah announced to the Jews was mainly confined to Galilee (Matt. 4:23; 11:1; Mark 1:14, 39; Luke 4:14)—i.e., gentile territory. Galilee was a major commercial hub marked by considerable migrant movement, and it was designated "Galilee of the Gentiles [or nations]" due to its majority non-Jewish, mixed, population. Thus, from a Jewish perspective, it was a land where people lived "in darkness," "the land of the shadow of death" (Isa. 9:1–2; Matt. 4:15). Galilee, in a word, epitomized foreignness or otherness. That it became the primary place of ministry for the (Jewish) Messiah points to the border-crossing, migrant-outsider status intrinsic to the divine mission. We should also note that Jesus chose to raise the crucial question about his identity, "who do people say the Son of Man is?" (Matt. 16:13), while in a gentile city (Caesarea Philippi). More important still, that he is pronounced "the Son of the Living God" in a setting marked by pagan worship and illustrative of human power portends its universal application.[142]

Jesus's migrant-outsider status is also evident in his origins. He hails not only from Galilee (outside the Jewish orbit) but from Nazareth: a little-known backwater town in Galilee that even fellow Galileans apparently despised (John 1:46). This fact has profound theological implications for our understanding of the subsequent spread of the Jesus movement and the church's mission. It is worth noting that the revolutionary ministry of John the Baptist, which bore witness to the appearance of the Messiah, also emerged on the margins. It began not in the temple (under the control of the Jewish authorities) but in the wilderness, that is, on the outer reaches or margins of society. Similarly, the long-awaited Messiah appears not in one of the notable cities of ancient Israel or the center of empire but in the obscurity of Nazareth. The same is true of the earliest witnesses. The Samaritan woman who proclaimed Jesus to her townspeople (John 4:1–30) did so potentially as an outcast, cer-

142. Caesarea Philippi (formerly Paneas) was a center of worship of Pan, the Greek god of the forest, and had elaborate temples devoted to various gods. The city was built and renamed for Augustus Caesar and Herod Philip by the latter's son, Herod the Great, who also erected a white marble temple dedicated to Augustus Caesar in the region.

tainly from a position of social marginality (a woman, many times widowed, probably childless, and in a fragile relationship).[143]

To put it plainly, *the mission of God starts on the margins*. In sociological terms, margins signify the vulnerability, powerlessness, and otherness intrinsic to migration and migrant existence. As we shall see, down the centuries, the faith birthed in the ministry of Jesus would chiefly spread through migration. Largely due to the role of Christian migrants in the cross-cultural transmission of the Christian message, it recurrently and inescapably penetrates new societies from the margins.

But the centrality of migration in the Gospel narratives is evident in other ways. Jesus spent his entire ministry as an itinerant preacher (Matt. 4:23; 9:35; Luke 8:1; 9:6); and the incessant movement of merchants, traders, and other migrants formed a backdrop to the social context. More likely than not, the "large crowds" often said to be traveling with, or following, him (Matt. 4:25; Mark 3:7; Luke 14:25; John 12:20–21) included gentiles. Jesus constantly crossed boundaries (ethnic, social, cultural), eschewed the exclusive claims of any particular social group, and gave much attention to those who were outsiders or on the margins. His teachings, exemplified in the "Good Samaritan" parable, condemned the cultural exclusivism of Jewish religion and categorically reaffirmed the injunction to love the foreigner-outsider.

Strikingly, his own life experiences included the pain of cultural rejection and the sense of homelessness fostered by itinerancy. The refusal of Samaritan villagers to extend hospitality to him and his followers elicited the moving declaration that "foxes have holes, and birds of the air have nests; but the Son of Man has nowhere to lay his head" (Luke 9:58). The physical travails of itinerancy in his day necessitated dependence on a support network of women (Luke 8:2–3); the indispensability of hospitality, or receptive welcome, for effective outreach was a constant consideration (Luke 9:3–5). Jesus the Messiah became the perennial outsider, even with respect to his own family and home community (Luke 8:19–21; Mark 6:2–4); he was forced into mini-exile by plots to take his life (John 11:54). In the Matthew 25 parable, the idea of the stranger is linked to God's eternal kingdom and the gathering of disciples from "all the nations" (Matt. 25:32). The Messiah-King is portrayed as a divine

---

143. Cf. Lynn H. Cohick, "The Real Woman at the Well," *Christianity Today* 59, no. 8 (2015): 66–69.

stranger, the unknown outsider seeking welcome and desperately in need of hospitality: "I was a stranger [*paroikos*] and you invited me in . . ." (Matt. 25:35). Thus, in a manner strongly evocative of the Old Testament covenant (cf. Deut. 10:19; Lev. 19:34), love and care for the foreigner-outsider as a hallmark of the people of God is explicitly affirmed in the new covenant.

In sum, the gospel writers not only depict Jesus as an itinerant who constantly crosses borders but also present him as the embodiment of the "stranger" (Matt. 25:35; also Luke 24:18). And believers are cautioned that their love for God or Christ is demonstrated in their treatment of the stranger-outsider (Matt. 25:40, 45): "whatever you did for one of the least of these brothers and sisters of mine, you did for me." The profoundly theological notion that the Messiah could be encountered in the stranger (the outsider seeking hospitality) no doubt carried deep resonance in an age when the community of faith comprised leaders and adherents who were frequently migrants and strangers. The Matthew 25 parable presents less a call to evangelism than an acknowledgment that fellow believers were often unknown outsiders. The exhortation explicitly invokes solidarity and mutual strengthening within the believing community ("these brothers and sisters of mine"). Nonbelievers are not in view.[144] Rather, the parable assails any effort to incorporate or replicate the sociopolitical divisions of the wider society within the community of faith. Within the Jesus movement no faithful individual or group should be mistreated simply because they were stranger-outsiders. Early growth quickly put this conviction to the test.

The Christian Movement as a Gentile Phenomenon

The Christian movement birthed through Jesus's ministry began as a decidedly Jewish phenomenon. Its growth into a dominant religious movement within the Roman Empire and a world movement by the end of the sixth century CE involved complex interpenetration among a vast array of diverse cultures and societies, aided by migration. As explained in the second chapter, historians have adopted a variety of explanatory concepts to account for the process of cross-cultural expansion and conversion; these included accultura-

---

144. The reference to "all the nations" in Matt. 25:32 points not to the entire human race but to the universal scope of the kingdom of God.

tion, adhesion or hybridity, syncretism, and transformation.[145] None of these, or any combination thereof, is convincing. In my view, the principle of translation propounded by Andrew Walls and Lamin Sanneh provides the most compelling construct.[146] Here, I examine its main assertions and arguments primarily in reference to the spread of Christianity within the Roman Empire; but the principle forms a key plank in the assessment of the role of migration in the globalization of the Christian faith that this study attempts.

Acts 6 and the Antioch Moment

The implacable divisions between Jews and gentiles that troubled the gospel's universal mandate are a dominant theme in the New Testament. But the primitive church that emerged in Palestine was already, in some ways, a multicultural entity; and the cultural frictions that inevitably accompany the incorporation of migrant-outsiders into the community of faith occurred before the Christian movement was launched in gentile territory. This is partly because Jerusalem, the cradle of the movement, was a multicultural city. The influence of Greek culture on the city was pervasive, exemplified by the presence of Greek-speaking schools and synagogues. But possibly no more than 20 percent of the population spoke Greek, while Latin was mainly confined to the tiny Roman segment.[147] The majority of the population interacted in Hebrew or Aramaic. More to the point, this culturally diverse city attracted immigrants from all over the Roman Empire, particularly diaspora (or Hellenistic) Jews from far-flung lands. Many were religious pilgrims; but some

145. Marc David Baer, "History and Religious Conversion," in *The Oxford Handbook of Religious Conversion*, ed. Lewis R. Rambo and Charles E. Farhadian (New York: Oxford University Press, 2014), 25–47.

146. Andrew F. Walls, *The Missionary Movement in the Christian History: Studies in the Transmission of the Faith* (Maryknoll, NY: Orbis Books, 1996), 26–42; Lamin Sanneh, *Translating the Message: The Missionary Impact on Culture*, 2nd ed. (Maryknoll, NY: Orbis Books, 2009). See also Kwame Bediako, *Christianity in Africa: The Renewal of a Non-Western Religion* (Maryknoll, NY: Orbis Books, 1995); C. René Padilla, "Hermeneutics and Culture—a Theological Perspective," in *Down to Earth: Studies in Christianity and Culture*, ed. Robert T. Coote and John R. W. Stott (Grand Rapids: Eerdmans, 1980), 63–78.

147. See Thorsten Prill, "Migration, Mission and the Multi-Ethnic Church," *Evangelical Review of Theology* 33, no. 4 (2009): 333.

(often those in their old age) returned to take up permanent residence since many devout Jews desired to be buried in Jerusalem.[148]

In the Acts 2 passage, Peter addresses the crowd as "fellow Jews and all of you who live in Jerusalem" (v. 14). No specific reference is made to gentiles; and, by all indications, the majority who responded to his message were *Hellenistic* Jews. Whether the numerical estimates in Acts are taken literally or not, *Hebraic* Jews who constituted the original members of the faith community were rapidly outnumbered. Outside a common faith and ancestry, the two groups had little in common. Born in Palestine and steeped in its culture, Hebraic Jews tended to be fiercely nationalistic. At the very least, they viewed themselves as the true Israel and the custodians of the Jewish way of life. They mainly spoke Aramaic and took great pains to restrict their interactions with non-Jews. In sharp contrast, Hellenistic or diaspora Jews were born (and lived) outside Palestine, spoke mainly Greek (many did not speak Aramaic), gave their children Greek names, married non-Jews, and fully absorbed Greek values and culture. Even though they represented diverse nationalities and were fluent in a variety of distinctive native languages (Acts 2:6, 11), Hellenism provided a common identity and had a greater impact on their religious life.[149] In Palestinian society most were sojourners and occupied the status of "outsiders"; stricter Jewish sects like the Pharisees considered them second-class Israelites.

By the nature of things, Hellenistic Jews brought distinctive cultural sensibilities to the primitive church and its mission; and their recruitment marked a significant development in the life of the Jerusalem fellowship of believers. Their multilingualism, diversity of cultural backgrounds, and foreign extraction transformed the fellowship into an immigrant community of faith and presented challenges to integration. While the believers "had everything in common" (Acts 2:44), the ideal of communal unity collided with inherent cultural divergences and social divisions. Whether or not the contention over the distribution of food was a one-off incident, it exposed underlying strains. We are left to imagine the subtle indignities that marked this native-outsider divide even as this community of believers pursued the

148. Prill, "Migration, Mission and the Multi-Ethnic Church," 333.
149. See Walter Woodburn Hyde, *Paganism to Christianity in the Roman Empire* (Philadelphia: University of Pennsylvania Press, 1946), 87–97.

ideal of unity in Christ.[150] Evidently, distribution of food was controlled by the Hebraic believers who, by the privileged treatment of their own widows, underscored the second-class status of the Hellenistic Jews within the community. Their marginalization within the community symbolized a stunning failure of hospitality rooted in cultural difference and social alienation.[151]

Remarkably, the story ends with the food distribution being placed in the care of seven Hellenistic Jews. All had Greek names, and were therefore "outsiders." But the resolution of a thorny issue was quickly overtaken by new developments.

Stephen, one of the seven, interpreted Jewish history and traditions from a decidedly non-Palestinian perspective that riled even his fellow Hellenistic Jews; and his views brought him to the attention of the Jewish authorities. In a lengthy unfinished speech to the Sanhedrin (the Jewish council), his devastating attack on the two most revered elements of national religion—the land and its temple—got him killed. Stephen contrasted the rebellious disobedience of the Jewish people living in the promised land with the faithful obedience of their migrant ancestors who encountered God in foreign lands. He asserted that since "the Most High" is present and active in all the world (Acts 7:44–50), his presence and power were clearly not confined to a single land, much less to a single edifice. God can be worshiped anywhere, as the mobile tabernacle built by Moses for the wandering Hebrews indicated. The existence or absence of a temple mattered little, since it was folly to think that mere mortals could build "a dwelling place for the God of Jacob" (Isa. 66:1–2; 1 Kings 8:27). The God of Israel cannot be localized or reduced to a tribal deity!

Stephen's death at the hands of enraged Jewish authorities and the threat of persecution triggered a dispersion of the new community of believers. In a notable demonstration of the link between migration and cross-cultural

150. The fact that they met in homes no doubt enhanced the dominance of the home-based Hebraic Jews. It also probably reinforced group consciousness. Some reason, based on the fact that the apostles had to "call a meeting of all the believers" (Acts 6:2, NLT), that the two groups "had their own social meetings." In any case, the marginalization of the migrant-outsiders (the Greek-speaking segment) became manifest in the discrimination against Hellenistic Jewish widows (Acts 6:1). See Prill, "Migration, Mission and the Multi-Ethnic Church," 334.

151. It is worth adding that as migrant-outsiders in a male-dominated society Hellenistic Jewish widows would have been especially in need of welfare support, since they were not likely to have relatives nearby to provide for them.

missionary action, the refugee movement instigated by his martyrdom became an itinerant missionary phenomenon that led to the establishment of new Christian congregations in various towns throughout the regions of Judea, Galilee, and Samaria. The cultural composition of the expanding community of faith changed even more radically due to the actions of boundary-crossing migrants. The Lucan account (Acts 8; 9:31; 10:1–48) records notable break-throughs: the evangelization of Samaritans, considered by some first-century Jews to be no better than gentiles; the conversion of the Ethiopian eunuch, a "God-fearer" emissary from the Kingdom of Meroë (in present-day Sudan); the preaching of the gospel to "the population of the eastern seaboard cities of Palestine" (from Azotus to Caesarea, Acts 8:40) that were predominantly gentile;[152] and the conversion of Cornelius, the Roman centurion and "God-fearer," in whose house the first recorded gentile Pentecost took place (Acts 10:44–46). But the migrant movement went beyond Palestine "as far as Phoenicia, Cyprus and Antioch" (Acts 11:19).

Antioch, founded by Greeks, the former capital of the Greek Seleucid Kingdom and the third-largest city in the Roman Empire, was a major commercial city in the Roman province of Syria and one of the most beautiful and prosperous cities in the Mediterranean region. It was subject to major influences from both East and West, marked by a great diversity of cultures and religious systems. Some of the unnamed Hellenistic Jewish Christian refugees (originally from Cyprus and Cyrene) who ended up in Antioch took the bold and unprecedented step of sharing their faith not only with fellow Jews (within the synagogue) but also with non-Jewish Greeks in the wider population, thus opening the way for the first Greek-speaking church. This innovative action arguably reflects instincts forged in diaspora existence, in contexts where the daily jostling of multiple nationalities and the constant interplay of religious ideas facilitated openness to outsiders. As William Ramsay puts it, these men "had been brought up in Greek lands and had a wider outlook on the world than Palestinian Jews."[153]

---

152. Themistocles A. Adamopoulo, "Elements of the Earliest Evangelisation of Gentiles in the Roman Empire: Caesarea Maritima, Antioch and Rome," *Phronema* 13 (1998): 71. Caesarea Maritima was a major urban center under direct Roman administration.

153. William M. Ramsay, *St. Paul: The Traveler and Roman Citizen* (Grand Rapids: Kregel, 2001), 50.

In Antioch then emerged the first gentile church, a multiethnic congregation with leaders from diverse cultural backgrounds (Acts 13:1). Given the radical change in religious allegiance involved, the conversion of these Greek-speaking believers was remarkable. It is quite possible that their receptivity reflects familiarity with the tenets of Hellenistic Judaism; which is to say, as Lewis Rambo suggests, that an established consonance between the two cultural systems aided conversion.[154] In the event, their new faith (and conduct?) was so strongly associated with the name of Christ that their neighbors labeled them "those who are connected with Christos," or "Chrestians."[155] What began as a popular slang for a strange new religious sect became permanent description—the vulgar Greek term subsequently Latinized as "Christians." The Antioch episode not only exemplified the capacity of Christian migrants to instigate defining moments in the history of Christianity but also demonstrated the vital role of migration for cross-cultural expansion and the fulfillment of the faith's core universal vision.

With the recognition that God "had opened the door of faith to the Gentiles" (Acts 14:27), the fledgling Christian movement crossed a major frontier; and this momentous development decisively transformed its prospects. Emerging in obscurity on the fringes of Palestinian Judaism, the early Christian community evinced little potential for expansion beyond a limited number of primarily Jewish adherents. The Antioch moment changed that. Compared to backwater Palestine, Antioch was a major center of commerce and communications that provided easy access to the wider Mediterranean world and beyond, by land and sea. With the establishment of the multicultural Antioch congregation, the new faith entered a new setting that allowed full access to the massive web of infrastructural and vibrant commercial interconnections that grew under Roman rule. Antioch acted as a gateway to the vast reaches of the Roman Empire (with its multitudes of cultures) and beyond. No other single individual epitomized and championed the international vision of the Jesus movement more assiduously than Saul (later Paul), the Jewish apostle to the gentiles whose missionary labors loom over the first generation of Christians.

154. Lewis R. Rambo, *Understanding Religious Conversion* (New Haven: Yale University Press, 1993), 41–42. See also Sherman E. Johnson, "Antioch, the Base of Operations," *Lexington Theological Quarterly* 18, no. 2 (1983): 70.

155. Ramsay, *St. Paul*, 54–55; Johnson, "Antioch," 64.

The Apostle Paul (ca. 5 CE–ca. 67 CE)

What little we know of Saul's background attests to an individual with multiple identities and a strong capacity for boundary crossing.[156] He was a deeply religious Hellenistic Jew with dual citizenship (Roman and Tarsian) who was fluent in at least three languages (Hebrew, Aramaic, and Greek).[157] Tarsus (in Cilicia), his city of birth, was decidedly cosmopolitan: a metropolis steeped in multicultural influences, situated at a crossroads of travel, and deeply connected to the international order.[158] Paul himself describes it as "no ordinary city" (Acts 21:39). His relocation to Jerusalem while still in his youth—"born in Tarsus . . . , but brought up in [Jerusalem]" (Acts 22:3)—where he trained under Gamaliel (one of the most esteemed rabbis of his day) contributed to Paul's transnational development. The two contexts, Palestine and Tarsus, had little in common with each other; but, in combination, they produced a multifaceted individual eminently capable of crossing cultural frontiers and maintaining transnational existence.

The tensions and seeming contradictions of transnational existence are readily apparent in Paul's life. He was a native of a cosmopolitan center of commerce who chose to settle as an immigrant in provincial Palestine.[159] An extremely devout Jew who was at home in the center of Judaism, Paul was also "trained to a far wider outlook on the world than the people of Jerusalem could attain to."[160] He was a zealous Pharisaic Jew yet intimately familiar with the Hellenistic (pagan?) world and its religious aspirations. In a dramatic turn of events, he became a follower of Christ and embraced a faith he had

156. See Caroline E. Johnson Hodge, "Apostle to the Gentiles: Constructions of Paul's Identity," *Biblical Interpretation* 13, no. 3 (2005): 270–88; Nicholas H. Taylor, "Conflicting Bases of Identity in Early Christianity: The Example of Paul," in *Handbook of Early Christianity: Social Science Approaches*, ed. Anthony J. Blasi, Paul-André Turcotte, and Jean Duhaime (Walnut Creek, CA: AltaMira, 2002), 577–97.

157. Roman citizenship hints at a family with at least modest social standing and affluence.

158. Tarsus is described as "a center of extensive commercial traffic with many countries along the shores of the Mediterranean, as well as with the countries of central Asia Minor"—M. G. Easton, *Baker's Illustrated Bible Dictionary* (Grand Rapids: Baker Book House, 1981), 537.

159. Admittedly, viewed from a religious perspective, this move constituted a relocation from the periphery to the center—a testimony to devoutness.

160. Cf. Ramsay, *St. Paul*, 45.

previously considered utterly repugnant to the Judaism he practiced. Still, he fully embraced the new faith without complete abandonment of his prior Jewish identity or loyalties. Undoubtedly, he viewed his new Christian identity (being "in Christ") as supreme. Yet, by his own confession, he "became like a Jew, to win the Jews" (1 Cor. 9:20, NTL). At the same time, and far more consequentially, his call to be "apostle to the Gentiles" required him (a Jew) to live like a gentile (Gal. 2:8–16; 1 Cor. 9:21)!

Whether the dramatic series of events that radically altered Saul's life and set him on a whole new career can be termed a "conversion" remains a matter of debate.[161] Intriguingly, some details of his postconversion activity provided in Acts are difficult to reconcile with Paul's own letters, notably the timing of the Jerusalem Council (Acts 15) and its significance for Paul's ministry. But the record is clear that sometime after his conversion, and before he embarked on his missionary journeys, Paul relocated to Antioch and made it his base of operations (Acts 11:26; Gal. 1:21). His lengthy stint with the multiethnic Antioch congregation probably afforded him the earliest opportunity to formulate his gospel to the gentiles. Even if we allow that subsequent opposition and competing ideologies radicalized his thinking,[162] the core tenets of Paul's message emerged early and remained unambiguous.[163]

Fundamentally, Paul repudiated the notion that "the door of the synagogue was the portal through which the nations must find their way into the church";[164] and on this issue his stance was clearly more uncompromising than that of other apostles like Peter (Gal. 2:11–16). Gentile Christians, he insisted, are "children of God through faith in Christ" (Gal. 3:26); and belonging to Christ, who is Abraham's seed, renders them inheritors of the same promises given to Israel (Gal. 3:16, 29). Thus, faith in Christ, not observance of the Mosaic Law and Jewish customs, or identification with the nation of Israel,

161. His "conversion" experience is perhaps best characterized as a radical form of *institutional transition* (to borrow Rambo's typology) involving a complex process of change from one community to another within a shared tradition.

162. See Taylor, "Conflicting Bases of Identity," 589–90.

163. Indeed, Nicholas Taylor hypothesizes that the creedal declaration in Gal. 3:28, "there is neither Jew nor Gentile, neither slave nor free, nor is there male and female," dates to Paul's earlier time in Antioch, since the contrast between Jew and gentile had little application to the predominantly gentile Galatian churches ("Conflicting Bases of Identity," 591).

164. Ramsay, *St. Paul*, 54.

was the basis of the new universal family that comprised God's household (Gal. 3:15–4:7; Rom. 3:21–31). Since there is "only one God" (Rom. 3:29–30), the God of the Jews is also the God of the gentiles; and there can therefore be only one household or community of faith—not one church for Jews and another for gentiles (cf. Eph. 2:14–16).[165] Moreover, within this new covenant community, "belonging to Christ" superseded other identities (Gal. 3:28).

By virtue of his transnational identity and capacity, Paul was exceptionally equipped to appreciate and champion the universality of the Christian message. With the gentile breakthrough at Antioch, the Christian message abolished the linguistic, cultural, and geographical confinement of Judaism and entered the international Mediterranean world. Antioch provided a natural springboard for empire-wide expansion. It also fittingly marked the starting point of Paul's public ministry. The conviction that "[God] had opened a door of faith to the Gentiles" (Acts 14:27) defined Paul's vision; and his extraordinary ministry embodied the first historic turning point in the spread of the Christian movement.

In a period of roughly twenty years the apostle Paul covered over 12,000 miles (by land and sea) from Syria to Asia Minor and eventually Europe.[166] By his own admission he was "constantly on the move" and "traveled on many long journeys" (2 Cor. 11:26). The biblical record only hints at the great dangers, extreme arduousness, and tremendous personal costs involved in the vast distances his missionary expeditions required.[167] Overland, Paul undeniably traveled on foot (with perhaps a donkey for his belongings), supporting himself with the valuable and highly mobile craft of tent making.[168] As his writings indicate, he was no less susceptible than other travelers to the liabilities and painful setbacks of overland travel or to the perilousness of sea voyages:

165. On this, see Andrew F. Walls, *The Cross-Cultural Process in Christian History: Studies in the Transmission and Appropriation of Faith* (Maryknoll, NY: Orbis Books, 2002), 76–78.

166. Stephen S. Gosch and Peter N. Stearns, *Premodern Travel in World History* (New York: Routledge, 2008), 39; Hyde, *Paganism to Christianity*, 167.

167. For a detailed overview, see Jerome Murphy-O'Connor, "Traveling Conditions in the First Century: On the Road and on the Sea with St. Paul," *Bible Review* 1, no. 2 (1985): 38–45.

168. Tent making equipped Paul to make and repair all leather goods, including sandals, gourds, cloaks, and harnesses, as well as tents—services that were much in demand among travelers. See Murphy-O'Connor, "Traveling Conditions," 3.

I have faced danger from rivers and from robbers. I have faced danger from my own people, the Jews, as well as from the Gentiles. I have faced danger in the cities, in the deserts, and on the seas.... I have been hungry and thirsty and have often gone without food. I have shivered in the cold, without enough clothing to keep me warm.... (2 Cor. 11:26-27, NLT)

As a long-distance traveler, incessantly on the move, constantly crossing boundaries, Paul the apostle became the perennial migrant-outsider. The experience of being a stranger was integral to his ministry and underlined his missionary consciousness. In innumerable cross-cultural encounters he embraced the vulnerability and marginalized status of the outsider as a strategic missionary necessity: "I have made myself a slave to everyone, to win as many as possible.... I have become all things to all people" (1 Cor. 9:19-22). He also compared apostles like himself (traveling preachers with no established status or power base in any city) to foreigners with no rights, comparable to criminals or captives "on display at the end of the procession, like those condemned to die in the arena" (1 Cor. 4:9).

Not for Paul, then, the posture of dominance and controlling authority that later became a hallmark of European foreign mission enterprise. He contended often with social alienation, spent a tremendous amount of time working to support himself (in a trade that allowed him to talk as he worked), and forfeited the privileged treatment that his apostleship merited. This approach reflected a determination to differentiate himself from those who collected fees for their preaching. But the lowliness of the migrant-outsider status also made it easier to proclaim that the power of God resided primarily in the message (Rom. 1:16), not the messenger.

The apostle Paul is the prime biblical example of the major role that transnational leaders (on which more in the next chapter) played in the spread of the early Christian movement. No other Christian leader did more for the spread of the new faith in the eastern (or Greek) half of the empire—Syria, Asia Minor, and Macedonia—where the Christian population was most heavily concentrated.[169]

But for all his extraordinary achievements, Paul was by no means the first

---

169. Hyde, *Paganism to Christianity*, 169; Rodney Stark, *The Rise of Christianity* (San Francisco: HarperSanFrancisco, 1997), 10.

to aspire to or achieve successful evangelization of non-Jewish communities. By the time he inaugurated his historic gentile mission, Christian communities had already emerged among gentile populations in major urban centers within the empire, notably Antioch (Acts 11), Caesarea (Acts 18:22), and Rome (Rom. 1:7).[170] These missionary efforts were mainly the work of Jewish Christian migrants such as Aquila (a native of Pontus and tentmaker), who with his wife Priscilla settled in Rome and was part of the church there (Acts 18:2–3).[171] In other words, Paul's extensive missionary travels and transnational activity were symptomatic of a broader manifestation: the recurrent migrant movement of individuals and groups that provided central impetus for the spread of the Christian message and the establishment of Christian communities within the Roman Empire—and beyond.

170. Cf. Adamopoulo, "Elements of the Earliest Evangelisation," 66–87. For instance, Paul wrote his letter (ca. 57 CE) to a well-established gentile Christian community in Rome that, by his own admission, he had not had an opportunity to visit (Rom. 1:11–13; 15:23) (see Adamopoulo, "Elements of the Earliest Evangelisation," 74–77, and John Behr, *Irenaeus of Lyons: Identifying Christianity* (Oxford: Oxford University Press, 2013), 22.

171. Behr explains that "Christians had made their way to Rome by the middle of the first century, as traders, immigrants, and travelers, establishing communities in an ad hoc manner" (*Irenaeus of Lyons*, 22).

Part Two

HISTORICAL ASSESSMENT

CHAPTER FOUR

Christianization of the Roman Empire:
The Immigrant Factor

> Though [Christians] are residents at home in their own coun-
> tries, their behavior there is more like that of transients; they
> take their full part as citizens, but that also submit to any-
> thing and everything as if they were aliens. For them, any
> foreign country is a motherland, and any motherland is a
> foreign country.
>
> —"Epistle to Diognetus" (second century CE)

How the Jesus movement grew from a little-known sect in an obscure corner
of the Roman realm to become the dominant religion of the empire in a matter of little over three centuries has long intrigued historians and scholars of
religion.[1] No other faith or new religion within the empire came even close to
matching this extraordinary achievement or rate of growth. Sociologist Rodney Stark calculates that the number of Christians rose from roughly 1,400
in 50 CE to over 40,000 in 150 CE and some 1.2 million in 250 CE.[2] This
momentum of growth escalated even further over the subsequent century.

---

1. Among the most comprehensive or insightful treatments are Kenneth Scott
Latourette, *The First Five Centuries*, vol. 1 of *A History of the Expansion of Christianity*
(Grand Rapids: Zondervan, 1970), 162–69; Ramsay MacMullen, *Christianizing the
Roman Empire: A.D. 100–400* (New Haven: Yale University Press, 1984); Rodney
Stark, *The Rise of Christianity* (San Francisco: HarperSanFrancisco, 1997); Anthony J.
Blasi, Paul-André Turcotte, and Jean Duhaime, eds., *Handbook of Early Christianity:
Social Science Approaches* (Walnut Creek, CA: AltaMira, 2002); Reidar Hvalvik, "In
Word and Deed: The Expansion of the Church in the Pre-Constantinian Era," in
Mission of the Early Church to Jews and Gentiles, ed. Jostein Ådna and Hans Kvalbein
(Tübingen: Mohr Siebeck, 2000), 265–87.

2. Stark, *Rise of Christianity*, 4–10.

By 300 CE, Christian adherents numbered around 6 million (slightly more than 10 percent of the empire's population)—though unevenly distributed, accounting for perhaps up to 50 percent of the population in Asia Minor.[3] Empire-wide, their numbers surged to 33.8 million (56.5 percent of the population) by 350 CE. Historian Ramsay MacMullen, whose estimate of about 5 million Christians by 300 CE is comparable, reckons that Christianity won adherents "on the order of half a million in each generation from the end of the first century up to [313 CE]."[4] The exactitude of these statistical claims is subject to debate; less so the general trend they portray, including the dramatic fourth-century shift (see figure 1).

The copious literature on the spread of Christianity in the Roman Empire mainly focuses on institutional or organizational development in the face of official opposition and competition with other religions or major philosophies. This often produces a preoccupation with the interrelated themes of major ecclesiastical councils, imperial edicts, and development of Christian thought (apologetics, doctrinal formulation, theological innovation, Christological controversies, etc.). The treatment provided in this chapter, however, is mainly concerned with how migration, migrant networks, and specific types of migrants provided significant impetus for the expansion of the faith within the Roman Empire.

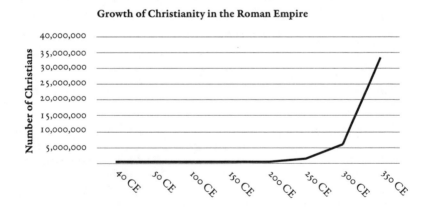

Growth of Christianity in the Roman Empire

3. Walter Woodburn Hyde, *Paganism to Christianity in the Roman Empire* (Philadelphia: University of Pennsylvania Press, 1946), 180.

4. MacMullen, *Christianizing the Roman Empire*, 32, 109–10.

An Ordinary Affair

The ascendancy of the Christian movement within the Roman Empire is even more astounding given the considerable tensions between Christian communities and the surrounding cultures (due to the former's distinctive identity), not to mention the relative "hiddenness" of the Christian movement prior to the fourth century. Attentiveness to the immigrant factor in the Christianization of the Roman Empire throws some light on these issues.

"A Holy Nation" and "Household of Faith"

There is scant evidence that early Christian believers and communities constituted a separatist, antisocial group, segregated from their fellow citizens or from the rest of the society. On the contrary, by all indications, Christians lived in daily interaction with their neighbors. Piqued by charges that Christian believers shirked their civic responsibilities, Tertullian (ca. 155–225), the Carthage-based African Christian apologist, insisted that

> we are not Indian Brahmins or Gymnosophists, who dwell in woods and exile themselves from ordinary human life. . . . So we sojourn with you in the world, abjuring neither forum, nor shambles, nor bath, nor booth, nor workshop, nor inn, nor weekly market, nor any other places of commerce. We sail with you, and fight with you, and till the ground with you; and in like manner we unite with you in your traffickings—even in the various arts we make public property of our works for your benefit. How it is we seem useless in your ordinary business, living with you and by you as we do, I am not able to understand.[5]

Admittedly, the necessity of refuting the charge that Christians were (in Tertullian's words) "useless in the affairs of life" strongly suggests that membership of the faith community engendered some degree of separation or alienation from the rest of society. But this requires explaining.

Some form of social alienation probably took place "through a voluntary

---

5. Tertullian, *Apology*, 42, in *The Writings of Tertullian*, vol. 1, ed. Anthony Uyl (Ontario: Devoted Publishing, 2019).

termination of, and conversion from, past familial, social and religious ties" (1 Pet. 1:14–16; 2:12; 3:15–17; 4:12–14),[6] actions which, in an age of tolerance, invited indignant hostility. At the very least, the view that conversion to Christ (followed by baptism) conferred a new identity and mandated distinctive codes of conduct was central to Christian commitment. Members of the community of faith were instructed to "live as servants of God" and to refrain from "doing what pagans choose to do" (1 Pet. 2:16; 4:3); and such strictures required shunning some associates and associations. Tertullian contended that Christians remained outstanding members of society who more than compensated for their nonparticipation in pagan festivals or religious ceremonies with other forms of generosity and compassion. But such abstention was liable to be interpreted as scornfulness or lack of patriotism (undermining Roman order);[7] and this engendered hostility and abuse, which in turn heightened an us-versus-them mentality among Christian believers.[8]

However, the boundary between believers and nonbelievers was not simply a matter of ethical standards, morals, ritual, or form of organization. Nor was it racial, ethnic, or sociopolitical (since adherents were drawn from all social categories).[9] It was profoundly theological; encapsulated in the conviction that believers were "a chosen people, a royal priesthood, a holy nation, God's special possession" (1 Pet. 1:3; 2:9). These claims betrayed Christianity's Jewish heritage; and in continuity with the Jewish tradition also, the Chris-

6. John Hall Elliott, *A Home for the Homeless: A Social-Scientific Criticism of 1 Peter, Its Situation and Strategy* (Minneapolis: Augsburg Fortress, 1990), 75.

7. Markus Mertaniemi, "From *Superstitio* to *Religio Christiana*: Christians as Others from the Third to the Fifth Century," in *The Faces of the Other: Religious Rivalry and Ethnic Encounters in the Later Roman World*, ed. Maijastina Kahlos (Turnhout: Brepols, 2011), 135–64. See also MacMullen, *Christianizing the Roman Empire*, 40; Hyde, *Paganism to Christianity*, 183–85; Peter Lampe, "Early Christians in the City of Rome: Topographical and Social Historical Aspects of the First Three Centuries," in *Christians as a Religious Minority in a Multicultural City: Modes of Interaction and Identity Formation in Early Imperial Rome*, ed. Jürgen Zangenberg and Michael Labahn (London: Continuum, 2004), 28.

8. Ramsay MacMullen even suggests that Christian congregations probably had "a rather repellant shell around them" (*Christianizing the Roman Empire*, 36; also pp. 32, 34–35).

9. However, the fact that nonmembers shared the same racial, social, and political profile as the believers possibly meant that the division elicited deeper resentments. See John Koenig, *New Testament Hospitality: Partnership with Strangers as Promise and Mission* (Eugene, OR: Wipf & Stock, 2001), 7.

tian community identified itself as the new "household of God" (1 Pet. 2:5; 4:17; also Eph. 2:19; 1 Tim. 3:15; Heb. 3:6). But, in contrast to the nationalistic exclusiveness that defined Israelite faith, or despite the ideals of the old covenant (see chapter 3), the new "people of God" (1 Pet. 2:10) intentionally amalgamated persons of diverse ethnicities and nations into a single community of faith.[10] The pluralism of the Christian movement, and its vision of a "new humanity" marked by racial and cultural equality (Eph. 2:14–18), gave it a distinctive religious identity in a world of multifarious sectarian groups (including Jews). And, as I argue below, by duplicating the familial bond and intimate association of the household, Christian churches held powerful appeal for the burgeoning immigrant population in Greco-Roman cities.

Hiding in Plain Sight

Not only did Christians lack temples, outdoor ceremonies, and spectacular processions; they also had good reason to avoid attention,[11] which may be one reason why they predominantly used pagan personal names until the 250s CE.[12] In the event, public evangelism receded by the early second century; and internal strife (precipitated by doctrinal differences) increasingly dominated the attention of church leaders. Anonymity was possible; and meetings were sometimes outlawed. As already noted, Christian withdrawal from social gatherings and pagan associations aroused ill feeling. But Christians were fully integrated within the general population. The author of the "Epistle to Diognetus" (usually dated to the second or third century) explained that "the difference between Christians and the rest of [humankind] is not a matter of nationality, or language, or customs. [For] Christians do not live apart in separate cities of their own, speak any special dialect, nor practice an eccentric way of life. . . . They pass their lives in whatever township—Greek

10. The recipients of 1 Peter were probably a multiethnic Christian community consisting of both former Jews and non-Jews (Elliott, *Home for the Homeless*, 82). As Adolf von Harnack notes, while the Christian religion had a "faculty for incorporating the most diverse nationalities . . . attracting to itself all popular elements, it repudiated only one, viz., that of Jewish nationalism." Adolf von Harnack, *The Mission and Expansion of Christianity in the First Three Centuries* (New York: Harper, 1962), book 2.9.

11. Hvalvik, "In Word and Deed," 280.

12. Lampe, "Early Christians," 31.

or foreign—each man's lot has determined; and conform to ordinary local usage in their clothing, diet, and other habits. . . ."[13]

All this should not be taken to mean that the church was invisible. Sporadic persecution and incidents of martyrdom brought the movement widespread attention and the courage of martyrs attracted potential recruits. Moreover, as the movement grew in different areas or communities and drew converts from competing religious guilds and associations, escaping public awareness would have been well-nigh impossible. By the second century, Christianity had begun to penetrate the higher social classes in Greco-Roman society, including the imperial household—mainly through the efforts of women.[14] It would have been harder for Christians at the higher social levels to maintain anonymity and the number of Christians in this category (disproportionately female) increased over time.

It is also misleading to conclude that Christian worship or fellowship was largely concealed because Christians predominantly gathered in private homes. In ancient societies, there was little privacy in daily life, and cities (where Christian communities were concentrated) were crushingly crowded. (The population density of second-century Antioch, for instance, is estimated to have been "roughly 75,000 inhabitants per square mile.")[15] The urban populace "lived in tiny cubicles in multistoried tenements," literally on top of each other; and entire families frequently occupied a single room.[16] Due to narrow roads (sometimes little wider than footpaths) tenants were even able to hold a conversation with neighbors across the "street" by leaning out of their windows. In such cramped living conditions (matched by jammed public spaces) everyone was alert or exposed to their neighbors' ideas and conduct. Needless to say, uncommon practices or a change of religious allegiance (there were innumerable deities to choose from) would have been difficult to conceal from family members and neighbors. At the very least, daily interaction between Christians and non-Christians was unavoidable.

13. Maxwell Staniforth, trans., "Epistle to Diognetus," in *Early Christian Writings: The Apostolic Fathers*, ed. Andrew Louth (New York: Penguin Books, 1987), 144.

14. Lampe, "Early Christians," 23–24. Lampe confirms that wealthy, higher-status Christians were disproportionately female. Two-thirds of the forty or more Christians among the senatorial class in the third century were women.

15. Stark, *Rise of Christianity*, 149.

16. Stark, *Rise of Christianity*, 150–51; see also MacMullen, *Christianizing the Roman Empire*, 39; Hvalvik, "In Word and Deed," 282.

This is an important fact, for the tremendous growth of Christianity in the Roman Empire was mainly due to the unregulated "missionary" effort of ordinary believers. "It is probably a misconception," wrote Kenneth Latourette, "to think of every Christian of the first three hundred years after Christ as aggressively seeking converts."[17] Undoubtedly, many faced discrimination or abuse and were keen to avoid attention. But the fact remains that face-to-face encounters—not public oratory or the circulation of Christian writings—were essential for evangelism. As such, even if most shirked this obligation, Christian missionary activity depended on the willingness of individual believers or groups to embody Christian teachings (knowledge of which no doubt varied) in their daily routines and/or share their beliefs with non-Christians whom they encountered or interacted with in everyday life.[18] Christians, declared the author of the "Epistle to Diognetus" matter-of-factly, "display to us their wonderful and confessedly striking method of life." Official missionary apparatus or agents played little role in the making of Christian converts after the first century of the church's existence. The mission, affirmed Adolf von Harnack, "was reinforced and actively advanced by the behavior of Christian men and women."[19]

Witness through With-ness

The pivotal role of ordinary believers in the spread of early Christianity may occasion surprise, since New Testament accounts attest to a number of official missionary agents such as apostles, evangelists, or itinerant preachers who pioneered the spread of the gospel and founded churches in new areas. However, by 200 CE, formal missionary outreach had waned considerably, and there is scant reference in the historical records to Christian missionary agents in the sense generally understood today.[20] "Apostle" (meaning "one who is sent" or a messenger) was the term used to describe the earliest missionary agents in

17. Latourette, *First Five Centuries*, 117.
18. For an overview of this scenario, see W. H. C. Frend, "The Missions of the Early Church, 180–700 A.D.," in *Miscellenea Historiae Ecclesiasticae* 3 (1970): 2–23.
19. Harnack, *Mission and Expansion*, book 3.2.
20. Hvalvik, "In Word and Deed," 265–87; MacMullen, *Christianizing the Roman Empire*, 33–35; Jack T. Sanders, "Conversion in Early Christianity," in *Handbook of Early Christianity: Social Science Approaches*, ed. Anthony J. Blasi, Paul-André Turcotte, and Jean Duhaime (Walnut Creek, CA: AltaMira, 2002), 634–35.

the early Christian community. It originally applied to Jesus's twelve disciples whom he commissioned to preach to Israel and the nations (Mark 3:14; 6:30) and was extended to the seventy (or seventy-two) other disciples sent out in Luke 10. Of these original apostles, however, only Peter is known to have left Jerusalem or preached the gospel to gentiles.[21] The designation was later applied to a broader group of influential Christian leaders—notably Paul, Barnabas, and James (the brother of Jesus). But its use, in the scriptural sense of a missionary, died out after the early second century.[22]

The Didache describes some itinerant ministers as "apostles," "prophets," and "teachers" (nos. 11, 13) and links their function to the community of faith—bishops, for instance, are described as "carrying out the ministry of the prophets and the teachers for you" (no. 15). But, as O'Loughlin explains, "the process of training and baptizing new members of the community is not assigned to any specially selected members of the community."[23] He also suggests that preaching of the gospel to outsiders "is assumed to belong to all the members of the community," though this is less clear.

Eusebius, who writes in the fourth century, reports that the successors of the early apostles "performed the office of evangelists, being filled with the desire to preach Christ to those who had not yet heard the word of faith."[24] By his day few of these evangelists were known by name and he identifies only two: Thaddeus, one of "the seventy disciples of Christ," who was sent as a preacher and evangelist to Edessa by the apostle Thomas (one of the twelve);[25] and Pantaenus (d. 200), head of the famous Catechetical School in Alexandria, who "displayed such zeal for the divine Word, that he was appointed as a herald of the Gospel of Christ to the nations in the East, and was sent

21. However, Acts 8 records that when the "apostles in Jerusalem" sent Peter and John to authenticate the faith of believers converted by Philip's outreach in Samaria, the two apostles preached the gospel "in many Samaritan villages" on their way back to Jerusalem (Acts 8:25).

22. For a thorough review, see Harnack, *Mission and Expansion*, book 3.1.1–6; Hvalvik, "In Word and Deed," 267–68; Sanders, "Conversion in Early Christianity," 635; MacMullen, *Christianizing the Roman Empire*, 34.

23. Thomas O'Loughlin, "The Missionary Strategy of the Didache," *Transformation* 28, no. 22 (2011): 81.

24. Eusebius, *Ecclesiastical History*, 3.37.2.

25. Eusebius, *Ecclesiastical History*, 1.13.4.

as far as India."[26] These "evangelists," explains Eusebius, extended the work of the apostles, by which he means that they "laid the foundations of the faith in foreign places . . . , preached the Gospel more and more widely and scattered the saving seeds of the kingdom of heaven far and near throughout the whole world."[27]

So evidence of officially sanctioned missionary sending and action in the early Church is not lacking; and these efforts, as Eusebius recognized, often involved considerable travel ("long journeys"). But, by the end of the second century, the term "apostle" was no longer in use in a missionary sense. Even the cognate term "evangelist," which occurs only three times in the New Testament (Eph. 4:11; Acts 21:8; 2 Tim. 4:5), drops out of usage and, from the third century, is used almost exclusively to describe the authors of the four Gospels. This does not mean that missionary work ceased. There was the rare instance of public discussion between a Christian and a non-Christian, such as transpired between Justin Martyr and Trypho the Jew about 135 at Ephesus.[28] Origen (ca. 185–254), writing in the third century, attests that some Christian believers "have made it their business to itinerate not only through cities, but even villages and country houses, that they might make converts to God."[29] So what died away were official missionary structures and institutional sending by congregations or ecclesiastical authority (which is interestingly how "missions" came to be understood almost exclusively in the modern period).[30]

As noted above, in the empire's overcrowded cities Christians lived cheek by jowl with non-Christians as family members, neighbors, and coworkers. Such intimate proximity is not sufficient by itself to explain the spread of the Christian faith; but it supports my view that Christian *witness* was a matter of *with-ness*. The closeness of contact between Christians and other people meant that the conduct, commitments, and practices of believers were readily observable. Small wonder that 1 Peter 2:11–12 exhorted believers to "live such

26. Eusebius, *Ecclesiastical History*, 4.10.2.

27. Eusebius, *Ecclesiastical History*, 3.37.1, 3.

28. Justin Martyr, *Dialogue with Trypho*.

29. Origen, *Against Celsus*, 3.9, trans. Frederick Crombie, in *Ante-Nicene Fathers*, vol. 4, ed. Alexander Roberts, James Donaldson, and A. Cleveland Coxe (Buffalo, NY: Christian Literature Publishing, 1885).

30. So, it is misleading to state, as MacMullen does, that "the church had no mission" (*Christianizing the Roman Empire*, 34).

good lives among the pagans that, though they accuse you of doing wrong, they may see your good deeds and glorify God." By the same token, they were to "always be prepared to give an answer to everyone who asks you to give the reason for the hope you have" (3:15).

Rodney Stark makes the compelling argument that "preexisting social networks" and the interpersonal attachments of converts were critical for the growth of Christianity because "typically people do not *seek* a faith," rather "they *encounter* one through their ties to other people who have already accepted this faith."[31] But he undercuts this "network growth" theory with the proposition that conversion was driven less by doctrinal appeal than by social conformity—i.e., the desire to bring one's religious behavior "into alignment with that of one's friends and family members."[32] Even if it is true that "social relationships are part of the tangible rewards of participating in a religious movement,"[33] this view of religious conversion reduces it to a social commodity; and the claim that ideology or doctrinal appeal plays little part devalues the religious element.[34] It is also unclear why the change is considered conversion if the motive is primarily to maintain social relationships. Conversion, observes MacMullen in his assessment of the same period, is "that change of

31. Stark, *Rise of Christianity*, 18–21, 55–70. He cites the rapid growth of Mormonism as a modern example.

32. Stark, *Rise of Christianity*, 14–17. See also Rodney Stark, "Why Religious Movements Succeed or Fail: A Revised General Model," *Journal of Mormon History* 11, no. 2 (1996): 142; Rodney Stark, "Why the Jehovah's Witnesses Grow So Rapidly: A Theoretical Application," *Journal of Contemporary Religion* 12, no. 2 (May 1997): 151–52.

33. Stark, "Why Religious Movements Succeed or Fail," 142.

34. Clearly, converts are more likely to share their faith with others within their social network than, say, with a random stranger. In Lewis Rambo's more robust analysis of conversion, interaction between the potential convert and the religious group (during which the former becomes more acquainted with the group's rituals, teachings, expectations, etc.) is a stage in the process. Lewis R. Rambo, *Understanding Religious Conversion* (New Haven: Yale University Press, 1993). However, in many instances conversion provokes severe tensions or conflicts within families and communities. Many believers were betrayed by friends and family (Justin, *Dialogue*, 35) and the stakes are often high in cross-cultural situations. In any case, changes in the life of a convert are most readily detected by family and friends; and it would be strange if no questions are asked (as 1 Pet. 3:15 surmises).

belief by which a person accepted the reality and supreme power of God and determined to obey him."[35]

But the crucial contribution of interpersonal attachments to the rapid spread of Christianity is noteworthy. Stark's claim that "the average convert [is] preceded into the church by many friends and relatives" supports the basic understanding articulated here that Christianity's missionary success was driven by the actions and decisions of ordinary believers.[36] At the same time, variable elements such as context and degree of engagement with the surrounding society probably had some impact on the church's recruiting potential.

In the face of disease epidemics, endemic poverty, widespread displacement and homelessness, Christian care for the sick and suffering (including prisoners), hospitality, and system of charity won over many to the faith.[37] Also, in a deeply religious world inundated with the worship of myriad deities and divinities, miracles and acts of divine power were taken quite seriously and widely reported.[38] Dating back to the ministries of Jesus and the early apostles, the performance of signs and wonders galvanized tremendous public interest and validated Christian teaching. In the Roman world, no other feature of Christian ministry had a greater missionary impact than demonstrations of spiritual power, notably in the form of miraculous healing and the driving out of spirits.[39] The intellectual class perhaps needed to be

35. MacMullen, *Christianizing the Roman Empire*, 5. We also do well to recall Rambo's contention that religious conversion is produced by multiple (interactive) elements and "is not one process" (*Understanding Religious Conversion*, 4, 5).

36. Stark, *Rise of Christianity*, 56.

37. Not to mention the fact that, by virtue of being immersed in caring communities, Christians fared better during social catastrophes and survived in greater numbers. Stark, *Rise of Christianity*, 83–93, 161; Harnack, *Mission and Expansion*, book 2.4.

38. Harnack claimed that even the church's "worship and its sacraments together represented a real energy of the divine nature." Harnack, *Mission and Expansion*, book 2, epilogue.

39. See MacMullen, *Christianizing the Roman Empire*, 22, 27–29, 109–10; Hvalvik, "In Word and Deed," 283–84; Dale T. Irvin and Scott Sunquist, *History of the World Christian Movement*, vol. 1, *Earliest Christianity to 1453* (Maryknoll, NY: Orbis Books, 2001), 38. The Christian religion, noted historian Adolf Harnack, "presented itself as something more than the gospel of redemption and of ministering love; it was also the religion of the Spirit and of power." *Mission and Expansion*, book 2.5.

won by persuasive argument and eloquent reasoning; but the lower classes whom the early Christian movement primarily attracted (or had access to) prior to the fourth century found miracles utterly compelling in matters of faith. The miraculous healing of a neighbor by ordinary believers (say, through the laying on of hands) would have electrified a neighborhood and authenticated Christian proclamation of the gospel and worship of a God superior to all other divinities.

But, while miracles and acts of charity undoubtedly attracted interest and potential recruits, some understanding of the gospel message (as opposed to Christian dogma) and congruence with the needs and aspirations of potential converts was arguably necessary for conversion. Christian demonstrations of the miraculous surpassed all others; but astonishment is not the same as acquiescence.[40] Conversion to a faith that demanded exclusive loyalty and enjoined denunciation of all other gods and cults as wicked and false took a certain amount of courage and conviction.[41] For most converts, personal transformation and grasp of Christian teachings would have been gradual, and old allegiances or convictions undoubtedly retained their hold even after baptism.[42] That said, there was also much about the Christian movement that would have been familiar to adherents of the many mystery religions; and, from the beginning, Christian apologists drew on Greek philosophical thought to present the gospel message. Elements of continuity and use of familiar ingredients inarguably facilitated the switch in religious allegiance. But, ultimately, as Rambo contends, the convert's aspirations, needs, and orientations were critical to the process.[43]

In this regard, the Christian message and identity had particular appeal for the empire's burgeoning immigrant population: its resident aliens, foreigners,

40. Indeed, the pervasive preoccupation with divine power and competing explanations for supernatural occurrences in the Roman world potentially worked against the efficacy of miracles in some instances.

41. MacMullen astutely comments on these points. MacMullen, *Christianizing the Roman Empire*, 5, 20–21.

42. Peter Lampe notes that in the city of Rome, Christians not only lived side by side with their pagan neighbors but also "often maintained pagan customs, particularly in the funeral domain" and (as noted earlier) used pagan personal names until the mid-third century. Lampe, "Early Christians," 30–31. See also MacMullen, *Christianizing the Roman Empire*, 78.

43. Rambo, *Understanding Religious Conversion*, 44–46.

and strangers. Before exploring this complex issue, however, it is necessary to provide an overview of mobility within the Roman Empire and examine the elements of cultural difference and social identity that framed outsider status or immigrant existence in the Roman world.

CONDITIONS IN THE ROMAN EMPIRE

At its height in the second century CE, the Roman Empire boasted a population of some 50–60 million spread over some 2–2.5 million square miles of territory.[44] The legendary Roman capacity for administration and engineering produced a magnificent transport and communications infrastructure that was matched (perhaps surpassed) only by the achievements of the Han Dynasty of China (ca. 200 BCE–200 CE).[45] Roman mastery of roadbuilding led to the construction of up to 48,000 miles of highly durable roads (including paved highways), replete with garrisons, stage posts, mileage posts, and inns to aid travel. Sea travel and the capacity of seagoing vessels also increased tremendously, in part due to the commercial needs of a rising population and the huge demand for various commodities.[46] Romans, however, were not sailors; their ships were built and operated by foreigners.[47] Indeed, for reasons explained below, the average Roman viewed sea voyages with considerable apprehension. But the Romans were the first and only rulers to unite the

44. This was about the same size as the contemporary, though admittedly less influential, Han Empire (206 BCE–220 CE), but a fraction of the size of later empires such as the Umayyad, Qing, Spanish, Russian, or British (the largest in history). In the event, the emergence of the powerful Sassanian (Persian) Empire to the east from the mid-third century CE placed severe limitations on the further extension of Roman rule. See Stephen S. Gosch and Peter N. Stearns, *Premodern Travel in World History* (New York: Routledge, 2008), 37; A. D. Lee, *Information and Frontiers: Roman Foreign Relations in Late Antiquity* (New York: Cambridge University Press, 2006), 24; C. R. Whittaker, *Frontiers of the Roman Empire: A Social and Economic Study* (Baltimore: Johns Hopkins University Press, 1994), 50–51.

45. See Lionel Casson, *Travel in the Ancient World* (Baltimore: Johns Hopkins University Press, 1994), 174; Gosch and Stearns, *Premodern Travel in World History*, 52–55.

46. Richard L. Smith, *Premodern Trade in World History* (New York: Routledge, 2008), 76–80.

47. Irene M. Franck and David M. Brownstone, *To the Ends of the Earth: The Great Travel and Trade Routes of Human History* (New York: Facts on File, 1984), 220.

Mediterranean world, cementing the region's emergence as a major center of world trade and transnational interaction.[48]

Travel and Mobility

Undeniably, the vast military resources and efficient administration of Roman rule transformed travel conditions. But the claim that *Pax Romana* "swept the seas clear of pirates and chased away most of the bandits from the main highways" during the first two centuries CE may be exaggerated.[49] Outside the ranks of government officials and high-ranking citizens, Rome's "protective umbrella" had limitations. In many areas, in both town and countryside, law and order were illusory and travelers were at the mercy of robbers and wild beasts.[50] The parable of the "Good Samaritan" hints at this reality; and the apostle Paul, who covered thousands of miles on land and sea, attested that he had been "in danger from bandits . . . , in danger in the city, in danger in the countryside" (2 Cor. 11:26).

Due to the exorbitant costs of transporting goods by road, mercantile traffic was mainly confined to waterways and seaways.[51] There were no passenger vessels in the ancient world, so sea travelers had to make use of available cargo vessels that "provided neither food nor services."[52] Passengers lived and slept on deck, so the more experienced brought small tents for protection.[53] The biggest ships of the day, known as clippers, accommodated up to 600 people—the Alexandrian ship that Paul took to Malta had 276 onboard (Acts 27:37). Weather permitting, a sea voyage could be most pleasant and was much preferable to the strenuousness of travel on land, which was principally

48. Franck and Brownstone, *To the Ends of the Earth*, 220; Casson, *Travel in the Ancient World*, 121.

49. Casson, *Travel in the Ancient World*, 122, 149.

50. Jerome Murphy-O'Connor, "Traveling Conditions in the First Century: On the Road and on the Sea with St. Paul," *Bible Review* 1, no. 2 (1985): 4–5.

51. Gosch and Stearns, *Premodern Travel in World History*, 37–38; Casson, *Travel in the Ancient World*, 65–66, 129–28; Maribel Dietz, *Wandering Monks, Virgins, and Pilgrims: Ascetic Travel in the Mediterranean World, A.D. 300/800* (University Park: Pennsylvania State University Press, 2005), 13–19.

52. Casson, *Travel in the Ancient World*, 153.

53. Murphy-O'Connor, "Traveling Conditions," 6–7; Casson, *Travel in the Ancient World*, 66, 152–53, 156. Not until the nineteenth century did sailing vessels designed for passengers first appear.

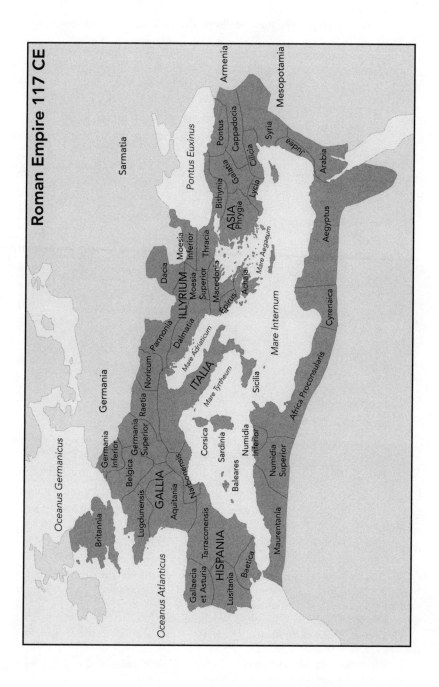

Roman Empire 117 CE

on foot.[54] But sea travel was quite perilous. The violence of winter storms limited most sea voyages to the period from May to October; and the duration of the voyage was largely dependent on the prevailing winds, type of vessel, and favorable omens. The acute discomfort of sea voyages in inclement weather conditions was heightened by the pervasive fear of shipwrecks. Farewells were made with the realization that the sea traveler may not be seen again.

But long-distance travel within the Mediterranean world frequently involved a combination of sea and road travel.[55] As noted in chapter 1, with prevailing winds, the voyage from Rome to Alexandria, a distance of some 1,000 miles, took ten to twenty days; but on the return (against headwinds) the journey lasted "as much as two months or more," or the same as the overland route.[56] Travel on land afforded greater flexibility but was time consuming and quite exhausting.[57] The traveler not only had to carry much more baggage to supply basic necessities (including kitchenware, bedding, a change of clothes, a tent, etc.) but also had to manage a mule or donkey if needed, contend with a variety of terrain or weather conditions, and strive to reach human habitation (for lodging at an inn or with an acquaintance) by nightfall each day of travel. Government officials and the wealthy could make use of passenger carts or carriages pulled by mules or horses, but the average traveler went on foot. Use of carriage allowed a traveler to cover 25–30 miles a day on average; but those who traveled on foot could only manage 15–20 miles a day and as little as 6 miles a day in mountainous terrain. Travel by land from Rome to Alexandria took up to two months.

For ordinary travelers and migrants, then, the first-class roads built by the Romans did little to alleviate the arduousness of travel. But the political unity, flourishing economy, and new levels of security established by the Romans generated an unprecedented volume of movement. Roman territorial expansion and subjugation of other nations or tribes contributed to population displacements, while economic opportunism and acute social inequalities

54. As Casson notes, "in cases where the length of a trip was the same over land as by sea, it was infinitely less wearing to pass the days lolling on a deck than walking or riding a mule or mule-drawn carriage" (*Travel in the Ancient World*, 148).

55. Murphy-O'Connor, "Traveling Conditions," 5.

56. Casson, *Travel in the Ancient World*, 151–52; see also Gosch and Stearns, *Premodern Travel in World History*, 41.

57. For details, see Casson, *Travel in the Ancient World*, 176–90; also Dietz, *Wandering Monks, Virgins, and Pilgrims*, 21–22.

generated a constant stream of cross-community migrants. Recurrent riots, disease epidemics, natural disasters, exile, and military service added to the flows. Long-distance travelers appeared on the roads and seaways in vast numbers. The most frequent travelers were merchants, soldiers, and government agents (such as governors, envoys, tax collectors, the couriers of the public post or *cursus publicus*, governors, and district officials).[58] But the throngs of travelers and migrants also included slaves, pilgrims, tourists, and holiday makers (mainly from the upper classes), entertainers, artisans, sick persons in search of healing remedies, priests, and missionaries.

In essence, not only did Roman rule incorporate a great multitude of peoples and cultures into a single polity but it also established the conditions for extensive travel throughout its realm. In the first two centuries of the Christian era, notes Casson, a traveler "could make his way from the shores of the Euphrates to the border between England and Scotland without crossing a foreign frontier, always within the bounds of one government's jurisdiction."[59]

Social Status and Identity

In the Greco-Roman world, status mattered greatly and fundamentally shaped daily life and experience. The primary and most definitive sociopolitical distinction was between citizen and foreigner (or noncitizen). In reality, however, these categories were fraught with ambiguities. To start with, the Romans inherited a Hellenistic system in which claims to multiple citizenships (some honorary) were common within the male elite class.[60] Roman citizenship— which bestowed the right to vote, own property, and hold public office— superseded all other identities or loyalties, but it was not tied to a fixed cultural or ethnic identity. It was also available to non-Romans through a variety of means such as military or other kinds of service to the state, political reward, or political treaties with conquered societies in an effort to secure the loyalty of entire groups in an age of rapid imperial expansion. The many paths to

58. Casson, *Travel in the Ancient World*, 127, 130–31; Gosch and Stearns, *Premodern Travel in World History*, 36.

59. Casson, *Travel in the Ancient World*, 122. See also Stark, *Rise of Christianity*, 135–37.

60. Benjamin H. Dunning, *Aliens and Sojourners: Self as Other in Early Christianity* (Philadelphia: University of Pennsylvania Press, 2009), 27–28.

citizenship also introduced gradations of status that made it a complicated category, and one with rather fluid boundaries that "varied according to time and place throughout the Empire."[61] For all this, however, citizenship was absolutely differentiated from other (and unquestionably lower) statuses such as barbarians, slaves, or foreigners.

To illustrate, the great stream of foreigners who flocked to the city of Rome from the provinces or distant lands were viewed with great disdain by its citizens (an elite class) and held to be a source of contamination.[62] Historian George La Piana reports that Roman dislike and contempt for the immigrant population appeared in "biting satires" that assailed "the stupidity of the Phrygians, the empty verbosity of the Persians, the criminal hypocrisy and maleficent arts of the Egyptians, the perfidy and superstition of the Africans, the selfishness and rapacity of the Jews, and the failings of all other races represented among the alien population of Rome."[63]

Whether these stereotypes were limited to elite intellectual circles—La Piana suggests the satires were "relished alike by plebeians and by persons of culture"[64]—they indicate the acute marginalization likely to accompany migrant-otherness. These immigrant peoples had little chance of gaining citizenship and some groups (including Jews) were objects of the periodic decrees of expulsion from the city, though enforcement was seldom pursued.[65]

In short, the distinction between citizen and noncitizen was well defined. But, outside this major sociopolitical demarcation, identifying the "other" was less clear cut. A range of terms was available in the Greek language for the foreigner-outsider: *allos, allotrios* (stranger); *xenos* (foreigner); *parepidē-mos* (transient or temporary visitor); *paroikos* (resident alien). The Romans, however, did not distinguish between temporary and permanent residents;

---

61. Dunning, *Aliens and Sojourners*, 27, 28.

62. George La Piana, "Foreign Groups in Rome During the First Centuries of the Empire," *Harvard Theological Review* 20, no. 4 (October 1927): 227–29; see J. P. V. D. Balsdon, *Romans and Aliens* (Chapel Hill: University of North Carolina Press, 1979), 14. See also Dunning, *Aliens and Sojourners*, 33–34.

63. La Piana, "Foreign Groups in Rome," 230; see also Balsdon, *Romans and Aliens*, 59–71; Dunning, *Aliens and Sojourners*, 33–34.

64. La Piana, "Foreign Groups in Rome," 194. Even Greeks, whose intellectual culture and customs many Romans embraced, were treated with disdain (p. 229).

65. Balsdon, *Romans and Aliens*, 13, 98–101, 106–8.

and Latin lacks a term that fully matches the meaning of "foreigner" or "immigrant" as used in English.[66] A foreigner could be described as *peregrinus/a* (someone who was free but not a Roman citizen), *provincialis* (inhabitants of provinces outside Italy), or *alienigenus/a* (someone born elsewhere, i.e., an alien). In the Greco-Roman world, *peregrinus/a* (Greek, *paroikos*) had the broadest application and conventionally represented all classes of noncitizens or foreigners.[67] This category of persons, though subject to taxes and other financial burdens, had no political rights and limited legal standing. They could not own land, hold high office, or inherit property from a Roman citizen. They represented the majority of the empire's population.

In addition to the "foreigner" status imposed by social structures, the vast array of societies and nationalities incorporated into Rome's *imperium* also multiplied the number of cultural boundaries. This, combined with increased mobility throughout the realm, significantly expanded the ranks of *paroikoi*, persons who were not at home or without native roots in the society, culture, or religious life of the people among whom they resided.[68] As noncitizens, they lacked the economic power afforded by land ownership and they mainly labored as farmers, merchants, traders, or artisans.[69] They also constituted the most mobile segment of the population.

Most important, the experience of being the "other," the outsider who does not belong, deepened social marginality and fostered receptivity to religious communities like Christianity that offered equality of members and a unique status.[70] At the same time, links to transnational or diaspora networks and/or involvement in long-distance travel made *paroikoi* active agents in the spread of religious ideas and practices.

---

66. David Noy, *Foreigners at Rome: Citizens and Strangers* (London: Duckworth, 2000), 1–3.

67. For a more technical overview, see Elliott, *Home for the Homeless*, 21–58. Noy also intimates that by the fourth century *peregrinus* came to be applied more broadly to "'foreigners' who were periodically expelled from Rome" (*Foreigners at Rome*, 1).

68. For an in-depth etymological analysis of the concept, see Noy, *Foreigners at Rome*, 24–37.

69. Noy, *Foreigners at Rome*, 68. On work, class, and occupation, see Robert M. Grant, *Early Christianity and Society: Seven Studies* (San Francisco: Harper & Row, 1977), 66–95.

70. Elliott, *Home for the Homeless*, 121–22.

THE MIGRANT FACTOR IN THE CHRISTIANIZATION OF EMPIRE

Our knowledge of the nature and extent of migrant movements in the first centuries CE is very limited; and concrete data connecting the migrant phenomenon to missionary activity are fragmentary. The massive hordes that thronged the roads and seaways of the Roman Empire left no trace of their movements or activities. There are enough data to construct a general picture of migration and travel in Roman times;[71] but records of individual migrants, even merchants, are rare. The case for the centrality of migration in the expansion of the Christian faith within the Roman Empire relies on deductive reasoning and, frankly, disciplined imagination. Christian writings after the New Testament period were mainly produced by and addressed to an elite (educated) class, who comprised a very small percentage of Christians in the first two and a half centuries.[72] Less than a quarter of the population was literate. But there is reasonable evidence to suggest that migrants or foreigners comprised a sizeable proportion, if not the majority, of adherents in the early Christian movement.

The prominence of "alien rhetoric"—language that captures the experience of foreignness, alien status, and otherness—in early Christian writings provides strong hints.[73] In many instances, such "alien rhetoric" is applied in a purely spiritual sense. For instance, the declaration that gentiles who were "excluded from citizenship in Israel and foreigners to the covenants of the promise" and "who once were far away have been brought near by the blood of Christ" (Eph. 2:12–13) clearly uses "foreigners" in a metaphorical sense, though reference to the change from an alien status to citizenship conveys the life-transforming nature of conversion.[74] Similarly, in Hebrews, the re-

---

71. Casson, *Travel in the Ancient World*, 190–218; Gosch and Stearns, *Premodern Travel in World History*, 36; Murphy-O'Connor, "Traveling Conditions," 1–2.

72. MacMullen, *Christianizing the Roman Empire*, 21, 33, 38.

73. Benjamin H. Dunning, "The Intersection of Alien Status and Cultic Discourse in the Epistle to the Hebrews," in *Hebrews*, ed. Gabriella Gelardini (Boston: Brill, 2005), 178–98.

74. Pauline authorship remains a matter of debate; but the letter's theological emphasis clearly reflects Paul's ideas. In any case, the writer equates the deprivations of noncitizenship in the Roman world to the alienation of nonbelieving gentiles from the promised blessings to the Jewish people. On authorship, see Harold W. Hoehner, *Ephesians: An Exegetical Commentary* (Grand Rapids: Baker Academic, 2002), 8–20;

cipients are exhorted to emulate heroes of faith who are identified as "aliens and strangers on earth" (11:13), which is to say that members of the believing community are to live like aliens or transients who maintain faithfulness to the covenant while looking forward to a promised hope.[75]

In 1 Peter, however, the addressees are pointedly described as "those who reside as aliens, scattered throughout Pontus, Galatia, Cappadocia, Asia, and Bithynia" (1:1) and as "aliens [*paroikoi*] and strangers [*parepidēmoi*]" (2:11, NASB). Traditional readings of this text favor a spiritual understanding. As such, many English translations replace "aliens and strangers" with more spiritually evocative terms like "sojourners" or "pilgrims." Based on this understanding, the letter's reference to aliens and strangers is treated not as a literal identification but as an allusion to the postconversion experience of all Christian believers—seen as "pilgrims" on earth (strangers in every society or nation where they live) because their true home is in heaven.

The matter remains open to debate; but there are cogent reasons to question this figurative understanding. In a thoroughgoing exegetical analysis that takes the political, economic, social, and cultural context into account (i.e., using social-scientific criticism), John Elliott contends that the terms "aliens" and "strangers" point to "the actual political, legal, and social status of the addressees *both before and after* their Christian conversion."[76] In other words, the letter was sent to "actual strangers and resident aliens who had become Christians." Elliott insists that in Asia Minor and throughout the Mediterranean world the early Christian movement recruited many members from among foreigners and visiting strangers.[77] Indeed, he argues, it was the recipients' concrete situation as *paroikoi* (resident aliens) that attracted them to

---

Stephen E. Fowl, *Ephesians: A Commentary* (Louisville: Westminster John Knox, 2012), 9.

75. Dunning, "Intersection of Alien Status," 189; William G. Johnsson, "Pilgrimage Motif in the Book of Hebrews," *Journal of Biblical Literature* 97, no. 2 (1978): 239–51.

76. Elliott, *Home for the Homeless*, xxviii, 39–49, 42–43, 129–31, 223–26. For scholarly response to Elliott's arguments, see David L. Balch, *Let Wives Be Submissive: The Domestic Code in 1 Peter* (Chico, CA: Scholars Press, 1981); Miroslav Volf, "Soft Difference: Theological Reflections on the Relation between Church and Culture in 1 Peter," *Ex auditu* 10 (1994): 15–30.

77. Elliott, *Home for the Homeless*, xxix, 131. The dating of the letter is also a subject of debate: Elliott dates the letter to the final decades of the first century (pp. 84–87); but a mid-first-century date is more common.

Christianity in the first place, even though conversion also intensified their social alienation and outsider status.[78]

Christianity as an Immigrant Religion

Like many other new religious movements in the Roman Empire, Christianity began as a religion of migrant-outsiders (*paroikoi*) or people on the margins;[79] and its astounding growth underscores the capacity of migrants and migrant movements to generate historical change.[80] The embeddedness of many immigrants in far-flung diaspora (or social) networks was a major factor in the rapid spread of Christianity. The Jewish population, for instance, formed a network of diaspora communities settled in most of the empire's provinces—about a million Jews resided in Egypt alone.[81] The spread of the Christian message by diasporan Jews (like Paul) who utilized an extensive network of synagogues laid the foundation for the emergence of Christian communities throughout the empire. The penetration of the gentile world produced multiethnic churches and even more rapid growth.[82] The rise of a predominant gentile membership also depended on "migrant communities who retained ties to their home locality, while traveling from one part of the [Roman] empire to another, for trade, or work, or some other reason."[83] In particular, Christian merchants from the Greek-speaking eastern regions of the empire who settled in western provinces were major agents in the spread of the faith.[84]

78. Elliott, *Home for the Homeless*, 72–78, 224.

79. La Piana confirms as much ("Foreign Groups in Rome," 184).

80. "There were no stronger influences in education and in administration than rapidity and ease of travelling and the postal service." William M. Ramsay, *St. Paul: The Traveler and Roman Citizen* (Grand Rapids: Kregel, 2001), 37.

81. Harnack, *Mission and Expansion*, book 1.1.

82. Multiethnic congregations were initially Jewish-gentile congregations along the lines of the Antioch model—a model Paul probably fostered among the churches he founded. Cf. Hyde, *Paganism to Christianity*, 167. Elliott also suggests that the recipients of 1 Peter were probably a multiethnic Christian community consisting of both former Jews and non-Jews (*Home for the Homeless*, 82).

83. Andrew F. Walls, "Mission and Migration: The Diaspora Factor in Christian History," *Journal of African Christian Thought* 5, no. 2 (2002): 4. Gentile communities were also "united by attachments" or connected to even wider social and transnational networks (Stark, *Rise of Christianity*, 56).

84. Frend, "Missions of the Early Church," 7.

The immigrant factor in early Christianity has been surprisingly over-looked in historical treatments. We have no historical record of the estab-lishment of particular churches within the vast mass of the Roman Empire. But Christianity's universal vision, the translatability of its message (or its "syncretist potential"[85]), the strength of its organization, and the predom-inantly urban location of its communities leave little room for doubt that foreigners and alien residents were heavily represented in its churches—col-lectively within a city, if not individual house congregations. Greco-Roman cities, confirms Stark, were peopled by foreigners because they "required a constant substantial stream of [immigrants] to maintain their populations" or offset high mortality rates.[86] The city of Rome was the seat of empire and, at least in the thinking of its intellectual class, the preserve of Roman life and culture. Yet, by the first century, the mass influx of foreigners had ren-dered residents of "old [Italian] Roman stock" a minority in the capital[87]—as Seneca observed:

> Look at the crowds . . . ; the majority of them are aliens in a sense. They have flooded in from the country towns of Italy, in fact from all over the world. . . . Most of them, you will find, have left home and come to Rome, the greatest and loveliest city in the world—but not theirs.[88]

If Elliott's analysis is correct, foreigners and visiting strangers formed a major segment of the burgeoning Christian communities in the East (Asia Minor and the Mediterranean world). This was also true in the West. The church in Lyons, Gaul, was possibly founded by and most certainly included many "immigrants from the East."[89] Similarly, Christians in the city of Rome (the largest Christian group in the empire by the third century) were mostly

---

85. Lamin Sanneh, *Translating the Message: The Missionary Impact on Culture*, 2nd ed. (Maryknoll, NY: Orbis Books, 2009), 49.

86. Stark, *Rise of Christianity*, 156.

87. La Piana, "Foreign Groups in Rome," 226–27, 232; see also Lampe, "Early Christians," 20. It is estimated that, by 44 BCE, some three-quarters of the city's population were of foreign ancestry. Balsdon, *Romans and Aliens*, 14.

88. Quoted in Balsdon, *Romans and Aliens*, 13.

89. John Behr, *Irenaeus of Lyons: Identifying Christianity* (Oxford: Oxford Uni-versity Press, 2013), 19. See also Morton Scott Enslin, "Irenaeus: Mostly Prolegom-ena," *Harvard Theological Review* 40, no. 3 (July 1947): 149; Paul Parvis, "Who Was

immigrants.[90] They resided in the areas populated by the flood of immigrants from the provinces, shared the low social status of the wider immigrant population, and reflected the considerable cultural mixture of the city's multitude of foreigners.[91] Prominent members like Justin Martyr, Valentinus, and Marcion were all immigrants from the East. Until the mid-third century, the dominant language of the church in Rome was Greek (the main language of immigrant culture), not Latin. The church's interconnection with the imperial capital's crucible of ethnicities and cultures facilitated symbiotic exchange and the extensive translation of the Christian message into Greek culture and philosophical thought.[92] The diverse origins of its members undoubtedly contributed to the theological pluralism that also flourished among Rome's scattered house churches.

The singular appeal that Christian communities had for foreigners and resident aliens (*paroikoi*) deserves further comment. Rome was not only the imperial capital; it was "the center of many of the empire's religious cults."[93] The constant influx of migrants produced a vibrant religious diversity in urban centers, so that even the old cults "were freshened by the influx of the new religions."[94] If the unprecedented travel and intermingling of displaced peoples in urban centers aided the unfettered spread of religious ideas, few religions were better equipped or positioned than Christianity to attract immigrants, due to its organizational structure and message.

Disconnected from their homelands and often separated from kinfolk, immigrants turned to voluntary associations such as trade guilds and mystery cults to meet their basic need for communal life and social integration.[95]

Irenaeus? An Introduction to the Man and His Work," in *Irenaeus: Life, Scripture, Legacy*, ed. Sara Parvis and Paul Foster (Minneapolis: Fortress, 2012), 15.

90. Though probably founded by migrant Jewish Christians, the Roman church was predominantly gentile by the time of Paul's letter to the Romans (late 50s CE).

91. See Lampe, "Early Christians," 20–32. See also La Piana, "Foreign Groups in Rome," 184–87; Behr, *Irenaeus of Lyons*, 22, 45. As La Piana points out, the massive sustained increase in the foreign element made straightforward absorption or assimilation into the minority "native" population a difficult proposition ("Foreign Groups in Rome," 201–2).

92. Lampe, "Early Christians," 28.

93. Balsdon, *Romans and Aliens*, 12.

94. Harnack, *Mission and Expansion*, book 2.9.

95. Political associations were forbidden, so these immigrant associations served

In a world where the household (*oikos*) functioned as "the basic economic unit of production and self-support," these associations became "homes for the homeless,"[96] often formed by "natives of the same town or province."[97] They offered "the possibility of at least a minimal degree of social security and of a psychological sense of belonging."[98] But few social organizations matched the recruiting power of the Christian movement, centered as it was on household units that replicated the close-knit intimacy and fraternal bonds of family life.

Up to the early fourth century, Christian households formed the focal point of ministry and the basic unit of mission. They catered to "the sustenance of itinerant missionaries, the hosting of strangers, the care of the needy, the assembling of worshippers, and the economic self-sufficiency of the movement."[99] Converts were mainly won in homes, not public spaces; and the conversion of entire households contributed greatly to the rapid growth of Christian communities. Christian households were also ideally suited to attract or recruit resident aliens and foreigners because they met practical needs of hospitality, social solidarity, and mutual support. The pull that Christian communities exerted on outsiders grew stronger as the church developed into a transnational religious and social organization that surpassed anything in the pagan Greco-Roman world. As Harnack noted:

> Here was a society which united fellow-believers, who were resident in any
> city, in the closest of ties, presupposing a relationship which was assumed
> as a matter of course to last through life itself, furnishing its members

social, economic, and religious needs. As La Piana explains, however, "the need of practicing in their new residence the religious cults of their land of origin is undoubtedly one of the leading causes which led immigrants to form associations of a religious character" ("Foreign Groups in Rome," 225).

96. For details, see Elliott, *Home for the Homeless*, 174–79. The "household ideology" was used at the state level to promote "subject unity and loyalty" (p. 174). Most important, "incorporation within an *oikos*, whether a natural local household or another form of social group which offered the protection and solace of a home, was a universal desire. This was especially true in an age of anxiety, turmoil and dislocation such as that of the Hellenistic Roman era" (p. 221).

97. La Piana, "Foreign Groups in Rome," 226.

98. Elliott, *Home for the Homeless*, 221.

99. Elliott, *Home for the Homeless*, 198; also 188.

... with a daily bond which provided them with spiritual benefits and imposed duties on them, assembling them at first daily and then weekly, shutting them off from other people, uniting them in a guild of worship, a friendly society, and an order with a definite line of life in view, besides teaching them to consider themselves as the community of God.[100]

The universal and egalitarian vision of the church further underlined its distinctiveness. As the dominant group, Romans regarded themselves as a superior class without rival in the world—"the gods' own people."[101] Their views of conquered nations or the vast diversity of cultures that populated distant provinces were derogatory.[102] With few exceptions, foreigners beyond its frontiers were objects of scorn and derided as "barbarians."[103] To the Roman mind, Gallican peoples were not so bad, but the English were barely civilized; Egyptians were generally regarded with hatred and contempt; Syrians, it was believed, made excellent slaves; and Arabs were disparaged as liars. It is highly unlikely that such cultural prejudice was absent from the church; but, by affirming all cultures, Christianity minimized the indignities of immigrant existence. At the very least, it accomplished a degree of solidarity and sense of belonging among the lower classes—regardless of regional origins and cultural distinctions—that were unusual in Roman society. By achieving such cohesion and collective consciousness, argues Peter Lampe, Christianity "contributed to the social integration of the Roman society as a whole."[104] And by so doing it also arguably helped pave the way for the incorporation of the multifarious barbarian tribes into Roman society.[105]

Displaced outsiders were attracted not only to the strong communal character of Christian communities but also to the uniqueness of the Christian message, which combined a universal vision (embracing all nationalities) with a strong emphasis on religious solidarity. In an environment where status mattered greatly, the Christian message asserted the superior status of

---

100. Harnack, *Mission and Expansion*, book 3.4.

101. Balsdon, *Romans and Aliens*, 2. In a manner echoed by later colonizing powers, Rome's empire "was proof enough of her enjoyment of divine favor" (p. 2); and foreign peoples were conquered for their "own good" (p. 4).

102. For more on this, see Balsdon, *Romans and Aliens*, 25–26, 59–71.

103. Balsdon, *Romans and Aliens*, 64–71, 79.

104. Lampe, "Early Christians," 25.

105. Cf. Whittaker, *Frontiers of the Roman Empire*, 199.

Christian believers. The believing community was represented as "a chosen people, a royal priesthood, a holy nation, God's special possession," a special brotherhood called to "be like-minded, be sympathetic, love one another, be compassionate and humble" (1 Pet. 1:3; 2:9; 3:8). To disadvantaged groups such as *paroikoi*, who were "estranged from the sources of political power, economic security and social mobility," and also faced hostility and rejection, the superior status claimed by Christians would have been greatly attractive,[106] all the more so because it was based not on blood ties or social class but on supernatural agency (divine election).[107]

By providing new believers with an alternative means of emotional sustenance and familial union, the household strategy made it possible for the believing community to overcome a major obstacle to attracting converts— namely, the vital importance of familial ties and support within the Roman world. In essence, the early Christian movement gained adherents and momentum partly because the familial and household character of the Christian community allowed it to compete with the foremost social institution of the Roman Empire.[108]

The Paradox of Otherness

Christianity in the Roman Empire was a predominantly immigrant phenomenon because adherents mainly comprised migrant-outsiders (foreigners and resident aliens). This led to what I would term the *paradox of otherness*: for while the solidarity of the house church alleviated the migrant's experience of alienation, the Christian community's immigrant ethos deepened the sense of otherness,[109] since the church was "an alternative and self-sufficient society where people could cultivate in common the values and ideals which were at variance with those of the society at large."[110] The prominence of foreigners

106. Elliott, *Home for the Homeless*, 79.
107. Elliott, *Home for the Homeless*, 79, 103, 122.
108. The household strategy also implies that the role of women within the movement was probably more influential than is often imagined. One could also argue that the household strategy was equally efficacious for outreach to citizens, since (as Matt. 10:34 indicates) potential converts to the new faith faced the prospect of estrangement (becoming strangers!) from kith and kin.
109. Cf. Irvin and Sunquist, *World Christian Movement*, 69.
110. Elliott, *Home for the Homeless*, 78.

and strangers among adherents in the early Christian movement meant that consciousness of an outsider status was likely ingrained in Christian identity and mission in the pre-Constantine era. Lacking a common homeland, shared nationality, or ties of blood and shaped by migrant experiences, Christian communities embraced the self-image of sojourning in the world, a self-perception poignantly depicted by the unknown second-century Christian apologist who explained that

> though they [Christians] are residents at home in their own countries, their behavior there is more like that of transients; they take their full part as citizens, but that also submit to anything and everything as if they were aliens. For them, any foreign country is a motherland, and any motherland is a foreign country.[111]

Far from inhibiting Christian growth, this paradox of otherness was relevant to missionary action. Otherness provided rationale for outreach.[112] Put differently, particularism (having a distinctive identity and message) was inseparable from pluralism (embrace of all nationalities and cultures) precisely because at the heart of Christianity's uniqueness was a universal vision. Illustratively, because the God Christians worshipped claimed to be the God of the whole earth, he countenanced no rivals and was antagonistic to all other supernatural powers (1 Cor. 8:5–6).[113] The "paradox of otherness" was integral to the church's missionary function because an outsider status was inseparable from a commitment to preach the Christian message to "outsiders." Thus, the author of 1 Peter counseled recipients that their status as foreigners and resident aliens presented an opportunity to demonstrate their unique religious identity and their faith in God alone (2:11–12): "live such good lives among

111. Staniforth, "Epistle to Diognetus," 144–45.

112. Recent research also confirms that "new religious movements are likely to succeed to the extent that they maintain [some] level of tension with their surrounding environment" (Stark, "Why Religious Movements Succeed or Fail," 137). Stark explains that evangelistic success depends on the new movement being "strict, but not too strict," by which he means that "strictness must be sufficient to exclude potential free-riders and doubters, but it also must be sufficiently low not to drive away everyone except a few misfits and fanatics" (p. 138).

113. MacMullen, *Christianizing the Roman Empire*, 18–19.

the pagans that, though they accuse you of doing wrong, they may see your good deeds and glorify God."[114]

Transnational Movement

As Eusebius noted, the early apostles and the evangelists (perhaps including itinerant preachers) who succeeded them covered long distances. But as the movement grew in numbers and organization, the categories of Christian migrants widened to include captives, refugees, and exiles (often made so by persecution), as well as increasing numbers of traders, artisans, soldiers, and church leaders. The growth of the church also saw the increasing use of migrants as messengers, tasked with the serious business of conveying important correspondence and copies of sacred texts, to support the vital interactive communication essential to building organizational cohesion and safeguarding unity.[115] Regardless of distance and form of migration, the movement of ordinary Christian migrants also carried a capacity for missionary activity.

This is not to suggest that every Christian migrant or traveler undertook evangelistic work. Rather, it reflects a recognition that the spread of the faith largely depended on the actions of ordinary believers. We recall Origen's third-century testimony that "Christians do not neglect, as far as in them lies, to take measures to disseminate their doctrine throughout the whole world."[116] The claim is perhaps exaggerated, but it would be odd, indeed, if Christian migrants or travelers did not act on the missionary impulse inherent in the Christian faith in the course of ordinary business.

In any case, in the first few centuries, the majority of Christian believers were recruited from the lower classes.[117] Many were lowly artisans; since their

114. They were also urged to "always be prepared to give an answer to everyone who asks you to give the reason for the hope you have" (1 Pet. 3:15).

115. Like the majority of inhabitants, Christians lacked access to couriers or the sophisticated government-funded mail service, the *cursus publicus*. The only recourse, writes Casson, "was to find some traveler who happened to be heading in the right direction" (*Travel in the Ancient World*, 220). For more on the vitality of personal and epistolary exchange between churches and Christian leaders, see Harnack, *Mission and Expansion*, book 3, excursus.

116. Origen, *Against Celsus*, 3.9.

117. The reference to "the wearing of gold jewelry and fine clothes" in 1 Pet. 3:3 perhaps hints at the inclusion of wealthier individuals; but, as Elliott points out, the

livelihood required movement, this class of persons had the most opportunity to spread the message of Christianity. Kenneth Latourette also affirmed that Christian missionaries were "men and women who earned their livelihood in some purely secular manner and spoke of their faith to those whom they met in this natural fashion."[118] Second- and third-century pagan critics of Christianity like Celsus and Porphyry depicted the new religion as superstitious delusion in part because, in their view, it was mainly spread by (and attracted) unlearned, lower-class groups.[119] Celsus, a second-century Greek writer, scornfully dismissed such Christian evangelists as "workers in wool and leather, and fullers, and persons of the most uninstructed and rustic character" who "are able to gain over only the silly, and the mean, and the stupid, with women and children."[120]

From the beginning, however, the growing ranks of Christian migrants who traveled long distances included prominent Christian leaders or teachers.[121] The Alexandria-based Origen, for instance, traveled extensively and visited, among other cities, Caesarea (in Palestine), Sidon, Tyre, Bostra, Antioch, Caesarea (in Cappadocia), Nicomedia, Athens, Nicopolis, and Rome.[122] He and many prominent teachers constituted "networks of mobile leaders" whose interactions and writings greatly influenced the development of the Christian movement.[123] Many were little more than migrant travelers who after visiting churches in various cities returned to their homelands. But of interest here are what I would term "transnational Christian leaders" who settled for extensive periods of time as foreigners in distant lands and whose concrete experience as migrant-outsiders shaped their contribution to the early church. The apostle Paul was an early example (see chapter 3). Despite the paucity of the historical records, the life and impact of these transnational Christian leaders (within and beyond the Roman Empire) underscores the significance of migration for the growth and development of the early Christian movement.

---

exhortation to slaves without a corresponding admonition for slave owners is also telling (*Home for the Homeless*, 70).

118. Latourette, *First Five Centuries*, 116.
119. Mertaniemi, "From *Superstitio* to *Religio Christiana*," 142–44.
120. Origin, *Against Celsus* 3.44, 55.
121. Harnack, *Mission and Expansion*, book 3, excursus, provides a list.
122. Harnack, *Mission and Expansion*, book 3, excursus, provides a list.
123. Irvin and Sunquist, *World Christian Movement*, 56.

Transnational Christian Leaders

Transnational leaders were individuals with dual citizenship or nationality who traveled long distances as part of their ministry and often occupied prominent positions within the community of faith in a particular city or region, despite being foreigners. These individuals were not only bilingual (or multilingual)—the ability to read or write more than one language was not uncommon among the educated elite in the Roman Empire—they were also, more importantly, bicultural. That is to say that they were assimilated into or had the ability to function effectively in different cultural contexts. Multiple citizenships (or plural belonging) also allowed them to function as *cultural brokers*, not least because they were often involved in efforts to translate the gospel message as it penetrated a new cultural environment or conducted their ministry in the intersection of two cultures.

Transnational leaders played a key role in the rise of Christianity as an international movement and its global expansion in a number of ways: first, their ministries or identities reflected Christianity's universal potential; second, transnational existence enhanced their capacity for sustained missionary action; third, teaching the tenets of the faith cross-culturally allowed them to contribute to theological development and understanding in unique ways; fourth, familiarity with the diversity of Christian experience made them more alive than most to the limitations of distinctively cultural expression of the faith and, thus, more perceptive of its essential unity. An outstanding example from the period under review was Irenaeus, bishop of Lyons.

Irenaeus of Lyons (ca. 135–ca. 202)

Irenaeus is recognized as the most important Christian theologian and controversialist to emerge "between the apostles and the third-century genius Origen."[124] Morton Enslin describes him as "the first systematic theologian which the new movement . . . produced, and its first systematic heresiologist."[125] But it is important to understand that it was as a transnational leader that the famed bishop of Lyons made his towering contributions to the devel-

---

124. Robert M. Grant, *Irenaeus of Lyons* (New York: Routledge, 1997), 1.
125. Enslin, "Irenaeus," 144.

opment of Christianity. The brief assessment that follows makes the case that Irenaeus's migrant identity and experience must be taken into consideration for a full examination of his historical significance.

Irenaeus's name points to a Greek identity and he was probably born in the city of Smyrna (Asia Minor), "a major center of sophistic culture and teaching."[126] Details of his life, mainly derived from Eusebius's *Ecclesiastical History* (written 312–324) and Irenaeus's own *Against Heresies* (written ca. 180), are tantalizingly sketchy.[127] Among other things, the exact nature of his relationship with Polycarp (ca. 80–155), Apostolic Father and bishop of Smyrna, is uncertain.[128] Irenaeus attested that he knew Polycarp in his youth, and the details he provides about Polycarp suggest that he was either a close follower or disciple of the venerable bishop. He may have accompanied Polycarp when the latter traveled to Rome around 154 CE or, just as likely, was already an immigrant in Rome at the time of Polycarp's arrival.[129] It is reasonably certain that Irenaeus resided in Rome before moving to the city of Lyons (Lugdunum) in southern Gaul; but how long he sojourned in Rome is a matter of conjecture.[130] Exactly when he arrived in Lyons is also unclear. But he settled there before 177 CE when the Christian communities in Lyons and Vienne came under intense persecution. How or why he escaped the cruel executions, even though he was a presbyter (or leading figure) in the church, is unknown. Pothinus, the ninety-year-old bishop of Lyons, was among the martyrs and Irenaeus was appointed his successor.

By the second century CE, migration and trade between Asia Minor and southern Gaul (land of the Celts) had been going on for several centuries.[131]

---

126. Jared Secord, "The Cultural Geography of a Greek Christian: Irenaeus from Smyrna to Lyons," in *Irenaeus: Life, Scripture, Legacy*, ed. Sara Parvis and Paul Foster (Minneapolis: Fortress, 2012), 25.

127. Some works of Irenaeus, mentioned by Eusebius, are no longer extant (see Eusebius, *Ecclesiastical History* 5.26; see also Parvis, "Who Was Irenaeus?," 13–14; Grant, *Irenaeus of Lyons*, 1–10).

128. For a detailed assessment, see Behr, *Irenaeus of Lyons*, 57–66; also, Enslin, "Irenaeus," 144–45. As reported by Eusebius, Irenaeus said of Florinus (a fellow Asian Christian who had migrated to Rome where he was a presbyter), "I saw thee when I was yet a boy in the lower Asia with Polycarp."

129. Behr, *Irenaeus of Lyons*, 66–67; Enslin, "Irenaeus," 148.

130. His stay lasted anywhere from a year or two up to over a decade. See Secord, "Cultural Geography," 32.

131. Enslin, "Irenaeus," 153–57; Behr, *Irenaeus of Lyons*, 17–18.

In Gaul, migrant traders spread Asian culture and religious cults while the establishment of Greek trading colonies facilitated the spread of Greek civilization among the native Celts.[132] After Roman colonization of Gaul in the first century BCE, Latin took root as the official language and enjoyed widespread usage. However, both Greek and Celtic culture persisted; and knowledge of Celtic is thought to have lasted into the fifth and sixth centuries.[133] Cities like Lyons became predominantly Latin but also cosmopolitan centers of trade and multicultural interaction.[134]

By the time Irenaeus was appointed bishop, the Gallican church was well established but probably in its infancy.[135] Given the enduring commercial ties and constant movement between Asia Minor and Gaul, it is quite possible that Christianity was introduced to southern Gaul by Greek-speaking migrants from the East. The two Christian communities maintained close relations and formal interaction. In the wake of the 177 persecution, Christians in Vienne and Lyons sent a detailed account of their tribulation to "the brethren throughout Asia and Phrygia, who hold the same faith and hope of redemption."[136] Importantly, many members of the church in Lyons were, like Irenaeus himself (and the martyred Bishop Pothinus), "immigrants from the East."[137] Lyons Christians, notes historian Paul Parvis, were "a Greek-speaking community in a Latin-speaking city nestled in the midst of a Celtic-speaking countryside. [And] they would in no small measure have been outsiders, strangers in a strange land, alienated culturally as well as religiously from the life of the city around them."[138] That the bloody persecution that overtook the church in 177 began with mob violence also fits the profile of a believing community mainly comprising despised immigrants.

Irenaeus acknowledged that "through [Roman] instrumentality the world is at peace, and we walk on the highways without fear and sail where

132. Grant, *Irenaeus of Lyons*, 4; Enslin, "Irenaeus," 154–55.
133. Lee, *Information and Frontiers*, 68.
134. Cf. Secord, "Cultural Geography," 32; Enslin, "Irenaeus," 155–56.
135. Behr, *Irenaeus of Lyons*, 18–19; Secord, "Cultural Geography," 30, 32. The founders of the church appear to have been among the martyrs (Eusebius, *Ecclesiastical History* 5.1.13).
136. Eusebius, *Ecclesiastical History*, 5.1.3.
137. Behr, *Irenaeus of Lyons*, 19. See also Enslin, "Irenaeus," 149.
138. Parvis, "Who Was Irenaeus?," 15.

we will."[139] But we have little knowledge of his actual travels. That said, his movement (from the East to "the land of the Celts" in the West) conformed to a wider pattern of migrations within the Roman Empire. He was also quite aware of his location and conscious of the disablements imposed by life and ministry in a foreign land, far from the culture of Asia in which he was most at home. After a few years as bishop he wrote:

> You will not expect from me, who am *resident among the [Celts]*, and am accustomed for the most part to use a *barbarous dialect*, any display of rhetoric, which I have never learned, or any excellence of composition, which I have never practiced, or any beauty and persuasiveness of style, to which I make no pretensions.[140] (italics added)

Irenaeus's native tongue was Greek, and he taught and wrote primarily in that language. The "barbarous dialect" that he had to acquire for the purposes of preaching and writing was either Latin or a local Celtic language. There is no scholarly consensus as to which one. Jared Secord rules out a Celtic language based on his view that Irenaeus's "voluminous body of correspondence [is] suggestive of a bookish existence," and that he did not have enough time to learn a Celtic language before leaving Rome.[141] He is convinced that Irenaeus learned or mastered Latin after he settled in Lyons as a matter of necessity. Lyons was after all a Latin city, the martyrs recorded in the 177 pogrom had mainly Greek and Roman names, and Latin possibly served as a means of communication between Greek and Celtic speakers.[142] As to why Irenaeus would have characterized Latin, the official language of the empire, as "barbarous," Secord argues that Irenaeus had an Eastern Greek view of the world and thus would have applied the term "barbarian" to any language other than Greek.

But the notion that a strategic and cosmopolitan Roman colony such as Lyons, "the religious and economic hub of the whole of Gaul," would be char-

---

139. Irenaeus, *Against Heresies*, 4.30.3, trans. Alexander Roberts and William Rambaut, in *Ante-Nicene Fathers*, vol. 1, ed. Alexander Roberts, James Donaldson, and A. Cleveland Coxe (Buffalo, NY: Christian Literature Publishing, 1885).

140. Irenaeus, *Against Heresies*, 1.3 (preface).

141. Secord, "Cultural Geography," 32.

142. Secord, "Cultural Geography," 25, 28, 29–31.

acterized as barbarian or that Irenaeus viewed the language of the empire he admired as a barbaric tongue seems quite far-fetched.[143] It is also hardly beyond the realm of possibility that the "bookish" Irenaeus already knew Latin. Irenaeus's choice of words, "resident among the Celts" (not simply resident in Lyons or Gaul) strongly denotes a Celtic-speaking environment, which was in fact the location of his largely immigrant flock. Montgomery Hitchcock probably overstates the case when he declares that "during his residence among the wild tribes of the Keltae . . . , [Irenaeus] had almost forgotten the use of Latin and Greek, having grown accustomed to the native dialects."[144] But Celtic language, rather than Latin, appears to be a more likely candidate.

We may never know for certain which "barbarous dialect" the bishop of Lyons learned as part of his cross-cultural ministry. But, regardless of whether it was a missionary calling that prompted Irenaeus to settle in the land of the Celts, as some suggest,[145] his rather rueful apology for expressing himself in an unsophisticated manner has strong missionary undertones. As bishop of a predominantly Greek-speaking flock, in a Latin city, surrounded by a non-Christian population, Irenaeus was in a missionary situation. There is no evidence for the belief (propagated by Gregory of Tours in the sixth century) that Irenaeus converted the whole city to Christianity. But it is noteworthy that imprisoned Gallican Christians awaiting execution extolled him as "zealous for the covenant of Christ."[146] In his quarter century as bishop, internal divisions instigated by heretical teachings within his flock consumed his time and energies. But it would have been strange indeed if an individual who chose to live outside the main centers of Christianity, who became leader of a diverse Christian community of disdained immigrants and took the trouble to learn the local language, was not fully alive to the missionary task. Indeed, a few centuries later, the highly respected Theodoret (393–457), bishop of Cyprus, commended Irenaeus as one "who enjoyed the teaching of Polycarp, and became a light of the western Gauls."[147]

---

143. Enslin, "Irenaeus," 157. See also Parvis, "Who Was Irenaeus?," 15; Grant, *Irenaeus of Lyons*, 4.

144. F. R. Montgomery Hitchcock, *Irenaeus of Lugdunum: A Study of His Teaching* (Cambridge: Cambridge University Press, 1914), 11.

145. Grant, *Irenaeus of Lyons*, 4; Enslin, "Irenaeus," 146, 157.

146. Eusebius, *Ecclesiastical History*, 5.4.2.

147. Theodoret, *Eranistes*, Dialogue 1.

Irenaeus is best known for his antiheretical writings in which he emphasized the role of the bishop and apostolic succession; and he condemned as dangerous heretics those who deviated from the teachings of the apostles.[148] Some modern scholars characterize his robust defense of the "true faith" as authoritarian, intolerant, and divisive.[149] But Irenaeus's theology was rooted in deeply pastoral concerns for the unity of the church and strong convictions about the universality of the Christian faith. His writings reveal a transnational perspective. He had the outlook of one who "in his own person united the major traditions of Christendom from Asia Minor, Syria, Rome, and Gaul, although his acquaintance with Palestine, Greece, and Egypt was minimal."[150]

Irenaeus envisioned one faith expressed in the various languages of humanity, so that "the Church . . . , although scattered throughout the whole world, yet, as if occupying but one house, carefully preserves it."[151] In this thinking, diversity of Christian life and existence are made possible by a shared faith. Thus, "although the languages of the world are dissimilar, yet the import of the tradition is one and the same."[152] The catholic church derives its unity not from uniformity or a monolithic ideal but by "lay[ing] hold of the tradition of the truth" to which the Spirit of God bears witness. In his words, the "*many nations of those barbarians* who believe in Christ do assent, having salvation written in their hearts by the Spirit, without paper or ink, and, *carefully preserving the ancient tradition*, believing in one God, the Creator of heaven and earth, and all things therein, by means of Christ Jesus, the Son of God" (italics added).[153] In actual fact, argues John Behr, it was the heretics he so vigorously denounced who are rigidly intolerant; for they proclaimed a single particular "truth" (different from what the apostles taught) based on which they differentiated themselves or withdrew from the majority of believers.[154]

Irenaeus's contribution as a transnational Christian leader was even more

148. Parvis, "Who Was Irenaeus?," 13. Teaching what the apostles taught, Parvis explains, was central to Irenaeus's understanding of the role of a bishop.

149. For a brief discussion, see Behr, *Irenaeus of Lyons*, 14–16; also Parvis, "Who Was Irenaeus?," 23–24.

150. Grant, *Irenaeus of Lyons*, 1.

151. Irenaeus, *Against Heresies*, 1.10.2.

152. Irenaeus, *Against Heresies*, 1.10.2.

153. Irenaeus, *Against Heresies*, 3.4.2.

154. Cf. Behr, *Irenaeus of Lyons*, 16, 46–47.

evident in his mediating effort during two major controversies involving the churches in Asia and in the West. The first was related to the ecstatic prophetic movement, known as New Prophecy or Montanism, that emerged in Phrygia (Asia Minor) in the second century.[155] The teachings and excesses of this movement divided the Asian church and led to its being banned by some local bishops. It seems, however, that the bishop of Rome was sympathetic to the movement; and it is possible that the Montanists appealed to Rome against their local bishops.[156] This potentially set the stage for grave ecclesiastical discord. The teachings of the new movement also caused dissent among Christians in Gaul, which suggests that at least some were attracted to its charismatic elements. Whether Irenaeus himself was receptive to the movement is difficult to say.[157] But, before their violent deaths, the Lyons martyrs wrote letters both to their Asian brethren and to Eleutherus, the bishop of Rome, that "set forth their own prudent and most orthodox judgment in the matter."[158] That Irenaeus was charged with delivering the correspondence on such a highly sensitive ecclesiastical matter involving distant Christian communities is very noteworthy. This undertaking gave him a role in "negotiating for the peace of the churches."[159]

The second instance involved the "quartodeciman [Easter] controversy."[160] It was believed that the Friday of the Jewish Passover week on which Christ was crucified fell on the fourteenth day of the month of Nisan (*quartusdecimus* is the Latin word for "fourteenth"). By long tradition, Asian churches commemorated Christ's death on this day, regardless of which day of the week it happened to be, and adjusted for Easter. The rest of the Christian world, according to Eusebius, celebrated the resurrection on Sunday (the first day of

155. Eusebius, *Ecclesiastical History*, 5.3.4; 5.14; 5.16.1–19.

156. Enslin, "Irenaeus," 150; Tertullian records that "the Bishop of Rome had acknowledged the prophetic gifts of Montanus, Prisca, and Maximilla." Tertullian, *Against Praxeas*, 1, trans. Peter Holmes, in *Ante-Nicene Fathers*, vol. 1, ed. Alexander Roberts, James Donaldson, and A. Cleveland Coxe (Buffalo, NY: Christian Literature Publishing, 1885).

157. Scholars disagree, based on differing interpretations of Eusebius's brief account, on the Lyons church's response to Montanism. See Parvis, "Who Was Irenaeus?," 23; Enslin, "Irenaeus," 149–50.

158. Eusebius, *Ecclesiastical History*, 5.3.4.

159. Eusebius, *Ecclesiastical History*, 5.3.4.

160. Detailed in Eusebius, *Ecclesiastical History*, 5.23.25; see also Enslin, "Irenaeus," 151–53.

the week) and consequently commemorated the crucifixion (and Passover) the preceding Friday. The disparity in observance of such a major Christian event had long been a source of friction. The conflict was heightened in major cities like Rome where the church comprised immigrants from all over the empire. Since both customs were followed, once every seven years Christians from Asia Minor commemorated Good Friday on the same day that their brethren celebrated Easter! In 189 when Victor became bishop of Rome he immediately sought to enforce the majority practice. When the Asian bishops reaffirmed their position, Victor peremptorily excommunicated them. These actions triggered a daunting crisis.

Irenaeus, writing "in the name of the brethren in Gaul over whom he presided," was one of the bishops who promptly admonished Victor.[161] His arguments, which Eusebius singles out, attest to his transnational character. Not only was he acquainted with Roman practices—indeed, the observance of Easter in Gaul conformed with that of Rome—but he was also familiar with the history and theology of churches in Asia Minor, his native land. He advocated peaceful accommodation and rejected the notion that uniformity of practice among churches could be imposed by any particular group or authority. His stance reveals a deep commitment to mutual acceptance and tolerant accommodation on matters of tradition and practice. From his perspective, the ability of the churches to live in peace with each other, despite such divergences in matters of custom, "confirms agreement in the faith." The outcome of his mediation is unknown. But, for Eusebius, our main source on the issue, "Irenaeus . . . became a peacemaker in this matter, exhorting and negotiating in this way in behalf of the peace of the churches."[162]

In sum, the spread and development of the faith in Roman domains remained strongly tied to migrant experiences or movements. In subsequent eras, the dominance of the institutional church within some societies or territories eclipsed the significance of the outsider status in Christian identity and mission. Even so, migration remained indispensable for cross-cultural expansion; and the principle of translation embedded in the Christian message rendered the missionary (regardless of status) an outsider in every encounter with non-Christian peoples. Successive translation of the gospel into new cul-

161. Eusebius, *Ecclesiastical History*, 5.24.11.
162. Eusebius, *Ecclesiastical History*, 5.24.18.

tural contexts, even within the empire, warranted pluralistic forms inherently subversive of efforts to absolutize the faith within a single cultural system, as Irenaeus apparently recognized. Ultimately, therefore, migration played a key role not only in Christianity's expansion but also, and by implication, in its theological development. The migrant element was crucial for the plurality of thought and expression that marked the growing Christian movement, often in the face of concerted efforts by powerful authorities to imprison Christian identity and understanding within a single, regulated cultural framework.

THE CONSTANTINE EFFECT

The conversion of Emperor Constantine I (272–337), followed by the Edict of Milan in 313 CE (which granted religious liberty throughout the empire),[163] dramatically transformed the fortunes of Christianity within the Roman realm. After decades of state persecution and proscription, Christianity—a minority faith that accounted for roughly 10 percent of the population[164]—entered a new era of unrestrained public presence and prominence in Roman domains. As self-appointed patron of the Christian faith, Constantine bestowed huge endowments of lands, wealth, and magnificent buildings on the church and pursued a religious policy that conferred great privileges on ecclesiastical authorities—so much so that the church "receiv[ed] a splendor far greater than that of the old ones which had been destroyed."[165] In his quarter of a century as Christian ruler (of the Western Roman Empire), Constantine forcefully inserted himself into ecclesiastical affairs and used his imperial authority to intervene in bitter theological divisions, based on his vision of a single unified Christian church. He also actively supported the propagation of the Christian faith within and beyond his territory.

Assessments of the impact of Constantine's public policies and his achievements as a Christian monarch are varied. But, whatever doubts persist about

---

163. Eusebius, *Ecclesiastical History*, 10.5.4–6.
164. Hyde, *Paganism to Christianity*, 180.
165. Eusebius, *Ecclesiastical History*, 10.2. See also Sverre Bagge, "Christianizing Kingdoms," in *The Oxford Handbook of Medieval Christianity*, ed. John Arnold (New York: Oxford University Press, 2014), 114; J. N. Hillgarth, *Christianity and Paganism, 350–750: The Conversion of Western Europe*, rev. ed. (Philadelphia: University of Pennsylvania Press, 1986), 46.

the strength of his personal faith, his reign marked a historic turning point in the development of the Christian movement. His actions and policies conferred a privileged position on the church, galvanized the Christianization of the empire, and actively promoted the spread of the faith beyond Roman territories.

Interestingly, the Christianization of the Roman Empire revived a long-standing Roman vision of an empire without limits. By the time of Julius Caesar (100–44 BCE), who is believed to have commissioned the first known map of the world, Romans had already embraced the idea that Rome was divinely ordained to rule the whole world.[166] However, ideology failed to match reality, either politically or culturally. The Roman Empire reached its height in the second century CE (extending perhaps up to 2.5 million square miles) and, while Roman tradition was cherished, Greek culture remained quite entrenched while myriad cultures flourished. However, the rise of Constantine and the establishment of Christianity as the official religion revitalized Roman notions of world domination. This is most evident in the writing of Eusebius, who effusively proclaimed Constantine a "divinely favored emperor" tasked with "the administration of this world's affairs" and "recalling the whole human race to the knowledge of God."[167] This universal mandate was adopted by a number of Constantine's successors, including Constantius II and, much later, the Byzantine Emperor Justinian.

More to the point, imperial patronage and endorsement presented the church with unprecedented opportunities for public expansion and propagation.[168] Meetings in private homes gradually gave way to dedicated church buildings. The household strategy, so effective in reaching immigrant populations or marginalized groups, became less essential. But imperial patronage did not by itself fully account for the extraordinary Christian accessions that accompanied and followed Constantine's rule. Some two-thirds of top officials in Constantine's government were non-Christian, and while his own profession of the Christian faith was zealous, it was not unambiguous—possibly due to political expediency, for instance, he "continued to pay honors to the

166. For more on this, see Whittaker, *Frontiers of the Roman Empire*, 31–38.

167. Eusebius, *Oration in Praise of Constantine*, 1.6, 2.4. Trans. Ernest Cushing Richardson, in *Nicene and Post-Nicene Fathers, Second Series*, vol. 1., ed. Philip Schaff and Henry Wace (Buffalo, NY: Christian Literature Publishing, 1890).

168. MacMullen, *Christianizing the Roman Empire*, 63–67.

sun."[169] Moreover, paganism and other religious cults continued to flourish during and long after Constantine's reign. Paganism prevailed in the army and remained the norm among "almost all Roman nobles" and other civil officials up to the fifth century.[170] Undoubtedly, the Christian movement gained tremendously from "conversions" induced by political, social, and economic pressures, presumably at the expense of pagan cults.[171] But the conversion of notable figures like Augustine of Hippo, however exceptional, point to the fact that the individual religious quest and the persuasiveness of the Christian message remained salient.

It is worth bearing in mind that about the time Constantine began his reign, non-Christians outnumbered Christians roughly 10:1, give or take. Additionally, the church was heavily concentrated in cities, which meant that large swaths of entire regions, including many with a sizeable Christian community, were strongholds of paganism. In Stark's assessment, Christians accounted for just over half of the empire's population by 350 CE; but MacMullen maintains that "the empire overall appears to have been predominantly non-Christian in AD 400."[172] More specifically, Rome was "more pagan than Christian until the 390s" and, as late as 500 CE, "the entire Levant from the Euphrates south to Egypt was not much more than half converted."[173] Imperial backing and largesse elevated Christianity to new heights of privilege and greatly enhanced its reach and appeal in a boisterous religious landscape. But pagan systems, structures, beliefs, traditions and practices could not simply be cast aside. Beyond numerical advantage—and numbers only reveal so much—non-Christians had much to cherish and protect. Many converts had to be won by preaching and persuasion; and demonstrations of spiritual power remained singularly effective.

But, most important for our analysis, the establishment of Christianity as the official religion of the Roman Empire contributed to a dramatic increase in travel among Christians. In short order, the throngs of government bu-

169. MacMullen, *Christianizing the Roman Empire*, 44.

170. MacMullen, *Christianizing the Roman Empire*, 47; Lampe, "Early Christians," 32.

171. See Jerry H. Bentley, *Old World Encounters: Cross-Cultural Contacts and Exchanges in Pre-Modern Times* (New York: Oxford University Press, 1993), 12–13.

172. MacMullen, *Christianizing the Roman Empire*, 83.

173. MacMullen, *Christianizing the Roman Empire*, 81, 83.

reaucrats, soldiers, and merchants on the roads and sea routes of the Roman Empire were joined by church leaders and their representatives. There were "bishops or churches to consecrate, Christians to confirm, synods [regional councils] to attend, or books or other objects to fetch."[174] The desire for political influence also prompted many prelates to make frequent journeys to the imperial court at Constantinople. Ecumenical councils (which convened bishops and church representatives from throughout the empire) also put large numbers of ecclesiastical dignitaries on the road; and many of them traveled considerable distances to attend.[175] The first council at Nicea, called by Constantine in 325, was attended by over three hundred bishops from provinces throughout the empire, each accompanied by a large staff that included priests, deacons, and acolytes. All were granted access to the vast imperial transportation network (or *cursus publicus*[176]) by the emperor.[177] Christian scholars or theologians, a group already prone to travel, joined clerics in synods and ecumenical councils; and swelling numbers of letter carriers or couriers (a role also performed by deacons, priests, and monks) covered great distances to transport the enormous amount of correspondence generated among churches and church leaders.[178]

With the rise of Constantine, cross-border movement precipitated by state-sanctioned persecution in the Roman Empire effectively ceased. But migration and the migrant-outsider experience remained central to cross-cultural expansion, most commonly, as we shall see, through recurrent warfare. But, from at least the third century, theological divisions led to the exile of prominent figures within the church and expulsions of Christian groups whose views or teachings were deemed heretical. Since exile typically meant

174. Norbert Ohler, *The Medieval Traveller* (Woodbridge: Boydell, 1997), 57.

175. Casson, *Travel in the Ancient World*, 300–302; Dietz, *Wandering Monks, Virgins, and Pilgrims*, 24.

176. A sophisticated and massive transport and dispatch service that required use of a government-issued *diploma*, the *cursus publicus* incorporated government-maintained facilities (including well-equipped inns and hostels), post stations generally 25 to 35 miles apart (for the exchange and replenishing of vehicles or draft animals), wagons, and light carriages. For more details, including abuse of the system, see Casson, *Travel in the Ancient World*, 182–88.

177. Indeed, clergy access to the *cursus publicus* for travel became routine and led to overindulgence. It also contributed to the widespread problem of clergy absenteeism that the church was forced to address.

178. Casson, *Travel in the Ancient World*, 302–4.

banishment from areas under the church's influence or control, many ended up residing among non-Christian populations. For some ecclesiastics, the pain and ignominy of exile came with opportunity for missionary action. Thus, when Dionysius of Alexandria (d. 264/265) was banished to the remote Libyan desert in the middle of the third century, his preaching led to a number of conversions among the inhabitants. Life in exile also allowed a bishop of Arbela (modern Erbîl, Jordan) to convert the population of the village in which he took refuge.[179] But, as an example of the unanticipated impact of exile on the transnational spread and progression of "unsanctioned" Christian ideas, few examples were more compelling than Arianism.

179. Latourette, *First Five Centuries*, 104.

CHAPTER FIVE

Frontier Flows: The Faith of Captives and the Fruit of Captivity

For whom have the nations believed—Parthians, Medes, Elamites, and they who inhabit Mesopotamia, Armenia, Phrygia, Cappadocia, and they who dwell in Pontus, and Asia, and Pamphylia, Tarriers in Egypt, and inhabiters of the region of Africa which is beyond Cyrene, Romans and sojourners, yes, and in Jerusalem Jews, and all other nations . . . inaccessible to the Romans, but subjugated to Christ . . . ?

—Tertullian, *An Answer to the Jews*, 7

From the time of Constantine, the exile of disfavored ecclesiastics and groups became even more common and consequential for the spread of the Christian faith, a powerful demonstration of the new patterns of collusion between Christian authority and political power. Roman emperors became deeply embroiled in explosive doctrinal controversies and sided with (or were co-opted by) one or the other of major ecclesiastical factions. In a vastly expanded church, bitter wrangling over doctrinal truth was invariably complicated by cultural difference, political resistance, and ecclesiastical rivalries. Political intrigue and the shifting position of individual emperors meant that the same groups on opposite sides of a major issue were alternatively ascendant and outlawed. Successive emperors supported or banished bishops on either side of the bitter and intractable Arian controversy in the fourth century. Athanasius, bishop of Alexandria, who was exiled four times (twice by pro-Arian emperors) was a notable and prominent victim of such deportations and testament to the vacillations of the new political order.

Only brief attention can be given here to the complex political and theological divisions that marked the rise and spread of Arianism in the fourth century. Political maneuvering, national identities, linguistic difference, and the East-West divide of the empire all played a part. But full grasp of the Arian controversy is impeded by the fact that public debate of the issues and other major developments continued more than half a century after the death of Arius (ca. 250–336), a theologian born in Libya (or Africa) who studied at Antioch and became a priest in Alexandria.[1] The debate had roiled the church in the Greek East for some two decades before it spread to the Latin West where it arguably had less of an impact but intensified the division between Eastern and Western theological traditions.[2] More to the point, it is far from clear which of the different theological strands in the prolonged and heated controversy can be directly traced to the teachings of Arius.

In the early fourth century there was no established Trinitarian doctrine in the church; and diverse theological views existed on the relationship between the persons of the godhead. About 318, a dispute erupted in Alexandria over Arius's Trinitarian beliefs. Arius elevated the divinity of God the Father above the other persons of the Trinity and taught that the Son was created by and subordinate to the Father. This position was rejected by Alexander, his bishop, who maintained that the Son was coeternal with the Father (i.e., not a created being). Arius and his followers were excommunicated. Exiled to the south of the South Danube region (in Illyricum), they won many supporters among younger bishops and spread their teaching in the region.[3] Arian views on the Trinity were subsequently condemned at the Council of Nicaea, convened by Emperor Constantine in 325. The Nicene declaration held the Son to be "same in substance/essence" (Greek, *homoousios*) with the Father. By then, however, the debate had widened in geography and substance—pun unintended.[4]

A major impediment to comprehension of the issues by the modern reader lies in the fact that the available sources were largely written after the victory of one particular entity, and those records "reduce what was in fact a very com-

1. P. J. Heather and John Matthews, *The Goths in the Fourth Century* (Liverpool: Liverpool University Press, 1991), 129.

2. Cf. Maurice Wiles, *Archetypal Heresy: Arianism through the Centuries* (New York: Oxford University Press, 1996), 35–40; Uta Heil, "The Homoians," in *Arianism: Roman Heresy and Barbarian Creed*, ed. Guido M. Berndt and Roland Steinacher (Burlington, VT: Ashgate, 2014), 90–115.

3. Adrian Ignat, "The Spread out of Arianism: A Critical Analysis of the Arian Heresy," *International Journal of Orthodox Theology* 3, no. 3 (2012): 120–22.

4. Cf. Heil, "Homoians," 88–89.

plicated matter into a simple bipartisan clash."[5] All opponents of the official "Catholic" doctrine were collectively labeled "Arian," regardless of key differences and bitter divisions among them. In the long run, the use of the Greek concept "same substance," which was vehemently rejected by some groups as contrary to Scripture, became a touchstone of orthodox belief.

By the mid-fourth century, a raft of conflicting Trinitarian traditions had emerged in the bitter, contentious climate of the Greek-speaking Eastern Church.[6] Among these were *homousians*, who believed the persons of the Trinity to be the "same substance" (the Nicene position); *homoiousians*, who maintained that the Son was distinct but "similar" to the Father, begotten not created; *homoians* (a modern term used to described a group that date to the Synod of Sirmium in 357), who rejected the "substance" language (as unscriptural), decried the homoiousian position for failing to differentiate between the natures of the persons of the Trinity, and pressed the (compromise) view that the Son was "like" the Father; and *anomoians* (or neo-Arians), who claimed that the Son was "unlike" or "unsimilar" to the Father since the former was begotten.

These different schools of thought enjoyed considerable support among church leaders who acted as powerful advocates at different synods. Some also enjoyed imperial favor for periods of time.[7] In 360, a synod in Constantinople, called by the emperor Constantius II, drew empire-wide representatives (drawn from two earlier synods meeting simultaneously in East and West[8]) and, with some imperial arm-twisting, adopted the *homoian* formulation.

---

5. Heather and Matthews, *Goths in the Fourth Century*, 127.

6. For details see Michel R. Barnes and Daniel H. Williams, eds., *Arianism after Arius: Essays on the Development of the Fourth Century Trinitarian Conflicts* (Edinburgh: T&T Clark, 1993); Heil, "Homoians," 85–115; Heather and Matthews, *Goths in the Fourth Century*, 127–28; Wiles, *Archetypal Heresy*, 28–34; Sara Parvis, "Was Ulfila Really a Homoian?," in *Arianism: Roman Heresy and Barbarian Creed*, ed. Guido M. Berndt and Roland Steinacher (Burlington, VT: Ashgate, 2014), 51–53; Knut Schäferdiek, "Ulfila and the So-Called 'Gothic' Arianism—English Summary," in *Arianism: Roman Heresy and Barbarian Creed*, ed. Guido M. Berndt and Roland Steinacher (Burlington, VT: Ashgate, 2014), 47.

7. Even Arius enjoyed some support from Constantine, whose successor, Constans, upheld the Nicene declaration. Emperors Valens and Constantius II supported the *homoian* position.

8. The two synods were held (in 359) in Rimini and Seleucia, and were attended by 400 and 150–60 bishops, respectively (Heil, "Homoians," 94–95).

Its declaration remained the official theological confession of the empire for twenty years. During this time, a significant segment of the church leadership (over 550 bishops had participated in the synods) and large segments of the empire's Christian population—including majorities in cities like Constantinople (East) and Milan (West)[9]—subscribed to non-Nicene beliefs. Many of these would be forgiven for thinking that the reinstatement of the Nicene declaration by the Council of Constantinople, summoned by Emperor Theodosius I in 381, was no more than another temporary reversal.

All this to say that it is only with the benefit of hindsight that the Nicene statement on the Trinity might be viewed as *the* Catholic position. This is less a commentary on its theological merits than an acknowledgment of the tangled political and ecclesiastical realities that attended the process. The term *Arian*, like other labels (such as *Donatist* and *Nestorian*) coined by the victorious side in the explosive theological debates of the fourth and fifth centuries, was wielded with powerful effect to impugn and delegitimize opponents. (See chapter 8 for a discussion of "Nestorianism.") Not only did the founders of these movements not call themselves by these given names but they also regarded themselves as orthodox Christians who were defending Scripture or theological truth.[10] In this instance, the leaders and groups branded "Arian" were deeply antagonistic to each other, claimed no loyalty to Arius, and gave no indication of indebtedness to his views.[11] Moreover, they fiercely denounced their Nicene opponents as heretics for unfaithfulness to Scripture and described themselves as "orthodox" or "catholic."[12]

After 381, the Nicene position was established as the religion of the empire; and Arianism was successfully suppressed within imperial domains by the end of the fourth century. By then, however, the theological strands associated with the Arian controversy had spread beyond the empire to Germanic tribes, among whom it survived well into the seventh century. How, when, and why particular Arian beliefs took hold among these groups (notably the

9. Wiles, *Archetypal Heresy*, 32, 36.

10. Robin Whelan, *Being Christian in Vandal Africa: The Politics of Orthodoxy in the Post-Imperial West* (Oakland: University of California Press, 2018), 11, 14.

11. When Bishop Palladius of Ratiaria (Illyricum) was accused of being an Arian by Ambrose of Milan, he "defended himself against this accusation, and emphasized that he knew neither Arius nor this text." Heil, "Homoians," 110.

12. Schäferdiek, "Ulfila," 45.

Vandals, Lombards, and Goths) is not clear in every instance. The context and circumstances in which the Vandals were converted to the Arian form of faith, for instance, is unknown.[13] But these developments were undoubtedly linked to the migrant movements and actions that shaped the intellectual currents and theological networks undergirding the rival ecclesiastical blocs within the empire itself.

This chapter examines the ways in which vast migrations and interactions of people across the Roman Empire's extensive frontier provided avenues and impetus for the spread of Christianity to nations and peoples beyond. After a brief overview, it mainly focuses on the establishment of the "Arian" form of Christianity as the dominant form of faith among the Goths, who were the first of the Germanic tribes to embrace Christianity in large numbers. (The story of the spread of Christianity into Persian realms is taken up in chapter 6.) The particular "Arian" theological tradition that was embraced by the Goths remains a matter of considerable debate. Of primary interest, however, is the missionary role of Christian migrants, specifically captives and exiles, in the establishment of the Gothic Church. Most important, careful examination of the migrant element yields important insights that are obscured by the traditional emphasis on political authority and imperial interests as key explanations for the Christianization of the Goths and other peoples beyond Roman dominion.

BEYOND FRONTIERS

Roman rule created a polyethnic empire and generated unprecedented levels of cross-community movements. Within the empire itself, migration was multidirectional: from the provinces to the metropolises, east to west, countryside to city, and (in each case) vice versa.[14] The borders of the Roman Empire extended over 3,700 miles and impacted a great diversity of peoples and places.[15]

---

13. Whelan, *Being Christian in Vandal Africa*, 11–13, 18–21. Whelan claims that it was *homoian* Christianity that the Vandals embraced. One possible explanation for its penetration of this group holds that it spread through recruitment in the Roman army. See also Ignat, "Spread out of Arianism," 117.

14. On the role of migration in the rise and decline of the Roman Empire, see Rey Koslowski, "Human Migration and the Conceptualization of Pre-Modern World Politics," *International Studies Quarterly* 46, no. 3 (2002): 375–99.

15. C. R. Whittaker, *Frontiers of the Roman Empire: A Social and Economic Study* (Baltimore: Johns Hopkins University Press, 1994), 133.

The eventual collapse of the western empire was also intertwined with considerable and quite consequential cross-border movements. Infiltration and occupation of Roman territory by Germanic tribes (the "barbarian" threat) in turn triggered waves of migrant-refugee movement as Roman inhabitants fled by land and sea to other regions or provinces.[16] Like the empire itself, frontier regions were marked by great demographic complexity. They were also fluid, indeterminate, and permeable—a reminder that "the very idea of the frontier as a line on a map is modern."[17] Ancient frontiers were zonal, not linear.

The rapid cross-cultural and transregional spread of the Christian movement among diversities of groups and ethnicities beyond the Roman Empire was well attested by prominent church leaders. As early as the early third century, Tertullian (ca. 155–ca. 240), the prolific African Christian apologist, claimed the presence of Christians among nations "inaccessible to the Romans."[18] Much later, in 403, Jerome (347–420), another prominent Christian theologian, reported:

> Already the Egyptian Serapis has been made a Christian; while at Gaza Marnas mourns in confinement and every moment expects to see his temple overturned. From India, from Persia, from Ethiopia we daily welcome monks in crowds. The Armenian bowman has laid aside his quiver, the Huns learn the psalter, the chilly Scythians are warmed with the glow of the faith. The Getæ, ruddy and yellow-haired, carry tent-churches about with their armies: and perhaps their success in fighting against us may be due to the fact that they believe in the same religion.[19]

It requires no leap of imagination to grasp that human migration played a huge role in the spread of Christianity among the tribes and peoples well beyond the Roman Empire. As was the case in the Christianization of Roman

16. Maribel Dietz, *Wandering Monks, Virgins, and Pilgrims: Ascetic Travel in the Mediterranean World, A.D. 300/800* (University Park: Pennsylvania State University Press, 2005), 22–23.

17. Whittaker, *Frontiers of the Roman Empire*, 71, 84, 140.

18. Tertullian, *An Answer to the Jews*, 7, trans. S. Thelwall, in *Ante-Nicene Fathers*, vol. 3, ed. Alexander Roberts, James Donaldson, and A. Cleveland Coxe (Buffalo, NY: Christian Literature Publishing, 1885).

19. Jerome, "Letter 107: To Laeta" (403 CE), accessed January 8, 2018, http://www.newadvent.org/fathers/3001107.htm.

domains, only more so, these missionary activities were disparate, haphazard, and unstructured. They also involved migrations of peoples on a vastly greater scale and scope. The point is that the transformation of the Christian movement into a transregional phenomenon required the transcultural, transnational, and transregional movement of Christian migrants, for a host of reasons and under a variety of circumstances. The migrants in question span a variety of categories: traders, soldiers, refugees, exiles, slaves, captives, emissaries, even self-designated or official missionaries. But no category of migrant was more prominent or consequential in the transregional spread of Christianity in the first five to six centuries than captives (or slaves).

"Involuntary Missionaries"

As noted earlier, the condition of servitude was common in the ancient world and the slave population within ancient societies was massive.[20] Within empires especially, a substantial proportion of the immigrant population were slaves, former slaves, or descendants of slaves. Accounts of the role that Christian captives played in the establishment and growth of the church among different tribes and kingdoms are among the most remarkable in the history of the Christian movement. Naturally, raids into Christian territory or the takeover of predominantly Christian provinces by enemy armies or invaders resulted in large numbers of Christians being carried off to foreign lands as captives or slaves.[21] By winning converts among the people in those lands, including their captors or other captives, these Christian captives became important agents of the interregional spread of Christianity in the first millennium. British historian Edward Gibbon memorably described them as "involuntary missionaries."[22]

The Christianization of Axum (part of modern Ethiopia) is an important case in point. This process, which began in the fourth century, had many

20. See J. P. V. D. Balsdon, *Romans and Aliens* (Chapel Hill: University of North Carolina Press, 1979), 77–113.

21. For an intimate account of the impact of such Germanic raids on provincial Christian communities, see Gregory of Pontus (or St. Gregory)'s *Canonical Letter*, in *A Select Library of Nicene and Post-Nicene Fathers of the Christian Church*, vol. 14, ed. Philip Schaff and Henry Wace (New York: Scribner's Sons, 1900), 602.

22. Edward Gibbon, *The History of the Decline and Fall of the Roman Empire* (London: A. Strahan & T. Cadell, 1789), book 3.37.

strands.[23] But a centerpiece involved the abduction and captivity of two young Syrian Christians, Frumentius and Aedesius, who were sold to the king of Axum after their ship was attacked and all adults aboard massacred. Due to their intelligence and education, the two foreign captives were appointed to important positions in the king's household. Over time, they won the respect and affection of the king, who entrusted them with the tutelage of his son, Ezana (d. 356). When (possibly after the death of the king) the queen subsequently granted them their freedom, Aedesius chose to return to his native land. But Frumentius remained and was invited to share in the responsibilities of ruling the kingdom. In an effort to lay the foundation of a Christian church, he sought out Christians among Axum's many Roman merchants and built places of Christian worship "in which they might gather for prayer in the Roman manner."[24] He also gave them "extensive rights, which he urged them to use." With the accession of Ezana to the throne, the Christianization of the kingdom began in earnest.

About 340 CE, Frumentius journeyed to Alexandria to request a bishop for the growing Christian community. Athanasius, the patriarch, promptly consecrated him bishop of Axum. But, for the next century or so, Christianity remained largely confined to the Axum court and the urban-based mercantile class. Extensive Christian penetration of the rural population began with the arrival of another group of migrant-foreigners in the late fifth and early sixth century. These were the "Nine Saints" or the *Sadqan* ("the righteous ones"), part of a larger group of learned monks and priests who came from the Byzantine world.[25] The long-standing view that the Nine Saints were of

23. The elites of Axum had quite possibly learned about Christianity from Christian merchants. For more, see Harold G. Marcus, *A History of Ethiopia* (Berkeley: University of California Press, 1994), 7; Rufinus of Aquileia, *History of the Church*, trans. Philip R. Amidon (Washington, DC: Catholic University of America Press, 2016), book 10; Christopher Haas, "Mountain Constantines: The Christianization of Aksum and Iberia," *Journal of Late Antiquity* 1, no. 1 (Spring 2008): 101–26.

24. Rufinus of Aquileia, *History of the Church*, book 10.9.

25. For more on the Nine Saints and evaluation of their impact, see Mary Anne Fitzgerald, *Ethiopia: The Living Churches of an Ancient Kingdom* (New York: American University in Cairo Press, 2017); María-José Friedlander and Bob Friedlander, *Hidden Treasures of Ethiopia: A Guide to the Remote Churches of an Ancient Land* (London: I. B. Tauris, 2015); Marcus, *History of Ethiopia*; and D. W. Phillipson, *Ancient Churches of Ethiopia: Fourth–Fourteenth Centuries* (New Haven: Yale University Press, 2009).

Syrian origin is now disputed, and whether they were fleeing persecution for non-Chalcedonian views remains an open question. But they evangelized the countryside, founded monasteries that revitalized the faith, established schools, and translated the Bible and other Christian writings into Ge'ez (the local vernacular that became the official language of the Ethiopian Church). The story of Ethiopian Christianity should not be reduced to outside influences.[26] Somehow, in a region marked by considerable movement, the inhabitants of the Axumite kingdom (a major African trading power) combined a "sense of collective identity" and distinctive culture with receptivity to outsiders.[27] In the event, the contribution of migrants to the establishment and early spread of Christianity in Axumite Ethiopia is undeniable.

Tradition traces the Christianization of the Kingdom of Georgia (or Iberia) on the Black Sea, north of Armenia, to the actions of a female Christian captive called Nino (or some variant thereof).[28] According to a fourth-century account, Nino's life of prayer piqued the curiosity of observers and when questioned she explained that she "worshipped Christ as God."[29] Shortly after, her prayers led to the healing of the queen, named Nana, "who was suffering from a bodily illness of the gravest sort and had been reduced to a state of absolute despair." The queen promptly converted to the Christian faith and entreated the king, Mirian III (d. 342 CE), to adopt the new religion. The king demurred. However, sometime later when he lost his way in the forest, the king too invoked the name of Christ and after he made his way back safely immediately summoned the female Christian captive. The monarchs made known their experiences and publicly professed their new faith. It is said that "the men believed because of the king, the women because of the queen, and with everyone desiring the same thing a church was put up without delay." The female captive provided basic instructions about

26. In fact, the Ethiopian Church was cut off from the wider church for long periods. Moreover, as Mary Anne Fitzgerald indicates, "indigenous traditions, developed over centuries . . . , particularly in matters of faith" hold the key to the Ethiopian Church's survival (in the face of formidable threats such as the rise of Islam) and help to explain its long history. Fitzgerald, *Ethiopia*, 1.

27. Fitzgerald, *Ethiopia*, 1.

28. See Rufinus of Aquileia, *History of the Church*, book 10; Ian Gillman and Hans-Joachim Klimkeit, *Christians in Asia before 1500* (Ann Arbor: University of Michigan Press, 1999), 90–91; also Haas, "Mountain Constantines," 101–26.

29. Rufinus of Aquileia, *History of the Church*, book 10.11.

Christian rituals and described the shape of a church. At her suggestion, an embassy was sent to Rome with a request for Christian priests—a request that Emperor Constantine eagerly fulfilled. Thus emerged one of the earliest Christian kingdoms.

In both the cases cited above, the spread of Christianity, at least the initial phase, rested on the actions of migrant actors and owed nothing to imperial ties or formal missionary enterprise. But probably the best known and most celebrated account of captivity as a crucial element in the Christianization of a people beyond Roman domains is that of Saint Patrick (ca. 387–ca. 460/493), the British migrant and apostle to the Irish. Much of what we know about Patrick's life and impact is a mixture of facts and fable; but his autobiographical *The Confession of St. Patrick* provides ample indication of the link between migration and mission.

Patrick, who was possibly a third-generation Christian born to wealthy parents in Roman Britain, was "taken into captivity in Ireland with many thousands of people" when he was about sixteen years of age ("almost a beardless boy").[30] By his own testimony, migration and the experience of captivity produced an intensification of faith, tantamount to religious conversion:[31]

> And there [in Ireland] the Lord opened my mind to an awareness of my unbelief, in order that, even so late, I might remember my transgressions and turn with all my heart to the Lord my God ... (no. 2)

> I used to pasture the flock each day and I used to pray many times a day. More and more did the love of God, and my fear of him and faith increase ... (no. 16)

The revitalization of his Christian faith fomented a strong missionary impulse in the young migrant—so strong, in fact, that after he managed to escape and made it safely to his parents' home in Britain (following six years in captivity), he felt constrained to return. His newfound sense of missionary vocation was fortified by "a vision of the night":

30. Unless otherwise stated, all quotations related to this story are taken from *The Confession of St. Patrick*, trans. John Skinner (New York: Image, 1998).
31. See Lewis R. Rambo, *Understanding Religious Conversion* (New Haven: Yale University Press, 1993), 2, 12–14.

> I saw a man whose name was Victorious coming as if from Ireland with innumerable letters, and he gave me one of them, and I read the beginning of the letter: The Voice of the Irish. . . . "They were crying as if with one voice: "We beg you, holy youth, that you shall come and shall walk again among us . . ." (no. 23)

There were already Christian communities in parts of Ireland prior to Patrick's captivity.[32] His is the only name we know; but it is highly unlikely that he was the only Christian who was carried off into captivity or the only Christian captive who developed a strong urge to share his faith with those he resided among. But it is significant that the missionary impulse compelled Patrick to return to the land of his captivity *after* he had regained his freedom, not to mention the fact that he was determined to labor among the Irish for the rest of his life. He was therefore not an "involuntary missionary" in the strictest sense; but captivity triggered missionary consciousness and presaged missionary action. As Dana Robert surmises, "Patrick's self-understanding as a wanderer under God's protection, and as someone who operated on the margins of society, was essential to his calling as a missionary."[33] Moreover, Patrick described himself (during his missionary labors in Ireland) as "first of all . . . an exile" (no. 13)—an intimation that he never lost his sense of being a foreigner-outsider or perhaps even the natural longing for homeland.

The precise nature and extent of Patrick's contribution may never be known. Paganism remained widespread in Irish society long after his death.[34] Still, *Confessions* portrays an extraordinary missionary career that led to the conversion of "many thousands of people" (no. 50) and the founding of the Irish church. "So, how is it that in Ireland," it claims, "where they never had any knowledge of God but, always, until now, cherished idols and unclean things, they are lately become a people of the Lord, and are called children of God; the sons of the Irish [Scotti] and the daughters of the chieftains are

32. Patrick's mission was to the still pagan northern part of the country. But by the late fourth or early fifth century, missionaries from the church in Gaul had won a sufficient number of converts in the southeastern region to justify the appointment of a bishop. See John Haywood, *The Celts: Bronze Age to New Age* (London: Routledge, 2004), 129; J. N. Hillgarth, *Christianity and Paganism, 350–750: The Conversion of Western Europe*, rev. ed. (Philadelphia: University of Pennsylvania Press, 1986), 118–19.

33. Dana L. Robert, *Christian Mission: How Christianity Became a World Religion* (Malden, MA: Wiley-Blackwell, 2009), 148.

34. Hillgarth, *Christianity and Paganism*, 118.

to be seen as monks and virgins of Christ" (no. 41). Intriguingly, the spirit of migration and mission that marked Patrick's remarkable career became a hallmark of Irish Christianity. As we shall see (chapter 7), within a century after his death, Irish missionary monks would adopt a life of travel and wandering that contributed enormously to the spread of Christianity in Britain and Europe.[35]

But long before a beardless Patrick was taken into captivity in Ireland (ca. 400 CE), other groups of captives were already instrumental in the spread and establishment of Christianity outside Roman domains. These movements occurred both northward—primarily among the Goths—and eastward into the lands under Parthian/Persian rule.

Barbarian Migrations

The term "barbarian" was of Roman origin. It basically meant non-Roman (in a derogatory sense) or signified the "other." In Roman discourse, it conveyed stereotypical images of lawlessness, a savage nature, and uncivilized existence.[36] By the third century, the Roman Empire faced increasing pressures from raids and incursions by various barbarian tribes including marauding Saracens (from Arabia), Franks, Alamanni, Goths (Germanic tribes), and Huns and Avars (nomadic Asiatic peoples).[37] In truth, centuries of cross-border movements and reciprocal interaction between Romans and barbarian groups such as the Goths arguably produced increasing congruence between the two groups.[38] Considerable barbarian settlement in frontier zones, combined with long-term economic and cultural cross-border exchange, also

35. Indeed, the church in Ireland would go on to play an outsized role in the worldwide spread of the Christian faith in succeeding centuries. One and a half millennia later, Ireland ranked second in the world in the number of missionaries sent per Christian population. Todd M. Johnson and Kenneth R. Ross, eds., *Atlas of Global Christianity 1910–2010* (Edinburgh: Edinburgh University Press, 2009), 259.

36. For a thorough overview, see Ralph W. Mathisen and Danuta Shanzer, eds., *Romans, Barbarians, and the Transformation of the Roman World: Cultural Interaction and the Creation of Identity in Late Antiquity* (Burlington, VT: Ashgate, 2011).

37. See Ralph W. Mathisen, "Catalogues of Barbarians in Late Antiquity," in *Romans, Barbarians, and the Transformation of the Roman World: Cultural Interaction and the Creation of Identity in Late Antiquity*, ed. Ralph W. Mathisen and Danuta Shanzer (Burlington, VT: Ashgate, 2011).

38. For detailed treatment, see Whittaker, *Frontiers of the Roman Empire*, 199–200, 219–35.

blurred the distinction between Roman territory and the lands beyond.[39] But notions of the "barbarian" as the savage other remained entrenched. This stereotype was prevalent even among Christian leaders and apologists;[40] and some speculate that it helps to explain the lack of official missionary activity among the various Germanic tribes beyond the empire's frontiers (or even within its northern provinces).[41]

At any rate, freedom of movement across the (northern) border of the empire allowed extensive immigration and settlement of Germanic groups within the empire itself. Some Germanic tribes were formally granted asylum by Roman authorities or incorporated into the Roman political system through negotiated treaties known as *foedus*, which bestowed an autonomous federate status.[42] The wholesale integration of barbarian units into the overstretched Roman army advanced the process of integration further; and the practice of rewarding military service with permanent settlement within the empire enlarged the Germanic immigrant population. About one million such immigrants were settled in Gaul.[43] In other words, long before the collapse of the Western Roman Empire, huge numbers of Germanic peoples were already part of Roman society.

Thus, the common notion of "barbarian invasions" as an explanation for the breakup of the Western Roman Empire is open to question.[44] "Invasion"

39. It is also noteworthy that some barbarian units within the Roman army were recruited from and stationed in frontier provinces where they maintained ties with kinfolk in their homelands. A. D. Lee, *Information and Frontiers: Roman Foreign Relations in Late Antiquity* (New York: Cambridge University Press, 2006), 76–77; Koslowski, "Human Migration," 393.

40. There are a few exceptions, such as St. Chrysostom (347–407), the Archbishop of Constantinople, and Pope Gregory I (ca. 540–604). Chrysostom, according to Edward Gibbon, sent missionaries who "converted great numbers of the Scythians, who dwelt beyond the Danube in tents and wagons" (*Decline and Fall of the Roman Empire*, book 3.34, n. 27)—and Gregory I commissioned the mission that led to the conversion of the Angles.

41. James C. Russell, *The Germanization of Early Medieval Christianity: A Sociohistorical Approach to Religious Transformation* (New York: Oxford University Press, 1994), 184.

42. Peter Heather, "The Crossing of the Danube and the Gothic Conversion," *Greek, Roman and Byzantine Studies* 27, no. 3 (1986): 290–91; also J. A. S. Evans, *The Age of Justinian: The Circumstances of Imperial Power* (New York: Routledge, 1996), 20–21; Ian Wood, *The Merovingian Kingdoms 450–751* (New York: Longman, 1994).

43. Koslowski, "Human Migration," 393.

44. Koslowski, "Human Migration," 393; Whittaker, *Frontiers of the Roman Empire*, 212–14; Lee, *Information and Frontiers*, 128–29.

suggests that the empire was overrun by substantial waves of people and armies. In fact, the size of the barbarian tribes involved in these incursions was small: the largest groups (such as the Franks or Vandals) had a total population of about 80,000; and, though the sources are vague on the scale of barbarian armies, estimates of the fighting men of most Germanic tribes vary from 5,000 to 40,000.[45] By comparison, the Roman Empire boasted approximately 248,000 frontier troops in 250 CE and over 434,000 total (land and fleet) by 280—though these included sizeable barbarian units.[46] The numbers shrank after the collapse of the western empire in the fourth century. But not even Persia, Rome's formidable military rival, attempted a full-scale invasion. Moreover, many Germanic tribes comprised clusters of clans and multiple rival rulers, a structure that made coordinated military campaigns difficult. Indeed, it is noteworthy that the establishment of the first barbarian kingdom on Roman territory in 410 was by Gothic groups (under a Christian leader) who were "allies" of the Roman state and had fought alongside its armies.

The long and complex process by which these barbarian groups gradually infiltrated the Western Roman Empire from the third to fifth centuries included acts of invasion and occupation;[47] but taken as a whole it is best characterized as *migrations*.[48] With this lens, it is easier to comprehend the multidirectional nature, the multiplicity of actors, and the multifarious outcomes involved. The bulk of the movement took the form of either *whole-*

45. Koslowski, "Human Migration," 393; Whittaker, *Frontiers of the Roman Empire*, 212; Lee, *Information and Frontiers*, 129.

46. Whittaker, *Frontiers of the Roman Empire*, 135 (also 288n); Evans, *Age of Justinian*, 48–52; Jane Burbank and Frederick Cooper, *Empires in World History: Power and the Politics of Difference* (Princeton: Princeton University Press, 2010), 66. Already in the second century BCE, the imperial army comprised around 130,000 men. Christopher Kelly, *The Roman Empire: A Very Short Introduction* (New York: Oxford University Press, 2006), 10.

47. Patrick Périn and Michel Kazanski, "Identity and Ethnicity During the Era of Migrations and Barbarian Kingdoms in the Light of Archaeology in Gaul," in *Romans, Barbarians, and the Transformation of the Roman World: Cultural Interaction and the Creation of Identity in Late Antiquity*, ed. Ralph W. Mathisen and Danuta Shanzer (Burlington, VT: Ashgate, 2011), 304.

48. This is not to endorse the notion of systematic, orchestrated, sustained movement implied in the concept of a "migration age" that has come under strong criticism. See Walter A. Goffart, *Barbarian Tides: The Migration Age and the Later Roman Empire* (Philadelphia: University of Pennsylvania Press, 2006), 12–22, 114–18. Indeed, my analysis explicitly eschews the idea of a single monolithic phenomenon.

community migration—the relocation of an entire group or tribe (such as the resettlement of the Goths in the Roman Empire in 376)—or the far more prevalent *cross-community migration*, the movement of select individuals or subgroups (typically young adult males) who leave one society to join another on a temporary or permanent basis (see chapter 1). Indeed, it is worth noting that these groups were themselves formed by prior movement and resettlement and therefore "neither ethnically nor culturally homogenous."[49] In any case, these cross-community migrations involved traders, refugees, soldiers, merchants, nomadic groups, spies, captives, slaves, smugglers, artisans, and others. Of central interest here is the degree to which Christian migrants contributed to the spread of Christianity among the Goths, who were the first of the Germanic peoples to settle on Roman territory en masse and also the first to convert to Christianity in large numbers.

CHRISTIANITY AMONG THE GOTHS

The Goths (identified in fourth-century sources as Thervingi and Greuthungi) are of obscure origins. It is no longer certain that they originated in southern Scandinavia, as once assumed. They had settled close to the Roman frontier, in the Pontic region, by the third century. One of the earliest references to their existence identifies them as a unit in the Roman army.[50] Within a matter of decades, however, Gothic groups also conducted attacks on Roman territory and established an independent kingdom in the region of Dacia (present-day Romania), formerly a Roman province, in the early 270s.[51] The Goths became one of the nearest and most familiar of the empire's northern neighbors. Gothic merchants were involved in transfrontier trade—primarily selling slaves in exchange for Roman goods[52]—and Gothic fighters were incorporated into the Roman military in huge numbers.

The available sources provide no indication that church authorities in the Roman Empire sent missionaries to evangelize Germanic peoples beyond the

49. Périn and Kazanski, "Identity and Ethnicity," 305.

50. Lee, *Information and Frontiers*, 26; also E. A. Thompson, *The Visigoths in the Time of Ulfila*, 2nd ed. (London: Duckworth, 2008), 1–3.

51. Dale T. Irvin and Scott Sunquist, *History of the World Christian Movement*, Vol. 1, *Earliest Christianity to 1453* (Maryknoll, NY: Orbis Books, 2001), 179.

52. Lee, *Information and Frontiers*, 71–73; Thompson, *Visigoths*, 40.

northern frontier; nor were clergy appointed to minister among the large communities of Christians carried off into captivity by barbarian raiders from the third century.[53] The Christianization of the Roman Empire was a long and uneven process that lasted well into the fifth century. But imperial patronage and support for the propagation of the Christian faith beyond Roman domains (at least by the emperor Constan) placed the church on a strong footing for missionary outreach to barbarian tribes. Yet, there is no evidence that the imperial government either sponsored or instigated missionary outreach among the barbarian groups it granted sanctuary on Roman territory, even though Germanic Christian converts were reportedly more peaceful and acquiescent than their non-Christian compatriots.[54]

The "Empire" Argument

The absence of official missionary efforts under the auspices of self-identified Christian Roman emperors or church authorities is partly responsible for the claim that the majority of Germanic tribes—including the Marcomanni, Heruls, Lombards, Goths, Gepids, Sueves, Vandals, and Burgundians—were converted to Christianity *after* they had settled on Roman territory.[55] E. A. Thompson, a major authority on Gothic history, contends that mass relocation to Roman territory was decisive for the conversion of barbarian tribes because "the act of crossing the imperial frontiers and settling down . . . on Roman soil necessarily and inevitably entailed the abandonment of pagan-

---

53. E. A. Thompson, "Christianity and the Northern Barbarians," in *The Conflict between Paganism and Christianity in the Fourth Century*, ed. Arnaldo Momigliano (Oxford: Clarendon, 1963), 63–68; W. H. C. Frend, "The Missions of the Early Church, 180–700 A.D.," in *Miscellenea Historiae Ecclesiasticae* 3 (1970): 13; Lee, *Information and Frontiers*, 74–75.

54. On the impact of Christian conversion on barbarian peoples, see Thompson, "Christianity and the Northern Barbarians," 67.

55. Thompson, "Christianity and the Northern Barbarians," 56–59, 62, 64–68, 77–78; also Thompson, *Visigoths*, xvii, 103–7. The Rugi, who adopted the Arian Christian faith while still living beyond the Roman frontier, are considered a major exception. Thompson, "Christianity and the Northern Barbarians," 76. Other Germanic tribes such as the Franks, Alamanni, and Frisians are excluded from the claim because they did not migrate into the Roman Empire in substantial numbers until after the western empire collapsed in 476.

ism and conversion to Roman religion [i.e., Christianity]."[56] He speculates that large-scale migration of Goths contributed to the disintegration of tribal organization and the decay of their tribal religion. Additionally, in his view, long-term settlement in a Roman environment elicited efforts to appropriate and approximate Roman structures and practices especially by the ruling class who, by becoming landowners, found their social interests increasingly aligned with the interests of the Roman landowners around them.[57] Essentially, "the move into a new economic and social world was necessarily followed by a move into a new spiritual world."[58]

In this assessment, Thompson primarily accounts for Germanic adoption of the Christian faith in terms of economic self-interest and proximity to imperial structures. He associates conversion with a change in the aspirations and allegiance of the ruling class and the supplanting of tribal organization. But, by making economic interest and political developments central to religious conversion, Thompson overlooks the role of nonelite actors and implicitly devalues initiatives by self-motivated individual Christian missionaries who acted independently of institutional authority.[59] For Thompson, efforts by Christian migrants were "haphazard and unorganized, and in themselves . . . won no major victories for the Church."[60] He also concludes that initiatives by individual churchmen ended in failure.[61]

But acceptance of this assessment requires endorsing the curious notion that the presence of sizeable migrant Christian communities (with their own bishops) among the Goths was inconsequential for their conversion to Christianity. Though he is at pains to depict the Christian community in Gothic lands as small and insignificant, Thompson concedes that the consecration of Ulfila (see "Bishop Ulfila," below) does confirm the existence "among the Visigoths [of] a Christian community which was sufficiently organized to

56. Thompson, "Christianity and the Northern Barbarians," 78.

57. Thompson, *Visigoths*, 107, 128.

58. Thompson, "Christianity and the Northern Barbarians," 78.

59. As Thompson himself notes, evangelistic work among Germanic groups *on Roman territory* appears to have been "purely local efforts" by individual churchmen, which is to say that efforts to win these groups to the Christian faith were not instigated by the official church." Thompson, "Christianity and the Northern Barbarians," 67.

60. Thompson, "Christianity and the Northern Barbarians," 56–59, 62.

61. Thompson, "Christianity and the Northern Barbarians," 67, 76–77.

make known to Constantinople that it required the services of a bishop."[62] Moreover, if the Goths "were still an essentially pagan people" when they entered the Roman Empire in 376,[63] and if living among Roman peoples prompted their conversion to Christianity, it is difficult to explain why they embraced the Arian version of the faith. For by the time of major Gothic settlement in the 380s, Arianism had long been outlawed within the Roman Empire and largely lost its appeal.[64] A determination to emulate Roman ways is difficult to reconcile with mass embrace of a religion outlawed by Roman authorities.

The absence of official missionary efforts to spread Christianity among barbarian peoples living beyond the empire's frontier does not mean that they lacked sustained contact with Christianity. In fact, the transfrontier movement of the Goths meant that they were exposed to a variety of Christian influences that filtered steadily across the frontier. Individual Latin- and Greek-speaking missionaries from Roman provinces crossed the frontier on their own initiative and made converts. The best known of the Gothic Catholics was Saint Saba, a Christian Goth martyred in 372.[65] Audius of Mesopotamia, an austere ascetic exiled by Constantius II to the province of Scythia Minor (for schismatic views), also crossed the frontier with missionary intentions and reportedly "made 'many converts' among the [Goths], and founded monasteries and convents."[66] Audians, as his followers were known, constituted a separate Christian sect distinct from Arians and Catholics. The latter, in turn, had separate bishops and ecclesiastical structures. Gothic Christianity as such had multiple strands.

Christian teachings and ideas also spread through a variety of sources: Christian captives acquired in raids on Roman provinces, barbarian soldiers in the Roman army who maintained contact with their kin across the border, large numbers of soldiers who returned to their homelands after serving with the imperial forces, and the throng of Roman merchants who pursued commercial activity across the border or settled permanently among the barbarian

---

62. Thompson, *Visigoths*, xvii.

63. Thompson, "Christianity and the Northern Barbarians," 58.

64. Frend, "The Missions of the Early Church, 180–700 A.D.," 13.

65. See *The Passion of St. Saba, the Goth*, in Heather and Matthews, *The Goths in the Fourth Century*, 102–10.

66. Thompson, *The Visigoths in the Time of Ulfila*, 82.

peoples.[67] These unstructured movements produced meaningful Christian communities in Gothic lands—communities that developed separately from the church in the Roman Empire.[68] By 376, when attacks by the Huns forced the Goths to settle on Roman territory, the church in Gothic lands had existed in some shape or form for over two hundred years; and though there is no record of mass conversions, its members included native Goths. That the impact of this immersive Christian presence would be discounted by scholars like Thompson is perplexing.

It defies logic to view the conversion of Gothic peoples to Christianity as a development wholly unconnected to the immigrant Christian communities that endured in Gothic lands for over two centuries. Granted, the paucity of the historical record precludes conclusive argument and leaves ample room for conjecture. But it is difficult to provide a satisfactory explanation for the spread of Christianity among the Goths and other Germanic tribes without attentiveness to the migrant element. Whatever their size, those communities paved the way for Gothic conversions through vernacular translation, cultural adaptation, missionary action, and the evocative witness of martyrdom. This is consistent with the view that the religious transformation of a society is a multigenerational process, subject to variations, shifts, and forms of resistance.[69] The Christianization of the Goths may have been incomplete prior to settlement on Roman territory in the late 370s; but the process was already underway for over a century and a half.

Actually, migration retains its explanatory relevance even if thoroughgoing Christianization came after these tribes settled within the empire, since whole-community relocation is a hugely disruptive process that can facilitate the crossing of religious boundaries. But the view taken here is that the roots of Gothic Christianity lay in the extensive cross-border movement that al-

67. See Thompson, "Christianity and the Northern Barbarians," 61; Thompson, *Visigoths*, 39.

68. The fact that the Gothic church sent a letter to the church in Cappadocia (along with Saba's martyred body) explaining the circumstances of his death provides evidence of contact; but this was well into the fourth century. The letter is referred to as *Passion of St. Saba*. See also Thompson, *Visigoths*, 64–77, 82.

69. As Bentley recognized, the transformation of whole societies involving the adoption of foreign cultural traditions—which he terms "social conversion"—takes place over centuries. Jerry H. Bentley, *Old World Encounters: Cross-Cultural Contacts and Exchanges in Pre-Modern Times* (New York: Oxford University Press, 1993), 8.

lowed Christianity to continuously filter across the frontier, with the result that the Gothic Church was founded and framed in the context of exile. This migrant factor also helps to explain why the "Arian" element became a feature of Christianity among the Goths prior to settlement in Roman territory.

Immigrant Christianity in Gothic Lands

In 258 CE, a group of Thervingian Goths invaded Asia Minor and carried off large numbers of Christian captives (including clergy) from Sadagolthina, a village in the Roman province of Cappadocia.[70] It is likely that subsequent Gothic raids into Roman territory further increased the number of Christian captives settled in Gothic lands. These Roman captives continued to practice their Christian faith and won converts from among the Goths.[71] In time, the Gothic Church also "sent missionaries to their kinsmen, the Ostrogoths in the Ukraine and the Gepids in the mountains north of Transylvania, preaching the gospel and trying to win them to the faith."[72] Thompson asserts that these efforts met with little success, and he portrays the Christian community in Thervingian lands as an insignificant group "scattered up and down the country, a handful in this village and a handful in that."[73] This portrayal is consistent with his view that Gothic peoples remained predominantly pagan prior to settlement on Roman territory.

In any case, if Gothic converts "were few and far between,"[74] it was not due to a lack of evangelistic endeavor. Conversion to Christianity would have

---

70. Photius, *Epitome of the Ecclesiastical History of Philostorgius, Compiled by Photius, Patriarch of Constantinople*, trans. Edward Walford, book 2.5. Philostorgius was an Arian Christian from Cappadocia and a historian who lived in the fourth and fifth centuries. His work is no longer extant. What we have is an epitome of it compiled by Photius, who was appointed to the patriarchal see of Constantinople in 853, and under whom the schism between the Eastern and Western churches was formally consummated. See also Charles Archibald Anderson Scott, *Ulfilas, Apostle of the Goths, Together with an Account of the Gothic Churches and Their Decline* (Cambridge: Macmillan and Bowes, 1885), 21–22; Kenneth Scott Latourette, *The First Five Centuries*, vol. 1 of *A History of the Expansion of Christianity* (Grand Rapids: Zondervan, 1970), 107, 211.

71. Photius, *Epitome*, book 2.5.

72. Thompson, *Visigoths*, 96.

73. Thompson, *Visigoths*, 96.

74. Thompson, *Visigoths*, 83.

taken a tremendous act of courage, given the hostile conditions. The church in Gothic lands labored under major disadvantages. It was established by "displaced foreigners living under Gothic rule" and comprised a largely poor and subjugated minority that worshipped in tents.[75] Additionally, Gothic rulers associated Christianity with a foreign power (imperial Rome), and "outbreaks of anti-Christian persecution by the Gothic authorities in the fourth century coincided with periods of military hostilities between Goth[s] and Roman[s]."[76]

But the church among the Thervingian Goths was no foreign outpost of Roman Christianity. The deep animosity felt by Goths toward the Roman Empire makes it improbable that Goths converted to Christianity because they were attracted to Roman culture. The church conducted its services in the Gothic language and, opposition notwithstanding, there is no indication that Goths who became Christian ceased to be Goths. The strength of this immigrant initiative is best judged by successful cross-cultural transmission of the Christian message, formation of Christian community outside the structures of empire, and persistent efforts to spread the faith to fellow Goths under fairly adverse circumstances.

At the very least, the establishment of worshipping communities in Gothic lands introduced new religious strands into the sociopolitical environment and opened the way for sustained engagement between the Christian and indigenous religious life. Conditions of servitude did not preclude social contact. Captives and their descendants enjoyed some degree of social interaction with the dominant population. In addition to the close ties fostered by intermarriage, some may have had special skills or training that ensured incorporation into local structures. Even incidents of open hostility toward Christians by Gothic rulers hint at cross-cultural impact, considering that opposition to the minority religion by tribal nobility originally stemmed as much from security concerns as from an awareness that Christian beliefs contradicted or threatened indigenous religion.[77] Whatever the considerations involved—

75. Richard Fletcher, *The Barbarian Conversion: From Paganism to Christianity* (New York: Holt, 1997), 76; Thompson, *Visigoths*, 96.

76. Fletcher, *Barbarian Conversion*, 76.

77. See *The Passion of St. Saba the Goth*, in Heather and Matthews, *Goths in the Fourth Century*, 102–10. Saba, a Gothic Christian known for his piety, was tortured and drowned by Gothic tribal authorities for refusing to eat sacrificial meat. He pub-

and there is no way of knowing conclusively—conversions to Christianity validated the Christian message and implied some degree of negotiation and exchange between two religious systems.

Bishop Ulfila (ca. 311–ca. 383)—"Apostle of the Goths"[78]

Even if the Gothic Church mainly comprised immigrants, the appointment of a bishop (in the 340s) to serve it points to a well-established Christian community.[79] The bishop in question was Ulfila (or Wulfila or Ulfilas), the most celebrated figure of the Gothic Church, who led the fledgling Gothic Christian community for some four decades. Though the church grew in strength and visibility, there is no evidence that Ulfila's ministry produced mass conversions among the pagan Goths.[80] Indeed, such an outcome was unlikely given the fact that Goths associated Christianity with the Romans, a dreaded military adversary with whom they fought four major wars during Ulfila's lifetime. This has led some to question the designation "Apostle to the Goths," frequently applied to him. But Thompson reasons astutely that "conversion must not be studied simply or mainly as an episode in the life of the individual missionary but as an episode in the general history of the converted people."[81] Ulfila's massive contribution to Gothic Christianity is best assessed in relation to the migrant identity of the Gothic Church and the unique effects of his intercultural outlook.

Details of Ulfila's background and early life are tantalizingly sketchy.[82] He was a descendant of the Cappadocian captives seized by Goths in the third century and member of a Christian community in a predominantly

---

licly defied the requirement and declined the protection offered by the non-Christians in the village who made an effort to hide or protect their Christian neighbors.

78. Gibbon, *Decline and Fall of the Roman Empire*, book 3.37.

79. Thompson, *Visigoths*, xvii.

80. Not even St. Patrick, whose pioneering ministry contributed to mass baptisms, is believed to have been single-handedly responsible for the conversion of the Irish.

81. Thompson, *Visigoths*, 125.

82. The main sources for Ulfila's life are a fragment of a fourth-century letter written by his pupil, Auxentius, bishop of Durostorum (in present-day Bulgaria) that survived in the writings of the fifth-century "Arian" bishop Maximinus—see *The Letter of Auxentius*, in Heather and Matthews, *Goths in the Fourth Century*, 135–43—and Photius, *Epitome*.

pagan society. He was born about 311; his Gothic name (which means "Little Wolf") suggests that "the family intermarried with Goths."[83] It also hints at the possibility that he was of mixed race; and not being a pure-blooded Goth means "he would not have been a member of any clan."[84] Thompson surmises that he was "the offspring of a very humble, though not servile, family in Gothia." How or when Ulfila became a Christian is unknown. He emerges in the historical record as a leader and teacher within "the Pontic church in exile,"[85] a predominantly immigrant church that worshiped in the language of the dominant pagan society. His background and gifts—he was fluent in Greek, Latin, and Gothic—made him distinctively capable to conduct an intercultural ministry and preach the Christian message to Goths.

Was the Gothic Church "Arian"?

For reasons that are unclear, Ulfila was included in a diplomatic mission sent to Constantinople by the Thervingian ruler sometime during the reign of Constantine. While in Constantinople he was consecrated bishop "of the Christians in the Gothic land" by Eusebius of Nicodemia (d. 342), an adherent of the *homoian* creed. This important step, probably at the request of the Gothic Christian community, took place in either 337 or 341.[86] Among Gothic Christians, Ulfila "was the sole spiritual leader of his people, their only bishop . . . [with] no clerical colleagues of equal standing with himself."[87] In other words, his elevation increased not only his labors but the consequences of his decisions and actions for the life of the church. His consecration by a Roman bishop in the "Arian" segment of the Roman Church is the main basis for the claim that the Gothic Christianity was "Arian."

As our earlier discussion makes clear, the label "Arian" was bestowed on diverse groups in the Roman Empire who opposed the Nicene declaration regarding the Trinity, rejected each other's doctrine, and claimed no loyalty to

83. Fletcher, *Barbarian Conversion*, 73.

84. Thompson, *Visigoths*, 75.

85. Andrew F. Walls, "Mission and Migration: The Diaspora Factor in Christian History," *Journal of African Christian Thought* 5, no. 2 (2002): 5.

86. See Thompson, *Visigoths*, xiv–xvii; also Parvis, "Was Ulfila Really a Homoian?," 54–56.

87. Thompson, *Visigoths*, 111. According to Thompson, the local Arian communities in Gothia "were led by presbyters."

Arius. Thus, applying the term "Arian" to the Gothic Church is problematic and unhelpful, since the label came to signify opposition to "catholic" orthodoxy and says little about how the Gothic Christians might have understood their Christian identity. Given the complexities of the Arian controversy, a more precise understanding of the particular set of beliefs that took root among Gothic Christians is called for.

While the centrality of migration to the rise of Gothic Christianity is unquestionable, the theological roots of the Gothic Church are less clear. The Christian migrants (including priests) who founded the church in Gothic lands were captured from Cappadocia in 258, long before the rise of the Arian controversy. This migrant Christian community, from whom Ulfila himself descended, was therefore neither "Arian" nor "Nicene." In the late 320s, however, a vibrant community developed around the exiled Arius in the South Danube region (a major intersection for migrant movement between the Roman Empire and Gothic lands); and some speculate that a youthful Ulfila may well have been aware of or found this migrant Arian community attractive.[88] At the same time, a bishop of Gothia, named Theophilus, was among the signatories at the Council of Nicaea in 325 (suggesting acceptance of the Nicene declaration among Gothic Christians), though little is known of him.[89]

The available record on Ulfila's associations and doctrinal beliefs provides better insight into his theological orientation and the religious character of the Gothic Church that he presided over and shaped for four decades. The scholarly consensus, based on this record (which is by no means incontrovertible), is that Ulfila subscribed to the *homoian* doctrine.[90] His associations appear to support this inference: he is consecrated bishop by Eusebius of Nicodemia, who is identified with the *homoian* position; he was present at the Synod of Sirmium (357), where some believe the *homoian* creed was first defined, and attended the Synod of Constantinople (held in 360) that produced the *homoian* declaration (though there is some suggestion that he was a reluctant backer); and he developed strong ties to the emperor Constantius II, a *homoian* advocate, who welcomed him and his refugee Christian flock into the Roman Empire (see "Bishop in Exile" below).

88. Parvis, "Was Ulfila Really a Homoian?," 58.
89. Wiles, *Archetypal Heresy*, 41; Parvis, "Was Ulfila Really a Homoian?," 56–57.
90. See Heather and Matthews, *Goths in the Fourth Century*, 130–31; Wiles, *Archetypal Heresy*, 42; Schäferdiek, "Ulfila," 45–47.

Ulfila's actual beliefs are portrayed in a fourth-century letter by his pupil Auxentius.[91] The letter makes no reference to a *homoian* doctrine (the term is of modern coinage); but it provides some support for the claim that Ulfila was of a *homoian* persuasion. Three strands stand out: belief in the strict differentiation between the persons of the Trinity (the Son is God, but begotten); insistence that his views are based on the authority of Scripture (a dig at the adoption of the "substance" language); and his vociferous denunciation of the *homousians* and *homoiousians* (who proclaim persons of the Godhead as "same" or "similar" in substance, respectively) as Antichrists and heretics.

Not all scholars are convinced by this argument. Sarah Parvis disputes the *homoian* claim on four counts: that the term *homoian* is a modern invention; that Ulfila's ecclesiastical alliances were not sufficiently well developed to support the assertion that he identified with a particular group; that his "terminology is closer to that of the early supporters of Arius (including Arius himself) than it is to the homoian creed of 360"; that the authors of the extant material on Ulfila, Auxentius and Philostorgius, were *anomoians* (or neo-Arians), a group that emphasized the created status of the Son.[92] These arguments are insightful but not compelling. *Anomoian* (like *homoian*) is also a twentieth-century construction; and the view that *anomoians* espoused a theology that was consciously based on the teaching of Arius is contested.[93] The teachings of Ulfila, depicted in Auxentius's letter, arguably lean more to the *homoian* than the more rigid *anomoian* doctrine.[94] The insistence that Ulfila remained faithful to Arius's teachings puts undue emphasis on influences that purportedly date to his youth (based on a conjecture that he encountered the early Arian community). This ignores the complex theological developments generated by the Arian controversy and minimizes the possibility that Ulfila's own views became more fully formed with the passage of time in a context of ministry far removed from divisive debates of Constantinople or Milan.

Perhaps the most that can be said is that Ulfila and the Gothic Church he led were non-Nicene, and that they adopted a distinctive Christian identity

---

91. Cf. *The Letter of Auxentius*, in Heather and Matthews, *Goths in the Fourth Century*, 135–43.

92. See Parvis, "Was Ulfila Really a Homoian?," 49–65.

93. See Wiles, *Archetypal Heresy*, 31–32.

94. Wiles, *Archetypal Heresy*, 43–44; Schäferdiek, "Ulfila," 45, 47.

shaped by both Roman and Gothic ingredients.[95] In what follows I use the term "Arian" as synonymous with "non-Nicene."

Bishop in Exile

Seven years into Ulfila's episcopate (ca. 348), the first full-blown persecution of Christians by Gothic rulers resulted in the martyrdom of many men and women. Ulfila and sizeable numbers of his Arian Christian community fled Gothic rule and crossed into Roman provinces. Not all the Gothic Christians left. Saba, mentioned above, was martyred in a subsequent wave of persecutions (369–372) that followed military defeat by the Romans. Meanwhile, the Gothic Arian refugees were welcomed by Emperor Constantius II and settled near the city of Nicopolis in Moesia (present-day Bulgaria). Arianism was still tolerated within the empire and Ulfila ministered as a bishop to his migrant flock for the next thirty-three years. It is a credit to his stature that his teaching ministry also extended to "Arian" Roman inhabitants of the Roman provinces.[96]

Ulfila spent the rest of his life in exile, as bishop of "a new Christian nation arising from a small-scale and quite involuntary migration."[97] Gothic Christians were viewed as outsiders by both the "Arian" and "catholic" communities within the Roman Empire.[98] Thus, even though Ulfila was recognized by Arian Roman inhabitants, he would arguably have been even more conscious of being a migrant-outsider while on Roman territory where he was undoubtedly viewed strictly as a Goth. He also became more fully a transnational leader, whose ministry was conducted in the intersection of cultures and greatly dependent on his linguistic gifts. At some point in exile, he embarked on the laborious task of translating the Bible into Gothic from Greek and Latin, a "vast undertaking that may well have occupied the entire forty years of his bishopric."[99] Since the Goths as a people were still pagan, this radical idea reflected a distinctly missionary commitment, one possibly fomented in the exigencies of migrant existence. As medieval historian

95. Cf. Wiles, *Archetypal Heresy*, 46–51; Schäferdiek, "Ulfila," 48.
96. Thompson, *Visigoths*, 117–18.
97. Walls, "Mission and Migration," 5.
98. Cf. Wiles, *Archetypal Heresy*, 49–50.
99. Thompson, *Visigoths*, xxii.

Richard Fletcher put it: "To no one had the notion occurred of translating the scriptures into a barbarian tongue which had never been written down before. Perhaps, as is often the case with simple but revolutionary and liberating ideas, it could only have come to one who was himself in some sense an outsider."[100]

Ulfila also produced material for his fellow clerics (in Greek, Latin, and Gothic), as part of an immense effort to support "those who proposed to study and preach from the translation of the Bible."[101] But the translation of the Bible into Gothic was his greatest achievement. In order to reduce the Gothic language to written form, he first had to compose a new alphabet of twenty-four letters, four of which he invented in order "to express the peculiar sounds of the Gothic language that were absent from Greek and Latin."[102] It is also well known that he omitted the books of Kings because he feared that the tales of military exploits would only fuel the passions of the Gothic tribes who "were especially fond of war."[103] In this Gothic translation, the word "sinner" is rendered "outcast" or "wanderer," presumably because "in the age and among the tribes, where every stranger was a foe, the simplest and the worst punishment an injured community could inflict was to drive the offender from their midst. Such a person became a wanderer on the face of the earth."[104] What proportion of the Goths were literate in the fourth century is uncertain;[105] but vernacular translation granted them better access to the truths of the Christian faith and added impetus to the spread of the gospel among the Germanic tribes.

After a long period of tolerance by Roman emperors, the tide turned against Arianism. In February 380, Theodosius I issued an edict against "Arian" heresies and all Arian churches were confiscated and handed over to Catholics. Ulfila was summoned to a council in Rome but fell ill and died there (ca. 381). By then, devastating attacks by the Huns (in 376) forced large

---

100. Fletcher, *Barbarian Conversion*, 77. On Ulfila's principles of translation, see Heather and Matthews, *Goths in the Fourth Century*, 145–62.

101. Thompson reports that some of his works perished when the Gothic king Reccared converted to Catholicism in 589 and "ordered all Arian books to be surrendered and burned." Thompson, *Visigoths*, 116.

102. Gibbon, *Decline and Fall of the Roman Empire*, book 3.37.

103. Photius, *Epitome* book 2.5.

104. Scott, *Ulfilas*, 135–36.

105. Thompson, *Visigoths*, 32.

numbers of Goths to cross the Danube River and seek refuge in the Roman Empire. Ill-treatment by the Romans provoked Gothic reactions that escalated into war in 378. The Goths defeated the Roman army, devastated the Dacia provinces, and killed the Roman emperor Valens. They then wandered about for four more years before Theodosius I settled them in Moesia (where they joined the earlier migrants led by Ulfila) and gave them federate status. Under this arrangement the Goths were required to defend the frontier in exchange for land. They also "became the first barbarian people to be accepted into the Empire *en bloc* and provided with land there by the imperial authorities."[106] It was during this period (382–395) that Goths converted to Arian Christianity in great numbers.

Why the Goths embraced Arian Christianity, at a time when it was proscribed (and certainly no longer common) in the Roman Empire, is a troublesome question. Such a move undermines the claim that Gothic conversion to Christianity took place after settlement on Roman territory because of the desire (or need) to emulate Roman structures and practices. Thompson advances three conjectural explanations for Gothic embrace of the "Arian" form of Christianity.[107] First, that the hierarchical understanding of the Trinity in Arianism "was readily comprehensible and acceptable to the tribesmen" whose social system required "the unqualified obedience of the lower members of it to the higher." Second, that acceptance of Catholicism would have meant incorporation into the organization of the Catholic Church "which in Theodosius' reign they would not all have cared to do, nor, if they had, would their followers have been likely to acquiesce in their action." Third, unlike Catholicism, the more decentralized ecclesiastical system of Arianism, which comprised "a number of essentially separate, local and independent churches . . . [was] more suited organizationally to a people who wished to preserve their social identity within the Roman empire."[108]

These explanations have merit; but Thompson omits an even more obvious

---

106. Thompson, *Visigoths*, v.
107. Thompson, *Visigoths*, 109–13.
108. Thompson adds that during Ulfila's time the structure (among Arians and Catholics alike) "was based on the hierarchical Roman practice" (Thompson, *Visigoths*, 110). Others also affirm that the Germanic kings "must have perceived some advantage in it relating to their public life to have been so determined to retain a faith pronounced heretical by the Roman clergy who monopolized religious governance in their newly acquired lands." Jo Ann McNamara, John E. Halborg, and E. Gordon

possibility: namely, the enduring influence and significance of the Christian community long formed by migrants in Gothic lands. His evident reluctance to give Ulfila much credit perhaps explains this, though his evaluation of the Gothic bishop has inconsistencies. For example, he insists that Gothic conversion in the years immediately following Ulfila's death had little to do with his "reputation and prestige," since Ulfila's influence was confined to the Christian communities and did not extend to Gothic leaders.[109] Yet, he accepts that Ulfila probably left behind "an active and able school of clerics who must have gone among the [Gothic leaders] in Moesia in 382–95 so as to explain to them the tenets of 'Arian' Christianity and to instruct them in the faith."[110] Thus, he allows, the conversion of the Goths "would scarcely have been achieved, at any rate in the form which it actually took, had it not been for [Ulfila's] preliminary work."[111]

Ulfila's monumental labor (including the production of a Gothic Bible and other material for Christian ministry) nurtured and shaped the Gothic Arian community—a community that provided the most intimate and credible exemplar of Christianity for potential Gothic converts. Under his leadership, Gothic Christians adapted their faith to Gothic culture, enshrined Christian practice in vernacular idiom, and established an independent Gothic church free from Roman control or domination. There is no indication that any of these developments were compromised after settlement on Roman soil. In exile, the Gothic Arian church had its own native clergy, was separate in language and organization, and was independent of the structures and religion of empire. So, while the "Apostle of the Goths" may not have played a direct role in the conversion of the majority of Goths to the Christian faith, his labor and legacy laid an indispensable foundation.

Thus it is strikingly odd that Thompson overlooks the importance of this older "Arian" community in the conversion of the larger group. Admittedly, the large-scale Gothic migration in the 380s disrupted the tribal structures

---

Whatley, *Sainted Women of the Dark Ages* (Durham, NC: Duke University Press, 1992), 38.

109. Thompson, *Visigoths*, 107. One could argue that Ulfila's inclusion (at the behest of the Gothic ruler) in a diplomatic mission to Constantinople in the early 340s suggests, at the very least, that he was held in some esteem by the ruling class even before he became bishop.

110. Thompson, *Visigoths*, 118.

111. Thompson, *Visigoths*, 119.

that underpinned ancestral religion and no doubt engendered greater receptivity to change. But, in the 380s, the war of 378 triggered by the brutalization of the Goths by Romans (after decades of hostility between the two groups) was still a fresh memory. So, the claim that Gothic conversion to Arianism (a faith outlawed by Roman authorities) was motivated by a desire among tribal nobility to emulate the ways of Romans is unconvincing. Far more crucial, the Gothic population that resettled in Moesia in 382 and converted to Christianity in large numbers did not do so in isolation. They joined a previously settled Gothic population that included the "Arian" Christian community led by Ulfila for over forty years, a group that had once lived among them as Christian migrants and maintained a distinctive Gothic Christian identity as refugees on Roman territory.

It is not unreasonable to assume that the encounter with an acculturated Gothic church (a powerful symbol of Gothicism) on Roman soil, following the traumatic experience of large-scale dislocation, was a significant factor in the Gothic conversions of the 380s and 390s. At the very least, the faith and practice of this long-standing Gothic Christian community, previously rejected as a foreign incursion into traditional Gothic existence, would have looked very different to Goths who were now migrant-outsiders themselves. If the structures of empire factored at all in this religious transformation, it was a matter of rejection rather than emulation.

Over the next two centuries, Gothic Christians were constantly on the move, "worshipping in tents or on wagons" as they traveled through the western European world to Italy, Gaul, and Spain. The "Arian" Christianity of the Goths eventually collapsed when the Gothic king Reccared converted to Catholicism in 589—perhaps further indication that Gothic Christianity was rooted less in doctrinal distinctiveness than in "the social role of a shared faith."[112]

In the event, the story of how the Goths turned to Christianity provides important glimpses into the role of migration in the global spread of the Christian movement in the first millennium. As was the case with the Goths, the spread of Christianity among the peoples of Europe took place against a backdrop of widespread invasions, population resettlement, seizure of Christian captives, piracy and pillage, expulsion or exile, expanding trade

---

112. Wiles, *Archetypal Heresy*, 50.

networks (connecting Scandinavia, eastern Europe, and the Arab world[113]), and extensive intertribal warfare (see chapter 7). Similarly, in many parts of Europe the dissemination of Christian ideas and practices to non-Christian populations began long before the arrival of official missionaries or formal efforts at Christianization.

But long before the centuries-long and hugely complex process of converting the pagan populations of Europe got under way—with Christian monarchs playing an increasingly central role—the eastward spread of Christianity into Persia, central Asia, and beyond was well underway. By the time the Frankish king Clovis I (ca. 466–511) converted to Christianity in the late fifth century, a major turning point in the conversion of Europe, the East Syrian Christian community in Persia numbered tens of thousands and constituted a full-fledged church, with scores of bishops and its own patriarch (or catholicos). In both contexts, the link between large-scale migrations, resettlement, and Christian missionary action is strongly evident. But the political realities and social conditions that framed the spread and establishment of the Christian faith were radically different.

113. See Anders Winroth, *The Conversion of Scandinavia: Vikings, Merchants, and Missionaries in the Remaking of Northern Europe* (New Haven: Yale University Press, 2012), 85–101.

CHAPTER SIX

Minority Report: From the Church in Persia to the Persian Church

The Christians are destroying our teaching. They are teaching people to serve only one God, not to worship the sun, not to honor fire, to defile the waters with despicable ablutions, not to marry women, not to produce sons or daughters, not to enter battle with the kings, not to kill, to slaughter and eat animals without murmuring [the ritual prayers], and to bury and to conceal the dead in the earth. . . .

—Martyrdom of Aqebshma

Unlike the western (or northern) frontier, which was bordered by loosely organized tribes and formless states, the eastern frontier of the Roman Empire adjoined highly developed urban civilizations—successively the Greek, Parthian, and Persian Empires. Yet, the eastern border was also indeterminate. Scholars variously identify the boundary as lying along "the course of the Euphrates River," following the Khabur and Nymphios Rivers, or running "from the Pontic shore to the Red Sea."[1] Samuel Moffett's contention that this was a political and cultural division perhaps reflects an overtly Christian perspective with its primary focus on an East-West ecclesiastical dynamic. In reality, political limits did not align neatly with cultural demarcation. Inhabitants of

---

1. C. R. Whittaker, *Frontiers of the Roman Empire: A Social and Economic Study* (Baltimore: Johns Hopkins University Press, 1994), 49–59. See also A. D. Lee, *Information and Frontiers: Roman Foreign Relations in Late Antiquity* (New York: Cambridge University Press, 2006), 49–66; Samuel H. Moffett, *A History of Christianity in Asia: Beginnings to 1500*, vol. 1 (Maryknoll, NY: Orbis Books, 1998), 7; J. A. S. Evans, *The Age of Justinian: The Circumstances of Imperial Power* (New York: Routledge, 1996).

the two empires did not face each other across accepted or administratively enforced boundaries. To reiterate, frontier regions were marked by unmanageable migrant flows as well as great linguistic, ethnic, and religious diversity.[2] The multiplicity of peoples and extensive interactions in the border zone produced cultures and identities that were mutable, overlapping, and adaptive.

This state of affairs did not preclude zones of homogeneity. Quite often substantial populations at the meeting point of imperial domains shared the same ethnicity or even a common faith. Sizeable communities of Christians and Jews straddled the Roman-Persian frontier; and, while a large variety of languages and dialects (including Greek) were used, Aramaic served as a lingua franca, only being replaced by Arabic after 637.[3] In particular, Syriac (an Aramaic dialect) was "the language of the whole Syrian and Mesopotamian world," providing a lubricating ingredient that facilitated trade and made communication and countless transactions between vastly diverse populations possible.[4] Syriac was also common in Sassanid Persia and usage spread as far as India and China with Christian missionaries.

The permeability of the Roman-Persian border and the demographic mosaic created by cross-border movements also rendered the distinction between citizen and foreigner, intruder and inhabitant, native and outsider quite fluid. Located as it was at the intersection of ancient civilizations and major centers of global commerce, the western frontier region (to take the Persian point of view) was a strategic hub of multidirectional movement and transnational exchange awash with migrants of all stripes: merchants, slaves, couriers, government officials, missionaries, refugees, captives, pilgrims, holy men and women, nomads, and more. But travel linked to religion or commerce accounted for the largest numbers of individuals crossing and recrossing the boundary between the two empires.[5] More to the point, such cross-border movement involved large numbers of Christians.

---

2. Whittaker, *Frontiers of the Roman Empire*, 75–78, 228–31; Lee, *Information and Frontiers*, 50–51, 66–71.

3. Aramaic was "widely spoken along the eastern coast of the Mediterranean and spread throughout the Middle East." Michael C. Howard, *Transnationalism in Ancient and Medieval Societies: The Role of Cross-Border Trade and Travel* (Jefferson, NC: McFarland, 2012), 23.

4. Moffett, *Christianity in Asia*, 74. See also Lee, *Information and Frontiers*, 50.

5. Lee, *Information and Frontiers*, 65; also Maribel Dietz, *Wandering Monks, Vir-*

This was because there were more Christians on *both sides* of the border than either Jews or Zoroastrians; and many of these Christian communities shared a common heritage that encouraged networks of communication. The exchange of letters and official documents between Christian leaders in Persian and Roman domains put large numbers of clerics on the road, some acting as official envoys or letter carriers.[6] Throngs of Persian Christians also traveled to Roman territory to visit holy sites, consult famous ascetics, or sojourn at centers of learning. Additionally, Christians on both sides of the border frequently embarked on long-distance travel for missionary activity. Added to these hordes of migrant travelers were tens of thousands of captives, refugees, and exiles, for some of whom the frontier region served as both a haven from religious oppression and fertile ground for missionary activity.

The story of Jacob Baradeus or Yaqub al-Barada'i (d. 578), the Syrian ascetic and Monophysite metropolitan of Edessa, is illustrative. Baradeus was consecrated bishop in 542, under the auspices of the Byzantine empress Theodora (500–548), a convinced Monophysite.[7] However, her husband, the emperor Justinian (482–565), was a staunch defender of Chalcedonian orthodoxy who had launched fierce persecution against Monophysites after his accession. Despite patronage by Theodora, who acted independently of her husband, Monophysite Christians and prelates were exiled from every large city by Byzantine authorities.[8] Baradeus spent over thirty-five years (from 542 to 578) in nomadic existence in the frontier region having to constantly evade imperial soldiers and spies.[9] His evangelistic, teaching, and pastoral

---

gins, and Pilgrims: Ascetic Travel in the Mediterranean World, A.D. 300/800 (University Park: Pennsylvania State University Press, 2005), 24.

6. Lee, *Information and Frontiers*, 56–78.

7. Theodora had received a request for "Monophysite missionary bishops" from the king of the Ghassanid Arabs, Harith ibn Jabadah, who "served Byzantine Rome as military governor of the provinces of eastern Syria." Moffett, *Christianity in Asia*, 245–47. In response, Theodora secretly had Baradeus and another monk, Theodore of Arabia, consecrated bishops. Theodore, an Arab, became a nomadic bishop among the Arab Ghassanids in Bostra, capital of the Roman province of Arabia. For more details, see Evans, *Age of Justinian*, 102–12, 185–86.

8. De Lacy O'Leary, *The Syriac Church and Fathers* (Piscataway, NJ: Gorgias, 2002), 119.

9. Evans, *Age of Justinian*, 185–86; Moffett, *Christianity in Asia*, 245; Jeanne-Nicole Mellon Saint-Laurent, *Missionary Stories and the Formation of the Syriac Churches* (Oakland: University of California Press, 2015), 98. The name Baradeus is

activities extended from Constantinople to the Persian border and as far as Egypt.[10] He is credited with ordaining twenty-seven metropolitan bishops and 100,000 priests! The wide-ranging ministry of this refugee bishop revived the movement and galvanized a host of Monophysite clergy, monasteries, and congregations that formed the Jacobite (or West Syrian) Orthodox Church. By 600, Jacobite churches "were found from the Aegean Sea to Armenia and across the border into Persian territory."[11]

EASTWARD CHRISTIAN MOVEMENT BEYOND ROMAN FRONTIERS

Just as in other parts of the world, as we have seen already, full understanding of the establishment of the church in Asia in the first and second centuries is beyond reach. The mists of tradition and the meager and contradictory accounts in the historical record, not to mention the inchoateness of Christian life and identity, all stand firmly in the way of meaningful recovery of the role of all but a few individuals. Still, what little evidence there is points to tantalizing possibilities. To start with, in contrast to the northern border of the Roman Empire, where significant Christian movement prior to the third century seems unlikely, there is high probability to near certainty that the Christian faith spread beyond the eastern frontier of the Roman Empire in the first generation.

In Acts chapter 2, those who heard and responded to the Christian message at the Pentecost event included Jews from Parthia, Media, and Elam (all provinces of the Parthian Empire). Whether they were included among those "who accepted [the] message" is unstated. But their presence confirms regular movement between the two domains and hints at the role of regular migrants in the early transmission of the Christian message. (It is difficult to imagine, unless one doubts its historicity, that those who witnessed this extraordinary event would have remained silent about it after they returned to their home-

---

derived from the nickname Barada'i (meaning "the patchwork man" or "man in rags") because he disguised himself as a beggar.

10. The scope of his travels and ministry led to the title "ecumenical metropolitan." John Binns, *An Introduction to the Christian Orthodox Churches* (Cambridge: Cambridge University Press, 2002), 147.

11. Dale T. Irvin and Scott Sunquist, *History of the World Christian Movement*, vol. 1, *Earliest Christianity to 1453* (Maryknoll, NY: Orbis Books, 2001), 249.

lands, whether they embraced the new faith or not.) In any case, the origins of the Jesus movement in the Asian region of the Roman Empire—that is, close to the eastern frontier—and the increase in the volume of trade between the Roman Empire and the Far East from the first century CE clearly favor early Christian expansion eastward.[12]

In addition to the well-known and enduring tradition that the apostle Thomas took the gospel to India (or, alternatively, to Parthia),[13] the earliest accounts of the establishment of Christianity in the east beyond the Roman Empire identify two major centers: Edessa (capital of the Kingdom of Osrhoene in eastern Syria) and Arbela (capital of the small border kingdom of Adiabene in Mesopotamia).[14] Tradition attributes the founding of the church in Edessa to Thaddeus, one of the seventy disciples mentioned in Luke 10, who subsequently sent two of his disciples to evangelize Arbela.[15] The capitals of the two border kingdoms, Edessa (today Urfa, Turkey) and Arbela (modern Erbîl in Iraq), emerged as centers of Christian growth by the end of the second century. Edessa became home to the first known church in Asia beyond the borders of the Roman Empire; and Osrhoene is celebrated as one of the earliest Christian kingdoms. The two areas also produced "Asia's first theologians":[16] Bardaisan (154–222), a philosopher born in Edessa to Persian migrants, and Tatian (120–180), a biblical scholar and student of Justin Martyr whose translation of the four gospels into Syriac spurred the spread of Christianity into the Asian countryside.

Under Parthian rulers, who allowed the practice of all faiths,[17] these flourishing Christianity centers beyond the Roman border provided refuge to large numbers of Christians fleeing persecution by Roman authorities. In 225 when Parthian rule ended with the rise of the Sassanian (or Sassanid) Dynasty, there were

12. Richard L. Smith, *Premodern Trade in World History* (New York: Routledge, 2008), 88–89. The role of Christian merchants in this expansive eastward movement is covered in chapter 8.

13. For an evaluation of the historicity of this tradition, see Moffett, *Christianity in Asia*, 29–36.

14. For a full account see Moffett, *Christianity in Asia*, 46–80.

15. Moffett, *Christianity in Asia*, 46–50, 57, 70; Kenneth Scott Latourette, *The First Five Centuries*, vol. 1 of *A History of the Expansion of Christianity* (Grand Rapids: Zondervan, 1970), 101.

16. Moffett, *Christianity in Asia*, 64–69, 72–77.

17. Howard, *Transnationalism in Ancient and Medieval Societies*, 44–45.

more than twenty bishoprics in the Tigris-Euphrates valley and on the borders of Persia.[18] By then, writes Moffett, Syrian Christians had carried the faith not just across the eastern frontiers of the Roman Empire but into Persia and "towards the steppes of the central Asiatic nomads and the edges of the Hindu Kush."[19] But within Persia itself Christians comprised small groups of mainly foreign migrants or non-Persians. Growth was slow. The church in Seleucia-Ctesiphon, capital of the Persian Empire and one of the largest cities in the world,[20] only gained its first bishop around 280. However, the intensification of conflict between Rome and the Sassanian rulers from the third to fifth centuries produced extensive migrant movements that bolstered the Christian population in Persia.

MIGRATION AND THE FORMATION OF PERSIAN CHRISTIANITY

At its greatest extent, the Sassanian Empire (224–651) stretched from the Euphrates River to the Indus River (in present-day Pakistan), incorporating Armenia and parts of Syria. The Sassanian rulers, who took the title of *Shāhanshāh* (King of Kings)—usually shortened to "shah"—claimed descent from the royal line of Medes and Persians and referred to their empire as *Erānshahr (Iranshæhr)*, meaning "Dominion of the Iranians (Aryans)."[21] They were determined to restore the glories of ancient Persia,[22] which meant winning back territory beyond their western frontier in Roman domains. Competi-

18. Latourette, *First Five Centuries*, 103.

19. Moffett, *Christianity in Asia*, 80.

20. Only Rome and Alexandria were larger. See Howard, *Transnationalism in Ancient and Medieval Societies*, 44.

21. Gianpaolo Savoia-Vizzini, "Iranian History: The Sasanian Dynasty," *The Circle of Ancient Iranian Studies* (2000). In most sources the names "Persia" and "Iran" are used interchangeably. Throughout this volume (except when quoting sources), I have used the name "Persia" rather than "Iran" to avoid confusion with the modern nation-state, which, though directly descended from ancient Persia, is territorially smaller. As Savoia-Vizzini notes, the Sassanian domain encompassed not only "all of today's mainland Iran" but also "Iraq, Armenia, Arran (also known as the republic of Azerbaijan), Georgia, Turkmenistan, Uzbekistan, Tajikistan, Afghanistan, UAE, Oman, Yemen, Bahrain, Kuwait, as well as eastern parts of Turkey, and parts of Syria and Pakistan."

22. Cf. Michael H. Dodgeon and Samuel N. C. Lieu, eds., *The Roman Eastern Frontier and the Persian Wars (AD 226–363): A Documentary History* (New York: Routledge, 1991), 16.

tion between the Roman and Sassanian powers for political control of the strategically located (and dominantly Christian) Armenia also fueled lasting hostilities.[23] Cities in Syria and Mesopotamia repeatedly changed hands.[24] For centuries, the strategic city of Edessa came alternately under the sway of one or the other of the two powers, though it remained largely within Persia's cultural orbit. In a predictable cycle, Persian invasions and territorial seizure inevitably provoked retaliatory Roman military action; and each power in turn extracted tactical concessions from the other. The demise of the Western Roman Empire in the fifth century left the Eastern Roman (Byzantine) Empire as Persia's main political adversary. In the long run, however, neither imperial power gained complete ascendancy. But Persian Christianity was a beneficiary of the numerous wars that roiled the wider region, its growth a by-product of the (ultimately futile) ambitions of rival imperial powers.

In this case, the structures of empire are integral to the story; but so are migrant movements and initiatives by ordinary people or nonstate actors. For one thing, the flow of human traffic between the two domains continued largely unabated throughout the centuries of Roman-Persian conflict.[25] Large-scale warfare intensified migration. Huge armies need provisions and large supplies of food, so their deployment invariably increased the volume of cross-border trade. Furthermore, military conflicts inevitably triggered a dramatic rise in the numbers of slaves, refugees, fugitives, evacuees, and defectors; and the extradition of prisoners or detainees added significantly to population transfer. The Christian element in these relentless migrations was substantial. The movement of Armenian Christians, Monophysite refugees, and Christian merchant communities all augmented the growth of Persian Christianity, deportees even more so. In the wake of military campaigns and invasions, Persian rulers frequently deported great numbers of captives from the eastern region of the Roman Empire (and also from Armenia)—areas with large Christian populations—into their own domains.[26]

---

23. Armenia was partitioned between the two powers in the fourth century but remained mainly under Persian control. Evans, *Age of Justinian*, 91.

24. For a succinct summary of Roman-Persian hostilities up to the reign of Constantine I, see Dodgeon and Lieu, *Roman Eastern Frontier*, 1–4.

25. See Whittaker, *Frontiers of the Roman Empire*, 141–43, 228–29; Smith, *Premodern Trade in World History*, 79.

26. Latourette, *First Five Centuries*, 227.

Crucially, the declining Western Roman Empire was vulnerable to Persian onslaught. Around 260 CE, the Persian ruler or shah Shāpur I (d. 272) invaded Roman territories for the third time in his reign. Antioch (the metropolis of Syria and a major Christian center) fell to the invading armies, and other major cities in the eastern provinces of the Roman Empire were laid waste. The Roman emperor Valerian was captured along with some 70,000 Roman soldiers.[27] When he finally returned to Persia, the shah also took with him a multitude of prisoners. Persian annals declare:

> On this third campaign . . . , we led away into captivity men from the empire of the Romans, non-Iranians, and settled them into our empire of Iranians, in Persia, in Parthia . . . , and in every other nation where our own and our fathers' and our forefathers' foundations were.[28]

The foreign deportees included many skilled individuals such as architects, engineers, craftsmen, and technicians.[29] A great number were also Christians,[30] including "priests who had been taken prisoner at Antioch."[31] Shāpur I built three towns to accommodate the large captive population and provided them "with homes and lands to till."[32] Such favorable treatment is illustrative of the impact of Persian-Roman hostility on the fortunes of Christianity in the Persian realm even before the conversion of Constantine. In the centuries when Christians faced persecution by Roman authorities, Persian rulers were fully disposed to treat them favorably.[33]

The religious dimension of this geopolitical rivalry also proved crucial

27. This calamity sent shock waves throughout the empire and inspired the rise of soldier-emperors considered better equipped to deal with the foreign threat.

28. Dodgeon and Lieu, *Roman Eastern Frontier*, 57.

29. Irene M. Franck and David M. Brownstone, *The Silk Road: A History* (New York: Facts on File, 1986), 145.

30. Christian communities were heavily concentrated in the eastern provinces of the Roman empire, accounting for perhaps up to 50 percent of the population in Asia Minor, so the proportion of Christians among these captives would have been fairly high. See Walter Woodburn Hyde, *Paganism to Christianity in the Roman Empire* (Philadelphia: University of Pennsylvania Press, 1946), 180.

31. *Chronicles of Se'ert* 2, in Dodgeon and Lieu, *Roman Eastern Frontier*, 297.

32. *Chronicles of Se'ert* 2, in Dodgeon and Lieu, *Roman Eastern Frontier*, 297.

33. Cf. S. P. Brock, "Christians in the Sasanian Empire: A Case of Divided Loyalties," in *Religion and National Identity*, ed. Stuart Mews (Oxford: Blackwell, 1982), 7.

in the long run. In an effort to unify their diverse and geographically extensive empire, the Sassanian rulers reinstituted and promoted Zoroastrianism (an ancient belief system over 1,200 years old).[34] Ardashir I, founder of the Sassanian Dynasty, was himself a Magian (or Magi, as the high priests of the Zoroastrian religion were known).[35] The subsequent elevation of Christianity as the official religion of the Roman Empire meant that competing religious systems became central to the imperial vision of the rival powers. The reinstitution of Zoroastrianism as the national religion of the Persian realm under the Sassanid Dynasty did not automatically translate into a policy of antagonism to other faiths. Recent scholarship, in fact, is inclined to stress the inherent tolerance of the Zoroastrian system. In the long run, however, the emergence of Christianity as the state religion of the Roman Empire, and promoted as such by Roman emperors, inserted a layer of deep religious discord into Roman-Persian hostilities.

Whereas the adoption and endorsement of Christianity by Constantine and his successors brought unprecedented advantages to Christians in the Roman Empire, for Christians in Persia the same development presaged major disadvantages and misfortune. Constantine's letter to the Persian ruler (ca. 315), commending Christian believers to the shah's care and protection,[36] possibly overestimated a Roman emperor's ability to influence internal Persian policy. But, even if Christians could not yet be identified "as agents of Rome," it would be odd indeed if, as Payne claims, such a letter failed to impress on the Persian court that Christianity was a largely Roman phenomenon.[37] In any case, the association did little to improve the fortunes of Christians in Persia. Sharing the faith of Persia's bitter adversary made Persian Christians—certainly those who were high-ranking officials or otherwise visible to Persian authorities—vulnerable to suspicion and accusations of political

34. Richard E. Payne, *A State of Mixture: Christians, Zoroastrians, and Iranian Political Culture in Late Antiquity* (Oakland: University of California Press, 2015), 6.

35. Dodgeon and Lieu, *Roman Eastern Frontier*, 10.

36. Eusebius, *Life of Constantine*, 4.9–13, trans. Ernest Cushing Richardson, in *Nicene and Post-Nicene Fathers, Second Series*, vol. 1, ed. Philip Schaff and Henry Wace (Buffalo, NY: Christian Literature Publishing, 1890).

37. Payne, *State of Mixture*, 39. There are no grounds to reject Eusebius's claim that, by then, "there were many churches of God in Persia, and . . . large numbers there were gathered into the fold of Christ." Eusebius, *Life of Constantine*, 4.8.

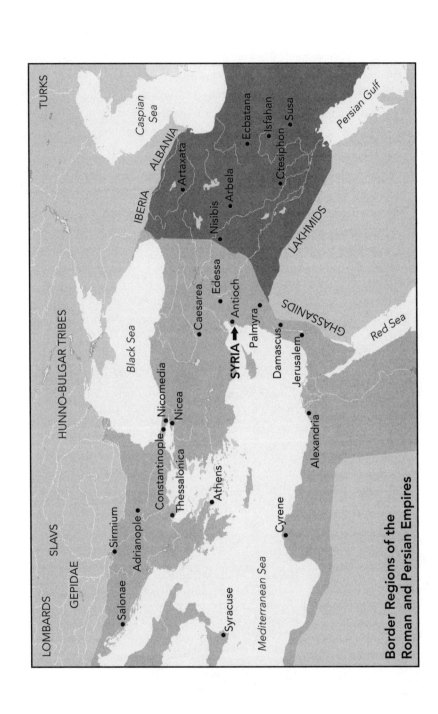

Border Regions of the Roman and Persian Empires

disloyalty.[38] Anyhow, widespread violence against Christians coincided with periods of intense conflict between the two empires—conspicuously so in the fourth century when the Persian Empire entered its golden age with the rise of Shāpur II (309–379), whose hostility to Christian believers was evidently shaped by political considerations. An imperial order (preserved in the annals of the afflicted church) categorically stated:

> the people of the Nazarenes . . . live in our territory [but] share the sentiments of Caesar our enemy.[39]

In three successive wars with the Romans, Shāpur II regained all the provinces that the Persians had ceded to Rome more than a decade earlier and briefly brought Armenia under Persian control. The reconquered lands included major Christian centers such as the city of Nisibis about forty miles from Edessa. The multitudes of prisoners, whom the shah resettled further east in Persia (in the cities of Isfahan and Susiana, hundreds of miles from the Roman frontier), "included almost a hundred thousand Christian families" who brought with them liturgical manuscripts and sacred books.[40] As such, the recurrent influx of captives bolstered not only the size of the Persian church but also its spiritual vigor. By the fifth century, the Christian communities in Persia predominated in the highlands (hill country) north of the large cities but spread as far east as modern Uzbekistan.

In other words, migration contributed immensely to the church's substantial growth and decisively shaped its existence. It is an undeniable fact that a major segment (likely the majority) of the Persian church arrived as *migrant-outsiders*. The Christian deportees of the early Sassanian era even adopted the label "captive" as a distinctive badge of identity, to distinguish themselves from the indigenous population.[41] This designation, whatever the spiritual undertones, evoked both separateness and suffering. To the extent that captives and displaced populations fueled the rise of Christian communities in Persia, the growth of the Persian church bore indirect testimony to the great devastation and ruin inflicted on eastern frontier regions by the

---

38. See Brock, "Christians in the Sasanian Empire," 8–12.
39. Quoted in Moffett, *Christianity in Asia*, 140.
40. Cf. Moffett, *Christianity in Asia*, 143.
41. Payne, *State of Mixture*, 66; Brock, "Christians in the Sasanian Empire," 3–4.

Romano-Persian wars. Lost territories could be regained, and treaties some-times provided for displaced inhabitants to rejoin their people on one side of the border or the other. But the majority of prisoners acquired in military campaigns were permanently settled on foreign soil, forever separated from their homelands. For migrant captives, this was a source of deep anguish; and the agony of displacement was invariably compounded by the distress and indignities of life as despised aliens in the land of their captors.

When captives joined an immigrant population with whom they shared the same nationality and religious heritage, the pain of migration was, we must suppose, somewhat mitigated. But permanent resettlement in a foreign land entailed cultural alienation and social deprivation that few captives relished. And, in the context of Roman-Persian hostilities, the prospect of religious opposition and social oppression could hardly have been far from the cap-tives' minds. A simple story illustrates this. About 362 CE, the Persian ruler besieged and ravaged border towns in Mesopotamia and took "roughly 9,000 prisoners."[42] This group included several priests, deacons, a community of holy men and women, and an aged Bishop Heliodorus. The bishop perished on the long journey to Persia. But, before he died, he consecrated Dausa, one of the older priests, as his successor. Threatened by his captors with death by the sword if he did not renounce the Christian faith, Dausa rejoiced at the pros-pect of martyrdom. Such courage was not uncommon; but Dausa's adamant response also conveyed something of the Christian captive's view of the life that awaited them in an unknown land:

> [Martyrdom] is for us an open rejoicing. With this, we are no longer taken captive and made aliens to our homeland, nor have we died in foreign parts, nor do we die as prisoners. Who will kill us? Let him neither stand still nor hesitate. . . .[43]

His wish was granted. The new bishop and hundreds of members of his cap-tive church were slain by the sword.

Bishop Dausa's conviction that martyrdom (the ultimate act of Christian

42. *The Acts of the Martyrs of Bezabde*, in Dodgeon and Lieu, *Roman Eastern Frontier*, 215.

43. *The Acts of the Martyrs of Bezabde*, in Dodgeon and Lieu, *Roman Eastern Frontier*, 217.

witness) was more desirable than life in captivity provides a hint of the dire forebodings that haunted the minds of the multitude of Christian captives who ended up in the Persian Empire. Yet, for those who survived such involuntary migration, the act of rebuilding their faith and traditions on Persian soil afforded the opportunity for a *living* witness that won converts to the Christian faith—even if large numbers also eventually paid the price of martyrdom during episodes of violence against Persian Christians by the Persian authorities.

THE "PEOPLE OF GOD" IN PERSIA

The church in Persia—referred to in most sources as the "East Syrian Church" or "Church of the East" (these two labels are used interchangeably here)—comprised gatherings of immigrants from foreign lands, whose numbers were periodically replenished by the arrival of deportees or captives. Though commonly referred to as East Syrian, the church was decidedly multicultural in its composition and multilingual in its practice, partly due to the diverse geographical, cultural, and racial origins of Christians in the Persian Empire.

Syriac, in fact, was only one of the many languages used in ecclesiastical life and worship during the Sassanid era.[44] The majority of Christian prisoners captured in Persian military campaigns were Greek speaking and therefore distinctive from the predominantly Syriac-Aramaic-speaking Christian communities whose presence dated back to the days of Parthian rule. The former, as noted above, called themselves "the captives" and apparently maintained a separate ecclesiastical identity and hierarchy (with their own bishops) until the early fifth century.[45] Greek was also the liturgical language of a growing population of Monophysite Christian refugees (including large numbers of Jacobites of the Syrian Orthodox Church). Persian control of all or parts of

---

44. Brock, "Christians in the Sasanian Empire," 3–4, 17–18; also Christopher Buck, "The Universality of the Church of the East: How Persian Was Persian Christianity?," *Journal of the Assyrian Academic Society* 10, no. 1 (1996): 54–95. The diversity of languages was in sharp contrast to the near universal usage of Latin in the Western church.

45. See also Wilhelm Baum and Dietmar W. Winkler, *The Church of the East: A Concise History* (London: RoutledgeCurzon, 2003), 9, 15.

Armenia (which became a "Christian nation" in the early fourth century[46]) added a strong Armenian element to the church; and by the sixth century, Armenian had replaced Syriac as the dominant ecclesiastical language. From the late fifth century onward, Persian (the official language of empire) was increasingly adopted in Christian writings; and "as the church expanded eastwards, yet more languages were adopted for ecclesiastical use."[47]

In short, the Christian communities in Persia had a multinational character and ethos—comprising diverse races, ethnicities, and geographical origins. This made for fractiousness and disunity, evident in the emergence of competing liturgies and loyalties and dual episcopal structures that the Synod of Isaac addressed (see "Becoming the Persian Church" below). The fact that bishops and even the catholicos (or patriarch) were allowed to marry further strengthened the tendency toward factionalism, dynastic succession, and monopoly of power.

For all this, East Syrian Christians referred to themselves collectively as the "People of God" (or "Nation of God"). This biblical concept expressed more than a strong sense of religious solidarity. It also conveys what might be described as a *theologizing of otherness*. It suggests that the predominantly immigrant members of the Church of God in Persia were strongly conscious of forming a reconstructed religious community and that they viewed this new community of faith—rather than the Persian or Roman Empire or any particular province—as their principal source of identity.[48] Implied also was the notion that the community of faith itself was the primary object of allegiance since it was perceived as a distinctive "nation." Appropriation of "people of God" as a badge of identity—along with the powerlessness and alienation conveyed by the "captive" label—signified an embrace of outsider existence that epitomized what I have termed the *paradox of otherness* (chapter 4), meaning that the otherness or outsider status of the Christian migrant sharpened religious identity (or coincided with religious boundaries) that provided the impulse and rationale for outreach. How these elements shaped the missionary fervor and impact of the church in the Persian context deserves careful examination.

---

46. Baum and Winkler, *Church of the East*, 11.
47. Brock, "Christians in the Sasanian Empire," 18.
48. Brock, "Christians in the Sasanian Empire," 12–13.

BECOMING THE PERSIAN CHURCH

East Syrian Christians were not the only minority religious group or immigrant community in Sassanian Persia. Sassanian domains encompassed vast territories and incorporated a multiplicity of religious groups. There were Monophysite, Armenian, and Jacobite (or West Syrian) Christian communities,[49] as well as sizeable groups of Manichaeans, Buddhists, and Jews. In the fifth and early sixth centuries, intense warfare between Persia and the Byzantine Empire witnessed further influx of hundreds of thousands of Christian prisoners, almost all of whom belonged to the Chalcedonian faith—that is, neither Nestorian nor Monophysite.[50] But East Syrian Christians constituted the largest non-Zoroastrian religious group in Persia and accounted for the majority segment of the Christian population, which, according to one estimate, grew from 35,000 in the early fourth century to well over one million by 650.[51]

The fortunes of the Church of the East changed dramatically under the Sassanian king Yazdgard I (r. 399–420) who pursued peaceful relations with the Roman Empire and adopted a more favorable posture toward the Christian communities in Persia, arguably a tacit recognition of their sizeable presence. Yazdgard I sponsored the building of churches, integrated Christians into Sassanian political structures and diplomatic endeavor, and granted the church protection during most of his reign. In 410, he authorized the first recorded council of the East Syrian Church, the Synod of Isaac. This gathering was attended by forty bishops, including the Armenian bishop Marutha (a Roman envoy to Persia who had good relations with the shah[52]) and prelates who

49. For more on the distinction of these categories, see "The Nestorian Label" below.

50. Moffett, *Christianity in Asia*, 246–47.

51. John C. England, *The Hidden History of Christianity in Asia: The Churches of the East before the Year 1500* (Delhi, India: ISPCK, 2002), 27; Buck, "Universality," 60; Laurence E. Browne, *The Eclipse of Christianity in Asia, from the Time of Muhammad Till the Fourteenth Century* (Cambridge: Cambridge University Press, 1933), 8–9. Christians and Jews numbered 1.5 million. Ian Gillman and Hans-Joachim Klimkeit, *Christians in Asia before 1500* (Ann Arbor: University of Michigan Press, 1999), 112.

52. Leo Duprée Sandgren, *Vines Intertwined: A History of Jews and Christians from the Babylonian Exile to the Advent of Islam* (Peabody, MA: Hendrickson, 2010), 521–22. Bishop Marutha may, in fact, have influenced the Persian emperor to convoke

traveled from as far east as Merv and Samarkand (in modern Turkmenistan and Uzbekistan, respectively).[53] Representation from such far-flung provinces confirms the extensive spread of East Syrian communities and the daunting challenge of ecclesiastical cohesion that the synod attempted to resolve.

The Synod of Isaac recognized the primacy of the bishop of Seleucia-Ctesiphon (the empire's capital) and ruled on the common celebration of major liturgical events (such as Easter and Lent). It also abolished the dual episcopal structure set up in major cities to serve separate groups of Aramaic- and Greek-speaking immigrant Christians.[54] This reorganization effort was only partially successful—internecine divisions persisted. But the transformation of the church in Persia into a Persian church was now underway. In 424, the Synod of Dadyeshu officially declared the Church of the East autocephalous, that is, a single church under a single head. This single head was the bishop of Seleucia-Ctesiphon, who was given the title "catholicos." Since the catholicos was equal to any ecclesiastical authority in the world, patriarchs in the West henceforth had no jurisdiction over the church in Persia and any appeal to their authority by Persian Christians was void.[55] The catholicos exercised the same authority in the East that the pope did in the Latin West.

The deeply cherished hope among East Syrian Christians for a Persian "Constantine"—a Persian Christian ruler who would champion the faith— never materialized.[56] There was never a fusion of church and state. Emboldened by Yazdgard I's auspicious overtures, some Christians (perhaps recent converts from Zoroastrianism) destroyed a Zoroastrian fire temple. This un-

---

the synod. Baum and Winkler, *Church of the East*, 15; also Moffett, *Christianity in Asia*, 153–54.

53. Baum and Winkler, *Church of the East*, 15; England, *Christianity in Asia*, 22; Brock, "Christians in the Sasanian Empire," 3. By then, according to Brock, the church encompassed six metropolitan sees and over thirty bishoprics; but England claims that the church was "organized in six provinces (under metropolitan bishops) which united approximately eighty bishoprics."

54. Baum and Winkler, *Church of the East*, 12, 15. The Greek-speaking congregations were absorbed by the Aramaic-speaking Christian population who apparently constituted the majority. See also Moffett, *Christianity in Asia*, 153–57.

55. Baum and Winkler, *Church of the East*, 19–20; Moffett, *Christianity in Asia*, 162.

56. It is highly doubtful "that any Sassanian emperor in a realm unified by a national religion ever at any time gave serious thought to conversion to the Christian faith." Moffett, *Christianity in Asia*, 154.

lawful act promptly turned the shah against the church and triggered state persecution.[57] Yet even if official recognition by the Persian ruler in the early fifth century failed to fulfill Persian Christian ambitions, it still enmeshed the official hierarchy of the church in political life. Future shahs would take active interest in synod decisions and intervene forcefully in the appointment of the catholicos to suit political priorities, exacerbating the problem of rival candidates.[58] But state recognition also meant that Persian shahs would, at the behest and on behalf of the church, send official requests to foreign governments. An official petition from Yazdgard III (624–651) to the T'ang emperor arguably explains the positive reception that Nestorian missionaries received in the 630s (chapter 8).[59] Thus, while recognition by the Persian state may have done little to support proselytization within empire, it somewhat paradoxically enhanced the East Syrian Church's foreign missions effort.

The Nestorian Label

By the mid-fifth century, the East Syrian Church had become a full-fledged, autonomous ecclesiastical entity. But the key role of migration in its growth and development remained unchanged. The process by which it gained a "Nestorian" identity, arguably the most transformative development in its history, is an important case in point. The Nestorian controversy, as Samuel Moffett notes, "was a Western, not an Asian dispute"; [60] yet it had the most profound impact on the Church of the East. A brief review of the Christological debate and the complex developments that led to the condemnation of the Nestorian position is warranted.[61]

---

57. Sandgren, *Vines Intertwined*, 522; Moffett, *Christianity in Asia*, 158–61.

58. Moffett, *Christianity in Asia*, 156; Buck, "Universality," 72–73.

59. See Glen L. Thompson, "Was Alopen a Missionary?," in *Hidden Treasures and Intercultural Encounters: Studies on East Syriac Christianity in China and Central Asia*, ed. Dietmar W. Winkler and Li Tang (Vienna: Lit, 2014), 274–76.

60. Moffett, *Christianity in Asia*, 186.

61. Among helpful accounts of the cultural and ecclesiastical issues surrounding the theological dispute and how Nestorianism came to define the Church of the East, see Baum and Winkler, *Church of the East*, 21–32, 39; Sandgren, *Vines Intertwined*, 594–95; Moffett, *Christianity in Asia*, 186–209, 248–51; Gillman and Klimkeit, *Christians in Asia*, 113–17; S. P. Brock, "The 'Nestorian' Church: A Lamentable Misnomer," *Bulletin of the John Rylands Library* 78, no. 3 (1996): 23–35.

What became known as Nestorian theology is traceable to Theodore of Mopsuestia or Antioch (ca. 350–428), a Syrian bishop who taught that the divine and human natures remained separate in Christ. This Antiochene theology (also referred to as the "two-nature" or Dyophysite doctrine) reflected the conviction that the divine or Godhead is unchangeable and that only a perfectly human Christ could save humanity. Opposed to this was the Alexandrian school of thought, which, in the Greek philosophical mold, upheld the unity (oneness) of divinity and humanity in Christ with a tendency to emphasize the divine. This doctrine became known as the "one nature" (or Monophysite) theology. In some respects, the two positions complemented each other; but, as is often the case, the differences mattered more.

Nestorius, whose name came to define the Antiochene or Syrian understanding, was patriarch of Constantinople (428–431) and a student of Theodore of Mopsuestia. Intervening in a local dispute over the depiction of the Virgin Mary, Nestorius insisted that Mary should be described as "Christbearer" (*christotokos*), not as "God-bearer" (*theotokos*), because a human person could only have begotten human nature (he referenced John 2:1). Almost bizarrely, a disagreement over the description of Mary triggered one of the most divisive and bitter theological disputes in the history of the Christian movement. Nestorius's view was vehemently opposed by Cyril, patriarch of Alexandria (412–444); and the row between the two ecclesiasts embroiled the whole Mediterranean world and fractured the wider Church. The controversy was marked by bitter ecclesiastical rivalry, fractious church politics, nationalist sentiments (in Syria and Egypt), and a healthy dose of cultural difference (manifest in linguistic misapprehensions involving Syriac and Greek terms). Both patriarchs were deposed; but the "compromise" declaration produced by the Council of Ephesus (431)—which actually comprised two separate synods, the first of which was convened by Cyril and technically illegal—satisfied neither side. Nestorius was banished and his teachings condemned.[62]

Twenty years later, the rancorous theological dispute and ecclesiastical divisions in the Roman Empire remained unresolved. The Council of Chalcedon (451) upheld the earlier condemnation of Nestorius but also dismissed Dioscorus of Alexandria (Cyril's successor), thus rejecting the Alexandrian

---

62. However, doubts and debates persist about how accurately Nestorius's teachings have been represented. See Moffett, *Christianity in Asia*, 175–77.

(Monophysite) position. While it endorsed the *theotokos* description, its Christological doctrine affirmed two natures in one person. Ultimately, and importantly, the Chalcedon formula failed to solve the theological controversy or heal the now implacable ecclesiastical division. Long before then, Monophysite teachings (already dominant in Egypt and Ethiopia) had spread to Syria, where they gave rise to what became known as the West Syrian Orthodox, or Jacobite, Church. In the end, three dominant doctrinal positions, each belonging to a major regional bloc, eventually emerged:

- *Monophysite* (also later known as non-Chalcedonian): Egypt, Ethiopia, West Syria, and Armenia;
- *Antiochene (or Nestorian)*: Persia, East Syria (or Church of the East), and India;
- *Chalcedonian*: the Western Roman Empire and the Byzantine (Eastern Roman) Empire (though the latter retained a major, often persecuted, Monophysite population).

"Nestorian," a derogatory catchall phrase for the Antiochene tradition, became unequivocally associated in the Western church with unorthodoxy or deviation from the definition of faith proclaimed at the Chalcedon meeting. Its application to the Church of the East is misleading for at least two reasons. First, whether Chalcedon's two-nature formula was acceptable to East Syrian Christians is a moot point. The Church of the East had declared complete ecclesiastical autonomy (in 424) over two decades before the Council of Chalcedon. As such, the theological decisions of Roman councils, including the controversial Ephesus meeting, had no bearing on its institutional life. (Over a century and a half later, in 586/7, when diplomatic efforts to end Roman-Persian hostilities brought Catholicos Isho'yahb I into direct contact with the patriarchs of Constantinople and Antioch, the latter pronounced the creed of the Church of the East, presented by the catholicos, to be "orthodox and without error.")[63]

Second, the church embraced Antiochene theology—spread eastward by migrants and refugees (see chapter 8)—not the specific teachings of Nesto-

---

63. Baum and Winkler, *Church of the East*, 36. The leaders of the two ecclesiastical blocs also commemorated this ecumenical agreement with a shared Eucharistic celebration.

rius, whose writings, with a single exception, were not translated into Syriac.[64] The name of Nestorius is conspicuously absent in the eight synods held by the Church of the East during the roughly 126-year period between 486 and 612.[65] To East Syrian Christians, notes S. P. Brock, Nestorius mattered less for his particular theological views than for his significance "as a martyr of the Antiochene Christological cause."[66] Ultimately, "Nestorian" became the designation for a major Christian movement that was only loosely linked to the ideas of Nestorius.[67]

In what follows, I use these different theological labels—Chalcedonian, Nestorian (more frequently, East Syrian), Monophysite—with no presupposition about the plausibility of claims to theological orthodoxy. There is much truth to L. E. Browne's observation that "a broad-minded observer ... [would] recognize the essential unity of belief of these ancient Churches."[68] My own view is that these different creeds or formulas represent contextual attempts to express timeless biblical truth. While each sought to articulate a confession of faith in a manner that has universal applicability, all are historically conditioned, that is, are shaped by cultural factors, ecclesiastical power structures, political dynamics, and social tensions. They are, ultimately, "local theologies addressing particular situations the church faced."[69] Due to the stronger and more enduring legacy of the Western Roman Church, the Chalcedon decision is often considered the standard-bearer of orthodoxy and universally normative. Not only are such assumptions about what constitutes orthodoxy dependent on Eurocentric understandings of history and theology but they

64. Brock, "'Nestorian' Church," 30. The work in question was only translated into Syriac ca. 539, long after the Church of the East reportedly adopted "Nestorianism."

65. Brock, "'Nestorian' Church," 29.

66. Brock, "'Nestorian' Church," 30.

67. After the fifth century, the label was applied to "a wide range of non-Latin Christian traditions native to Syria, Persia, Central Asia and India"; and it became synonymous with "Church of the East" and "East Syrian." In more recent times the church is more often referred to as "Chaldean" or "Assyrian." See England, *Christianity in Asia*, 4–5.

68. Browne, *Eclipse of Christianity*, 7.

69. Steve Strauss, "Creeds, Confessions, and Global Theologizing: A Case Study of Comparative Christologies," in *Globalizing Theology: Belief and Practice in an Era of World Christianity*, ed. Craig Ott and Harold A. Netland (Nottingham: Apollos, 2007), 154.

also "often prevent any adequate study of Eastern Christianity in terms of its own historical and cultural setting."[70]

While churches across all ages may choose to adopt the decisions of one "ecumenical" council or the other, it is worth bearing in mind that such theological formulations were produced by ecclesiastical authorities for churches within a specific political sphere and had no direct impact on Christian communities outside whose voices and particular concerns were not taken into consideration. As Dietmar Winkler puts it,

> despite the process of acceptance, one cannot assume a priori that a synod which has achieved "ecumenical" validity in the history of the Christianity of the Roman empire is necessarily an ecumenical council for the Church as a whole. . . . Even these councils had first a local character, that is, they were reacting to political and theological events within the Roman empire.[71]

The bitter doctrinal controversies that divided major communities of Christian believers in the first five centuries teach us not that there is only one way to express biblical truth but that frank disagreements among sincere believers—whose "divisions . . . are seen to be trivial compared with the truths held in common"[72]—require genuine effort at compromise and accommodation with forbearance for human limitations.

In this instance, the suspicion and hostility engendered by theological disagreements endured all the more because they became enshrined in cultural distinction and geographical distance.[73] Centuries later, when Rabban bar Sauma (ca. 1220–1294), an East Syrian monk and Mongol-Turk, led a delegation to western Europe as an ambassador to the pope (sent by Catholicos Yaballaha III at the behest of the Mongol ruler Ilkhan Arghūn), he was questioned by the cardinals in Rome regarding his tradition and Christian heritage.[74] In this historic encounter between the two Christian traditions

70. England, *Christianity in Asia*, 2–3.
71. Baum and Winkler, *Church of the East*, 18.
72. Browne, *Eclipse of Christianity*, 7.
73. For an overview, see Francis M. Rogers, *The Quest for Eastern Christians* (Minneapolis: University of Minnesota Press, 1962), 13–27.
74. See James A. Montgomery, trans., *The History of Yaballaha* (New York: Columbia University Press, 1927), 57–59.

(Eastern and Western), differences in the niceties of theological doctrine were manifest; but so were shared truths rooted in apostolic tradition. On his return to Rome, after a trip to England and France, Sauma expressed his "desire to consecrate [the Eucharist] that you too may see our custom." The newly elected Pope Nicholas IV (one of the cardinals who had previously interviewed him) readily consented.[75] The poignancy of this brief moment, in which a Chinese-born "Nestorian" Christian official celebrated the East Syrian liturgy in Rome with the pope and cardinals in attendance, can only be imagined. Sauma reported that a great congregation assembled to see how the ambassador of the Mongols consecrated. And when they saw it they rejoiced and said: "*The language is different, but the rite is one*" (italics added).[76]

It was Lenten season and a week later, on Palm Sunday, Sauma "rejoiced greatly to receive Communion from the hand of the Reverend Pope" in front of thousands of congregants.[77] And when Sauma departed, the pope sent him back with "letters patent which contained authorization of [Catholicos Yaballaha's] patriarchate over all the Orientals."

Alas, this thirteenth-century incident of unfettered Christian communion that transcended theological divide and ecclesiastical separation was all the more striking because it was anomalous—attributable to the unique ecumenical vision of Nicholas IV's papacy. To view it as an indication that the bitter doctrinal dispute between Eastern and Western Christianities "had now become half-forgotten" overstates the case.[78] When Mongol expansion and extensive migration brought renewed contact between the two traditions, the old antagonisms were fully evident in the encounter between representatives of Western Christendom (such as William of Rubruk) and East Syrian communities. Indeed, the refusal of Western missionaries to view Eastern Christians as coreligionists arguably doomed their evangelistic efforts in the East.[79]

75. Earlier in his travels, at the request of King Edward I of England, Rabban Sauma had celebrated the Eucharist with "the King and his courtiers attending"; and the king had received the Communion from him. Montgomery, *History of Yaballaha*, 66.

76. Montgomery, *History of Yaballaha*, 68.

77. Sauma, in his own words, "received the Communion with tears and weeping, acknowledging the grace of God." Montgomery, *History of Yaballaha*, 69.

78. Christopher Dawson, *Mission to Asia* (Toronto: University of Toronto Press, 1980), xxix.

79. James D. Ryan, "Christian Wives of Mongol Khans: Tartar Queens and Missionary Expectations in Asia," *Journal of the Royal Asiatic Society* 8, no. 3 (1998): 421.

The School of Nisibis

Those Antiochene bishops and clergy who rejected the Ephesus compromise and the Chalcedon decision lost their positions in the Roman Empire and migrated across the border to join the East Syrian Church in Persia. Essentially, Antiochene theology and the teachings of Theodore of Mopsuestia spread to Edessa and Nisibis (centers with historic ties to Persian Christianity) through refugees and exiles banished as heretics by Roman churches. In Edessa was located the famous and prestigious "School of the Persians" (founded ca. 200), so called because large numbers of students from the Persian church studied the Bible and theology there—crossing into "Roman territory" to do so when Edessa came periodically under Roman control. The church in Edessa became increasingly Dyophysite, gaining a Dyophysite bishop around 435; and, under the leadership of Narsai (399–502), a celebrated Persian theologian (see "Continuity and Challenge" below), the School of the Persians at Edessa became a center of Antiochene theology.[80] How the Church of the East became Nestorian—that is, how it came to embrace the Antiochene teaching of two "distinct" natures in one person—has to do with the oversized influence of the theological school at Edessa on East Syrian Christianity.[81]

Sometime around 457, when Monophysite elements gained ascendancy at Edessa, Narsai fled to Nisibis inside the Persia border.[82] As the Chalcedon position became more entrenched in Roman domains, the existence of the school at Edessa became increasingly precarious. In 489, the Byzantine Roman emperor Zeno expelled the remaining Nestorians from his domain and closed the School of the Persians. The school's teachers and students resettled in Nisibis—a town captured from Byzantium by the Persians in 361—and reestablished the school as the School of Nisibis, under Narsai's directorship. The School of Nisibis attracted gifted students from near and far, and its student body grew to over a thousand.[83] It became "one of the most influential centers for theological education in the ancient Christian world," generating

---

80. Baum and Winkler, *Church of the East*, 25, 27–28; see also Arthur Vööbus, *History of the School of Nisibis* (Louvain: Secrétariat du CorpusSCO, 1965), 57–121.

81. In the brief account that follows, I draw mainly from Arthur Vööbus's *History of the School of Nisibis* (1965), which remains the most definitive treatment to date.

82. Vööbus, *School of Nisibis*, 45.

83. Vööbus, *School of Nisibis*, 55, 143; also, Latourette, *First Five Centuries*, 230; Baum and Winkler, *Church of the East*, 26; Sandgren, *Vines Intertwined*, 593.

a stream of scholarship in biblical studies that "was known and used in the Middle Ages all over the continent of Europe."[84]

Even more importantly, the School of Nisibis was the chief training center for the Church in the East and "functioned as the heart of spiritual life in East Syrian Christianity."[85] Arthur Vööbus asserts that its "structural contribution to that wealth of religious expression characteristic of East Syrian Christianity" is difficult to exaggerate; for "nearly all the great luminaries, church leaders, authors and teachers drew light, inspiration, knowledge and spiritual energy from the institution."[86] As the foremost intellectual center, it "continuously produced contingents of teachers for the educational institutions of the church," trained men for various positions in the church, and regenerated the monastic tradition.[87] In this way, the School of Nisibis not only invigorated East Syrian Christianity for centuries but also made it fully Nestorian, as generations of alumni steeped in its Antiochene theology rose to prominent positions in the Persian Church. More than that, it "instilled zeal for active propagation of the Christian faith,"[88] providing the training and theology that contributed to the extraordinary expansion of Nestorian missions from the fifth century.

In 486, the Synod of Aqaq (or Acacius) (486), the fourth general synod of the East Syrian Church, officially endorsed Antiochene theology and produced the first preserved Christological statement of the East Syrian Church.[89] This creed affirmed Christ's two natures ("perfect God and perfect man") as concrete, distinct, unmixed, and inseparable. It is noteworthy that the synod makes no reference to Nestorius or to earlier theological pronouncements of the Roman Councils of Ephesus (431) and Chalcedon (451) for that matter.[90]

84. Vööbus, *History of the School of Nisibis*, 191, 195.
85. Vööbus, *History of the School of Nisibis*, 310.
86. Vööbus, *History of the School of Nisibis*, 5.
87. Vööbus, *History of the School of Nisibis*, 204–6.
88. Vööbus, *History of the School of Nisibis*, 208.
89. The creed also confessed faith in "a single Lordship and to a single (object of) worship." How distinct this is from the two "persons" formula associated with Nestorianism is hardly worth pursuing, especially given the tangled linguistic semantics involved and the challenge of understanding how different individuals at different times applied the relevant nonbiblical terms in Syriac or Greek. Similarly, how this formula is different from the Chalcedonian creed depends on how "nature" is understood.
90. In addition to the fact that its theological position did not quite reflect the extreme views attributed to Nestorius, this does suggest that the Church of the East ironically placed less importance on the "Nestorian controversy" than its counterpart

Like all conciliar statements, the timing and wording was prompted by contextual concerns. In this case, the dramatic increase in Monophysite groups within the Persian Empire was a primary issue.[91] But, far more important from a contextual point of view, the association of the East Syrian Church with Nestorian teachings (outlawed in the Roman Empire or in Greek territory) made the Persian Church more acceptable to Persian authorities, for whom it signaled the weakening of religious loyalty by its Christian subjects to the Roman state. Awareness of this benefit may in turn have motivated East Syrian Christian leaders to strengthen the Nestorian identity of the Church of the East.[92] This is to say that, like the Roman Church, the theological identity of the Persian Church was shaped to a certain extent by local concerns and the immediate political context.

PERSIAN CHRISTIANITY AND THE PERSIAN WORLD

The extent to which the Christian communities in Persia were identified with or incorporated into Persian society, especially after the East Syrian Church became autocephalous in the fifth century, remains a difficult question. Clearly, imperial cognizance of the institutional church did not automatically translate into social incorporation. Antiapostasy laws (though intermittently enforced) ensured that Christian communities remained demarcated from Zoroastrians and the wider Persian society. Indeed, since Zoroastrianism was the religion of the Persian state, official recognition of Christianity possibly meant that the Christian communities throughout Persia now formed a *millet*, a legally recognized religious minority confined to separate settlements in the various cities.[93] This would further support the notion that, though widely

---

in the West. In fact, the Church of the East accepted the creeds of Nicea and Chalcedon, albeit based on their own interpretation. See Baum and Winkler, *Church of the East*, 7, 18, 30; Moffett, *Christianity in Asia*, 250.

91. Intense military conflict between the Persian and Byzantine empires in the fifth century had witnessed a dramatic rise in Persia's Monophysite population. Moffett, *Christianity in Asia*, 246–47. The Monophysite one-nature theology, which implied that divinity experienced change and suffering, was repugnant to East Syrian Christians.

92. So much so that the imprisonment of Catholicos Babowai (457–484) was probably due to his apostasy from the Nestorian faith. Sandgren, *Vines Intertwined*, 593.

93. England, *Christianity in Asia*, 23.

spread throughout the empire, East Syrian Christian communities remained insular in their social existence, a minority faith vulnerable to local antagonism and the vicissitudes of Sassanian rule.

But separation is not the same as insularity. Though Christianity never became a dominant faith in Persia by any means, a number of considerations trouble the notion of a largely sequestered church. Periodic royal support of Christian institutional life, intermarriage (which was actively encouraged by monarchs), the strong representation of East Syrians in artisan and merchant guilds, and the appointment of Christians to important royal posts, not to mention the strong evangelistic orientation of East Syrian Christians, all indicate broad interaction with the indigenous Persian (Iranian) population.

It is noteworthy that full identification of the Church of the East with the Persian realm (from the early fifth century) coincided with the incorporation of leading Christians into Persia's political aristocracy. But the minority status of East Syrian Christian communities still raises a number of complex questions about the nature of the encounter with the wider Persian society, especially given the formidable challenges posed by Zoroastrianism and the fact that Christianity was the official religion of a rival power (though the Persian Church's adoption of Nestorianism altered the equation somewhat). If there was a significant degree of cross-cultural interaction, as we must suppose, how were the East Syrian Christians able to maintain a distinctive religious existence that allowed a foreign faith to flourish? Put differently, if the Church of the East was marked by a unique religious identity, how did it manage to gain adherents (presumably at the expense of Zoroastrianism) and spread so extensively?[94]

These questions cannot be answered fully. For one thing, on matters of religious conversion and exchange, Zoroastrian and Christian accounts are not easily reconcilable, leaving ample room for interpretative bias. That there were Christian conversions to the Zoroastrian faith is certain. But what the rest of this chapter seeks to examine are the factors and considerations that influenced or facilitated the cross-cultural accessions to Christianity in Persian society prior to the Arab invasion in the mid-seventh century.

As elsewhere in this volume, I will make the case that the experience of mi-

94. By most accounts, the institutional church grew vigorously, though this cannot always be equated with numerical increase. By the mid-seventh century it comprised ten metropolitan sees and ninety-six bishoprics. Brock, "Christians in the Sasanian Empire," 3.

gration and the outlook of migrant-outsiders shaped the religious encounter with the dominant culture—basically, that migrant identity informed missionary commitment. Insofar as it attributes significant agency to marginalized groups and nonelite or nonstate actors in the cross-cultural spread of the Christian faith, this argument goes against the grain of traditional analyses of historical change, which typically favor political structures or interests and elite contribution as the principal instruments. Richard Payne's *A State of Mixture: Christians, Zoroastrians, and Iranian Political Culture in Late Antiquity* (2015), an impressive study that describes the integration of East Syrian Christians into the Persian imperial structure, exemplifies this latter approach.

Payne challenges at least three commonplace suppositions about Christianity in Sassanian Persia. First, he dismisses the commonplace view that the Persian state, often at the behest of antagonistic Zoroastrian high priests (or *mobeds*), episodically persecuted Christians as a group. Indeed, he strenuously objects to the traditional view that religious conflict pervaded Persia's hugely diverse multiethnic society. His portrayal of Sassanian rulers and Zoroastrian authorities is strikingly laudatory, to the point where acts of violence against Christians are rationalized as essential for cooperation and coexistence.[95] Moreover, he insists that state-sanctioned violence against Christians (laity or leaders) was directed only at specific individuals—such as converts from Zoroastrianism, Christians who assaulted fire temples, and elite Christians who violated state policy.[96] Discounting vivid descriptions of extensive persecution in Christian sources, he makes the astounding claim that the story of the "Great Persecution"—a forty-year pogrom (from 339 to 379) under Shāpur II, attested in "upward of forty works"[97]—is a myth perpetuated by East Syrian hagiographers.[98] He argues that, far from being implacably hostile to other faiths (as commonly believed), Zoroastrianism had a capacity for tolerance and inclusion that facilitated coexistence and collaboration between the two faiths.

95. Payne, *State of Mixture*, 56.

96. Not until the early fifth century, Payne insists—when Christians had been incorporated into Persia's political aristocracy (serving at court as scribes, diplomatic envoys, intermediaries, etc.) and therefore subject to imperial discipline for acts of disloyalty—were they consistently exposed to imperial violence. Even then, in his view, the number of martyrs is modest.

97. Payne, *State of Mixture*, 38.

98. For details of the persecution, see Moffett, *Christianity in Asia*, 139–45; also Latourette, *First Five Centuries*, 228–29.

Second, he rejects the view that East Syrian Christians formed discrete and unintegrated religious communities. His "model of mixture" thesis contends that, contrary to the conventional view that Christian communities maintained an insular ethnoreligious existence, leading Christians in Persia were incorporated into the political order by Persian rulers and not only "cooperated with a Zoroastrian ruling elite" but also "participated in Zoroastrian institutions."[99] Moreover, he insists, sustained interaction between Zoroastrians and Christians necessitated adaptation and innovation on both sides; and this produced a comingling of cultures that allowed Christianity to flourish.

Third, Payne rejects the notion that the growth of Christianity in Persia came at the expense of Zoroastrianism. He determines that a "fluidity of religious boundaries" prevailed in elite circles and that encounters between Christians and Zoroastrians from the fifth century produced "vacillation rather than straightforward conversion." "There is no reason to believe," he surmises, "that Zoroastrians abandoned their religion in any significant numbers at any point in Sassanian history."[100] And even if elite members converted to Christianity in large numbers "there may have been as many Christians who apostatized in favor of the Good Religion."[101]

As an evaluation of the interplay between ruling elites and the religious structures of empire, Payne's *State of Mixture* presents valuable insights. And by demonstrating extensive Christian participation in the structures of empire, he effectively challenges the conventional view of East Syrian Christian communities as segregated, persecuted minorities. But the treatment as a whole is revisionist. The case for full integration of Christian elites into a Zoroastrian political system comes with ideological blind spots and sweeping conclusions. His assessment focuses on elite networks and the structures of empire in a way that leaves little room for the voices or representation of nondominant groups, while implicating them in the arguments.

The nature and outcomes of the encounter between Christians and the prevailing Zoroastrian culture is a case in point. Within bureaucratic structures and the higher echelons of Persian society, religious interaction was a high-stakes affair. Christians who adopted Zoroastrian practices improved

99. Payne, *State of Mixture*, 1–2.
100. Payne, *State of Mixture*, 49.
101. Payne, *State of Mixture*, 193.

their social standing but apostates from Zoroastrianism were liable to be "expropriated and executed." Conversion to Christianity by elite members of society was the most visible (to imperial or Zoroastrian authorities) and also the least tolerable, because such defections undermined the synthesis of religion and Sassanian rule.[102] Even pro-Christian rulers like Yazdgard I (or later successors like Husraw I and Husraw II), who patronized Christianity or befriended influential Christian leaders, vigorously persecuted Zoroastrian apostates. Thus, the high costs of apostasy among members of the privileged class in Zoroastrian society (even if punishments varied across time) help to account for the vacillation in religious identification that Payne refers to. Christian authorities and elites, for their part, were ambivalent or reticent about high-profile Zoroastrian conversions to Christianity for somewhat similar reasons: it invited imperial disfavor, which endangered their aristocratic status and threatened the peaceful existence of the institutional church.[103]

There is no reason to assume that such fluidity and vacillation in religious identification also prevailed in *the wider society*. Payne, to his credit, concedes that despite fears of adverse repercussions, proselytism "was a Christian practice that East Syrian leaders could restrict only with difficulty."[104] We do well to remember that the degree of volition that potential converts exercise in conversion decisions has significant bearing on the outcomes.[105] Since "there was no systematic enforcement of a law of apostasy within the general population," it stands to reason (all things being equal) that conversions to Christianity among the ordinary inhabitants, especially its more mobile segments, were likely to be more definitive. Payne does allow that "regulation of conversion will not . . . have restricted the spread of Christianity among the subordinate populations of the empire that were—and continue to be—largely invisible." Since there were conversions even among high-ranking members of society in the face of severe punishment,[106] it is reasonable to conjecture that, given the

102. However, Payne argues that highly placed apostates were only punished in certain political circumstances and could practice their Christianity in the open for years before facing persecution.

103. Payne infers that "ecclesiastical leaders accepted these limitations [on Christian expansion] as the terms of integration." Payne, *State of Mixture*, 56.

104. Payne, *State of Mixture*, 48.

105. Robert L. Montgomery, "Conversion and the Historic Spread of Religions," in *The Oxford Handbook of Religious Conversion*, ed. Lewis R. Rambo and Charles E. Farhadian (New York: Oxford University Press, 2014), 165, 166.

106. Payne notes the proliferation in "accounts of Zoroastrians who converted to

relative freedom within the general population to cross and recross religious boundaries, the rate of conversion among ordinary citizens was likely to be higher, not lower. As Payne also attests, "Christianity gained its adherents among the largely invisible, middling inhabitants of the villages, towns, and cities in Mesopotamia and Khuzestan and along the transregional mercantile routes that extended into Central Asia through Khurasan and into the Indian Ocean through the Persian Gulf."[107]

Payne's strong predilection for Zoroastrian sources, combined with explicit distrust of Christian hagiographical material, is also troubling—especially considering the fact that the latter shed the most light on the experiences and views of marginalized groups. Persian martyrologies do incorporate legendary elements and tend toward exaggeration; but they furnish enough details to substantiate large-scale persecution.[108] Yet, Payne dismisses Christian (East Syrian) description of Zoroastrian destruction of churches and shrines as untrustworthy on the grounds that the sources fail to specify "the sites and dates at which such acts were supposed to have occurred"! He also considers it far more conclusive that the vast Zoroastrian literature contains "not a single injunction to destroy" Christian institutions.[109] This wholesale rejection of East Syrian Christian sources further accounts for his conviction that violence against Christians by Persian authorities was provoked not by their religious identity or association with imperial Rome but by internal Persian politics.

The inequitableness of this approach raises serious questions about interpretative objectivity. Ultimately, no historical source is completely reliable; but the arbitrary rejection of "hagiographical literature" betrays perspectival bias. One can present sensible arguments to refute "accounts of Christianity's inevitable diffusion at the expense of the Good Religion" without resorting to cavalier dismissals of particular sources. Payne's strongly professed skepticism about high rates of Christian conversion also reflects unqualified validation of Zoroastrian sources at the expense of the Christian record. Middle Persian sources, he notes, depict conversion as ambiguous and treat religious identities as open-ended (i.e., "converts joined the Good Religion as commonly as

---

Christianity and were martyred for apostasy" from the fifth to early seventh centuries. Payne, *State of Mixture*, 48.

107. Payne, *State of Mixture*, 11.
108. Baum and Winkler, *Church of the East*, 11.
109. Payne, *State of Mixture*, 34.

they departed it").[110] East Syrian hagiographical literature, on the other hand, attests to large-scale conversion and depicts individual conversion as unequivocal. Payne discounts this latter testimony, again citing "lack of substantive details such as names, dates and places." Excluding all but *documented cases* of conversion to Christianity—an unfathomable restriction—allows him to conclude that the number of converts was quite low.[111] He expresses concern that Christian assessments downplay "religious encounters that did not lead to the clear crossing of religious boundaries" but tellingly disregards the possibility that Zoroastrian sources were just as likely to minimize rates of apostasy.

The precise extent to which Christianity penetrated Persian society will never be known. From a historical perspective, the paucity of empirical data, the highly subjective nature of the process, and the implicit bias in available records all but preclude definitive conclusions. But an approach that privileges particular historical sources and concentrates on high-profile segments of the Persian realm is unlikely to provide a clear picture. The nature or outcome of religious encounter and exchange produced in the wider social context is typically absent from the historical record, perhaps especially so in a context where religious tensions made it unwise to publicly celebrate or encourage proselytizing activities. Either way it is misguided to expect detailed documentation of the haphazard and unpredictable crossing of religious boundaries that transpired in daily life.

Religious conversion in contexts of cross-cultural encounter—or *"traditional transition,"* as Rambo terms it[112]—is a hugely complex process. Most important (as explained in chapter 2), the social context in which religious encounters and conversion take place furnishes particular insights into potential outcomes, because it "shapes the nature, structure, and process of conversion."[113] In this regard, attentiveness to the issue of migration and migrant experiences as critical elements of the Christian encounter with Sassanian Persia is essential. While it affirmed religious distinctiveness or tacit resistance to total assimilation, the conflation of Christian identity with the dis-

---

110. Payne, *State of Mixture*, 192.

111. "Scarcely a dozen" in the sixth and early seventh centuries. Payne, *State of Mixture*, 192–93.

112. This type of religious conversion entails "moving from one worldview, ritual system, symbolic universe, and lifestyle to another." Lewis R. Rambo, *Understanding Religious Conversion* (New Haven: Yale University Press, 1993), 14, 38.

113. Rambo, *Understanding Religious Conversion*, 22–35.

paraged status of the foreigner-outsider did not necessarily imply segregated existence. On the contrary, this *theologizing of otherness* is consistent with regular interaction and permeable boundaries between religious communities. A segregated or secluded community would hardly need to make a case for a distinctive identity. In a context of multiple (intersecting) faiths, therefore, distinctive presence and practice became a form of proclamation. Otherness was a prerequisite for outreach. It formed part of a strategy of survival that refused to compromise religious belonging.

Migration and Mission

The *Chronicle of Se'ert*, an eleventh-century Nestorian document, affirms that "the Christians . . . multiplied in Persia, building churches and monasteries."[114] Estimates suggest that they numbered well over one million by the end of the seventh century.[115] Over time, they also grew in influence; and their wider learning, industry, and international contacts "earned them a rising reputation in the service of the empire."[116] The shahs' personal physicians were invariably Christian; and, by the sixth century, Christians were well represented within the civil service and served the emperor's court as interpreters and secretaries of state.[117] Still, East Syrian Christians who attained high social status or became members of the aristocratic order were a tiny segment of the church. The vast majority of Persian Christians were immigrants who belonged to mercantile, artisan, and agricultural classes—that is, middle class or below.[118] They constituted a troublesome but largely marginalized minority that wielded very little political power. Even at the height of their influence, they remained vulnerable to repressive policies. Whether or not the church's leaders gained political clout, they exercised no authority outside the Christian community. As Moffett puts it, Christians "were not the equals of their Zoroastrian counterparts; officially they were inferior."[119]

114. Complied in the early eleventh century and written in Arabic, this document draws on early Syriac material. The quote here is taken from Dodgeon and Lieu, *Roman Eastern Frontier*, 297 (see also note 4). See also Brock, "Christians in the Sasanian Empire," 3.

115. England, *Christianity in Asia*, 27; Buck, "Universality," 60.

116. Moffett, *Christianity in Asia*, 221.

117. Moffett, *Christianity in Asia*, 153, 221; England, *Christianity in Asia*, 18.

118. Moffett, *Christianity in Asia*, 222.

119. Moffett, *Christianity in Asia*, 222.

The Christian encounter with Zoroastrianism defined the fortunes of the church and the nature of its mission. Zoroastrianism was a monotheistic religion promoted by adherents and authorities as the only "Good/True Religion"—the only religion that could perfect the world order.[120] Central elements of its belief system included a radical dualism (founded on the notion of a cosmic conflict between good and evil), the importance of ethical behavior/choices as the basis for salvation, and a pronounced emphasis on ritual purity as part of the struggle against the forces of evil (indeed, the all-encompassing nature of this struggle meant that a system of purification rites was applied to adherents and nonbelievers alike).

As the state religion of Sassanian Persia, Zoroastrianism was inseparable from national life and was the mainstay of the sociopolitical order. Zoroastrian beliefs, institutions, and practices were nurtured and upheld by priests (known as *mobeds*, called *magi* by the Greeks and Romans) who exerted considerable influence in Persian society. Such was the synthesis of religion and political rule that the *mobadan-mobed*, or chief priest, arguably wielded as much authority as the Persian ruler. Not only were Zoroastrian practices prevalent throughout the Persian realm but its norms were also viewed by the ruling class as indispensable for the well-being of empire and the integration of its diverse populations. Zoroastrian fire temples were immediately built upon the capture of new territories.

The precise tenets or variants of Zoroastrian religion in the Sassanid era are open to debate; and how widely particulars of the faith were followed within the indigenous (Persian) populace is not entirely certain. Popular observances encompassed ceremonial rites (notably initiations for children), specific burial practices, adherence to extensive purity laws,[121] and participation in feast days and special religious festivals. Family life and the home were central to the religion. The Zoroastrian emphasis on fertility and productivity meant that having many children and even multiple wives (for the purposes of procreation) were considered virtues; and the home was a key site of religious commitment.[122] But fire was the most important element in Zoroastrian religious practice. Fire was considered the essence of life. It represented the energy and

120. Payne, *State of Mixture*, 30.
121. For more, see Scott Sunquist, "Narsai and the Persians: A Study in Cultural Contact and Conflict" (Ann Arbor: UMI Dissertation Services, 1990), 83–98.
122. Sunquist, "Narsai and the Persians," 86, 99–101; also Robin E. Waterfield,

visible symbol of the creator and was "seen as a gateway through which the divine comes to earth."[123] Maintenance of sacred fires was viewed as "a cosmic necessity and a duty laid upon believers."[124] Fire temples (sacred buildings that housed well-tended fires) formed the centerpiece of the Zoroastrian system. In communities and villages throughout the Persian realm, local fire temples were tended by magian priests who wielded considerable local influence.[125] The faithful also kept sacred (hearth) fires in their homes; and, since fire was revered in every form, sun worship was common.

As members of a minority religion, ordinary Christian believers practiced and propagated their faith in a religious environment pervaded by the purification rites and sacred rituals of Zoroastrianism. Migration engendered sustained interaction between the two faith communities. Since the requirements of the Zoroastrian belief system penetrated deeply into ordinary life and influenced daily routine, tensions between East Syrian Christian ideals and Zoroastrian norms were inescapable and readily apparent in the commonplace interactions and transactions of daily life.[126] Many East Syrian religious practices—including celibacy, asceticism, acceptance of virginity, and burial of the dead (which polluted the earth)—were deeply abhorrent to the Zoroastrian mind. By the same token, Zoroastrian teachings on basic matters such as marriage and family were irreconcilable with Christian beliefs; and many aspects of Zoroastrian devotion, including the deification of fire and reverence for celestial entities, were idolatrous from an East Syrian Christian perspective. Fire was also associated with purification in the Christian tradition; but, for Christians, it was more commonly a symbol of divine judgment and destruction, for example, "our God is a consuming fire" (Heb. 12:29; Deut. 4:24).

From a Zoroastrian perspective, however, the issues at stake extended beyond theological difference and conflicting ritual observances to matters of national identity and security. As previously noted, association of Christianity

Christians in Persia: Assyrians, Armenians, Roman Catholics and Protestants (London: George Allen and Unwin; New York: Barnes & Noble, 1973), 32.

123. Sunquist, "Narsai and the Persians," 93.

124. James Barr, "The Question of Religious Influence: The Case of Zoroastrianism, Judaism, and Christianity," *Journal of the American Academy of Religion* 53, no. 2 (1985): 227.

125. Sacred regional fires may also have been instituted as a unifying strategy for highly diverse populations.

126. Sunquist, "Narsai and the Persians," 99.

with the national religion of a rival power invited persistent suspicion about the true political loyalty of the immigrant Christian community. In Zoroastrian thought, also, violation of purity laws (intrinsic to the fight against evil) undermined the well-being of the state and threatened the natural order. Beliefs and practices of East Syrian Christianity jeopardized this Zoroastrian order in fundamental ways.[127]

In many areas and arenas, therefore, there was ample room for misunderstanding and resentment between adherents of the two faiths. But it was the zealousness with which East Syrian Christians propagated their faith and sought converts that generated the most hostility. Apostasy or turning away from the "True Religion" was a punishable offense (more so for magians and elites[128]). Death (the ultimate punishment) was seldom imposed except during periods of intense persecution; but imprisonment, eviction from homes, and destruction of livelihood were not uncommon.[129] Yet, convinced about the superiority of their faith,[130] Christian believers in Persia actively proselytized. The collision between the two faiths in theological thought and religious practice is conveyed in the following magian complaint:

> The Christians are destroying our teaching. They are teaching people to serve only one God, not to worship the sun, not to honor fire, to defile the waters with despicable ablutions, not to marry women, not to produce sons or daughters, not to enter battle with the kings, not to kill, to slaughter and eat animals without murmuring [the ritual prayers], and to bury and to conceal the dead in the earth. They say that God created serpents and scorpions together with vermin, not Satan. They impair many of the servants of the king and teach them the sorcery that they call books.[131]

Despite tremendous theological differences, however, the Christian captives in Persia established flourishing churches, propagated their faith within the Persian Empire, and won many converts. "It is not sufficiently realized by

---

127. For more on the clash of religion, see Moffett, *Christianity in Asia*, 106–12.

128. As noted above (see "Persian Christianity and the Persian World"), religious encounters and exchange in local communities were conceivably less visible to religious authorities and therefore less constrained.

129. England, *Christianity in Asia*, 23; Moffett, *Christianity in Asia*, 195.

130. As Payne also attests (*State of Mixture*, 57).

131. From the *Martyrdom of Aqebshma*, quoted in Payne, *State of Mixture*, 38.

modern scholars," writes Alphonse Mingana, "that the immense majority of the members of the Nestorian Church living east of the Tigris were of Persian, and not Semitic or Aramean birth and extraction."[132] He adds that many were second-generation Christians, "born of Christian parents who originally belonged to the Zoroastrian faith" while many others were converts from Zoroastrianism. Christopher Buck notes that ethnic Persians probably "formed the most visible and important ethnic minority of Christianity in Persia."[133] Such cross-cultural expansion was the more remarkable given the fact that Christian communities had to contend with restrictive policies and religious hostility. Clearly, whatever the converts' motivations, material gain and social advancement were not among them. Even in this hostile climate, some Christian converts from Zoroastrianism adopted Christian names at the time of baptism to conform with their new faith, though some retained their Iranian names.[134]

But missionary success raises a number of questions. What made the faith of these migrant Christian communities attractive to adherents of Zoroastrianism? What factors contributed to Christian conversion in a context where the transmission of the Christian message encountered a full-fledged and entrenched state religion whose authorities responded with a mixture of patronage and persecution? How was the Christian message translated into the Persian context and religious milieu so as to facilitate acceptance and appropriation?

It is, of course, impossible to recover the finer details of the intimate encounters and layers of symbiotic exchange that shaped processes of conversion in such an environment. Repressive state policy was only one of many variables that had a bearing on the decision of potential converts. Zoroastrian converts to Christianity also wrestled with crucial social and cultural dilemmas, such as "how to extricate oneself from a disapproving family, what to do with one's Zoroastrian spouse, whether to continue observing Zoroastrian regulations of purity."[135] Two key considerations throw some light on the encounter between East Syrian Christianity and Zoroastrianism in Sassanian Persia and help to explain the growth of the minority faith: first, cross-cultural religious conversion is more likely when areas of affinity exist that provide conceptual footholds for navigating the boundary between different belief systems; sec-

---

132. Alphonse Mingana, *The Early Spread of Christianity in Central Asia and the Far East: A New Document* (Manchester: University Press, 1925), 6.

133. See Buck, "Universality," 54

134. Mingana, *Early Spread of Christianity*, 6.

135. Payne, *State of Mixture*, 193.

ond, successful cross-cultural missionary outreach requires translation and cultural adaptation to facilitate transmission and appropriation.

Continuity and Challenge

Despite diametrically opposed religious ideals and practices, East Syrian Christianity and Sassanian-era Zoroastrianism shared areas of affinity that aided exchange and reception. Put differently, the formidable dialectical differences between the two belief systems did not preclude areas of conceptual similarity and theological convergence. In a fascinating study that examined the homilies of the Persian thinker Narsai (399–502), possibly the foremost theologian of the East Syrian Church, Scott Sunquist identifies several areas of theological convergence or "selective affinity" between the two faiths:[136]

- a creation story in which the "first man" is ancestor of the future savior figure (of the world);
- accounts of "the fall" (or "death") of the original couple through temptation;
- comparable notions of incarnation: the strong emphasis on the humanity of Jesus in Nestorian theology cohered with the portrayal of the savior figure in Zoroastrianism (*Saoshyant*) as human messenger in whom the divine is present;
- a savior whose work leads to a resurrection of the dead and victory over death—which in Zoroastrian belief is "the greatest evil, or impurity, in this world";[137]
- an understanding of purification through fire (the Holy Spirit as a *purifying fire* in the Syrian tradition has some correspondence with the fundamental concern for purification in Zoroastrian worship and its supreme focus on fire—in Narsai's writings, the purifying attribute of the Holy Spirit is evidenced in baptism, worship, and Christian service); and
- an understanding of salvation that extends beyond human existence to all of creation.

136. Sunquist, "Narsai and the Persians," See passim, 174–75, 182–83, 219–21, 234, 236, 245–54, 267–70, 294.
137. Sunquist, "Narsai and the Persians," 269.

Strikingly also, according to the Zoroastrian tradition, the savior [*Saoshyant*] was "to be born of the prophet's seed from a virgin mother"[138]— not to mention the presence (in the Gospel narrative) of magi "from the east" who were guided by a star to pay homage to the newly born Messiah, which provided evocative association with Zoroastrian religion.[139]

Efforts to explain how these noteworthy affinities between the two faiths came about are mainly conjectural. Did familiarity with Zoroastrian salvation beliefs shape the birth story of Christ? Or were two distinct, but comparable, traditions melded in early Syrian Christian traditions by Zoroastrian converts?[140] In a major study that traces the spread of Zoroastrian doctrines in the Greco-Roman world, Mary Boyce and Frantz Grenet propound the controversial view that the two faiths shared striking similarites because Zoroastrian thought contributed to early Christian beliefs via Judaism.[141] They contend that Jewish sectarian movements assimilated the teachings of Zoroaster (during the intertestamental period) and bequeathed certain essential Zoroastrian doctrines to Christianity that are revealed in early Christian writings—namely, "a struggle between good and evil, an end of time, a coming World Savior, and a last judgment."[142] However, by focusing on a few isolated elements, Boyce and Grenet minimize the huge discrepancies in beliefs and doctrine between the

138. Mary Boyce and Frantz Grenet, *A History of Zoroastrianism* (New York: Brill, 1991), 451.

139. Marco Polo, who journeyed through Persia around 1292, reported: "In Persia is the city of Saba [now Sāveh, located 60 miles southwest of Tehran], from which the three Magi set out when they went to worship Jesus Christ; and in this city they are buried in three very large and beautiful monuments, side by side." He gives the names of the magi as Jaspar, Melchior, and Balthasar, though he found that the people of the city had no idea who the "Three Magi" were. See Marco Polo, *The Book of Ser Marco Polo, the Venetian: Concerning the Kingdoms and Marvels of the East*, trans. Henry Yule (London: Murray, 1871), 79.

140. Boyce and Grenet note the prevalence of Syrian sources in the oldest known Christian commentaries and noncanonical material concerning the visit of the magi (*History of Zoroastrianism*, 448–53). See also Brock, "Christians in the Sasanian Empire," 15n65.

141. Boyce and Grenet, *History of Zoroastrianism*, 440–56. However, they admit the difficulty of extracting real knowledge of Zoroastrianism from meager sources that incorporate legend and superstition.

142. In their view, some ideas expressed by the apostle Paul, such as the entire creation groaning to be free "from its slavery to decadence" (Rom. 8:19–23), are of Zoroastrian inspiration and derived either from his reflections on Jewish apocalyptic literature or from lingering Zoroastrian influences among the Jewish circles in Tarsus. Boyce and Grenet, *History of Zoroastrianism*, 444.

religions; and the claim that key ideas in Judaism and Christianity ultimately originate in Zoroastrianism has been convincingly refuted by James Barr.[143]

The most that can be said is that the comparable elements in the two faiths provided a modicum of continuity that helps to account for Persian receptivity to the Christian message. As Boyce and Grenet explain, East Syrian Christians may have gained converts among Zoroastrians because the Christian message "embodied doctrines taught by their own faith."[144] But the existence of (theological) affinity is only one side of the coin. The differences also mattered. Insofar as it involves choice and commitment, the switching of religious allegiance typically denotes a conviction on the part of the convert that the new faith more adequately addresses particular needs, aspirations, or dilemmas. As Sunquist puts it, if "the similarities in the two systems made communication possible . . . the challenges [i.e., areas of conflict and contestation] made conversion a necessity."[145]

In their efforts to persuade Zoroastrian believers that the new religion was superior to theirs, Christian missionaries quite possibly depicted the story of the magi as the old religion paying homage to the new.[146] Sunquist also argues that the Christian message (as portrayed in Narsai's theology) was compelling because it introduced new dimensions to the Zoroastrian worldview in at least two major areas.[147] First, in contrast to the radical dualism of Zoroastrian thought, in which the cosmic struggle between good and evil pervades daily life and necessitates endless purification, Christian teachings depict a created order that, despite dualistic forces, is fully under the control of the One God. The Christian world image "of harmony and fullness" in contradistinction to "conflict and separation" may have been more appealing to some. Second, in both religious systems, creation is an act of God. In Zoroastrianism, however, God is limited by the presence of an opposing (evil) power and this forms the

143. Barr, "Question of Religious Influence," 201–35. Barr notes, among other things, the striking indifference to the religion of ancient Persia in the Hebrew Scriptures and rejects the notion that recognition of comparable elements or common concepts is tantamount to acceptance of another religion or submission to its ideas. Acceptance of comparability, he contends, may well have motivated Jews to express their own religion in terms that were intelligible or meaningful to the other "even while resisting all the time the actual claims of that other" (229–30).

144. Boyce and Grenet, *History of Zoroastrianism*, 441.

145. Sunquist, "Narsai and the Persians," 294.

146. Boyce and Grenet, *History of Zoroastrianism*, 453.

147. Sunquist, "Narsai and the Persians," 289–95.

basis for eternal conflict. By contrast, Persian Christianity presented "a full-blown redemption story" in which God is sovereign over all time and space and brings about the renewal of all creation.

But meaningful cross-cultural impact requires give and take. If comparability between the two religious systems aided Christian evangelistic efforts, Christian life and practice were also affected over time by the prevailing Zoroastrian environment. Adaptation of Christian practices to Persian culture was inevitable. Migrant communities can never fully replicate the systems they leave behind; and, in this case, the political realities as well as the pervasive influence exerted by Zoroastrianism on national identity and popular consciousness imposed insurmountable constraints. Institutional survival and effective missionary outreach required strategic adaptation to the Sassanian world. In the long run, the transformation of the (predominantly East Syrian) church in Persia to the Persian Church involved more than institutional or ecclesiastical reform. It also entailed concessions or contextualized responses to Zoroastrian beliefs and practice.

In a hugely momentous decision, the Aqaq synod that issued the earliest known doctrinal statement of the East Syrian Church (establishing its Nestorian identity) also ruled that all Christians, laity and clergy alike, had the right to marry. Scriptural rationale or moral concerns may have informed this pronouncement; but it was quite likely inspired by a pressing need to conform to Persian cultural norms, under the influence of the growing number of Persian Christians.[148] Persians regarded marriage as imperative and held procreation to be of foremost importance. Asceticism in any form was considered a "blasphemy against life";[149] and celibate clergy were held in contempt. The synod's validation of marriage effectively suppressed celibacy and curbed the monastic strands so integral to East Syrian Christianity.[150] This secured a unique East Syrian Christian identity—at least in comparison to the growing Monophysite movement in Persia, which was heavily monastic.[151] But, perhaps more important, it brought Christian practice more in line with

---

148. Clearly, the growing number of ethnic Persians who joined the church also brought unique cultural sensibilities into an already diverse Christian community. See Moffett, *Christianity in Asia*, 198–99; Buck, "Universality," 80–81; Waterfield, *Christians in Persia*, 32.

149. Waterfield, *Christians in Persia*, 32.

150. Baum and Winkler, *Church of the East*, 32, 35.

151. Sandgren, *Vines Intertwined*, 640.

Zoroastrian culture and gave the church a place within the fabric of Persian society. It also removed a significant impediment to Christian mission in the Persian domain. For good measure, the ruling also underlined the church's distinctiveness from the Roman world in which it had originated.[152] The church in Persia had for all intents and purposes become the Persian Church.

This act of indigenization did not eliminate conflict with Zoroastrianism. Zoroastrian marital norms—which endorsed "the marriage of brother and sister, of father and daughter, or of other equally proximate kin" as cosmologically beneficial[153]—were irreconcilable with Christian standards. Whether to eat meat at Zoroastrian social functions (feasts and festivals) was another profoundly thorny issue. In Persian culture, consumption of food was steeped in religious ritual, and meat offered at feasts was associated with Zoroastrian rites (which Christians viewed as idolatrous). Yet, refusal to consume meat offended Persian sensibilities; and since participation in banquets at festivals was a prerequisite for maintaining political standing, Christian elites were faced with a difficult quandary.[154] As the church grew in wealth and influence, acquiescence to Persian norms and social expectations became more common; and the lines between conformity and compromise more easily blurred. Christian ideals and practice at the popular level were clearly susceptible to the mutual borrowing and exchange that marks multicultural existence.

Thus, in the sixth century, newly elected catholicos Mar Aba I (r. 540–552), himself a convert from Zoroastrianism, initiated extensive reform of unsanctioned practices and corruption within the church. Among other things, his 544 synod condemned the eating of meat used in pagan worship, proscribed the union of a Christian man and an unbelieving woman, and issued a prohibition against a Christian man marrying the wife of his father or uncle, his aunt, his sister, his daughter, or his granddaughter, "like the Magians."[155]

In the Persian context, also, successful cross-cultural missionary outreach required translation of the Christian message into Persian language and

---

152. Brock, "Christians in the Sasanian Empire," 12–19.

153. Payne, *State of Mixture*, 108.

154. "For Christian officeholders," writes Payne, "participation in festive banquets was an inevitable and indispensable component of their political practice, and a failure to partake of Magian meat would have insulted their peers, disappointed their inferiors, and caused irreparable damage to their status." Payne, *State of Mixture*, 122.

155. Payne, *State of Mixture*, 108.

concepts.[156] Christian communities in Persia were mainly Greek- or Syriac-speaking. Syriac, as we have noted, was a trade lingua franca and widely spoken in Persia; but it was not the main language. The reading public in Persia was small, so translation of Christian texts or apologies into Persian arguably had limited evangelistic value.[157] But whether Syriac remained the language of liturgy and worship of the East Syrian Church is an important issue. If so, it would mean that many Persian converts to Christianity had to adopt Syriac, a necessity that would arguably have inhibited Persian receptiveness. The evidence suggests, however, that "Syriac was not the exclusive language of liturgy and instruction in the Persian Church."[158] Christian worship was adapted to local vernaculars and Persian became the medium of Christian instruction.[159] Also, "the ecclesiastical Canons of the Nestorian Church were sometimes written in Persian."[160] From the fifth century, notes Christopher Buck, "Persian became an increasingly important vehicle for Christians" and a "subsidiary Christian vernacular."[161] An extensive body of Christian literature in Persian developed, including religious works, canticles, hymns, and even (in some regions) the canons of the church.[162] All of this confirms the church's dual commitment to missionary propagation and a Persian identity.

PERSIAN CONVERSIONS

The historical record furnishes few personal details about conversion to Christianity within Persia. Accounts of notable figures like Mar Aba I (who, at the time of his conversion, was a high-ranking Persian government official) appear to combine fact and folklore.[163] By the nature of things, also, most

156. See Buck, "Universality," 81–86.

157. Latourette, *First Five Centuries*, 227–28. However, even in the Roman Empire, Christian writings were mainly consumed by Christians.

158. Buck, "Universality," 54. See also Brock, "Christians in the Sasanian Empire," 17–18.

159. Buck, "Universality," 83–87.

160. Mingana, *Early Spread of Christianity*, 6.

161. Buck, "Universality," 57, 82, 88.

162. Brock, "Christians in the Sasanian Empire," 18; Waterfield, *Christians in Persia*, 32.

163. At the time of his dramatic conversion, through the kindness of a Jewish-Christian believer, Mar Aba was "secretary to the governor of the province of Beth Garmai and . . . a member of the magian clan." Sandgren, *Vines Intertwined*, 626.

attempts at proselytization failed. Despite bitter complaints that Christians were destroying Zoroastrian teaching, more Persians rejected the Christian message than were persuaded by its claims. Some allowance must be made for the fact that East Syrian Christians maintained and proclaimed their faith in a religious environment where the level of resistance was formidable. As Moffett notes, "sixth century Zoroastrianism held a far stronger patriotic and religious hold on the Iranian population than paganism had ever exerted in Constantine's Rome."[164] Punishments for apostasy and proselytizing were enforced even in situations where leading Christians gained the trust and respect of Persian rulers.[165]

That said, the Church of the East was by most accounts a missionary church whose members took the evangelistic obligations of their faith seriously. Even Payne, who is manifestly disinclined to credit Christian conversions, notes the proliferation in "accounts of Zoroastrians who converted to Christianity and were martyred for apostasy" from the fifth to early seventh centuries.[166] "Even if one takes a minimalist view of rates of conversion," he adds, "there were likely many more apostates than the paltry number of documented martyrs."[167] Ultimately, it appears that native Persians converted to Christianity in significant numbers, though the details are scanty.[168]

East Syrian communities were more heavily concentrated in some areas than others; but as many as eighteen provinces within the empire (approximately 68 percent of Sassanian territory) may have been evangelized.[169]

---

164. Moffett, *Christianity in Asia*, 232.

165. Bishop Marutha's medical skill reportedly cured Yazdgard I of a violent headache and earned the shah's high regard; but his influence (which the powerful Zoroastrian elite immediately tried to counter) did little more than improve relations between the shah and the empire's Christian minority. See Moffett, *Christianity in Asia*, 153; Sandgren, *Vines Intertwined*, 521–22. It is worth reiterating Moffett's observation that it is highly unlikely "that any Sassanian emperor in a realm unified by a national religion ever at any time gave serious thought to conversion to the Christian faith." Moffett, *Christianity in Asia*, 154.

166. Payne, *State of Mixture*, 48

167. Payne, *State of Mixture*, 51.

168. See Buck, "Universality," 75–81; Brock, "Christians in the Sasanian Empire," 4–6; Johan Ferreira, *Early Chinese Christianity: The Tang Christian Monument and Other Documents* (Strathfield, New South Wales: St. Pauls Publications, 2014), 66–67.

169. Buck, "Universality," 67, 69, 76–78, 87. Christian missionary activity even

Importantly, the Persian policy of distributing captives throughout Persian territory—many of whom were settled along the Silk Road and in newly built towns—had the unintended consequence of facilitating missionary outreach. The policy was obviously intended to foster assimilation and prevent heavy concentration of foreign populations in regions close to their homelands. The ensuing interaction of migrant Christians with the indigenous population may well have facilitated cultural assimilation. But, contrary to design, it contributed to the proliferation of churches and aided the propagation of Christianity. The *Acts of Pusai*, which tells the story of Pusai, a fourth-century descendant of Roman prisoners of war, records that

> when Shāpur (II) had built the city of Karka de Ladan and settled their captives from various places, he also thought of bringing and settling about thirty families apiece from each of the ethnic groups living in the various cities of his empire among them, so that as a result of inter-marriage, the captives would be bound by family ties and affection, and it would therefore not be as easy for them to flee gradually back to their homeland. This was Shāpur's clever plan; but God in his mercy used it to the good, so that through this mixing of those deported with the pagans, the latter were caught in the recognition of truth and converted to the knowledge of the faith.[170]

Acts of Pusai does carry a hint of Christian propaganda; but it conveys the sense that Persian conversion to Christianity was largely a product of regular associations and interactions between migrant Christians and the indigenous population. Since proselytization was illegal, personal interaction and association presumably provided the primary means for Christian evangelism. The prohibition of marital union between Christian believers and non-Christians at Mar Aba's 544 synod suggests that intermarriage (at least when freely practiced by Christian men) came to be regarded as a source of corruption in the church. But it is also apparent that *compulsory* intermarriage, implemented by Persian authorities with the express purpose of promoting cultural integration, provided an avenue for winning converts. According to the *Acts of Pusai*,

---

penetrated regions in central and eastern Persia that were predominantly Zoroastrian; and it is worth noting that indigenous converts "figure prominently" in martyrologies.

170. *Acts of Pusai* 2, p. 209, in Dodgeon and Lieu, *Roman Eastern Frontier*, 163.

Pusai himself "took a Persian wife . . . , converted her, baptized his children, and brought them up in and taught them Christianity."

Other than intermarriage, the associations formed by traders and artisans to maximize their resources arguably provided another avenue for Christian proselytization. The Roman captives who were settled in different regions within the empire included architects, engineers, technicians, physicians, and other trained individuals. Practically all physicians were Christian, which gave them some influence in both the imperial circles and the wider society. Christians also dominated the mercantile and artisan classes and are named in contemporary documents as "chief of the artisans," "head of the guild of silversmiths," and "president of the merchants."[171] Many Christian captives, in other words, came with highly desirable skills.

Pusai, who is described as "an excellent craftsman and an expert in weaving and embroidering gold ornaments," was "among those craftsmen whom the king gathered from the various ethnic groups . . . and whom he formed into an association with many sub-divisions and for whom he fitted out a workshop next to his palace in Karka de Ladan." Since Pusai was commended to the king for his skill and made chief craftsman "after a short time," it is obvious that his Christian identity was not a liability or hindrance to advancement. Moreover, in keeping with Persian resettlement policy, Pusai's entire household (including his brothers and sisters) was resettled with him in Karka de Ladan. This approach accounts for the emergence of large Christian communities in various regions of the empire with a greater capacity (compared to isolated individuals or families) to maintain their faith in the new environment.

In this context, however, few professions afforded more opportunity for missionary action than trade. Many Syrian Christian captives were merchants; and they had the capacity, experience, and international networks to exploit the empire's strategic location. Indeed, even Christians in Persia who were not merchants apparently turned to trade as a means of supporting themselves.[172] This was because Sassanian Persia occupied a strategic position within the global economy, exercising powerful control over trade on the Silk Road and the Spice Route. Persian ships and merchants extended their reach as far as China, exporting pearls and textiles and transmitting Chinese paper and silk and Indian spices to Europe.

171. See Moffett, *Christianity in Asia*, 222.
172. Howard, *Transnationalism in Ancient and Medieval Societies*, 143.

In merchant groups, especially those regularly engaged in long-distance travel, evangelistic-minded Syrian Christians would have had ample opportunities to share their faith. Within Persia itself, imperial resettlement policy, combined with the heavy concentration of Christians in trade associations or guilds, allows the conjecture that some conversions of native Persians to Christianity involved what historian Jerry Bentley termed *voluntary association* (see chapter 2).[173] This is to say that indigenous individuals or groups may have been motivated to associate with or accommodate the immigrant community because the latter offered superior skills, much-needed experience, and access to trade networks with the potential for economic profitability. Syrian merchants possessed resources and economic potential that were attractive to Persians. Based on the "voluntary association" model, some Persians may have adopted the foreign group's unfamiliar ways and practices because it eased access and because participation in "a [shared] code of ethics and values" contributed to success. At least for some, sustained engagement and close collaboration may have produced greater receptivity to the Christian message and ultimately opened the way to religious conversion.

When all is said and done, at precisely what point Persian Christianity ceased to be almost exclusively a religion of the Syriac-Aramaic–speaking immigrant population is impossible to say. But the remarkable growth of the Church of the East is beyond question.[174] By the mid-seventh century, it "far surpassed its Western counterparts in geographical reach."[175] Between 410 and 650 ecclesiastical leadership expanded from 43 prelates (five metropolitans and thirty-eight bishops) to 105 (nine metropolitans and ninety-six bishops). Internal strife and bitter feuds often hobbled Christian vitality. But from the fifth century Christianity increasingly penetrated the upper classes of Sassanian society. Members of the royal household and some high officials were included among its members. The personal retinue of Shah Kavadh I (488–531) included many Christians who carried out missionary activities

173. In Bentley's model, indigenous groups and rulers associate with diaspora merchant communities and ultimately adopt their "foreign ways" because of the opportunities this offers for political and economic benefit. Jerry H. Bentley, *Old World Encounters: Cross-Cultural Contacts and Exchanges in Pre-Modern Times* (New York: Oxford University Press, 1993), 9–10.

174. Brock, "Christians in the Sasanian Empire," 3; Moffett, *Christianity in Asia*, 255.

175. Payne, *State of Mixture*, 203.

during his brief exile in central Asia. Khusrau (or Chosroes) II had two Christian wives.[176] In the turbulent and chaotic half century or so that preceded the Arab invasion, various catholicoses served as an international embassy in negotiations between Persian and Byzantine courts. By then also, the majority of the population in northern Mesopotamia, including the aristocracy, was Christian.[177]

To the very end, wars, negotiated treaties, military truces, and concessions between the Persian and Roman (Byzantine) powers shaped the fortunes of the Church of the East. Intense wars resumed in the fifth and early sixth centuries. Religious concerns remained integral to political conflict. The Persian-Byzantine treaty of 562 that inaugurated a fifty-year peace included provisions intended to safeguard the rights of Persian Christians (to build churches and worship freely) as long as they refrained from converting magians to their faith.[178] In the early seventh century, Persian forces eventually conquered and incorporated Syria, Anatolia, Palestine, and Egypt into the Persian realm. The religious implications were no less distressing than the economic or political ramifications. Conquest of Jerusalem (in 614) and the capture of the highly venerated True Cross by a pagan ruler dealt a devastating blow to Roman imperialism and threatened its claim to being a Christian empire, even if Persian rulers subscribed the True Cross's supernatural potency.[179] Eventually, in 627, the Byzantine emperor Heraclius (575–641) invaded Persia during a time of political turmoil. He killed the Persian ruler, regained conquered territories, and secured the return of captives. Most important, the True Cross was restored to the Church of the Holy Sepulchre in Jerusalem (in 630), to rapturous acclaim.

How Byzantine conquest might have affected the circumstances of the Church of the East will never be known. Within a matter of decades, Sassanian Persia was crushed by Arab armies. By then, Christians constituted

176. Maria, who was thought to be of Roman descent, and Shirin (the emperor's favorite), an Aramean convert to Monophysitism.

177. Baum and Winkler, *Church of the East*, 32, 36; Sandgren, *Vines Intertwined*, 642; Payne, *State of Mixture*, 136; Brock, "Christians in the Sasanian Empire," 3.

178. Sandgren, *Vines Intertwined*, 628. Whether these provisions were adhered to is unknown.

179. Payne, *State of Mixture*, 169–70. The True Cross was a relic believed to be the actual cross on which Christ died, reportedly discovered and installed in Jerusalem by Helena, mother of Constantine I.

a significant minority in Persian society, heavily concentrated in some areas and enjoying modest influence in the higher echelons of government. Wearied by prolonged warfare, political volatility,[180] and the heavy burdens of taxation, many Persian Christians welcomed Arab rule. Their status as a religious minority remained unchanged; indeed, the restrictions of the Persian *melet* system formed the basis of the Arab *dhimmi* system.[181] But Arab rule brought improved status and more favorable conditions. Increased demand for their learning and professional skills (as accountants, scribes, physicians, teachers, translators, and interpreters) also gave Christians considerable influence.

In sharp contrast, Zoroastrians were vigorously repressed by the Arab invaders. Not only were they identified with Persian political leadership, and therefore a potential source of nationalist rebellion, but they were also (unlike Christians) considered pagan idolaters. In the wake of Islamic conquest, Zoroastrianism declined precipitously through widespread conversion to Islam; and "[its] religious structures of high priests and *mobeds* all but disappeared."[182] Thus, under Islamic rule, the faith of an immigrant minority flourished, at least in the short term, while the state religion that had held sway over it for centuries foundered. Such were the complexities and contradictions of the interconnections between empire and the spread of religion.

180. In a space of four years, five shahs and two queens followed each other in quick succession. Baum and Winkler, *Church of the East*, 40; Gillman and Klimkeit, *Christians in Asia*, 124–27; Buck, "Universality," 73.

181. This means that they were treated as a "protected community," who "had their own residential sectors, and, under the general suzerainty of Muslim law, were left to order their own affairs, not only ecclesiastical but also, to a considerable degree, their own legal system." Gillman and Klimkeit, *Christians in Asia*, 125. See also, Moffett, *Christianity in Asia*, 337–38; Browne, *Eclipse of Christianity*, 45, 63.

182. Moffett, *Christianity in Asia*, 379.

CHAPTER SEVEN

Christ and Odin: Migration and Mission
in an Age of Violence

I worshipped the quick-witted lord of Hlidskjalf [Odin],
before everything altered in the fortunes and fates of men.
All my lineage shaped lines praising Odin's reign;
I remember precious poems, the work of my ancestors' age;
reluctantly—for Odin's rule always pleased the poet—
I show hostility to the husband of Frigg, for I follow Christ.

—The Troublesome Poet (tenth century)[1]

In a manner strikingly similar to assessments of post-1500 European encounters with the non-European world, the spread of Christianity among the
peoples of Europe, especially in Scandinavia (from roughly 500–1200 CE),
is generally depicted in terms of political motivation or state building.[2] Expla-

---

1. Icelandic poet (or skald) Hallfred Ottarson, who lived in the tenth century, was
named "the troublesome poet" by King Olaf Tryggvason of Norway (r. 995–1000) for
his reluctance to relinquish worship of Odin, "the god who had blessed him and his
ancestors with the gift of poetry." Quoted in Angus A. Somerville and R. Andrew Mc-
Donald, eds., *The Viking Age: A Reader*, 2nd ed. (North York: University of Toronto
Press, 2014), no. 91 (pp. 393–94); on Odin's attributes, see no. 10 (pp. 55–57). See also
Anders Winroth, *The Conversion of Scandinavia: Vikings, Merchants, and Missionaries
in the Remaking of Northern Europe* (New Haven: Yale University Press, 2012), 1–4.

2. However, it must be said that the ferocity of violence applied in the conversion of northern Europeans far surpassed the brutal destructiveness of subsequent
European colonization projects in the Americas or modern Africa and Asia. Equally
important, the gap between Christians and pagans, especially in terms of technology
and culture, was considerably less in the early Middle Ages than was the case in the
early modern era between Europe and the vast lands Europeans colonized. Also, as
Andrew Walls points out, whereas in Europe the pre-Christian gods were displaced,
in the diverse societies of the non-Western world "the Christian preachers found God

nations as to why military initiatives by Christian kings and chieftains often took precedence to the preaching and persuasion of official missionaries generally emphasize political expedience.[3] Among the most common arguments are the following: the encounter with pagan religion took place in a setting where use of violence for political ends and a warrior culture (in which exchange of gifts to ensure group loyalty was central) were prominent elements; tribal chieftains constantly competed for political ascendancy and, to some, Christianity offered greater prestige and advantages than ancestral religion; and the interpenetration of the ecclesiastical sphere and political structures that marked the formation of medieval Christendom produced a top-down approach to religious expansion that favored coercion. "In this violent world," avers Jacques Le Goff, "the chief form of violence was conversion."[4]

It is important to clarify that this assessment does not apply to medieval missionary efforts in eastern Europe, where Byzantine emperors took full responsibility for organizing missions. In Europe's eastern regions, pagan peoples were subject to "political pressure and cultural penetration"; but use of violence was largely absent in efforts to spread the Christian faith. Long before the arrival of missionaries, diplomatic means and other forms of cultural engagement were used to make Christianity desirable to pagan nations like the Slavs (at least to the aristocracy); and the establishment of the church was generally accompanied by thoroughgoing Christian instruction.[5]

In western and northern Europe, the use of brute force in vicious campaigns against pagan religion and the bloodied savagery that characterized many efforts to make Christian converts are a matter of record. Armed re-

---

already there," and the vernacular names of God were retained. Cf. Andrew F. Walls, *The Missionary Movement in the Christian History: Studies in the Transmission of the Faith* (Maryknoll, NY: Orbis Books, 1996), 70–72; Sverre Bagge, "Christianizing Kingdoms," in *The Oxford Handbook of Medieval Christianity*, ed. John Arnold (New York: Oxford University Press, 2014), 122.

3. See, among others, Winroth, *Conversion of Scandinavia*, 138–42; Anders Winroth, *The Age of the Vikings* (Princeton: Princeton University Press, 2014), 198–99; Jacques Le Goff, *Medieval Civilization, 400–1500* (New York: Blackwell, 1988), 147–49.

4. Le Goff, *Medieval Civilization*, 149.

5. Leading historian Richard Sullivan explains that the powerful pull of Byzantine, or "Greek," culture and the projection of imperial power meant that, unlike their Western counterparts, Eastern missionaries operated "under nearly ideal conditions." Richard E. Sullivan, "Early Medieval Missionary Activity: A Comparative Study of Eastern and Western Methods," *Church History* 23, no. 1 (1954): 17–20.

sistance by pagans in response to attacks on ancestral religion, especially as the faith spread northward, further intensified the cycle of violence.[6] But the centuries-long, uneven, often opaque, and decidedly fluid process of religious change that marked the Christianization process defies easy analysis. Indeed, at what stage the conversion from paganism to Christianity became complete is a fraught question.[7] There were reversions to pagan religion and reconversions aplenty; and the overlap between old and new beliefs in daily life often continued long after the establishment of the church.[8] Most important, the selection and interpretation of the historical sources present particular challenges that deserve brief attention.

TEXTS AND CONTEXTS

There is no shortage of primary source accounts of the spread of Christianity among European peoples. But the modern historian must reckon with deliberate omission or misrepresentation and with the absence of records that convey the views or responses of the pagan tribes themselves. Moreover, the historical value and reliability of medieval narratives of conversion, such as the *Lives of Saints* and the Icelandic sagas (which date to the twelfth and thirteenth centuries), both of which are indispensable for understanding the Christian conversion of Europe, have long inspired vigorous and contentious debate.[9] The sagas

6. On pagan protests against Christian mission more broadly, see Ramsay Mac-Mullen, *Christianity and Paganism in the Fourth to Eighth Centuries* (New Haven: Yale University Press, 1997), 18–20.

7. Winroth probes the issue with deft insight, noting the latent bias of medieval conversion narratives as well as the limitations of archeological material. In my view, however, his analysis is weakened somewhat by a rather simplistic view of religious conversion and a static understanding of religion. Winroth, *Conversion of Scandinavia*, 103–4, 121–40.

8. The fact that Western European peoples joined the church as clans, tribes, and nations meant that knowledge of the new religion lagged well behind outward conformity to its rituals. At the same time, the coexistence of pre-Christian beliefs and tenets of the new faith underscores the critical role of indigenous appropriation and religious adaptability in the Christianization process. Here, as in every major cross-cultural transmission of the faith, the principle of translation was fully operative (see chapter 2).

9. Renowned Scandinavian medievalist Theodore M. Andersson provides a compelling overview of the close to a century of debate around Icelandic sagas in *The Growth of the Medieval Icelandic Sagas (1180–1280)* (Ithaca, NY: Cornell University

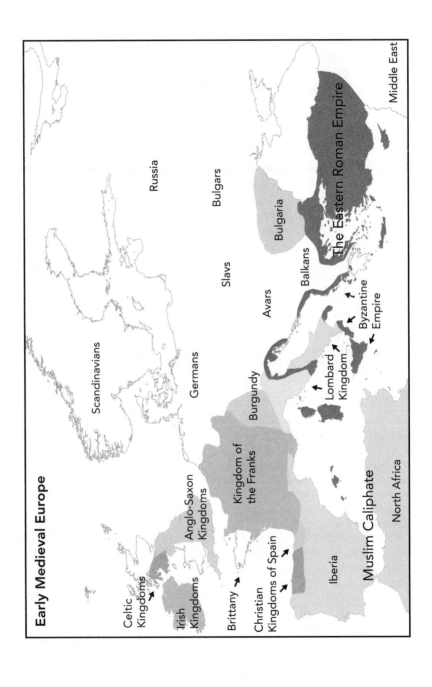

Early Medieval Europe

Celtic Kingdoms

Irish Kingdoms

Brittany

Christian Kingdoms of Spain

Anglo-Saxon Kingdoms

Kingdom of the Franks

Burgundy

Iberia

Muslim Caliphate

North Africa

Lombard Kingdom

Byzantine Empire

Germans

Scandinavians

Russia

Slavs

Avars

Bulgars

Bulgaria

Balkans

The Eastern Roman Empire

Middle East

draw on both oral and literary traditions, incorporate rich symbolism and stylized prose, and provide valuable cultural perspectives, while the corpus of saints' *Lives* emerged out of monastic traditions and provide unique insights into contemporary views of missions and missionaries.[10] But the abundance of miracle stories and supernatural occurrences in these sources—not to mention their providential view of historical events, depictions of conversion as the instantaneous transformation of individuals or multitudes, and hagiographical content (unbridled exaltation of missionary figures)—offend the intellectual sensibilities of many modern Western scholars and readers.[11]

This has encouraged unrepentant selectivity by individual historians in their reconstruction of these events, in a manner that invites readers to give greater credence to modern interpretative bias than to the primary sources themselves.[12] Outright rejection of some sources on the basis of incompatibility with modern scientific views raises more questions than it solves. Given the world in which these sources were produced, the absence of miracle stories and other supernatural occurrences such as healing or prophecy would be more adequate grounds for questioning the trustworthiness of the accounts. In any case, as others note, our chroniclers "were closer to the events than we

Press, 2006); see also Oddr Snorrason, *The Saga of Olaf Tryggvason*, trans. Theodore M. Andersson (Ithaca, NY: Cornell University Press, 2003), 1–27; Somerville and McDonald, introduction to *Viking Age*, xv–xix; Winroth, *Conversion of Scandinavia*, 121–37; Winroth, *Age of the Vikings*, 229–32.

10. I. N. Wood, *The Missionary Life: Saints and the Evangelisation of Europe, 400–1050* (Harlow: Longman, 2001), 58.

11. It is perhaps necessary to note that in non-Western contexts where religious worldviews are much closer to that of these medieval sources, such narratives are read with very different lenses and appreciation. By and large, many outside the Western world are untroubled by the wonderful demonstrations of supernatural power related in Christian missionary encounters—not to mention that these elements, as well as the tacit view of conversion as instantaneous, are validated by Christian Scripture (the cardinal reference point for Christian thought and expectation). The sagas have been variously designated by different Western scholars as "literary fictions," imaginative inventions, or products of an institution of storytelling that draw on a historical tradition.

12. Winroth, for instance, seizes on the permission granted Icelanders (after conversion) to continue select pagan practices as indication that "they did not in any real way embrace a new system of beliefs"; yet he arbitrarily rejects the same writer's assertion that this official accommodation of pagan practices ended after a few years. Winroth, *Conversion of Scandinavia*, 139.

are, and we must concede to their writing, if not factuality, a high degree of plausibility."[13]

Medieval conversion narratives were shaped by the outlook and imagination of their Christian writers in such a way that they cannot be treated in their entirety as historically factual. (However, it is noteworthy that some of these writers were at pains to affirm the veracity of their accounts and the credibility of their sources).[14] More to the point, the medieval writers' worldviews and the traditions they drew on (Christian or pagan) were marked by a profound consciousness of the transcendental. They and their audiences shared an abiding sense of inhabiting a sacramental universe, one in which the divide between the spiritual and temporal was notional or nonexistent. Natural explanations were not ruled out; but Christians, no less than the pagans they sought to convert, were conditioned to discern spiritual significance behind events. Both were convinced of the existence of a supernatural world that for all its profound mysteries was a source of important human benefits.

In this context, religious conversion was fundamentally a matter of confrontation and competition (though sometimes accommodation) between powers that staked a claim to all of life, including land and people. By the nature of things, observes Henry Mayr-Harting, "it was up to Christianity to show that [religious change] could be done without loss of the old benefits, that Christian medicine could work as well as pagan magic."[15] Such expecta-

13. Somerville and McDonald, *Viking Age: A Reader* (Introduction), xviii.

14. See Andersson, *Medieval Icelandic Sagas*, 7–12, 21–26. This is true, for instance, of Adamnan (*Life of St. Columba*), as Richard Sharpe explains in his excellent introduction to *Life of St. Columba* (New York: Penguin Books, 1995), 56–57. Also, in a moment of critical self-reflection, Snorrason, author of *The Saga of Olaf Tryggvason*, acknowledges that "the sort of tales about such phantoms and prodigies as have just been related may surely seem less than credible"; and he goes on to explain that "the matters that we have related with respect to such tales and exempla we do not judge to be true in the sense that they happened, but rather we believe that they appeared to happen because the devil is full of deceit and evil" (no. 45, p. 97). Willibald, the eighth-century author of *Life of Saint Boniface*, was curiously not one of the saint's many disciples, which is perhaps why he makes a point of noting that he "[made] the most careful investigation in my power, from the narration of his disciples who had long tarried with [Boniface]." Willibald, *The Life of Saint Boniface*, trans. George W. Robinson (Cambridge: Harvard University Press, 1916), 24.

15. Henry Mayr-Harting, *The Coming of Christianity to Anglo-Saxon England*, 3rd ed. (London: B. T. Batsford, 1991), 47; see also Richard Fletcher, *The Barbarian Conversion: From Paganism to Christianity* (New York: Holt, 1997), 244–53.

tions were not incompatible with thoughtful reflection and moral principles. Indeed, supernatural demonstrations of power were efficacious insofar as they authenticated the message and moral virtues of the Christian agents. Holy men and women were celebrated and idolized precisely because "miracles were indicative of moral worth and spiritual advancement."[16]

None of this, of course, nullifies the complex and important task of ascertaining historical validity and application. Our sources were not written, constructed, or produced with modern historical sensibilities in mind; but neither are they free from the grievous errors, deliberate omissions, or parochial designs (latent or manifest) of historical sources of all ages. As such, whether modern Western historians choose to believe that the events happened as reported, our sources impose analytical constraints that preclude a complete picture.

Ultimately, however, analysis is closely tied to the historian's interpretative assumptions. The central focus on migration adopted in this study contrasts sharply with the proclivity in Western scholarship for explaining major historical change, including the transregional spread of religion, in terms of state action or formal structures of political power and economic self-interest—what I term the "empire" argument. Empire and migration are major features of human history and are perennially linked. But the analytical yield is radically dissimilar when one or the other shapes historical perspective. This is primarily because one is top-down, the other bottom-up. To restate my central thesis, human migration has played an indispensable role in the cross-cultural spread of the Christian faith principally because migrants who are Christian inevitably fulfill a missionary function in their encounters with non-Christian peoples and societies. Official or planned missionary initiatives are not precluded in this view. Actually, the foreign missionary, regardless of official status or nature of reception, is typically a migrant and invariably an outsider. The key issue is that the migrant movements in any epoch, in their multitudinous forms and multiplicity of impact, hold important clues about the nature and fashion of Christian expansion. This means that, when applied as an analytical lens, migration arguably affords a broader understanding of the range of missionary actors and the variety of missionary activity.

16. Mayr-Harting, *Coming of Christianity*, 49.

Missionary Action and Migrant Agency
in the Christianization of Europe (500–1000)

The collapse of the Western Roman Empire left road networks in disrepair; and local folk ripped up the stones to use as building material.[17] In the fifth and sixth centuries, surging movements, recurrent warfare, and large-scale resettlement by barbarian peoples (the Lombards, Saxons, Jutes, Goths, Franks, and more) were major causes of social upheaval and unsettling transformations.[18] The costly wars initiated by the Byzantine emperor Justinian (482–565), in an ultimately futile effort to renew the Roman Empire by reconquering territories lost to Germanic tribes, added to the turbulence of the era.[19] We must reiterate that travel was dreadfully slow. Topographically, western Europe was an expanse of forests "perforated by relatively fertile cultivated clearings."[20] This erected great barriers and dangers (real and imagined) to travel. The majority of people traveled on foot (covering 20–25 miles a day); and many went barefoot, by choice (usually for religious reasons) or necessity.[21] If many set out easily in medieval Europe, it was mainly because they lacked a strong sense of homeland and had little to leave behind by way of material possessions or property.[22] Further east, the downfall of the Han Empire in China in the mid-third century was followed by four centuries of tumultuous rule by warring states,[23] while increasing raids on trade routes by nomadic tribes undermined security on overland routes across central Asia.

With the emergence of the Islamic and Mongol empires conditions for

17. Smith, *Premodern Trade in World History*, 82.

18. For helpful treatment, see Ralph W. Mathisen and Danuta Shanzer, eds., *Romans, Barbarians, and the Transformation of the Roman World: Cultural Interaction and the Creation of Identity in Late Antiquity* (Burlington, VT: Ashgate, 2011); Walter A. Goffart, *Barbarian Tides: The Migration Age and the Later Roman Empire* (Philadelphia: University of Pennsylvania Press, 2006).

19. The Justinian Wars lasted from 536 until his death in 565. For details, see J. A. S. Evans, *The Age of Justinian: The Circumstances of Imperial Power* (New York: Routledge, 1996), 126–82.

20. Le Goff, *Medieval Civilization*, 131.

21. Norbert Ohler, *The Medieval Traveller* (Woodbridge: Boydell, 1997), x, 29, 97.

22. Le Goff, *Medieval Civilization*, 134.

23. Louise Levathes, *When China Ruled the Seas: The Treasure Fleet of the Dragon Throne, 1405–1433* (New York: Oxford University Press, 1996), 34. According to a 2 CE census, the population of Han China was 58 million. Johan Ferreira, *Early Chi-*

long-distance travel rapidly improved. From this period, the growth of urban centers, lowered costs of food production (which made it easier to provide for travelers), proliferation of hospices and inns, extension of road networks, increase in bridge building, and greater use of ferries all extended the range of travel and mobility substantially.[24] By the ninth and tenth centuries, slightly faster speeds became possible due to an increasing number of post stations, quicker horses with improved harnesses, and better bred draft animals (donkeys, mules, and camels).[25] A mounted rider could manage 30–35 miles a day, slightly less over long journeys (due to delays, rest, and terrain). Improved conditions for land travel allowed the "hypermobile" Frankish emperor Charlemagne to average over 620 miles (1,000 km) a year between 794 and 804.[26] Medieval monarchs mainly traveled on horseback and had even faster advance riders. But riding animals were scarce among the general population and were typically used by women, children, and the infirm, or for heavy loads.

Still, the modest increases in the pace of travel intensified networks of long-distance exchange and encouraged greater numbers of travelers. Travel by sea remained much faster than travel by land and also allowed travelers to take much more on the journey.[27] Vast numbers of migrants who played a role in the Christianization of Europe—including Irish monks, Anglo-Saxon nuns, Viking captives, and royal princesses—covered great distances over sea routes.

Even so, travel (whether by land or sea) was grueling and perilous; and the obstacles that confronted long-distance travelers remained formidable.[28] These included the challenge of dealing with unfamiliar languages (an issue

---

nese Christianity: The Tang Christian Monument and Other Documents (Strathfield, New South Wales: St. Pauls Publications, 2014), 97.

24. Ohler, *Medieval Traveller*, 15–41, 97–101.

25. Ohler, *Medieval Traveller*, 29, 97–99, 107–17.

26. In 800 and 801 alone, Charlemagne reportedly covered an estimated 3,035 miles (involving some 162 days of travel) on the road. See Rosamund McKitterick, *Charlemagne: The Formation of a European Identity* (New York: Cambridge University Press, 2008), 178–86; Winroth, *Conversion of Scandinavia*, 12; Ohler, *Medieval Traveller*, 153.

27. John Haywood, *The Great Migrations: From the Earliest Humans to the Age of Globalization* (London: Quercus, 2008), 105.

28. For a detailed overview, see Ohler, *Medieval Traveller*, 74–78, 97–140.

even for educated travelers in an era when most people were illiterate[29]); the heavy physical toll exacted by the hardships of climate and harsh terrain; the unpredictability and interminable delays of sea voyages, in addition to the ever-present dangers of piracy and shipwrecks; the constant threat to life and limb posed by robbers or warfare on the roads; and the harsh penalties imposed by local authorities when unwitting travelers failed to pay tolls or ran afoul of unwritten local laws. Naturally, few set out alone if they could help it; and most knew to avoid carrying anything of value if possible. But, even for large groups or caravans, safe arrival (of people and goods) at a distant destination was never a foregone conclusion.[30] Death was ever present. Hunger, adverse weather, disease and sickness, armed conflict, exhaustion, piracy and pillage, and other perils of the journey often exposed long-distance migrants to greater risks of dying than the community they left behind.

Historical sources by their very nature recount the experiences and exploits of notable travelers and make no mention of the countless "ordinary" individuals who perished on the journey (along with their knowledge and discoveries). Needless to say, the lives of countless migrants were cut short in complete obscurity. Up to the sixteenth century and for long after, long-distance travelers embarked on their journeys acutely aware that they may never return. This made even planned departures poignant events. Generally, such travelers made a will before parting, had a Mass said, put their house in order, made peace with their enemies, elicited the prayers of friends and relations (monks asked for the prayers of their brother monks), and sought letters of introduction to take on the journey.[31] For those left behind, there was little to mitigate the wretched emotional anguish of minds consumed by the sheer uncertainty surrounding a loved one's safe return. Thus, the safe return of a traveler was celebrated with as much ceremony as his departure. All this mattered because in addition to substantial monastic movement, the medieval period witnessed a great escalation of religious travelers.

In fact, migration was a perennial and pervasive element throughout the medieval era in Europe, an indispensable lubricant in the wheels of encoun-

29. Ohler, *Medieval Traveller*, 131.

30. Richard Foltz, *Religions of the Silk Road: Premodern Patterns of Globalization* (New York: Palgrave Macmillan, 2010), 11; Irene M. Franck and David M. Brownstone, *The Silk Road: A History* (New York: Facts on File, 1986), 174–75.

31. Ohler, *Medieval Traveller*, 132.

ter and exchange that shaped economic development, state formation, and ongoing Christian expansion. In the necessarily abbreviated assessment that follows, the aim is not to recount or reexamine the multifarious initiatives and complex processes that led to the Christianization of Europe over many centuries, but rather to highlight a number of aspects that illustrate the efficacy of the migrant element. Three main categories of missionary actors deserve attention: Christian queens, monks, and monarchs.

Christian Wives and Queen Mothers

The emphasis on formal initiatives and political action in assessments of the Christianization of Europe has produced an almost exclusive focus on *male* agents—be they representatives of the institutional church or powerful pagan chieftains. This male-centered approach is encouraged, if not reinforced, by the blood-soaked sagas of the era in which warfare, murderous pillage, and savage conflicts are dominant themes. In medieval Europe, and throughout the entire period covered by this volume for that matter, women were, generally speaking, less mobile than men and more vulnerable on the roads. Even so, they naturally featured in invasions, resettlement, displacement, political change, and long-distance cultural exchange. But their stories and contributions are typically overlooked.[32] The role of women in the Christianization of European societies arguably comes more readily into view when migration functions as a primary lens. In the period under review, the main categories of migrants included not only monks and rulers or public officials but also slaves, soldiers, merchants, captives, nomadic invaders, and royal brides. Royal brides, who, unlike peasant women, often journeyed to a new home in distant lands to marry foreign husbands, form the focus here.

The historical records provide only the most tantalizing glimpses into activities of women as long-distance travelers and cross-cultural migrants. However, as we have seen, instances of female Christian captives who be-

---

32. For more on the role and contribution of women in this era, see Lisa M. Bitel, *Women in Early Medieval Europe, 400–1100* (New York: Cambridge University Press, 2002), 46–94; also Jo Ann McNamara and Suzanne Wemple, "The Power of Women through the Family in Medieval Europe, 500–1100," in *Women and Power in the Middle Ages*, ed. Mary Carpenter Erler and Maryanne Kowaleski (Athens, GA: University of Georgia Press, 1988).

came missionaries in distant lands are well known, though the obscurity of captivity severely limits historical data. The missionary contribution of Christian women who became the wives of foreign rulers was less anonymous and achieved greater impact (see also chapter 8). This is not to suggest that the role that women played in the conversion of Europe was limited to migrant action. Historian Jo Ann McNamara notes that they acted as missionary agents in three major ways: as a bridge between the local Christian community and barbarian invaders; as "patrons, foundresses and rulers of monastic communities" that contributed to the conversion of other women; and in their function "as supply bases for the heroic individuals who ventured out over long distances to carry the Gospel to new tribes."[33]

Yet, it was often as migrants or in contexts of migration that many women had an outstanding missionary impact. The most detectable and dramatic incidents involve Christian women from royal families who traveled great distances or crossed cultural boundaries as part of marital arrangements or diplomatic outreach. This was because in the premodern world, royal marriages were frequently used to consolidate imperial expansion, cement political alliances between different powers, or strengthen diplomatic ties.[34] In the Byzantine Empire, where elite women benefited from exceptional legal protections and enjoyed considerable independence, women were routinely used to further political alliances.[35] It was common practice to send women "out of their family homes to make a new life among un-Christian people"; and, when married to a foreign ruler, they were "accompanied by large numbers of Byzantine courtiers, diplomats, Orthodox priests, and ladies-in-waiting."

33. Jo Ann McNamara, "Living Sermons: Consecrated Women and the Conversion of Gaul," in *Medieval Religious Women: Peaceweavers*, ed. Lillian Thomas Shank and John A. Nichols (Kalamazoo, MI: Cistercian Publications, 1987), 19.

34. See Pauline Stafford, *Queens, Concubines, and Dowagers: The King's Wife in the Early Middle Ages* (Athens, GA: University of Georgia Press, 1983), 32–49. As Bitel notes, such long-distance marital arrangements among the ruling class were in contrast to peasant women who married locally. Bitel, *Women in Early Medieval Europe*, 81.

35. Imperial princesses, explains Judith Herrin, were specifically trained to perform vital diplomatic service through marriage. She adds that "even though the empire shared an overwhelmingly patriarchal culture and forms of male domination and female marginalization found in all premodern societies, women can frequently be seen to exercise power." Judith Herrin, *Unrivalled Influence: Women and Empire in Byzantium* (Princeton: Princeton University Press, 2013), 1–4.

The Byzantine practice was probably the most highly developed. On the other end of the spectrum, some royal Christian women adamantly refused to marry pagan rulers precisely because they feared for their faith.[36] The point, however, is that it was not uncommon for women from elite or aristocratic families to marry across cultural or national boundaries or end up in distant territories as part of broader political developments.

In addition to holding potential political influence, Christian women who moved to foreign lands as diplomats or wives were also, like other Christian migrants, prospective agents of mission. As wives they sometimes won pagan husbands to the Christian faith; as queen mothers they shaped the faith of the royal line and household; as confidantes or members of the ruling elite they were in a position to exert some influence in religious policy; and access to considerable wealth allowed them to act as patrons of religious activity and programs or use their position to exercise power over the church.[37] Royal marriages, as the Mongols' experience attests (chapter 8), did not always secure long-term missionary success. But, at the very least, a pattern whereby Christian women left their family homes to make a new life among non-Christian people, as part of wider cross-community migrations, played a unique role in Christian missions and the spread of religious ideas.

Dynastic or royal marital alliances occurred with great frequency in medieval Europe, though not every instance commanded the interest of contemporary writers. The reliability of relevant historical sources varies greatly, and the personal lives and personalities of royal women are often overlooked.[38] The lascivious lifestyle and wandering affections of kings meant that many royal marriages were short-lived or ended tragically. Foreign queens and princesses, who were often pawns in diplomatic relations or dynastic alliances, were also liable to end up as victims of court intrigue or political tensions.[39] Neverthe-

---

36. It is recorded, for instance, that when the tenth-century Danish princess Þyri (or Tyra), the sister of King Sveinn of Denmark, learned that she had been betrothed to the much older Wendish king Burislav as part of a peace agreement, her response was that "she would rather die than live with a heathen king and compromise her Christianity." Snorrason, *Saga of Olaf Tryggvason*, no. 46.

37. McNamara and Wemple, "Power of Women," 94–97.

38. Bitel, *Women in Early Medieval Europe*, 93.

39. Ian Wood, *The Merovingian Kingdoms 450–751* (New York: Longman, 1994), 120–23. Also Stafford, *Queens, Concubines, and Dowagers*, 38–44; Bitel, *Women in Early Medieval Europe*, 81–92; McNamara and Wemple, "Power of Women," 91–94.

less, the late fifth century witnessed a number of significant marriages among the powerful dynastic houses established in Europe by barbarian tribes.[40] The greatest of these was the Merovingian kingdom established by the Franks, which lasted from the fifth to eighth centuries. The marriage between the Burgundian princess Clotilda or Chlothild (d. 545) and the Merovingian king Clovis I (d. 511), who assumed the throne in 483, exemplifies the immense contribution of royal women as missionary agents.[41]

The Burgundians, like the Franks, settled in Gaul. During what might have been a succession struggle, Gundodad (one of the royal princes) murdered his brother Chilperic II, Clotilda's father, and drowned her mother. He then exiled Clotilda and her older sister. Frankish diplomatic envoys to Burgundy encountered Clotilda and brought her to the attention of the Frankish king Clovis I, who requested her hand in marriage.[42] Clotilda was a devout catholic Christian, whereas Clovis is depicted as a pagan ruler whose troops had a habit of plundering churches. But this was also a complex religious world in which paganism coexisted and overlapped with "Arian" (or non-Nicene) strands of Christianity and catholic belief systems.[43] Antagonistic relations between Arian and catholic Christians remained an issue; but the different religious beliefs also coexisted. While the Burgundian royal household may have been Arian, Clotilda and Gundodad's own wife were catholic. Similarly, Clovis held fast to ancestral religion, but one of his sisters, Lanthechild (or

40. Wood, *Merovingian Kingdoms*, 42; Stafford, *Queens, Concubines, and Dowagers*, 44, 46. Wood notes that the structure of Merovingian politics allowed some royal women to exert great influence through their marriage relationships and access to considerable wealth.

41. See Gregory of Tours, *The History of the Franks*, trans. Lewis Thorpe (Baltimore: Penguin, 1974), book 11.27–31; also Jo Ann McNamara, John E. Halborg, and E. Gordon Whatley, *Sainted Women of the Dark Ages* (Durham, NC: Duke University Press, 1992), 38–50. *The History of the Franks* by the sixth-century bishop and historian Gregory of Tours (ca. 538–594) provides the most details. This lengthy work (misleadingly titled, since it is not a nationalist history) surveyed the complex political landscape of Gregory's time with an eye on major religious developments. It perhaps overemphasizes Clotilda's role in the ensuing story. See Wood, *Merovingian Kingdoms*, 28–32.

42. Gregory of Tours, *History of the Franks*, book 2.28.

43. James C. Russell, *The Germanization of Early Medieval Christianity: A Sociohistorical Approach to Religious Transformation* (New York: Oxford University Press, 1994), 148–50.

Lenteild), was an Arian Christian and some Franks in his kingdom had converted to catholicism.

In this setting also, political considerations often factored in a ruler's religious inclination, though the extent to which this was true in Clovis's case remains a matter of debate.[44] James Russell suggests that the harmonious relationship between the Franks and the Romans, compared with intermittent hostilities between the Franks and other Germanic tribes, may have made the Frankish ruling class more predisposed toward Roman catholic religion.[45] Yet, given the proclivity for Arianism among Germanic rulers, Clovis, who gained the Frankish throne in 481, may well have opted to convert to the Arian faith. In such a complicated religious and sociopolitical world, multiple interactive elements no doubt shaped the outcome. What seems clear is that Clovis retained strong allegiance to paganism even after marrying a catholic wife; and a strong case can be made that Clotilda played a singularly influential role in his conversion to catholic Christianity.

The *History of the Franks* by Gregory of Tours (538–94), which I follow here, is comprehensive but not unbiased. Queen Clotilda is portrayed as a determined and intelligent transmitter of her catholic faith, a royal wife whose prayers and intervention were instrumental in her husband's conversion and baptism. Even if Gregory amplifies her role in the king's conversion, there are no grounds for doubting the value of Clotilda's influence. She defended her faith in the face of Clovis's strictures (when their first child died soon after his baptism) and boldly questioned his religious allegiance to gods that "are carved out of stone or wood or some old piece of metal . . . [and] certainly not worthy of being called divine."[46] She also remained in continual prayer "that her husband might recognize the true God and give up his idol-worship." In Gregory's record, Clovis's conversion eventually took place on the battlefield in dramatic fashion (accompanied by miraculous signs); and his prayer for deliverance, in the face of catastrophic military defeat, appealed to Jesus Christ "who *Clotild* maintains to be the Son of the living God."[47] He was subsequently baptized by Bishop Remigius of Rheims, though the exact year is uncertain. Gregory's claim that he was joined by three thousand of his men

44. Russell, *Germanization of Early Medieval Christianity*, 150–54.
45. Russell, *Germanization of Early Medieval Christianity*, 150–51.
46. Gregory of Tours, *History of the Franks*, book 2.29.
47. Gregory of Tours, *History of the Franks*, book 2.30.

is open to question. But Clovis's baptism marked a significant turning point in the Christianization of western Europe.

McNamara hails Queen Clotilda as "the first link in a chain of queens who secured the conversions of both pagan and Arian monarchs in succeeding centuries."[48] Her daughter (with the same name) married the Visigothic king of Spain, Amalaric; her granddaughter, Theodelinda, married Alboin (king of the Lombards). Also, Clovis's sisters, Albofted and Lanthechild (an Arian Christian), converted to the catholic faith at the same time as their brother; and Albofted married the Arian king Theodoric of the Ostrogoths. We lack any specific details about the contribution of these Christian queens. But, whether she evangelized anyone other than Clovis, Queen Clotilda's missionary actions arguably bore lasting fruit in other Christian women who became "Catholic female missionaries to the courts of the pagan and Arian kings they married."[49]

Sixth-century England also provides notable examples of the role of Christian queens in the cross-cultural spread of Christianity in Europe. Sometime around 580, the pagan Anglo-Saxon prince Æthelbert (r. 560–616) of Kent (England) married Bertha (539–ca. 612), the catholic Christian daughter of the Merovingian King Charibert I of Gaul.[50] The marriage was sanctioned "on condition that she be allowed to practice her faith and religion unhindered."[51] Christianity was definitely not unknown in Saxon Kent (see "Anglo-Saxon Missions and the Papacy" below). But Queen Bertha most probably brought Christian belief and practice to the Kentish court. She traveled with her own bishop and used an abandoned church in Canterbury (originally built by the Romans in honor of St. Martin) for worship.[52]

The historical records, including Bede's account, are completely silent on the impact of this immigrant Christian queen on the spiritual or political affairs in Kent; and her missionary contribution can only be indirectly discerned. All things considered, Queen Bertha's piety and practice almost certainly played

48. McNamara, "Living Sermons: Consecrated Women," 24.
49. McNamara, Halborg, and Whatley, *Sainted Women*, 38.
50. See Wood, *Merovingian Kingdoms*, 176–77. There are varying estimations of the precise date of their marriage. On the ca. 580 date, see http://www.canterbury-archaeology.org.uk/bertha/4590809451 (accessed June 20, 2019). Mayr-Harting suggests an even earlier date—possibly 570. Mayr-Harting, *Coming of Christianity*, 63.
51. Bede, *The Ecclesiastical History of the English People*, ed. Judith McClure and Roger Collins (New York: Oxford University Press, 1994), book 1.25.
52. Bede, *Ecclesiastical History*, book 1.26.

a vital role in the establishment of Christianity among the Anglo-Saxons of England. We have no way of knowing why King Æthelbert did not embrace his Frankish wife's faith (prior to the Gregorian mission). The suggestion that this was possibly due to his political concerns about Frankish influence has merit.[53] Regardless, Queen Bertha's devout Christian presence preceded the arrival of Roman missionaries and undoubtedly prepared the ground for King Æthelbert's conversion and the Christianization of Kent. In fact, some speculate that Pope Gregory I's decision to send missionaries to Kent in 597 may well have been in response to a request from the queen.[54] In any case, a letter from Pope Gregory I to Queen Bertha conveys something of the Christian influence she brought to bear on her husband as well as her singular contribution to the conversion of Kent.[55] In a notable passage, the pope wrote:

> You have been to the English what Helena, the mother of Constantine, was to the Romans. But you ought already to have brought your influence *further to bear* on our glorious son your consort [i.e., Æthelbert], so that through him the conversion of the whole English nation may be brought about. . . . Delay not then to *strengthen your glorious husband's love of the gospel* by continual exhortation, and inflame his zeal for a complete conversion of the whole nation. So may the good things spoken of you be found in all respects true, and increase. You are already known and prayed for at Rome, nay your fame has reached Constantinople and even the ears of the most serene emperor: your Christianity already fills us on the earth with joy. . . . (italics added)[56]

Elsewhere in the Anglo-Saxon world, the conversion of King Edwin of Northumbria (r. 616–633) bears strikingly similar motifs.[57] Edwin's marriage

53. Mayr-Harting, *Coming of Christianity*, 63.

54. Edward L. Smither, *Gregory the Great and Augustine of Canterbury* (Eugene, OR: Cascade Books, 2016). The fact that Gregory maintained correspondence with many potentates and prelates in Frankish Gaul forms the main basis for this conjecture.

55. Pope Gregory I wrote to a number of Christian queens and showed particular confidence in their ability to exert influence on non-Christian or newly baptized husbands.

56. Quoted in James Barmby, *Gregory the Great* (New York: SPCK, 1879), 124.

57. Bede, *Ecclesiastical History*, book 2.9–12; see also Mayr-Harting, *Coming of Christianity*, 66–67.

(in 625) to Æthelburh, the Christian daughter of King Æthelbert, was approved on the condition that he would in no way interfere with his wife's practice of the Christian faith and permit all who came with her (including a bishop and priests) to worship freely. Again, our source provides no evidence of Queen Æthelburh's direct role in her husband's conversion, which took place after many years of procrastination.[58] As with other rulers, Edwin's decision to accept Christianity undoubtedly included political calculation. But a letter from Pope Boniface V (r. 619–625) to Queen Æthelburh, prior to Edwin's conversion, conveys the prelate's hope that God, through her faith, "could the more easily inflame with His Love not only the mind of your illustrious husband but of all the nation that is subject to you."[59] The pope perhaps exaggerates the queen's influence, especially considering that Christianity in Northumbria was still the faith of outsiders and possibly associated with the Celts, who were bitter rivals of the Anglo-Saxons.[60] But he expressed strong confidence in Queen Æthelburh's missionary commitment and endeavor:

> We have been informed . . . that your Majesty . . . continually shines in pious works pleasing to God and diligently avoids the worship of idols and the enticements of shrines and soothsaying; that with unimpaired devotion, you occupy yourself so much with the love of your Redeemer that *you never cease from lending your aid in spreading the Christian faith.* . . . Therefore . . . , we urge you that, being imbued with the Holy Spirit, you should not hesitate, in season and out of season, to labor so that, through the power of our Lord and Savior Jesus Christ, [the king] may be added to the number of Christians" (italics added).[61]

Much later (in the ninth century), far removed from the Anglo-Saxon world, the marriage (against her wishes) of Anna, daughter of Byzantine emperor Romanos II, to Vladimir, the Russian prince of Kiev, led to the latter's conversion to the Christian faith and the Christianization of his people. Queen Anna is credited with playing a leading role in this process.[62] Anna's

---

58. Bede's account stresses the role and contribution of Bishop Paulus, who accompanied Æthelburh to Northumbria in 625 and labored vigorously to seek converts.

59. Bede, *Ecclesiastical History*, book 2.11.

60. Bagge, "Christianizing Kingdoms," 116.

61. Bede, *Ecclesiastical History*, book 2.11.

62. Herrin, *Unrivalled Influence*, 8–9.

daughter, Theophana, who was trained in the Byzantine imperial tradition in which elite women served in foreign lands, also carried Christianity north when she was sent to marry the ruler of Novgorod. Additionally, in 964, Boleslav I (the duke of Bohemia) married his daughter Dobrava, a pious Christian, to Duke Miesco of Poland. Dobrava reportedly converted her husband; and in 966, in part due to growing ties with Germany, the country converted to Christianity.[63]

The missionary actions of all these Christian queens and their descendants did not always bear immediate fruit in the form of conversion and sometimes provoked open rejection. Amalaric, the Arian king of Spain, had requested the hand of Queen Clotilda's catholic daughter in marriage. But he heaped such violent abuses on her that her brother Childebert invaded Spain with an army to rescue her.[64] Invariably, the missionary efforts of these women (even when it led to mass baptisms) represented merely the initial step in a long process of conversion that lasted centuries and often required the painstaking work of instruction and institutional reinforcement by generations of men and women, mostly from monastic orders. In Kent and Northumbria, the Christianization process suffered major (if temporary) setbacks after the deaths of Æthelbert and Edwin. But the stories of these Christian queens provide powerful illustration of the missionary potential and religious exchange inherent in migrant movement.

Monastic Migration and Christian Mission

The medieval period witnessed the rise of the religious traveler (including pilgrims, holy men and women, clerics, missionaries, and mystics) as a significant category of migrant, though they constituted, throughout, "only a small fraction of the total" migrant population.[65] Pilgrims accounted for the majority of religious travelers due mainly to the fact that Jews, Christians, and Muslims (adherents of the three Abrahamic faiths) share a tradition of pilgrimage to the Holy Land. In fact, the number of religious pilgrims on

63. Bagge, "Christianizing Kingdoms," 118.
64. Gregory of Tours, *History of the Franks*, book 3.1, 10.
65. Maribel Dietz, *Wandering Monks, Virgins, and Pilgrims: Ascetic Travel in the Mediterranean World, A.D. 300/800* (University Park: Pennsylvania State University Press, 2005), 23.

the road increased exponentially with the rise of Islam. Pilgrimage is central to Islam, and visiting holy shrines in Mecca at least once in a lifetime is an obligation for every Muslim. But religious pilgrimage (Latin *peregrinatio*, meaning "journey" away from home, or "residing abroad") also emerged as a key feature of Latin Christianity.[66] Islam produced no equivalent of the monastic movement that, in the West, promoted the religious value of travel and endorsed a life of permanent wandering or perpetual "pilgrimage." Other than trade, however, pilgrimage was the principal cause of long-distance travel from the eighth to the fourteenth century. Maribel Dietz describes it as "the quintessential form of religiously motivated travel."[67]

We must note, however, that until the fourth century, travel to the Holy Land as an expression of pious devotion was only sporadically practiced among Christians.[68] Visits to sacred sites escalated steadily following Emperor Constantine's extensive building efforts in Palestine (which included the erection of the Church of the Holy Sepulchre[69]) and the famed journey to Jerusalem in 327 by his elderly mother, Helena.[70] In 333, the unknown Christian "Bordeaux pilgrim" covered the 3,400 miles from Gaul to Jerusalem in about six months or so.[71] Christian pilgrims to Palestine burgeoned thereafter. A great proportion

---

66. See Edith L. B. Turner and Victor W. Turner, *Image and Pilgrimage in Christian Culture* (New York: Columbia University Press, 1978), 187–88; Marcus Bull, "Pilgrimage," in *Oxford Handbook of Medieval Christianity*, ed. John Arnold (Oxford: Oxford University Press, 2014), 204.

67. Dietz, *Wandering Monks, Virgins, and Pilgrims*, 27. See also Ohler, *Medieval Traveller*, 57.

68. The destruction of Jerusalem by the Romans in 70 CE limited pilgrimage. But the Christian life as a pilgrimage was the dominant understanding and a centerpiece of spirituality from early beginnings. See Craig G. Bartholomew and Fred Hughes, *Explorations in a Christian Theology of Pilgrimage* (Burlington, VT: Ashgate, 2004), 94–95, 98.

69. Khusraw (the eleventh-century Muslim pilgrim), who confirmed that the Church of the Holy Sepulchre was particularly venerated by Christians, described it as "large enough to hold 8,000 people inside . . . extremely ornate, with colored marble and designs and pictures . . . arrayed with Byzantine brocades." W. M. Thackston, trans., *Nasir-I Khusraw's Book of Travels* (Costa Mesa, CA: Mazda, 2001), 27, 48.

70. For detailed treatment, see Dietz, *Wandering Monks, Virgins, and Pilgrims*, 109–20; also Lionel Casson, *Travel in the Ancient World* (Baltimore: Johns Hopkins University Press, 1994), 305–7.

71. Stephen S. Gosch and Peter N. Stearns, *Premodern Travel in World History* (New York: Routledge, 2008), 43; Casson, *Travel in the Ancient World*, 307–9, 315.

were women. Indeed, noble or wealthy women were among the most dedicated Western pilgrims. Perhaps the best known is Egeria (possibly from Spain), whose journey to the Holy Land in the 380s, largely alone, lasted over three years.[72] Over time, the number of Christian pilgrims on the roads grew immensely; and a vast network of hostels specifically for Christian travelers (*xenodochia*), monastic hospices, and inns (many run by immigrants) were established to serve the needs of the multitude of religious travelers and pilgrims.[73]

The connection between pilgrimage, migration, and the Crusades is discussed in chapter 9. The rest of this section focuses on religious travel linked to missionary motives or outcomes. We must note that a spiritual understanding of travel existed in the church from early beginnings. Early Christian teaching linked Christian identity to the concrete experience of being a "stranger" or "foreigner" (Latin, *peregrinus*) and endorsed the view of the Christian life as involuntary pilgrimage or exile (*peregrinatio*) away from the spiritual heavenly home. These ideas gained new currency in the medieval era along with a form of piety that emphasized physical embodiment of spirituality. In a world where the distinction between the native and the foreigner was a fundamental feature of daily existence, travelers abroad were painfully aware of their outsider status and vulnerability. Regardless of motivation or destination, the alienation and physical adversities involved in life as a *peregrinus* or sojourner invested journeys with spiritual or religious meaning for Christians.[74] The great dangers and considerable hardships of medieval travel also made journeying conducive to acts of penance. Long-distance travel allowed even wealthier citizens to experience the ordeal of homelessness and temporary exile.[75]

Thus, despite intrinsic association with seclusion and separation from the world, medieval monasticism produced a significant proportion of religious

72. Egeria, who journeyed in the 380s, was one of the few early pilgrims to provide a detailed travel account—see John Wilkinson, *Egeria's Travels*, 3rd ed. (Warminster: Aris & Phillips, 1999); Dietz, *Wandering Monks, Virgins, and Pilgrims*, 43–54.

73. Ohler, *Medieval Traveller*, 79–96; Gosch and Stearns, *Premodern Travel in World History*, 43–44; Casson, *Travel in the Ancient World*, 320–24.

74. Dietz, *Wandering Monks, Virgins, and Pilgrims*, 43. This was true not only of Christians but also of Muslims and Buddhists. As we have noted, pilgrimage is a core requirement of the Islamic faith. By the tenth century CE, Islamic Sufi masters and Buddhist monks were also energetic foreign missionaries—see Foltz, *Religions of the Silk Road*, 12.

75. Turner and Turner, *Image and Pilgrimage*, 193–96.

travelers.[76] For many monks, the act of migration and the deprivations of physical travel mirrored the "interior spiritual journey . . . , the journey of the soul toward God."[77] Many also adopted wandering as ascetic practice.[78] But large numbers of monastic men and women routinely embarked on long journeys for other reasons such as refugee movement, evangelism, pilgrimage, study, itinerant preaching, monastic business, works of charity, and attendance at formal church gatherings. ˙ So common was the movement of medieval monks that from the fourth century church authorities passed laws and decrees to govern ascetic travel and regulate the growing numbers of wandering monks, especially the much-derided *gyrovague* (the false, or unsupervised, traveling monk).[79]

Among the most dedicated and determined group of monastic migrants, however, were those driven by the desire to propagate the Christian faith in foreign lands. Their missionary ventures were generally planned or intentional; but the circumstances and motivations that governed their initiatives varied considerably: some were propelled by independent conviction, others were commissioned by ecclesiastical authority, and still others were appointed by Christian sovereigns. In an era of escalating movement, monastic missionaries were a paltry segment of the swelling migrant population. Yet, their contribution to the spread of Christianity in Europe was substantial and in many respects decisive. The country of Ireland, home to Celtic-speaking peoples,[80] and largely outside Roman dominion or influences, provided the earliest and most extensive examples of monastic missionary migration.

Irish Monasticism and Missionary Exile

Much of Ireland remained pagan long after Patrick's mission (chapter 5). But the conversion of the country was more or less complete by the close of the sixth century. Irish Christianity was overwhelmingly monastic, and its mon-

76. Travel was so much a part of medieval monastic life that the sixth-century (pre-Benedictine) *Regula Magistri* stipulated that a monk who refused to go on a journey was punishable by excommunication—see Dietz, *Wandering Monks, Virgins, and Pilgrims*, 97–99.

77. Dietz, *Wandering Monks, Virgins, and Pilgrims*, 3.

78. Dietz, *Wandering Monks, Virgins, and Pilgrims*, 23–34.

79. For thoroughgoing treatment, see Dietz, *Wandering Monks, Virgins, and Pilgrims*, 69–72, 78–80, 88–100.

80. Haywood, *Great Migrations*, 46–51.

asteries earned a reputation for high standards of scholarship and literary production.[81] Uniquely, the vast Irish monastic structure duplicated the indigenous tribal system of kinship groups, kings, and overking, along with tribal inheritance conventions.[82] Since groups of monasteries (*paruchia*) remained under the control of the founder's family, abbots (heads of monasteries) had a status akin to tribal leaders, which made them more powerful and influential than territorial bishoprics.[83] Over time also, Irish monasteries acquired considerable wealth (through landownership and bequests) and attracted merchants and artisans, whose presence and activities contributed to commercial growth and linked the monasteries to networks of trade in the larger Mediterranean world.[84] The largest monasteries became the nucleus of small towns and strategic centers of trade and travel.

Irish missionary migration was stimulated by indigenous factors.[85] The Irish desire for wandering was legendary. Also, roaming and banishment or imposed exile (becoming a *peregrinus*) were common practices in Irish society, serving as a means of penitence, judgment, and purification of land and people.[86] The Irish tradition of wandering found ready expression in monasticism. Confederations of monasteries (established by a common

81. John Haywood, *The Celts: Bronze Age to New Age* (London: Routledge, 2004), 131.

82. See Kathleen Hughes, *The Church in Early Irish Society* (Ithaca, NY: Cornell University Press, 1966), 70–78; Haywood, *Celts*, 130; J. N. Hillgarth, *Christianity and Paganism, 350–750: The Conversion of Western Europe*, rev. ed. (Philadelphia: University of Pennsylvania Press, 1986), 118–19.

83. Hughes, *Church in Early Irish Society*, 79–90. "Once a confederation of monasteries was founded," writes Hughes, "the position of the abbot of the major church corresponded to the position of an over-king" (p. 78). See also Thomas Charles-Edwards, *Early Christian Ireland* (New York: Cambridge University Press, 2000), 241–81.

84. Haywood, *Great Migrations*, 133.

85. For more, see Thomas Charles-Edwards, "The Social Background to Irish *Peregrinatio*," in *The Otherworld Voyage in Early Irish Literature: An Anthology of Criticism*, ed. Jonathan M. Wooding (Portland, OR: Four Courts, 2000), 95–100. Hillgarth, *Christianity and Paganism*, 118–19; Haywood, *Celts*, 130–34; Charles-Edwards, *Early Christian Ireland*; Hughes, *Church in Early Irish Society*; Alexander O'Hara, "*Patria, Peregrinatio*, and *Paenitentia*: Identities of Alienation in the Seventh Century," in *Post-Roman Transitions: Christian and Barbarian Identities in the Early Medieval West*, ed. Walter Pohl and Gerda Heydemann (Turnhout: Brepols, 2013), 89–124.

86. For instance, an individual could be removed from a kin group as punishment for murder of another member. Such a person became an outsider to their kin, an outcast and a wanderer. See Charles-Edwards, "Irish *Peregrinatio*," 100.

founder or patron) were often widely dispersed, sometimes over areas larger than dioceses in western Europe. This necessitated wide-ranging travel by the large communities of monks, who made use of Ireland's extensive waterways. Monastic vocation essentially emulated isolation or alienation from kinfolk; and the ascetic ideal of exile replicated abandonment of society.[87] The pursuit of solitude and isolation inspired Irish monks to travel over land and sea to remote locations (such as deserts) and build their monasteries in uninhabited islands. Irish monks became the first Europeans to reach Iceland (by 800).[88] In addition to strenuous asceticism, Irish monasticism also developed a strong tradition of religious traveling or self-imposed perpetual exile ("traveling for God," *peregrinatio*) that produced "wandering monks" (*peregrini*).[89] Unlike religious pilgrims, *peregrini* permanently resided abroad without returning home.

For some monks self-imposed permanent exile was not simply a matter of rigorous asceticism and isolation. Travel to distant lands and residing abroad as foreigners among non-Christian peoples triggered missionary action or served an evangelistic purpose. The missionary zeal of wandering Irish monks led many to evangelize without staying long enough in one place to instruct new converts or build churches. This sowed important seeds; but often it produced nominal converts and necessitated reconversions. The link between *peregrinatio* and mission became more fully developed in the work of eighth-century English missionaries Willibrord (ca. 658–737) and Boniface (ca. 680–754).[90] But its roots are traceable to missionary impulses within Irish monasticism that exerted a profound influence on English Christianity.

87. As Charles-Edwards explains, the monastic vocation based on "renunciation of kindred and wealth" cohered with Irish social custom and legal processes. Charles-Edwards, "Irish *Peregrinatio*," 100.

88. They reached Iceland long before the Vikings; and the practice of remote travel continued until the twelfth century. See Haywood, *Celts*, 133–34; Seymour Phillips, "The Medieval Background," in *Europeans on the Move: Studies on European Migration, 1500–1800*, ed. Nicholas P. Canny (New York: Oxford University Press, 1994), 15; Somerville and McDonald, *Viking Age*, no. 68.

89. Hughes, *Church in Early Irish Society*, 91–92; Dietz, *Wandering Monks, Virgins, and Pilgrims*, 194.

90. John-Henry Clay, however, views "mission as *peregrinatio*" as a uniquely Anglo-Saxon concept epitomized in the work of the English missionary Boniface and his companions. John-Henry Clay, *In the Shadow of Death: Saint Boniface and the Conversion of Hessia, 721–754* (Turnhout: Brepols, 2010), 242–48.

In 563, Columba or Colum Cille (ca. 521–597), an Irish monk, sailed from Ireland to the west coast of Scotland and founded a monastic community at Iona.[91] Little is known about the first forty years of Columba's life. The *Life of St. Columba*, the most authoritative source on Columba—written by Adamnan (679–704), ninth abbot of Iona—states that he was born of noble lineage (to Princess Eithne) in a family that was part of the powerful Uí Néill (O'Neill) group in northwest Ireland.[92] The circumstances and motivations for Columba's resolve to leave his homeland are open to question.[93] But his stated objective, to become a "pilgrim for Christ" (*peregrinus*), reflected a long-standing Irish tradition of religiously motivated exile—in this case, with a focus on missionary activity. Columba's aristocratic lineage also conferred advantages of leadership and, from the beginning, he commanded a significant following.[94]

The specific details of Columba's contacts, travels, and mission to Britain are sketchy. He left with twelve companions, and the total number of monks at Iona reportedly grew to 150 during his lifetime.[95] But exactly how many churches he founded is subject to conjecture; and while as a foreigner-outsider he relied on political alliances for the protection and patronage his work needed, *Life of St. Columba* provides no concrete details.[96] From his base in Iona, in a ministry that lasted thirty-four years, Columba established

91. Columba's date of birth is uncertain. My brief assessment of his missionary contribution here draws mainly on *Life of St. Columba* and Richard Sharpe's splendid introduction to the 1995 Penguin Books publication. On the difficulty surrounding Columba's birth date, see Adamnan, *Life of St. Columba*, trans. Richard Sharpe (New York: Penguin Books, 1995), 9–12.

92. *Life of Columba* is a complex combination of history and legend, made up almost entirely of miracle stories. On its veracity and historical reliability, see Sharpe's analysis in Adamnan, *Life of St. Columba*, 1–8, 55–65.

93. The suggestion that the decision was prompted by penitential exile, for participation in the bloody battle of Cúl Drebene, is unconvincing, as Sharpe shows (Adamnan, *Life of St. Columba*, 12–15); see also John R. Walsh and Thomas Bradley, *A History of the Irish Church, 400–700 AD*, 2nd ed. (Dublin: Columba, 2003), 100.

94. He reportedly left with twelve companions. *Life of St. Columba*, book 3.3. See Sharpe's commentary (p. 19, n. 356).

95. James Thayer Addison, *The Medieval Missionary: A Study of the Conversion of Northern Europe, A.D. 500–1300* (Philadelphia: Porcupine, 1976), 77.

96. See Adamnan, *Life of St. Columba*, 1–8, 30–34; see also Douglas Dales, *Light to the Isles: Mission and Theology in Celtic and Anglo-Saxon Britain* (Cambridge: James Clarke, 2010), 56.

a vast network of monasteries in Ireland and Scotland and (according to Bede) converted the Picts of Scotland to Christianity.[97] Iona became a major missionary-sending center after his death. In particular, missionaries from Iona reestablished Christianity in Northumbria (England) at the request of King Oswald, who had sheltered at Iona while in exile.[98]

But the Irish monastic migration was not one single movement, and Irish migrant missionary activities in Britain and on the European continent were not limited to the Iona missions. Fursa (d. 650), a monk and popular preacher in Ireland, also chose to leave his native land as a *peregrinus* and ended up in East Anglia. He was well received by King Sigbert, converted many unbelievers to Christ, and built the northeast monastery of Lastingham at Yorkshire, before traveling to Gaul.[99] Other Irish missionaries in England founded Christian communities at Malmesbury, Glastonbury, and as far south as Mercia.[100]

On the European continent, the best known and most celebrated example of Irish monastic migration is St. Columbanus (d. 615).[101] Columbanus, like Columba, came from a wealthy family and made a decision to become a "pilgrim for Christ" (*peregrinus*)—although he was already a migrant-exile by virtue of the fact that he had left his home province to study and enter monastic life.[102] Columbanus set out from his monastery in Bangor (in the province of Ulster) around 590 with twelve companions and spent some twenty-five years in Merovingian France and northern Italy.[103] By then the Merovingian kingdom was largely Christian and there was an established tradition of royal sponsorship of monasteries.[104] He settled in Burgundy; and, with crucial sup-

---

97. Bede, *Ecclesiastical History*, book 3.4.
98. Bede, *Ecclesiastical History*, book 3.4–6.
99. Bede, *Ecclesiastical History*, book 3.19.
100. Dales, *Light to the Isles*, 99–100.
101. Details of the ministry and impact of many notable figures of the period come from a corpus of saints' *Lives*. Much of what is known about Columbanus's extensive work is recorded in *Life of Columbanus*, written in the mid-seventh century by Jonas of Bobbio, an Italian monk (and a notable figure in his own right and missionary) who joined the Bobbio monastery three years after the saint's death in 615. For a helpful summary of Columbanus's achievements and controversies surrounding his legacy, see Charles-Edwards, *Early Christian Ireland*, 344–90.
102. Charles-Edwards, *Early Christian Ireland*, 344.
103. Hillgarth, *Christianity and Paganism*, 122.
104. Wood, *Merovingian Kingdoms*, 183–84.

port from Merovingian kings (Childebert II and Theuderic II) and Frankish aristocrats, he founded a number of monasteries in Annegray, Luxeuil, and Bobbio. Columbanus achieved great stature; and the monasteries he founded "precipitated a fundamental change in Frankish Christianity."[105]

But his status as an alien outsider remained unchanged.[106] In fact, being an Irish *peregrinus* accentuated his foreignness and contributed to cultural conflict and ecclesiastical tension, evident in his appeal to Irish customs during bitter disputes over the celebration of Easter. Long-standing disagreements with Burgundian bishops (over his refusal to conform to local Christian practice) and the complicated politics of the Merovingian era led to his expulsion by Theuderic II (the king of Burgundy) in 610.[107]

The unique Irish monastic structure, bound up in tribal divisions, was not replicated elsewhere.[108] Indeed, while Irish monastic migrants played a significant role in the Christianization of Europe, Irish Christianity was itself affected by influences flowing the other way through the establishment or reinforcement of networks of communication and exchange between Ireland and the wider world.[109] According to Bede, Egbert, a nobleman from Northumbria who became a *peregrinus* in Ireland (essentially moving in the reverse direction of Irish *peregrini*) was influential in convincing the Ionan monks and the Picts to adopt the Roman Easter.[110] But Columbanus and other Irish missionaries brought innovative influences to bear on Christianity in Europe—notably, a more rigorous monasticism and use of the Penitentials (detailed but adaptable guidelines for penance that reformed the system and introduced the practice of private penance).[111] However, the uncompromising and punishing asceticism that marked Columbanian monasticism was

---

105. Charles-Edwards, *Early Christian Ireland*, 344.

106. He described himself in a letter to Pope Gregory as "more a stranger than a scholar." O'Hara, *"Patria, Peregrinatio,* and *Paenitentia,"* 99 (see note 44).

107. Charles-Edwards, *Early Christian Ireland*, 356–71, 389–90; Wood, *Merovingian Kingdoms*, 192–202; also O'Hara, *"Patria, Peregrinatio,* and *Paenitentia,"* 93.

108. Addison, *Medieval Missionary*, 116–17.

109. Charles-Edwards, *Early Christian Ireland*, 345. Both Columba and Columbanus, it is worth noting, visited Ireland after adopting lives of ascetic exile.

110. Bede, *Ecclesiastical History*, book 3.4, 27; also Mayr-Harting, *Coming of Christianity*, 265.

111. Wood, *Merovingian Kingdoms*, 191; Hillgarth, *Christianity and Paganism*, 122–23.

combined with, and ultimately replaced by, the more moderate Rule of St. Benedict, which the Irish monastic movement then helped to spread.[112]

Assessing the missionary impact of the Irish monastic movement also requires recognition that the effects of its diverse strands extended well beyond the activities or achievements of original Irish *peregrini* like Columba and Columbanus. The latter's missionary work, in the sense of converting pagans to the faith, was probably negligible at best; and assessing his legacy requires a wider perspective. To start with, the ideals of monastic asceticism and the extraordinary works attributed to its most outstanding figures represented a forceful repudiation of paganism—which is partly why the many saints' *Lives* emphasize the performance of miracles. In this regard, the establishment and expansion of Irish monasticism in foreign lands had great impact on the religious landscape. Furthermore, the monasteries founded by these movements became major centers of evangelistic endeavor. Columbanian monasteries as well as Columbanus's successors accomplished important missionary work.[113] The influential Luxeuil monastery founded new monasteries and nunneries in largely pagan rural areas in Merovingian France and played a significant role in the Christianization of the countryside. Columbanus's successor, Eurasius, undertook a mission to Bavaria; and Jonas, his biographer, was sent from Luxeuil to help Bishop Amand (ca. 584–679), the celebrated seventh-century missionary of Flanders (present-day Belgium) who also worked among the Slavs and Basques.[114] Above all, Irish monasticism exemplified the vast potential of migration as a potent source of missionary expansion.

112. Whether the initial mixing of the two rules dates to Columbanus himself is debated. Among other things, the Rule of Columbanus called for monks to fast daily (except on Sundays and feast days), eat once a day, subsist on a vegetarian diet, confess sins of thought and action once a day, and live in absolute subjugation to their superiors. This extreme asceticism is generally associated with Irish monasticism. But Hughes suggests that the ferocious self-abnegation and absolute obedience mandated by the Rule of Columbanus matched the violence and insecurity of Merovingian society. See Charles-Edwards, *Early Christian Ireland*, 383–89; Hughes, *Church in Early Irish Society*, 57–59; Wood, *Merovingian Kingdoms*, 188–89.

113. See Wood, *Merovingian Kingdoms*, 191; Charles-Edwards, *Early Christian Ireland*, 378–90; Addison, *Medieval Missionary*, 88–89; O'Hara, "*Patria, Peregrinatio, and Paenitentia*," 117.

114. Cf. Hillgarth, *Christianity and Paganism*, 137–49.

Anglo-Saxon Missions and the Papacy

Astonishingly, the papacy—the medieval Latin Church's highest authority and principal guardian of the Christian faith—played a limited role in the centuries-long effort to convert western Europe to Christianity. This, it is important to note, was in sharp contrast to the extensive missionary involvement and accomplishments of the patriarchs of the Church of the East (chapter 8).[115] There are plausible explanations:[116] the collapse of the Western Roman Empire left the office of pope severely weakened; the constant threat to the city of Rome (the papal see) in the centuries of tumultuous disorder and violent upheaval that accompanied barbarian settlement was no small distraction; moreover, while in theory the medieval papacy represented universal spiritual authority, papal jurisdiction outside the city of Rome was quite restricted and often eclipsed or usurped by ambitious political rulers. These circumstances forestalled papal missionary initiative or active engagement with evangelistic projects, though various popes provided detailed responses to questions raised by the conversion of pagans to Christianity. All said and done, medieval Christian missions were chiefly initiated by monks and monarchs. The mission to the Anglo-Saxon kingdom of Kent (England), commissioned in 596 by Pope Gregory I, was a major and historic exception to this state of affairs.

Pope Gregory I (590–604) is celebrated as one of the greatest popes of the medieval era;[117] and his Kentish mission represented the first time that a Latin pope orchestrated the conversion of a pagan people in a foreign land.

115. Papal involvement in missions to Asia during the period of this study was also minimal and often (as was the case among the Mongols) reactive. See James D. Ryan, "To Baptize Khans or to Convert Peoples? Missionary Aims in Central Asia in the Fourteenth Century," in *Christianizing Peoples and Converting Individuals*, ed. I. N. Wood and Guyda Armstrong (Turnhout: Brepols, 2000), 247–57.

116. For a helpful overview, see Kathleen G. Cushing, "Papal Authority and Its Limitations," in *Oxford Handbook of Medieval Christianity*, ed. John Arnold (New York: Oxford University Press, 2014), 515–28. Cushing observes, for instance, that the most authoritative pronouncements of the period (dating back to the early Church) came from ecumenical councils, while substantive ecclesiastical legislation was typically produced by or at the behest of Roman emperors and Christian monarchs (p. 516). See also Richard E. Sullivan, *Christian Missionary Activity in the Early Middle Ages* (Brookfield, VT: Variorum, 1994), 46–106.

117. On the nature and significance of his papacy, see Bronwen Neil, "The Papacy in the Age of Gregory the Great," in *A Companion to Gregory the Great*, ed. Bronwen

The exact reasons for his choice of the Anglo-Saxons, a people about whom he had scant knowledge, are unknown and attract debate.[118] As mentioned above (see "Christian Wives and Queen Mothers"), a request from Queen Bertha of Kent, a devout Frankish Christian, is not beyond the realm of possibility. In the event, there is little doubt that Gregory's primary purpose was the propagation of the Christian faith.

England had a Christian population before it was conquered and settled by pagan Anglo-Saxons (from northern Europe) as early as the fourth century.[119] With time, these earlier Christian communities were reduced to an insignificant remnant, with disused church buildings serving as poignant symbols of hollowed existence. Saxon religion supplanted Christianity and transformed the landscape. Major elements included temples, a professional priesthood, shrines and groves dedicated to various deities (such as Thor or Tiw), and magical arts.[120] Prior to the Gregorian mission, however, there was growing Christian penetration of Saxon kingdoms from at least two sources. By the sixth century, the Irish monastic movement had spread as far as southern Britain, though Anglo-Saxons regarded the Celts as rivals.[121] Southern England also had substantial commercial and cultural ties with nearby Merovingian Gaul, which had a large Christian population and a strong monastic tradition dating back to the late fourth century. Merovingian hegemonic inclinations complicated relations;[122] but Anglo-Saxon rulers had much to gain from strong ties with the Frankish power. The marriage between the Kentish king Æthelbert (r. 560–616) and the Frankish princess Bertha (539–ca. 612) bears this out. Needless to add, Queen Bertha's public piety and Christian devotion preceded and undoubtedly provided a foundation of sorts for Gregory's Kentish mission.

Bede's *Ecclesiastical History* (completed in 731), our main source on the Kentish mission, provides important details about the initial effort and its

---

Neil and Matthew Dal Santo (Boston: Brill, 2013), 3–28; Mayr-Harting, *Coming of Christianity*, 51–64.

118. For a brief but helpful review, see Mayr-Harting, *Coming of Christianity*, 57–61.

119. Mayr-Harting, *Coming of Christianity*, 13–16, 30–39; Haywood, *Great Migrations*, 100–105. Christian presence in Britain dated to the period when it served as a Roman province—roughly 43–410 CE.

120. Mayr-Harting, *Coming of Christianity*, 22–30.

121. Bagge, "Christianizing Kingdoms," 116.

122. Wood, *Merovingian Kingdoms*, 176.

immediate aftermath, though there are significant gaps.[123] The original mission comprised several monks from Pope Gregory's own monastery in Rome under the leadership of Augustine, the monastery's prior.[124] The undertaking was almost aborted before it began when the group, discouraged by the arduousness of the journey and unnerved by the daunting prospect of preaching "to a barbarous, fierce, and unbelieving nation," resolved to return home. Augustine was sent back to Rome to request abolishment of the mission. Pope Gregory's response, though expressed with pastoral sensitivity, was unyielding. He admonished the group "to carry out the task you have begun under the guidance of God with all constancy and fervor" and strengthened Augustine's authority by appointing him abbot. He also, importantly, made arrangements for Frankish interpreters to be added to the group, presumably from the church in Gaul.

Augustine's group of Roman monks and their Frankish interpreters, some forty in total, arrived in Saxon Kent in 597. Shortly after their arrival, they were granted audience with King Æthelbert. The king, who had been married to a Christian queen for at least two decades, was no doubt familiar with Christian belief and practice. As to why he had refrained from converting to his wife's faith, Mayr-Harting's conjecture that he feared increased political dependence on the Franks is quite plausible.[125] Queen Bertha's role is muted in the records. Whether she had a hand in prompting the pope's commissioning of the mission, she undoubtedly welcomed the missionaries. At the very least, her influence would explain Æthelbert's extremely cordial reception of the foreign missionaries and his eagerness to hear them preach. Pope Gregory, in a letter to Bertha, commended the "kindness and charity your Glory has displayed towards our most reverend brother and fellow-bishop Augustine."[126] King Æthelbert is portrayed by Bede as not only bound to superstitious beliefs—he took the precaution of meeting with the foreign missionaries in the open air to avoid being deceived by magic arts—but also mindful of the hold of ancestral beliefs on his people. For all this, the missionaries were provided

---

123. Bede, *Ecclesiastical History*, book 1.23–33. See also Mayr-Harting, *Coming of Christianity*; Addison, *Medieval Missionary*, 106–17.

124. See the explanatory notes by Judith McClure and Roger Collins in Bede, *Ecclesiastical History*, 370.

125. Mayr-Harting, *Coming of Christianity*, 63.

126. See Barmby, *Gregory the Great*, 123–24.

with a place to live and granted freedom to preach everywhere. While the king wavered, many of his subjects became Christian converts.

The role of the Frankish interpreters in the mission is unstated but difficult to overemphasize. The language barrier was a principal cause of the Roman missionaries' earlier decision to abandon the mission, an acknowledgment of the futility of attempting to propagate the Christian faith to a foreign nation "whose language they did not even understand."[127] Without interpreters and vernacular translation, Latin-speaking monks from Rome stood little chance of communicating the Christian message to pagan Angles who spoke a Germanic dialect. Absent translation of the message, the permission to preach everywhere in the kingdom would have been useless. Thus, the addition of Frankish interpreters, whose native (Germanic) language was more intelligible to Anglo-Saxon people,[128] was as vital to the mission as its initial omission is perplexing. It represented a crucial strategic adjustment, without which the Gregorian mission was well-nigh inconceivable.

More than ten thousand Anglo-Saxons were reportedly baptized by the end of 597. The consecration of Augustine as bishop sometime before 578 attested to a growing Christian population. In time, at an unknown date, King Æthelbert was also baptized along with a number of his nobles. Bede identifies spiritual reasons for the king's decision;[129] but, as was the case with almost all powerful rulers, political self-interest—in this case, the prestige and influence afforded by closer relations with the Roman world—was a probable factor. Æthelbert's conversion opened the way for lesser kings to accept the new faith and galvanized the spread of Christianity in the Anglo-Saxon world. His nephew and political subordinate, King Sabert (d. ca. 616) of the East Saxons, also became a Christian. In June 601, Pope Gregory dispatched another group of missionaries to England under the abbot Mellitus to support the growing work and the organization of the church.

It is crucial to note that the mission to England was undertaken by un-

127. Bede, *Ecclesiastical History*, book 1.23.
128. Cf. Anna Maria L. Fadda, "The Vernacular and the Propagation of the Faith in Anglo-Saxon Missionary Activity," in *Missions and Missionaries*, ed. P. N. Holtrop and Hugh McLeod (Rochester, NY: Boydell, 2000), 1–15.
129. He mentions the strict moral life of the monks, the effectiveness of their preaching, and the performance of many miracles (though no examples are given) as particularly effective. Bede, *Ecclesiastical History*, book 1.26.

armed monks and without the use of force. Bede avers that King Æthelbert "compelled no one to accept Christianity," having been informed that "the way of salvation . . . was voluntary and ought not to be compulsory." This statement is striking because Pope Gregory, the architect of the mission, favored the use of coercion in the conversion of pagans to Christianity.[130] In a letter delivered to King Æthelbert by Mellitus, the pope urged the king to use his power to "hasten to extend the Christian faith among the people . . . subject to [him]" and to "increase [his] righteous zeal for their conversion, suppress the worship of idols, overthrow their buildings and shrines."[131] A month later, however, the pope (in another letter to Mellitus) sent instructions for Augustine that contradicted his earlier letter to the Kentish king in both tone and injunction. He admonished Augustine that "the idol temples of [the English people] should by no means be destroyed, but only the idols in them"; that well-built shrines should be converted "from the worship of devils to the service of the true God"; and that animal sacrifice, commonly used in pagan worship, should not be abolished—rather that meat from the slaughter of animals was to be joyously consumed during the great feasts of the church.[132]

We have no way of knowing the specific considerations that convinced Pope Gregory that the cross-cultural mission in distant Kent was better served by caution and compromise than by combativeness and coercion. An admission in his Mellitus letter—"tell [Augustine] what I have decided *after long deliberation* about the English people" (italics added)—strongly implies that his volte-face was prompted by further reflection on the report he had received about the Kentish mission.[133] His reasoning that "it is doubtless impossible to cut out everything

130. In Sicily, the pope requested the help of civil authority in seeking out and punishing heathens; and in Sardinia, landowners, bishops, local military commanders, and the local governor were all encouraged to use coercive measures (landowners were exhorted to make rent burdensome for pagan tenants) to bring pagans to the faith. See R. A. Markus, "Gregory the Great and a Papal Missionary Strategy," in *The Mission of the Church and the Propagation of the Faith*, ed. G. J. Cuming (London: Cambridge University Press, 1970), 29–44; R. A. Markus, "Gregory the Great's Pagans," in *Belief and Culture in the Middle Ages*, ed. Richard Gameson and Henrietta Leyser (New York: Oxford University Press, 2001), 23–34.

131. Bede, *Ecclesiastical History*, book 1.32.

132. Bede, *Ecclesiastical History*, book 1.30.

133. For a helpful analysis, see Markus, "Gregory the Great," 29–38; also George Demacopoulos, "Gregory the Great and the Pagan Shrines of Kent," *Journal of Late Antiquity* 1, no. 2 (Fall 2008): 353–69.

at once from their stubborn minds" and hints at renewed appreciation of the tenacity of pagan religion, despite the large number of English converts, with an eye on the rewards of patient Christian instruction. This readiness to discard his earlier policy in the light of reports from a new and developing situation reveals the pope's conscious engagement with the complexities of a foreign mission.

Translation in View

Gregory's new conception emphasized a more sensitive and accommodating approach to religious conversion that reflects the principle of translation (see chapter 2). The disavowal of the use of force by religious or political authorities was not merely a concession to the gradual, and often prolonged, process of conversion and Christianization. Viewed from the perspective of the translation principle, this Gregorian approach carried two noteworthy implications. First, it signaled the limitations of the reach and resources of the foreign missionary as an outsider. Taken at face value, the Kentish mission was from the center (Rome) to the periphery (pagan Anglo-Saxons in England). It was also, for all intents and purposes, top-down, insofar as it was commissioned by a prestigious authority whose emissaries enjoyed the patronage of a powerful local ruler. But, like all missionary initiatives involving foreigners or the crossing of a cultural frontier, the evangelistic effort started from the margins, in a cultural if not political sense. Despite their training and social status, Augustine and his missionaries were *disempowered* to a certain extent by their identity as foreigners and representatives of an alien culture. Even with the benefit of interpreters and the backing of local authority they could not simply dictate the outcomes of the mission. As outsiders, notes Anna Maria Fadda, they "were forced to adapt themselves to the ways and expressions of the people they came to instruct."[134]

Second, the Gregorian approach allowed that key ingredients of indigenous culture were valid building blocks in the creation of a new Christian community; that some pre-Christian practices could be preserved, "with changed hearts," for the worship of the true God.[135] This implicated the re-

134. Fadda, "Vernacular and the Propagation of the Faith," 5.
135. Bede, *Ecclesiastical History*, book 1.30. The pope cited the example of the Israelites in Egypt, whose practice of animal sacrifice was preserved in the worship of Yahweh.

ceiving culture in the process of conversion and confirmed the agency of the converts. It also discredits the entrenched notion of pagan converts as passive recipients. Put more directly, vernacular translation renders recipients of the message (and, by extension, the indigenous apparatus of the pagan world) active collaborators in the conversion process.[136]

The value of these missionary principles was also evident elsewhere in the medieval English context. The first Irish missionary sent to Anglo-Saxon Northumbria from Iona at King Oswald's request was unsuccessful in his work because "the people were unwilling to listen to him." This individual's harsh disposition and cultural prejudice (he viewed the English as intractable and uncivilized) led to mission failure, even with royal backing.[137] His successor, Bishop Aidan (d. 651), is described pointedly as "a man of outstanding gentleness . . . and moderation," that is, one given to patient instruction. Aidan "was not completely at home in the English tongue"—King Oswald, who had acquired the Irish language during his long period of exile in Iona, acted as his interpreter! Yet, he became one of the most effective Irish missionaries in England; and the monastery he established at Lindisfarne became a leading missionary and ecclesiastical center.[138]

The vital importance of usage of the local language, with its unique sounds and concepts, in conversion and Christianization is more humorously demonstrated by a story involving King Cenwealh (d. 672) of the West Saxons. Cenwealh had appointed Bishop Agilbert, a Frankish-speaking monk, to preside over the church. Over time, however, he grew tired of the bishop's "barbarous speech" and unceremoniously replaced him with a bishop from Gaul "who spoke the king's tongue"![139] This whimsical historical vignette clearly suggests that the gifts and contribution of foreign Christian leaders remained subject

---

136. It is worth reiterating that though political pressure by the Byzantine government and the appeal of Greek culture (deemed a superior civilization) were key features in the conversion of the Slavs and Moravians, the missionaries had to be able "to converse fluently in pagan languages" to ensure the successful transmission of Christian tenets. See Sullivan, "Early Medieval Missionary Activity," 26–27.

137. Bede, *Ecclesiastical History*, book 3.5.

138. Aidan perhaps acquired greater fluency in English; for he reportedly "traveled everywhere in town and country, not on horseback but on foot," conversing with those he met—rich or poor, believer or unbeliever. Bede, *Ecclesiastical History*, book 3.5.

139. Bede, *Ecclesiastical History*, book 3.8.

to the sensibilities and vernacular requirements of the indigenous Christian community long after the establishment of a church.

The Kentish missionaries brought with them the rich heritage and re-sources of Roman Christianity, including much paraphernalia for the worship and organization of the Roman church.[140] In England, however, they encountered unfamiliar local institutions, customs, and expressions.[141] The application of Christian tradition (as they knew it) to the day-to-day realities of Anglo-Saxon society inevitably raised new questions. Augustine sought papal guidance and authority on a range of issues pertaining to Christian practice in the English context, including how one who robs a church should be punished, whether two brothers may marry two sisters from a different family, and whether it is lawful to marry a stepmother or a sister-in-law.[142] Thus, while external materials from Roman and Gaulish churches were utilized in the establishment of the English Church, the spread of Christianity into the Anglo-Saxon world through foreign agents expanded the range and application of Christian teaching beyond those earlier traditions. This central dynamic to migration and mission would be repeated with the successive Christian penetration of new pagan domains.

Despite auspicious beginnings in Kent, the conversion of the Anglo-Saxons to Christianity was a prolonged and often troublesome process.[143] Pope Gregory's mission was confined to the Kentish kingdom; but Irish monks, chiefly from Iona, evangelized Northumbria and much of southern England.[144] Everywhere, rulers played a key role in the advancement or retrenchment of missionary enterprise. In a number of situations, Christian monarchs were succeeded to the throne by pagan sons, with calamitous consequences for budding churches. King Æthelbert's own son, Eadbald, and King Sabert's three sons remained pagan. Similarly, in Northumbria, King Edwin, a Christian, was succeeded by pagan rulers before the reign of King Oswald

140. Bede, *Ecclesiastical History*, book 1.29.

141. For a helpful assessment, see Fadda, "Vernacular and the Propagation of the Faith," 8–15.

142. Bede, *Ecclesiastical History*, book 1.27; also Walls, *Missionary Movement*, 74–75.

143. Mayr-Harting, *Coming of Christianity*, 29. Hillgarth's claim that "by the 680s all the Anglo-Saxon kingdoms were converted to Christianity" is perhaps a narrow reference to the ruling class. Hillgarth, *Christianity and Paganism*, 150.

144. Bede, *Ecclesiastical History*, book 3.3; Hillgarth, *Christianity and Paganism*, 150.

(from 635), who had converted to Christianity during a period of exile in Iona. In all, the conversion of the Anglo-Saxon ruling class took nearly ninety years, with recurrent relapses into paganism. The spread of Christianity into the countryside lasted many more centuries.[145]

Boniface and the German Mission: In Brief

In the long run, the medieval English Church, so deeply influenced by Irish monastic missionaries and the legacy of Pope Gregory's Kentish mission, produced missionaries who set out to evangelize other pagan tribes, notably the Germanic peoples of northern Europe. The limits of space prohibit coverage here; but that story also showcases the themes of migration and mission central to this volume. The best known and most outstanding of these English missionaries was Boniface (originally named Wynfryth), whose missionary career lasted from around 719 until his death at the hand of robbers in 754.[146] No European missionary of the medieval period has been the subject of more scholarly production and documentation.

Inspired by the Irish practice of voluntary permanent exile (*peregrinatio pro Christo*), Boniface spent almost forty years continually journeying as a missionary, "travers[ing] immense portions of the earth,"[147] and never returned to his homeland. He labored in Frisia for three years alongside Willibrord (ca. 658–737), another Anglo-Saxon missionary monk also inspired by Irish *peregrinatio*. In 722 he was commissioned by Pope Gregory II as missionary bishop for all of Germany. Thereafter, he devoted his life to both the propagation of the gospel and the organization of the church among German peoples in Hesse, Thuringia, and Bavaria, founding scores of monasteries.

With no episcopal see, Boniface lived as a migrant bishop. However, he gathered a large group of Anglo-Saxon supporters and followers. Since Anglo-Saxons "could learn South German without much difficulty, and spoke the same language as the Saxons," the need for interpreters was low.[148] Uniquely

145. Mayr-Harting, *Coming of Christianity*, 29.

146. Much of what is known about Boniface comes from his biography, *Life of Saint Boniface*, written ca. 768 (within a few years after his death) by Willibald, one of his disciples, and Boniface's large corpus of extant letters.

147. Willibald, *Life of Saint Boniface*, 43.

148. Hillgarth, *Christianity and Paganism*, 169. See also Willibald, *Letters of Saint Boniface*, 15–16.

at the time, this band of missionaries included a large group of women, nota-bly Leoba, an English nun from Wessex and Boniface's relative, who crossed the sea to join Boniface in his mission and became a pillar of his work.[149] Boniface, like Willibrord, depended on the protection of powerful Frankish rulers like Charles Martel (r. 732–741) for his extensive mission work and church-building project. Abrasive by temperament, he pursued the destruc-tion of paganism with singular intensity.[150] The well-known Geismar episode, in which he felled the sacred Oak of Jupiter, associated with worship of Thor, epitomized this confrontational approach.[151] However, heeding the counsel of Bishop Daniel of Winchester, who recalled the Gregorian missionary policy in England, Boniface apparently began to give greater emphasis to preaching and accommodation in his ministry;[152] however, he remained dependent on Frankish protection and papal endorsement.[153]

149. The main primary source for Leoba is Rudolf of Fulda's *Life of Leoba* (ca. 836). On the strategic importance of Leoba and the contribution of female supporters to Boniface's mission, see Eleanor Shipley Duckett, "Saint Boniface; Saint Lull; Saint Leoba," in *The Wandering Saints of the Early Middle Ages*, ed. Eleanor Shipley Duck-ett (New York: Norton, 1964), 193–228; Mary Ellen Rowe, "Leoba's Purple Thread: The Women of the Boniface Mission," *Magistra* 17, no. 2 (Winter 2011): 3–20; H. P. Hyland, "Missionary Nuns and the Monastic Vocation in Anglo-Saxon England," *American Benedictine Review* 47 (1996): 141–74; C. E. Fell, "Some Implications of the Boniface Correspondence," in *New Readings on Women in Old English Literature*, ed. Helen Damico and Alexandra Hennessey Olsen (Bloomington: Indiana Univer-sity Press, 1990), 29–43. See also Charles H. Talbot, *The Anglo-Saxon Missionaries in Germany: Being the Lives of Ss. Willibrord, Boniface, Sturm, Leoba, and Lebuin, Together with the Hodoeporicon of St. Willibald and a Selection from the Correspondence of St. Boniface* (New York: Sheed & Ward, 1954); also Wood, *Missionary Life*, 67–68.

150. In one of the more recent studies, John-Henry Clay argues that in Hessia and Thuringia Boniface endeavored to confront and convert both the pagan landscape and pagan inhabitants. Clay, *In the Shadow of Death*, 279–397.

151. Willibald, *Life of Saint Boniface*, 63–64; see also Clay, *In the Shadow of Death*, 344–47; Carole M. Cusack, "Pagan Saxon Resistance to Charlemagne's Mission: 'Indigenous' Religion and 'World' Religion in the Early Middle Ages," *Pomegranate* 13, no. 1 (2011): 36–42.

152. Cf. Bishop Daniel Winchester's letter to Boniface (723–724), in Ephraim Emerton, trans., *The Letters of Saint Boniface* (New York: Norton, 1976), 48–50. The bishop argued, for instance, that comparing pagan superstition to Christian doctrine was necessary, "so that the pagans, thrown into confusion rather than angered, may be ashamed of their absurd ideas and may understand that their infamous ceremonies and fables are well known to us" (49).

153. C. H. Talbot, "St. Boniface and the German Mission," in *The Mission of the Church and the Propagation of the Faith*, ed. G. J. Cuming (London: Cambridge Uni-

Predictably, Christian penetration of German populations produced new and perplexing questions about Christian belief and practice that required papal response—on matters ranging from marital relations to use of sacrificial meat and lepers.[154] Boniface conducted three journeys to Rome and corresponded with four successive popes. His European mission received unwavering papal support; correspondingly, his missionary enterprise significantly extended the reach and authority of the papacy in Europe.[155] Some note that he spent a greater portion of his career in organization and reform of the church (in Bavaria and the Frankish kingdom) than in mission to pagans.[156] Yet, his promotion to missionary archbishop by Pope Gregory III (ca. 732) was based on recognition that "multitudes have been converted by you from paganism and error to a knowledge of the true faith."[157] In fact, Boniface and his large community of foreign monks and nuns remained fully motivated to propagate the Christian faith among pagans. In 754, at roughly seventy-four years of age and in the face of dire warnings, Boniface, accompanied by a group of companions, traveled to still largely pagan Frisia to evangelize. Many thousands were baptized and churches were built. But on the morning of the day newly baptized converts were to be confirmed, Boniface and his party were attacked and killed by a band of armed robbers.

Boniface's death confirmed the great perils of medieval travel and the enduring strength of paganism in the face of Christian expansion. It also exposed the limits of state protection in an age of endemic conflict. Yet, in the period following his demise, political authorities assumed an even greater role in mission to pagans—either sending missionaries to pagan lands or taking up the cause of converting pagan nations by military means. About 826, for example, the Frankish emperor Louis the Pious (d. 840) sent Benedictine monk Anskar (801–865) as missionary first to Denmark, then later to Sweden.[158]

---

versity Press, 1970), 48–49; also James C. Russell, *Germanization of Early Medieval Christianity*, 192–98.

154. For details, see Pope Gregory's letter to Boniface (November 22, 726) responding to his questions. Emerton, *Letters of Saint Boniface*, 53–56.

155. Mayr-Harting, *Coming of Christianity*, 268–73.

156. Wood, *Missionary Life*, 58–60.

157. Cf. Emerton, *Letters of Saint Boniface*, 57.

158. *The Life of Saint Anskar*, in Angus A. Somerville and R. Andrew McDonald, *The Viking Age: A Reader*, 2nd ed. (Toronto: University of Toronto Press, 2014), no. 88 (pp. 372–83). This source notes, interestingly, that Anskar was the only monk "willing to undertake [the] dangerous journey [to Denmark] for the name of

Anskar's labor in Denmark and Sweden produced many converts. The fact that he met many Christian captives in Sweden undermines the claim that he was the first to proclaim the Christian faith in this land.[159] In the event, the Christianization of Scandinavia in subsequent centuries involved forcible actions by political rulers often matched by resolute pagan resistance, which largely explains the recurrent violence in medieval conversion narratives.

MEDIEVAL MONARCHS:
POLITICAL VIOLENCE AND MISSIONARY VISION

It bears reiterating that medieval Europe was a world of extensive migrant movements. Other than religious pilgrims, the best-known migrants were the Vikings (a word meaning "sea-borne pirate" or "raider") or Norsemen (i.e., "men of the North," with the connotation of "foreigner" or "heathen").[160] Viking movements were wide ranging. By 870, Norsemen from Sweden and Norway had rediscovered uninhabited Iceland,[161] which was quickly occupied by substantial populations from Scandinavia (especially Norway).[162] So many Norwegians migrated that King Harald I banned the practice, to avoid depopulation. Within sixty years population pressures in newly occupied Iceland led to the discovery and colonization of nearby Greenland from the tenth century. The seafaring Norsemen were also the first Europeans to

---

Christ." See also Winroth, *Conversion of Scandinavia*, 103–12; Addison, *Medieval Missionary*, 29–30, 100–102.

159. Despite lingering questions about whether Christianity survived in Denmark and Sweden beyond Anskar's death (in 865), there is evidence to suggest that Christian beliefs and practices endured amid the violence of the Viking age. A later medieval source—Adam of Bremen's *History of the Archbishops of Hamburg-Bremen* (dated to the 1070s)—refers to efforts to "completely destroy Christianity in Denmark" in the late tenth century. See Somerville and McDonald, *Viking Age*, no. 89 (p. 384).

160. For helpful treatment, see Somerville and McDonald, *Viking Age*, and Winroth, *Age of the Vikings*; also Winroth, *Conversion of Scandinavia*, 14–31, 54–60; Le Goff, *Medieval Civilization*, 43–45.

161. Iceland was first discovered by the Irish before 800.

162. But migrants also came from as far as Scotland and Ireland. See Winroth, *Conversion of Scandinavia*, 54–55; Phillips, "Medieval Background," 15; Haywood, *Great Migrations*, 112–13; Somerville and McDonald, *Viking Age*, nos. 70–76 (pp. 297–311). It is estimated that the population totaled about 20,000 by 930 and subsequently rose to around 60,000 by the twelfth century.

reach North America; and Scandinavian trading activities drove expansion in the east, leading to sustained contacts with Muslim Arabs.[163] Viking trade, driven by competition for goods among chieftains, contributed to the vast networks of trade that extended from western Europe to Asia in the ninth and tenth centuries.[164]

As was the case with the spread of Christianity among the Goths and other Germanic groups, Christian beliefs and practices penetrated Scandinavian tribes long before the arrival of official missionaries. The evidence, even with corroboration by archeological findings, is scanty and requires some conjecture;[165] but the prominence of migration is undebatable. Long before the Viking age, Scandinavia had multiple cultural and commercial interconnections with the rest of Europe that facilitated the multidirectional flow of goods and religious artifacts or ideas (Christian and non-Christian). Scandinavian mercenaries served in the Roman army, and returning or retired soldiers (like their Gothic counterparts) brought back with them material and intellectual components of Roman culture. Many would have encountered Christianity; and converts doubtless carried Christian beliefs back to their original homelands. From around the mid-ninth century, many Vikings gave up raiding for permanent settlement in the British Isles and other parts of Europe.[166] These Scandinavian settlers joined Christian populations and became assimilated into the politics, armies, and cultures of those societies.

More importantly, Christian beliefs and practices traveled north and spread among Scandinavian tribes through the growing numbers of Christian captives brought back from Viking raids. Some of these captives attained positions of influence among the ruling and warrior class. When Anskar arrived at the Swedish port town of Birka in the early ninth century, he met many Christian captives, some of whom—including Herigar, the prefect of the town and a counselor of King Biorn II—had not yet been baptized.[167] Shortly after his baptism, Herigar "built a church on his own ancestral property and served God with the utmost devotion." Whether or not these Christian immigrant

---

163. Somerville and McDonald, *Viking Age*, nos. 63, 65–66 (pp. 274–79, 282–88).

164. Winroth, *Conversion of Scandinavia*, 85–101.

165. Winroth, *Conversion of Scandinavia*, 129–37.

166. Somerville and McDonald, *Viking Age*, nos. 52–58 (pp. 236–58); Winroth, *Conversion of Scandinavia*, 54–58; Phillips, "Medieval Background," 23–25.

167. Somerville and McDonald, *Viking Age*, no. 88 (p. 375).

communities gained converts among their captors, their presence and inter-action with the general population brought Christian faith into sustained contact with pagan religion.[168] Archeological discovery of the combination of Christian and pagan religious symbols in burial sites—notably the cross and the hammer (Mjöllnir) of Thor, the pagan god of war and lightning—attests to the contestation and ambiguity that mark the encounter between two religious systems during the long process of conversion.[169] In late medi-eval Europe, however, that process was attended by complex migrations and considerable violence.

The Context of Conversion

To put it bluntly, the spread of Christianity among the tribes of Scandinavia took place against a backdrop of endemic warfare and bloodshed. The Viking age, which lasted from the late eighth to mid-twelfth centuries, was a time of widespread conflict and wanton destruction. Scandinavian Vikings set forth on pillaging raids and murderous rampages over much of Europe in search of wealth. The swiftness of the Vikings' hit-and-run attacks (using fast ships that materialized with little warning) struck terror among local populations. Viking raiders plundered churches and monasteries (which were undefended) and sought captives to be enslaved or ransomed.

Yet, the ferocious and destructive Viking invasions were but one mani-festation of the prevalent violence and warfare in an age that culminated in the Crusades. Importantly, the Viking age coincided with the vastly more de-structive rampages of the Frankish emperor Charlemagne (r. 768–814), who spent almost his entire reign (a period of forty-six years) engaged in bloody warfare against other Germanic tribes. As Anders Winroth observes, with a large well-organized army at his disposal, Charlemagne "was able to inflict much more violence, seize more booty, and demand greater tributes than the Vikings could ever dream of."[170] In the ninth and tenth centuries, also, Arab Muslims or Saracens conquered Sicily, attacked Spain, and tormented vast numbers of inhabitants with pillaging attacks, while nomadic Magyars from

168. Addison, *Medieval Missionary*, 31.
169. Winroth, *Conversion of Scandinavia*, 134–35.
170. Winroth, *Age of the Vikings*, 43.

Asia launched devastating raids on western Europe before settling down in present-day Hungary.

Much of the violence had little to do with religious conversion, but religious existence was implicated. Group solidarity, a warrior ideology, and deadly tribal competition were core features of Scandinavian societies; and the ability of rulers to command loyalty and sustain kinship bonds was key to survival and success.[171] Shared religion was central to tribal solidarity, and tribal leadership incorporated both religious and political dimensions. Religion was "intensely personal, so that there was a strong connection between attachment to a leader and attachment to his gods."[172] As such, a change in religious affiliation had deep implications for tribal allegiance and even national existence.

The conversion of Iceland in 1000 CE illustrates the point.[173] Initially, only a segment of the Icelandic people and chieftains accepted Christian baptism. This generated religious division that posed a grave threat to the solidarity of the nation. When the pagan lawmaker Þorgeirr (or Thorgeir) was consulted on the solution, he affirmed, and all agreed, that "we should have *one law and one religion*" (italics added). Asked to make the decision on behalf of the community, Þorgeirr withdrew to his booth, where he spent a whole day and night, in complete silence, with his cloak over his head. When he emerged, he summoned all the people and announced that everyone should become Christian. He deemed it much better to abandon the old gods than open the door to the devastation of tribal disunity. However, in a shrewd concession to the disorderliness of wholesale religious change, the lawmaker permitted some pagan practices to continue—namely, the exposure of children, eating horseflesh, and sacrifices done in secret. The record states, however, that these "heathen practices" were rescinded a few years later.

Such peaceful resolution of religious disruption was unusual. In most instances, the enforcement of "one law, one religion" in the face of Christian penetration was conflictual and fraught precisely because of the profound political implications. In other words, the bloody violence that attended the

171. Addison, *Medieval Missionary*, 21–22; Winroth, *Conversion of Scandinavia*, 41–51; also Walls, *Missionary Movement*, 19–20.

172. Bagge, "Christianizing Kingdoms," 122.

173. This story appears in the Icelandic sagas. Here, I have followed the account provided in Snorrason, *Saga of Olaf Tryggvason*, no. 41.

protracted process of Christian conversion in Europe had a lot to do with the fact that, from the perspective of converted rulers or tribal chieftains, pagan or competing belief systems had to be eradicated because they could form a basis for rival centers of power. In this sense, the sustained and often ferocious campaigns against pagan religion by medieval authorities were partly motivated by political consideration or ambition. Yet, by the nature of things, political motivation and religious intention were inextricably mixed. Whether or not it was viewed as prestigious, Christianity (in sharp contrast to ancestral religion) demanded a stark choice between old and new; and faithful adherence to its precepts required the dethronement of the ancestral gods. As such, the outlawing of practices associated with the old religion by a political leader marked a critical step in the conversion process. Not only did the institution of Christianity as a new religion with a powerful structure have a centralizing effect, but by facilitating the abolition of all protagonists (political and religious) its monopolistic character also bolstered autocratic rule.[174]

Nonetheless, it is problematic to evaluate the reach and results of Christian mission in medieval Europe wholly in terms of political expediency. In some respects, the prominence of political motivation in the conversion of European peoples reflects the principles of adaptation and translation intrinsic to the cross-cultural spread of the Christian faith. For Christian preaching and penetration were more likely to be successful when the encounter introduced ideas and concepts that appealed to influential segments of society or fulfilled indigenous aspirations more broadly. It is argued, for instance, that missions to England were successful in part because Christianity brought a new way to conceptualize authority: an idea of kingship that fused Roman command structures with the Old Testament models suitable to tribal realities.[175] This held considerable appeal for local rulers like King Æthelbert who were growing in power and influence.

However, it is one thing to say that the Christian encounter with medieval European societies *was fundamentally shaped by* the latter's preexisting sociopolitical structures—this was also true of Christian engagement with Sassanid Persia, Japan, and the Mongol empires—and another thing entirely

174. Cf. Bagge, "Christianizing Kingdoms," 124–25.
175. Geoffrey Koziol, "Christianizing Political Discourses," in *Oxford Handbook of Medieval Christianity*, ed. John Arnold (New York: Oxford University Press, 2014), 475.

to assume or allege that Christianity spread among European peoples *because of* or *in service to* the existing political order. Such a claim seems reductionist and possibly reflects a desire to circumvent the salience of religious experience and convictions in social transformations. In his thoroughgoing analysis of Scandinavian conversions, for instance, Winroth distinguishes between the earlier unregulated seepage of Christian ideas and practices into Scandinavia (mainly through migration) and subsequent "institutional conversion" that involved the violent destruction of pagan temples by local rulers and the establishment of the church. He characterizes the latter as "more a political event than a spiritual process,"[176] and he makes the astonishing claim that Scandinavian conversion "was not about [religious] beliefs . . . [but] all about community and practices."[177]

In the first place, this implies that the process cannot be both at the same time—strategic and spiritual, religious and realistic. Religious conversion, as we have noted (chapter 2), brings several dimensions of the context (social, political, economic, cultural, religious, etc.) into play and typically involves decisions based on the potential converts' aspirations. The prevailing belief in a supernatural world was by no means incompatible with calculated self-interest, not to mention the fact that the medieval worldview permitted no sharp demarcation between the sacred and secular. The conversion of Iceland involved no demonstration of supernatural power and no intellectual debate or military conquest, merely the pragmatic decision by a pagan leader with provision for religious compromise.

Admittedly, the medieval political landscape dictated group conversions and a top-down approach to religious change—rulers were either primary targets or key architects of Christianization. But this did not reduce Christianization to state building or render every act of conversion a political event. Icelanders converted en masse because it was, as the sagas reveal, vital to "have one law and *one religion*" (italics added). The permission of pagan practices— individuals being allowed to sacrifice "in secret"—more likely indicates a pragmatic religious concession than an artful political ploy. In the sagas, as Theodore Andersson points out, the enemies of Olaf Tryggvason (ca. 964–1000), the indefatigable missionary-ruler of Norway, are "defined not just as political

176. Winroth, *Conversion of Scandinavia*, 103–4.
177. Winroth, *Conversion of Scandinavia*, 139.

opponents but also as religious antagonists."[178] Also, while political protection and patronage (notably by Frankish rulers) were essential for the monastic missions, the piety, spiritual outlook, and religious commitment of the monks themselves were central to evangelistic objectives and outcomes.

The Anglo-Saxon exception is particularly noteworthy. The use of political violence was conspicuously lacking in the conversion of England. King Æthelbert of Kent may have showed greater affection for believers after he was baptized in the seventh century, but he *"compelled no one* to accept Christianity" (italics added).[179] Among pagan Anglo-Saxons, patient instruction, not coercion, laid the foundation for remarkable missionary success. Boniface and his large Anglo-Saxon missionary group largely eradicated paganism without the use of military force (though under Frankish Carolingian patronage). Centuries later, Alcuin, an Anglo-Saxon cleric of York (based at the Frankish court) admonished Charlemagne that "faith is a voluntary matter, not one of coercion."[180]

In the final analysis, the use of force was seldom decisive in the process of Christianization. There are at least four reasons for this: first, when religious motives are conflated with political goals, eradication of existing institutions and authority takes priority over the instruction and institution building required for the more long-term transformation in religious life that conversion entails; second, violent compulsion was typically aimed at alteration of outward religious behavior rather than change in religious belief or convictions; third, physical assaults on pagan religion inevitably produced violent revolt or entrenched resistance, since target communities linked ancestral religion to independence and the new religion with subjugation; and fourth, coerced mass baptisms of adult populations were liable to be negated by mass apostasy (reversion to pagan traditions).[181] Even if a goodly number of medieval Christian rulers used brutal military campaigns and unrestrained violence to

178. Andersson, *Medieval Icelandic Sagas*, 31.

179. Bede, *Ecclesiastical History*, book 1.26.

180. Luitpold Wallach, *Alcuin and Charlemagne: Studies in Carolingian History and Literature* (New York: Cornell University Press, 1959), 27.

181. The tragic efforts to subjugate the Wends (Slavic tribes in present-day eastern Germany) were a major case in point—cf. Addison, *Medieval Missionary*, 53–56, 148. Even when the process of Christianization under the patronage of a baptized monarch was peaceful, as was the case in many parts of England including Kent and Northumbria, the new religion thrived only as long as the monarch was alive or retained power.

compel pagan rivals and subject groups to accept the Christian faith, force had limited geographic scope (proximity was a strategic necessity) and the immediate results were decidedly mixed. Two brief examples must suffice.

The Frankish emperor Charlemagne was the greatest of Europe's medieval rulers and the foremost builder of the short-lived Carolingian Empire.[182] He was also a tireless itinerant. It is estimated that the total distance he covered in his forty-six years of rule (768–814) "would equal the distance around the world several times over."[183] By the time of his reign, Christianity was fused with Frankish nationalism and the spread of the faith bound up with Frankish hegemony.[184] The longer prologue to the Frankish Salic Law (eighth century) claimed "God" as founder of the "famous race of Franks . . . , now converted to the Catholic Faith."[185] His relentless military campaigns aimed at expanding the Frankish realm combined brutal conquest with a glorious vision of Christian mission in which annexation of territory and conversion of pagan peoples became one and the same thing. Military conquest acquired religious legitimacy under his rule. Subjugation of pagan rulers was immediately followed by mass baptism, the baptismal vow also serving as an oath of allegiance to the Christian ruler.[186] But for adversaries, the prospect of losing both political independence and ancestral religion inspired strenuous resistance.

For complex reasons, Charlemagne embarked on a relentless and vicious campaign against neighboring pagan Saxons from 772.[187] Pagan temples and physical symbols, like the cultic Irminsul tree, were destroyed; and bestowal of the benefits of the Frankish Christianity involved mass baptisms at the point of the sword as well as extensive deportations of the population into Frank-

182. For a helpful review of his expansionist efforts, see McKitterick, *Charlemagne*, 103–36.

183. Ohler, *Medieval Traveller*, 153.

184. Hillgarth, *Christianity and Paganism*, 75, 89–90.

185. Quoted in Hillgarth, *Christianity and Paganism*, 93.

186. This also confirmed that clerics accompanied the conquering forces. Ohler, *Medieval Traveller*, 157.

187. This campaign is well covered in the relevant literature. For perhaps the most comprehensive assessment, see Bernard S. Bachrach, *Charlemagne's Early Campaigns (768–777): A Diplomatic and Military Analysis* (Leiden: Brill, 2013); also Alessandro Barbero, *Charlemagne: Father of a Continent*, trans. Allan Cameron (Berkeley: University of California Press, 2004), 43–57; Matthias Becher, *Charlemagne* (New Haven: Yale University Press, 2003), 59–79; Yitzhak Hen, "Charlemagne's Jihad," *Viator* 37, no. 1 (2006): 33–51.

ish realms. But conquest and conversion met with resolute, equally brutal, Saxon resistance,[188] producing a vicious cycle of conquest, spirited rebellion, and ruthless reprisals. In one notorious instance (in 782), 4,500 Saxons were slaughtered in retaliation for Frankish military losses. Subjugation of the Saxon peoples took thirty-two years of savage warfare and ended with their forcible incorporation into the Carolingian empire (considered Christian territory).[189] It is possible to argue that Saxon conversion came as much by conquest as by forcible assimilation of land and peoples. Geographical proximity was also key. Not even a leader of Charlemagne's military capabilities and lofty missionary vision attempted to spread Christianity to distant lands by military force.[190] His use of Christian religion as a tool of political subjugation received widespread adulation in the Christian world of Europe; but contemporary critics were not lacking. As the cleric Alcuin, the emperor's close friend and confidant, averred, "a person might be compelled to baptism but never to faith."[191]

The *Saga of Olaf Tryggvason*, written between 1180 and 1200 by Benedictine monk Oddr Snorrason, provides the most comprehensive account of the zealous efforts of King Olaf Tryggvason (r. 995–1000) to Christianize Norway.[192] Born after his father, a chieftain in southeastern Norway, was killed by the Norwegian king, Olaf spent his earliest years in exile in Russia where he trained to become a Viking warrior. During his Viking years, he conducted raids on the

188. The Saxons destroyed Christian churches, pillaged monasteries, and sacrificed prisoners of war to their gods.

189. This was far shorter in duration than the two-hundred-year violent campaign against the Wends by the German emperors (from the tenth to twelfth centuries); but, nonetheless, it was an astonishing feat of sustained military aggression that invoked the name of Christ. See McKitterick, *Charlemagne*, 103–6; Addison, *Medieval Missionary*, 48–52.

190. For distant areas, such as the mission to the Slavs, diplomacy was the preferred option. Bagge, "Christianizing Kingdoms," 118.

191. Douglas Dales, *Alcuin—Theology and Thought* (Cambridge: James Clarke, 2013), 115; Eleanor Shipley Duckett, *Alcuin, Friend of Charlemagne* (New York: Macmillan, 1951), 132. See also, Hen, "Charlemagne's Jihad," 40, 42–44.

192. Scholars continue to debate the historical reliability or factual elements of this largely biographical account that incorporates legend, oral anecdotes, hagiographic literature, and supernatural elements. See Snorrason, *Saga of Olaf Tryggvason*; Andersson, *Medieval Icelandic Sagas*, 25–42; Somerville and McDonald, *Viking Age*, no. 90; Sverre Bagge, "The Making of a Missionary King: The Medieval Accounts of Olaf Tryggvason and the Conversion of Norway," *Journal of English and Germanic Philology* 105, no. 4 (October 2006): 473–513; also Addison, *Medieval Missionary*, 31–33.

coasts of Scotland, England, and Ireland, acquiring wealth and followers. He converted to Christianity somewhere close to Ireland,[193] and he subsequently returned to Norway to seize the throne. As king of Norway, Olaf pursued the Christianization of the country with relentless determination, driven by a combination of missionary fervor and political ambition. His efforts began in Vik, a part of Norway (previously ruled by his father) that had earlier converted to Christianity before reverting to paganism. He forcibly imposed Christianity on the population, inflicting terrible punishments on recalcitrant subjects.

Accompanied by a large army, Olaf Tryggvason converted other territories using ferocious violence. Efforts at persuasion through eloquent preaching are recorded, as are peaceful means—in Hordaland, for instance, marriage alliances (between Olaf's sisters and local chieftains) paved the way for conversion of the population.[194] But, more typically, conversion was compelled: adversaries were overpowered, sorcerers slain or banished, pagan temples destroyed, and mass baptisms imposed. The words of Hallfred Ottarson, a court poet in King Olaf's day who struggled with the decision to turn his back on Odin, captures the stark choice imposed by his royal mission:

> I worshipped the quick-witted lord of Hlidskjalf [Odin],
> before everything altered in the fortunes and fates of men.
> For followers of the faith of [King Olaf], sacrifices are banned;
> we must shun most of all the age-old ordinances of the norns;
> all men throw Odin's tribe to the tempest;
> I am forced to forsake Njord's kin to pray to Christ.[195]

King Olaf's missionary campaign lasted around four years and ended with his defeat at the Battle of Svold by a coalition of pagan kings that included rebellious Norwegian chieftains. He is credited with the conversion of Norway, Shetland, Orkney, the Faroe Islands, Iceland, and Greenland. But the chronicler admits that the communities that he left behind in Norway were more pagan than Christian. The explanation is telling: "It was not to be expected that the people would be compliant in their ways and their total faith in God, because the time was short and the people recalcitrant and hardened in false belief and

193. Snorrason, *Saga of Olaf Tryggvason*, no. 14.
194. Snorrason, *Saga of Olaf Tryggvason*, no. 31 [S22–24].
195. Somerville and McDonald, *Viking Age*, no. 91 (p. 394).

reluctant to abandon the religion of their kinsmen. There was also a great lack of clerics, and those who were available were hesitant *because of a lack of intelligence or learning in the use of the Norse language*" (italics added).[196] Mission through use of force and intimidation was ineffectual precisely because it sought instantaneous results and reduced conversion to a single act of submission. Christianization required much more, including the painstaking effort of instruction and vernacular translation (or learning in the use of the Norse language).

The contrast with the mission to Iceland, undertaken by a Saxon priest at the behest of Olaf Tryggvason, could not be more stark. The Iceland mission was bereft of military action or use of force and depended almost exclusively on proclamation. The Saxon missionary "instructed the people . . . in the faith and baptized those who accepted it."[197] This approach not only won converts but led to the adoption of Christianity by the entire nation through an indigenous process of deliberation and decision making (see above). In Norway, meanwhile, the process was fitful and protracted, despite heavy application of political violence. The Christianization of Norway was later completed under Olaf Haraldsson (ca. 995–1030), who became king of Norway fifteen years after the death of Olaf Tryggvason.

The vivid tales of dramatic religious change among European kings and chieftains (on occasion from paganism to Christian piety in one bound!), wholesale conversions, and miraculous occurrences that validated the triumph of Christ over Odin or Thor deserve attention and invite critical appraisal. But the fact remains that the Christianization of Europe was a prolonged, multistage, multigenerational process of transformation that lasted until at least the twelfth century. The phenomenal complexity of the diverse elements that contributed to the outcomes complicates straightforward assessment. But few elements were more central or constant than migration.

---

196. Snorrason, *Saga of Olaf Tryggvason*, no. 52. Moreover, he adds, in remote settlements and mountains throughout Norway, paganism remained quite entrenched.
197. Snorrason, *Saga of Olaf Tryggvason*, no. 41.

CHAPTER EIGHT

To the Ends of the East: The Faith of Merchants

The meaning of the teaching has been carefully examined: It is mysterious, wonderful, calm; it fixes the essentials of life and perfection; it is salvation of living beings, it is the wealth of man. It is right that it should spread through the empire. Therefore, let the local officials build a monastery in the I-ning quarter with twenty-one monks. . . .

—T'ang Emperor Taizong[1]

Christianity began as an Asian (non-Western) religion, and its spread eastward along the Silk Road into central Asia, as far as China and India, is one of the most remarkable chapters in the annals of the world Christian movement. It is a story of extraordinary missionary endeavor in which "empire" was unessential and state sponsorship (including the use of force) as an evangelizing strategy was conspicuously absent. The seven-hundred-year period following the demise of Sassanian Persia witnessed the rise of Christian communities in the east that far exceeded western Christendom in size, missionary zeal, and spiritual vigor. For many centuries, notes John England, "the Church of the East included greater numbers over vastly greater distances than the Churches of Rome or Byzantium . . . without colonial or imperial domination."[2] About the midpoint of this period, in the early ninth century, the Latin Church in

---

1. Decree issued by the Chinese emperor in reference to Nestorian Christianity, which spread to China in 635 CE. Ian Gillman and Hans-Joachim Klimkeit, *Christians in Asia before 1500* (Ann Arbor: University of Michigan Press, 1999), 279.

2. John C. England, *The Hidden History of Christianity in Asia: The Churches of the East before the Year 1500* (Delhi, India: ISPCK, 2002), 2. See also Erica C. D. Hunter, "The Church of the East in Central Asia," *Bulletin of the John Rylands Library* 78, no. 3 (1996): 130.

the West was "a shrunk remnant"[3] confined by the spread of Islamic rule. In Rome, a beleaguered Pope Leo III (d. 816) looked to the military conquests of Charlemagne (r. 768–814) and the ultimately short-lived Frankish Empire to consolidate papal authority.[4] Meanwhile, at Baghdad under Abbasid rule (then the greatest cultural center in the world), the patriarch of the Church of the East, Timothy I (779–823), presided over a rapidly expanding church, with nineteen metropolitan provinces, eighty-five bishops, and countless clergy, covering an area many times the size of Europe.[5]

In addition to their phenomenal growth and remarkable endurance, the churches of the east produced the earliest Christian kingdoms, functioned in a variety of languages (though not Latin), developed rich liturgies and powerful intellectual traditions, mounted impressive missionary efforts to distant lands, thrived in contexts of religious diversity, engaged in dialogue with other world religions, and successfully translated the faith into the fabric of life outside the Greek East and Latin West. Thoughtful consideration of the experiences and exploits of Eastern Christians troubles commonplace understandings of the Christian story because it affords critical insights into a range of issues pertinent to the life and witness of the church that are muted to varying degrees in Western accounts. These include the deeply contextual nature of theological production, the exigencies of Christian life and proclamation when the church exists as a minority religion (or the faith of foreigners), models of missionary action devoid of state or political power, the capacity of the faith to thrive in polyreligious contexts, and the pivotal role of migrants as missionary agents in the cross-cultural expansion of the Christian faith (which is this study's primary focus).

The reasons for the neglect of this rich history within Western historical

3. John Foster, *The Church of the T'ang Dynasty* (London: SPCK, 1939), 34. See also Wilhelm Baum and Dietmar W. Winkler, *The Church of the East: A Concise History* (London: RoutledgeCurzon, 2003), 79–80.

4. Charlemagne's empire fragmented within decades of his death, by 890. See Jane Burbank and Frederick Cooper, *Empires in World History: Power and the Politics of Difference* (Princeton: Princeton University Press, 2010), 83–87.

5. Johan Ferreira, *Early Chinese Christianity: The Tang Christian Monument and Other Documents* (Strathfield, New South Wales: St. Pauls Publications, 2014), 75; Foster, *Church of the T'ang Dynasty*, 34; England, *Christianity in Asia*, 27. In 804, writes England, Patriarch Timothy, who served under five caliphs, established six new provinces.

scholarship are complex but decipherable.[6] In addition to weak coverage of the church outside the Roman Empire, Western assessments have persistently disparaged Eastern Christian communities as unorthodox. The general view is that "anything east of Antioch was 'heretical' from the second century on, or unworthy of study even if it did survive!"[7] Most notably, the term "Nestorian" became emphatically associated with doctrinal fallacy. This understanding, as already noted (chapter 6), is problematic; and the picture of a fifth-century "ecumenical" consensus rejected by a radical minority is patently false. S. P. Brock denounces this portrayal as "an utterly pernicious caricature" rooted "in a hostile historiographical tradition which has dominated virtually all textbooks of church history from antiquity down to the present day."[8]

The egregious dismissal of all Christian presence and mission in Asia prior to 1500 is also self-serving. The Western historical tradition treats the Christian experience and theological heritage of European peoples as universally normative. The shallowness of this position is more patently manifest when the fascinating record of the Church of the East, a major and once dominant segment of the world Christian movement, is actually taken into account. Clearly, "criteria or methodologies developed to interpret the familiar fields of Western church history cannot . . . be applied unchanged" to Christian writings from the Asian

---

6. It is noteworthy that Eusebius's *Ecclesiastical History* (fourth century), a prime source for the history of the church up to the time of Constantine, is confined to Christianity within the Roman Empire and makes no reference to the Church of the East; and his panegyric *Life of Constantine* (also fourth century) treats "large numbers of Christians" in Persia as distant associates of the Roman state—see S. P. Brock, "Christians in the Sasanian Empire: A Case of Divided Loyalties," in *Religion and National Identity*, ed. Stuart Mews (Oxford: Blackwell, 1982), 1–3. Kenneth Latourette's seven-volume *A History of the Expansion of Christianity* provides minimum coverage: the first volume (on the first five centuries) primarily focuses on developments within the Roman Empire and the rise of Constantine; however, three of the ten chapters in volume 2, titled *The Thousand Years of Uncertainty: A.D. 500–A.D. 1500*, cover Eastern Christianity. More recent global histories have largely avoided this imbalance—e.g., Dale T. Irvin and Scott Sunquist's two-volume *History of the World Christian Movement* (2001 & 2012); Dana L. Robert, *Christian Mission: How Christianity Became a World Religion* (2009); and Douglas Jacobsen, *The World's Christians: Who They Are, Where They Are, and How They Got There* (2011).

7. England, *Christianity in Asia*, 2.

8. S. P. Brock, "The 'Nestorian' Church: A Lamentable Misnomer," *Bulletin of the John Rylands Library* 78, no. 3 (1996): 23.

region.[9] In fairness, it is worth noting that even when there is academic interest, thoroughgoing research and study of early Asian Christianity is daunting. These Christian communities expanded vigorously and successfully beyond Sassanian and Islamic rule for almost a millennium and in a multiplicity of contexts. Effective assessment requires expertise in a range of academic disciplines and substantial knowledge of ancient cultures and languages.[10]

In this regard, claims about the paucity of historical record for Christian expansion in the East have long ceased to be credible. In truth, much of the rich deposits of pre-1500 Christian missions in Asia, documented and nondocumented, remain undiscovered or little studied (if unearthed).[11] But a growing body of material sources is allowing a more detailed picture to emerge. Archeological evidence and surviving Christian documents, most of which were discovered in the early twentieth century, confirm the existence of considerable, highly developed Christian communities in Asia. A brief survey is in order.

EASTERN CHRISTIAN MISSIONARIES: A NOTE

The full extent of the extensive "Nestorian" missions in Asia may never be known or fully reconstructed. Data on the nature and duration of many of the metropolitanates established in central Asia are lacking; and the particular approaches adopted in a vast array of cross-cultural contexts by the innumerable migrant missionaries remain beyond reach. However, significant archeological discoveries from the late nineteenth century have shone substantial light on the lost Christianities of Asia. A thorough review is impossible here; but some findings are worth noting:[12]

9. England, *Christianity in Asia*, 3. He adds that serious study of Eastern Christianity is liable to expose "culturally-defined criteria in scholarship" and "present sharp challenges . . . to our understandings of theology, human community and historical process." See also Philip Jenkins, *The Lost History of Christianity: The Thousand-Year Golden Age of the Church in the Middle East, Africa, and Asia—and How It Died* (New York: HarperOne, 2008), 1–44.

10. England, *Christianity in Asia*, 2, 4; Ferreira, *Early Chinese Christianity*, 2–3. For England, "the diverse nature of the evidence, and of the cultural contexts within which it is shaped, will yield their secrets only to approaches which are fully cross-cultural and interdisciplinary."

11. See England, *Christianity in Asia*, 4–9.

12. Among publications that provide detailed assessment, see Alphonse Mingana, *The Early Spread of Christianity in Central Asia and the Far East: A New Document*

- Nestorian cemeteries with more than 630 gravestones bearing Syriac and Turkic inscriptions, discovered in 1885 near the towns of Pishpek and Tokmak (in the Russian province of Semiryechensk in South Siberia). The gravestones date from the mid-ninth to mid-fourteenth centuries. Many are of women; but the remains of "nine archdeacons, eight doctors of ecclesiastical jurisprudence and of Biblical interpretation, twenty-two visitors, three commentators, forty-six scholastics, two preachers and an imposing number of priests"[13] indicate a vibrant, well-established Christian community.
- a thirteenth-century Syriac lectionary of the Gospels inscribed in letters of gold upon a blue background, written for Queen Arangul, the sister of King Georges Ganatu-Uriyang of the Christian Turks.
- Nestorian liturgical manuscripts and artifacts, as well as medical treatises and medical works (dating from the fifth to fourteenth centuries), that were discovered in the early 1900s in East Turkestan, particularly in Turfan and Dunhuang—major centers of commercial interchange between China and the western regions along the Silk Road.
- in Turfan (a wealthy district successively incorporated into Hun, Chinese, Uighur, and Mongol realms):
    - some fragments of a lectionary of the Gospels used in the Nestorian community, dated no later than the tenth century, mostly written in the Sogdian dialect of Middle Persian (using Syriac characters) but interspersed with complete sentences in the Syriac language.
    - extensive Christian relics, including ruined churches, large Christian murals, remains of monasteries, and what appear to be Christian tombs.
- Dunhuang (an important oasis city and multinational trading center in northwestern China, situated at the confluence of major trade routes

---

(Manchester: University Press, 1925), 36–58; England, *Christianity in Asia*; Gillman and Klimkeit, *Christians in Asia*, 223–27; Ferreira, *Early Chinese Christianity*; Dietmar W. Winkler and Li Tang, eds., *Hidden Treasures and Intercultural Encounters: Studies on East Syriac Christianity in China and Central Asia*, 2nd ed. (Vienna: Lit, 2014); Jean-Pierre Charbonnier, *Christians in China: A.D. 600 to 2000* (San Francisco: Ignatius Press, 2007), chapter 3.

13. England, *Christianity in Asia*, 48.

and successively incorporated into the Tibetan, Tangut, Mongol, and Ming empires):

- a major library of Nestorian writings dating from the eighth and ninth centuries that includes Christian manuscripts containing biblical, historical, and liturgical teachings.

- two T'ang Christian documents: (1) the *Hymn for Obtaining Salvation to the Trinity of the Luminous Religion* (or *Hymn to the Trinity*), dated ca. 800; and (2) *Saints and Scriptures*, dated to the tenth century, in the period immediately following the T'ang Dynasty.[14]

- composed for liturgical use in the Chinese church, the *Hymn to the Trinity*, which is based on the *Gloria in Excelsis Deo* but makes use of contemporary Buddhist and Daoist terminology. Johan Ferreira concludes that it "expresses traditional or standard Christian theology, albeit in Chinese clothing."[15]

- the document titled *Saints and Scriptures*, which includes a list of saints (including biblical figures) and a catalogue of Scriptures presumably used in the T'ang church.

As Alphonse Mingana asserts, there are no credible grounds for denying the fact that "in an amazingly short space of time, [Nestorian pioneers] introduced their religious convictions literally into the remotest confines of ancient Asia."[16] We may lack details about specific means or approaches; but it is clear that the hordes of East Syrian Christian migrants (laity and clergy) who traveled great distances along trade routes became agents of Christian expansion. Their missionary endeavors required uncommon determination and a willingness to brave all manner of predicaments, including the hazards of long-distance travel, the vulnerability and marginalization inherent in encountering new societies as migrant-outsiders, and suffering at the hands of hostile state powers or actors. As traders, artisans, wandering monks, captives, and other types of migrants, few of these missionary agents could boast economic advantage—wealthy merchants like Thomas of Cana were notable

14. For a brief summary, see Ferreira, *Early Chinese Christianity*, 287–90.
15. Ferreira, *Early Chinese Christianity*, 261.
16. Mingana, *Early Spread of Christianity*, 5.

exceptions—and most sustained themselves by their own labors. Rolf Syrdal, perhaps with Nestorian monks in mind, submits that "the missionaries themselves were poor, adapting themselves to the conditions of the people among whom they labored.... They received gifts—among them some large grants from the rulers of various tribes. They did not keep what they received, except what could be used directly for the extension of their work."[17]

There was also a linguistic factor. The widespread use of the Syriac and Persian languages contributed immensely to Nestorian missionary success. Syriac, the main language of the Church of the East, was widely used or understood along trade routes. Nestorian missionaries and merchants contributed to the widespread use of Syriac, and "the Syriac characters as used by the Nestorians gave rise to many Central Asian and Far Eastern alphabets such as the Mongolian, the Manchu, and the Sogdian."[18] By the fifth century, Persian—which also became a "subsidiary Christian vernacular" in Nestorian communities and served as a medium of Christian instruction[19]—had emerged as the language of the overland trade routes in central Asia and remained so long after the rise of Islam.[20]

Even more critical than the use of trade languages were vernacular translations of Christian Scriptures and liturgy that allowed Christianity to take root among local populations. Archeological findings suggest that it was principally in Sogdian that Nestorian Christianity spread across Asia.[21] But Nestorian manuscripts, discovered across Asia and dating as far back as the fifth century, include seventeen different languages in addition to Syriac and Sogdian.[22] The growing population of Christian Turks and Mongols in central

17. Rolf A. Syrdal, *To the End of the Earth: Mission Concept in Principle and Practice* (Minneapolis: Augsburg, 1967), 74.

18. Mingana, *Early Spread of Christianity*, 47; Baum and Winkler, *Church of the East*, 77–78.

19. Christopher Buck, "The Universality of the Church of the East: How Persian Was Persian Christianity?," *Journal of the Assyrian Academic Society* 10, no. 1 (1996): 57, 82–88; also Brock, "Christians in the Sasanian Empire," 18; Robin E. Waterfield, *Christians in Persia: Assyrians, Armenians, Roman Catholics and Protestants* (London: George Allen and Unwin; New York: Barnes & Noble, 1973), 32.

20. Richard Foltz, *Religions of the Silk Road: Premodern Patterns of Globalization* (New York: Palgrave Macmillan, 2010), 16–18.

21. Foltz, *Religions of the Silk Road*, 68. The discovery of Christian Sogdian manuscripts in Turfan and Dunhuang (Eastern Turkestan) confirms the activity of Sogdian Christians.

22. England, *Christianity in Asia*, 53.

Asia, Persia, and Mesopotamia, for instance, necessitated the composition of hymns in Mongolian for their use by Nestorian hymn writers.[23]

In the long run, the spread of Islam ultimately countered and constrained Christianization of central Asian societies. From the eighth century, Muslim armies gradually conquered lands in central Asia, including Sogdiana. The entire region was absorbed into the expanding Islamic empire and over the next few centuries the general populace converted to Islam in vast numbers. But the Christian churches, schools, and monastic units in Samarkand lasted for almost a thousand years, surviving Islamic rule and the 1220 Mongol invasion.[24] When he visited the city around 1272, Marco Polo estimated that over one hundred persons, about a tenth of its inhabitants, were Christians.[25] Turkish tribes converted to Christianity through Nestorian missions in Transoxiana or West Turkestan retained their faith up to the fourteenth century, long after the faith had died elsewhere.[26]

No matter the limitations of the historical sources, the commonplace tendency to portray Christianity in Asia as a relatively recent development linked to the arrival of Western missionaries—a product of empire, no less!—is an egregious misconstruction. And it is one that the eventual eclipse of vast and vibrant Christian communities in central Asia (in the face of Islamic expansion and Mongol invasions) in no way justifies. Indeed, the complex reasons for their demise warrants close study, as Philip Jenkins demonstrates.[27] In any case, robust communities of Christians that have historical links to the East Syrian Church and claim a heritage that dates back to the apostolic era are present in India to this day. Moreover, a good many of those Christian communities in Asia, "founded long before the time of Clovis, King of the Franks, and Boniface, the Apostle of Germany, long before Augustine and Aidan in England . . . , persisted uninterruptedly" to the mid-twentieth century.[28]

---

23. Mingana, *Early Spread of Christianity*, 44.

24. England, *Christianity in Asia*, 45; Gillman and Klimkeit, *Christians in Asia*, 218.

25. England, *Christianity in Asia*, 45.

26. Gillman and Klimkeit, *Christians in Asia*, 218.

27. Jenkins, *Lost History of Christianity*. If omission of catastrophic setbacks in the history of Christianity was a governing principle, the extensive treatment of Western Christendom's catastrophic encounters with the Islamic world, epitomized by the crusades, would be difficult to justify.

28. G. Francis S. Gray, "The Spread of Christianity in Asia (in Early Christian Period)," *International Review of Mission* 42, no. 167 (1953): 269.

Of primary concern here, however, is the fact that an exclusive focus on post-1500 Christianity in Asia obscures a key fact—namely, that the missionary accomplishments and the spread of Christian presence in the Asian region fully demonstrate that, while empire building or imperial interest can provide structures and resources that facilitate missionary action, state sponsorship or political power is by no means a requirement for the successful spread of religion across cultural frontiers. In certain instances, in fact, endorsement by or association with local political authority can prove detrimental to foreign missions in the long run—as was arguably the case with Nestorian missions in China during the T'ang and Yuan (Mongol) Dynasties. To put it differently, the spread of Christianity in Asia was wholly dependent on migration and the missionary capacity of Christian migrants. These missionary endeavors, principally of East Syrian Christians, lasted for centuries and involved largely unstructured outreach aided by the unprecedented levels of intercultural interaction generated through expanding networks of long-distance travel. The primary missionary agents were unnamed migrants whose missionary function was inseparable from the vulnerabilities and unpredictable dilemmas of the migrant experience. Many were refugees, medics, or monks. But, as the story of T'ang Christianity demonstrates, the great majority were merchants propelled along the Silk Road by wider historical forces.

The Faith of Merchants

Once again, we must acknowledge that while there is rich historical record, at least enough to plot the general outlines of extensive missionary movement, the evidence is limited and much of it is ambiguous.[29] This is the bane of social history. We may glimpse the broad sweep and impact of groups or collectives in the shifting sands of time, but the subtle qualities of the human spirit and enterprise go unrecorded. The vastly different realities of distant times and distinct cultures also add to the dense fog that inhibits perception. Imaginative and sympathetic reconstruction is needed if the historical contribution of nondominant actors and vulnerable or marginalized persons is to be accounted for, however imperfectly. That said, even primary historical evidence

29. England, *Christianity in Asia*, 3; Hunter, "Church of the East," 130; Foltz, *Religions of the Silk Road*, 20–21.

or testimony can be equivocal and subject to conflicting interpretation. As a case in point, the translations of the T'ang Christian Monument into a variety of European languages are quite divergent, producing contradictory understandings of the most important source of early Chinese Christianity.[30]

That said, the role of merchants in the transnational spread of religious ideas and traditions in the period from 500 to 1500 is difficult to overemphasize; and the relevance to the extraordinary missionary activity of the Church of the East is indisputable. Admittedly, the missionary dynamism of the East Syrian Church was fostered by its theology, spiritual outlook, a migrant identity, and existence as a minority faith within a powerful state. The theological training provided by the School of Nisibis, in particular, "instilled zeal for active propagation of the Christian faith."[31] Moreover, "the 'missionaries' in this Asia-wide movement for over a thousand years included many who had been trained in the Christian monasteries and academies of Mesopotamia and Persia; institutions which were at their height from the fourth to ninth centuries."[32] Yet, there is no discounting the fact that geographical location and connections to global trade rendered the activity of merchants critical to the church's missionary success.

For much of human history, long-distance merchants have been among the world's most prominent migrants. Up to at least the fifteenth century, trade diasporas and commercial networks formed the basis for interregional linkages and mediated the most important modes of cultural contact,[33] though there are caveats. In some ancient societies, notably Greece and China, commercial activity (the business of trade and profit) was derided as inherently deceitful, and long-distance merchants were viewed with distrust and suspicion (usually because they were mainly foreigners).[34] In most societies, the

---

30. See Ferreira, *Early Chinese Christianity*, 148–54. First discovered in 1623, the inscription comprises 1,800 Chinese characters, sixty-three Syriac words, and seventy Syriac names.

31. Arthur Vööbus, *History of the School of Nisibis* (Louvain: Secrétariat du CorpusSCO, 1965), 208.

32. England, *Christianity in Asia*, 47.

33. Philip D. Curtin, *The World and the West: The European Challenge and the Overseas Response in the Age of Empire* (New York: Cambridge University Press, 2000), 3.

34. Philip D. Curtin, *Cross-Cultural Trade in World History* (New York: Cambridge University Press, 1984), 6, 75–77; Richard L. Smith, *Premodern Trade in World*

unpopularity of foreign merchants increased with their wealth, in much the same way that wealthy immigrant communities invariably incur the hostility of the indigenous population. But, as long-distance travelers, merchants were vital to religious life: they transported, sometimes over thousands of miles, the products needed by countless religious communities for religious ceremonies: for Christians "wine for mass, oil for consecration and incense for religious celebration."[35] It is no coincidence, affirms Richard Foltz, "that throughout history ideas and technologies have spread along trade routes, and that merchants have been among their prime transmitters."[36]

The point is that long-distance commerce, incorporating trade routes (overland or maritime) and networks of trading centers, constituted the main arteries for cultural expansion and interchange in the ancient world. The ambitions and activities of merchants or specialist traders produced transregional networks of roads, ports, and diaspora communities that became conduits for the spread of religious beliefs and cultural influences along with trade commodities. By the seventh century CE, the famous Silk Road (comprising major trade routes), which began to take shape several centuries before Christ, extended some 4,000 miles from the Mediterranean Sea in the west to the city of Xi'an (earlier Chang'an) in northwestern China. These networks of roads "provided a means of cultural exchange that connected peoples over much of the world, conveying not just goods but fashions, traditions, and ideas."[37]

The main centers of trade between East and West lay in the eastern provinces of the Roman Empire, principally the province of Syria, a major source of the Christian captives whose numbers and gifts swelled the ranks of the Church of the East. The nation of Syria was even better known for its mercantile activities and networks than for its skilled artisans who (as captives) were so attractive to Sassanian rulers (chapter 6). Few peoples, it is noted, demonstrated a greater instinct for trade than the Syrians.[38] Not only was the mercantile profession a prominent feature in the life and mission of the East Syrian

---

History (New York: Routledge, 2008), 51–52; Norbert Ohler, *The Medieval Traveller* (Woodbridge: Boydell, 1997), 63.

35. Ohler, *Medieval Traveller*, 61.
36. Foltz, *Religions of the Silk Road*, 8.
37. Foltz, *Religions of the Silk Road*, 4, 5.
38. M. P. Charlesworth, *Trade-Routes and Commerce of the Roman Empire* (New York: Cooper Square, 1970), 54.

Church but the spread of its communities throughout Persia also spurred mercantile activity—so that even nontrading Christian families turned to long-distance trade as a means of supporting themselves.[39] Furthermore, since many East Syrian Christians were merchants, merchants or merchant groups would arguably have been primary recipients of their proselytizing efforts; and even minimal success would have generated a cumulative increase in the numbers of Persian merchants who were Christian.

There is little doubt, however, that a good proportion of Persian merchants were Christians or that Christians dominated the mercantile class. The movement and trading activities of these Christian merchants—a group that combined the means and mettle for hazardous journeys over great distances with religious fervor—helped to expand the faith eastward into Asia.[40] So integrated were mercantile activity and missionary outreach that, among Syrian Christians, the word "merchant" became a metaphor for "missionary." The words of the fourth-century Syriac poet Cyrillona, evoking Christ's charge to his disciples, portray the apostolic functions attributed to the merchant figure:

> Travel well girt like merchants,
> That we may gain the world.
> Convert men to me,
> Fill creation with teaching.[41]

In other words, if the missionary ventures of Eastern Christians "exceeded the much more celebrated missionary successes in Europe,"[42] it was because hordes of widely traveled merchants supplemented the evangelistic outreach of clergy and "wandering monks."[43]

39. Michael C. Howard, *Transnationalism in Ancient and Medieval Societies: The Role of Cross-Border Trade and Travel* (Jefferson, NC: McFarland, 2012), 143.

40. Charbonnier, *Christians in China*, 43.

41. Robert Murray, *Symbols of Church and Kingdom: A Study in Early Syriac Tradition* (Piscataway, NJ: Gorgias, 2004), 174–75. Cyrillona was a younger contemporary of Ephrem the Syrian (ca. 306–373), the ascetic theologian and prolific Syriac hymn writer.

42. Jenkins, *Lost History of Christianity*, 10.

43. Samuel H. Moffett, *A History of Christianity in Asia: Beginnings to 1500*, vol. 1 (Maryknoll, NY: Orbis Books, 1998), 100.

It was through both Syrian merchants and monks that Nestorian Christianity penetrated as far east as China and south Asia.[44] Admittedly, the earliest beginnings of Christianity in India are enveloped by a shadowy mist in which the efforts of elusive figures left barely discernible traces—just enough to ensure perennial disputations among historians! But trading ties between Persia and India fostered an early link between the East Syrian Church and the local Christian communities in Kerala. One of the most persistent traditions reports that Thomas of Cana, a Syrian Nestorian merchant, arrived on the Malabar Coast in southwestern India "bringing with him a group of Christian families, perhaps as many as four hundred people, including deacons, priests, and a bishop."[45] The Persian immigrants were welcomed by the local rulers, formed a mercantile class within the Hindu caste system in Kerala, and invigorated a weakened church. Such a major influx of immigrants from distant lands was probably not uncommon, and archeological evidence supports the reception and integration of such groups. But, despite its plausibility, the precise date of this particular event is elusive. Different assessments support either a fourth- or eighth-century date.[46] Whether this group of immigrants had a missionary impact—Thomas of Cana apparently used his wealth to purchase land on which he built a church—this tradition exemplifies the extensive eastward movement of Christian (mainly Nestorian) merchants who, while engaged in trade, contributed to the growth of Christian communities across Asia.

East Syrian Christians also had other motivations for migrant movement. State recognition from the early fifth century gave the Church of the East a relatively more settled presence in Persia. But Christians in the Sassanian realm remained a vulnerable minority, perennially under suspicion, and subject to adversities. Proselytizing remained a capital offense (though enforcement was inconsistent) and intermittent outbreaks of state persecution continued as late as the mid-sixth century. Political and economic pressures made eastward migration by Persian Christians a regular occurrence. Many individual Christians and families sought escape from suffering and debilitating circumstances;

---

44. Charbonnier, *Christians in China: A.D. 600 to 2000*, 42–43.

45. Moffett, *Christianity in Asia*, 266–67, 275. See also Gillman and Klimkeit, *Christians in Asia*, 160–65.

46. Scholars who favor the fourth century date, like Samuel Moffett, associate the emigration of such a considerable body of migrants with the great Persian persecution under Shāpur II.

and, though the numbers were probably inconsequential relative to the size of the church, periods of prolonged political strife or religious persecution would have caused dramatic escalation of such movement.[47] Anyhow, the relentless conflicts and political volatility that accompanied the demise of Sassanian rule, followed by the uncertainties of Islamic rule, intensified migrations by East Syrian Christians.[48]

For such Christian emigrants, especially wealthier segments looking for better economic prospects as well as religious freedom, eastward movement was the logical and most favorable option.[49] To the south lay Arabia, which had close proximity to a heavy concentration of Syriac- and Greek-speaking captives on the Persian side of the border and attracted refugees fleeing Sassanian persecution.[50] But the Arab Desert held little promise for long-term settlement. To the west lay the Byzantine Empire, which was resolutely hostile to the East Syrian Christian form of faith and whose repressive policies had contributed to the East Syrian movement toward Persia in the first place. To the north, the mountainous ranges and steppes (stretching from present-day Hungary to Mongolia) had no appeal for city dwellers or people accustomed to living in plains.

Ultimately, despite considerable challenges, eastward travel was well established. From the seventh to thirteenth centuries flourishing long-distance trade along the Silk Road attracted hordes of migrants; and other than for specifically missionary purposes, few Persian Christian emigrants would have considered other options. Crucially, eastward migrations far outstripped westward movement from China and central Asia precisely because Western demand for Eastern goods always exceeded Eastern demand for Western commodities.[51] This

47. Glen L. Thompson, "Was Alopen a Missionary?," in *Hidden Treasures and Intercultural Encounters: Studies on East Syriac Christianity in China and Central Asia*, ed. Dietmar W. Winkler and Li Tang (Vienna: Lit, 2014), 269.

48. In a space of four years, five shahs and two queens followed each other in quick succession. Baum and Winkler, *Church of the East*, 40. Thompson, "Was Alopen a Missionary?," 268–69.

49. Thompson, "Was Alopen a Missionary?," 269.

50. Cf. Buck, "Universality?," 63; J. Spencer Trimingham, *Christianity among the Arabs in Pre-Islamic Times* (New York: Longman, 1979), 188–202. The Arab Lakhmid Dynasty immediately beyond the Persian border was Christian, indeed strongly Nestorian. But it was under the sway of the Sassanian state and caught up in the unremitting Roman-Persian conflicts.

51. Smith, *Premodern Trade in World History*, 95; Curtin, *Cross-Cultural Trade in World History*, 94.

also means that while merchants were not the only migrants traveling eastward, they formed a major segment of the eastward movement that dramatically intensified in the early seventh century with Byzantine and Arab invasions.

EASTWARD MIGRATION AND NESTORIAN MISSIONS

Due in part to the Sassanian policy of resettling captives in towns at ever greater distances from the Persian-Roman border (chapter 5), East Syrian Christian communities were widely dispersed in Persia. The presence of Christians is reported in the eastern province of Bactria (modern-day Afghanistan, Tajikistan, and Uzbekistan) by the end of the second century.[52] Persistent evangelistic efforts also contributed to the spread of Christianity across the Persian heartland to its eastern provinces in the Oxus region.[53] In 424 when the Church of the East declared itself an autocephalous body (independent of Byzantine authority), four major cities in the vicinity of the Oxus River were recognized as bishoprics: Ray, Naishabur, Herat, and Merv.[54] Synods of the Church of the East held in the fifth and sixth centuries list up to twenty-one bishops in the region encompassing the eastern provinces of Persia up to the Oxus River.[55] Christopher Buck estimates that of the eighteen administrative provinces evangelized by Christians (out of a total of twenty-five in the Persian realm), eight were located in eastern Persia.[56] Merv, "the administrative seat of the Sassanian province of Margiana" close to its northeastern border, had become a metropolitanate by the mid-sixth century.[57]

Severely constrained in its Persian heartland by Islamic rule, the missionary spirit of the Church of the East was channeled through escalating transnational networks of long-distance trade along myriad land and sea routes that connected various cosmopolitan towns and trading centers. Each

52. Mingana, *Early Spread of Christianity*, 7–8.
53. Ferreira, *Early Chinese Christianity*, 72; Gillman and Klimkeit, *Christians in Asia*, 221–22.
54. Mingana, *Early Spread of Christianity*, 4.
55. Mingana, *Early Spread of Christianity*, 24–26; also, Thompson, "Was Alopen a Missionary?," 270.
56. Buck, "Universality," 61–70.
57. Hunter, "Church of the East," 132.

successive center of East Syrian Christianity provided a base for new evangelistic initiatives among diverse cultures. There were failures, setbacks, and defections, to be sure. But this phenomenal, largely unplanned, missionary movement that lasted over a thousand years has no parallels in the history of the world Christian movement. In Mingana's oft-quoted description, the Nestorian Church was "by far the greatest missionary Church that the world has ever produced."[58]

There were planned East Syrian missionary initiatives too, such as those orchestrated by the missionary-minded Patriarch Timothy I or by lesser-known prelates such as Bar Shabba (bishop of Merv in the fifth century), or Metropolitan Elijah (or Elias), also of Merv, in the seventh century. In his historical account *The Book of Governors* (840 CE), the East Syrian bishop Thomas of Marga records that Timothy I ordained many monks as bishops and "sent them to convert the heathens of the Far East."[59] It also appears that, at least in some instances, prelates were ordained or appointed with their capacity for cross-cultural Christian missions in mind. Bishop Shubba-lishō (metropolitan of the Dailamites in northern Persia, southeast of the Caspian Sea), was ordained by Patriarch Timothy with the express purpose of "evangelizing the primitive peoples inhabiting the countries lying beyond Central Asia." He is said to have been especially fitted for the task because "he was versed not only in Syriac but also in Arabic and Persian." The bishop lived up to expectations:

> He taught many cities and thickly peopled districts, and baptized [their inhabitants], and brought them near to the doctrine of Divine life. And he built churches, and established priests and deacons in them, and he set apart some of the brethren who were with him to teach them psalms and spiritual praises, and he himself went further and further into the country, until [he arrived at] the ends of the East in the great teaching which he made among the heathen, and Marcionites, and Manichees, [against] every object of worship and every impure thing; and he sowed among them the glorious light of the doctrine of the Gospel, the mother of life and peace.[60]

58. Mingana, *Early Spread of Christianity*, 53.

59. Thomas of Marga, *The Book of Governors: The "Historia Monastica" of Thomas Bishop of Margâ*, trans. E. A. Wallis Budge (London: K. Paul, Trench, Trübner, 1893), 181n3; also Mingana, *Early Spread of Christianity*, 13.

60. Cf. Thomas of Marga, *Book of Governors*, 480–812.

On the whole, however, the wide-ranging Nestorian missionary movement was mainly unregulated. It involved many monks who became willing itinerants along the multiple paths and passageways of the Silk Road. But it was dominated by unknown laypersons, primarily merchants, traversing the extensive trade routes. Trading activities allowed them to carry the gospel to far-flung regions of Asia often on "year-long journeys by camel, by ass or even on foot . . . or by equally lengthy sea-trips along the many routes of Arab, Persian or Indian traders."[61] Most, it seems, "travelled on foot wearing sandals, a staff in their hands, and on their backs a basket filled with copies of the Scripture and other religious books."[62] Migration was inseparable from mission; and these missionary migrants, clergy and laity, "literally explored all the corners of the Eastern globe in order to sow in them the seed of what they firmly believed to be the true religion of God."[63] Missionary migration was a prominent characteristic of the Church of the East.[64]

Persia's Eastern Frontier: Gateway to the East

Eastern Persia was located in a vast region west of the Oxus River known as Khorasan (a Persian name that literally means "land where the sun rises"). Like its western frontier on the border with the Roman Empire, Persia's eastern provinces were marked by immense diversity and extensive migrations involving captives, mercenaries, couriers, nomads, and merchants. Most important, Persia's eastern provinces, a major zone of cross-cultural interactions intimately connected to long-distance trade routes, formed the gateway to the East. Thus the eastern frontier acted as a natural launching ground for the missionary endeavors of Eastern Syrian Christians in central Asia (the immense territory between eastern Persia and China). Major Christian centers like Merv (north of Khorasan) that were strategically located close to the Persian northeastern border and on the Silk Road became natural bases of missionary outreach beyond the Oxus by the Church of the East.[65]

61. England, *Christianity in Asia*, 46.
62. Syrdal, *To the End of the Earth*, 74.
63. Mingana, *Early Spread of Christianity*, 53.
64. As Walls also notes. Andrew F. Walls, "Mission and Migration: The Diaspora Factor in Christian History," *Journal of African Christian Thought* 5, no. 2 (2002): 6.
65. Hunter, "Church of the East," 133.

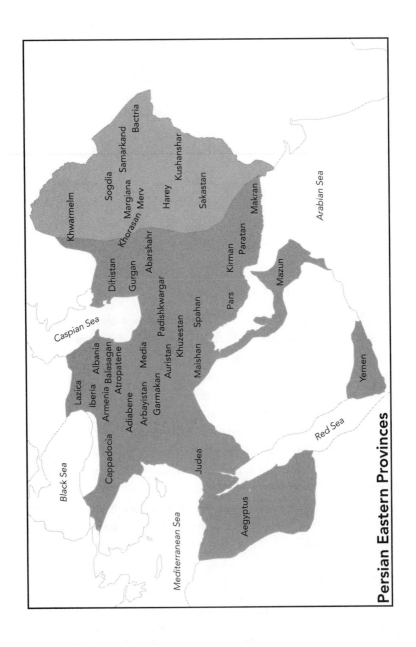

Persian Eastern Provinces

How or when exactly Christianity reached the nomadic tribes just beyond the Persian eastern border is not known. From about the fifth century, Persia's eastern provinces were increasingly infiltrated and settled by the Hephthalite Huns and Turkic-speaking nomads.[66] Merchant groups had extensive contact and interaction with nomadic tribes; and the latter were probably exposed to Christianity as the faith of merchants before they interacted with settled Christian populations. Marauding nomads like the White Huns also encountered Christian beliefs among Byzantine captives acquired in raids.[67] In the long run, Turkic-speaking tribes and the Hephthalite Huns were exposed to sustained Christian influence and missionary action after they overran and settled in the towns and rural areas of Sogdiana and Bactria where East Syrian communities were already established.[68]

We have noted in connection with the Goths (chapter 5) that dislocation and migration of settled communities often create receptiveness to new religious belief systems in part because kinship ties and tribal structures are severely disrupted.[69] In all likelihood, the transition from nomadic existence to the fresh challenges of long-term residential settlement similarly impacted tribal life sufficiently to accommodate a shift in religious attitudes and an attendant receptivity to institutional religion. Ian Gillman and Hans-Joachim Klimkeit explain that there were various instances in which "Turkish tribes, once dislocated from their homeland, gave up their indigenous religion and turned to a world religion like Christianity, which gave a more encompassing answer to the problems of life in the new social and political situation."[70] Whatever the scenario, migration and migrant action were crucial elements.

In 498, when the Sassanian shah Kavadh I (488–531) took refuge among the nomadic White Huns in Bactria he found Christians (Byzantine cap-

---

66. Despite defeats by the Persian army, the Hunnic threat persisted throughout the fifth century, bringing instability and chaos to the empire. In 483, the White Huns invaded and plundered parts of eastern Persia for two years and "exacted heavy tribute for some years thereafter." Gianpaolo Savoia-Vizzini, "Iranian History: The Sasanian Dynasty," *The Circle of Ancient Iranian Studies* (2000). See also Hunter, "Church of the East," 132–33.

67. Laurence E. Browne, *The Eclipse of Christianity in Asia, from the Time of Muhammad Till the Fourteenth Century* (Cambridge: Cambridge University Press, 1933), 93.

68. Gillman and Klimkeit, *Christians in Asia*, 218.

69. See also Gillman and Klimkeit, *Christians in Asia*, 233.

70. Gillman and Klimkeit, *Christians in Asia*, 229.

tives) among them. Christians in the exiled shah's entourage ministered to the captives and also engaged in evangelism.[71] Two of these were Christian laymen who reportedly stayed among the Huns for over thirty years, during which time they also married and had children. Their missionary labors were subsequently augmented by the arrival of a Nestorian bishop and four priests. In a remarkable instance of ecumenical collaboration, an Armenian (Monophysite) bishop also joined the missionary effort.[72] Within a matter of decades, the Huns sent a letter to the Nestorian patriarch Mar Aba I requesting a bishop. This implicit acknowledgment of the patriarch's authority confirms that they credited East Syrian Christians with the spread of the faith among them. A bishop was ordained for the Hephthalite kingdom in 549.

Nestorian missionaries also "taught the Turks the art of writing in the Turkish language, and evangelized and baptized a considerable number of them."[73] A century later, when the Hephthalite kingdoms were overrun by Turkic-speaking nomads,[74] large numbers of Turks were converted to Christianity through the missionary initiative of Elijah, the metropolitan of Merv.[75] In one account, the ecclesiastic encountered a Turkic chieftain and his troops while traveling in the Oxus region (in 644). After demonstrating the power of the Christian faith by using a sign of the cross to dispel a hurricane conjured up by the chieftain's pagan priests, Elijah baptized the leader and his entire army in a nearby stream. He also recruited clergy to work among them. Christian expansion among these groups remained vigorous at least up to the ninth century. Additionally, Patriarch Timothy, who gave considerable impetus to Nestorian missions in central Asia, also converted a number of Turkic kings to the Christian faith and maintained correspondence with them to impart

71. Mingana, *Early Spread of Christianity*, 8–10.
72. Foster, *Church of the T'ang Dynasty*, 10.
73. Mingana, *Early Spread of Christianity*, 9.
74. The terms "Turkic" and "Turkish" are sometimes used interchangeably in the literature but they have distinct application. "Turkic" (used of both language and peoples) is much broader and applicable to Turks everywhere; "Turkish" (in terms of language, people, and culture) is mainly associated, in English-language usage at least, with the Turkish Republic (Turkey). Thus, for instance, the "Turkish" language is only one of many "Turkic" languages. See Carter V. Findley, *The Turks in World History* (New York: Oxford University Press, 2005), 6.
75. Mingana, *Early Spread of Christianity*, 11–12. Hunter, "Church of the East," 133; Gillman and Klimkeit, *Christians in Asia*, 216–17.

Christian doctrine. About 781, he reported that "the king of the Turks, with nearly all (the inhabitants of) his country, has left his ancient idolatry, and has become Christian, and he has requested us in his letters to create a Metropolitan for his country; and this we have done."[76]

Samarkand

In central Asia, halfway between the Mediterranean and China, lay Sogdiana (modern Tajikistan and Uzbekistan), an ancient civilization whose inhabitants were of Persian or Iranian descent. Its capital was Samarkand. Sogdiana was a principal trading center and its merchants dominated the trade routes connecting East and West.[77] In keeping with their transnational trading activities, Sogdian merchants acquired many foreign languages and often served as interpreters and translators in commercial transactions. They were de facto "middlemen between the great empires of China and Persia."[78] Their trading colonies established all along the Silk Road as far as China acted as major conduits for the transmission not only of technology and cultural traditions but also of religious texts, ideas, and practices. Sogdians became fervent converts to a variety of faiths—Manichaeanism, East Syrian Christianity, and Islam among them—and in every case they used their extensive trading activities to spread one religious faith or another along the Silk Road.

The details of how the sizeable Christian communities—East Syrians, Jacobites, Melkites, and Armenians among them—emerged in Sogdiana are obscure. Evidence of Christian presence in Sogdiana dates to the fourth century, and by the fifth century there were translations of Christian literature into Sogdian.[79] It is highly probable that the wide-ranging Sogdian merchants were among the first converts in the province.[80] The province became a major center of Nestorianism: archeological excavations have uncovered several churches and monasteries, a large number of Syriac Christian rock inscriptions, coins

76. Quoted in Mingana, *Early Spread of Christianity*, 12, 14.

77. Curtin, *Cross-Cultural Trade in World History*, 107; Foltz, *Religions of the Silk Road*, 14–16, 65–66; Ferreira, *Early Chinese Christianity*, 117.

78. Ferreira, *Early Chinese Christianity*, 117.

79. Thompson, "Was Alopen a Missionary?," 270; England, *Christianity in Asia*, 45; Foltz, *Religions of the Silk Road*, 66. Indeed, some of the Sogdian versions are older than the extant Syriac equivalent and there are no known Syriac versions for others.

80. Foltz, *Religions of the Silk Road*, 65.

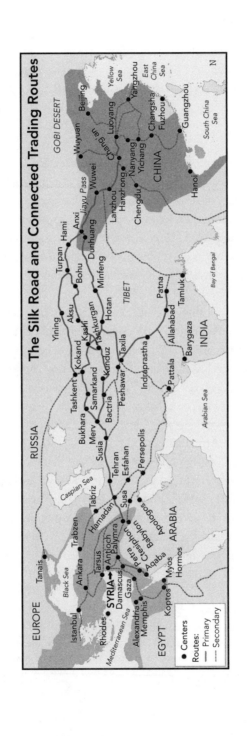

The Silk Road and Connected Trading Routes

with crosses, mural paintings of biblical scenes from the late seventh to the ninth century, and the remains of Nestorian Christian village settlements.[81] Samarkand was made a metropolitan see of the East Syrian Church perhaps as early as the seventh century.[82] This move was arguably in a strategic acknowledgment of the province's missionary significance as "a natural base for proselytism amongst the Iranian communities settled in the region, as well as amongst the westward moving [Turkic] nomadic groups."[83] It is also possible that Samarkand "may have helped consolidate the Church of the East in Tibet where it had already made inroads by the end of the seventh century."[84] In the event, Sogdian merchants from Samarkand, who "had a string of settlements on the Central Asian routes leading to China and Mongolia," helped to spread the Christian faith further east, translating Syriac texts into their own language.[85]

"They Lightened All the Ends of the East"[86]

The eastward spread of the Christian faith through indigenous converts, merchants, and varieties of migrants was an Asia-wide phenomenon. The establishment of East Syrian Christian metropolitanates in a number of major cities in central Asia and the Far East makes evident the scope and impact of this missionary effort. Substantial Christian populations emerged in far-flung societies and cultures among diverse peoples about whose ways of life and ethnographic characteristics Persia-based Christians and clergy had little knowledge.[87]

The speed and scope of travel in this era steadily improved; but long-distance travel remained hazardous and grueling. Traversing the vast distances between cosmopolitan centers in East Turkestan, Mongolia, or China and the center of the patriarchate in Seleucia-Ctesiphon (or Baghdad, from 775 CE) involved daunting year-long journeys. As a practical matter, the metropoli-

81. Ferreira, *Early Chinese Christianity*, 73; England, *Christianity in Asia*, 45; Gillman and Klimkeit, *Christians in Asia*, 224–27.

82. Mingana, *Early Spread of Christianity*, 29.

83. Hunter, "Church of the East," 135.

84. Hunter, "Church of the East," 136.

85. Gillman and Klimkeit, *Christians in Asia*, 218.

86. Thomas of Marga, *Book of Governors*, 493.

87. Mingana, *Early Spread of Christianity*, 27.

tans of Samarkand, India, and China (and presumably other remote prelates) were exempted from regular attendance at official synods. In one correspondence, Patriarch Isho'yahb III (650–660) explained that there were "more than twenty bishops and two archbishops in the East" (in Samarkand and Kashgar) who had not visited Persia for many years. He added,

> nor did we ask them to come. But we know that, in spite of the long distance that separates them from us they fulfil the obligations of their episcopacy in strict conformity with the Church of God, while the rights of episcopal jurisdiction are duly received from us. We write to them and they write to us.[88]

In addition to the metropolitanates of China and India, which possibly date to the seventh century, five other principal cities beyond the Oxus were elevated into metropolitanates, each with six to twelve bishops under them:[89] Samarkand (which became a metropolitan seat by the seventh century); Tangut, in the vicinity of Tibet (elevated ca. 790); Kashgar, in Eastern Turkestan (elevated ca. 1180); Khatai, in northern China (possibly elevated in the eleventh century); and Khān Bālik (present-day Beijing) in China. The energetic Patriarch Timothy I, who pursued a vigorous policy of expansion, established six metropolitanates during his tenure (779–823). One of these was for Tibet; and archeological evidence shows that the Tibetan church survived at least to the tenth century.[90]

It is evident that these metropolitans "played an integral role in the expansion of the Church of the East, simultaneously consolidating and maintaining its dioceses in Central Asia."[91] Located in remote territories, and confronted by large non-Christian populations, these bishops "enjoyed widespread powers when proselytizing."[92] Working among nomadic tribes, theirs was an incredibly

88. Quoted in Foster, *Church of the T'ang Dynasty*, 63. Mingana explains that the distant prelates "had to write a letter of submission to the Patriarch once every six years, in order to inform him of the spiritual and moral needs of their dioceses." Mingana, *Early Spread of Christianity*, 27, 73–74.

89. Mingana, *Early Spread of Christianity*, 29–36, 73–76.

90. England, *Christianity in Asia*, 55–56.

91. Hunter, "Church of the East," 141.

92. Hunter, "Church of the East," 139. Patriarch Timothy, for instance, gave distant metropolitans permission to appoint bishops of newly evangelized populations

mobile ministry—so much so that the episcopal seats of some "were probably only tent chapels mounted on wagons."[93] Everywhere, they constantly endeavored to extend the missionary work in the face of intense competition from Islam, Manichaeanism, Buddhism, and even other Christian traditions. But our knowledge of these ecclesiastics is scanty; and details about the precise nature of the pioneering missionary activities that gave rise to flourishing Christian communities in the various cosmopolitan centers and trading posts across Asia are scarce. Writing in the ninth century, Thomas of Marga admitted that, due to the number and remoteness of the countries in which the "mighty deeds" of these bishops were completed, it was not possible "to distinguish clearly how it was worked, or in what village or city, or in whom a healing was performed, or from whom devils and sicknesses were expelled."[94]

But while the specific details of their actions are lost in the mists of time, there is some indication that the formal missionary initiatives of church officials benefited from the movement, contacts, and influence of Christian merchants. The events that led to mass conversion among the Kerait Turks in 1007 (see "Christianity among the Mongols," chapter 9) are a case in point. But the complementary interplay between the activities of foreign merchants and official action by the Persian Church is more fully demonstrated in the establishment of Christianity in T'ang China. The expansion and eclipse of T'ang Christianity also showcases the distinctive challenges, including shifting political winds and unexpected nationalist (or antiforeigner) reactions, that confronted the extensive missionary efforts of East Syrian Christians.

ALL ROADS LEAD TO CHANG'AN

Exactly when Christianity first reached China is not clearly evident. But there is general agreement that Christian presence in the Middle Kingdom predates the early seventh century when the arrival of Syrian missionaries is recorded.[95]

---

without the requirement of having three persons present. In place of a third bishop (presumably in the first few instances), they were instructed to place "the Book of the Gospels . . . on the [episcopal] throne on the right hand." Thomas of Marga, *Book of Governors*, 490.

93. Moffett, *Christianity in Asia*, 448–49.
94. Thomas of Marga, *Book of Governors*, 491.
95. There are indirect or oblique references in sundry ancient records to mission-

Even the eighth-century T'ang Christian Monument that documents this event hints at prior Christian settlement. It declares that "the Way was *recovered*" and that "Luminous Religion [i.e., Christianity] *returned* to our Tang dynasty" (italics added). Others note that the highly favorable reception that Alopen received from the T'ang emperor and the great success (in evangelistic scope and institutional development) achieved by his mission are difficult to account for without prior Christian existence.

In all probability, given the fact that merchants and other migrants were crucial agents in the eastward spread of Christianity in Asia, the earliest Christian contacts came through the settlement of Christian immigrants in China. Despite Confucian suspicion of outsiders, the Chinese often displayed a natural curiosity about foreigners and a general attitude of tolerance toward foreign cultures.[96] In addition to the economic interactions necessitated by China's size and prominence, the numerous states and nations on its frontiers required various kinds of engagement that ensured a constant flow of people and ideas. In any case, China, like other major civilizations or empires, was a pluralistic entity, home to a diversity of peoples and cultures, a virtual melting pot for much of its history. Chinese authorities played constant host to diplomats and trade missions from many nations; and Chinese society attracted a host of immigrants (foreign students, merchants, refugees, artisans, etc.). It is estimated that "some two hundred thousand Persians, Arabs, Indians, Malays, and others lived in seventh-century Guangzhou as traders, artisans, and metal workers."[97]

Economic factors were key. The Chinese and Romans were aware of each other's existence by the first century CE.[98] Chinese sources refer to the Roman Empire, perhaps more specifically its eastern region (undoubtedly Syria), as *Daqin*. Contact between the two was mainly economic—though Romans

---

ary activity in China as early as the third century—helpfully summarized by Ferreira, *Early Chinese Christianity*, 287–88; see also Foster, *Church of the T'ang Dynasty*, 1–15.

96. Louise Levathes, *When China Ruled the Seas: The Treasure Fleet of the Dragon Throne, 1405–1433* (New York: Oxford University Press, 1996), 34; Ferreira, *Early Chinese Christianity*, 97, 115–20.

97. Levathes, *When China Ruled the Seas*, 39.

98. Cf. Yoshirō Saeki, *The Nestorian Documents and Relics in China* (Tokyo: The Toho bunkwa gakuin: The Academy of Oriental Culture, 1937), 40–42; also Lionel Casson, *Travel in the Ancient World* (Baltimore: Johns Hopkins University Press, 1994), 123–26.

had no idea as to how the silk came to them.[99] Governmental interaction was rare. However, the existence of an integrated system of routes, by land and sea, linking the two extremities of the Eurasian landmass means that Christian missionary contact with China was quite possible in the first few centuries. In the seventh and early eighth centuries (specifically in 643, 667, 701, and 719), rulers of the Byzantine Empire sent four embassies to Chang'an to seek Chinese help in the face of the expanding Islamic empire.[100]

The close commercial connection between Sassanian Persia and China presents even stronger possibilities. Persia was strategically located on the historic silk routes that extended from Syria to Beijing and played an important role within the global economy. Persian ships and merchants extended their reach as far as China, exporting pearls and textiles and transmitting Chinese paper and silk and Indian spices to Europe. Persia and China not only "benefited from trade along the Silk Road, and shared a common interest in preserving and protecting that trade" but they also "cooperated in guarding the trade routes through central Asia, and both built outposts in border areas to keep caravans safe from nomadic tribes and bandits."[101]

The Sassanians sent at least thirteen diplomatic missions to China and sought Chinese military assistance in the face of Muslim-Arab aggression.[102] The common security interests, strong commercial ties, long-running diplomatic relations, and military collaboration between Sassanian and Chinese authorities contributed greatly to the conditions that sustained long-distance trade and travel. Persian officials were not an unfamiliar sight at the Chinese imperial court; and, given the incorporation of Christians within Persia's political hierarchy from the fifth century (especially as diplomats), Chinese officials were probably aware of Christianity. Following Islamic invasion, the last Sassanian ruler, Piroz II, fled with other Persian nobles to China in 677 and took refuge in the imperial court.[103]

99. Smith, *Premodern Trade in World History*, 136; Ferreira, *Early Chinese Christianity*, 290.

100. Ferreira, *Early Chinese Christianity*, 119.

101. Savoia-Vizzini, "Iranian History." See also Ferreira, *Early Chinese Christianity*, 294.

102. Ferreira, *Early Chinese Christianity*, 119.

103. Ferreira, *Early Chinese Christianity*, 294. When efforts to restore Sassanian rule failed, T'ang emperor Gaozong appointed Piroz "governor of a newly created Persian enclave on the western border of China"; and many Persian refugees took

Most important, China's economic stature and dominance of the trade routes made it a magnet for merchants. Persian merchants, for instance, dominated the porcelain route that spanned 6,000 miles, from Guangzhou on the south coast of China all the way to the Persian Gulf.[104] Thus, Persian and Sogdian Christian merchants, who traversed the Silk Road and settled over much of central Asia from the fourth century, were almost certainly well represented in the sizeable foreign merchant population that flourished in major Chinese cities whose huge markets marked the terminus of the trade routes.

THE STORY OF T'ANG CHRISTIANITY

The so-called Nestorian stele (or Nestorian Monument), discovered in 1625, describes the establishment of Christianity in China with the arrival of a Christian leader named Alopen in 635. The timing of Alopen's mission—less than two decades into T'ang dynastic rule (618–907)—was central to the success of his mission. After centuries of political instability and social turmoil, China was reunited by Yang Jian, a Chinese-Turkish general who rebuilt the old capital Chang'an (now Xian) and established the short-lived Sui Dynasty (581–618). This transitory regime paved the way for the T'ang Empire, a period of rule considered the most successful and creative in the history of China—its golden age. Its founding emperor, Li Yuan, who was half Turk, seized power with the help of Turkish nomadic horsemen. Under the early T'ang emperors, China expanded its territory westward toward central Asia and reestablished control over large sections of the Silk Road, reaching as far as Bukhara and Samarkand in 659.[105] Concurrent Arab Islamic conquests moving eastward limited T'ang expansion and ended its control of central Asia. But, by 750, the T'ang ruled over more than 50 million people.[106]

The T'ang Dynasty lasted for a period of 289 years and produced twenty-one rulers. Its expansionist policies, in tandem with the spread of Islamic trade networks, galvanized foreign trade and long-distance travel. Long-distance

---

up positions in the Chinese government. According to Savoia-Vizzini, Piroz's son, Narseh, rose to the position of the commander of the Chinese imperial guards "and his descendants lived in China as respected princes."

104. Levathes, *When China Ruled the Seas*, 35.

105. Ferreira, *Early Chinese Christianity*, 116.

106. Howard, *Transnationalism in Ancient and Medieval Societies*, 77.

merchants could travel by land and sea from the Atlantic to the Pacific.[107] Most important, the T'ang rulers' openness to foreign trade saw the growth of a sizeable foreign population of merchants in China.[108] Inevitably, the encouragement of foreign trade intensified foreign influences. Chang'an, the T'ang capital, became the largest city in the world, a multiethnic and cosmopolitan center "with nearly two million people in the [main] urban area and a million [taxable residents] within the city walls."[109] By way of comparison, Constantinople had a population of 500,000 to 750,000 people at its height.[110] A third of the population in Chang'an were foreigners.[111] "Fondness for foreign objects," writes Louise Levathes, "touched every class—even simple household objects used in the most humble dwellings were decorated with figures of bearded, long-nosed foreigners."[112]

If the mixed culture (Turkic-Chinese) heritage of the T'ang emperors helps to explain their remarkable openness to outside influences, it also arguably accounts for their policy of religious tolerance. Daoism (the indigenous religion) and Confucianism remained entrenched; but Christianity and Buddhism (the latter also introduced to China by merchants and migrants via the Silk Road[113]) enjoyed imperial favor under different T'ang rulers. Whatever the status of Christianity in the pre-T'ang period, such receptiveness to the foreign and unfamiliar created auspicious conditions for the establishment and spread of the Christian faith.

107. Curtin, *Cross-Cultural Trade in World History*, 105.

108. Unprecedented economic prosperity under the T'angs went hand in hand with political reform, improved education, and the introduction of a more equitable legal system. It also "encouraged individual industry and large scale production of consumer goods such as silk, lacquer ware, jade, and ceramics." Ferreira, *Early Chinese Christianity*, 99–100.

109. Howard, *Transnationalism in Ancient and Medieval Societies*, 77; Curtin, *Cross-Cultural Trade in World History*, 105; Levathes, *When China Ruled the Seas*, 34–35; Ferreira, *Early Chinese Christianity*, 101, 119–20.

110. Cf. Ferreira, *Early Chinese Christianity*, 120.

111. Ferreira, *Early Chinese Christianity*, 101.

112. Levathes, *When China Ruled the Seas*, 38.

113. Indeed, many early Buddhist preachers in China came from Persia—the first Buddhist missionary identified in Chinese sources was a Parthian monk—and some speculate that this helps to account for the favorable reception accorded to East Syrian Christians, who originated from the same region and travelled along the same routes. Xinru Liu, *The Silk Road in World History* (New York: Oxford University Press, 2010), 60; Foltz, *Religions of the Silk Road*, 49–51.

The story of T'ang Christianity is well documented.[114] The Nestorian (or T'ang Christian) Monument, which was created in 781, is the main primary source. Its broad narrative history chronicles the arrival of Nestorian monks in the seventh century, imperial endorsement of the Christian faith as "a true religion," efforts at vernacular translation, and the spread of Christianity in China's multireligious context. The monument does not present a complete account of the church in the T'ang era, in part because it only tells the story of the first 146 years of the 271-year history of T'ang Christianity. Scholars fill the gaps from other sources, such as the Dunhuang documents. This, combined with differing translations of the inscription, means that there are competing interpretations of the story of Christianity in T'ang China.[115] The brief analysis that follows primarily focuses on two aspects: the role of migration and the mixed rewards of state sponsorship.[116]

T'ang Christianity, in keeping with the spread of Christianity throughout central Asia, was rooted in migration. According to the inscription on the T'ang Christian Monument, Christian monks from "the country of *Daqin* [Syria]" arrived in T'ang China, in 635, after a long and difficult journey.[117] The leader of the group, identified as Alopen or Aluoben (a Chinese rendering of either a biblical, Semitic, or Iranian name), possibly originated from Sogdi-

---

114. Among the most useful, see Saeki, *Nestorian Documents*; Foster, *Church of the T'ang Dynasty*; Moffett, *Christianity in Asia*, 288–323; Gillman and Klimkeit, *Christians in Asia*, 274–314; Charbonnier, *Christians in China*; Winkler and Tang, *Hidden Treasures*; Ferreira, *Early Chinese Christianity*.

115. To a large extent, the variety of analyses among scholars reflects not only different understandings of the actual text (itself an effort to express Syriac expressions in the Chinese language of the period) but also different perspectives on the nature of the encounter between East Syrian Christianity and T'ang Chinese context. Some emphasize Christian meanings, while others focus on Buddhist or Daoist connotations.

116. In areas where argumentation utilizes details provided by the Nestorian Monument, I have depended mainly on Johan Ferreira's interpretative approach, which has the modern Christian reader in view. As Ferreira admits, this might lower the modern reader's appreciation of the cross-cultural challenges that the Syrian missionaries faced; but it more readily clarifies their "decidedly Christian perspective." Ferreira, *Early Chinese Christianity*, 148–258.

117. Unless otherwise stated, direct quotations from the Nestorian Monument are from "How Many Roman Catholics Are There in the World?," BBC News, March 14, 2013, in which the translation of the text has been modernized.

ana.[118] Alopen was received in Chang'an by the chief minister, Fang Xuanling, at the behest of the Emperor Taizong (Tai-tsung). This state-level reception has long puzzled scholars, given Alopen's foreign missionary status. One possible explanation is that the missionary group was part of a larger delegation from the Sassanian government, which raises the possibility that the favorable reception was in response to a specific request from the Sassanian court.[119] The absence of any reference to such an embassy in the annals of the Sassanian state is not necessarily conclusive. There is no mention of Alopen's mission in the available records of the East Syrian Church either![120] But for a Sassanian ruler to sanction a mission to China aimed at propagating Christianity in that land stretches credibility—not to mention the fact that the political turmoil and widespread insecurity that characterized Sassanian Persia around this period all but precluded routine diplomatic missions.[121]

More plausibly perhaps, Alopen's mission was favorably received by the T'ang government because it was solicited by prominent Christian (Sogdian, Persian, and Turkic) merchants in China who wanted episcopal oversight for the growing immigrant Christian community.[122] Over time, as Jerry Bentley explains in his *conversion through voluntary association* model,[123] well-

---

118. Baum and Winkler, *Church of the East*, 47—"since the imperial courtiers were able to converse with him in his native tongue." Earlier attempts to identify Alopen with biblical or Semitic names such as Abraham are no longer considered persuasive. Max Deeg argues that it probably rendered an Iranian name such as Ardabān. Max Deeg, "Ways to Go and Not to Go in the Contextualisation of the Jingjiao Documents of the Tang Period," in *Hidden Treasures and Intercultural Encounters: Studies on East Syriac Christianity in China and Central Asia*, ed. Dietmar W. Winkler and Li Tang (Vienna: Lit, 2014), 147–48; see also Foster, *Church of the T'ang Dynasty*, 43.

119. Cf. Thompson, "Was Alopen a Missionary?," 274–75.

120. Ferreira, *Early Chinese Christianity*, 295.

121. The assassination of Khusrau (or Khosrow) II in 628 was followed by a fourteen-year period of chaos and civil war, during which twelve rulers (including two daughters of previous shahs) followed each other in quick succession. Savoia-Vizzini, "Iranian History."

122. Thompson, "Was Alopen a Missionary?," 273–74, 275. If this was the case, the additional influx triggered by Islamic expansion could have made the need even more pressing. Ferreira also speculates that Fang Xuanling, possibly due to Christian sympathies, "orchestrated the visit following a request from the Christian centers at Merv and Balkh, both of which had thriving Christian communities." Ferreira, *Early Chinese Christianity*, 295.

123. Discussed in chapter 2; see Jerry H. Bentley, *Old World Encounters: Cross-*

established merchant diaspora communities sought to bring over religious authorities such as priests or monks whose ministry consolidated cultural traditions and even contributed to religious expansion. This was a likely scenario in T'ang China, since "merchants from abroad were allowed a large measure of self-government and the free exercise of their own religion."[124] It is also noteworthy that Sogdians, who were leading merchants, formed the majority in the church of the T'ang Dynasty.[125] A favorable response from the T'ang emperor to the Christian merchants' request is also understandable. The T'ang policy of religious tolerance aside, China derived substantial benefits from the cultural, political, and trade networks of its immigrant merchant population. Moreover, at a time of Islamic expansion from the west, it served the T'ang authorities' strategic interests to cultivate a strong alliance with neighboring Christian tribes.[126] Accommodating the immigrant Christian population at this time made both economic and strategic sense.

At any rate, a favorable reception by the T'ang government was key. Even if Alopen's mission was supported by the Sassanian court, it could only have proceeded or succeeded with the explicit approval of the T'ang authorities, for "the sanction and management of religious communities came under the control of the state."[127] Such dependence on imperial patronage, as a prerequisite for the establishment and spread of Christianity, would have been all too familiar to East Syrian Christians whose religious establishments had flourished in Sassanian Persia under the auspices of the state for over two centuries. Moreover, throughout central Asia, East Syrian missionaries had established minority Christian communities in a variety of domains and multireligious contexts where freedom of action was contingent on political accommoda-

Cultural Contacts and Exchanges in Pre-Modern Times (New York: Oxford University Press, 1993), 9–10.

124. Foster, *Church of the T'ang Dynasty*, 77.

125. Huaiyu Chen, "The Encounter of Nestorian Christianity with Tantric Buddhism in Medieval China," in *Hidden Treasures and Intercultural Encounters: Studies on East Syriac Christianity in China and Central Asia*, ed. Dietmar W. Winkler and Li Tang (Vienna: Lit, 2014), 200.

126. Ferreira, *Early Chinese Christianity*, 301; see also Foster, *Church of the T'ang Dynasty*, 56–58, 72–74.

127. Ferreira, *Early Chinese Christianity*, 296. He adds that "it was unthinkable for any religious community to function underground or outside the oversight of the government, for the scope of governmental authority and control was universal."

tions. Such adaptability was crucial for cross-cultural missionary expansion and essential for Christian engagement with multifaith societies. But it by no means guaranteed long-term success. The establishment of Christianity in T'ang China demonstrated both the rewards and limitations of mission under imperial aegis.

IMPERIAL AEGIS AND CHRISTIAN MISSION

According to the inscription on the Nestorian Monument, the "sacred books" that Alopen carried were translated into the Chinese language and carefully studied by Emperor Taizong (r. 626–649). Earlier assessments insisted that such translations (into a language that had no Christian vocabulary) would have been greatly deficient, due to the immense amount of time required to master literary Chinese.[128] But that view fails to take into account the preparation and involvement of the multilingual Christian merchant community long resident in China.[129] Reportedly impressed by the soundness and truth of the new religion, the emperor issued an edict three years later (in 638) authorizing the dissemination of Christianity. The edict stated in part:

> Having examined the principles of this religion, we find them to be purely excellent and natural; investigating its originating source, we find it has taken its rise from the establishment of important truths; its ritual is free from perplexing expressions, its principles will survive when the framework is forgot; it is beneficial to all creatures; it is advantageous to mankind. Let it be published throughout the Empire. . . .[130]

Chinese authorities associated Christianity with Persia and referred to it as the "Persian religion" or "the Luminous Religion." Taizong sanctioned the building of a Syrian monastery on donated land in Chang'an with funds

128. Foster, for instance, maintains that, even with some knowledge of the Chinese language, the foreign missionaries "had little chance even to make intelligible all that they wanted to write," though he concluded that "beneath the makeshift terminology and the execrable style, they do manage to set forth the main historical facts and the most fundamental doctrines of the Christian Church." Foster, *Church of the T'ang Dynasty*, 44–50.

129. Cf. Ferreira, *Early Chinese Christianity*, 298.

130. Yoshirō Saeki, *The Nestorian Monument in China* (London: SPCK, 1916), 210.

from the imperial treasury; and court officials were dispatched to inscribe the emperor's portrait on the monastery's walls.[131] State sponsorship, combined with the freedom to propagate the faith throughout the empire, inaugurated an era of vigorous Christian growth. Taizong's son and successor, Emperor Gaozong/Kau-tsung (650–683), also promoted Christian teachings and reportedly allowed churches to be built in each of China's ten provinces.[132]

The inscription on the T'ang monument, which is eulogistic in tone and written in "the obsequious style of the Chinese court,"[133] makes hyperbolic claims—for instance, that "every city was full of churches"[134]—but does not provide specific details about the actual process of expansion within and beyond the capital. Nor, for that matter, does it relate the nature and content of the Christian message that was proclaimed by the Christian missionaries. We are also left in the dark about other crucial elements of the cross-cultural encounter: the degree to which the hordes of Christian merchants contributed to the establishment of churches; how outreach to local inhabitants in the towns and villages was conducted; how new converts were instructed and organized into Christian communities;[135] and whether (or to what extent) local authorities gave needed support to Christian institutions (imperial fiat notwithstanding). Still, given the fact that the seventy missionaries identified on the monument had Syriac names, it is all but certain that "Christianity was spread primarily by foreigners, especially Persian merchants."[136]

In a society where the religious field was marked by competition and coexistence among many faiths, all vying for imperial patronage, changes in political leadership were liable to impact religious existence. T'ang policy and the conditions of the era meant that many different religious systems enjoyed

131. The portrait was a seal of imperial patronage and a reminder that prayers were to be offered for the sovereign's success. See Foster, *Church of the T'ang Dynasty*, 53–54.

132. He also honored Alopen as "the Great Patron and Spiritual Lord of the Empire." Saeki, *Nestorian Monument in China*, 167; see also Ferreira, *Early Chinese Christianity*, 301–2.

133. Charbonnier, *Christians in China*, 38.

134. This suggests the unlikely scenario of 358 Christian monasteries or churches being erected in each of the empire's prefectures—cf. Foster, *Church of the T'ang Dynasty*, 60–61.

135. Foster speculates that wandering monks possibly set out from the Christian monasteries and settled in areas where there was local support and interest in the new faith. Foster, *Church of the T'ang Dynasty*, 62.

136. Baum and Winkler, *Church of the East*, 47–48; Ferreira, *Early Chinese Christianity*, 200–208, 314; Saeki, *Nestorian Documents*, 42.

official support. But such support was a prerogative of individual rulers and, as such, variable. During the reign of Empress Wu Zetian (683–705), a usurper and devoted promoter of Buddhism, Buddhist influences became ascendant at the royal court, and royal patronage of Christianity swiftly gave way to long-term persecution. Some churches were destroyed and many foreign priests fled back to their homelands or abandoned their vocation.[137] Hostility from Daoist priests may also have provoked mob action against the Christian monastery in the capital in 712/13.[138]

The patronage and protection of the Christian movement was restored with the rise of Emperor Xuangzong (712–755), the longest reigning of the T'ang rulers. Xuangzong ardently promoted Confucianism but allowed both Buddhism and Christianity to thrive. The former's extravagant gains under the previous regime were curtailed, and the destroyed Christian monasteries were rebuilt. But it appears that imperial recognition of Christianity was not officially reestablished until 742, two decades into Xuangzong's rule, when the T'ang court made a large donation of "a hundred pieces of silk" to the church and had five portraits of previous T'ang rulers installed in the Chang'an monastery. These endowments confirmed "Christian loyalty to the restored Tang royal family."[139] Why exactly royal patronage was so long delayed is unexplained. Xuangzong presided over the dynasty's most glorious era (an acme of political influence and cultural prominence) and may well have been otherwise occupied.[140] But there is perhaps also a hint that royal patronage was no longer a foregone conclusion.[141]

Still, the height of T'ang rule coincided with vigorous Christian expansion. The revitalization of the T'ang Church in the first half of the eighth century was bolstered by the return of exiled priests and a fresh influx of foreign

137. Ferreira, *Early Chinese Christianity*, 304.
138. Foster, *Church of the T'ang Dynasty*, 68–69; Ferreira, *Early Chinese Christianity*, 238, 302.
139. Ferreira, *Early Chinese Christianity*, 305. Acceptance of the emperor's gifts, which included the portraits of three deceased rulers, certainly suggests an act of cultural accommodation, since the church now had to pray "not only for the well-being of the ruling monarch but [also] for his dead ancestors": "Seven times a day," records the inscription, the monks "have worship and praise for the benefit of the living and the dead."
140. See Foster, *Church of the T'ang Dynasty*, 70–78.
141. Foster, *Church of the T'ang Dynasty*, 76, 82.

missionaries from Christian centers in central Asia. These developments also coincided with the appointment of a metropolitan for China, by Patriarch Saliba (714–728).[142] In 744, the arrival of another Christian delegation from "the kingdom of Syria," under Bishop Jihe/Kih-ho, further energized the missionary effort in China. The group paid homage to the emperor and, at the latter's behest, a Christian service was conducted at the royal palace. Whether this should be taken to mean that members of the royal family became Christian is a matter of speculation; but it marked the height of Christian influence at court. This new standing may have emboldened Christian leaders to press the emperor for an important change in the designation of Christian churches in China. In 745, an imperial decree declared that

> in order that all men might know the (real and true) origin of what are commonly known as 'Persian monasteries' in the two capitals (the names) are henceforth to be changed to the Ta-ch'in [Daqin, i.e., Syrian] Monasteries.[143]

The change from "Persian" to "Daqin" was significant. The designation "Persian" religion blurred the distinction between Christianity, Zoroastrianism, and Manichaeanism, at least in popular Chinese thinking.[144] Moreover, Persian converts to Islam now formed part of the immigrant merchant population,[145] adding Islam to the number of Persian religions. The "Daqin" label gave the church the distinctive identity it needed in a pluralistic context. "Daqin" was the Chinese name for the eastern reaches of the Roman Empire (or the Far West), specifically the province of Syria.[146] The new name revealed the T'ang Church's "real and true" beginnings because it referenced the birthplace of Christianity—since, as the inscription puts it, "a virgin gave birth to the Holy One in Syria." Importantly, also, the name change clarified

142. Baum and Winkler, *Church of the East*, 47.

143. Quoted in Saeki, *Nestorian Documents*, 51; Foster, *Church of the T'ang Dynasty*, 213.

144. See Foster, *Church of the T'ang Dynasty*, 119–20.

145. Islam entered China in the early eighth century through Arab and Persian merchants. Saeki, *Nestorian Documents*, 51; Foster, *Church of the T'ang Dynasty*, 77.

146. Baum and Winkler, *Church of the East*, 48; Ferreira, *Early Chinese Christianity*, 306; Saeki, *Nestorian Documents*, 39–40; Foster, *Church of the T'ang Dynasty*, 87–89.

that T'ang Christianity was a religion unconnected to any political state and unassociated with imperial expansion.

In the mid-eighth century, a rebellion headed by An Lu-shan, a Turkish (non-Chinese) general, upended China's long period of peace and stability and led to devastating civil war. The upheaval precipitated the abdication of Xuangzong, who was succeeded by his son, Su Zong (756–762). Though an ardent Buddhist, Su Zong maintained the policy of religious tolerance and rebuilt churches. The next two rulers—Daizong (763–779) and Dezong (780–805)—similarly supported Christianity and the work of Christian mission. In the wake of the civil war, at least one Christian, Priest Yisi/I-sz' (originally from the city of Balkh), attained a prominent position in the T'ang administration and military bureaucracy. The inscription attests that Yisi used his prominence and financial resources to perform "deeds of benevolence" and bolster the spread of "the Luminous Religion."

The T'ang Christian Monument, which was produced during this time (in 781), mirrors the optimism and confidence of the T'ang Church and marks the apogee of Christian prosperity in this era. Built at considerable expense, and erected in public, the monument served several objectives:[147] it commemorated the spread of Christianity, affirmed imperial support for Christianity in China, contextually proclaimed the content of the Christian faith to the wider public, and corroborated imperial patronage. In sum, it promoted Christianity as compatible with Chinese culture, as a respectable religion that had acquired a legitimate place in Chinese society.

The author of the inscription is identified as Adam (whose Chinese name was Ching-Ching), then bishop of China, described as "among the most striking personalities of the Church of the East in China."[148] Well versed in the Chinese classics, Adam translated several Christian texts into Chinese and famously collaborated with an Indian Buddhist to translate Buddhist sutras into Chinese; however, the latter endeavor ended in failure due to his ignorance of Sanskrit and Buddhist teachings. Clearly, such interreligious collaboration befitted the religious pluralism of the T'ang era. The assumption that this offers proof of the syncretistic nature of T'ang Christianity is blunted not

147. Ferreira, *Early Chinese Christianity*, 143, 309.
148. Baum and Winkler, *Church of the East*, 49; see also Foster, *Church of the T'ang Dynasty*, 107–14.

only by the orthodoxy of the inscription on the T'ang Monument but also by the fact that the strongest opposition came from Buddhists who, writes John Foster, feared that Adam "was trying to make Buddhism too Christian."[149]

By the end of the ninth century, the once glorious T'ang Dynasty had passed its heyday. The upsurge in antiforeign sentiments precipitated by the mid-eighth-century civil war was a major factor in the deterioration of T'ang authority. This conflict, instigated by a non-Chinese military commander, exposed China to foreign incursions—Tibetan forces briefly occupied the capital—and gave impetus to latent forces of xenophobic isolationism. The climate of suspicion stoked smoldering resentments and bred violence. In 758, discontented foreign (Arab and Persian) traders started a riot in Guangzhou that caused widespread damage and forced the governor to flee.[150] In retaliation, Chinese ports were closed to foreigners for fifty years. Violent clashes with the Uighurs, once reliable allies of the Chinese state, also produced retaliatory measures and state suppression of Manichaeanism (strongly associated with the Uighur presence).[151] An assertive cultural patriotism, aided by the revival of Confucianism, eventually triggered a forceful crackdown on Buddhism and all foreign religions in 845.[152] The imperial edict stated in part:

> As for the Ta Ch'in [Syrian] and Muh-hu [Zoroastrian] forms of worship, since Buddhism has already been cast out, these heresies must not alone be allowed to survive. People belonging to these also are to be compelled to return to the world, belong again to their own districts, and become taxpayers. As for foreigners, let them be returned to their own countries, there to suffer restraint.[153]

At the time of the edict, T'ang Christians reportedly numbered about 260,000.[154] Over a period of twenty months, more than 4,600 monasteries

149. Foster, *Church of the T'ang Dynasty*, 114.

150. Levathes, *When China Ruled the Seas*, 39.

151. Levathes, *When China Ruled the Seas*, 39; Foster, *Church of the T'ang Dynasty*, 118–20.

152. Foster, *Church of the T'ang Dynasty*, 120–27; Ferreira, *Early Chinese Christianity*, 310–13.

153. Quoted in Foster, *Church of the T'ang Dynasty*, 123; see also Charbonnier, *Christians in China*, 63–67; Saeki, *Nestorian Documents*, 47–48.

154. Baum and Winkler, *Church of the East*, 50.

and 40,000 hermitages (private temples) were demolished; and at least 3,000 Christian and Zoroastrian monks were "compelled to return to the world, lest they confuse the customs of China."[155] Reprieve came in 847 when a new emperor issued a new edict that restored the policy of toleration. But the multiculturalism that marked the T'ang period was irreparably damaged and the forces of xenophobic hostility were not easily assuaged. In 878, antagonism toward foreigners contributed to a major uprising, during which most of the resident foreigners in Canton were killed.[156] An Arab account records that "one hundred and twenty thousand persons, Muslims, Jews, Christians, and Zoroastrians, who had settled in the city for the sake of trade" perished, along with an unknown number of Chinese natives.[157] The uprising was quelled with the help of foreign troops, at great cost of life; but it epitomized the disorder, insecurity, and misrule that marked a waning empire. Internal dissension eventually brought the T'ang Dynasty to an end in the early tenth century amid political turmoil and more brutal attacks on foreign religious communities.

The decline of the T'ang church coincided with the collapse of T'ang authority. But the prolonged anarchy that accompanied the end of T'ang rule precludes accurate record of Christian presence in China after 900. According to an Arabic record that dates to the late tenth century, an East Syrian monk sent to China in 987 to assess the state of the church found Christianity extinguished and not a single surviving Christian.[158] Other accounts suggest, however, that East Syrian Christian communities and structures persisted in China until at least the eleventh century.[159] But, to all intents and purposes, the East Syrian Church had ceased to exist as a public institution in China by the mid-eleventh century.

There is no shortage of explanations for the demise of T'ang Christianity.[160] Almost all are conjectural or less than persuasive. In his detailed analysis, Moffett identified four major areas of assessment: religious, theological, missiological, and political. Religious explanations focus on the fierce backlash

155. Foster, *Church of the T'ang Dynasty*, 125.
156. Curtin, *Cross-Cultural Trade in World History*, 108.
157. Quoted in Foster, *Church of the T'ang Dynasty*, 130.
158. Foster, *Church of the T'ang Dynasty*, 115; Baum and Winkler, *Church of the East*, 51.
159. See England, *Christianity in Asia*, 74; Baum and Winkler, *Church of the East*, 51.
160. The most comprehensive examination is provided by Moffett, *Christianity in Asia*, 302–14. See also Ferreira, *Early Chinese Christianity*, 313–15.

against foreign religions combined with state-led persecution in the ninth century that devastated the Chinese church. However, the survival (and growth) of Christian communities in the Roman and Sassanian realms in the face of vigorous state persecution limits the force of this argument, even if, in this context, imperial patronage (a practical necessity) was a double-edged sword that heightened the church's vulnerability to state action. Theological reasons are the most contentious. T'ang Christianity has been derided by some as heretical or unpardonably "syncretistic" on account of its Nestorian heritage, ecclesiastical isolation, and uncritical appropriation of Confucian and/or Buddhist categories.[161] But more recent assessments, based on close study of T'ang documents and better understanding of the T'ang cultural milieu, largely reject earlier Western diatribes. Foster was among the first scholars to denounce "the savage condemnation" of T'ang Christianity as unwarranted.[162] Moffett, who quotes Foster, also ascertains that Nestorianism is virtually absent from the T'ang Christian documents and that "the Christology of the documents is essentially orthodox."[163] Ferreira similarly dismisses charges of syncretism and asserts that T'ang Christian documents are "distinctively Christian."[164]

The missiological explanation asserts that the T'ang Church's foreignness (or Persian character) and limited cross-cultural impact were major factors in

---

161. See Kenneth Scott Latourette, *A History of the Expansion of Christianity*, vol. 2, *The Thousand Years of Uncertainty* (Grand Rapids: Zondervan, 1970), 280; Bishop Adam's collaboration with an Indian Buddhist to translate Buddhist sutras into Chinese, for instance, is decried by some Western Christian scholars as confirmation of the syncretistic nature of T'ang Christianity, while others commend it as consistent with the missionary task—an effort to establish Christianity as a Chinese faith. See Foster, *Church of the T'ang Dynasty*, 112–14; Ferreira, *Early Chinese Christianity*, 309–10; Moffett, *Christianity in Asia*, 309–13.

162. As he explains, the borrowing of terminology from non-Christian sources to express Christian truth in the far-eastern environment was no different from "the debt owed by the Church in the West to Greek philosophy." Foster, *Church of the T'ang Dynasty*, 112–13.

163. Moffett, *Christianity in Asia*, 312. He adds that even the earliest inchoate efforts at vernacular translation (such as the "Jesus-Messiah Sutra") "managed remarkably well to transmit the core of the biblical Christian message" (pp. 306–9).

164. Ferreira, *Early Chinese Christianity*, 315 (also pp. 151, 261, 314). Gillman and Klimkeit are content to describe the documents as "examples of a new religious and spiritual synthesis between Christian thought and Chinese tradition." Gillman and Klimkeit, *Christians in Asia*, 292.

its ultimate demise. Some see the predominantly Syriac names on the T'ang Monument as proof positive that T'ang Christianity remained the faith of foreigners or wholly confined to non-Chinese inhabitants. This view is unpersuasive. Whether in fact the names on the monument indicate foreign extraction is open to debate; and it has been tenably argued that the erection of the monument was actually motivated by a determination to contextualize the Christian message in the Chinese environment. The extent to which Christianity was embraced by the indigenous population, amid competing faiths, is unknown. But the missionary commitment of T'ang Christians is evident in extensive efforts at vernacular translation and the indigenization of teaching and worship.[165] T'ang documents not only expressed the Christian message in a Chinese philosophical framework but also made extensive use of the Chinese language in liturgy, revealing impressive knowledge of Chinese traditions.[166] The church's rootedness in Chinese culture is also indicated by the fact that all the extant documents of T'ang Christianity are in the Chinese language, not Syriac. By this token, the T'ang Church was arguably more indigenous than the much older Indian Church, which survives to this day.[167]

From a different analytical standpoint, Ferreira argues that the most serious missiological shortcoming of the T'ang Church was not lack of contextualization but the failure to develop *indigenous leadership*. He states that, after almost two centuries of existence in China, "most of the church's leadership, if not all, were of foreign extraction [i.e., non-Chinese] . . . appointed from Baghdad."[168] This conclusion is difficult to reconcile with England's finding, based on the extant documents and inscriptions, "that significant numbers of Chinese were active in the leadership of the Chang-an Christians during the

165. England, *Christianity in Asia*, 71.

166. Ferreira, *Early Chinese Christianity*, 314.

167. In the Indian context, vernacular translation efforts came centuries after the church's establishment and, despite the Indian Church's integration into the Hindu upper class, the church's extensive use of Syriac in liturgy and theology is reflected in hordes of manuscripts. See Aprem Mar Mooken, "Reference to China in Syriac Sources," in *Hidden Treasures and Intercultural Encounters: Studies on East Syriac Christianity in China and Central Asia*, ed. Dietmar W. Winkler and Li Tang (Vienna: Lit, 2014), 184–85.

168. Ferreira, *Early Chinese Christianity*, 315.

Tang Dynasty."[169] He adds that the list of names prior to 781 includes "forty-nine monks, sixteen priest-monks, an abbot, an archdeacon and a bishop." But the argument that a dearth of Chinese leadership was a key reason for the decline of T'ang Christianity also fails to convince because Christian communities in South India survived for many centuries without indigenous leadership. Not until the seventeenth century was the first Indian bishop consecrated.[170]

The political explanation holds that the fortunes of Christianity in China were so inextricably tied to the patronage and protection of the T'ang Dynasty that the fall of the T'ang state sealed the church's fate. Moffett, who subscribes to this view, avers that "dependence on government is a dangerous and uncertain foundation for Christian survival."[171] Be that as it may, this reasoning pits political expediency against missiological necessity, since it seems highly doubtful that the church would have been established in the first place without imperial support. Christian loyalty to the T'ang Dynasty may have been compromising at a certain level;[172] but, to migrant missionaries, this probably seemed a small price to pay for the state-sanctioned opportunity to proclaim the Christian faith in the Chinese context. Indeed, eschewing royal patronage would have made more sense if the Christian immigrant community had little interest in cross-cultural mission.

T'ang Christianity lasted over two centuries and its eventual demise is best seen as an ill-fated outcome produced by a complex combination of inherent weaknesses and historical happenstance. No definitive explanation appears possible. In the end, neither vigorous indigenization nor imperial support nor, for that matter, peaceful coexistence with other faiths gained the church a more enduring foothold. State sponsorship was a double-edged sword that

169. England, *Christianity in Asia*, 72–73.

170. Like the T'ang Church, the church in South India was also under the jurisdiction of the "Patriarch of the East" headquartered in Baghdad, and this ongoing ecclesiastical connection was "marked by the occasional visits of bishops, monks, and other holy men and by acquiring holy oil from the patriarch." David Chidester, *Christianity: A Global History* (New York: HarperCollins, 2000), 454.

171. Moffett, *Christianity in Asia*, 313.

172. It is important to note that this was quite different from emperor worship. As Ferreira explains, honoring the imperial dynasty was a cultural requirement, an expression of loyalty in exchange for the court's patronage. Ferreira, *Early Chinese Christianity*, 147.

guaranteed missionary access but left the church all the more vulnerable to the vicissitudes of political life. What one imperial edict bestowed another could destroy; and the institutional visibility encouraged by official support rendered church structures all the more vulnerable to attack when that support was lost. On one issue, however, there can be little doubt. No matter the degree of cultural adaptation and Chinese participation, Christianity never transcended its status as an immigrant religion,[173] and it perhaps even remained centered in merchant centers. So migration was both the chief source of mission and a probable cause for its collapse.

Weakened by brutal massacres, decimated by the expulsion of foreigners, and cut off from other Christian communities (by China's new isolationism and the disruption to long-distance travel that accompanied the fall of the T'ang Empire), the Christian community in China withered away. But the church survived in central Asia; and mass expulsion may have served to spread Christian influence. As it turned out, further migrations triggered by the rise of the Mongols contributed to the rebirth of Christianity in China by the early thirteenth century and reshaped the religious landscape in much of Asia.

173. Even Buddhism, with a larger Chinese following and much longer presence in China (possibly already there before the birth of the Christian movement), was still perceived as a foreign religion.

CHAPTER NINE

Gaining the World: The Interlocking Strands of Migration, Imperial Expansion, and Christian Mission

> If I were to turn to the faith of Christ and become a Christian, then my barons and others who are not converted will say, "What has moved you to be baptized and to take up the faith of Christ? What powers or miracles have you witnessed on His part . . . ?"
>
> — Kublai Khan

From the seventh to the fifteenth centuries, the networks of contact and exchange between Africa, Europe, and Asia expanded rapidly and consequentially. From the late seventh century, Islamic rulers established an imperial communication network that linked Damascus to other major cities in the growing empire. Under the Abbasids, this system (re-centered on Baghdad) extended some 4,000 miles from Algiers (North Africa) to present-day Kabul and included hundreds of post stations spaced 6 to 12 miles apart.[1] The network was primarily designed for government-related business and allowed mounted couriers to cover up to 50 miles a day.[2] This road building connected new lands and peoples, and greatly expanded the numbers and movement of travelers. In the ninth century, Arab emissary Tamīm ibn Bahr traversed the 3,500 miles from Baghdad to Mongolia and covered the last 2,000 miles (in Uighur territory in central Asia) in forty days.[3] Further east, the Mon-

---

1. Stephen S. Gosch and Peter N. Stearns, *Premodern Travel in World History* (New York: Routledge, 2008), 112–13.

2. Norbert Ohler, *The Medieval Traveller* (Woodbridge: Boydell, 1997), 101.

3. Gosch and Stearns, *Premodern Travel in World History*, 112–13; V. Minorsky, "Tamīm Ibn Bahr's Journey to the Uyghurs," *Bulletin of the School of Oriental and African Studies, University of London* 12, no. 2 (1948): 283.

gols also constructed vast road networks and established a relay system that reportedly allowed couriers to cover up to 235 miles in twenty-four hours.[4] In the north, a vast arc of trade networks developed in the ninth to tenth centuries linked western, northern, and western Europe with western Asia via the Baltic Sea.[5]

Sea travel also changed dramatically. By the ninth century, Persian seamen and merchants could sail from Basra, a multicultural port city close to the Persian Gulf, to the Chinese port of Guangzhou, a distance of over 6,000 miles (referred to as "the porcelain route"), in six months.[6] A round trip with stops for trade could be completed in about eighteen months.[7] The ships on which these merchants sailed possibly carried up to six hundred men and were navigated by the stars.[8] From the twelfth century, however, long-standing Persian and Arab dominance of the Indian Ocean was swiftly overtaken by Chinese naval supremacy. This started with rulers of the Song Dynasty (960–1279), who turned to overseas trade after they were driven out of China's rich agricultural north to the south in the twelfth century. Political and economic incentives spurred inventions of new maritime technology and navigational aids (such as the magnetic compass and fixed rudder) that improved the speed and comfort of sea travel.[9] The Song built ships that could carry up to one thousand men and cover 300 miles in one day.[10] After defeating the Song in

4. Ohler, *Medieval Traveller*, 97.

5. Anders Winroth, *The Conversion of Scandinavia: Vikings, Merchants, and Missionaries in the Remaking of Northern Europe* (New Haven: Yale University Press, 2012), 86, 100. Among other things, this extensive trade system brought large quantities of Arab silver to European markets.

6. Gosch and Stearns, *Premodern Travel in World History*, 114–15; Louise Levathes, *When China Ruled the Seas: The Treasure Fleet of the Dragon Throne, 1405–1433* (New York: Oxford University Press, 1996).

7. Philip D. Curtin, *Cross-Cultural Trade in World History* (New York: Cambridge University Press, 1984), 108, 119.

8. Levathes, *When China Ruled the Seas*, 35–36.

9. Levathes, *When China Ruled the Seas*, 41–48; Richard L. Smith, *Premodern Trade in World History* (New York: Routledge, 2008), 140.

10. In time, the Chinese produced vessels of increasing size and splendor that included watertight compartments (six hundred years ahead of European efforts) and "no fewer than sixty individual cabins for merchants." See Levathes, *When China Ruled the Seas*, 49, 81; Michael C. Howard, *Transnationalism in Ancient and Medieval Societies: The Role of Cross-Border Trade and Travel* (Jefferson, NC: McFarland, 2012), 19; Gosch and Stearns, *Premodern Travel in World History*, 72, 107–8, 145–46.

the 1270s, Kublai Khan intensified the shipbuilding effort. By 1281, Kublai was able to assemble the largest armada in the world: a force of 4,500 ships and 150,000 men.

These developments corresponded with exponential increases in the numbers of travelers and the distances covered in journeys. Propelled by a variety of motivations and myriad forces, merchants, adventurers, missionaries or religious specialists, pilgrims, diplomatic envoys, scholars, slaves and captives, soldiers, nomads, and hordes of refugees traversed road arteries and sea routes. The intensification of cross-community migrations facilitated intercultural exchange between more distant and more diverse societies.[11] A global web of interconnections emerged between societies and regions from eastern China to western Africa, "reconnecting communities . . . which had developed distinct cultures over tens of thousands of years."[12] In an era marked by considerable political turbulence, thick interconnections developed due to long-distance trade, empire building, and religious travel (for missionary purpose or pilgrimage). Even more so than earlier periods, these interlocking strands galvanized cross-cultural exchange and decisively shaped religious propagation.

Interestingly, the interaction between imperial powers, trade, and merchants could be both conflicting and complementary. The stability and security provided by imperial rule inevitably bolstered commercial activity, while the profits of trade provided political authorities with revenues needed to finance the needs of the state.[13] Merchants were also valued because they epitomized the reach and resources of cross-cultural contact and exchange. Precisely because foreign trade "bound together through the exchange of goods people of different races, religions and cultures,"[14] long-distance traders often spoke several

11. Patrick Manning, *Migration in World History* (New York: Routledge, 2005), 92–106; Gosch and Stearns, *Premodern Travel in World History*, 73–74.

12. Ian Goldin, Geoffrey Cameron, and Meera Balarajan, *Exceptional People: How Migration Shaped Our World and Will Define Our Future* (Princeton: Princeton University Press, 2011), 3. See also Nayan Chanda, *Bound Together: How Traders, Preachers, Adventurers, and Warriors Shaped Globalization* (New Haven: Yale University Press, 2007), 48–50.

13. Conversely, governing authorities can implement policies that are harmful to trade: some implement excessive taxes and dues to exploit lucrative trades; and in some situations, government can take over the business of trade (as was the case in Song China) or promote the commercial activities of particular groups at the expense of others.

14. Ohler, *Medieval Traveller*, 63–64.

languages and were the best sources of information about foreign peoples, customs, and innovations.[15] But there is no fixed correspondence between imperial expansion and commercial growth.[16] The structures of empire can enhance the reach of commercial activity, but the growth of lucrative trade networks or centers can provide powerful incentive for destructive conquest or plunder. Also, while military conquests can inflict serious damage on commercial life and disrupt trade routes, territorial acquisition can also "open new routes, create new demands, and introduce new commodities." Nor does the collapse of empire necessarily translate into the cessation of thriving commercial activity, especially if long-distance trading activity contributed to the rise of empire in the first place. In sum, while mercantile activities and reach sometimes derived impetus from imperial expansion, they often exceeded the reach of empire.

The relationship between empire and religious expansion was even more fraught. As we have noted (chapter 2), almost all the major religions were adopted as the official religion of an imperial state at some stage in their histories, and their global expansions were facilitated in part by conquest or colonization of extensive territories. This has convinced some scholars that state sponsorship is vital for the spread of religion across cultural frontiers. Jerry Bentley, for instance, insisted that the absence of political power is the main reason for the eventual breakdown of Nestorian communities in Asia that were established by merchants, in stark comparison to the successful spread of Christianity in Europe where monastic missions enjoyed the benefits of organizational leadership and sponsorship by powerful monarchs.[17] But this argument fails to take into account the radically dissimilar European and Asian contexts, vastly greater distances involved in East Syrian missions, and the presence of other major faiths among Asian civilizations. Most important, it underestimates the degree to which broader migratory flows shape long-term religious engagement and even contributed to the rise of empires. This chapter examines the complex interactions between vast migrations, empire building, and the fortunes and fate of Christian communities in Islamic and Mongol domains.

---

15. Ohler, *Medieval Traveller*, 59, 75. The prophet Isaiah (23:3) memorably described Tyre (the ancient Phoenician port city) as the "marketplace of the world" (NLT).

16. Smith, *Premodern Trade in World History*, 52–53.

17. Jerry H. Bentley, *Old World Encounters: Cross-Cultural Contacts and Exchanges in Pre-Modern Times* (New York: Oxford University Press, 1993), 100–109.

How nomadic tribes such as Arabs and Mongols managed to not only overcome the armies of long-standing empires but also establish sophisticated civilizations in their place is an intriguing question.[18] Part of the answer lies in the nature and militaristic advantages of nomadic existence. Nomadic groups participated in long-distance trade and sometimes controlled critical trade routes, even as their mobility allowed them to profit from pillaging raids on commercial rivals or trade caravans. By any reckoning, nomadic armies were formidable fighters and potent adversaries,[19] in part because pastoral nomadism made such groups excellent breeders of horses and exceptional horse riders, which meant that "the whole society could be mobilized for war."[20] Highly mobile, boasting an exceptionally skilled warrior class, and able to acquire advanced technologies from settled populations, nomadic groups troubled imperial domains whose large sedentary populations made them vulnerable to highly organized marauding attacks. Imperial powers sometimes responded by forging temporary alliances with powerful nomadic tribes on their borders and even recruited their fighters into overstretched armies.[21] More to the point, when such tribes formed confederacies and combined military forces, their capacity for territorial invasion increased dramatically. Indeed, nomadic tribes could cause greater disruption than regular armies

18. For a helpful assessment, see Jane Burbank and Frederick Cooper, *Empires in World History: Power and the Politics of Difference* (Princeton: Princeton University Press, 2010), 43–45, 71, 94–99; also Smith, *Premodern Trade in World History*, 125–26, 139.

19. Over time, militaristic nomadic groups gained experience in challenging and exploiting the weaknesses of empires. What they lacked in numbers they more than made up for in military tactics, fighting skills, and the rugged determination imbued by nomadic existence.

20. Arab and Mongol tribes were renowned for their superior horsemanship. All Mongols, writes Charbonnier, "learned to ride when they were three or four years old, girls as well as boys," and "every tribesman between sixteen and sixty was a warrior." Jean-Pierre Charbonnier, *Christians in China: A.D. 600 to 2000* (San Francisco: Ignatius Press, 2007), 71. They also "controlled about half the world's horses in the thirteenth century." Burbank and Cooper, *Empires in World History*, 99; Irene M. Franck and David M. Brownstone, *The Silk Road: A History* (New York: Facts on File, 1986), 176.

21. By the sixth century, for instance, the rank and file of the Byzantine army was made up of soldiers from Germanic tribes. J. A. S. Evans, *The Age of Justinian: The Circumstances of Imperial Power* (New York: Routledge, 1996), 51. A similar strategy failed to prevent the collapse of the Western Roman Empire (chapter 5).

because conquest was followed by large-scale migration and settlement within the local population.[22]

The prevalence of illiteracy among nomadic tribes is often mistakenly equated with lack of intelligence or political acumen. Tribal politics incorporated strategic alliances, diplomatic skills, tactical mindedness, and treaty making that produced strong leaders—not to mention the fact that proximity to great powers made nomadic leaders familiar with the systems and strategies of imperial rule, which they adopted or adapted to once conquest was complete. More often than not, the intensely personalized forms of leadership prevalent among nomadic tribes fueled blood feuds and bitter internal rivalries; and it was this, rather than lack of capacity for complex political organization, that frequently caused the undoing of empires created by nomadic peoples.

THE ISLAMIC (UMAYYAD AND ABBASID) EMPIRES

Mohammed had been a trader and Islam originated in a trading center. Medina, the oasis from which he conquered all of Arabia, was still no more than "a town on the edge of a salty, barren desert" in the eleventh century.[23] The link between religion and trade within the new religion, and the role of merchants in its vigorous spread, was emphatic. Muslim domination of the Silk Routes that extended from the western Mediterranean all the way to China accelerated the Islamization of central Asia and extended its influence eastward. By the end of the eleventh century, a major trading network had emerged in the Mediterranean region (centered at Cairo) that involved "perhaps 8,000 traveling merchants" conducting trade by ships and caravans between Tunis and Sicily and even further west.[24] As "the principal agency for contact between the discrete cultures of this period," Islamic rule facilitated the transmission of religious ideas and cultural practices, as well as inventions (such as the Chinese

22. Nehemia Levtzion, "Conversion to Islam in Syria and Palestine and the Survival of Christian Communities," in *Conversion and Continuity: Indigenous Christian Communities in Islamic Lands, Eighth to Eighteenth Centuries*, ed. Michael Gervers and Ramzi Jibran Bikhazi (Toronto: Pontifical Institute of Mediaeval Studies, 1990), 291.

23. W. M. Thackston, trans., *Nasir-I Khusraw's Book of Travels* (Costa Mesa, CA: Mazda, 2001), 76.

24. Curtin, *Cross-Cultural Trade in World History*, 111–15.

compass and European artillery), between distant societies.²⁵ It also had major implications for the shape, survival, and spread of Christian communities.

By the time of Mohammed's death (632), the religious movement he founded had secured the "submission" (*islām* in Arabic) of most of the Arabian tribes. His successors (or *caliphs*) consolidated political rule of the Arabian peninsula and Arab Muslim armies embarked on successive military campaigns that created a world empire to rival that of the Romans. Western Arabia, the cradle of the new movement, was part of a trading network connected to the Sassanian and Byzantine Empires and lands beyond. By the seventh century the two empires were waning, exhausted by centuries of debilitating and costly wars. The better-defended Byzantine Empire remained a bulwark against Islamic advancement and lasted until the fifteenth century. But in the 630s its armies suffered crushing defeats, and valuable territories in Egypt, Palestine, Syria, North Africa, and Armenia were wrested from its control.²⁶ Between 632 and 642, the Sassanian Empire, which had endured decades of political instability, rapidly collapsed. Both empires harbored vast disaffected populations or oppressed minority groups that collaborated with or welcomed conquering Muslim armies. More often than not, bitter religious (nationalistic) divisions, internal strife, and political rivalries played into the hands of Muslim conquerors. For millions of Copts, Syrians, and Armenians, Arab invasion and occupation did not end minority status; but it heralded more favorable treatment in the medium term.

Victories over imperial armies galvanized the expansion of Arab Islamic rule. By the end of the Umayyad Caliphate (661–750), the Islamic empire incorporated 60 million people, including *half of the world's Christian population*.²⁷ It also encompassed 7 million square kilometers of territory, including "most of the Middle East with the exception of western Turkey . . . , North Africa from Egypt to Morocco, most of Spain and Portugal, parts of southwestern Central Asia that included Bukhara and Samarkand, and most

25. Curtin, *Cross-Cultural Trade in World History*, 107.

26. In the famous six-day Battle of Yarmouk (636), a woefully outnumbered Muslim army of 40,000 decisively defeated a Byzantine force numbering over 100,000 (according to Arab sources), thus permanently ending Byzantine rule south of Asia Minor.

27. Dale T. Irvin and Scott Sunquist, *History of the World Christian Movement*, vol. 1, *Earliest Christianity to 1453* (Maryknoll, NY: Orbis Books, 2001), 270.

of modern Pakistan and Afghanistan."[28] From 750 to at least 1500, Muslim civilization emerged as the most dynamic and successful heir to the Roman and Sassanian civilizations.

The Limitations of Arab Christianity in the Face of Rising Islam

The Arabian peninsula was wedged between the Byzantine and Sassanian Empires and populated by nomadic tribes that lived on the trade routes.[29] Some were settled in semiautonomous kingdoms on the borders that became vassal states of the two powers. The spread of Christianity to the region probably dates to the first century (Acts 2:11; Gal. 1:15–17);[30] and the available record confirms the presence of bishoprics in the mid-third century. By 500 CE at least, large indigenous populations of Monophysites and Nestorians were present among the tribes of Arabia.[31]

Local merchants and Arab women played a significant role in spreading the faith. About 400 CE, a Najrani merchant named Hayyan stopped in Persia on his return journey from a trade mission in Constantinople and was converted to the Nestorian faith. He became a vigorous evangelist among his people.

28. Howard, *Transnationalism in Ancient and Medieval Societies*, 73.

29. Prior to the seventh century, the inhabitants of Arabia did not share a common identity, and "Arab" was not a reference to a distinctive cultural group. J. Spencer Trimingham, *Christianity among the Arabs in Pre-Islamic Times* (New York: Longman, 1979), 2–3.

30. Christianity was transmitted through Jewish merchant networks, Syrian ascetics, or the waves of persecuted Christians (from the Roman and Persian domains) who sought refuge in the desert and became missionaries. For treatment of Christianity in Arabia prior to the rise of Islam, see Trimingham, *Christianity among the Arabs*; Ian Gillman and Hans-Joachim Klimkeit, *Christians in Asia before 1500* (Ann Arbor: University of Michigan Press, 1999), 75–86; Samuel H. Moffett, *A History of Christianity in Asia: Beginnings to 1500*, vol. 1 (Maryknoll, NY: Orbis Books, 1998), 273–84; Laurence E. Browne, *The Eclipse of Christianity in Asia, from the Time of Muhammad Till the Fourteenth Century* (Cambridge: Cambridge University Press, 1933), 11–13; John C. England, *The Hidden History of Christianity in Asia: The Churches of the East before the Year 1500* (Delhi, India: ISPCK, 2002), 27–30; John Stewart, *Nestorian Missionary Enterprise: The Story of a Church on Fire* (Trichur, India: Mar Narsai Presss, 1961), 51–76.

31. Trimingham, *Christianity among the Arabs*, 159–202, 259, 308. Only a few Arab tribes (in western Syria and Palestine) were associated with the Chalcedonian communion.

The western Tanukhs, a Syrian Arab federation (and vassals of Rome), became Christian in the late fourth century and their queen, Māwiyya, requested a bishop for her people as a condition for peace with the Romans.[32] Also, both the mother and wife (Queen Hind) of al-Mundir III (ca. 505–554), the most powerful ruler of the Lakhmid Dynasty centered at Hira (a vassal state of Persia), were Christians. Their rivals, the Ghassanid Arabs, were tied to Byzantium and within the Monophysite fold.[33] A number of tribes in central Arabia, including the Kinda ruling clan, also professed Christianity.[34] The Council of Chalcedon (451) was attended by eighteen Arab metropolitans and bishops.

However, the Christian faith mainly took root among sections of the population with strong ties to the wider world such as townspeople, merchants, and soldiers. In the obscure town of Mecca, for instance, Christians were mainly non-Meccans. Most Arab Christian communities were part of settled populations subject to Byzantine or Persian domination.[35] Furthermore, Arab churches were shaped by tribal rivalries; and the combination of geographical separation and strategic ties to adjacent empires allowed various groups to use adherence to one competing Christian community or the other as "an assertion of . . . ethnic independence."[36] All in all, this reduced Arab Christians to "religious clients" and produced a form of Christianity that "was no more than a surface influence" among the nomad tribes of the interior.[37]

The outsized role played by foreign powers and external influences in Arab Christianity subverted its ability to penetrate Arab life and helps to account for the failure of an indigenous church to fully develop. In addition to espousing cultic and creedal expressions of faith derived from Christian

32. Trimingham, *Christianity among the Arabs*, 7, 96–101, 254. That she was able to set such terms bespoke both military and political prowess.

33. Trimingham, *Christianity among the Arabs*, 171–202. According to Trimingham, relations between the Byzantines and Arabs were characterized by disagreement and mistrust because they never understood each other, while the Persians were more successful in their dealings with the latter (p. 184).

34. Trimingham, *Christianity among the Arabs*, 267–79.

35. Trimingham, *Christianity among the Arabs*, 308–9. The African kingdom of Ethiopia also wielded some influence in southern Arabia and intervened forcefully with its armies in 525 CE to avenge murderous persecution of Christians in Najran.

36. Trimingham, *Christianity among the Arabs*, 7.

37. Trimingham, *Christianity among the Arabs*, 206, 250, 260. Lamin O. Sanneh, ed., *Disciples of All Nations: Pillars of World Christianity* (New York: Oxford University Press, 2008), 63.

centers outside the Arab world, Arab Christians were also content to worship in Syriac, a language tied to Aramaic culture. In essence, even though the Arabic script of the Quran had developed centuries before the rise of Islam, "Christian Arabs found no role for it in relation to their beliefs."[38] There was no translation of the Bible into Arabic prior to Islamic expansion—an omission that is especially noteworthy given the translation of the Scriptures into the local vernaculars of other Asian peoples.[39] To Arabs, Christianity was a foreign faith enshrined in an unfamiliar language. The disparate and bitterly divided Arab Christian communities, closely related to foreign powers, and lacking deep roots in the indigenous culture, were no match for the powerful movement of religious reform that emerged in the early seventh century out of the obscure Arabian town of Mecca. With its strong appeal to Arab unity and identity, Islam exposed the limitations of Arab Christianity's social and cultural achievement.[40]

Migration, Islamic Rule, and Non-Arab Christian Populations

The Arab nomads created an empire that encompassed large sedentary populations. But migration and conquest went hand in hand. Everywhere, Islamic conquest and occupation triggered mass migrations of Christians that over time left some Christian centers (like Roman North Africa, Syria, and Palestine) depopulated. Still, by uniting all of Persia, Mesopotamia, Syria, Palestine, Egypt, and Roman North Africa under one political authority, Muslim rule achieved what neither Persian nor Roman military domination had accomplished.[41] Additionally, since Islamic rulers treated the variety of Christian groups within their domain (Jacobite, Monophysite, East Syrian,

38. Trimingham, *Christianity among the Arabs*, 226 (see, more broadly, pp. 223–38). Translations of Christian writings from Syriac into Arabic came after the sixth century; and Arab Christian scholarship continued to thrive well into the eleventh century.

39. Explanations for this lack of vernacular translation include cultural prejudice or insensitivity toward less sophisticated Arab peoples; widespread use of Aramaic (a language with strong affinity to Arabic); and the limitations of Arabic, which, before it was universalized by Islam, "remained undeveloped, a limited linguistic code, intractable to conceptual expression." Trimingham, *Christianity among the Arabs*, 224. See also Moffett, *Christianity in Asia*, 281, 332; Sanneh, *Disciples of All Nations*, 63–64.

40. Sanneh, *Disciples of All Nations*, 70.

41. Irvin and Sunquist, *World Christian Movement*, 272–73.

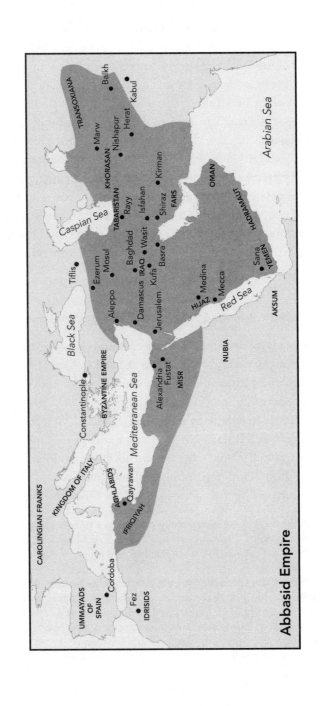

Abbasid Empire

Chalcedonian, etc.) as a single religious collective over whom they appointed a sole religious leader, Muslim administration paradoxically created an institutional unity that centuries of Christian conflict and debate had failed to achieve. But even in societies where Christian groups had originally welcomed the invading Muslim armies, centuries of Muslim political rule, often accompanied by successive waves of Arab immigration, produced degrading dhimmitude (segregated minority status) and active repression. Aggressive Islamization, heavy taxation, and violent persecution by Muslim authorities triggered further Christian emigrations and refugee movement that accelerated the religious transformation of the Middle East and western Asia.

Under the Abbasids, a Persian dynasty (750–1258), the Islamic political order reached its fullest extent, and Arab prestige and wealth achieved its greatest height.[42] The Abbasid Empire stretched from Iberia and Morocco in the west to sub-Saharan Africa in the south and as far east as northern India and integrated a multitude of peoples, ethnicities, and cultures. In 762, the Abbasids, who promoted a global vision, built a new capital in the city of Baghdad that effectively shifted the political center of power of Islam from Arabia to a more strategic location, though Mecca's status as the spiritual center of the Muslim faith remained unchanged. But, for all its achievements, Abbasid rule utterly failed to bring unity to *dar al Islam*.

From its beginnings, the Islamic movement was bedeviled by a volatile mixture of national rivalries, bitter theological controversies, and bloody succession disputes. Potent sectarian impulses incessantly troubled centralized control of the large multinational empire. The Abbasid government was based in Persia, dominated by non-Arabs, and dependent on foreign fighters (especially Turks) for security.[43] In southern Spain a remnant of the Umayyad Dynasty overthrown by the Abbasids retained a strong foothold. By the tenth century, localized centers of power and autonomous non-Arab dynasties with competing political ambitions had emerged throughout Muslim lands.[44]

---

42. Moffett, *Christianity in Asia*, 377. The stories of Sinbad the sailor date to this period.

43. Richard Foltz, *Religions of the Silk Road: Premodern Patterns of Globalization* (New York: Palgrave Macmillan, 2010), 89; Burbank and Cooper, *Empires in World History*, 75–77; Howard, *Transnationalism in Ancient and Medieval Societies*, 74.

44. Howard, *Transnationalism in Ancient and Medieval Societies*, 74; Moffett, *Christianity in Asia*, 375–85.

Among the strongest were the Samanids in Persia (819–999), the Fatimids in Egypt (909–1171), and the Seljuk Turks (1037–1157).[45] The rise of disparate and competing dynastic houses arguably helped to spread the reach and influence of Islam; but the clash of imperial projects also produced major incidents of destructive intrafaith violence.

As a case in point, the conversion of Turkish-speaking peoples propelled the Islamic faith across the trade routes into central Asia and among nomadic Eurasian peoples—a good number of whom were Christian—and generated a Turkish Islamic dynasty. In pursuit of their own imperial ambitions, the Seljuk Turks captured Baghdad in 1055 and decimated Abbasid power. Thereafter, they inflicted major defeats on the Byzantine army, seized parts of Turkey from Byzantine rule, and conquered Christian Armenia. Their invasion and occupation of Palestine after 1077 sent shock waves throughout western Christendom and triggered the ferocious but futile military campaigns by Western powers known as the Crusades.

Meanwhile, the structures of the Islamic empire indirectly aided the spread of Christianity among *non-Muslim* peoples in western Asia and beyond. Since Islamic rule strictly forbade Christian proselytization of Muslims, Eastern Christians channeled their missionary energies beyond Muslim domains. As a result, from about 640 to 820, Christian churches in central Asia expanded from nine to nineteen metropolitan provinces.[46] Patriarch Timothy I (r. 780–823), a major architect of this expansion, survived five caliphs. In 804, he established six new provinces beyond Persian frontiers "for Armenia, Damascus, Rai, Dailam, Turkestan and Tibet."[47] By the beginning of the eleventh century the Christian communities under the East Syrian patriarch "extended from China to the Tigris and from Lake Baikal to Cape Comorin."[48]

---

45. The multiple dynastic centers undermined but did not nullify the core Islamic vision of a single religious community (the *umma*). More to the point, the divided political landscape reflected the incorporation of large populations of non-Arabs (or outsiders) into the world of Islam.

46. England, *Christianity in Asia*, 27; also Alphonse Mingana, *The Early Spread of Christianity in Central Asia and the Far East: A New Document* (Manchester: University Press, 1925), 12–14.

47. England, *Christianity in Asia*, 27.

48. Stewart, *Nestorian Missionary Enterprise*, 167.

Pilgrimage and Religious Encounter

The idea of migration is profoundly integral to the Islamic faith, inviting comparisons to Judaism and Christianity. For Muslims, the Arabic term *hijra* (to migrate, abandon, or break ties with another) is rooted in historical events and enshrined in doctrine.[49] Religious pilgrimage, as we have noted, became a pillar of Latin (medieval) Christianity.[50] But the practice of pilgrimage is even more central to Islam. Visiting holy shrines in Mecca at least once in a lifetime is an obligation for every Muslim; and the rise of Islam caused a phenomenal increase in religious pilgrims. Among the earliest and most prominent Muslim pilgrims was Nasir-i Khusraw, a Persian administrative official for the Seljuk Turks, who went on a pilgrimage to Mecca (from central Asia) in the mid-eleventh century and covered some 4,000 miles in about fifteen months.[51] He reported that some 20,000 Muslims visited Jerusalem every year, along with large numbers of Christians and Jews. As a major form of migration, religious pilgrimage contributed to some of the most consequential developments in the period under review. The violent mistreatment of Western pilgrims in Jerusalem after it was overrun by the Seljuk Turks in the eleventh century was a major contributing factor to the Crusades.

The ordeals and costs of travel meant that pilgrimages were not undertaken lightly; and many perished on the journey.[52] Armed conflict and hostilities often made routes dangerous; and the advantages and relative security of group travel were easily offset by the fact that groups of pilgrims provided

49. The Qur'an and Islamic tradition prescribe *hijra* or migration as an obligation under certain circumstances (to move from non-Muslim lands and resettle in Islamic society, for instance), though the doctrinal warrant and specific conditions for migration are now a matter of vigorous debate. See Muhammed Khalid Masud, "The Obligation to Migrate: The Doctrine of *Hijra* in Islamic Law," in *Muslim Travellers: Pilgrimage, Migration, and the Religious Imagination*, ed. Dale F. Eickelman and James P. Piscatori (London: Routledge, 1990).

50. See Edith L. B. Turner and Victor W. Turner, *Image and Pilgrimage in Christian Culture* (New York: Columbia University Press, 1978), 187–88; Marcus Bull, "Pilgrimage," in *Oxford Handbook of Medieval Christianity*, ed. John Arnold (Oxford: Oxford University Press, 2014), 204.

51. Thackston, *Nasir-I Khusraw's Book of Travels*; also Gosch and Stearns, *Premodern Travel in World History*, 115–17.

52. For examples, see Matti Moosa, *The Crusades: Conflict between Christendom and Islam* (Piscataway, NJ: Gorgias, 2008), 141–55.

ready cover for vagabonds and criminals. Among Christians, the practice was debased by outrageous abuse and exploitation by the church hierarchy.[53] Yet, the pilgrimage tradition represented an expression of piety and penance that transcended theological difference and geographical distance. Extended travel for religious purpose engendered a form of social and spiritual solidarity that defied otherwise rigid barriers of language, social status, gender, and nationality.[54] It also contributed to religious interrelatedness, insofar as the communal worship of saints, shrines, and sacred places in Palestine and elsewhere provided unique opportunities for contact and interaction between Christians of all persuasions and backgrounds. In this regard, religious pilgrimages demonstrated the international character and multifariousness of the Christian movement more vividly than any synod or "ecumenical" council.

The global reach and ecumenical possibilities of Christian pilgrimage were demonstrated in the remarkable journey of two East Syrian Turkic monks, Rabban Sauma and Rabban Marcus, who set out from Mongolia to visit the Holy Land in the 1270s.[55] Traveling east to west, the two Chinese pilgrims were fully cognizant of "the difficulty of the way and the fatigue of the journey and the danger of the roads and the obstacles one might find in a foreign land." After months of arduous travel, they arrived in Baghdad, where they were received by the catholicos (Mar Denha). Thereafter, they visited holy places in Armenia and proceeded to the Holy Land with the intention of visiting Jerusalem; but the roads were too dangerous. When they returned to Baghdad, Marcus was consecrated Metropolitan of the Church in China (with the name Yaballaha) and Mar Sauma was appointed to serve him as Vicar-General. But their return to China was blocked for more than two years by an outbreak of war. When the catholicos died in 1281, Mar Yaballaha was unanimously elected as his successor on the basis that "the rulers of the whole empire were Mongols, and there was none who was acquainted at all with their customs and policies and language but he."[56] The East Syrian prel-

---

53. See Turner and Turner, *Image and Pilgrimage*, 192–97; Jacques Le Goff, *Medieval Civilization, 400–1500* (New York: Blackwell, 1988), 135–36.

54. Ohler, *Medieval Traveller*, 57; Turner and Turner, *Image and Pilgrimage*, 189, 192–93.

55. For details of this journey, see *The History of Yaballaha*.

56. James A. Montgomery, trans., *The History of Yaballaha* (New York: Columbia University Press, 1927), 44.

ates presented the new head of their church to the Mongol ruler as "one who came from the East to go to Jerusalem."

His transformation from pilgrim to patriarch made Mar Yaballaha the premier Christian authority in the Islamic world and a major influence at the court of the ilkhans in Persia. The Mongol ruler Arghūn (1284–1291), for instance, consulted Mar Yaballaha on the choice of an emissary to send to Christian monarchs in Europe, whose military support he needed to conquer Muslim-controlled Syria and Palestine. The catholicos recommended Rabban Sauma as one who was "acquainted with the languages" of Europe (presumably Greek and Latin). It was during this diplomatic mission that Sauma was given the opportunity to celebrate the Eucharist in Rome in the presence of the pope and cardinals, marking a historic communion between Eastern and Western Christianity (see chapter 7).

THE CRUSADES AS MIGRATION

The Persian author of *The History of Yaballaha* is believed to be a contemporary who composed his account in the early fourteenth century. The absence of reference in his account to the bitter conflicts between Latin Christendom and Islam is striking. He was, in all likelihood, aware that in 1263, a decade or so before Rabban Sauma and Marcus set out from their region for Jerusalem, the Egyptian Mamluks had overrun Palestine, laid waste to the land, and brought an end to crusader control.[57] Yet, his account gives no indication that the two pilgrims (or their fellow Christians who warned them about the hardships of their proposed pilgrimage) were aware of the Crusades or Muslim occupation of Palestine. He mentions that the Metropolitan of Jerusalem (who resided in Tripoli, Syria) was one of the prelates who participated in Mar Yaballaha's consecration.[58] But he makes no reference to the East Syrian Christian population in Syria and Palestine whose presence predated Islamic conquests and whom Islamic policy distinguished from the invading crusad-

---

57. The utter destruction of Nazareth left hardly any site or shrine for Christian pilgrims to visit or pray in. Raphael Israeli, *Green Crescent over Nazareth: The Displacement of Christians by Muslims in the Holy Land* (London: Frank Cass, 2002), 8.

58. Montgomery, *History of Yaballaha*, 45–46; see Montgomery's note. See also Israeli, *Green Crescent over Nazareth*, 6.

ers.[59] The lack of allusion to Muslim rule by the Persian writer perhaps reflects a mind attuned to a long history of minority existence and accommodation to foreign domination that made such details unremarkable. If so, it was an outlook far removed from the implacable hatred and apocalyptic dread fomented within Latin (Western) Europe toward Islam.

The historical study of the Crusades has generated a mountain of literature, and little can be added here. Of interest, however, is the correspondence between the Crusades and migration. Initially triggered by loss of the Holy Land and its sacred sites to Muslim control, the Crusades (in the Middle East) were a composite of expeditions, popular movement, territorial occupation, resettlement, and invasion. Though grounded in theological appeal, participation in the Crusades (including female involvement[60]) derived impetus from material causes and was driven by complex individual motives. Whether or not the crusading movement provided an outlet for the pressures of excessive population growth, it reflected migratory impulses of the era.[61] As Le Goff argues, in a feudal world where the vast majority of inhabitants had few land rights or material possessions, emigration was easy for masses of peasants "because they barely had a homeland to leave" and little of worth to keep them at home.[62] Most crucially, however, the Crusades had roots in the pilgrimage tradition. Not only were the terms used by contemporaries to denote pilgrimage (*peregrinatio*) and traveler (*peregrinus*) applied to the crusading army but also the phenomenon shared many distinctive features of pilgrimages.[63] Scholars

---

59. The latter were considered enemies to be annihilated. Israeli, *Green Crescent over Nazareth*, 6.

60. For an assessment of female participation in the Crusades, see Helen J. Nicholson, "Women's Involvement in the Crusades," in *The Crusader World*, ed. Adrian Boas (New York: Routledge, 2015), 54–67.

61. In the period between 600 and 1350 CE, the population in western Europe almost quadrupled—from 14.7 million (ca. 600) to 22.6 million (in 950) to 54.4 million (by 1350). This trend generated large-scale internal migrations and provided powerful catalyst for external expansion. Le Goff, *Medieval Civilization*, 59–66; also Sverre Bagge, "Christianizing Kingdoms," in *The Oxford Handbook of Medieval Christianity*, ed. John Arnold (New York: Oxford University Press, 2014), 127.

62. Le Goff, *Medieval Civilization*, 134. So great were the numbers of people who "had left their work, homes, and lands, even neglected their families" to undertake pilgrimage to the Holy Land that the church intervened with regulations. Moosa, *Crusades*, 152.

63. See Léan Ní Chléirigh, "*Nova Peregrinatio*: The First Crusade as a Pilgrim-

have variously characterized the Crusades as "armed pilgrimage"[64] or "a special kind of pilgrimage made by armed men."[65]

The first and most successful of the Crusades (1096–1099) was an international undertaking that assembled some 60,000 men.[66] The majority were Franks, and they followed well-known pilgrimage routes. This First Crusade led to the establishment of the so-called Latin kingdoms (or Crusader states) in Jerusalem, Edessa, Tripoli, and Antioch.[67] Latin Christian conquest and occupation were major acts of cross-community migration. The process infused a new nation of foreigners into the incredibly diverse population of the Levant, the Eastern Mediterranean region that already boasted a vibrant sociocultural mix (of indigenes and foreigners, denizens and nomads) and vigorous religious plurality. Prior to the Crusades, long-term inhabitants included Muslims of different sects, Jews, Samaritans, Greek Orthodox Christians (including a Melkite community), and Eastern Christians (comprising East Syrian, Jacobite, Armenian, and Maronite groups), as well as Ethiopian and Coptic ascetics. In essence, the large numbers of Latin (western European) Christians who settled in Palestine after the First Crusade were the latest immigrants in a long and recurrent cycle of incursions that had produced a multifarious religious landscape.

Within a matter of decades the vast majority of the residents of European descent were themselves born in the Holy Land, and therefore nei-

---

age in Contemporary Latin Narratives," in *Writing the Early Crusades: Text, Transmission and Memory*, ed. Marcus Bull and Damien Kempf (Woodbridge: Boydell, 2014); Moosa, *Crusades*, 131–33; Paul E. Chevedden, "Pope Urban II and the Ideology of the Crusades," in *The Crusader World*, ed. Adrian Boas (New York: Routledge, 2015); M. Cecilia Gaposchkin, "From Pilgrimage to Crusade: The Liturgy of Departure, 1095–1300," *Speculum* 88, no. 1 (2013): 44–91; Hunt Janin, "'A Pilgrimage in Arms': The First Crusade and Its Aftermath," in *Four Paths to Jerusalem: Jewish, Christian, Muslim, and Secular Pilgrimages, 1000 BCE to 2001 CE* (Jefferson, NC: McFarland, 2002).

64. Chléirigh, "*Nova Peregrinatio*," 63.

65. Moosa, *Crusades*, 131.

66. To this were added large numbers of noncombatants, including women, children, and regular pilgrims. In all, an estimated 100,000 Europeans may have been involved in some way. See Janin, "Pilgrimage in Arms," 90–93; Chléirigh, "*Nova Peregrinatio*," 68.

67. Some 3,000 Franks (including 300 knights) stayed behind in Jerusalem after the First Crusade. Janin, "Pilgrimage in Arms," 99.

ther crusaders nor, strictly speaking, immigrants. They were also a small minority compared to the indigenous population. The European inhabitants of the Crusader kingdom of Jerusalem, for instance, numbered 120,000 to 140,000 or 25 percent of the total population.[68] The degree of integration between the Franks (who controlled the Crusader states until the last European stronghold was annihilated in 1291) and the mass of inhabitants is debated.[69] One view holds that the Franks formed a ruling class or military aristocracy that treated the native population as subject peoples with whom they had limited interaction. Linguistic dissimilarity is proffered as the main evidence, which is to say that since the Franks retained French, whereas the majority of the inhabitants spoke Arabic or some other dialect, language essentially became "a key marker of difference between the rulers and the ruled."[70] But the notion of a strict binary or segregated divide between European newcomers and the native population appears simplistic. The Franks were confronted by a diversity of religious communities, and their attitude to or interaction with each group was determined by the latter's degree of religious affinity to Latin Christianity and pragmatic self-interest.[71] This arguably produced a hierarchy of relationships in which "indigenous Christians clearly enjoyed a more privileged position than Saracens, Bedouins, Jews, or Samaritans."[72]

For the Franks, in any case, proximity and practical necessity fostered attitudinal adjustments as well as religious realignments in dealings with the manifold Christian communities. Greek Orthodox Christians, with whom they felt the strongest religious kinship, were incorporated into a newly es-

---

68. Seymour Phillips, "The Medieval Background," in *Europeans on the Move: Studies on European Migration, 1500–1800*, ed. Nicholas P. Canny (New York: Oxford University Press, 1994), 19.

69. See Alan V. Murray, "Franks and Indigenous Communities in Palestine and Syria (1099–1187): A Hierarchical Model of Social Interaction in the Principalities of Outremer," in *East Meets West in the Middle Ages and Early Modern Times: Transcultural Experiences in the Premodern World*, ed. Albrecht Classen (Boston: de Gruyter, 2013); Johannes Pahlitzsch and Daniel Baraz, "Christian Communities in the Latin Kingdom of Jerusalem (1099–1187 CE)," in *Christians and Christianity in the Holy Land: From the Origins to the Latin Kingdoms* (Turnhout: Brepols, 2006), 205–35.

70. Murray, "Franks and Indigenous Communities," 299.

71. On Frankish attitudes and interactions with the different Christian groups, see Pahlitzsch and Baraz, "Christian Communities."

72. Murray, "Franks and Indigenous Communities," 309.

tablished Latin patriarchate of Jerusalem and accorded a high status. The fact that Greek Orthodox structures and clergy were subordinated to Latin ones (and Greek Orthodox patriarchs ended in exile) made for complex relations. The variety of Eastern Christians who had inhabited Syria and Palestine continuously long before and after Islamic conquest (though their numbers gradually declined thereafter[73]) were utterly alien to the Franks. These non-Chalcedonian groups remained objects of conversion to Latin Christianity; but concerns about their "orthodoxy" weakened sufficiently for intermarriages between Latins and the Armenian nobility.[74] Also, while the Franks avoided areas with predominantly Muslim populations, many reportedly settled in the countryside "almost exclusively . . . near [Eastern] Christians."[75]

Most important, in a milieu so radically shaped by migrant movement, other forces were at work. Generally speaking, long-term migrants or settlers inevitably acquire new customs, practices, and mindsets that, no matter the strength of their affection for a distant homeland, create some cultural distance from those they leave behind. The early crusaders set out for the Middle East as liberators (of subjugated Christian populations and territories), but they and their descendants settled as subjugators and rulers of those same people and places. The society in the short-lived Latin kingdoms may not have been fully integrated, and the hierarchical gap between the rulers and ruled must be acknowledged. Yet, predictably, the migrants who set out from Europe intent on transforming a distant society were themselves changed by the vibrant setting in which they and their descendants resettled. Fulcher de Chartres (ca. 1059–ca. 1127), the French chaplain who accompanied the First Crusade, conveys the social transformation and radical change in cultural identity that was evident even within the first generation of European migrants in a well-known passage:

73. By one estimate, for instance, the majority Christian population of Palestine that numbered at least one million in the sixth century was reduced to 300,000 (a third of its size) by 1500, with Christians forming a small minority—cf. Levtzion, "Conversion to Islam," 289–90; see also Philip Jenkins, *The Lost History of Christianity: The Thousand-Year Golden Age of the Church in the Middle East, Africa, and Asia—and How It Died* (New York: HarperOne, 2008), 178–79, 211–13.

74. Pahlitzsch and Baraz, "Christian Communities," 228; Murray, "Franks and Indigenous Communities," 308–9.

75. Pahlitzsch and Baraz, "Christian Communities," 232.

Consider, I pray, and reflect how in our time God has transferred the [West] into the [East]. For *we who were Occidentals now have been made Orientals*. He who was a Roman or a Frank is now a Galilaean, or an inhabitant of Palestine. He who was a citizen of Rheims or of Chartres now has been made a citizen of Tyre or of Antioch. We have already forgotten the places of our birth; already they have become unknown to many of us, or, not mentioned anymore. . . . Some have taken wives not only of their own people but Syrians or Armenians or even Saracens who have obtained the grace of baptism. . . .

Words of different languages have become common property known to each nationality, and mutual faith unites those who are ignorant of their descent. . . . *He who was born a stranger is now as one born here; he who was born an alien has become a native.*[76] (italics added)

This process of cultural indigenization also had religious dimensions. In the Crusader states, the ingrained intolerance that prevailed in the Latin West toward groups deemed heretical gave way to accommodation and relatively peaceful coexistence between Latin and Eastern Christian communities. At the very least, the absence of persecution or systematic effort to proscribe non-Latin forms of worship is noteworthy.[77] Physical proximity and the novel experience of religious intermingling arguably engendered greater tolerance for doctrinal difference and ecclesiastical pluralism. Such a change in perception may not have been widespread and possibly reflected consciousness of a common adversary in Islam. But it is wholly consistent with the effects and experience of migration. In Europe, too, the Islamic threat produced a strong desire for union with the Christian communities of the East (often centered on the legendary "Prester John"). In the aftermath of the Crusades, however, this outlook was replaced by implicit rejection of the distinctive and diverse Eastern Christianity and renewed emphasis on "a distinction between the familiar (or Latin) and the unfamiliar (or anything Oriental, whether Eastern Christian, Saracen, or pagan)."[78]

76. Fulcher de Chartres, *A History of the Expedition to Jerusalem, 1095–1127*, translated by Frances Rita Ryan (Knoxville: University of Tennessee Press, 1969), book 3.37 (pp. 271–72).

77. Pahlitzsch and Baraz, "Christian Communities," 235.

78. Francis M. Rogers, *The Quest for Eastern Christians* (Minneapolis: University of Minnesota Press, 1962), 180.

In Sicily and Spain, where military action by Catholic Europe against the forces of Islam began in the late tenth century, subjugation and conversion went hand in hand, and the reconquest of Muslim territories was accompanied by large numbers of Muslim conversions to the Christian faith.[79] In the Middle East, where Muslims outnumbered Christians five to one,[80] conversion of Muslims was not initially an explicitly stated objective, though it had emerged as a crusading aim by the mid-twelfth century.[81] In any case, conversions (coerced and voluntary) did result from the crusading effort.[82] Some Muslims embraced Christian baptism for fear of their lives; and many Muslim slaves became Christian converts as a way to earn their freedom (in sufficient numbers that the loss of labor became a concern for the crusader lords). Many Muslim converts to Christianity also joined the crusader army. But there were no mass conversion movements or systematic efforts to evangelize the subject non-Christian population. Indeed, the Frankish nobility evinced a distinct "lack of enthusiasm for Muslim conversion."[83] Ultimately, however, the boundaries of religious existence were permeable; and conversion went both ways.[84] If Muslim warriors joined the crusader armies, Christian recruits also joined Muslim forces.[85]

Despite the latent antagonisms and divisions, the various religious groups in the political domains set up by the Franks achieved a certain level of coexistence. The Crusader states were politically fragile but formed part of a strategic and flourishing trade network.[86] Their existence encouraged large numbers of Western pilgrims, facilitated commercial and intellectual exchange between

79. B. Z. Kedar, *Crusade and Mission: European Approaches toward the Muslims* (Princeton: Princeton University Press, 1984), 42–57; also Bentley, *Old World Encounters*, 149–56.

80. Mark Cartwright, "Crusader States," Ancient History Encyclopedia, November 1, 2018.

81. Kedar, *Crusade and Mission*, 57–72.

82. Kedar, *Crusade and Mission*, 62, 74–85.

83. Kedar, *Crusade and Mission*, 82.

84. Bentley, *Old World Encounters*, 152–53.

85. Michael Lower, "Christian Mercenaries in Muslim Lands: Their Status in Medieval Islamic and Canon Law," in *The Crusader World*, ed. Adrian Boas (New York: Routledge, 2015), 383–95.

86. Edna J. Stern, "Maritime Commerce in the Latin East as Reflected in the Import of Ceramics," in *The Crusader World*, ed. Adrian Boas (New York: Routledge, 2015), 474–96.

the Islamic world and Western Christendom, and contributed to the growing knowledge of Africa and Asia among Western Europeans.[87] However, by the mid-thirteenth century, the inhabitants of the Holy Land were confronted by a rapidly rising Eurasian power—the Mongols.[88] Mongol armies subjugated the Muslim Seljuk Turks (in 1243) and steadily advanced westward. In 1258, they conquered Baghdad, sacked the city, slaughtered nearly all its population, and killed the caliph.[89] Their armies closed in on the Middle East and began to conduct raids on Jerusalem. The Mongol westward advance was ultimately stopped by the Egyptian Mamluks. But the massive Mongol Empire that emerged out of Mongol military conquests had momentous consequences for travel and trade and decisively shaped the fortunes of Christianity. Here too the migrant element was emphatic.

THE MONGOL EMPIRE

The term "Mongol" was originally used by the Chinese T'ang to describe a number of dispersed tribes outside their borders in what is now Mongolia.[90] Due to Turkish influence, various Eurasian peoples including Mongol clans adopted the title "khan" (the Turkish word for "supreme ruler") or variations thereof for their leaders.[91] About 1190, Temujin (ca. 1167–1227), a rising leader among the nomads, was elected khan by other clan leaders and took the name Chinggis Khan. After consolidating his rule over Mongol tribes, through elimination of rivals, strategic alliances, and royal marriages, Chinggis embarked on further conquests. In an extensive military campaign, during which recalcitrance was brutally punished, he expanded his rule over territories in northern China, central Asia, and westward into Persia. His troops went on to conquer Armenia, Azerbaijan, and Georgia. They also inflicted defeats on the

---

87. Le Goff, *Medieval Civilization*, 146–47; Bernard Hamilton, "The Impact of the Crusades on Western Geographical Knowledge," in *Eastward Bound: Travel and Travellers, 1050–1550*, ed. Rosamund Allen (New York: Manchester University Press, 2004), 15–34.

88. Israeli, *Green Crescent over Nazareth*, 8.

89. Browne, *Eclipse of Christianity*, 149. Various figures are given for the number of city residents killed—ranging from 200,000 to 800,000. See Burbank and Cooper, *Empires in World History*, 105.

90. Howard, *Transnationalism in Ancient and Medieval Societies*, 81.

91. Burbank and Cooper, *Empires in World History*, 96.

Rus of Kiev and Bulghars of the Volga region. After Chinggis Khan's death, his four sons (Jochi, Chagatai, Ögetei, and Tolui) by his first wife, Borte, and their dynastic descendants pushed the frontier of the empire well into Islamic domains and extended Mongol authority as far as Syria. In Persia, Mongol rulers were referred to as *Il-khans* (Persian for "subordinate khan").

By the mid-thirteenth century, the Mongols had created the greatest empire in human history: a vast transcontinental multiethnic domain that stretched from Korea to Moscow and from northern China to the edge of Constantinople. Whereas Roman empire building took more than four centuries, the formidable Mongol khans, using mobile armies of mounted archers, fashioned an even larger empire in seven decades.[92] Like the Romans, the Mongols established peace (and stability) through horrific violence. *Pax Mongolica* was short-lived (roughly 1250–1350); but the lands conquered by the various khanates stretched across a distance of about 6,000 miles by 1250.[93] It expanded even further when Kublai (1215–1294), son of a Christian princess married to Chinggis's son Tolui, brought the whole of China (a territorial expanse some 4,000 miles across[94]) under Mongol rule in the 1270s and established the Yuan Dynasty (1206–1368). He astutely adopted the Chinese title of emperor in place of the honorific "khan."

The Mongol political order unified all of central Asia for the first time and generated commercial and cultural connections between East and West, bringing hitherto separate worlds into close interaction. The building of roads and bridges and the vast network of trade routes and highways that connected khanates (including an extensive postal relay system) produced a dramatic rise in the mobile population, though facilitating military movement was the primary aim. In all, Mongol "maintenance of a high-speed transit and communications system across Eurasia, protection of merchants and artisans, and practices of dispute resolution all expanded the horizons of possibility and imagination for long distance trade."[95] It also "enabled an enormous transfer of knowledge, ideas, and techniques across long distances."[96]

Mongol rule collapsed after a matter of decades. Bitter rivalry and feuding

92. Burbank and Cooper, *Empires in World History*, 94.
93. Gosch and Stearns, *Premodern Travel in World History*, 108.
94. Levathes, *When China Ruled the Seas*, 48–49.
95. Burbank and Cooper, *Empires in World History*, 111.
96. Burbank and Cooper, *Empires in World History*, 110.

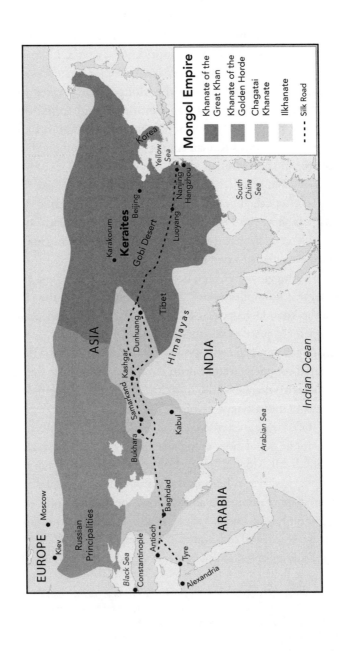

Mongol Empire

- Khanate of the Great Khan
- Khanate of the Golden Horde
- Chagatai Khanate
- Ilkhanate
- ---- Silk Road

EUROPE

Moscow

Kiev

Russian Principalities

ASIA

Karakorum

Keraites

Beijing

Gobi Desert

Korea

Yellow Sea

Luoyang

Nanjing

Hangzhou

South China Sea

Tibet

Himalayas

Dunhuang

Kashgar

Samarkand

Bukhara

INDIA

Kabul

Baghdad

Antioch

Constantinople

Black Sea

Tyre

Alexandria

ARABIA

Arabian Sea

Indian Ocean

between the four khanates, unresolved ethnic and tribal tensions, debilitating succession struggles, reprisals by subjugated groups, and attacks by external foes contributed to rapid disintegration of the vast empire. By 1400, the majority of the khanates had dissolved; the last to fall, the great Yuan-Chinese Empire, collapsed in 1368. But, the volume and variety of travelers on the Silk Routes during this period exceeded any previous age.[97] As already noted, migrants moving eastward from Europe to central Asia and China far exceeded those traveling westward from China and central Asia toward Persia and the Mediterranean.[98] To this period belong the stories of some of the most heroic and celebrated travelers of the pre-1500 period, including the Franciscan William of Rubruck (ca. 1215–1270), the Muslim scholar Abdallah ibn Battuta (1304–1368/69), and Venetian merchant Marco Polo (1254–1324).[99] Also among the mass of travelers were throngs of religious pilgrims and East Syrian missionaries.

Christianity among the Mongols

The presence of large Christian communities throughout the Mongol realm was confirmed in the chronicles of prominent European travelers and Franciscan missionaries in the thirteenth to fourteenth centuries—particularly Marco Polo (traveled 1271–1295), William of Rubruck (traveled 1253–1255), John of Plano Carpini (traveled 1245–1247), and John of Montecorvino (traveled 1289–1328).[100] Unsurprisingly, their descriptions of the East Syrian Christian

97. Gosch and Stearns, *Premodern Travel in World History*, 109.

98. Gosch and Stearns, *Premodern Travel in World History*, 109. The imbalance existed in part because, dating back to the early Roman Empire, Western demand for Eastern goods always exceeded Eastern demand for Western commodities. Smith, *Premodern Trade in World History*, 95; Curtin, *Cross-Cultural Trade in World History*, 94.

99. Battuta and Marco Polo—the two best-known travelers of the period—spent twenty-five and twenty-four years, respectively, outside their homelands. However, in a blurring of migrant categories, their "travels" also included extended periods spent as settlers in distant locales. Battuta spent six years in India at one point, while Marco Polo, who had planned a journey of a few years, lived some seventeen years among the Mongols.

100. See Christopher Dawson, *Mission to Asia* (Toronto: University of Toronto Press, 1980) for John of Plano Carpini's "History of the Mongols," letters of John of Montecorvino, and "The Journey of William of Rubruck." See also Marco Polo, *The Book of Ser Marco Polo, the Venetian: Concerning the Kingdoms and Marvels of the East*, trans. Henry Yule (London: Murray, 1871), books 1, 2; William of Rubruck,

communities they encountered reflect perspectives and preconceptions filtered through the prism of the Latin Christian heritage and experience. This mental conditioning is evident even in Marco Polo, who traveled (with his two uncles) to Mongol China not as a missionary or official representative of the Latin Church but as a merchant-traveler. Far removed from the familiar Latin Mass and the relative homogeneity of Latin Europe, he lamented that Jacobites and Nestorians were not Christians "in the fashion enjoined by the Pope of Rome" and was convinced that "they come short in several points of Faith."[101]

The Polos' journey from the ports of Venice to Shangdu (the capital of Kublai's Yuan Dynasty in China) lasted about three years (roughly from 1271 to 1274/75) and covered over 9,000 miles. Their expedition mainly followed overland routes that took them through Persia and central Asia and across China. They spent about sixteen years in China in Kublai's employ before returning home, having been away from Europe for twenty-four years. Marco Polo's report, which was not free from errors, provided valuable accounts of Christian presence among the Mongols.[102] Among other things, he notes "a very great number of Christians" (Jacobite and East Syrian) living among the Arabs in the city of Mosul, Persia; the East Syrian Christian communities throughout central Asia, along the Silk Road, who were mingled with Muslims and "idolaters"; and the "many Nestorian Christians, who have churches of their own" in Kashgar and the city of Samarkand among Muslims.[103]

Christianity had already been reestablished in China—perhaps through Kerait missionaries—by the time of Kublai's conquest in the 1270s.[104] Kublai, whose mother was a devout Christian, had requested (in a previous encounter

---

The Mission of Friar William of Rubruck: His Journey to the Court of the Great Khan Möngke, 1253–1255, trans. Peter Jackson (Indianapolis: Hackett, 2009). Also useful is Ohler, *Medieval Traveller*, 199–220.

101. Marco Polo, *Book of Ser Marco Polo*, book 1.5. For more on the attitudes of Latin Christians toward Eastern Christianity, see Rogers, *Quest for Eastern Christians*.

102. The inaccuracies and embellishments in Marco Polo's book (and the absence of any reference to the Great Wall of China) have fueled considerable debate for centuries; but most scholars accept his vivid eyewitness account of the sixteen or so years he spent in Mongolia. For a helpful summary of the debate, see Gosch and Stearns, *Premodern Travel in World History*, 140–43, 152–55.

103. Marco Polo, *Book of Ser Marco Polo*, book 1.5, 33.

104. See Browne, *Eclipse of Christianity in Asia*, 103; Moffett, *Christianity in Asia*, 430–31. The Turkic-Mongol Christians Mark (the future Yaballaha III) and his older companion Bar Sauma were born in China in the 1240s and 1230s, respectively.

with Marco Polo's uncles) that the pope send one hundred missionaries.[105] The emperor's desire for skilled Westerners may have been genuine enough; but the assurance he gave that he and his men would become Christian if Western missionaries would prove that Christianity was the best religion is generally regarded as a clever ruse. By the time of the Polos' arrival around 1274, Christianity in China was experiencing a new period of prosperity and expansion under Mongol rule. Marco Polo documents the presence of East Syrian Christians and churches in many Chinese cities, including "three very fine [Nestorian] churches" in the city of Kanchau.[106] He also remarked that in the city of Ching-Hianfu (which had two Nestorian churches), Mar Serghis, a Nestorian Christian, had served as governor for three years.[107] The appointment of Christian governors (and assistant governors) was common practice in the Mongol era.

But the story of the Mongol encounter with Christianity predates the Mongol Empire. As noted in chapter 8, Turkic nomadic tribes close to Persia's eastern frontier began converting to Christianity from the early sixth century. Much later, East Syrian Christian merchants in central Asia spread the faith among the Mongol Turks.[108] In 1007, the Turkish Keraits became the first of the Mongolian tribes to become Christian. According to the main account, the Kerait king lost his way in a violent storm while out hunting and "had given all hope of safety" when Mar Sergius (a popular saint who hailed from Samarkand) appeared to him in a vision.[109] The saint told the king that if "he believed in Christ" he would be shown the way and not perish. Once he returned safely, the monarch summoned Christian merchants who instructed him in the Christian faith and informed him of the importance of baptism.[110] After the king's conversion "the number of those that believed with him reached 200,000." At the urging of the Christian merchants, the king sent an

105. Marco Polo, *Book of Ser Marco Polo*, book 1.7.
106. Marco Polo, *Book of Ser Marco Polo*, book 1.44. See also Moffett, *Christianity in Asia*, 447–48.
107. Marco Polo, *Book of Ser Marco Polo*, book 2.73.
108. Browne, *Eclipse of Christianity in Asia*, 103.
109. The account of this incident is drawn from two sources, a twelfth-century Nestorian chronicler and a thirteenth-century Jacobite historian. For more, see Mingana, *Early Spread of Christianity*, 14–15; Browne, *Eclipse of Christianity*, 101–3; Gillman and Klimkeit, *Christians in Asia*, 237–40; Moffett, *Christianity in Asia*, 400–401.
110. The summoning of the merchants confirms that their religious identity was already known.

emissary to the metropolitan of Merv requesting a priest who would baptize them and teach them Christian rites. The East Syrian catholicos (in Baghdad) instructed the metropolitan "to send two persons, a priest and a deacon, and with them the requisites of an altar, who should go there and baptize as many as believed and teach them the Christian rites."[111] The entire tribe became Nestorian, and some Kerait khans adopted Christian names.[112]

Over the next century or so, Christianity spread in Mongolia through the missionary activities of merchants and monks. Many other Turkic tribes such as the Naiman, Uighur, Tartar, Ongut, Kitai, and Merkit became Christian or partly Christian.[113] The number of bishoprics of the Church of the East in Eastern Turkestan and China doubled from ninety-six (in 1000 CE) to about two hundred (by 1300 CE).[114] Kashgar, an important trading entrepôt in Eastern Turkestan, was made a metropolitanate around 1180. In 1287, when questioned by incredulous cardinals in Rome about his ministry, Rabban bar Sauma's response left little doubt about the importance of the church in Mongolia. He declared:

> Know my fathers, that many of our fathers went to the lands of the Mongols and Turks and Chinese and taught them. And today there are many Mongol Christians. Indeed, some of the children of the King and Queen are baptized and confess Christ. And they have churches in the camp. And they honor the Christians greatly, and there are also many believers among them.[115]

---

111. Browne, *Eclipse of Christianity*, 102. The metropolitan also inquired about what the Turks should eat during Lent "as they had no corn." The catholicos responded that Kerait Christians were to "abstain from eating meat, but they should be allowed to drink milk, if indeed, as they say, Lent food is not found in their land."

112. Baum and Winkler, *Church of the East*, 77. Some scholars have questioned whether "the Turks" in the account were actually the Keraits (in distant Mongolia), since the Metropolitan of Kashgar was much closer and a more logical contact. It is also believed that the Keraits only became known to Syrian writers during the Mongol invasions that took place much later. One view holds that the tribe in question was possibly the Oghuz, a confederation of Turkish groups in Transoxiana (literally "beyond the Oxus"—a Western viewpoint). Hunter, "Church of the East," 139.

113. Mingana, *Early Spread of Christianity*, 17–23; England, *Christianity in Asia*, 78–80; Foltz, *Religions of the Silk Road*, 66–68; Browne, *Eclipse of Christianity*, 104–8; Baum and Winkler, *Church of the East*, 76–79; Dawson, *Mission to Asia*, xxiv; Charbonnier, *Christians in China*, 75–77.

114. Baum and Winkler, *Church of the East*, 79.

115. Montgomery, *History of Yaballaha*, 56–57.

The largely illiterate Mongols practiced shamanism, a primal religious system (common in nomadic societies) centered on healer-diviners, without an institutionalized structure.[116] Whether or not they embraced one of the major faiths, the khans maintained an official policy of religious openness that treated all religious practitioners with equal respect and accommodated the different religions (Christianity, Islam, Buddhism, Manichaeanism, etc.) within their sprawling empire. This tolerance of religious plurality was enshrined in a written law, the *yasa*, believed to have been established by Chinggis Khan himself.[117] In theory, it reflected a worldview that genuinely saw value in all forms of religious practice; in the real world, it reflected the political pragmatism necessary to administer a realm that incorporated large publics with long-standing religious systems that were intimately tied to cultural existence.[118] Even though Mongol rulers were dependent on practitioners of the major religions they encountered to provide the advanced skills needed to maintain the empire, astute khans used preferential treatment of one religion or the other as a political strategy. Most important, tolerance for all religions precluded Mongol subordination to a single religious authority or tradition, thus preventing "religious leaders from developing any political structures that might grow to rival the emperor's power."[119]

Even so, Christianity enjoyed a particularly strong position within the Mongol Empire in terms of influence and missionary capacity. To start with, the tribes and territories initially incorporated into the empire founded by Chinggis Khan (ca. 1167–1227) contained large populations of Christians. Additionally, East Syrian Christians (from among the various Mongol tribes) occupied high positions in the army and administration of successive khans; and many of the physicians in the royal courts were Christian.[120]

---

116. For more on the nature of Mongol shamanism, see John of Plano Carpini's account in Dawson, *Mission to Asia*, 8–14. See also Bruno de Nicola, *Women in Mongol Iran: The Khātūns, 1206–1335* (Edinburgh: Edinburgh University Press, 2017), 183–85.

117. Cf. Moffett, *Christianity in Asia*, 401–2; also James D. Ryan, "Christian Wives of Mongol Khans: Tartar Queens and Missionary Expectations in Asia," *Journal of the Royal Asiatic Society* 8, no. 3 (1988): 416.

118. As John of Plano Carpini observed, since the Mongols "observe no law with regard to the worship of God they . . . compelled no one to deny his faith." Dawson, *Mission to Asia*, 10.

119. de Nicola, *Women in Mongol Iran*, 183.

120. Gillman and Klimkeit, *Christians in Asia*, 297–99. Among these were Chinkai, a Kerait, who became secretary of state; Qadaq, an army leader; Kitbugha,

Importantly, Chinggis's rise as Mongol leader was largely due to the support of Toghrul, the Christian ruler of the dominant Kerait tribe. (Toghrul may well have been the fabled Prester John, a Christian ruler or priest-king rumored in medieval Europe to hold sway in the Far East, beyond the Islamic domains).[121] When Toghrul turned against his protégé, Chinggis Khan crushed the Keraits and absorbed the Christian nation into his growing realm. A contemporary Jacobite historian reports that "having seen very much modesty (or, chastity) and other habits of this kind among the Christian people, certainly the Mongols loved them greatly at the beginning of their kingdom."[122]

Mongol Wives and Queen Mothers as Migrant Missionaries

Many family members of the khans and ruling elites among the Mongols professed the Christian faith, including Alaghai Beki, daughter of Chinggis Khan by his first wife. Also, a good number of the wives or mothers of Mongol khans (called *khātūns*) were Christians who hailed from the families of foreign rulers.[123] Royal marriages often served political purposes and, not infrequently, required elite women of marriageable age to leave their homelands to take up a new life among non-Christian peoples in foreign societies. Mongol rulers made extensive use of royal marriages as a political strategy, to safeguard control of newly acquired lands and reinforce diplomatic or military alliances. Such royal marriages typically involved migration and represented a

---

a military commander who became governor of Damascus; and Sama, a district commander in China. See also England, *Christianity in Asia*, 80.

121. Moffett, *Christianity in Asia*, 401–2; Dawson, *Mission to Asia*, xi. This almost mythical figure loomed in the European imagination as a crucial ally for repelling the Islamic threat. In all likelihood, however, the rumor stemmed from a conflation of two realities: Mongol victory over Islamic armies in central Asia and the presence of Christian khans among Mongol peoples.

122. Bar Hebraeus, *The Chronography of Gregory Abû'l Faraj, the Son of Aaron, the Hebrew Physician, Commonly Known as Bar Hebraeus*, trans. Ernest A. Wallis Budge (London: Oxford University Press, 1932), 411. Bar Hebraeus or Gregory Abû'l Faraj (1225–1286) was a prominent Syrian (Jacobite) Christian cleric of the thirteenth century.

123. For coverage of Christian *khātūns*, see Ryan, "Christian Wives of Mongol Khans," 411–21; de Nicola, *Women in Mongol Iran*; see also England, *Christianity in Asia*, 82–83; Moffett, *Christianity in Asia*, 402.

potential source for spreading the Christian faith or strengthening Christian presence in the Mongol realm. (On the missionary contributions of Christian women in Europe who became the wives of foreign rulers, see chapter 7.)

It is relevant to note that Mongolian women, generally speaking, enjoyed considerable influence in domestic affairs and participated fully in economic, military, political, and religious life.[124] They owned property (including the family's mobile tent) and bore primary responsibility for the socialization and training of the younger members of the family. Elite women ruled over the *ordu* (the camp associated with each Mongolian noble that functioned as a center of social life). Female involvement in political affairs was a natural extension of the authority women wielded within the family structure. It seems that Mongol invasion of Asian societies that already had a tradition of female regents and rulers also contributed to the institutionalization of female rule in Mongol politics and allowed women to play a major role in the development of the Mongol Empire.[125] This was true whether the women were Mongol or belonged to a subjugated group.[126] In a notable case, Töregene Khatun (d. 1246), a woman from the Merkit tribe defeated by Chinggis Khan,[127] ruled the entire Mongol Empire for twenty years. Not only did she gain the throne with shrewd political skill but she also restructured the administration, implemented political reform, and appointed other women to political leadership.

No Christian *khātūn* ruled the Mongol Empire, which, in any case, fragmented into four khanates by 1260. But the capacity of leading women to wield political power and pursue personal interests within the expanding Mongol confederacy was significant. Women "occup[ied] high positions at court, participated in the election of the new ruler by establishing alliances in support of their sons, and acted as counsellors to their male counterparts (sons or husbands)."[128] Such a high degree of political agency meant that Christian

124. See Adam Berger, "Overview of Women in Medieval Mongol Empire," in *Medieval Central Asia*; de Nicola, *Women in Mongol Iran*, 34–50, 130–35.

125. de Nicola, *Women in Mongol Iran*, 50–89. On the dominant position of Mongol queens, see also Montgomery, *History of Yaballaha*, 6–7.

126. de Nicola, *Women in Mongol Iran*, 50.

127. She was originally the wife of one of the Merkit chiefs but was given in marriage to Chinggis Khan's son Ögetei when the Merkits were integrated into the expanding Mongol Empire.

128. de Nicola, *Women in Mongol Iran*, 104.

wives and mothers were uniquely positioned to advance the cause of Christianity within the broader context of Mongol rule.

After Chinggis Khan subdued the Christian Keraits, he and his sons married aristocratic Christian Kerait women. Sorkaktani-beki (or Sorqoqtani Begi), Toghrul's niece, married Tolui (Chinggis's fourth son) and became the mother of three khans: Möngke of the Mongols (r. 1251–1259), Kublai of China (r. 1260–1294), and Hülegü Ilkhan of Persia (r. 1260–1265).[129] Her older sister became Chinggis Khan's wife and another sister married his oldest son, Jochi. Both Möngke and Hülegü (two of Sorkaktani's sons) also married Christian women.[130] Hülegü (1258–1265), who conquered Persia and became the first ilkhan, married Doquz-khatun, a Kerait princess and devout Christian. Hülegü's son, Abaqa (1265–1282), remained a shamanist but had Christian sympathies. Abaqa confirmed the newly elected Catholicos Mar Yaballaha III in office and also married several Christian wives, one of whom, Despīna Ḳātūn (or Maria Palaeologina) was daughter of the Byzantine emperor and an Orthodox Catholic Christian. His son, Arghūn (1284–1291), also wed East Syrian women and engaged in active diplomacy with western Europe in an effort to secure Christian alliance against the Muslim Mamluks in Egypt. These initiatives failed to bear fruit; but he had one of his sons baptized and named Nicholas (after Pope Nicholas IV with whom he corresponded).

Mongol tolerance for religious plurality, upheld by law (the *yasa*), generally allowed all faiths to flourish once conquest was complete. But the Christian women who were integrated into the militaristic Mongol khanates as wives (and mothers) evidently used their position and authority to influence Mongol occupation of other lands in ways that were favorable to Christianity and supportive of Christian mission. In the history of the Mongol Empire, two Christian *khātūns* achieved remarkable importance and impact: Sorkaktani-beki (1190–1252) and Doquz-khatun (d. 1264).

Sorkaktani, an East Christian Kerait, married Chinggis Khan's son Tolui and became one of the most formidable and influential women in Mongolia. With her husband largely absent on incessant military campaigns, she raised their children and, when he died in 1233, took charge of his vast territories

---

129. She bore a fourth son, Ariq Böke.

130. According to William of Rubruck, Cotota-khatun, Mangu's wife, fully participated in Eastern Christian worship, "fasted along with her household" during Lent, and supported the church. William of Rubruck, *Mission*, 189, 304.

in Mongolia and northern China.[131] In the difficult succession struggle that followed the death of the Great Khan in 1248, Sorkaktani used her high status and diplomatic skills to have her son Möngke promoted to the khanate. Under Möngke Khan, Christian presence at the royal court grew; and, though rumors of his conversion to Christianity appear unfounded, Möngke attended Christian ceremonies and married Christian women. John of Plano Carpini (a Franciscan friar and papal envoy to the Mongols in the late 1240s) reported that "among the Tartars, [Sorkaktani] is the most renowned, with the exception of the Emperor's mother, and more powerful than anyone else except Bati."[132] More importantly, as the Christian mother of three khans, she directly contributed to the development of the Mongol Empire and played a unique role in shaping this extraordinary Asian dynasty.[133]

The vast Mongol army under Hülegü that embarked on the conquest of the Abbasid caliphate in 1258 included large numbers of Christians from various tribes in central Asia. Hülegü's "most gifted general," Ked-Buka, was a Christian.[134] The Mongols besieged Baghdad, killed the caliph, and slaughtered hundreds of thousands of the city's Muslim residents. The city's Christians, who gathered into one of the East Syrian churches, were spared. This blanket clemency probably had something to do with the strong connections between the Mongols and Christianity. In addition to the Christians within the invading Mongol army, there were Christians also in Hülegü's own family. This essentially means that Christians were involved in the establishment of the Persian Ilkhanate. But it is also quite likely that Baghdad's Christians were protected during the bloody destruction of the city because Doquz-khatun, Hülegü's wife, exerted considerable influence on Mongol policy.

Doquz was a Kerait princess and an East Syrian Christian of fervent faith. She was first married to Tolui (Sorkaktani-beki's husband) and, on his death, became the chief wife of Hülegü. These successive marriages to Mongol khans placed her in a position of great prominence and influence within the Mongol hierarchy. As a Christian queen, Doquz intervened in political affairs and used

---

131. de Nicola, *Women in Mongol Iran*, 73.

132. In Dawson, *Mission to Asia*, 26. The powerful and enormously wealthy Bati (or Batu) was Chinggis's grandson through Jochi Khan, who founded the Golden Horde Khanate and ruled it from 1242 to 1255.

133. Moffett, *Christianity in Asia*, 402, 443–44.

134. Moffett, *Christianity in Asia*, 422, 423.

her influence to revitalize Christianity in Persia. Her *ordu* included a church, and her tent became a portable chapel where Mass was celebrated daily when she traveled. Incidentally, the other Christian women who accompanied Hülegü's campaign also "adapted tents into churches where priests, monks and Mongol *khātūns* could worship."[135] But Doquz's influence was unequalled.

Hülegü reportedly declared himself a Christian. If true (there is no evidence that he was ever baptized), this was the first time in the history of the East Syrian Church that it was under a political ruler who called himself a Christian.[136] Regardless, Hülegü's munificence toward Christians was evidently motivated by a desire to please his wife.[137]

After six centuries of largely oppressive Muslim rule, the minority Christian population in Persia unexpectedly found itself on the ascendancy. Under Doquz's influence the various Christian communities in Persia enjoyed imperial protection and were allowed to build places of worship. This change of fortunes came largely at the expense of Islam.[138] One of the palaces belonging to the caliphs, for instance, became the new abode of the catholicos, who had a church built in it. Christians gained a profound sense of liberation. But centuries of hostile rule and painful discrimination had crystallized into deep-seated religious acrimony, and many Christians used their newfound freedom to assault or ill-treat Muslims, essentially demonstrating the same capacity for intolerance as their erstwhile persecutors.[139]

The authority of the Nestorian patriarch over the East Syrian Christians in Persia was unsurpassed. But Doquz's political authority and personal standing, as Christian queen and as kingmaker (she bore no children), shaped the tenor and trajectory of Christianity in Persia for at least a generation. She exercised authority in ways that approximated that of a Christian ruler, such as when she "caused the temples of the Saracens to be utterly destroyed, and put the Saracens into such slavery that they dared not show themselves any more."[140] Given the pesky ecclesiastical rivalries that dogged Persian Christianity, it is notewor-

135. de Nicola, *Women in Mongol Iran*, 193.
136. Browne, *Eclipse of Christianity*, 149.
137. Moffett, *Christianity in Asia*, 426.
138. Browne, *Eclipse of Christianity*, 149–51.
139. However, when Christians in Takrit plundered and killed Muslims, they in turn, on Hülegü's orders, were slaughtered and their children taken captive. See Browne, *Eclipse of Christianity*, 150; Moffett, *Christianity in Asia*, 426.
140. Browne, *Eclipse of Christianity*, 151.

thy that she demonstrated a spirit of ecumenicity. Though steeped in the East Syrian tradition, she used her authority to serve all the Christians in Persia. Sources from the period note that she "very much loved all Christians, Armenians and Syrians."[141] When Maria Palaiologina (Despīna Ḵātūn) married Hülegü (to cement the diplomatic alliance between the Byzantine and Mongol powers), she brought a Christian bishop with her and founded a new bishopric. Doquz was, therefore, "chief wife" in a multifaith imperial household.

But the fact remains that none of the Mongol khans became a baptized Christian or endorsed Christianity as a state religion. Both Hülegü and Arghūn possibly considered Christian baptism; but the sincerity of their intentions remains open to question. Despite their traditional support for all faiths, other Mongol rulers did convert to other religions. Kublai Khan, though raised by a Christian mother, favored Buddhism;[142] and Tegüder Ahmad Ilkhan (r. 1282–1284), the third ilkhan (son of an East Syrian mother and a baptized Christian[143]), became the first Mongol ruler to convert to Islam within a generation after the death of Doquz-khatun.[144]

In Europe, where devout Christian wives of pagan rulers had been instrumental in the spread of Christianity, the potential for Mongol Christian queens to play a role in the conversion of their husbands and sons excited the minds of Christian leaders.[145] Pope Nicholas IV (r. 1288–1292), in particular, entertained high hopes that the Christian *khātūns* would perform such a proselytizing role in Asia. He sent letters to the Christian queens of Ilkhan Arghūn in which he encouraged them to prod the ilkhan toward Christian baptism. Arghūn reportedly "loved the Christians with all his heart" and even had a church built in close proximity to his throne "in order to encourage all who believe in Christ";[146] but he stopped short of becoming a Christian. Thus, while Mongol

141. Quoted in de Nicola, *Women in Mongol Iran*, 193.
142. Ironically, perhaps, his preference for Buddhism was due to the influence of his principal wife, Queen Chabi, a devout Buddhist—though Christians attained high ranks in his administration, and his five sons all bore Christian names. Moffett, *Christianity in Asia*, 452–54, 456.
143. Moffett, *Christianity in Asia*, 432.
144. However, his conversion to Islam placed him at odds with the Mongol elites and contributed to his downfall two years later. See Browne, *Eclipse of Christianity*, 156; de Nicola, *Women in Mongol Iran*, 94–98.
145. See Ryan, "Christian Wives of Mongol Khans," 417–21.
146. Montgomery, *History of Yaballaha*, 51, 74.

queens may have "traditionally enjoyed a position of authority within their society unrivalled in the western Byzantine, Chinese or Arab worlds,"[147] this prestige yielded little by way of discernible or enduring missionary results.

Again, this was in sharp contrast to well-known examples of Christian queens in medieval Europe (such as Clotilda or Bertha) who influenced their pagan husbands to embrace Christianity, thus setting in motion the conversion of entire nations. But a straightforward comparison between Mongol wives and European queens is misguided; and, although well meaning, the expectations of Latin pontiffs, based on the European experience, that Christian wives could convince Mongol rulers to accept Christian baptism was understandable but imperceptive. In his superb treatment of the subject, James Ryan concludes that the brief papal hope that these women would use their influence "to promote the spread of the Roman Church in Asia" proved futile because that era's Roman Catholic missionaries failed to recognize "the potential resource for proselytization" that Christian *khātūns* represented.[148] There is some validity to this assessment; but contextual factors play a critical role in religious conversion, and attentiveness to major differences between the Asian and European contexts is called for. Even the most cursory examination indicates that the missionary function of Mongol Christian women in the thirteenth and fourteenth centuries was constrained by context-specific elements that were absent from medieval Western Christendom.

In addition to the challenges of adapting to a new culture, Christian *khātūns* joined polygamous households that had multiple wives from diverse cultures and religious backgrounds. Their ability to influence the khans to accept one religion over others was subject to obvious limitations. Even if the other wives were less inclined to exert the same influence or were indifferent to the khan's religion, they would surely have been alive to the fact that the wife whose religion got adopted by the khan would acquire unmatched influence and become the recipient of disproportionate affection.[149] Kublai's special affinity for

147. Ryan, "Christian Wives of Mongol Khans," 420.

148. Ryan, "Christian Wives of Mongol Khans," 421. In his view, "the failure to pursue the support of Christian women at the Tartar courts is illustrative of the short-sightedness of that era's missionaries, who were unwilling or unable to work with Greek, Nestorian or other schismatic Christians in the east."

149. In theory, greater affection for any one of the wives gave the wife in question greater influence over the ruler's decisions.

Buddhism, for instance, is generally attributed to the sway of his principal wife, Chabi, who was a devout Buddhist.[150] Also at stake in such matters was the issue of succession. Royal sons were presumably trained in different religious traditions by their respective mothers. Given the bitter factional rivalries that routinely erupted in khanate successions, it was never a foregone conclusion that a Christian son would succeed a pagan or non-Christian khan.[151]

It is also noteworthy that none of the Mongol Christian wives boasted external political connections of the kind that would provide additional leverage in proselytization of the powerful Mongol rulers—as was the case, for instance, with Frankish princesses. Legendary *khātūns* like Sorkaktani-beki and Doquz hailed from Christian ruling houses, as did Maria Palaiologina (from Byzantium); but their status and prestige depended on personal traits or their intrinsic status within the Mongol ruling class, not on ties of blood to a powerful Christian monarch. The Mongols considered their empire to be the most powerful in the world and, with few exceptions, Christian wives came from subjugated nations. James Ryan seems to suggest that greater and more sustained support for the Christian *khātūns* from popes and Roman Catholic missionaries would have provided the necessary leverage. That is open to question. A positive response by Christian powers in Europe to Ilkhan Arghūn's repeated appeals for an alliance against Mamluk Egypt seems far more likely to have bolstered the efforts by his Christian wives to urge his conversion.

In Europe, generally speaking, Christian missionaries confronted tribal religion, a single system of beliefs binding on the whole society. Conversion to Christianity often involved the entire tribe; and the wholesale change of allegiance from one religious system to the other, however gradual or fitful, was often initiated by the ruler. There were similar occurrences in Asia among Turkic tribes such as the Keraits. However, in the case of Mongol khanates, the situation was fundamentally different in terms of both religious life and the potential for conversion of the ruler. The Christian women who became wives of the khans joined imperial families that presided over religiously pluralistic

---

150. Moffett, *Christianity in Asia*, 451–52, 453.

151. There were no limits on the number of wives a man might have. John of Plano Carpini reported that Mongol marriage customs allowed men to marry close relations "with the exception of their mother, daughter and sister by the same mother," that sons may take their father's wives after his death, and that a younger brother may marry his brother's wife after his death. See Dawson, *Mission to Asia*, 7.

societies in which Christians (or varieties of Christian traditions) typically constituted one religious group among many. Christians were invariably a minority within the various khanates. Other faiths (Islam in Persia, Confucianism in China) were dominant among the population and, prior to Mongol rule, functioned as state religions. An active policy of religious tolerance made the khanates governable and, as explained above, the majority of Mongol khans had pragmatic reasons for avoiding the elevation of one religious tradition above all others. In these circumstances, the conversion of a ruler based on the entreaties of a Christian queen was far less probable. When a Mongol khan converted to Islam and reinstated Islamic rule, the process was greatly influenced by the fact that Islam was the faith of the majority of the population. The emergence of a Mongol "Clovis" is difficult to imagine, no matter how pious and persuasive the Christian wives were!

Perhaps most important, assessing the missionary impact of Christian *khātūns* in terms of familiar Western accounts of the conversion of European rulers is liable to obscure the significant role that these (foreign) women played in the dramatic change of fortune that vast Christian populations in Asia enjoyed under Mongol rule. The prosperity of the church in the Mongol Empire—especially in Islamic lands where they had been an oppressed minority, or in China where the church had previously all but disappeared—was due in no small measure to the great influence and zealous faith of Christian *khātūns*. It would be misguided to discount the tremendous gains (in the form of church building and revitalization of ministry, for instance) or profound sense of reprieve that political favor or imperial patronage mediated by these Christian queens brought to beleaguered Christian communities in Mongol Asia.

Under the influence of successive Christian Ilkhan wives in Muslim Persia "both the Nestorian and Jacobite churches flourished, and western missionaries had a free hand."[152] Throughout the Mongol Empire, Christian *khātūns* interacted closely with Christian priests, participated in religious ritual, and influenced state religious policy. On the face of things, they contributed to Christian mission principally through exemplary lives, political intervention to secure freedom of Christian worship and expansion, sponsorship of Christian projects, support for foreign missionaries, and, less tangibly, the increased popularity that Christian rituals gained as a result of endorsement

152. Ryan, "Christian Wives of Mongol Khans," 416.

by the nobility. They contributed to the missionary cause through a number of public activities and through the authority and influence that they exercised at the courts of the Mongol rulers (especially Kublai Khan and Ilkhan Hülegü). It is not unreasonable to assume that they sought to proselytize at a personal level through direct persuasion and piety. England claims that under their influence, "an unknown number of others were also Christian, as members and chieftainesses of tribes or clans."[153] Moffett adds, more importantly, that "throughout the whole span of Mongol royal history the major channel of continuous Christian influence, apart from the patriarchate itself, runs through the blood of royal women from Sorkaktani to Uruk-khatun."[154]

Turning Tides

Mongols in western Asia ultimately rejected Christianity in favor of Islam. It is futile now to speculate how the history of Christianity (indeed, of the world) would have turned out had the Western Mongols become Christian. Indeed, this prospect is rendered even more tantalizing in hindsight given the favorable attitudes toward Christians by successive khans and Ilkhan Arghūn's eagerness for an alliance with Christian Europe against Islam. The fourteenth-century author of *The History of Yaballaha* was convinced that had Arghūn "won over the West to his plan of a Crusade against the Mamluk power, the centre of Islam's resistance, he might have become the Constantine of his Mongols."[155] A review of the complex factors that shaped this historic turning point, including the decisive defeat of Western Christian powers after two centuries of Crusades against Islam, is outside the purview of this study. The brief comments that follow focus on Persia and China where the turning of the tides was most dramatic.

In Persia, the creation of the Ilkhanate was accompanied by mass immigrations that included Christian groups; and, as we have seen, the Christian communities enjoyed imperial favors under successive Mongol rulers. Equally important, from 1281 to 1317, the patriarch of the East Syrian Church was for the first time a Turkish Mongol. This was the celebrated Mar Yaballaha III,

153. England, *Christianity in Asia*, 83.
154. Moffett, *Christianity in Asia*, 478. Uruk-khatun was Ilkhan Arghūn's third wife and mother of his son Nicholas.
155. Montgomery, *History of Yaballaha*, 17.

who was made patriarch while on a pilgrimage from Peking to Jerusalem. Mar Yaballaha's ecclesiastical jurisdiction and spiritual authority extended well beyond Persia; and having a Mongol patriarch in a land under Mongol rule was of incalculable advantage to the widespread East Syrian Christian communities. For all this, the precarious position of Christians as a religious minority in a region where Islam was the dominant faith remained unaltered. Persia had been ruled solely by Muslim rulers for six hundred years; and the Mongols themselves were greatly outnumbered by a majority Muslim population. They also had reason for concern on the military front. The Mamluks of Egypt had proven to be formidable adversaries, stopping Mongol advance and twice defeating them in battle.[156] Indeed, it may well be that the militaristic and highly superstitious Mongols had for this reason come to regard Islam as the most powerful religion.[157]

The resurgence and triumph of Islam in the Ilkhanate appears sudden; but, as the conversion to Islam of the third ilkhan (Tegüder Ahmad, r. 1282–1284) suggests, Islam was slowly making headway within the Mongol population. The competing forces of Christianity and Islam came to a head in a predictably acrimonious struggle for the Ilkhanate throne in 1295. By then, such was Islam's growing popularity that the two claimants were compelled to confess the Muslim faith to garner support. In the end Baidu, the claimant most favorable to Christians, was slain by his rival Ghazan Khan (r. 1295–1304), who ascended the throne as a Muslim ruler. With Ghazan's accession the tide turned against Christianity, and "the hordes of the Arabs roused up to avenge themselves upon the Church and her children for their losses."[158] Bar Hebraeus, the thirteenth-century Jacobite historian, painted a violently graphic picture:

> And there was great sorrow among the Christians in all the world. The persecutions, and disgrace, and mockings, and ignominy which the Christians suffered at this time, especially in Baghdad, words cannot describe. Behold, according to what people say, "No Christian dared to appear in the streets (or, market), but the women went out and came in and bought and sold, because they could not be distinguished from the Arab women,

156. Browne, *Eclipse of Christianity*, 154–56.
157. Browne, *Eclipse of Christianity*, 154.
158. Montgomery, *History of Yaballaha*, 80.

and could not be identified as Christians, though those who were recognized as Christians were disgraced, and slapped, and beaten and mocked. And behold, all the Christians who were in these regions were tortured with punishment of this kind; I would not say abandoned by God."[159]

The decades that followed witnessed widespread atrocities against Christian communities and extensive efforts to extirpate the church in Persia and elsewhere.[160] The breakup of the Persian Ilkhanate in 1335 loosened any remaining restraints on the persecution of Christians.[161] By the end of the fourteenth century, relentless repression under Muslim rulers had reduced the Church of the East to a shadow of its former self. This turning of the tide against Christians in the Ilkhanate was a harbinger of things to come throughout the Mongol Empire.

In China, where Christianity also prospered under Mongol rule, the faith was mainly confined to foreigners (Turks and Mongols). Moffett argues that if the turning point in the Ilkhanate was reached in 1294 with the conversion of Ghazan to Islam, the critical moment occurred in China when Kublai died a year later in 1295. Mongol rule was deeply unpopular. The social and cultural gap between Mongols and Chinese was wide—intermarriage between the two groups, for instance, was uncommon.[162] Kublai, who distrusted the Chinese, placed authority within his administration in the hands of foreigners (Mongols, Muslims, and Christians) who constituted a tiny minority in the populous empire.[163] After his death, his faction-ridden Yuan (Mongol) Empire went into terminal decline. Eventually, the smoldering embers of entrenched Chinese resentment and animosity erupted into open rebellion that led to the crushing defeat of the last Mongol emperor in 1368.

For the church in China, history repeated itself. Some four hundred years earlier, the demise of the T'ang Dynasty had signaled the downfall of T'ang Christianity, despite rootedness in Chinese culture. To be sure, the church of the

159. Bar Hebraeus, *Chronography*, 595–96.
160. In Egypt also, Christians suffered prolonged and vicious persecution. See Browne, *Eclipse of Christianity*, 163–78; see also Moffett, *Christianity in Asia*, 475–80.
161. Browne, *Eclipse of Christianity*, 171.
162. Gosch and Stearns, *Premodern Travel in World History*, 152; see also Moffett, *Christianity in Asia*, 454.
163. Marco Polo reported that being treated by foreigners "as slaves" was the main reason "all the Cathayans detested the Great Kaan's rule." Marco Polo, *Book of Ser Marco Polo*, book 2, chapter 23.

Mongol era was more emphatically linked to a foreign power than T'ang Christianity ever was. But, in a striking echo of the previous era, the fall of the Yuan Dynasty was followed by the expulsion of Mongols (a disliked foreign regime) and the collapse of the Church (both East Syrian and Roman Catholic) associated with their rule. The Yuan Dynasty was the last of the Mongol khanates to fall.

The disintegration of the Mongol Empire was accompanied by widespread chaos and insecurity. In western and central Asia, the void was largely filled by expanding Islam. The brief but extremely bloody campaign of Tamerlane or Timur the Great (1336–1405), the Turkish-speaking Muslim Mongol who emerged out of Samarkand with a vision of a worldwide Islamic caliphate, wreaked indescribable devastation on Christian communities in Asia from Persia to northern India.[164] But the imperial domain that Tamerlane created through devastating violence and wanton slaughter quickly fragmented after his death. By 1500, the church in Asia that only three centuries earlier had derived great energy and boost from expansive Mongol rule and its vast transcontinental networks was reduced to "shattered remnants . . . left isolated in ever smaller pockets of desperation."[165] Within a matter of centuries, Christianity in Asia suffered an "eclipse" where only centuries earlier it had been experiencing a period of dynamic expansion, aided by Mongol domination. Only in southern India, beyond the Islamic and Mongol Empires, did a large population of Asian Christians survive.

With the disintegration of the khanates, insecurity and anarchy once again bedeviled long-distance travel along the overland trade routes through central Asia. Towns along the Silk Routes decayed or disappeared, the lively commercial activity of the Mongol era declined, and the migrant flows between West and East dwindled.[166] China, a civilization whose economic and cultural riches had for centuries provided gravitational pull for much long-distance trade and travel, also found itself in crisis in the short term. Similarly, the old centers of Islamic civilization in Persia and the Arab world lost their vitality and took a long time to recover.

164. Tamerlane sought Christian allies when it suited his purposes, and "Muslims who opposed him suffered as severely as did Christians of all persuasions." Gillman and Klimkeit, *Christians in Asia*, 139. For an overview, see Moffett, *Christianity in Asia*, 480–88.

165. Moffett, *Christianity in Asia*, 471.

166. Smith, *Premodern Trade in World History*, 139; Curtin, *Cross-Cultural Trade in World History*, 121.

Moreover, in the mid-fourteenth century, amid widespread disintegration and economic stagnation, the bubonic plague (the Black Death), transmitted from the east by travelers, spread with devastating impact along the trade routes to Europe. The human toll was catastrophic. In China, the Middle East, and Europe, large sections of the populations, "half, two-thirds, three-fourths, and in isolated cases even larger proportions," succumbed.[167] Europe's population is estimated to have declined from some 73 million by 1300 to 45 million around 1400.[168] The ramifications were also ruinous: acute labor shortages produced steep decline in production, which compounded the financial crises. Struggling institutions were decimated, major centers of trade shriveled, and interregional encounters declined sharply.

Yet, the tragic misfortune that befell East Syrian Christian missions in Asia ought not to distract from its striking historical significance. Unaided by political authority, cultural power, or social status, East Syrian Christian migrants depended on their individual skills or mercantile activity to participate in diverse societies. It was a mission, writes England, "largely by lay people through education, medical care, state service and trade, and of friendly coexistence—even mutual borrowing—with, in particular, Buddhists, Manicheans, and Muslims."[169] The success of these diverse and wide-ranging missionary endeavors also owed something to the spirit of East Syrian Christianity: a religious community defined by migrant existence, habituated to life as a minority faith, attuned to outsider witness, and shaped by ethnic plurality (an attribute that became even more pronounced as it spread among the peoples of central and eastern Asia). Everywhere, East Syrian clergy and laity acknowledged, even celebrated, the authority of non-Christian authorities and built communities that combined missionary-mindedness with religious coexistence and interdependence. The contrast with the Roman Church or Western Christendom, with its distinctive vision of religious uniformity and intimate alliance of cross and crown, could not be more striking.

In the centuries that followed, changes in travel and patterns of migration continued to shape the story of global Christianity even more powerfully. By the end of the Mongol period a long-term shift in long-distance trade was already

167. Bentley, *Old World Encounters*, 163. See also Phillips, "Medieval Background," 21.
168. Le Goff, *Medieval Civilization*, 245.
169. England, *Christianity in Asia*, 49–50.

underway. Due to its precariousness and the limitations of draft animals, over-land trade was confined to luxury items (like silk) and small bulk goods. Chinese innovations in shipbuilding and navigational technology dating back to the Song Dynasty produced larger and faster ships as well as improvements in safety that allowed enormous increases in the volume of shipping cargo along the maritime route between China, Southeast Asia, South Asia, and the Middle East.[170] The capacity to transport bulk goods for mass consumption, such as rice, textiles, and timber, generated an unprecedented boom in maritime trade and sea travel. China emerged as the dominant maritime power and leading trading nation.

The height of Chinese shipbuilding came in the early fifteenth century, when Ming emperor Zhu Di ordered the construction of an imperial fleet comprising trading vessels and warships.[171] This immense effort produced the largest ocean-going vessels anywhere (over four hundred feet in length, sporting nine masts and twelve sails) with watertight bulwark compartments, stern posts, and balanced rudders.[172] European shipbuilders would only emulate these innovations some four hundred years later. The emperor's treasure fleet of 317 vessels and 28,000 men, under the command of Admiral Zheng He (a Muslim eunuch), embarked on trade expeditions between 1405 and 1433. The fleet sailed as far as Mogadishu and Mombasa on the eastern coast of Africa in 1418.[173] These developments laid the foundation for a new age of migration and overseas exploration that transformed the world and ushered in a new era of global Christian expansion.

170. Howard, *Transnationalism in Ancient and Medieval Societies*, 84; Smith, *Premodern Trade in World History*, 140; Curtin, *Cross-Cultural Trade in World History*, 119–20.

171. Levathes, *When China Ruled the Seas*, 73–106.

172. The most luxurious ships contained "grand cabins for the imperial envoys" and "windowed halls and antechambers . . . festooned with balconies and railings." Levathes, *When China Ruled the Seas*, 81–82. As often pointed out, these magnificent vessels were more than four times the length of Columbus's flagship *Santa Maria* (which was 85 feet). The smallest ship in Zheng's flotilla, a highly maneuverable five-masted, 165-foot-long warship, was still almost twice as large as the legendary Spanish galleon.

173. Levathes, *When China Ruled the Seas*, 149–50. Chinese foreign influence, notes Louise Levathes, reached its peak during this period, when "all the important trading ports in the Indian Ocean basin and China seas—from Korea and Japan throughout the Malay Archipelago and India to the east African coast—were at least nominally under Chinese authority" (142).

In short, from the late fifteenth century onward, ocean travel generated new intercontinental connections and new encounters between the world's peoples. The bigger capacity of ocean vessels greatly increased the number of migrants and vastly expanded cross-cultural interactions. The advances in shipbuilding also ushered in a new era of colonization. For the first time in history, humans had the capacity to travel around the world or, figuratively speaking, to the ends of the earth. The continents of the world were brought into closer contact than at any time previously. Overseas exploration and intercontinental voyages, as well as the new age of naval warfare, contributed to the development of "a worldwide system of plantations, mines, empires, and colonies" that intensified the exchange of goods, ideas, and people. More than any other development, aggressive European colonization fostered the penetration of the vast interior landmasses of Africa and Asia, producing immense intercultural exchange. Massive migration movements of Europeans, Africans, and Asians (males and females[174]) transformed whole societies and "led ultimately to a large-scale redistribution of the world's population" by the end of the nineteenth century.[175]

And so the story continues.

New thresholds of globalization have ushered in astonishing change and transformations that have progressively caused the world to shrink dramatically. How these unprecedented changes are connected to the extraordinary spread of the Christian faith in the last five to six centuries requires multidisciplinary approaches and the use of a range of conceptual tools to analyze fully.[176] For the discerning historian, however, the inextricable link between migration and mission (or escalating cross-cultural religious encounters) became even more obvious and compelling, not less.

---

174. With increasing family migrations, in the period 1550–1750, "women dominated in short-distance migrations, while men predominated in long-distance migrations." Manning, *Migration in World History*, 124.

175. Manning, *Migration in World History*, 110.

176. See Jehu J. Hanciles, *Beyond Christendom: Globalization, African Migration, and the Transformation of the West* (Maryknoll, NY: Orbis Books, 2008).

CHAPTER TEN

Beyond Empire

> Consider, I pray, and reflect how in our time God has trans-
> ferred the [West] into the [East], for we who were Occiden-
> tals now have been made Orientals. He who was a Roman or
> a Frank is now a Galilaean, or an inhabitant of Palestine. . . .
> Words of different languages have become common property
> known to each nationality, and mutual faith unites those who
> are ignorant of their descent. . . . He who was born a stranger
> is now as one born here; he who was born an alien has become
> a native.
>
> —Fulcher de Chartres

The willful amnesia about the unparalleled missionary expansion of Christianity among the diverse polyglot cultures of Asia (prior to 1500) has produced distorted mental maps of the Christian world in the first 1,500 years
among generations of Christians and theology students. Without knowledge
of the unique and fascinating elements of Christian presence in Asia in the
Islamic age, historical understanding of the life and faith of Christian communities worldwide or the process by which Christianity became a global faith
is deeply flawed. Major studies that buck this trend are not lacking;[1] but the

---

1. Notably, Jenkins, *The Lost History of Christianity* (2008); England, *The Hidden History of Christianity in Asia* (2002); Dana L. Robert, *Christian Mission: How
Christianity Became a World Religion* (2009); Gillman and Klimkeit, *Christianity in
Asia before 1500* (1999); Moffett, *A History of Christianity in Asia: Beginnings to 1500*
(1998); Jacobsen, *The World's Christians: Who They Are, Where They Are, and How
They Got There* (2011); Irvin and Sunquist, *History of the World Christian Movement*,
vol. 1 (2001). Much older publications include Stewart, *Nestorian Missionary Enterprise* (1961) and Foster, *The Church of the T'ang Dynasty* (1939).

discrepancy persists. It matters that the Mongol patriarch of the East Syrian Church, Mar Yaballaha III (1245–1317), "exercised ecclesiastical sovereignty over more of the earth's surface than even the pontiff in Rome"[2] and that East Syrian Christianity remained the dominant branch of the faith in Asia until the early fifteenth century. These historical details matter because they help to convey the immense diversity, multiplicity of expressions, and polycentric nature of world Christianity from the early centuries.[3]

The narrow historiography of the Western tradition largely focuses on particular segments of the world Christian movement and precludes a full account. The conceptual frameworks or interpretative lenses that underpin its treatment are more subtle but no less constraining. The "empire argument" discussed in this study is a major example. The fact that imperial projects loom large over the history of the world and have played a major role in the integration of the world's peoples easily masks the pervasive use of the empire argument as a rubric of historical analysis. Yet, even the reality of empire is complicated.

Empires have been characterized as "the normal way in which political power is exercised, not the exception."[4] But this does not mean that they are inevitable. The conditions that produce empire building are far from predictable; and empires do not simply emerge on an evolutionary political continuum. They have generally developed haphazardly rather than through grand design, emerged in multiple ways with great variation in form and impact, and come in a variety of shapes and sizes.[5] The Islamic and Mongol Empires, for

2. Samuel H. Moffett, *A History of Christianity in Asia: Beginnings to 1500*, vol. 1 (Maryknoll, NY: Orbis Books, 1998), 434.

3. Klaus Koschorke, "Transcontinental Links, Enlarged Maps, and Polycentric Structures in the History of World Christianity," *Journal of World Christianity* 6, no. 1 (2016): 28–56.

4. John Isbister, *Promises Not Kept: The Betrayal of Social Change in the Third World*, 5th ed. (Bloomfield, CT: Kumarian, 2001), 78. This characterization is a testament to the deep inequalities and exceptional levels of organized violence that have characterized processes of globalization from ancient times. See also David Held, Anthony McGrew, David Goldblatt, and Jonathan Perraton, *Global Transformations: Politics, Economics and Culture* (Stanford, CA: Stanford University Press, 1999), 87, 89–90; Nayan Chanda, *Bound Together: How Traders, Preachers, Adventurers, and Warriors Shaped Globalization* (New Haven: Yale University Press, 2007), 177.

5. Lord Palmerston's well-known quip that the British Empire was acquired in a "fit of absent-mindedness" underscores the point that empire building (the orga-

instance, unlike the Han or Roman Empires, were formed by nomadic tribal groups. And, regardless of size, sophistication, or duration, empires are also balancing acts of control and concession.[6]

Empire building has been a driving force of historical change from ancient times; and it is useful as a concept because it epitomizes supreme political domination and the exercise or projection of superior power in ways that effect large-scale transformation. But empires should not be assessed in isolation from other historical forces such as large-scale migration. As a case in point, the "Crusader states" established through conquest and occupation in the Levant ought to be examined not only in terms of political domination but with particular attentiveness to the powerful processes of cultural change and integration that its Latin architects and immigrants were subjected to—so much so that, in the words of Fulcher de Chartres (a contemporary observer), "we who were Occidentals now have been made Orientals," and "he who was born an alien has become a native."

In Western thought, an emphasis on the *nation-states* as a major symbol of political dominance and control seemingly detracts from the focus on empire in historical study. But the difference between the two embodiments of organized power—empire viewed as expansionist and pluralistic; the nation-state considered more singular, exclusive, and homogenizing—is less significant than often assumed.[7] It is noteworthy, for instance, that the nation-state of Japan presently has greater global influence and impact than it did when it was, in the words of Inoue Kaoru (foreign minister of Japan, 1885–1887), a "European-style empire on the edge of Asia."[8] Empire and nation-state exist

nization of extensive territories, peoples, or nations under a single rule or supreme authority) is often an unintended consequence. See Brian Stanley, *The Bible and the Flag: Protestant Missions and British Imperialism in the Nineteenth and Twentieth Centuries* (Leicester: Apollos, 1990), 34; Philip D. Curtin, *The World and the West: The European Challenge and the Overseas Response in the Age of Empire* (New York: Cambridge University Press, 2000), 38–41, 48–51.

6. Generally, reliance on local authorities in subjugated areas is a pragmatic necessity; the economic burden of maintaining massive armies and bureaucratic structures ultimately conflicts with economic progress; and, by the very nature of things, hegemonic power inevitably triggers organized resistance. For a brief commentary on the British experience, see Curtin, *World and the West*, 15–17.

7. Jane Burbank and Frederick Cooper, *Empires in World History: Power and the Politics of Difference* (Princeton: Princeton University Press, 2010), 8.

8. Burbank and Cooper, *Empires in World History*, 302.

on a spectrum; and, though there is "no single path from empire to nation" or vice versa, either can be "transformed into something like the other."[9] In any case, the commonplace use of the nation-state as a unit of analysis also hints at the conceptual appeal of the empire argument.

In the final analysis, the Western appetite for totalizing explanations centered on structures of dominance, especially when assessing global realities, remains alive and well.[10] When applied as an analytical construct, "empire" conveys the conviction that major social transformations and historical change are best understood in terms of hegemonic power, superior material resources, and expansionist political forces. This understanding accounts for explanations that focus on major events, great nations and civilizations, political ambition, the activities of great men, and the role of institutional agents. These are legitimate rubrics or tools of analysis; but they have acquired a primacy in historical interpretation that is seldom contested. In histories of Christianity, this "empire" argument accounts for marked emphasis on institutional authority and intellectual elites and conceptions of global Christianity as largely a product of one-directional processes of change originating in Western centers.

EMPIRE AND RELIGIOUS CONVERSION

In the popular mind, empire is inextricably linked to religious expansion because of what Bentley terms *conversion induced by political, social, or economic pressure*.[11] This describes contexts of mass migration or imperial conquest in

---

9. Burbank and Cooper, *Empires in World History*, 9. These authors argue that not only do nation-states "share space with empires" but some also mimic the hegemonic ambitions and reach of empires—as both the United States and Russia arguably do presently.

10. See A. G. Hopkins, "Back to the Future: From National History to Imperial History," *Past and Present*, no. 164 (1999): 198–243; Philip Pomper, "The History and Theory of Empires," *History and Theory* 44, no. 4 (2005): 1–27; Patrick Wolfe, "History and Imperialism: A Century of Theory, from Marx to Postcolonialism," *American Historical Review* 102, no. 2 (1997): 388–420; James W. Cook, "The Kids Are All Right: On the 'Turning' of Cultural History," *American Historical Review* 117, no. 3 (June 2012): 746–71.

11. Jerry H. Bentley, *Old World Encounters* (New York: Oxford University Press, 1993), 12–13.

which the dominant authorities apply particular measures (such as punitive taxation, prohibition of unsanctioned religious practices, or social exclusion based on religious adherence) to induce conversion of subjugated peoples to the state religion. In this view, regardless of forms of resistance, large-scale conversion ultimately ensues when painful discriminatory measures are applied over two or more generations. To be sure, even in the absence of coercive state action, hegemonic domination can produce lasting sociocultural transformations in distant societies that impact religious life[12]—though such large-scale "religious conversion" is essentially a *social* process, synonymous to a large degree with acculturation.[13]

Importantly, empires in which a monotheistic faith invested the imperial project with a universal vision and legitimized singular rule—one empire, one ruler, one god[14]—appear more likely to sanction the use of force in the spread of religion as an integral component of empire building. This is not always straightforward, for the alliance of political rule and religious legitimization neither guarantees imperial unity nor precludes the rise of competing centers of power.[15] But claims that empire building has been crucial for the transregional spread of religion, or that state sponsorship was indispensable for successful cross-cultural missionary expansion, typically have such empires in view.

12. Colonization, for instance, is frequently accompanied by some degree of integration into the colonizer's cultural system through the institution of a foreign language and new customs, and the restructuring of society to privilege particular classes of people.

13. With reference to the British Empire, some go as far as to argue that "colonization . . . of indigenous modes of perception and practice" was so thoroughgoing that even indigenous resistance and protest was of necessity expressed in terms and categories set by the invading culture. Jean Comaroff and John Comaroff, "Christianity and Colonialism in South Africa," *American Ethnologist* 13, no. 1 (1986): 2, 16–17. This essentially implies that indigenous societies "have no option but to reformulate their identity in response to major changes in the scale and contours of their social environment." Brian Stanley, "Conversion to Christianity: The Colonization of the Mind?," *International Review of Mission* 92, no. 366 (2003): 317.

14. Burbank and Cooper, *Empires in World History*, 17.

15. Also, which entities have authority to speak on behalf of the one "god" can be a major source of contention in a manner that is disruptive to religious unity and propagation. Burbank and Cooper, *Empires in World History*, 18.

The Limits of Empire

From a broader sociohistorical perspective, the common supposition that state sponsorship or the projection of empire is necessary for the successful establishment of religious communities across cultural frontiers fails to hold up well under scrutiny. This point of view has been challenged at various points throughout this study. A more focused appraisal is in order, though my examples are limited to Christianity and Islam.

First, the focus on hegemonic action and dominant structures implicitly downplays the extent to which the aspirations, needs, and free volition of the prospective converts themselves shape the outcome of religious encounter. Even in situations of conquest, different sections of the society respond differently to conversionist pressure. Elites generally make entirely different calculations from the majority population and are often more vulnerable to use of state instruments or inducements. The reverse is sometimes true. In some situations, oppressed groups or lower-class communities within the beleaguered society may be attracted to the prestige of the invader's religion and the resources it provides for social advancement. Thus, in the face of expanding Islam, many local authorities and members of the higher classes resisted Islamic rule while oppressed minorities rallied to the new faith based on different expectations or aspirations. Monophysites, Jacobites, and Nestorians, for instance, welcomed Arab governments in expectation of relief from Roman and Sassanian authorities.[16] Thus, in the messy complexity of the human condition, it was reprieve from one empire that sometimes motivated the embrace of another.

Second (and relatedly), while conquest and coercion limit the convert's agency, it is worth considering that *resistance* "is the normal or typical reaction of both individuals and societies to conversion attempts."[17] Importantly, the converts' capacity for resistance is especially strong in situations where a cultural frontier is involved, which usually happens with the spread of empire. Belief cannot be compelled; and even in situations of mass conversion, whether as a result of repressive measures or not, a substantial proportion (if

16. Moffett, *Christianity in Asia*, 336–48; Browne, *Eclipse of Christianity*, 39–43.
17. Lewis R. Rambo, *Understanding Religious Conversion* (New Haven: Yale University Press, 1993), 35.

not the majority) of people generally repudiate the new religion. This is why, when the application of force is a major factor, the process of conversion takes place over centuries, as was the case with large-scale conversions to Islam in the Middle East.[18] Even in the European context "culture-based resistance to Christianity continued for a long time indeed."[19] The point, however, is that resistance is normal and frequently enduring. History is replete with instances of minority groups preserving their religious tradition and sustaining their faith over many centuries under antagonistic imperial rule.[20] In many societies where Islamic rule was exercised for centuries (such as the Iberian Peninsula, Sicily, Greece, the Balkans, and much of India), the Islamic faith failed to gain full acceptance.[21]

Third, state sponsorship of religion and religious propagation is a double-edged sword. It may contribute to the spread of religion in some situations; but in many instances association with imperial patronage or state power actually works *against* the long-term success of religious expansion across cultural frontiers. In Asia, where Christianity was mainly spread by merchants (not monks, as in the case of Europe), the fortunes of East Syrian Christian communities were strongly tied to the support and patronage of local political authority. In the long run, this *association with ruling powers* contributed to retrenchment. In T'ang China, where the earliest East Syrian missionaries on record were welcomed and supported by Emperor Taizong, the church quickly collapsed after over two and a half centuries of flourishing presence and influence when the T'ang Dynasty ended.[22] (Much later, in the sixteenth to eighteenth centuries, burgeoning Christian communities in Japan and

18. Marcia Hermansen, "Conversion to Islam in Theological and Historical Perspectives," in *The Oxford Handbook of Religious Conversion*, ed. Lewis R. Rambo and Charles E. Farhadian (New York: Oxford University Press, 2014), 632–33, 638.

19. Jerry H. Bentley, *Old World Encounters: Cross-Cultural Contacts and Exchanges in Pre-Modern Times* (New York: Oxford University Press, 1993), 103.

20. Jewish communities survived various empires; Christianity withstood vicious Roman persecution in the early centuries of its existence and thrived in Sassanian Persia under adverse conditions; Nestorian communities did relatively well under Muslim and Mongol rule for many centuries.

21. See Robert L. Montgomery, "Conversion and the Historic Spread of Religions," in *The Oxford Handbook of Religious Conversion*, ed. Lewis R. Rambo and Charles E. Farhadian (New York: Oxford University Press, 2014), 172–76.

22. For helpful analysis, see Moffett, *Christianity in Asia*, 302–14; Aprem Mar Mooken, "Reference to China in Syriac Sources," in *Hidden Treasures and Intercul-*

China collapsed in part because local authorities took vigorous action against a foreign faith that they came to associate with the projection of political authority from distant lands.)

Fourth, the empire or state sponsorship argument strongly implies that the cross-cultural expansion of religion is a one-directional process of transformation—that the threat or application of superior force allows foreign agents to neatly supplant indigenous religious culture with the faith and traditions of the invading culture. In reality, even in situations of conquest, the sustained cross-cultural encounter between religious systems is inevitably marked by mutual exchange and borrowing. As Bentley acknowledges with great insight:

> By no means . . . did efforts at cultural expansion result in the replication of a given tradition in a new region; when crossing religious boundaries, beliefs and values necessarily adapted and made accommodations to the political, social, and economic, as well as cultural traditions of different peoples. Thus, when it occurred on a large scale, cross-cultural conversion followed a process of syncretism rather than wholesale cultural transformation, or the refashioning of one people according to the cultural standards of another.[23]

As a case in point, while Islam overran Arabia and displaced Christianity, the language of transmission for the spread of Islam across the Silk Road was Persian, not Arabic.[24] Moreover, Islam did not simply sweep all before it. Features associated with Islam, such as "veiled women . . . , set hours or chanted prayers and offices, and a prostrate posture, facing east for prayer," actually existed among Christians before the time of Mohammed.[25] In fact, winning converts to a new religion across cultural frontiers tends to be achieved more

---

tural Encounters: Studies on East Syriac Christianity in China and Central Asia, ed. Dietmar W. Winkler and Li Tang (Vienna: Lit, 2014), 183–93.

23. Bentley, *Old World Encounters*, 110.

24. Richard Foltz, *Religions of the Silk Road: Premodern Patterns of Globalization* (New York: Palgrave Macmillan, 2010), 17–18.

25. Ian Gillman and Hans-Joachim Klimkeit, *Christians in Asia before 1500* (Ann Arbor: University of Michigan Press, 1999), 79; see also Philip Jenkins, *The Lost History of Christianity: The Thousand-Year Golden Age of the Church in the Middle East, Africa, and Asia—and How It Died* (New York: HarperOne, 2008), 179–206.

readily with translation and cultural adaptation rather than through state-sponsored coercion. Certainly, in the case of Christianity, the translatability of the core message privileges the recipient culture (albeit to varying degrees depending on historical circumstance) in a way that imposes limits on external control by missionary agents or a conquering power. This leads to the next point.

Fifth, where large-scale cross-cultural conversion is linked to political power or use of repressive measures, complex contextual factors often have great bearing on the outcome. In situations where political instability, social disorder, or widespread dislocation prevail, receptiveness to cultural change or a new religion is likely to be higher. As such, the extensive upheavals and tragic displacements that often accompany imperial conquests arguably contribute as much to wholesale conversions as state coercion (if not more). The degree of consonance between the two cultural systems is also of great relevance, since cross-cultural conversion is more probable when two groups already share cultural affinities.[26] In this regard, the territorial and cultural proximity that characterized missionary efforts in Europe, including those associated with military conquest by prominent Christian monarchs like Charlemagne, was pertinent to outcomes. In sharp contrast, not only did East Syrian missionary endeavor in China involve vast distances but the cultural chasm between the two cultures also presented unique challenges.

The nature of religious life and organization in the local context is also relevant since it shapes the response of potential converts to the religious message and new religious forms. That Christian missions have historically enjoyed their greatest success in the encounter with primal religious societies (in Europe and elsewhere) and much less so in the direct encounter with other major faiths or outreach to competitive multifaith societies reflects this simple fact.

Sixth, in certain situations, the exigencies of empire and the mandate for conversion actually collide. In the early stages of the Islamic Empire, for instance, Islamic rulers extracted revenue for the upkeep of empire mainly by imposing extra taxes and tributes on nonbelievers (since, for reasons of national security, they were exempt from military service). This created a vicious cycle: the financial pressures increased conversions to Islam (decreasing the pool of taxpayers), and the increased burden of taxation on the shrinking non-

26. Rambo, *Understanding Religious Conversion*, 41–42.

Muslim population induced even more conversions. Alarmed rulers felt the need to lower incentives for conversion for fear of the financial consequences of losing a large tax base of nonbelievers, even as the burden for supporting the army increased.[27] In British colonial Africa, the spread of empire brought large Muslim populations under British rule; and, to the chagrin of foreign missionaries, dependence on local Islamic rulers or Islamic structures of governance led colonial authorities to preclude predominantly Muslim areas from Christian missionary activity.[28]

Seventh, all the major faiths have enjoyed their greatest successes in situations where coercion or imperial domination played little or no role. These include conversion of the Mongols and Turks to Islam, the Islamization of Indonesia (the world's most populous Muslim country), the spread of Buddhism in China, the embrace of Christianity by most western Europeans, and the extraordinary accessions to Christianity in Africa and Asia in the postcolonial period. As we have seen, the rulers of the massive Mongol Empire eschewed the elevation of any one religious system in their vast domains and allowed the multiplicity of faiths within their conquered territories to flourish—apparently due to the recognition that the authority invested in a state religion would pose a threat to political power (chapter 9). Various khans converted to different religions, some to more than one over the course of time, and some used religious favoritism as a political tool. But none of the khanates officially subscribed to a state religion until the late thirteenth century when the ilkhans of Persia converted to the Muslim faith.[29] This gave Islam a new power base within the empire; yet the Ilkhanate of Persia was the first of the Mongol dynasties to collapse.

Eighth, adopting the empire explanation for the spread of religion reflects a theoretical approach that advances functionalist explanations for religious conversion to the exclusion of religious or spiritual rationale. The role of self-interest and personal aspirations cannot be denied. Under nor-

---

27. Chanda, *Bound Together*, 184; Moffett, *Christianity in Asia*, 344–46.

28. Roland A. Oliver, *The African Experience* (London: Pimlico, 1994), 202. As Andrew Walls points out, by the end of the nineteenth century the queen of England had become "the world's leading Islamic ruler." Andrew F. Walls, *The Cross-Cultural Process in Christian History: Studies in the Transmission and Appropriation of Faith* (Maryknoll, NY: Orbis Books, 2002), 219.

29. In China, Khublai Khan converted to Buddhism, which was not a state religion.

mal circumstances converts embrace change or switch allegiance because it adds value to their lives; and, as the conversion of Iceland indicates, the process can be attended by compelling logic. From the vantage point of the true convert, however, conversion to a different belief system tends to be a decidedly religious experience. Supernatural displays of healing and miracles or charismatic preaching by a foreign missionary agent were frequently more effective in winning converts cross-culturally than political domination or interests. When asked why he did not convert to Christianity, Khublai Khan reportedly responded:

> If I were to turn to the faith of Christ and become a Christian, then my barons and others who are not converted will say, "What has moved you to be baptized and to take up the faith of Christ? What powers or miracles have you witnessed on His part?" . . . But now you shall go to your Pope, and pray him on my part to send hither an hundred men skilled in your law, who shall be capable of rebuking the practices of the idolaters to their faces . . . , and so control the idolaters that these shall have no power to perform such things in their presence. When we shall witness this we will denounce the idolaters and their religion, and then I will receive baptism; and when I shall have been baptized, then all my barons and chiefs shall be baptized also, and their followers shall do the like, and thus in the end there will be more Christians here than exist in your part of the world![30]

Finally, the great religions have surpassed empires in transcontinental reach, cultural longevity, and capacity for large-scale mobilization. The global communities united by the Islamic faith and practices (including the Arabic language and elements of Arabian culture) did not revert back to their old ways with the waning of the Islamic empires. The Islamic traditions and culture established in Europe under the Ottoman Turks in the sixteenth century still exist today within sizeable Muslim populations.[31] In the case of Christianity,

30. Quoted in Laurence E. Browne, *The Eclipse of Christianity in Asia, from the Time of Muhammad Till the Fourteenth Century* (Cambridge: Cambridge University Press, 1933), 153.

31. The Muslims in Bosnia and Kosovo are descendants of the Ottoman presence in Europe.

elements of the transplanted European forms have endured in the non-Western world, notably the use of European languages. More strikingly, not only did the faith take on new expressions in former colonies but it also experienced its most vigorous growth *after* the end of colonial rule. In short, while some connection between empire and the spread of religion across cultural frontiers is detectable, it is certainly not predictable. Quite simply, the myriad probabilities and paradoxes of religious encounter and intercultural exchange render the theoretical leap from correlation to causation deeply problematic.

The Foreign Missionary as an Agent of Empire

Formally planned or institutionally commissioned missionary activity is more prominent in Christianity than other missionary faiths like Buddhism and Islam. Central to the notion that empire is indispensable for religious expansion is the implicit assumption that foreign missions are more likely to succeed when the missionaries' efforts benefit from state sponsorship or association with a superior political power. This perspective is quite pronounced in accounts of the global spread of Christianity in tandem with European colonial expansion from the late fifteenth century.[32] In the pre-1500 period covered in this volume, this assertion is somewhat blunted by the fact that cultural exchanges linked to extensive migrant movements typically allowed Christian forms and ideas to penetrate non-Christian societies or peoples *long before* the arrival of missionaries. State control and regulation of religious ideas were operative (quite notably within the Byzantine and Islamic Empires); but porous political boundaries, the transcontinental sweep of nomadic groups, and the prevalence of merchants in long-distance travel helped to sustain expansive

---

32. This supposes that the global spread of Christianity in the post-1500 world was a one-directional movement from the centers of economic and political power in the West; and, thus, as Lamin Sanneh put it, "essentially a phase of Europe's worldwide ascendancy." Lamin Sanneh, "World Christianity and the New Historiography: History and Global Connections," in *Enlarging the Story: Perspectives on Writing World Christian History*, ed. Wilbert R. Shenk (Maryknoll, NY: Orbis Books, 2002), 97–98. Also noteworthy is the conviction that the work of the foreign missionary, as primary agent of "the subtle inculcation of European values," was particularly crucial for colonialism in Africa. Comaroff and Comaroff, "Christianity and Colonialism in South Africa," 15.

webs of cultural interaction and exchange that far surpassed the role and reach of institutional authorities and agents.

But this still leaves the key question of whether the association or identification of foreign missionary agents with empire or a superior political power was critical to the success of Christian missions. In many instances, particularly in medieval Europe, political patronage and protection safeguarded missionary outreach to foreign lands, and association with a superior power served the interests of Christian propagation. As this study has shown, however, the impact and implications of association with a foreign or distant political power on the work of the missionary and the outcomes of missionary outreach were complex and unpredictable.

There are many reasons for this complexity. State protection does not guarantee the safety or survival of foreign missionary agents in the face of entrenched hostility. The response of local authorities to foreign missions was typically shaped less by the designs of distant political powers than by local needs and aspirations. Foreign missionary initiatives that were principally rooted in political ambition and state policy were invariably limited in scope, required geographical proximity, and provoked powerful resistance from inhabitants faced with the simple choice of Christian conversion or political autonomy. Successful propagation of the Christian message and church planting in foreign lands solely under the auspices of local authority in the recipient society was rarely long lasting (especially if the local authority was also of foreign extraction)—not to mention that the piety, demeanor, and message of the missionary were almost frequently crucial for a fruitful outcome.

In the final analysis, at least three fundamental facts must be acknowledged: (1) the planned initiatives of individual missionaries (or groups) sent by a religious body, or under the auspices of state authority, to foreign territories with the primary aim of winning converts and establishing a church, were the exception, not the rule; (2) the foreign missionary, regardless of links to empire or state power, is a *migrant-outsider*; and (3) the most extraordinary missionary accomplishments in the first 1,500 years of the world Christian movement had nothing to do with empire or state sponsorship.

It is also significant that many foreign missionaries experienced their own "conversions"—a significant change in worldview or radical rethinking of the norms or beliefs they previously held—after full immersion in a foreign culture for extended periods of time. Put differently, the most effective foreign missionaries were those who adapted their message and methods to the exigencies of the local environment. This means that "conversion on a significant scale has usually taken place only when . . . [foreign] missionaries have been prepared to allow their encounters with indigenous peoples to change both them and the formulation of their message."[33] The celebrated Boniface, despite his dependence on the protection of Frankish rulers (an arrangement that did not prevent his martyrdom), was persuaded to moderate his bellicose approach to paganism and make preaching more central to his mission among the Germans. Whether or not they failed to denounce European colonialism, the foreign missionaries who left a lasting legacy were generally those who were able to distance themselves from the designs of empire at least sufficiently to grasp the efficacy of indigenous agency and local initiatives.

In sum, the empire argument distorts historical understanding not only because it places disproportionate emphasis on formal structures, official agency, and state resources that played a minimal role in Christian expansion but also because it minimizes the importance of the recipient societies and the agency of potential converts. The primacy of indigenous culture and local resources for Christian conversion in contexts of cross-cultural engagement is fully exposed by the "translation principle" (chapter 2). For proponents like Lamin Sanneh, "mission as translation is the vintage mark of Christianity," because the indispensable need to convey the sense and meaning of the message using the language (ideas, categories, and idioms) of the recipient indigenous culture establishes the compatibility of the Christian faith with all cultures.[34] Whether in Europe or among the multitudes in the vast reaches of Asia, vernacular translation made potential converts active collaborators in

33. Stanley, "Conversion to Christianity," 323. Incidentally, the cross-cultural contacts created by European colonial expansion also led to a number of European conversions to Islam, apparently motivated in part by disaffection with the nature of colonial rule. Hermansen, "Conversion to Islam," 643–644. See also, Birgit Herppich, *Pitfalls of Trained Incapacity: The Unintended Effects of Integral Missionary Training in the Basel Mission on Its Early Work in Ghana (1828–1840)* (Eugene, OR: Pickwick, 2016), which explores the downsides of foreign missionary training and preparation in the face of unanticipated cross-cultural challenges.

34. Lamin Sanneh, *Translating the Message: The Missionary Impact on Culture*, 2nd ed. (Maryknoll, NY: Orbis Books, 2009), 34.

the conversion process and underlined the indispensability of local resources for religious change.

The translation principle effectively alerts the historian to the limits of political power and the inherent limitations of the cultural resources of foreign missionary agents. In every epoch, and in the encounter with every successive cultural context, missionary pioneers must perforce "concede the primacy of indigenous influence and materials."[35] As I have argued, cross-cultural missionary engagement inevitably starts at the margins, meaning that the foreign missionary agent must reckon with an outsider status, even when rulers are among the first converts. Such a person may well revel in religious otherness as a badge of cultural superiority and extol outsider status as a symbol of dominance; but those whom they seek to reach or persuade across religious boundaries are no less conscious of the otherness of the foreign missionary agent. In the long run, effective cross-cultural religious transmission requires local converts or agents to play an outsized role in the evangelistic process.

THE MIGRANT FACTOR

Migration is a defining feature of human existence and a significant force of historical change, even if the historical record is often scanty, and analyzing the impact or imprint of human migration in specific contexts or periods often requires imaginative reasoning. This is all the more remarkable given that migrants "have always been a minority of the human race."[36] In the period under review, most people never left their province or region of birth in their lifetime. But, as this study emphatically demonstrates, the impact of migrants on destination societies is often out of all proportion to their numbers. Despite the tremendous human costs and foreboding hardships of long-distance travel, the scale and scope of migration steadily increased (from the biblical era

---

35. Sanneh, *Translating the Message*, 29. Greater awareness of the degree to which the preexisting religious heritage shapes indigenous appropriation invites the view that the indigenous religious heritage and resources require as much attention as the advent of the foreign missionary. Ogbu Kalu, "Introduction: The Shape and Flow of African Christian Historiography," in *African Christianity: An African Story*, ed. Ogbu Kalu (Trenton, NJ: Africa World Press, 2007), 12.

36. John Haywood, *The Great Migrations: From the Earliest Humans to the Age of Globalization* (London: Quercus, 2008), 6.

up to 1500) and contributed directly to the escalation of cultural interactions between more distant and more diverse societies. The types of migration and the categories of migrants cover the full range. But cross-community migrations, involving individuals and groups who leave one community to join another (with variation in distance and duration), are the most prevalent and most frequently referenced in this study.

Intriguingly, migration was inescapably linked to empire, for the simple reason that empire building is inconceivable without human migration or increased mobility. The very act of conquest or territorial expansion required substantial migration and resettlement. The movement of large conquering forces was unavoidably disruptive; and the subjugation of whole populations inevitably caused mass movement (of refugees, captives, deportees, defectors, etc.). At the same time, effective administration of vast domains required speed and efficiency of movement, which prompted heavy investment in building road networks or communications infrastructure. This, combined with the improved security provided by imperial domination, invariably stimulated high levels of mobility. Similarly, imperial rule fostered interregional connections and trade networks that intensified long-distance travel. Inevitably also, the collapse of imperial structures or the contraction of imperial power occasioned mass migrations precipitated by economic insecurity, political instability, and armed incursions.

It could be argued, therefore, that the intensification of migration engendered by imperial projects does more for cross-cultural religious expansion and encounter than political action or economic incentives. In this regard, it is worth restating that borderlands and frontier regions were environs of lively cultural exchange and religious innovation. This is because such unregulated spaces between or beyond the boundaries of empire were marked by unmanageable migrant flows as well as great linguistic, ethnic, and religious diversity.[37] There is abundant historical evidence that neither imperial structures nor institutional hierarchies nor formal systems of control are requisites for religious systems to thrive or expand.

The interconnection between religious expansion and human migration is

---

37. C. R. Whittaker, *Frontiers of the Roman Empire: A Social and Economic Study* (Baltimore: Johns Hopkins University Press, 1994), 75–78, 228–31; A. D. Lee, *Information and Frontiers: Roman Foreign Relations in Late Antiquity* (New York: Cambridge University Press, 2006), 50–51, 66–71.

inescapable and indisputable. In the period covered by this study, all aspects of culture were transported by human persons.[38] At least until the early nineteenth century (when the discovery and use of electric signals fundamentally transformed long-distance communication), the spread of cultural objects, practices, and ideas to different societies and distant communities required physical human interaction and depended almost exclusively on human movement or migration. Not only were religious ideas and practices disseminated mainly through migrant interaction but also over time an increasing proportion of migrants engaged in long-distance travel for religious reasons. No other single factor or feature of human existence correlates more closely with the transregional or global spread of religion than human migration. The link between migration and global Christian expansion is as pivotal and profound as its neglect in the historical study of Christianity is perplexing.

This state of affairs has something to do with the "top-down" view that prevails in much historical study, with its near exclusive focus on dramatic events and the contribution of elites. In this regard, the "bottom-up" perspective of sociohistorical inquiry, with its predilection for exploring the impact and power of ordinary people or routine occurrences, provides a much-needed corrective. The limitations of the historical record, and the concurrent need to "reconstruct the past with imagination," have been repeatedly acknowledged. Important gaps remain, to be sure. But this volume's wide-ranging assessment of the role of migration in the global spread of the Christian movement from its earliest beginnings substantiates the thesis that *every Christian migrant is a potential missionary*.

Since human migration is a fact of history, adherents of all religions become migrants at one point or another.[39] The absence of formal missionary structures in other major religions like Islam or Buddhism arguably renders the role of migration in the spread of those faiths more readily evident. But the centrality of migration in transnational Christian outreach and propagation is incontro-

38. Exceptions include the much cruder and chancier methods of long-distance communication in ancient societies such as drums, trumpets, or smoke signals.

39. However, it is interesting to note that in the opening decade of the twenty-first century, Christians constituted nearly half (49 percent) of the world's international migrants, with Muslims representing the second-largest religious group of migrants (27 percent). Phillip Connor and Catherine Tucker, "Religion and Migration around the Globe: Introducing the Global Religion and Migration Database," *International Migration Review* 45, no. 4 (2011): 994.

vertible, in a way that is not fully accounted for by merely acknowledging the historical significance of migration. Escalating transnational networks of contact and exchange, facilitated by long-distance trade and travel, and stimulated by the growth of empires, are integral to the story. Also crucial, as this study explains, is the fact that the Christian faith and Scriptures invest migration and the migrant experience with particular theological significance, with vast implications for Christian identity and witness down the centuries.

From the start, members of the Jesus movement claimed the mantle and mandate of divine election and proclaimed themselves the "people of God," a biblical reference steeped with migrant connotations. Early Christian teaching also linked Christian identity to the concrete experience of being a "stranger" or "foreigner" and endorsed the view of the Christian life as involuntary exile. Whether the writer of the "Epistle to Diognetus" merely intended to portray the concrete experiences of the Christian communities of his day, his words conveyed a timeless truth about the essential migrant-outsider nature of Christian life and witness. For Christian believers, he observed, "any foreign country is a motherland, and any motherland is a foreign country."

The inextricable link between migration and the propagation of the Christian faith has a lot to do with the fact that a migrant-outsider existence (or "otherness") accentuates distinctive presence and practice—or "lived faith." If "migration is a theologizing experience," this is in part because the encounter with unknown lands and peoples implicitly widens the horizons of religious understanding and often (though not always) intensifies religious commitment. Even in the absence of evangelistic activity, the otherness of the migrant status connotes a distinctive religious identity that is de facto a form of proclamation. For countless communities of Christian migrants down through the ages to the present day, a lived faith not only forms part of a strategy of survival (meeting the need for solidarity and belonging) but it also shapes interaction and engagement with the wider society. The migrant experience makes poignantly manifest what may otherwise be muted in the life of the church: *otherness is foundational to outreach*.

Thus, from the earliest beginnings, the cross-cultural spread of the Christian faith and progressive fulfillment of its core universal vision were sustained by the largely unstructured, boundary-crossing movements of Christians in countless migrant flows. "Empire" does feature in the story: a few Christian monarchs in Europe sponsored or orchestrated Christian missionary enterprise among pagan populations; and various empires (Persian, T'ang, Islamic, Mongol) shaped the nature and outcome of Christian missionary endeavor in distinct ways. Ecclesiastical authority also played a role: the sixth-century mission to the Anglo-Saxons commissioned by Pope Gregory I was exceptional (in the West) but historically significant; and East Syrian patriarchs like Timothy I also commissioned several "foreign" missions from the late eighth century.

But this volume has laid out in great detail the extensive and primary role of multitudes of Christian migrants, of all stripes and categories, in the global spread of the Christian faith. Taken as a whole, the cross-cultural expansion of the Christian faith to societies and peoples throughout the world—from Scandinavia to the Sassanian realm, from Constantinople to Chang'an—in the pre-1500 period owed little or nothing to state sponsorship or the projection of empire. Institutional authority and agents, that are commonly considered indispensable for global Christian expansion, also played a minimal role. When all is said and done, the rise of Christianity as a world movement has been predominantly through the agency and activity of migrants—individuals and communities living as strangers and outsiders in foreign lands.

Bibliography

Adamnan. *Life of St. Columba.* Translated and with an introduction by Richard
  Sharpe. New York: Penguin Books, 1995.
Adamopoulo, Themistocles A. "Elements of the Earliest Evangelisation of Gen-
  tiles in the Roman Empire: Caesarea Maritima, Antioch and Rome."
  Phronema 13 (1998): 65–87.
Addison, James Thayer. *The Medieval Missionary: A Study of the Conversion of
  Northern Europe, A.D. 500–1300.* Perspectives in European History, no. 1.
  Philadelphia: Porcupine, 1976.
Anderson, Bernhard W. *From Creation to New Creation: Old Testament Perspec-
  tives.* Overtures to Biblical Theology. Minneapolis: Fortress, 1994.
Andersson, Theodore M. *The Growth of the Medieval Icelandic Sagas (1180–1280).*
  Ithaca, NY: Cornell University Press, 2006.
Arnold, John, ed. *Oxford Handbook of Medieval Christianity.* New York: Oxford
  University Press, 2014
Asen, Bernhard A. "From Acceptance to Exclusion: The Stranger in Old Testa-
  ment Tradition." In *Christianity and the Stranger,* edited by Francis W.
  Nichols, 16–35. Atlanta: Scholars Press, 1995.
Ashcroft, Bill, Gareth Griffiths, and Helen Tiffin. *The Post-Colonial Studies
  Reader.* 2nd ed. New York: Routledge, 2006.
Augustine. *The Confessions of St. Augustine.* Translated by J. G. Pilkington. New
  York: Boni & Liveright, 1927.
Bachrach, Bernard S. *Charlemagne's Early Campaigns (768–777): A Diplomatic
  and Military Analysis.* Leiden: Brill, 2013.
Baer, Marc David. "History and Religious Conversion." In Rambo and Farhadian,
  The Oxford Handbook of Religious Conversion, 25–47.

Bagge, Sverre. "Christianizing Kingdoms." In Arnold, *Oxford Handbook of Medieval Christianity*, 114–31.

———. "The Making of a Missionary King: The Medieval Accounts of Olaf Tryggvason and the Conversion of Norway." *Journal of English and Germanic Philology* 105, no. 4 (October 2006): 473–513.

Balch, David L. *Let Wives Be Submissive: The Domestic Code in 1 Peter.* Chico, CA: Scholars Press, 1981.

Balsdon, J. P. V. D. *Romans and Aliens.* Chapel Hill: University of North Carolina Press, 1979.

Barbero, Alessandro. *Charlemagne: Father of a Continent.* Translated by Allan Cameron. Berkeley: University of California Press, 2004.

Bar Hebraeus. *The Chronography of Gregory Abû'l Faraj, the Son of Aaron, the Hebrew Physician, Commonly Known as Bar Hebraeus.* Translated by Ernest A. Wallis Budge. London: Oxford University Press, 1932.

Barmby, James. *Gregory the Great.* New York: SPCK, 1879.

Barnes, Michel R., and Daniel H. Williams, eds. *Arianism after Arius: Essays on the Development of the Fourth Century Trinitarian Conflicts.* Edinburgh: T&T Clark, 1993.

Barr, James. "The Question of Religious Influence: The Case of Zoroastrianism, Judaism, and Christianity." *Journal of the American Academy of Religion* 53, no. 2 (1985): 201–35.

Bartholomew, Craig G., and Fred Hughes. *Explorations in a Christian Theology of Pilgrimage.* Burlington, VT: Ashgate, 2004.

Baum, Wilhelm, and Dietmar W. Winkler. *The Church of the East: A Concise History.* London: RoutledgeCurzon, 2003.

Baylis, Phillipa. *An Introduction to Primal Religions.* Edinburgh: Traditional Cosmology Society, 1988.

BBC News. "How Many Roman Catholics Are There in the World?" March 14, 2013. http://www.bbc.com/news/world-21443313.

Becher, Matthias. *Charlemagne.* New Haven: Yale University Press, 2003.

Bede. *The Ecclesiastical History of the English People.* Edited with an introduction by Judith McClure and Roger Collins. New York: Oxford University Press, 1994.

Bediako, Gillian. "Christianity in Interaction with the Primal Religions of the World—a Historical and Global Perspective." Paper presented at Calvin-FTS Religious Plurality Project Consultation, Pasadena, CA, 2005.

Bediako, Kwame. *Christianity in Africa: The Renewal of a Non-Western Religion.* Maryknoll, NY: Orbis Books, 1995.

———. "Understanding African Theology in the 20th Century." In *Issues in African Christian Theology,* edited by Samuel Ngewa, Mark Shaw, and Tite Tienou, 56–72. Nairobi: East African Educational Publishers, 1998.

Behr, John. *Irenaeus of Lyons: Identifying Christianity.* Christian Theology in Context. Oxford: Oxford University Press, 2013.

Bellwood, Peter S. *First Migrants: Ancient Migration in Global Perspective.* Malden, MA: Wiley-Blackwell, 2013.

Bentley, Jerry H. *Old World Encounters: Cross-Cultural Contacts and Exchanges in Pre-Modern Times.* New York: Oxford University Press, 1993.

Berger, Adam. "Overview of Women in Medieval Mongol Empire." In *Medieval Central Asia,* 1–1. January 2011. http://connection.ebscohost.com/c/articles/52534002/overview-women-medieval-mongol-empire.

Berlin, Adele. "Psalms and the Literature of Exile: Psalms 137, 44, 69 and 78." In *The Book of Psalms: Composition and Reception,* edited by Peter W. Flint and Patrick D. Miller, 65–78. Boston: Brill, 2005.

Berndt, Guido M., and Roland Steinacher, eds. *Arianism: Roman Heresy and Barbarian Creed.* Burlington, VT: Ashgate, 2014.

Bidegain, Ana Maria. "Rethinking the Social and Ethical Functions of a History of World Christianity." *Journal of World Christianity* 1, no. 1 (2008): 88–119.

Binns, John. *An Introduction to the Christian Orthodox Churches.* Cambridge: Cambridge University Press, 2002.

Bitel, Lisa M. *Women in Early Medieval Europe, 400–1100.* Cambridge Medieval Textbooks. New York: Cambridge University Press, 2002.

Blasi, Anthony J., Paul-André Turcotte, and Jean Duhaime, eds. *Handbook of Early Christianity: Social Science Approaches.* Walnut Creek, CA: AltaMira, 2002.

Blenkinsopp, Joseph. "Second Isaiah—Prophet of Universalism." *Journal for the Study of the Old Testament* 41 (1988): 83–103.

Boas, Adrian, ed. *The Crusader World.* New York: Routledge, 2015.

Böhning, W. R. "International Migration and the Western World: Past, Present, Future." *International Migration* 16, no. 1 (1978): 11–22.

Boyce, Mary, and Frantz Grenet. *A History of Zoroastrianism.* New York: Brill, 1991.

Brettell, Caroline. "Theorizing Migration in Anthropology: The Social Construction of Networks, Identities, Communities, and Globalscapes." In Brettell and Hollifield, *Migration Theory*, 97–136.

Brettell, Caroline, and James Frank Hollifield. "Migration Theory." In Brettell and Hollifield, *Migration Theory*, 1–26.

Brettell, Caroline, and James Frank Hollifield, eds. *Migration Theory: Talking across Disciplines*. New York: Routledge, 2000.

Bright, John. *A History of Israel.* 4th ed. With an introduction and appendix by William P. Brown. Westminster Aids to the Study of the Scriptures. Louisville: Westminster John Knox, 2000.

Brock, S. P. "Christians in the Sasanian Empire: A Case of Divided Loyalties." In *Religion and National Identity*, edited by Stuart Mews, 1–19. Vol. 18 of Studies in Church History. Oxford: Blackwell, 1982.

———. "The 'Nestorian' Church: A Lamentable Misnomer." *Bulletin of the John Rylands Library* 78, no. 3 (1996): 23–35.

Brown, William P. Introduction to *A History of Israel*, 4th ed., by John Bright. Westminster Aids to the Study of the Scriptures. Louisville: Westminster John Knox, 2000.

Browne, Laurence E. *The Eclipse of Christianity in Asia, from the Time of Muhammad Till the Fourteenth Century.* Cambridge: Cambridge University Press, 1933.

Bryant, M. Darrol. "Conversion in Christianity: From Without and from Within." In *Religious Conversion: Contemporary Practices and Controversies*, edited by Christopher Lamb and M. Darrol Bryant, 177–90. New York: Cassell, 1999.

Buck, Christopher. "The Universality of the Church of the East: How Persian Was Persian Christianity?" *Journal of the Assyrian Academic Society* 10, no. 1 (1996): 54–95.

Bull, Marcus. "Pilgrimage." In Arnold, *Oxford Handbook of Medieval Christianity*, 201–15.

Burbank, Jane, and Frederick Cooper. *Empires in World History: Power and the Politics of Difference.* Princeton: Princeton University Press, 2010.

Burke, Aaron A. "An Anthropological Model for the Investigation of the Archeology of Refugees in Iron Age Judah and Its Environs." In Kelle, Ames, and Wright, *Interpreting Exile*, 41–56.

Cabrita, Joel, David Maxwell, and Emma Wild-Wood, eds. *Relocating World*

Christianity: Interdisciplinary Studies in Universal and Local Expressions of the Christian Faith. Boston: Brill, 2017.

Carroll, Robert P. "Deportation and Diasporic Discourses in the Prophetic Literature." In *Exile: Old Testament, Jewish, and Christian Conceptions*, edited by James M. Scott, 63–85. New York: Brill, 1997.

———. "Exile! What Exile? Deportation and the Discourses of Diaspora." In Grabbe, *Leading Captivity Captive*, 62–79.

Carroll R., M. Daniel. *Christians at the Border: Immigration, the Church, and the Bible*. Grand Rapids: Baker Academic, 2008.

———. "Portraits of People on the Move in the Bible." In *Thinking Christianly about Immigration*, edited by M. Daniel Carroll R., 1–12. Denver, CO: Grounds Institute of Public Ethics, 2011.

Cartwright, Mark. "Crusader States." Ancient History Encyclopedia. November 1, 2018. https://www.ancient.eu/Crusader_States/.

Casson, Lionel. *Travel in the Ancient World*. Baltimore: Johns Hopkins University Press, 1994.

Castles, Stephen, and Mark J. Miller. *The Age of Migration: International Population Movements in the Modern World*. 4th ed. New York: Guilford, 2009.

Chambers, Clarke A. "The 'New' Social History, Local History, and Community Empowerment." *Minnesota History* 49, no. 1 (1984): 14–18.

Chanda, Nayan. *Bound Together: How Traders, Preachers, Adventurers, and Warriors Shaped Globalization*. New Haven: Yale University Press, 2007.

Charbonnier, Jean-Pierre. *Christians in China: A.D. 600 to 2000*. San Francisco: Ignatius Press, 2007.

Charles-Edwards, Thomas. *Early Christian Ireland*. New York: Cambridge University Press, 2000.

———. "The Social Background to Irish *Peregrinatio*." In *The Otherworld Voyage in Early Irish Literature: An Anthology of Criticism*, edited by Jonathan M. Wooding. Portland, OR: Four Courts, 2000.

Charlesworth, M. P. *Trade-Routes and Commerce of the Roman Empire*. 2nd rev. ed. New York: Cooper Square, 1970.

Chen, Huaiyu. "The Encounter of Nestorian Christianity with Tantric Buddhism in Medieval China." In Winkler and Tang, *Hidden Treasures and Intercultural Encounters*, 195–213.

Chevedden, Paul E. "Pope Urban II and the Ideology of the Crusades." In Boas, *The Crusader World*, 8–36.

Chidester, David. *Christianity: A Global History*. New York: HarperCollins, 2000.

Chléirigh, Léan Ní. "*Nova Peregrinatio*: The First Crusade as a Pilgrimage in Contemporary Latin Narratives." In *Writing the Early Crusades: Text, Transmission and Memory*, edited by Marcus Bull and Damien Kempf, 63–74. Woodbridge: Boydell, 2014.

Christian, David. *Maps of Time: An Introduction to Big History*. The California World History Library. Berkeley: University of California Press, 2004.

Clay, John-Henry. *In the Shadow of Death: Saint Boniface and the Conversion of Hessia, 721–754*. Cultural Encounters in Late Antiquity and the Middle Ages 11. Turnhout: Brepols, 2010.

Cohick, Lynn H. "The Real Woman at the Well." *Christianity Today* 59, no. 8 (2015): 66–69.

Collins, John J. "The 'Historical Character' of the Old Testament in Recent Biblical Theology." In Long, *Israel's Past in Present Research*, 150–69.

Comaroff, Jean, and John Comaroff. "Christianity and Colonialism in South Africa." *American Ethnologist* 13, no. 1 (1986): 1–22.

Connor, Phillip, and Catherine Tucker. "Religion and Migration around the Globe: Introducing the Global Religion and Migration Database." *International Migration Review* 45, no. 4 (2011): 985–1000.

Coogan, Michael David. "In the Beginning: The Earliest History." In Coogan, *The Oxford History of the Biblical World*, 3–31.

———, ed. *The Oxford History of the Biblical World*. New York: Oxford University Press, 1998.

Cook, James W. "The Kids Are All Right: On the 'Turning' of Cultural History." *American Historical Review* 117, no. 3 (June 2012): 746–71.

Couvares, Francis G. "Telling a Story in Context; or, What's Wrong with Social History?" *Theory and Society* 9, no. 5 (1980): 674–76.

Cox, James L. "The Classification 'Primal Religions' as a Non-Empirical Christian Theological Construct." *Studies in World Christianity* 2, no. 1 (1996): 55–76.

Crüsemann, Frank. "'You Know the Heart of a Stranger' (Exodus 23:9). A Reflection of the Torah in the Face of New Nationalism and Xenophobia." In *Migrants and Refugees*, edited by Dietmar Meith and Lisa Sowle Cahill, 95–109. Maryknoll, NY: Orbis Books, 1993.

Cuming, G. J., ed. *The Mission of the Church and the Propagation of the Faith.* London: Cambridge University Press, 1970.

Curtin, Philip D. *Cross-Cultural Trade in World History.* Studies in Comparative World History. New York: Cambridge University Press, 1984.

———. *The World and the West: The European Challenge and the Overseas Response in the Age of Empire.* New York: Cambridge University Press, 2000.

Cusack, Carole M. "Pagan Saxon Resistance to Charlemagne's Mission: 'Indigenous' Religion and 'World' Religion in the Early Middle Ages." *Pomegranate* 13, no. 1 (2011): 33–51.

Cushing, Kathleen G. "Papal Authority and Its Limitations." In Arnold, *Oxford Handbook of Medieval Christianity*, 515–28.

Dales, Douglas. *Alcuin—Theology and Thought.* Cambridge: James Clarke, 2013.

———. *Light to the Isles: Mission and Theology in Celtic and Anglo-Saxon Britain.* Cambridge: James Clarke, 2010.

Davies, Philip R. "Exile? What Exile? Whose Exile?" In Grabbe, *Leading Captivity Captive*, 128–38.

Dawson, Christopher. *Mission to Asia.* Medieval Academy Reprints for Teaching. Toronto: University of Toronto Press, 1980.

Deeg, Max. "Ways to Go and Not to Go in the Contextualisation of the Jingjiao Documents of the Tang Period." In Winkler and Tang, *Hidden Treasures and Intercultural Encounters*, 135–52.

De La Torre, Miguel A. *Genesis.* Belief: A Theological Commentary on the Bible. Louisville: Westminster John Knox, 2011.

Demacopoulos, George. "Gregory the Great and the Pagan Shrines of Kent." *Journal of Late Antiquity* 1, no. 2 (Fall 2008): 353–69.

de Nicola, Bruno. *Women in Mongol Iran: The Khātūns, 1206–1335.* Edinburgh: Edinburgh University Press, 2017.

Dietz, Maribel. *Wandering Monks, Virgins, and Pilgrims: Ascetic Travel in the Mediterranean World, A.D. 300/800.* University Park: Pennsylvania State University Press, 2005.

Diner, Hasia R. "History and the Study of Immigration." In Brettell and Hollifield, *Migration Theory*, 27–42.

Dodgeon, Michael H., and Samuel N. C. Lieu, eds. *The Roman Eastern Frontier and the Persian Wars (AD 226–363): A Documentary History.* New York: Routledge, 1991.

Dorsey, David A. *The Roads and Highways of Ancient Israel.* The Asor Library of

Biblical and Near Eastern Archaeology. Baltimore: Johns Hopkins University Press, 1991.

Duckett, Eleanor Shipley. *Alcuin, Friend of Charlemagne*. New York: Macmillan, 1951.

———. "Saint Boniface; Saint Lull; Saint Leoba." In *The Wandering Saints of the Early Middle Ages*, edited by Eleanor Shipley Duckett, 193–228. New York: Norton, 1964.

Dunning, Benjamin H. *Aliens and Sojourners: Self as Other in Early Christianity*. Philadelphia: University of Pennsylvania Press, 2009.

———. "The Intersection of Alien Status and Cultic Discourse in the Epistle to the Hebrews." In *Hebrews*, edited by Gabriella Gelardini, 178–98. Boston: Brill, 2005.

Easton, M. G. *Baker's Illustrated Bible Dictionary*. Grand Rapids: Baker Book House, 1981.

Elliott, John Hall. *A Home for the Homeless: A Social-Scientific Criticism of 1 Peter, Its Situation and Strategy*. Eugene, OR: Wipf & Stock, 2005.

Ellwood, Robert S. *Many Peoples, Many Faiths: An Introduction to the Religious Life of Mankind*. Englewood Cliffs, NJ: Prentice-Hall, 1976.

———. *Readings on Religion: From Inside and Outside*. Englewood Cliffs, NJ: Prentice-Hall, 1978.

Emerton, Ephraim, trans. *The Letters of Saint Boniface*. New York: Norton, 1976.

England, John C. *The Hidden History of Christianity in Asia: The Churches of the East before the Year 1500*. Delhi, India: ISPCK, 2002.

Enslin, Morton S. "Irenaeus: Mostly Prolegomena." *Harvard Theological Review* 40, no. 3 (July 1947): 137–65.

Eusebius. *Life of Constantine*. Translated by Ernest Cushing Richardson. In *Nicene and Post-Nicene Fathers, Second Series*, vol. 1, edited by Philip Schaff and Henry Wace. Buffalo, NY: Christian Literature Publishing, 1890.

———. *Oration in Praise of Constantine*. Translated by Ernest Cushing Richardson. In *Nicene and Post-Nicene Fathers, Second Series*, vol. 1., edited by Philip Schaff and Henry Wace. Buffalo, NY: Christian Literature Publishing, 1890.

Evans, J. A. S. *The Age of Justinian: The Circumstances of Imperial Power*. New York: Routledge, 1996.

Fadda, Anna Maria L. "The Vernacular and the Propagation of the Faith in Anglo-

Saxon Missionary Activity." In *Missions and Missionaries*, edited by P. N. Holtrop and Hugh McLeod, 1–15. Rochester, NY: Boydell, 2000.

Fagan, Brian M. *The Journey from Eden: The Peopling of Our World*. New York: Thames & Hudson, 1990.

Farb, Peter. *The Land, Wildlife, and Peoples of the Bible*. New York: Harper & Row, 1967.

Fell, C. E. "Some Implications of the Boniface Correspondence." In *New Readings on Women in Old English Literature*, edited by Helen Damico and Alexandra Hennessey Olsen, 29–43. Bloomington: Indiana University Press, 1990.

Ferreira, Johan. *Early Chinese Christianity: The Tang Christian Monument and Other Documents*. Strathfield, New South Wales: St. Pauls Publications, 2014.

Findley, Carter V. *The Turks in World History*. New York: Oxford University Press, 2005.

Fisher, Humphrey J. "Conversion Reconsidered: Some Historical Aspects of Religious Conversion in Black Africa." *African Affairs* 43, no. 1 (1973): 27–40.

Fitzgerald, Mary Anne. *Ethiopia: The Living Churches of an Ancient Kingdom*. New York: American University in Cairo Press, 2017.

Fletcher, Richard. *The Barbarian Conversion: From Paganism to Christianity*. New York: Holt, 1997.

Flight, John W. "The Nomadic Idea and Ideal in the Old Testament." *Journal of Biblical Literature* 42, no. 3/4 (1923): 158–226.

Foltz, Richard. *Religions of the Silk Road: Premodern Patterns of Globalization*. New York: Palgrave Macmillan, 2010.

Foster, John. *The Church of the T'ang Dynasty*. London: SPCK, 1939.

———. "The Sailor's Share in the Spread of the Gospel." *Expository Times* 70, no. 4 (1959): 110–13.

Fowl, Stephen E. *Ephesians: A Commentary*. The New Testament Library. Louisville: Westminster John Knox, 2012.

———. "Texts Don't Have Ideologies." *Biblical Interpretation* 3, no. 1 (1995): 15–34.

Franck, Irene M., and David M. Brownstone. *The Silk Road: A History*. New York: Facts on File, 1986.

———. *To the Ends of the Earth: The Great Travel and Trade Routes of Human History*. New York: Facts on File, 1984.

Frank, Isnard Wilhelm. *A History of the Medieval Church.* Translated by John Bowden. London: SCM, 1995.

Frend, W. H. C. "The Missions of the Early Church, 180–700 A.D." *Miscellanea Historiae Ecclesiasticae* 3 (1970): 2–23.

Friedlander, María-José, and Bob Friedlander. *Hidden Treasures of Ethiopia: A Guide to the Remote Churches of an Ancient Land.* London: I. B. Tauris, 2015.

Fulcher de Chartres. *A History of the Expedition to Jerusalem, 1095–1127.* Translated by Frances Rita Ryan. Knoxville: University of Tennessee Press, 1969.

Gaposchkin, M. Cecilia. "From Pilgrimage to Crusade: The Liturgy of Departure, 1095–1300." *Speculum* 88, no. 1 (2013): 44–91.

Gibbon, Edward. *The History of the Decline and Fall of the Roman Empire.* London: A. Strahan & T. Cadell, 1789.

Gillman, Ian, and Hans-Joachim Klimkeit. *Christians in Asia before 1500.* Ann Arbor: University of Michigan Press, 1999.

Global Slavery Index. "Findings: Executive Summary." Accessed July 22, 2019. https://www.globalslaveryindex.org/2018/findings/executive-summary/.

Goffart, Walter A. *Barbarian Tides: The Migration Age and the Later Roman Empire.* Philadelphia: University of Pennsylvania Press, 2006.

Goldin, Ian, Geoffrey Cameron, and Meera Balarajan. *Exceptional People: How Migration Shaped Our World and Will Define Our Future.* Princeton: Princeton University Press, 2011.

Goldingay, John. "The Patriarchs in Scripture and History." In Long, *Israel's Past in Present Research*, 485–91.

Goodpasture, H. McKennie. *Cross and Sword: An Eyewitness History of Christianity in Latin America.* Maryknoll, NY: Orbis Books, 1989.

Gosch, Stephen S., and Peter N. Stearns. *Premodern Travel in World History.* New York: Routledge, 2008.

Grabbe, Lester L., ed. *Leading Captivity Captive: "The Exile" as History and Ideology.* Sheffield: Sheffield Academic, 1998.

Grant, Robert M. *Early Christianity and Society: Seven Studies.* San Francisco: Harper & Row, 1977.

———. *Irenaeus of Lyons.* The Early Church Fathers. New York: Routledge, 1997.

Gray, G. Francis S. "The Spread of Christianity in Asia (in Early Christian Period)." *International Review of Mission* 42, no. 167 (1953): 266–74.

Green, Nancy L. "The Comparative Method and Poststructural Structuralisms:

New Perspectives for Migration Studies." In Lucassen, Lucassen, and Manning, *Migration, Migration History, History*, 57–72.

Gregory of Tours. *The History of the Franks*. Translated with an introduction by Lewis Thorpe. Baltimore: Penguin, 1974.

Haas, Christopher. "Mountain Constantines: The Christianization of Aksum and Iberia." *Journal of Late Antiquity* 1, no. 1 (Spring 2008): 101–26.

Hallo, William W. "Biblical History in Its Near Eastern Setting: The Contextual Approach." In Long, *Israel's Past in Present Research*, 77–97.

———. "The Limits of Skepticism." *Journal of the American Oriental Society* 110, no. 2 (April–June 1990): 187–99.

Hamilton, Bernard. "The Impact of the Crusades on Western Geographical Knowledge." In *Eastward Bound: Travel and Travellers, 1050–1550*, edited by Rosamund Allen, 15–34. New York: Manchester University Press, 2004.

Hanciles, Jehu J. *Beyond Christendom: Globalization, African Migration, and the Transformation of the West*. Maryknoll, NY: Orbis Books, 2008.

———. "New Wine in Old Wineskins: Critical Reflections on Writing and Teaching a Global Christian History." *Missiology: An International Review* 35 (July 2006): 361–82.

Harnack, Adolf von. *The Mission and Expansion of Christianity in the First Three Centuries*. Harper Torchbooks. New York: Harper, 1962.

Harvey, Graham. Introduction to Harvey, *Indigenous Religions: A Companion*, 1–19.

———, ed. *Indigenous Religions: A Companion*. New York: Cassell, 2000.

Harzig, Christiane, Dirk Hoerder, and Donna R. Gabaccia. *What Is Migration History?* Malden, MA: Polity, 2009.

Haywood, John. *The Celts: Bronze Age to New Age*. London: Routledge, 2004.

———. *The Great Migrations: From the Earliest Humans to the Age of Globalization*. London: Quercus, 2008.

Heather, P. J., and John Matthews. *The Goths in the Fourth Century*. Translated Texts for Historians. Liverpool: Liverpool University Press, 1991.

Heather, Peter. "The Crossing of the Danube and the Gothic Conversion." *Greek, Roman and Byzantine Studies* 27, no. 3 (1986): 289–318.

Hefner, Robert W. *Conversion to Christianity: Historical and Anthropological Perspectives on a Great Transformation*. Berkeley: University of California Press, 1993.

Heil, Uta. "The Homoians." In Berndt and Steinacher, *Arianism*, 85–116.

Held, David, Anthony McGrew, David Goldblatt, and Jonathan Perraton. *Global Transformations: Politics, Economics and Culture*. Stanford, CA: Stanford University Press, 1999.

Hen, Yitzhak. "Charlemagne's Jihad." *Viator* 37, no. 1 (2006): 33–51.

Hermansen, Marcia. "Conversion to Islam in Theological and Historical Perspectives." In Rambo and Farhadian, *The Oxford Handbook of Religious Conversion*, 632–66.

Herodotus. *The Histories*. Translated by Aubrey de Sélincourt. Baltimore: Penguin Books, 1954.

Herppich, Birgit. *Pitfalls of Trained Incapacity: The Unintended Effects of Integral Missionary Training in the Basel Mission on Its Early Work in Ghana (1828–1840)*. American Society of Missiology Monograph Series. Eugene, OR: Pickwick, 2016.

Herrin, Judith. *Unrivalled Influence: Women and Empire in Byzantium*. Princeton: Princeton University Press, 2013.

Hiebert, Theodore. "The Tower of Babel and the Origin of the World's Cultures." *Journal of Biblical Literature* 126, no. 1 (2007): 29–58.

Hillgarth, J. N. *Christianity and Paganism, 350–750: The Conversion of Western Europe*. Rev. ed. The Middle Ages. Philadelphia: University of Pennsylvania Press, 1986.

Hitchcock, F. R. Montgomery. *Irenaeus of Lugdunum: A Study of His Teaching*. Cambridge: Cambridge University Press, 1914.

Hodge, Caroline E. Johnson. "Apostle to the Gentiles: Constructions of Paul's Identity." *Biblical Interpretation* 13, no. 3 (2005): 270–88.

Hoehner, Harold W. *Ephesians: An Exegetical Commentary*. Grand Rapids: Baker Academic, 2002.

Hoffmeier, James K. *The Immigration Crisis: Immigrants, Aliens and the Bible*. Wheaton, IL: Crossway, 2009.

———. *Israel in Egypt: The Evidence for the Authenticity of the Exodus Tradition*. New York: Oxford University Press, 1997.

Hopkins, A. G. "Back to the Future: From National History to Imperial History." *Past and Present*, no. 164 (1999): 198–243.

Horner, Thomas M. "Changing Concepts of the 'Stranger' in the Old Testament." *Anglican Theological Review* 42, no. 1 (1960): 49–53.

Horton, Robin. "African Conversion." *African Affairs* 41, no. 2 (1971): 85–108.

Houten, Christiana van. *The Alien in Israelite Law*. Sheffield: Sheffield Academic, 1991.

Howard, Michael C. *Transnationalism in Ancient and Medieval Societies: The Role of Cross-Border Trade and Travel*. Jefferson, NC: McFarland, 2012.

Hughes, Kathleen. *The Church in Early Irish Society*. Ithaca, NY: Cornell University Press, 1966.

Humphreys, Colin J. "The Number of People in the Exodus from Egypt: Decoding Mathematically the Very Large Numbers in Numbers I and XXVI." *Vetus Testamentum* 48, no. 2 (1998): 196–213.

———. "The Numbers in the Exodus from Egypt: A Further Appraisal." *Vetus Testamentum* 50, no. 3 (2000): 323–28.

Humphreys, W. Lee. "A Life-Style for Diaspora: A Study of the Tales of Esther and Daniel." *Journal of Biblical Literature* 92, no. 2 (1973): 211–23.

Hunter, Erica C. D. "The Church of the East in Central Asia." *Bulletin of the John Rylands Library* 78, no. 3 (1996): 129–42.

Hvalvik, Reidar. "In Word and Deed: The Expansion of the Church in the Pre-Constantinian Era." In *Mission of the Early Church to Jews and Gentiles*, edited by Jostein Ådna and Hans Kvalbein, 265–87. Tübingen: Mohr Siebeck, 2000.

Hyde, Walter Woodburn. *Paganism to Christianity in the Roman Empire*. Philadelphia: University of Pennsylvania Press, 1946.

Hyland, H. P. "Missionary Nuns and the Monastic Vocation in Anglo-Saxon England." *American Benedictine Review* 47 (1996): 141–74.

Ignat, Adrian. "The Spread out of Arianism: A Critical Analysis of the Arian Heresy." *International Journal of Orthodox Theology* 3, no. 3 (2012): 105–28.

Irenaeus. *Against Heresies*. Translated by Alexander Roberts and William Rambaut. In *Ante-Nicene Fathers*, vol. 1, edited by Alexander Roberts, James Donaldson, and A. Cleveland Coxe. Buffalo, NY: Christian Literature Publishing, 1885.

Irvin, Dale T. "World Christianity: An Introduction." *Journal of World Christianity* 1, no. 1 (2008): 1–26.

Irvin, Dale T., and Scott Sunquist. *History of the World Christian Movement*. Vol. 1, *Earliest Christianity to 1453*. Maryknoll, NY: Orbis Books, 2001.

Isbister, John. *Promises Not Kept: The Betrayal of Social Change in the Third World*. 5th ed. Bloomfield, CT: Kumarian, 2001.

Isichei, Elizabeth A. *A History of Christianity in Africa: From Antiquity to the Present.* London: SPCK, 1995.

Israeli, Raphael. *Green Crescent over Nazareth: The Displacement of Christians by Muslims in the Holy Land.* London: Frank Cass, 2002.

Janin, Hunt. "'A Pilgrimage in Arms': The First Crusade and Its Aftermath." In *Four Paths to Jerusalem: Jewish, Christian, Muslim, and Secular Pilgrimages, 1000 BCE to 2001 CE*, 86–109. Jefferson, NC: McFarland, 2002.

Jastrow, Morris. *The Study of Religion.* Classics in Religious Studies Series of Scholars Press and the American Academy of Religion. Chico, CA: Scholars Press, 1981.

Jenkins, Philip. *The Lost History of Christianity: The Thousand-Year Golden Age of the Church in the Middle East, Africa, and Asia—and How It Died.* New York: HarperOne, 2008.

———. *The Next Christendom: The Coming of Global Christianity.* Oxford: Oxford University Press, 2011.

Johnson, Sherman E. "Antioch, the Base of Operations." *Lexington Theological Quarterly* 18, no. 2 (1983): 64–73.

Johnson, Todd M., and Kenneth R. Ross, eds. *Atlas of Global Christianity 1910–2010.* Edinburgh: Edinburgh University Press, 2009.

Johnsson, William G. "Pilgrimage Motif in the Book of Hebrews." *Journal of Biblical Literature* 97, no. 2 (1978): 239–51.

Juergensmeyer, Mark. "Thinking Globally about Religion." In *The Oxford Handbook of Global Religions*, edited by Mark Juergensmeyer, 3–12. New York: Oxford University Press, 2006.

Kalu, Ogbu. "Introduction: The Shape and Flow of African Christian Historiography." In *African Christianity: An African Story*, edited by Ogbu Kalu, 3–22. Trenton, NJ: Africa World Press, 2007.

Kedar, B. Z. *Crusade and Mission: European Approaches toward the Muslims.* Princeton: Princeton University Press, 1984.

Kelle, Brad E., Frank Ritchel Ames, and Jacob L. Wright, eds. *Interpreting Exile: Displacement and Deportation in Biblical and Modern Contexts.* Atlanta: Society of Biblical Literature, 2011.

Kelly, Christopher. *The Roman Empire: A Very Short Introduction.* New York: Oxford University Press, 2006.

King, Russell. *Atlas of Human Migration.* Buffalo, NY: Firefly Books, 2007.

Kitagawa, Joseph Mitsuo. *The History of Religions: Understanding Human Experience.* Atlanta: Scholars Press, 1987.

Kitchen, K. A. *On the Reliability of the Old Testament.* Grand Rapids: Eerdmans, 2003.

Kling, David W. "Conversion to Christianity." In Rambo and Farhadian, *The Oxford Handbook of Religious Conversion,* 598–631.

Koenig, John. *New Testament Hospitality: Partnership with Strangers as Promise and Mission.* Eugene, OR: Wipf & Stock, 2001.

Kollman, Paul V. "Understanding the World-Christian Turn in the History of Christianity and Theology." *Theology Today* 71, no. 2 (2014): 164–77.

Koschorke, Klaus. "New Maps of the History of World Christianity: Current Challenges and Future Perspectives." *Theology Today* 71, no. 2 (2014): 178–91.

———. "Transcontinental Links, Enlarged Maps, and Polycentric Structures in the History of World Christianity." *Journal of World Christianity* 6, no. 1 (2016): 28–56.

Koslowski, Rey. "Human Migration and the Conceptualization of Pre-Modern World Politics." *International Studies Quarterly* 46, no. 3 (2002): 375–99.

Koziol, Geoffrey. "Christianizing Political Discourses." In Arnold, *Oxford Handbook of Medieval Christianity,* 473–89.

Lacocque, André. *The Captivity of Innocence: Babel and the Yahwist.* Eugene, OR: Cascade, 2010.

———. "The Stranger in the Old Testament." In *The Newcomer and the Bible,* edited by André Lacocque and Francisco Ruiz Vasquez, 9–16. Staten Island, NY: Center for Migration Studies, 1971.

Lampe, Peter. "Early Christians in the City of Rome: Topographical and Social Historical Aspects of the First Three Centuries." In *Christians as a Religious Minority in a Multicultural City: Modes of Interaction and Identity Formation in Early Imperial Rome,* edited by Jürgen Zangenberg and Michael Labahn, 20–32. London: Continuum, 2004.

La Piana, George. "Foreign Groups in Rome during the First Centuries of the Empire." *Harvard Theological Review* 20, no. 4 (October 1927): 183–403.

———. "The Roman Church at the End of the Second Century: The Episcopate of Victor, the Latinization of the Roman Church, the Easter Controversy, Consolidation of Power and Doctrinal Development, the Catacomb of Callistus." *Harvard Theological Review* 18, no. 3 (1925): 201–77.

Latourette, Kenneth Scott. *A History of the Expansion of Christianity*. Vol. 1, *The First Five Centuries*. Grand Rapids: Zondervan, 1970.

———. *A History of the Expansion of Christianity*. Vol. 2, *The Thousand Years of Uncertainty, A.D. 500–A.D. 1500*. Grand Rapids: Zondervan, 1970.

Lee, A. D. *Information and Frontiers: Roman Foreign Relations in Late Antiquity*. New York: Cambridge University Press, 2006.

Le Goff, Jacques. *Medieval Civilization, 400–1500*. New York: Blackwell, 1988.

Lenchak, Timothy. "Israel's Refugee Ancestors." *Bible Today* 35, no. 1 (January 1997): 10–15.

Levathes, Louise. *When China Ruled the Seas: The Treasure Fleet of the Dragon Throne, 1405–1433*. New York: Oxford University Press, 1996.

Levison, John R., and Priscilla Pope-Levison, eds. *Return to Babel: Global Perspectives on the Bible*. Louisville: Westminster John Knox, 1999.

Levtzion, Nehemia. "Conversion to Islam in Syria and Palestine and the Survival of Christian Communities." In *Conversion and Continuity: Indigenous Christian Communities in Islamic Lands, Eighth to Eighteenth Centuries*, edited by Michael Gervers and Ramzi Jibran Bikhazi, 289–311. Toronto: Pontifical Institute of Mediaeval Studies, 1990.

Liu, Xinru. *The Silk Road in World History*. The New Oxford World History. New York: Oxford University Press, 2010.

Long, V. Philips, ed. *Israel's Past in Present Research: Essays on Ancient Israelite Historiography*. Winona Lake, IN: Eisenbrauns, 1999.

Lower, Michael. "Christian Mercenaries in Muslim Lands: Their Status in Medieval Islamic and Canon Law." In Boas, *The Crusader World*, 383–95.

Lucassen, Jan, Leo Lucassen, and Patrick Manning. "Migration History: Multidisciplinary Approaches." In *Migration History in World History: Multidisciplinary Approaches*, edited by Jan Lucassen, Leo Lucassen, and Patrick Manning, 3–35. Boston: Brill, 2010.

———, eds. *Migration, Migration History, History: Old Paradigms and New Perspectives*. New York: Lang, 1997.

MacMullen, Ramsay. *Christianity and Paganism in the Fourth to Eighth Centuries*. New Haven: Yale University Press, 1997.

———. *Christianizing the Roman Empire: A.D. 100–400*. New Haven: Yale University Press, 1984.

MacRaild, Donald M., and Avram Taylor. *Social Theory and Social History*. New York: Palgrave Macmillan, 2004.

Manning, Patrick. *Migration in World History*. Themes in World History. New York: Routledge, 2005.

Marcus, Harold G. *A History of Ethiopia*. Berkeley: University of California Press, 1994.

Markus, R. A. "Gregory the Great and a Papal Missionary Strategy." In Cuming, *The Mission of the Church and the Propagation of the Faith*, 29–44.

———. "Gregory the Great's Pagans." In *Belief and Culture in the Middle Ages*, edited by Richard Gameson and Henrietta Leyser, 23–34. New York: Oxford University Press, 2001.

Masci, David. "An Uncertain Road: Muslims and the Future of Europe." The Pew Research Center. October 19, 2005. https://assets.pewresearch.org/wp-content/uploads/sites/11/2005/10/muslims-europe-2005.pdf.

Masud, Muhammed Khalid. "The Obligation to Migrate: The Doctrine of *Hijra* in Islamic Law." In *Muslim Travellers: Pilgrimage, Migration, and the Religious Imagination*, edited by Dale F. Eickelman and James P. Piscatori, 29–49. London: Routledge, 1990.

Masuzawa, Tomoko. *The Invention of World Religions, or, How European Universalism Was Preserved in the Language of Pluralism*. Chicago: University of Chicago Press, 2005.

Mathisen, Ralph W. "Catalogues of Barbarians in Late Antiquity." In Mathisen and Shanzer, *Romans, Barbarians, and the Transformation of the Roman World*, 17–32.

Mathisen, Ralph W., and Danuta Shanzer, eds. *Romans, Barbarians, and the Transformation of the Roman World: Cultural Interaction and the Creation of Identity in Late Antiquity*. Burlington, VT: Ashgate, 2011.

Mayr-Harting, Henry. *The Coming of Christianity to Anglo-Saxon England*. 3rd ed. London: B. T. Batsford, 1991.

McComiskey, Douglas S. "Exile and Restoration from Exile in the Scriptural Quotations and Allusions of Jesus." *Journal of the Evangelical Theological Society* 53, no. 4 (2010): 673–96.

———. "Exile and the Purpose of Jesus' Parables (Mark 4:10–12; Matt 13:10–17; Luke 8:9–10)." *Journal of the Evangelical Theological Society* 51, no. 1 (2008): 59–85.

McKitterick, Rosamond. *Charlemagne: The Formation of a European Identity*. New York: Cambridge University Press, 2008.

McNamara, Jo Ann. "Living Sermons: Consecrated Women and the Conversion of Gaul." In *Medieval Religious Women: Peaceweavers*, edited by Lillian Thomas Shank and John A. Nichols, 19–37. Kalamazoo, MI: Cistercian Publications, 1987.

McNamara, Jo Ann, John E. Halborg, and E. Gordon Whatley. *Sainted Women of the Dark Ages*. Durham, NC: Duke University Press, 1992.

McNamara, Jo Ann, and Suzanne Wemple. "The Power of Women through the Family in Medieval Europe, 500–1100." In *Women and Power in the Middle Ages*, edited by Mary Carpenter Erler and Maryanne Kowaleski, 83–101. Athens, GA: University of Georgia Press, 1988.

McNeill, William H. "Human Migration in Historical Perspective." *Population and Development Review* 10, no. 1 (March 1984): 1–18.

Mertaniemi, Markus. "From *Superstitio* to *Religio Christiana*: Christians as Others from the Third to the Fifth Century." In *The Faces of the Other: Religious Rivalry and Ethnic Encounters in the Later Roman World*, edited by Maijastina Kahlos, 135–64. Turnhout: Brepols, 2011.

Míguez-Bonino, José. "Genesis 11:1–9: A Latin-American Perspective." In Levison and Pope-Levison, *Return to Babel*, 13–16.

Millard, A. R. "Israelite and Aramean History in the Light of Inscriptions." In Long, *Israel's Past in Present Research*, 129–40.

———. "Where Was Abraham's Ur? The Case for the Babylonian City." *Biblical Archaeology Review* 27, no. 3 (May/June 2001): 52–57.

Mingana, Alphonse. *The Early Spread of Christianity in Central Asia and the Far East: A New Document*. Manchester: University Press, 1925.

Minorsky, V. "Tamīm Ibn Baḥr's Journey to the Uyghurs." *Bulletin of the School of Oriental and African Studies, University of London* 12, no. 2 (1948): 275–305.

Moch, Leslie Page. "Dividing Time: An Analytical Framework for Migration History Periodization." In Lucassen, Lucassen, and Manning, *Migration, Migration History, History*, 41–56.

Moffett, Samuel H. *A History of Christianity in Asia: Beginnings to 1500*. Vol. 1. Maryknoll, NY: Orbis Books, 1998.

Montgomery, James A., trans. *The History of Yaballaha*. New York: Columbia University Press, 1927.

Montgomery, Robert L. "Conversion and the Historic Spread of Religions." In Rambo and Farhadian, *The Oxford Handbook of Religious Conversion*, 164–89.

Mooken, Aprem Mar. "Reference to China in Syriac Sources." In Winkler and Tang, *Hidden Treasures and Intercultural Encounters*, 183–93.

Moosa, Matti. *The Crusades: Conflict between Christendom and Islam.* Publications of the Archdiocese of the Syrian Orthodox Church in the Eastern United States 5. Piscataway, NJ: Gorgias, 2008.

Murphy-O'Connor, Jerome. "Traveling Conditions in the First Century: On the Road and on the Sea with St. Paul." *Bible Review* 1, no. 2 (1985): 38–45.

Murray, Alan V. "Franks and Indigenous Communities in Palestine and Syria (1099–1187): A Hierarchical Model of Social Interaction in the Principalities of Outremer." In *East Meets West in the Middle Ages and Early Modern Times: Transcultural Experiences in the Premodern World*, edited by Albrecht Classen, 291–301. Boston: de Gruyter, 2013.

Murray, Robert. *Symbols of Church and Kingdom: A Study in Early Syriac Tradition.* Piscataway, NJ: Gorgias, 2004.

Neil, Bronwen. "The Papacy in the Age of Gregory the Great." In *A Companion to Gregory the Great*, edited by Bronwen Neil and Matthew Dal Santo, 3–28. Boston: Brill, 2013.

Nicholson, Helen J. "Women's Involvement in the Crusades." In Boas, *The Crusader World*, 54–67.

Nock, Arthur Darby. *Conversion: The Old and the New in Religion from Alexander the Great to Augustine of Hippo.* Oxford: Clarendon, 1933.

Northrup, David. *Africa's Discovery of Europe, 1450–1850.* 3rd ed. New York: Oxford University Press, 2014.

Noy, David. *Foreigners at Rome: Citizens and Strangers.* London: Duckworth, 2000.

O'Hara, Alexander. "*Patria, Peregrinatio*, and *Paenitentia*: Identities of Alienation in the Seventh Century." In *Post-Roman Transitions: Christian and Barbarian Identities in the Early Medieval West*, edited by Walter Pohl and Gerda Heydemann, 89–124. Turnhout: Brepols, 2013.

Ohler, Norbert. *The Medieval Traveller.* New ed. Woodbridge: Boydell, 1997.

Okorocha, Cyril C. "Religious Conversion in Africa: Its Missiological Implications." *Mission Studies* 9, no. 18 (1992): 168–80.

O'Leary, De Lacy. *The Syriac Church and Fathers.* Piscataway, NJ: Gorgias, 2002.

Oliver, Roland A. *The African Experience.* London: Pimlico, 1994.

O'Loughlin, Thomas. "The Missionary Strategy of the *Didache*." *Transformation* 28, no. 22 (2011): 77–92.

O'Reilly, Karen. *International Migration and Social Theory.* New York: Palgrave Macmillan, 2012.

Origen. *Against Celsus.* Translated by Frederick Crombie. In *Ante-Nicene Fathers*, vol. 4, edited by Alexander Roberts, James Donaldson, and A. Cleveland Coxe. Buffalo, NY: Christian Literature Publishing, 1885.

Padilla, C. René. "Hermeneutics and Culture—a Theological Perspective." In *Down to Earth: Studies in Christianity and Culture*, edited by Robert T. Coote and John R. W. Stott, 63–78. Grand Rapids: Eerdmans, 1980.

Pahlitzsch, Johannes, and Daniel Baraz. "Christian Communities in the Latin Kingdom of Jerusalem (1099–1187 CE)." In *Christians and Christianity in the Holy Land: From the Origins to the Latin Kingdoms*, 205–35. Turnhout: Brepols, 2006.

Parvis, Paul. "Who Was Irenaeus? An Introduction to the Man and His Work." In Parvis and Foster, *Irenaeus: Life, Scripture, Legacy*, 13–24.

Parvis, Sara. "Was Ulfila Really a Homoian?" In Berndt and Steinacher, *Arianism*, 49–65.

Parvis, Sara, and Paul Foster, eds. *Irenaeus: Life, Scripture, Legacy.* Minneapolis: Fortress, 2012.

Patrick. *The Confession of St. Patrick.* Translated by John Skinner. New York: Image, 1998.

Payne, Richard E. *A State of Mixture: Christians, Zoroastrians, and Iranian Political Culture in Late Antiquity.* Transformation of the Classical Heritage. Oakland: University of California Press, 2015.

Périn, Patrick, and Michel Kazanski. "Identity and Ethnicity During the Era of Migrations and Barbarian Kingdoms in the Light of Archaeology in Gaul." In Mathisen and Shanzer, *Romans, Barbarians, and the Transformation of the Roman World*, 299–329.

Phan, Peter C. "Migration in the Patristic Era." In *A Promised Land, a Perilous Journey: Theological Perspectives on Migration*, edited by Daniel G. Groody and Gioacchino Campese, 35–61. Notre Dame: University of Notre Dame Press, 2008.

Phillips, Seymour. "The Medieval Background." In *Europeans on the Move: Studies on European Migration, 1500–1800*, edited by Nicholas P. Canny, 9–25. New York: Oxford University Press, 1994.

Phillipson, D. W. *Ancient Churches of Ethiopia: Fourth–Fourteenth Centuries.* New Haven: Yale University Press, 2009.

Photius. *Epitome of the Ecclesiastical History of Philostorgius, Compiled by Photius, Patriarch of Constantinople.* Translated by Edward Walford. London: Henry G. Bonn, 1855.

Pitard, Wayne T. "Before Israel: Syria-Palestine in the Bronze Age." In Coogan, *The Oxford History of the Biblical World,* 33–77.

Polo, Marco. *The Book of Ser Marco Polo, the Venetian: Concerning the Kingdoms and Marvels of the East.* Translated by Henry Yule. London: Murray, 1871.

Pomper, Philip. "The History and Theory of Empires." *History and Theory* 44, no. 4 (2005): 1–27.

Prill, Thorsten. "Migration, Mission and the Multi-Ethnic Church." *Evangelical Review of Theology* 33, no. 4 (2009): 332–46.

Provan, Iain W. "Ideologies, Literary and Critical: Reflections on Recent Writing on the History of Israel." *Journal of Biblical Literature* 114, no. 4 (1995): 585–606.

Provan, Iain W., V. Philips Long, and Tremper Longman. *A Biblical History of Israel.* Louisville: Westminster John Knox, 2003.

Rambo, Lewis R. *Understanding Religious Conversion.* New Haven: Yale University Press, 1993.

Rambo, Lewis R., and Charles E. Farhadian, eds. Introduction to Rambo and Farhadian, *The Oxford Handbook of Religious Conversion,* 1–22.

Rambo, Lewis R., and Charles E. Farhadian, eds. *The Oxford Handbook of Religious Conversion.* New York: Oxford University Press, 2014.

Ramírez Kidd, José E. *Alterity and Identity in Israel: The גר in the Old Testament.* New York: de Gruyter, 1999.

Ramsay, William M. *St. Paul: The Traveler and Roman Citizen.* Rev. and updated ed. Grand Rapids: Kregel, 2001.

Redmount, Carol A. "Bitter Lives: Israel in and out of Egypt." In Coogan, *The Oxford History of the Biblical World,* 79–121.

Rendtorff, Rolf. "The Paradigm Is Changing: Hopes—and Fears." In Long, *Israel's Past in Present Research,* 51–68.

Richmond, Anthony H. "Sociological Theories of International Migration: The Case of Refugees." *Current Sociology* 36, no. 2 (June 1, 1988): 7–25.

Robert, Dana L. *Christian Mission: How Christianity Became a World Religion.* Blackwell Brief Histories of Religion Series. Malden, MA: Wiley-Blackwell, 2009.

————. "Shifting Southward: Global Christianity Since 1945." *International Bulletin of Missionary Research* 24 (April 2000): 50–58.

Rogers, Francis M. *The Quest for Eastern Christians*. Minneapolis: University of Minnesota Press, 1962.

Rowe, Mary Ellen. "Leoba's Purple Thread: The Women of the Boniface Mission." *Magistra* 17, no. 2 (Winter 2011): 3–20.

Rufinus of Aquileia. *History of the Church*. Translated by Philip R. Amidon. Washington, DC: Catholic University of America Press, 2016.

Ruiz, Jean-Pierre. *Readings from the Edges: The Bible and People on the Move*. Maryknoll, NY: Orbis Books, 2011.

Russell, James C. *The Germanization of Early Medieval Christianity: A Sociohistorical Approach to Religious Transformation*. New York: Oxford University Press, 1994.

Ryan, James D. "Christian Wives of Mongol Khans: Tartar Queens and Missionary Expectations in Asia." *Journal of the Royal Asiatic Society* 8, no. 3 (1988): 411–21.

————. "To Baptize Khans or to Convert Peoples? Missionary Aims in Central Asia in the Fourteenth Century." In *Christianizing Peoples and Converting Individuals*, edited by I. N. Wood and Guyda Armstrong, 247–57. Turnhout: Brepols, 2000.

Saeki, Yoshirō. *The Nestorian Documents and Relics in China*. Tokyo: The Toho bunkwa gakuin: The Academy of Oriental Culture, 1937.

————. *The Nestorian Monument in China*. London: SPCK, 1916.

Saint-Laurent, Jeanne-Nicole Mellon. *Missionary Stories and the Formation of the Syriac Churches*. Transformation of the Classical Heritage. Oakland: University of California Press, 2015.

Samuel, Raphael, Keith Hopkins, John Breuilly, Joyce Youings, David Canadine, Royden Harrison, and J. C. D. Clark. "What Is Social History?" *History Today* 35, no. 3 (1985): 34–44.

Sanders, Jack T. "Conversion in Early Christianity." In Blasi, Turcotte, and Duhaime, *Handbook of Early Christianity*, 619–41.

Sandgren, Leo Duprée. *Vines Intertwined: A History of Jews and Christians from the Babylonian Exile to the Advent of Islam*. Peabody, MA: Hendrickson, 2010.

Sanjek, Roger. "Rethinking Migration, Ancient to Future." *Global Networks* 3, no. 3 (2003): 315–36.

Sanneh, Lamin. *Translating the Message: The Missionary Impact on Culture.* 2nd ed. Maryknoll, NY: Orbis Books, 2009.

———. *Whose Religion Is Christianity? The Gospel beyond the West.* Grand Rapids: Eerdmans, 2003.

———. "World Christianity and the New Historiography: History and Global Connections." In Shenk, *Enlarging the Story,* 94–114.

———, ed. *Disciples of All Nations: Pillars of World Christianity.* New York: Oxford University Press, 2008.

Sarna, Nahum M. "Exploring Exodus: The Oppression." *Biblical Archaeologist* 49, no. 2 (June 1986): 68–80.

Savoia-Vizzini, Gianpaolo. "Iranian History: The Sasanian Dynasty." *The Circle of Ancient Iranian Studies* (2000). http://www.cais-soas.com/CAIS/History/Sasanian/sasanid.htm.

Schäferdiek, Knut. "Ulfila and the So-Called 'Gothic' Arianism—English Summary." In Berndt and Steinacher, *Arianism,* 45–48.

Schaff, Philip, and Henry Wace, eds. *A Select Library of Nicene and Post-Nicene Fathers of the Christian Church.* Vol. 14. New York: Scribner's Sons, 1900.

Schniedewind, William M. *How the Bible Became a Book: The Textualization of Ancient Israel.* New York: Cambridge University Press, 2004.

Scott, Charles Archibald Anderson. *Ulfilas, Apostle of the Goths, Together with an Account of the Gothic Churches and Their Decline.* Cambridge: Macmillan and Bowes, 1885.

Secord, Jared. "The Cultural Geography of a Greek Christian: Irenaeus from Smyrna to Lyons." In Parvis and Foster, *Irenaeus: Life, Scripture, Legacy,* 25–33.

Sharp, Carolyn J. "Sites of Conflict: Textual Engagements of Dislocation and Diaspora in the Hebrew Bible." In Kelle, Ames, and Wright, *Interpreting Exile,* 365–76.

Shenk, Wilbert R. *Enlarging the Story: Perspectives on Writing World Christian History.* Maryknoll, NY: Orbis Books, 2002.

———. "Toward a Global Church History." *International Bulletin of Missionary Research* 20 (April 1996): 50–57.

Smart, Ninian. *The Religious Experience.* 4th ed. New York: Macmillan, 1991.

Smith, Daniel L. *The Religion of the Landless: The Social Context of the Babylonian Exile.* Bloomington, IN: Meyer-Stone Books, 1989.

Smith, Richard L. *Premodern Trade in World History*. Themes in World History. New York: Routledge, 2008.

Smith, Timothy L. "Religion and Ethnicity in America." *American Historical Review* 83, no. 5 (December 1978): 1155–85.

Smith-Christopher, Daniel L. *A Biblical Theology of Exile*. Minneapolis: Fortress, 2002.

Smither, Edward L. *Gregory the Great and Augustine of Canterbury*. Eugene, OR: Cascade Books, 2016.

———. *Missionary Monks: An Introduction to the History and Theology of Missionary Monasticism*. Eugene, OR: Cascade Books, 2016.

Snorrason, Oddr. *The Saga of Olaf Tryggvason*. Translated by Theodore M. Andersson. Ithaca, NY: Cornell University Press, 2003.

Snow, Dean R. "The Multidisciplinary Study of Human Migration: Problems and Principles." In *Ancient Human Migrations: A Multidisciplinary Approach*, edited by Peter N. Peregrine, Ilia Peiros, and Marcus W. Feldman, 6–20. Salt Lake City: University of Utah Press, 2009.

Soggin, J. Alberto. "History as Confession of Faith—History as Object of Scholarly Research." In Long, *Israel's Past in Present Research*, 207–19.

Somerville, Angus A., and R. Andrew McDonald, eds. *The Viking Age: A Reader*. 2nd ed. North York: University of Toronto Press, 2014.

Song, Choan-Seng. "Genesis 11:1–9: An Asian Perspective." In Levison and Pope-Levison, *Return to Babel*, 27–33.

Southern, R. W. *Western Society and the Church in the Middle Ages*. Harmondsworth: Penguin, 1990.

Spina, Frank Anthony. "Israelites as Gērîm, 'Sojourners,' in Social and Historical Context." In *The Word of the Lord Shall Go Forth*, edited by Carol L. Meyers, Michael Patrick O'Connor, and David Noel Freedman, 321–35. Winona Lake, IN: Eisenbrauns, 1983.

Stafford, Pauline. *Queens, Concubines, and Dowagers: The King's Wife in the Early Middle Ages*. Athens, GA: University of Georgia Press, 1983.

Staniforth, Maxwell, trans. "Epistle to Diognetus." In *Early Christian Writings: The Apostolic Fathers*, revised and edited by Andrew Louth, 137–51. New York: Penguin Books, 1987.

Stanley, Brian. *The Bible and the Flag: Protestant Missions and British Imperialism in the Nineteenth and Twentieth Centuries*. Leicester: Apollos, 1990.

————. "Conversion to Christianity: The Colonization of the Mind?" *International Review of Mission* 92, no. 366 (2003): 315–331.

Stark, Rodney. *The Rise of Christianity*. San Francisco: HarperSanFrancisco, 1997.

————. "Why Religious Movements Succeed or Fail: A Revised General Model." *Journal of Mormon History* 11, no. 2 (1996): 133–46.

————. "Why the Jehovah's Witnesses Grow So Rapidly: A Theoretical Application." *Journal of Contemporary Religion* 12, no. 2 (May 1997): 133–57.

Stearns, Peter N. "Social History and History: A Progress Report." *Journal of Social History* 19, no. 2 (Winter 1985): 319–34.

Stern, Edna J. "Maritime Commerce in the Latin East as Reflected in the Import of Ceramics." In Boas, *The Crusader World*, 474–96.

Stewart, John. *Nestorian Missionary Enterprise: The Story of a Church on Fire*. Trichur, India: Mar Narsai Press, 1961.

Strauss, Steve. "Creeds, Confessions, and Global Theologizing: A Case Study of Comparative Christologies." In *Globalizing Theology: Belief and Practice in an Era of World Christianity*, edited by Craig Ott and Harold A. Netland, 140–56. Nottingham: Apollos, 2007.

Sullivan, Richard E. *Christian Missionary Activity in the Early Middle Ages*. Brookfield, VT: Variorum, 1994.

————. "Early Medieval Missionary Activity: A Comparative Study of Eastern and Western Methods." *Church History* 23, no. 1 (1954): 17–35.

Sunquist, Scott. "Narsai and the Persians: A Study in Cultural Contact and Conflict." PhD diss., Princeton Theological Seminary, 1990. Ann Arbor: UMI Dissertation Services.

Syrdal, Rolf A. *To the End of the Earth: Mission Concept in Principle and Practice*. Minneapolis: Augsburg, 1967.

Talbot, Charles H. *The Anglo-Saxon Missionaries in Germany: Being the Lives of Ss. Willibrord, Boniface, Sturm, Leoba, and Lebuin, Together with the Hodoeporicon of St. Willibald and a Selection from the Correspondence of St. Boniface*. New York: Sheed & Ward, 1954.

————. "St. Boniface and the German Mission." In Cuming, *The Mission of the Church and the Propagation of the Faith*, 45–57.

Taylor, John B. *Primal World-Views: Christian Involvement in Dialogue with Traditional Thought Forms*. Ibadan, Nigeria: Daystar, 1976.

Taylor, John V. *The Primal Vision: Christian Presence Amid African Religion*. London: SCM Press, 1963.

Taylor, Nicholas H. "Conflicting Bases of Identity in Early Christianity: The Example of Paul." In Blasi, Turcotte, and Duhaime, *Handbook of Early Christianity*, 577–97.

Tertullian. *Against Praxeas.* Translated by Peter Holmes. In *Ante-Nicene Fathers*, vol. 1, edited by Alexander Roberts, James Donaldson, and A. Cleveland Coxe. Buffalo, NY: Christian Literature Publishing, 1885.

———. *An Answer to the Jews.* Translated by S. Thelwall. In *Ante-Nicene Fathers*, vol. 3, edited by Alexander Roberts, James Donaldson, and A. Cleveland Coxe. Buffalo, NY: Christian Literature Publishing, 1885.

———. *The Writings of Tertullian.* Vol. 1. Edited by Anthony Uyl. Ontario: Devoted Publishing, 2019.

Thackston, W. M., trans. *Nasir-I Khusraw's Book of Travels.* Costa Mesa, CA: Mazda 2001.

Thomas of Marga. *The Book of Governors: The "Historia Monastica" of Thomas Bishop of Margâ.* Translated by E. A. Wallis Budge. 2 vols. London: K. Paul, Trench, Trübner, 1893.

Thompson, E. A. "Christianity and the Northern Barbarians." In *The Conflict between Paganism and Christianity in the Fourth Century*, edited by Arnaldo Momigliano, 56–78. Oxford: Clarendon, 1963.

———. *The Visigoths in the Time of Ulfila.* 2nd ed. London: Duckworth, 2008.

Thompson, Glen L. "Was Alopen a Missionary?" In Winkler and Tang, *Hidden Treasures and Intercultural Encounters*, 267–78.

Tilly, Louise A. "Social History and Its Critics." *Theory and Society* 9, no. 5 (1980): 668–70.

Trimingham, J. Spencer. *Christianity among the Arabs in Pre-Islamic Times.* New York: Longman, 1979.

Turner, Edith L. B., and Victor W. Turner. *Image and Pilgrimage in Christian Culture.* New York: Columbia University Press, 1978.

Vaux, Roland de. "The Hebrew Patriarchs and History." In Long, *Israel's Past in Present Research*, 470–79.

Verkuyl, Johannes. *Contemporary Missiology: An Introduction.* Edited by Cooper Dale. Grand Rapids: Eerdmans, 1978.

Volf, Miroslav. "Soft Difference: Theological Reflections on the Relation between Church and Culture in 1 Peter." *Ex auditu* 10 (1994): 15–30.

Vööbus, Arthur. *History of the School of Nisibis.* Corpus Scriptorum Christianorum Orientalium, V 266 Subsidia, T 26. Louvain: Secrétariat du CorpusSCO, 1965.

Wallach, Luitpold. *Alcuin and Charlemagne: Studies in Carolingian History and Literature*. New York: Cornell University Press, 1959.

Walls, Andrew F. *The Cross-Cultural Process in Christian History: Studies in the Transmission and Appropriation of Faith*. Maryknoll, NY: Orbis Books, 2002.

———. "Eusebius Tries Again: The Task of Reconceiving and Re-Visioning the Study of Christian History." In Shenk, *Enlarging the Story*, 1–21.

———. Introduction to Baylis, *An Introduction to Primal Religions*.

———. "Mission and Migration: The Diaspora Factor in Christian History." *Journal of African Christian Thought* 5, no. 2 (2002): 3–11.

———. *The Missionary Movement in the Christian History: Studies in the Transmission of the Faith*. Maryknoll, NY: Orbis Books, 1996.

———. "Scholarship, Mission and Globalisation: Some Reflections on the Christian Scholarly Vocation in Africa." *Journal of African Christian Thought* 9, no. 2 (December 2006): 34–37.

———. "Structural Problems in Mission Studies." *International Bulletin of Missionary Research* 15 (October 1991): 146–55.

Walsh, John R., and Thomas Bradley. *A History of the Irish Church, 400–700 AD*. 2nd ed. Dublin: Columba, 2003.

Waterfield, Robin E. *Christians in Persia: Assyrians, Armenians, Roman Catholics and Protestants*. London: George Allen and Unwin; New York: Barnes & Noble, 1973.

Waweru, Humphrey. *The Bible and African Culture: Mapping Transactional Inroads*. Eldoret, Kenya: Zapf Chancery, 2011.

Whelan, Robin. *Being Christian in Vandal Africa: The Politics of Orthodoxy in the Post-Imperial West*. Oakland: University of California Press, 2018.

Whittaker, C. R. *Frontiers of the Roman Empire: A Social and Economic Study*. Baltimore: Johns Hopkins University Press, 1994.

Wiles, Maurice. *Archetypal Heresy: Arianism through the Centuries*. New York: Oxford University Press, 1996.

Wilkinson, John. *Egeria's Travels*. 3rd ed. Warminster: Aris & Phillips, 1999.

William of Rubruck. *The Mission of Friar William of Rubruck: His Journey to the Court of the Great Khan Möngke, 1253–1255*. Translated by Peter Jackson; introduction, notes, and appendices by Peter Jackson with David Morgan. Indianapolis: Hackett, 2009.

Willibald. *The Life of Saint Boniface*. Translated with notes and introduction by George W. Robinson. Cambridge: Harvard University Press, 1916.

Wilson, Robert R. "Forced Migration and the Formation of the Prophetic Literature." In *By the Irrigation Canals of Babylon: Approaches to the Study of the Exile*, edited by John J. Ahn and Jill Anne Middlemas, 125–38. New York: T&T Clark, 2012.

Winkler, Dietmar W., and Li Tang, eds. *Hidden Treasures and Intercultural Encounters: Studies on East Syriac Christianity in China and Central Asia*. 2nd ed. Vienna: Lit, 2014.

Winroth, Anders. *The Age of the Vikings*. Princeton: Princeton University Press, 2014.

———. *The Conversion of Scandinavia: Vikings, Merchants, and Missionaries in the Remaking of Northern Europe*. New Haven: Yale University Press, 2012.

Wolde, E. J. van. *Words Become Worlds: Semantic Studies of Genesis 1–11*. Biblical Interpretation Series. New York: Brill, 1994.

Wolfe, Patrick. "History and Imperialism: A Century of Theory, from Marx to Postcolonialism." *American Historical Review* 102, no. 2 (1997): 388–420.

Wood, I. N. *The Missionary Life: Saints and the Evangelisation of Europe, 400–1050*. Harlow: Longman, 2001.

Wood, Ian. *The Merovingian Kingdoms 450–751*. New York: Longman, 1994.

Yan, Yu Suee. "The Alien in Deuteronomy." *Bible Translator* 60, no. 2 (April 2009): 112–17.

Yü, Dan Smyer. "Buddhist Conversion in the Contemporary World." In Rambo and Farhadian, *The Oxford Handbook of Religious Conversion*, 465–87.

Zakovitch, Yair. "'My Father Was a Wandering Aramean' (Deuteronomy 26:5) or 'Edom Served My Father'?" In *Mishneh Todah: Studies in Deuteronomy and Its Cultural Environment in Honor of Jeffrey H. Tigay*, edited by Nili Sacher Fox, David A. Glatt-Gilad, and Michael J. Williams, 133–37. Winona Lake, IN: Eisenbrauns, 2009.

Index

Page numbers in boldface indicate maps.